KV-576-843

PRAISE FROM OUR READERS

Mastering HTML 4

"This is THE book!! If you can't find what you are looking for or learn HTML from this book, then there is no hope. This is the most comprehensive HTML book I have ever seen! Well worth the money and time to read it!"
Martha Rich, Arkansas

"Fantastic, Comprehensive, Easy-to-Read! I've thumbed through, and read thoroughly, many HTML books, but this one just grabs your brain, rattles out your neurons and implants the goodies you need to slam-dunk a great Web site. The authors provide an easy-to-read format with just the right amount of examples and details that won't leave you asking more questions or bore you with too many arcane details."
Sabrina Hanley, North Carolina

Mastering XML

"Got XML questions? This book has the answers. For implementers: detailed tips and techniques used by the experts. For XML users: clear explanations of the XML family of standards and XML applications. For managers: case studies of successful XML implementations. This book deserves a place on your bookshelf."
Eric Freese, Director of Consulting Services, ISOGEN International Corp., http://www.isogen.com

"Mastering XML provides a solid introduction to the concepts essential for mastering, and applying, XML. Navarro, White, and Burman offer details on various XML vocabularies, which are critical elements of any XML effort."
Laura Walker, Executive Director, OASIS, http://www.oasis-open.org/, http://xml.org

SYBEX
www.sybex.com

MASTERING™ MAYA® COMPLETE™ 2

Perry Harovas

John Kundert-Gibbs

Peter Lee

SYBEX®

San Francisco • Paris • Düsseldorf • Soest • London

Associate Publisher: Cheryl Applewood
Contracts and Licensing Manager: Kristine O'Callaghan
Acquisitions & Developmental Editor: Cheryl Applewood
Editors: James A. Compton, Marilyn Smith, Jeff Gammon,
Pat Coleman, Pete Gaughan
Project Editor: James A. Compton
Technical Editors: Mark Smith, Mike Stivers
Book Designers: Patrick Dintino, Catalin Dulfu,
Franz Baumhackl
Graphic Illustration: Publication Services
Electronic Publishing Specialists: Robin Kibby, Grey Magauran,
Nila Nichols
Project Team Leader: Lisa Reardon
Proofreaders: Jennifer Campbell, Molly Glover
Indexer: Nancy Guenther
Companion CD Compilation: Mark Smith
Companion CD Production: Keith McNeil, Kara Schwartz,
Ginger Warner
Cover Designer: Design Site
Cover Illustrator: Sergie Loobkoff

Library of Congress Card Number: 99-66406
ISBN: 0-7821-2521-2

Manufactured in the United States of America

10 9 8 7 6 5 4

To our families and friends (especially Philip, Michele, Kristin, Joshua, and Kenlee), whose love, insight and countless hours of sacrifice have made this book possible.

Acknowledgments

A book like this doesn't appear by smoke and mirrors, but by the hard work and dedication of a great number of people. While everyone who had any part in this book deserves credit, we have room to mention only a special few.

First, we'd like to thank the hard-working, inspired people at Alias|Wavefront for making such fantastic tools for us. We are especially indebted to Chris Ford, Mark Sylvester, Duncan Brinsmead, Russell Owen, Jackie Farrell, Sharon Zamora, Mike Stivers, Katriona Lord-Levins, Tracy Hawken, and Vic Fina. Their contributions to this book have been invaluable.

We are privileged to thank Ellen Pasternack and Habib Zargarpour from Industrial Light & Magic, who were always willing to help, and went beyond the call of duty with their time and effort, and also Don Davidson of New Jersey Newsphotos, for his eternal faith and patience.

We would also like to thank the acquisitions, editorial, and production team assembled by Sybex for their insightful, timely, and professional management of the evolving work, especially Jim Compton, Cheryl Applewood, Mark Smith, and Adrienne Crew. Marilyn Smith, Jeff Gammon, Pat Coleman, and Pete Gaughan also contributed greatly to the editing. On the production side, Robin Kibby, Lisa Reardon, Teresa Trego, Molly Glover, and Jennifer Campbell displayed their usual skill and resourcefulness in turning the edited manuscript into a finished book. Keith McNeil, Kara Schwartz, and Ginger Warner made the companion CD-ROM a reality.

Thanks also to our agency, Studio B Literary Agency, who made the contracts go smoothly and were our champions from day one, especially Neil Salkind and Sherry Rogelberg.

Without the generous support and freedom our employers have given us, this book could never have been written. A special thanks to Richard Silver of Cambridge Electronics and the staff at The Lighthouse. We would also like to thank the faculty and staff of two fine universities, California Lutheran University, and the University of North Carolina at Asheville, especially the late Dr. Jonathon Boe, Michael Arndt, Mike Adams, Joan Wines, Tom Cochran, and Jim Pitts.

Our loved ones have been with us throughout this book's production, and have given their time and energy to this work as much as we have. From this large group, we would like to give special thanks to Joan and Lee Gibbs, Michele Harovas, Marilyn Harovas, and the late Philip Harovas, Peter Lee's parents, David Lee, Tim, Hee Sun, Sharon and Danny, Melanie and Jim Davis, and Kristin, Joshua, and Kenlee Kundert-Gibbs.

Contents at a Glance

Table of Contents

Foreword

Welcome to the wonderful world of Maya. Little did I realize fifteen years ago that I would be writing the foreword to a book about a product that is the result of an idea I had in 1984—to do something with computers and art.

I can imagine how excited you must be. You have the book, the software, and a hot computer; and now you are going to get busy and educate yourself in the many disciplines that it takes to be an accomplished Maya animator. Good luck to you. The investment you are about to make in yourself is worth every minute you put into it—and every hour, week, weekend, and holiday that you work through as you babysit that final render or rush to make a 9 A.M. deadline. There are thousands of people just like you who have dedicated themselves to becoming world-class experts at Maya. This book is now a part of your continuing education program.

When we started Wavefront in 1984, we had a vision of how an artist would use our tools to create amazing images. That vision attracted many like-minded people to our way of doing things. Coincidentally, during that same spring in 1984, two other companies were having the same conversations: in Paris the early developers of Explore from Thomson Digital Images (TDI), and in Toronto the founding team at Alias Research. Each of the companies had attracted like-minded artists and animators that gravitated to our approach to the computer graphics problem. Now those various methodologies, features, functions, and workflows are represented in our next-generation application, Maya.

Maya is the combination and, in many ways, a culmination of hundreds of man years of effort at creating a computer graphics system that meets the demanding requirements of users from the ultrahigh-end film studios to the start-up animation companies that are springing up in garages around the planet. Maya effectively brings together the best thinking of all three systems plus new technologies, workflow, and usability features that were impossible to imagine fifteen years ago. There is a lot here to learn. Nevertheless, diligence, patience, and an open attitude will help you succeed as you go through the exercises in this book. Challenge yourself.

Learning Maya is a lot like learning the Japanese game of GO. They say it takes minutes to learn and a lifetime to master. You can get through the Alias|Wavefront tutorials in a couple of days. However, that just gets you to beginner status. You obviously want to improve your skills beyond this—you purchased *Mastering Maya Complete 2* to move beyond Maya's beginning tutorials. Your ability to utilize the skills that you learn in this book in creative ways will enable you to develop unique solutions to your future graphics problems. It is only after years of grappling with tough visual problems that you achieve expert status. Remember, there are usually more than a few ways to solve the same problem within Maya. Everything can be combined with everything else, and this is one of the most powerful aspects of the software.

This book will get you acquainted with Maya Complete Version 2. When we started work on Maya in 1995, after the merger of Alias and Wavefront, we wanted to deliver a software system that would change the way computer animation was created by challenging established ways of working—even those we pioneered ourselves. In Version 1, we set our goals high, and we met most of them. Version 2 now completes our original design plans for the software and its architecture. Software is never actually done, just as a great painting always seems to need "just a little more—if I only had the time."

I had the chance to review a few of chapters of this book while they were still being edited, somewhat like getting a look at Alpha software. The great thing about a book not written by a product's manufacturer is that certain liberties can be taken by the authors. They can have fun with the lessons and their comments. I am sure you will appreciate the tone the book uses as you are led though lessons that will reinforce your knowledge of each of the various aspects of Maya. The lessons build upon themselves, which is great for taking you through the process incrementally. I have always enjoyed learning this way. The best part of the book is the enclosed CD. This way, you know you have a safety net; if you make a mistake, you can always reload the lesson examples.

Once you have gotten a good feel for the software and its potential, it will be time to meet others who share your enthusiasm for Maya. Internet news groups, online chats, Maya rings, and the various Alias|Wavefront and Maya Web sites are all good forums to meet others and discuss specific aspects of the software, its uses, and how much this book helped you in getting more out of the software. I encourage you to take time regularly to interact with other users. See if there is a user group in your community and make sure you plan a trip to SIGGRAPH each year for the Global Users Association's annual meeting.

Well, enough about how great life will be once you have learned Maya; it is time to get to work and start exercising your gray cells. I hope that this book becomes just one more part of your investment in lifelong learning and continuing education. This is just the beginning. Have fun. I still do—every day!

Ride the wave,
Mark Sylvester
Ambassador
Alias|Wavefront
Santa Barbara, California
November, 1999

Introduction

Maya—a word full of mystery, wonder, and power. It conjures up all sorts of imagery. Not coincidentally, so does the software, which can be a magical imaging tool. But as with any other tool, making magic requires an artist who knows the proper way to use that tool.

In *Mastering Maya Complete 2*, you will learn how to use Maya to create images that the rest of us have never seen before. How can we be sure of that? Because you are unique, with your own life experiences, point of view, and artistic flair. We can guarantee that no one has seen the images you will create, because they come from YOU.

The point to reading this book is to give yourself the knowledge you need to use this tool called Maya to the best of your ability. Then, and only then, will the imagery you create come closer to what you see in your mind.

What You Will Learn from This Book

Maya Complete is an incredibly rich, full-featured 3D graphics and animation program that encapsulates tremendous computational power. As you'll see in this book, Maya's dynamics engines literally put the laws of physics at your fingertips to make objects behave in perfectly realistic ways—or not-so-realistic, if that's where your imagination takes you. Maya presents this power through a user interface that is both logical and consistent enough for you to learn quickly and flexible enough to adapt to the needs of any user or project.

Mastering Maya Complete 2 is a comprehensive, practical guide to every aspect of the program. You'll begin with a tour of the user interface and its tools for optimizing your workflow. Then you'll learn the basics of computer modeling and the major types of modeling available in Maya: NURBS, polygon, and organic. You'll work through the stages of animation and rendering, and you'll learn to use the MEL scripting language. In the last group of chapters, you'll work with some of Maya's most advanced tools, including its particle dynamics. Finally, you'll be introduced to the amazing Paint Effects module, which is new in Maya 2.5.

What's the Best Way to Use This Book?

Mastering Maya 2 Complete is not just a reference manual. As working animators and 3D artists, we knew from the beginning that simply marching through the menus and dialog boxes would not be an effective way for you to learn how to use the software or for us to share our insights and experiences. We knew that "hands-on" is always the best approach for learning software, and nowhere is that more true than with 3D modeling and animation. So we've built each chapter around examples and tutorials that let you try out each new feature as you're studying it.

To implement this approach, we've created a fully integrated book and CD-ROM. The companion CD includes working files—Maya project files, sketches, TIF images, and MEL scripts—that will get you started with each exercise, as well as rendered images and animations you can use to check your progress as you go. (The CD also includes some illustrations that are best viewed in color, and bonus material, as described at the back of the book.)

Nearly every exercise is intended to create production-quality finished work, but most of them can be done by anyone who has a little experience with 3D software—and some patience and persistence. You don't need to be an accomplished draftsperson, but you do need to work with care. And you should be willing to step away from a project and come back to it when you are ready. A few exercises are intended for more advanced users and are identified that way.

Even though some projects begin in one chapter and continue in another, you don't need to read the whole book straight through from beginning to end. (Of course, we like to think that once you start, you'll find it hard to stop.) As with any how-to book, you can focus on the subjects that interest you or the tasks you need to accomplish first, particularly if you are already working at an intermediate level.

Who Should Read This Book

This book is intended for a range of Maya users, from beginners to experts, but we expect that most readers will be in the "advanced beginner" or intermediate range. We assume that most people who invest in a professional-quality 3D graphics program (and the hardware to run it) have already begun working with some modeling/ animation software and now want to hone their skills and take advantage of the breakthroughs in software technology that Maya makes available. You may be working in a production environment already, or in a training program, or working in a related field and preparing to make the jump to 3D modeling and animation. Of course, few people are experts in all things; so everyone should be able to learn something useful or cool here, or at least learn a new way of doing things.

If you are a relative beginner, or if you are self-taught and feel that your background in the fundamentals has a few holes in it, you should start from the beginning and work through the first half of the book. Here you will learn how to create a human model from the ground up, texture it, add a skeletal control system (IK) to it, and animate and render it. You will also learn how to populate your world with objects that behave as they do in the real world.

Users at the intermediate level will find plenty of interest beyond the fundamentals. Two chapters introduce the MEL scripting language, giving you enough of a foundation to get started learning how to harness the full power of Maya and make the software handle repetitive operations for you. As you'll see, you don't need to learn the entire scripting language in order to customize your workspace for automation and efficiency. The last five chapters provide an in-depth look at the advanced topic of particle dynamics and a hands-on introduction to Maya's newest and most powerful tool, Paint Effects.

In fact, if you're beyond the "absolute beginner" stage, you can find valuable information in practically every chapter. Scan through the Table of Contents to find the topics you're most interested in, or check the "What's New in Maya 2" notes to see what new features are covered in a chapter. Again, everyone who tries out the exercises will find a wealth of fun, useful, educational, and sometimes dazzling projects.

 N O T E   As an added attraction, and to inspire you to create dazzling work of your own, we've collected 16 pages of some of the most beautiful color illustrations created in Maya. You'll see artwork developed in the exercises, along with pictures and animation stills created by the authors and other Maya artists, with hints about the Maya tools they used.

How This Book Is Organized

Depending on your interests and skill level, you can either study each chapter from beginning to end or start with what you need to know first. Here's a quick guide to what each part and chapter covers.

Part I: Maya Fundamentals introduces Maya and its tools with the following topics:

Chapter 1: Your First Maya Animation uses a hands-on example—building and launching a rocket ship—to introduce the basic elements of Maya: modeling, texturing, lighting, animation, dynamics and rendering. This provides a good foundation if you aren't accustomed to using Maya.

Next we explore the Maya interface further in **Chapter 2: The Maya Interface**. We look in depth at the elements that make up models and windows, and the various menus and interfaces you'll work with.

In **Chapter 3: Techniques for Speeding Up Workflow**, we introduce Maya tools that allow you to work efficiently, with the largest amount of screen real estate and in the fastest way.

Chapter 4: The Hypergraph: Your Roadmap to a Scene shows how the Hypergraph (or dependency graph) gives Maya its power. The Hypergraph is the heart of Maya, bringing together all of its elements. Don't underestimate its power and simplicity.

Part II: Modeling offers a detailed exploration of Maya's modeling techniques:

Chapter 5: Modeling Basics uses simple objects to introduce basic modeling concepts and Maya's way of implementing them. The example projects are a great way to learn about construction history.

In **Chapter 6: NURBS Modeling** we open up the world of NURBS modeling, showing what elements make up a NURBS surface, how to edit them, and finally how to apply these concepts by modeling an aftershave bottle. As we introduce more tools, you'll create a more advanced aftershave bottle, and finally a human face.

Chapter 7: Polygon Modeling explores the basic ingredients that make up a polygonal model and how to edit them. Extrusions, UV mapping, edge smoothing and model smoothing are also explored. The hands-on project is the creation of a human hand in polygons.

All the work you've done so far leads up to **Chapter 8: Organic Modeling**. In this chapter, we show you how to take a dog from a sketch to a finished model.

Chapter 9: Working with Artisan, is a guided tour of Artisan. You'll learn why it's such a useful set of tools and what you can do with it besides just "denting" your models, and you'll get a preview of MEL scripting in Artisan's MEL script painting function.

Part III: Animation shows how to add motion to models you've created:

In **Chapter 10: Animating in Maya** you will get started creating, controlling, and editing animation in Maya. We take our human model further by using Set Driven Keys to control our polygonal human hands' fingers.

In **Chapter 11: Paths and Bones** you are introduced to setting up skeletons correctly the first time, and you'll learn how to animate cameras and objects properly and quickly, with motion paths.

Chapter 12: Deformers and **Chapter 13: Skinning and Character Setup** show you how to use deformers to add secondary animation to your Inverse Kinematics (IK) characters, and also how to use these deformers to create facial expressions and phonemes.

Chapter 14: Character Animation: a Walk Cycle and More introduces and explains walk cycles, showing how to add emotion to your character's movements. You'll also learn how to animate run cycles, catching and throwing a ball, and more complex movements such as somersaults.

In **Chapter 15: Working with Rigid Body Dynamics** you will learn what rigid bodies are and how to control them, how to use fields and forces for different results, and how to "bake" the animation when you are done, speeding up interactivity and ensuring that no discrepancies occur while batch rendering.

Part IV: Working with MEL shows how to make the Maya Embedded Language work for you, even if you're not a programmer:

Chapter 16: MEL Basics is a jumping-off point for beginning MEL users, ending with examples that put the theories into practice.

Chapter 17: Programming with MEL takes MEL scripting further, showing you how to create, debug, and edit MEL scripts and MEL interfaces.

Part V: Rendering takes you through the details of producing rendered images and animations:

Chapter 18: Rendering Basics explores the way Maya defines a rendered image, how to use Interactive Photorealistic Rendering (IPR), image planes, and Depth of Field. You will also learn how to set up renders that allow for changes to be made quickly and without rerendering the entire animation.

With **Chapter 19: Shading and Texturing Surfaces** you will learn how to texture surfaces right the first time, and how to create effects with layered shaders that would be hard or impossible without them. The examples used are those of texturing the dog model and the clothing and skin of the child model.

Chapter 20: Lighting examines the Maya lighting system, the shadow types available, effects you can add to lights, and proper studio lighting of your subjects. You will learn how to balance speed and quality with depth-mapped shadows and when to use raytraced shadows, as well as fog, light color, glows and halos.

Part VI: Advanced Maya Effects extends your Maya skills to work with particles and soft bodies, as well as the new Paint Effects tool:

In **Chapter 21: Particle Basics** we show you how and when to use particles, how to control them, and give you several examples of uses for them.

Then, in **Chapter 22: Particle Rendering**, we show you the different ways to render particles, and why each has its own place in your rendering pipeline.

With **Chapter 23: Using Particle Expressions and Ramps** we really get our hands wet with particles, as we show you how to add expressions to grow and move the particles, as well as to define their lifespan and what happens to them at death.

Chapter 24: Dynamics of Soft Bodies takes the particle and rigid body knowledge you have gained, and puts it to use in soft body simulation. We cover Goal Weights, springs, constraints and more. The chapter concludes with two great uses of soft bodies: simulated water ripples from a fountain and a water tentacle out of science fiction.

Chapter 25: Paint Effects takes you into the world of the newest Maya tool. You will learn what it can do and what its hundreds of attributes mean, to help you immediately understand and start using Paint Effects. The tutorial that ends the chapter takes you step-by-step into adding real hair to the child model, explaining how to approach it and why each step is taken.

Finally, the **Appendix** offers some food for thought as Perry Harovas and John Kundert-Gibbs interview four of the leading lights in animation and computer graphics. You'll learn about how Maya was created and the challenges it may tackle next; how the new Paint Effects tool was developed; the philosophy behind the Maya user interface; and how Maya was used in the latest *Star Wars* movie.

Hardware and Software Considerations

Maya 2 Complete is available for both Windows NT and IRIX platforms. Alias|Wavefront has been able to implement the same feature set and user interface on both platforms, so all of the information in this book applies to both NT and IRIX. The CD-ROM accompanying this book, however, has been tested only on NT; so we cannot guarantee that all parts of it will work exactly as described on IRIX systems.

Alias|Wavefront provides a Qualification Chart in the printed documentation and on its Web site (www.aliaswavefront.com/qual_charts), certifying particular combinations of processors, operating system versions, graphics cards, and drivers for operation with Maya NT. Be sure to check this chart for your configuration.

Alias|Wavefront lists the following *minimum* hardware requirements for running Maya Complete on Windows NT; to work at a comfortable pace, you'll probably want more processor speed, RAM, and disk space:

- Pentium processor, at least 200MHz
- 128MB RAM
- CD-ROM drive
- High-performance graphics card. See the Qualification Chart for current recommendations.
- Hardware lock provided by Alias|Wavefront with the Maya shipment
- Three-button mouse with mouse driver software. The Microsoft Intellimouse is not supported in this release.
- Sound card (optional)
- Wacom tablet (optional)
- Magellan Spaceball (optional)
- Disk space as follows for an NTFS file system (for a FAT file system, space requirements would be approximately doubled)
  - 220MB for Maya Complete
  - Up to 15MB temporary space on the C: drive to start the installation program
  - 4 MB for Invigorator
  - 45 MB for Fusion Lite

The minimum software requirments are as follows:

- Windows NT 4.0 (with Service Pack 5)
- TCP/IP network protocol software (for Maya batch rendering and other features)
- Web browser: Netscape Navigator 3.0 or Internet Explorer 3.0 (or higher)
- Graphics card driver software (available from the card manufacturer's web site)
- Appropriate driver software for optional hardware
- Appropriate networking software and hardware if you plan to use and share files on IRIX workstations

What's Next?

By the time you finish this book, you'll be well on your way to mastery of Maya 2. A number of chapters offer suggestions for further reading related to animation and 3D graphics, and the accompanying CD contains links to some of the most important Web sites in the field. Be sure to check the sites maintained by Perry Harovas (www .lighthousepost.com) and Sybex (www.sybex.com) for updates and bonus material as Maya evolves.

As you work through this book and begin exploring Maya on your own, you'll probably think of topics you'd like us to cover further and other improvements we can make. You can use the Sybex Web site to provide feedback (click the Contact link and then the Book Content Issues link to display a form where you can type your comments) or send e-mail directly to Perry Harovas (perry@ce.com), John Kundert-Gibbs (jkundert@bulldog.unca.edu), or Peter Lee (peter3d@home.com).

Now it's up to you to make the most of the tools that Maya offers. Have fun, and remember that the most important tool is your own imagination!

PART I

MAYA FUNDAMENTALS

Create your first Maya animation

Use the Maya interface

Speed up your workflow

Use the Hypergraph tool effectively

chapter 1

YOUR FIRST MAYA ANIMATION

Featuring

- Setting the scene: modeling

- Texturing your models using the Hypershade

- Lighting the scene

- Animating the rocket

- Creating a follow camera

- Rendering the animation

- Advanced topic: adding exhaust

YOUR FIRST MAYA ANIMATION

Welcome to *Mastering Maya 2 Complete*! Although this book will give you a great deal of in-depth knowledge about all aspects of Maya Complete, if you're like us, you'd probably like to get your feet wet before bothering with the nuts and bolts of the program. Well that's what this chapter is here for: you'll try out modeling, keyframing, texturing, and using Maya's built-in dynamics, all in one animation that shows off the power of Maya's interface and renderer. You'll also learn the basics of maneuvering around a Maya scene, and you'll start to see where adjusting various options would lead to different results.

While we won't deal with theory or do a lot of explaining in this chapter (that's what the rest of the book is for!), if you follow along, you should get a very good idea of what Maya is about and how you can use it in your future endeavors.

Before you start the animation in this chapter, take a few minutes to read through the Introduction to this book. It contains information that will make it easier to work through the tutorials, and it will give you an overview of how to best use the book to get the results you want.

If you are already familiar with other 3D animation packages, going through this chapter should get you ready to use Maya proficiently. If you are new to the whole world of 3D animation, or if you would like a little more grounding in the fundamentals of Maya, you may want to read Chapters 2 and 3 before reading this chapter. Those two chapters will get you up to speed on both the Maya interface and many of the conventions of 3D animation.

But enough talk—let's do some animating!

Setting the Scene: Modeling

In this chapter, we're going to build, texture, light, and animate a little rocket ship that takes off, loses power after a couple of seconds, and crashes back to earth.

While this modeling and animation project is a bit simplified, it is definitely a "real world" example of work you can do in Maya. Don't get discouraged if things don't turn out well immediately (especially if you are new to 3D modeling and animation). Remember that you can return to this project as you progress through the book, refining your work. Given a bit of time and practice, you should be able to get this project looking very good—even if you've never done 3D work before! To give you an idea of what you're working toward, here's a still shot from the completed animation. (To get the full effect, see the Chapter 1 Color Gallery on the CD).

The first step to almost any animation in Maya is to build your scene elements; therefore, we'll build the rocket (and ground) as our first step. To build our little ship, we'll use just a couple of the many different modeling techniques Maya has available for you.

1. First, let's create a project and save our file, so it has a home. Open Maya by double-clicking its desktop icon. Now, from the File menu, choose File ➤

Project ➤ New. In the New Project options window, click the Use Defaults button, type in a name for your project (something like **rocketProject**) in the Scene File Locations text box, and click Accept to accept these choices. You now have your project saved in your default directory on your hard drive. To save your actual *scene,* you need to choose File ➤ Save Scene As, and then choose an appropriate name for the file (like rocket1.ma).

T I P Your project consists of several folders (or directories) of information about the scene (which is where your scene file is stored), any rendering jobs, source images, output images, textures, and so forth. Whenever you first create a new scene in Maya, there are *two* steps to saving: first, save your project (which contains all the proper places for Maya to store your project's information), and then save the actual scene file.

W A R N I N G Maya is based on the Unix operating system, which means you *must never* use spaces in your filenames—even if you're running the NT version of Maya. If you do, Maya will give you an error when you try to open your scene later, and you won't be able to access your earlier work! The operating system will allow you to save according to its filename conventions, but Maya's file system won't recognize any names with spaces.

T I P It is a very good idea to append a number to the name of every scene (for example, **rocket1**). As you work, you will want to save your scene often, in case you run into any problems, and, rather than just saving over your old scene, you should save a new scene each time, numbered sequentially (**rocket2**, **rocket3**, and so on). Every time you are told to save in this project, remember to save a new file with a higher number. If you are concerned about disk space on your hard drive, you can erase earlier versions of your project as you work through later ones. We generally save about the last four or five versions, and then start trashing the earlier ones.

2. One you have saved your project and file, look over the interface for a moment (see Chapter 2 for a tour of the interface if you have never used Maya before). Then change your scene window from the default perspective view to a "four view" of the scene by first clicking in the scene (big) window and then pressing and releasing the spacebar quickly. Your scene window should change to four smaller panes, each labeled for its view angle (top, side, front and persp—perspective). Select the side view by clicking your mouse inside this pane, then

press and release the spacebar quickly again to make the side view take up the entire viewing pane.

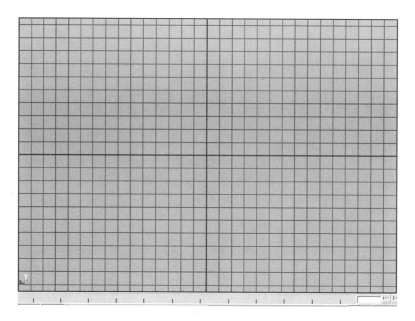

N O T E   If switching between panes is difficult for you (or if you are completely new to Maya), you should read through Chapter 2 to learn about the Maya interface, before continuing in this chapter.

To create the body of the rocket, we'll use an EP (Edit Point) curve tool to define four points that make up the rocket's outline, and then "revolve" this curve into a surface.

3. Pick the EP Curve tool (Create ≻ EP Curve Tool); your cursor should turn into a cross, indicating that you're now using the EP Curve tool. Because we want the first (top) point of the curve to lie directly on the Y axis (the thick vertical line at the center of the pane), we need to turn on the "snap to grid" button before we create the first point on the curve—click the Snap to Grid button on the Status Line in Maya (the topmost toolbar).

PART 1

4. A little below the top of the window, where the X axis meets one of the other grid lines, click once (with your left mouse button) to create your first point. Now turn off the Snap to Grid button (click it again), and create three more points, approximately like the following image. If you hold down the mouse button when you click to create a point, you can move that point around until you like its positioning; you can also hit the backspace key to remove the last point you made. When you are satisfied with the shape of the ship, hit the Enter key to save the points (the curve will turn green).

5. Our next step is to create an actual surface from our outline. Be sure Modeling is showing on the Status Line (at the far left top of the screen). If not, choose it from the pop-up menu there. Now revolve the curve by choosing Surfaces ➤ Revolve ❑.

T I P   The ❑ symbol in Maya is known as an *option box*. Selecting this box with your mouse will open a window where you can change the options of your command—in this case, the Revolve command.

6. In the Revolve options window, click the Reset button and then set the segments to 16 (instead of the default 8). Click the Revolve button and close the options window. You should now see your curve transformed into a squat looking rocket ship body! To see your rocket ship shaded, hit the 3 key (on the main keyboard; not the numeric keypad) and the 6 key—the 3 key changes your view to high-resolution, while the 6 key turns on flat shading mode (instead of wire frame).

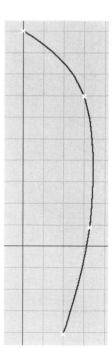

7. Rename your object (shown in the Channel box, at the right of the main window) from revolvedSurface1 to something more appropriate, like **body**: click once on the name (revolvedSurface1) and type in your new name, replacing the old one. Save your work now.

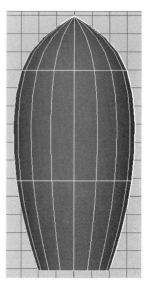

 T I P   If you don't see the object name listed (and a Channels menu directly above it), try holding down the Ctrl key and pressing the A key. This should change your view to the Channel box view.

 T I P   If something goes wrong on this or any step in the project, remember that you can always hit the Z (undo) key to move back one or more steps in your work.

8. Now we need to build our rocket engine exhaust nozzle. We'll use the same method we learned to create the rocket itself: Choose the EP curve tool (or hit the Y key, which will reselect the last used tool for you), and then click several points in the shape of an exhaust cone.

 T I P   To make the size (scale) of the curve easier to see, try creating the exhaust nozzle directly below the rocket body.

9. When you are satisfied with the look of your exhaust nozzle, hit the Enter key and, while the engine is still selected (green), choose Surfaces ➢ Revolve to revolve the engine (note that we don't have to use the options this time; this revolve operation will use the same options you set for the rocket body last time). Hit the 3 key to smooth out the view of the engine nozzle; then rename the object (in the Channel box) from revolvedSurface2 to **nozzle** and save your work.

10. We now need to move the engine into the base of the rocket. Choose the engine (if it's not green, click or drag a selection marquee on the engine—be sure not to highlight the rocket body), then press the W key to bring up the Move tool. You should see several colored arrows (above the engine) around a yellow box. Click and drag up on the green arrow until the nozzle is where you want it to be.

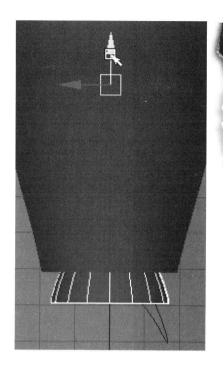

Maya Shortcut Keys

The QWERTY keys (across the top left of your keyboard) are shortcut keys. Memorize these keys now—using shortcut keys is one secret to getting work done in Maya quickly! Here's the function for each one:

- The Q key puts Maya into "select" mode (where you can only select, not modify, scene elements).
- The W key places Maya in Move mode.
- The E key places Maya in Rotate mode.
- The R key places Maya in Scale mode (not rotate mode!).
- The T key places Maya in Manipulator mode (we won't deal with this tool in our work here).
- Finally, the Y key places Maya in whatever mode—besides Move, Scale, and Rotate—was last chosen (the EP Curve Tool, in our work).

11. Now let's create a cockpit for our ship from a default sphere. Click the sphere (ball) button on your tool shelf, or choose Create ➤ NURBS Primitives ➤ Sphere (remember to press the 3 key to display the sphere in hi-res mode). You won't be able to see the sphere, as it is currently inside the rocket body, so change to Move mode (press the W key) and move the sphere to the right of the rocket body. Now change to scale mode (the R key) and stretch the sphere up until it is about twice as tall as it is thick, by pulling the green scale handle up. Finally, change back to Move mode (the W key) and move the sphere into position near the front end

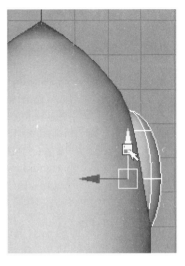

of the rocket body. Be sure to change the name of the object (in the Channel box) from nurbsSphere1 to **cockpit**, and save your work.

N O T E   If you are not familiar with shelves, see Chapter 2 for an introduction to them.

12. No space ship would be complete without some fancy fins on it. We'll create one fin using a default cone, and then adjust its points to make it look more like a fin. Choose Create ➤ Polygon Primitives ➤ Cone ❏, set the Subdivisions along Height option to 5 (instead of 1), click Create and close the Cone Options window; then name the cone **fin1**. Set Maya to Move mode, and then move the cone out so it is below the cockpit. Now change to Rotate mode (the E key) and rotate the cone so it points away from the side of the ship. To do this, grab the outermost ring of the Rotate tool and drag to the right.

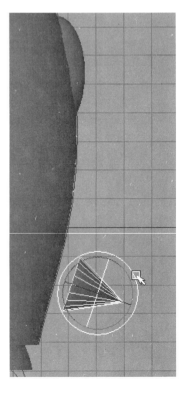

13. The fin is almost correctly placed, but it's currently much too small. Change to scale mode (the R key), and then scale the whole cone out (click the yellow box in the center, and then drag to the right) until it is the right size. We're getting closer, but now the cone has been scaled out in all directions. To fix this, change to four-view mode (press the spacebar quickly), and, in front or top view, click on the red (X axis) scale button and scale the fin so it is thin in that dimension.

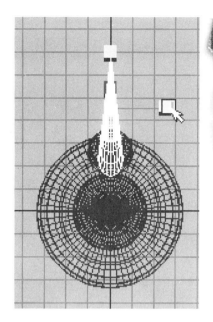

14. Now that the cone/fin is thin, return to the side view (click in the side view, and then press and release the spacebar). Highlight the fin so it is green; then press the F8 key to go into Component selection mode. Drag a selection marquee around the point at the tip (it will turn yellow), and then move that point down so it is about as low as the exhaust nozzle—don't worry that it looks very angular right now. Next, draw a selection marquee around the second row of points in from the tip (be sure to select only this row), and move them down some as well. Finally, choose the bottom set of points on the next two rows in (toward the body), and move them up a bit. You should now have a curved fin. Save your work.

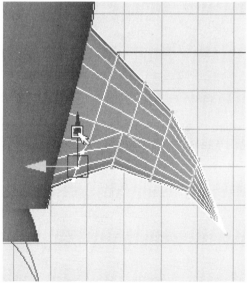

15. When you like the shape of the fin, press the F8 key again to return to Object mode. While the fin is nice, it could use some smoothing. Be sure the fin is still selected (green), and then choose Edit Polygons ➤ Smooth to smooth out the angles between polygon facets. At this point, you might wish to move the fin in toward the body more, so there is no gap between the fin and body.

16. Great, we have one fin. Now we need to make two more. Rather than model these new fins, let's make Maya do the work. First, we need to move the pivot point of the fin (the point around which it rotates) to 0 on the X and Z axes, then we'll just tell Maya to make two duplicates and rotate them.

17. Click on the fin to highlight it, press the Insert key on your keyboard, click the blue handle (it may be difficult to see), and drag it to the center line. To see if the pivot point is close to 0, look at the feedback line (just above the scene panel) and watch the Z component move. Stop when you are as close to 0 as you can 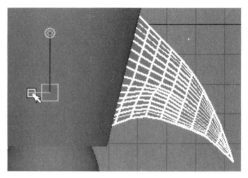 get. When the pivot point has been moved, press the Insert key again to return to Normal mode.

18. Now choose Edit ➢ Duplicate ❑ and, in the options window, click the Reset button, and then set Rotate Y (the middle box) to 120 (120 degrees, or one third of a circle), and Set Number of Copies to 2. Press Duplicate and close the window. You will now have three fins spaced evenly around the body of the ship—Maya even names the other fins *fin2* and *fin3* for you!

19. As a last step, we need to make some ground for our rocket to take off from. Choose Create ➢ NURBS Primitives ➢ Plane ❑, click the Reset button (in the options window), and then set the Width to 1000 (so the ground is very big). Click Create and Close; then rename the plane **ground**. You'll note that the plane is right in the middle of the rocket. Using the Move tool, move the plane down until it is *a significant* distance below the ship—don't let the rocket body, fins, or nozzle touch the plane, or you will have big problems later in this chapter!

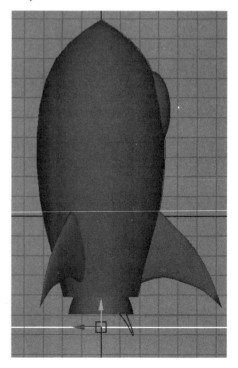

20. Now that we have all of our pieces, we need to get rid of the construction history for each of them, and then erase the curves that generated them (otherwise we'll have problems later on in the animation process). First, select everything in the scene (or RM choose Select All in the scene window); then choose Edit ➤ Delete by Type ➤ History. Now find the curves you used to build the body and nozzle of the rocket (you can choose any component of the rocket and then use the right and left arrow keys to "scroll" through all the components—or you can use the outliner or hypergraph to find the curves). When you have each curve selected, just hit the Backspace key to delete it.

N O T E   If the phrase "RM choose" is unfamiliar, see the list of Maya three-button mouse operations in Chapter 2.

21. As a last step, we need to make all our rocket components into one group (we'll call it *rocket*), and move the pivot point of our rocket down to the ground plane (the reason for this will be apparent as we animate the ship).

22. Drag a selection marquee around the ship and all its components (be sure *not* to include the ground, though!); then hold down the Ctrl key and press G. This creates a new group (called *group1*) that contains all the pieces of the rocket we have modeled. Rename this group rocket.

T I P   In the future, if you click on any component of the rocket (the body, say) and press the up-arrow key, Maya will automatically move up the group's hierarchy and choose the rocket group for you.

23. Be sure the rocket group is still selected (check to see that its name is showing in the Channel box); then press the Insert key. Move the pivot point down (using the green handle) until it is below the bottom of the nozzle. Moving the pivot point will be important when we animate the scale of the ship (otherwise the ship will scale around its middle, instead of its bottom). Be sure to press the Insert key again when you are done moving the pivot point. Save your work.

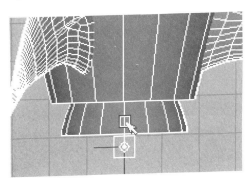

24. Let's take a look at our handiwork. Change to perspective view in the scene panel (remember the spacebar trick), change to shaded mode (press the 6 key), and then rotate around your ship by holding down the Alt key and left mouse button (LM button) and dragging around the scene window.

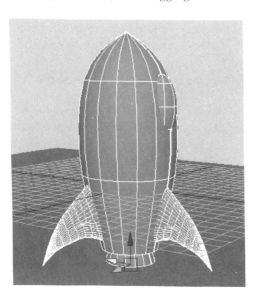

If your results are very different from those you see in the book, you may wish to return to the area that is different and rework it until you are satisfied with the results. Save your work and take a break—good job so far!

Texturing Your Models Using the Hypershade

You might find the model you've created so far a bit... well... gray. Let's remedy that situation now by adding materials to the different model elements, giving them a bit more color and interest. To create these materials, we'll use the new Hypershade in version 2 of Maya (if you have a copy of Maya 1, try to follow along as best you can using the Multilister instead of the hypershade).

N O T E *Materials* in Maya are the general container for a shading network, which gives an object its color, transparency, reflectivity, and so forth. Normally, you create a material, then edit the material's settings or add textures (images or procedural textures) to it to get the look you want. Think of materials in Maya as your own virtual paint can.

1. Select the cockpit and then choose Window ➤ Hypershade, opening the Hypershade window.

2. To create a new material, look down the left-hand side of the Hypershade until you find the Create section. Choose the Phong shader (the very center sphere) and, with your middle mouse button, drag (MM drag) the phong material into the window on the right. Name the window **cockpitPhong** by holding down the Ctrl key, double-clicking the default name (**phong1**), and then typing in the new name.

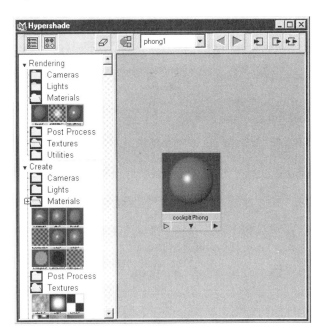

3. To assign this new material to the cockpit, just MM drag the material ball onto the cockpit in the scene window. Because the phong material is still gray, you won't see much difference yet.

4. To adjust the color of the new material, double-click it in the Hypershade. This will open the Attribute Editor (to the right of the scene panel or in its own floating window), with several options you can control for color and other attributes.

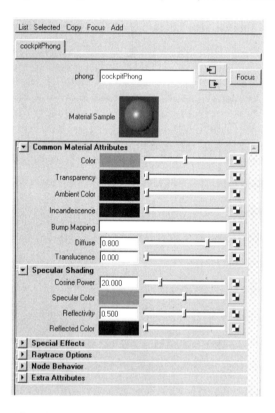

5. All we're interested in for the cockpit is its color. Click on the gray rectangle next to the word *color*, and, in the color picker that pops up, choose a very dark blue (almost black) color. You can watch the cockpit itself change as you adjust the color. When you get a color you like, click the Accept button.

6. Let's make another phong material for the body of the rocket. MM drag a phong material onto the right side of the Hypershade window, and then rename this material **bodyPhong**. Now MM drag the material ball onto the body of the rocket.

7. First, adjust the color of the new material to a very pale blue-gray (the color of brushed aluminum). To make this work right, you'll need to set the saturation of your color very low (we set it to 0.075).

8. When you accept the color, you'll probably notice that the highlights on the rocket body are big and ugly. Fortunately, we can compensate for this. In the

Attribute Editor, set the Cosine Power (the size of the highlight) to a large number, like 75, and set the Specular color to a darker gray (drag the slider to the left). When you finish, you should have a more pleasing highlight.

9. To create the ground shade (we don't want a highlight on the ground!), let's use the lambert shader, which cannot create a highlight. MM drag a lambert material (top right) onto the right side of the Hypershade; then rename it **groundLambert**. Then MM drag the new material onto the ground plane, assigning it to the plane.

10. In the Attribute Editor, set the color of the ground plane to a dusty orange-yellow (a desert dirt color).

11. The last two materials we'll make will be a bit more interesting. First, let's create a material with a procedural texture for the nozzle. Create a new phong shader, name it **nozzlePhong**, and assign it to the nozzle.

12. Instead of assigning a color to the new material, click the little checkerboard next to it (to the right of the color slider). This will bring up the Create Render Node window. Click on the Checker button, and your material will have a checker pattern to it.

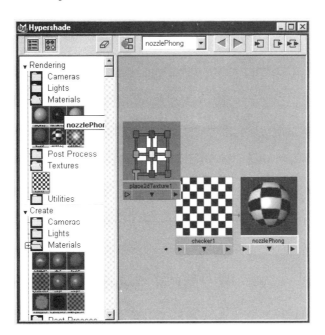

13. While this texture as it currently looks might be all right for playing checkers, it's not what we're after. In the Attribute Editor, make both of the colors in the checker pattern a shade of gray (drag the sliders next to the color swatches).

Finally, decrease the Contrast setting to about 0.7. These changes will make the pattern much subtler.

14. Now click on the place2Dtexture1 tab (at the top of the Attribute Editor) and set the Repeat UV to 16 and 0.5, respectively. This will give the nozzle the ringed appearance common to rocket nozzles.

15. Finally, let's create the fin material, using a ramp to get our effect. First, create a new phong material (called **finPhong**), and assign it to all three fins—you will probably have to rotate the scene panel in order to see all three fins so you can do this.

16. In the Attribute Editor, click the checker box next to Color again to bring up the Create Render Node window. Choose Ramp from the list of 2D textures. You should see a default ramp appear, and all the fins should have the colors applied to them.

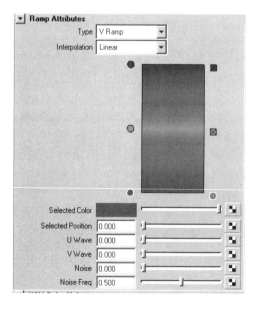

17. While the smooth transitions of the default ramp are nice, they're not what we need for our fins. From the Interpolation pop-up menu, choose None. This turns off the smooth interpolation of the colors, making the ramp a series of color bars.

18. To change the ramp colors, select the ramp node (the circle to the left of the color bar) and then click on the Selected Color swatch to bring up the color picker. To create a new color node, just click in the color swatch where you want it. To move a color up or down, drag the circle on the left of the color bar. Finally, to remove a color, click on the box to the right of the color bar. You can use whatever colors you like for the ramp, but when you are finished, you should have something like the following.

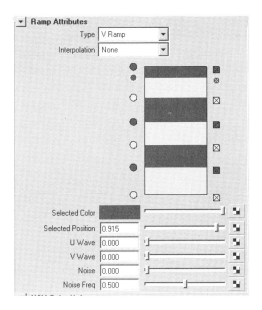

We now have a fully textured ship and ground plane. While none of these materials is terribly complex, they give the ship some color, and add to the cartoonish feel of the world we're creating. To be able to see our ship when we render it, we'll next need to add some lights to the scene.

Lighting the Scene

To light this scene, we'll add four lights: one ambient light to shade the whole scene, and three spotlights. This lighting setup will give the scene a night-time quality, which is a bit more fun than one big light for the sun. Additionally, we'll make two of the lights "track" (or aim toward) the ship at all times.

1. First, let's create our ambient light. Select Rendering from the pop-up menu at the top left of the screen. Then, choose Lights ➤ Create Ambient Light ❏. In the options box, set the intensity to 0.2, and then click Create and Close.

T I P   To see how the scene is lit so far, press the 7 key on your keyboard to go into lighted mode (the scene should be almost dark). Press the 6 key to return to flat shaded mode.

2. Now let's create our spotlights. From the shelf, choose Lights ➤ Create Spot Light ❏. In the option window, click the Reset button, and then set the penumbra angle to 10 (this fades the edges of the spotlight). Click Create and Close. Rename this light **frontSpot** (if the Channel box isn't open, press Ctrl+A to toggle it back on). Press the W key to get into Move mode, and then move the light up and away from the ship, toward the camera. Be sure the light is above the rocket by a significant amount; otherwise, it won't light the ground below the ship (which gives depth and solidity to the scene).

TIP To move your lights, you will need to use the top and side views (use the spacebar to see these views), and scale these views out by holding down the Alt key, along with the left and middle mouse buttons, and dragging to the left in each window pane.

3. Because we want this spotlight to aim at the ship at all times, let's add an aim constraint to it. First, click on any part of the ship; then press the up-arrow key (be sure the Channel box says *rocket* in its title area). Then, holding down the Shift key, click (or drag around) the light, highlighting it as well. Finally, from the Animation menu set (choose Animation from the top-left pop-up menu), choose Constrain ➤ Aim. The focus of the spotlight will now be locked onto the rocket, wherever it goes.

4. We now need to create another light, this one off to the right side of the ship. Create a new spotlight (Lights ➤ Create Spot Light), call it **rightSideSpot**, and move it off to the right of (and above) the ship.

5. We want this light to follow the ship as well, so we'll do the same trick again: First, select the rocket (remember to press the up-arrow), then Shift+select the rightSideSpot light. Finally, choose Constrain ➤ Aim to force the light to look at the ship.

6. Finally, let's create our last spotlight (which will stay pointed at the launch area). Once again, create a spotlight; then name the new light **leftSideSpot**, and move it to the left and above the rocket.

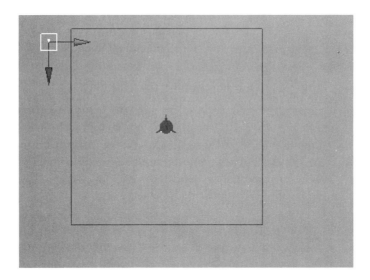

7. As we won't be auto-aiming the light, we'll need to do it manually. In the top view (with the light still selected), from the panel menu at the top of the top view panel, choose Panel ➤ Look Through Selected to change the view to show what the light sees (nothing at this point). Rotate the view until the rocket is centered in the view (hold down the Alt key and drag with the left mouse button). To return to top view, choose Panel ➤ Orthographic ➤ Top.

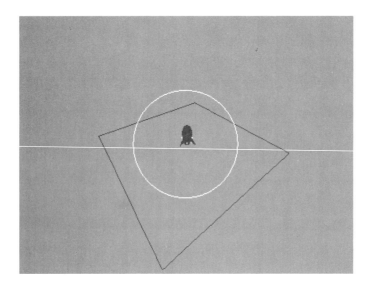

8. To see how your scene is lit, press the 7 key again. It should be well (and evenly) lit across the ship and the ground near it. If not, try moving your lights around, or increasing their intensity.

9. Save your work and take a break. Good job so far!

TIP   It is often difficult to see how well lit your scene is using the flat (openGL) renderer. To get a better view of your scene, choose Render ➢ Render into New Window from the Rendering menu set (the top-left pop-up menu). This will create a quick little rendering of your scene.

Animating the Scene

If things haven't been fun and interesting enough so far, we're really going to have fun here: We'll animate our little ship, and use some of the power of Maya's dynamics engine to bring it back to earth.

Keyframed Animation

First we need to create a keyframe animation of the ship about to take off. For our simple animation, we'll only animate the scale of the ship as it squashes, getting ready for takeoff, and then stretches as it "leaps" off the ground. This is classic cartoon anticipation and overshoot—you'll recognize the effect from any old Tex Avery cartoons you run across.

NOTE   *Keyframe* is an old animation term for important moments in an animation (key frames). In digital animation, you tell the computer which frames are important (the keyframes), and the computer "in-betweens" the rest of the frames between these key frames, creating an animation.

1. To create the initial keyframe, first be sure you're on the first frame of the animation (use the VCR-like controls at the bottom-right of the screen, and check to see that the timeline marker is at 1).

2. Next, select the rocket (be sure it's the whole rocket, and not just the body); then, in the Channel box, drag your mouse over the names of the three scale channels (scale X, Y, and Z). Then, with the right mouse button over the

selected channels, choose (RM choose) Key Selected from the pop-up menu. The channels for scale should turn orange, indicating that they're now keyframed.

3. Once you have created your first keyframe manually, you can make Maya automatically keyframe your channels from that point on. Check to be sure the auto-keyframe option is on by verifying that the key icon at the bottom-right of the screen (below the VCR-like time controls) is red. If it's not, simply click on it to turn it red.

4. Now we need to make our animation longer (it defaults to 24 frames, or one second of animation). In the number field for the end time (to the right of the time range slider), set the frame range to 100 frames—a bit over four seconds.

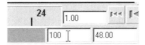

N O T E   Maya defaults to 24 frames per second—film speed. Thus, 24 frames are one second, and 96 frames are four seconds.

5. Move the time marker (the gray bar in the time slider) out to 48 frames (2 seconds) by dragging it across the time slider—or just click about where the 48th frame would be. Be sure your rocket is still selected, and then enter scale mode (R key) and scale down the Y (green) axis so that the rocket becomes shorter (a scale of about 0.7 on the Y axis channel should do). You may notice that this simply shrinks the rocket; we also need to scale out the X and Z axes to make the rocket appear more squashed. While we could do this via the X and Z scale handles, it is easier to do so in the Channel box itself. Click in the scale X box, and then enter a value of 1.4. Do the same in the scale Z box. Your rocket should now look squashed.

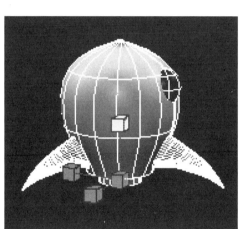

6. We now need to hold this squashed look for some frames (a *hold keyframe*). Move the time marker to frame 60, select the scale X, Y, and Z channel names again, and RM choose Key Selected (alternatively, you could reenter the numbers you had before, forcing Maya to create a new keyframe via the auto-keyframe option).

7. At this point, it's a good idea to play back your animation to see how it looks so far. Click the Rewind button on the VCR-like controls (or press Alt+Shift+V); then click the Play button (or press Alt+V) to play the animation. The rocket should squash down and then hold its appearance—and then the animation loops and repeats itself.

8. Now let's make the rocket stretch out, as if stretching to take off from the ground (don't worry for now that it's not moving up). Move to frame 70 and set the X, Y, and Z scales to 0.7, 1.4, and 0.7, respectively (the rocket should look stretched out now).

9. We need another hold keyframe (with the rocket stretched out), so move to frame 78, choose the scale channels, and RM choose Key Selected once again.

10. Now move to frame 90 (close to four seconds), and reset all the scale channels to 1—the ship will now return to its original shape at 90 frames. When you play back the animation, you should see the rocket squash, preparing for takeoff, then stretch up (as it takes off—don't worry, we'll take care of that next!), and finally return to its original shape. If you don't like how the animation runs, you can Shift+click on any keyframe (highlighting it in red), and then drag that keyframe left or right on the timeline, thereby adjusting the speed of the animation between each keyframe.

Using Dynamics for Animation

We've completed our keyframed animation for this project. Now let's make Maya do the rest of the work. We'll make the ship rise into the air by giving it a force (or impulse), and then drag it back down using gravity. Finally, we'll make the ground and rocket collide. To do all this, we'll use what is known as *rigid body dynamics* to tell Maya what forces act on our object (the rocket). As explained in Chapter 15, Maya (specifically, its *dynamics engine*) will use our input to do all the calculations necessary for realistic movement.

1. First, we need to make both the rocket and ground rigid bodies, so they'll react to each other and the forces we apply to them. Select the ground plane, and then change to the Dynamics menu set (from the pop-up menu at the top left of your screen). Choose Bodies ➤ Create Passive Rigid Body ❑. (Be sure not to select Active!) In the options window, set the Static and Dynamic Friction to 0.5, and set the Bounciness to 0.2. Click Create and Close to create the rigid body.

2. Now let's make the rocket a rigid body. Select any of the rocket's body parts and press the up-arrow (be sure *rocket* is the name selected in the Channel box). Choose Bodies ➤ Create Passive Rigid Body ❑. In the options window, set the rocket's mass to 1000, set the Impulse Y to 5000, and set the Impulse Position Y to 12 (this forces the impulse to be above the rocket's body, so the rocket won't spin around when you launch it). Click Create and Close.

T I P   If you get an error when you try to create the rocket's rigid body, check (using the hypergraph or outliner) to be sure you have erased the two curves for the nozzle and body of the rocket. If you haven't, do so—this should take care of any error messages.

3. With the rocket still selected, choose Fields ➤ Create Gravity ❏. In the options window, set the magnitude of gravity to 25 (this setting is far heavier than Earth's gravity, which is 9.8, but it makes the animation look better!), and then click Create and Close. Because the rocket was selected when you created the gravity field, it will be "attached" to gravity (that is, affected by it).

4. If you play back the animation now, you will see that it looks just the same as before. That's because our rocket is still a passive rigid body (meaning that no forces can affect it). What we have to do is keyframe the rocket to be an active rigid body just at the frame where it should take off. Be sure the rocket is selected, and then move to frame 62. Under the Shapes node (in the Channel box), you should see a channel called Active (toward the bottom) that is set to off. Click once on the text (the word Active), and then RM choose Key Selected to set a keyframe. Now move to frame 63, click in the text box that says *off*, and type in the word **on**. This will set a keyframe, turning the rocket's rigid body on, so it can now be affected by forces.

5. Before you play back the animation, you'll want it to run longer. Set the playback length to 1000 instead of 100. (Type **1000** in the end-time number box just to the right of the time range slider.) The frame range should now go from 1 to 1000. Rewind and play back the animation: you should see the rocket zoom off into parts unknown.

T I P   If the rocket gets stuck in the ground, you've got a *rigid body interpenetration error*, a problem you'll learn more about in Chapter 15. To fix it, move the ground down a bit and run the animation again.

W A R N I N G   When playing back dynamics animations, it is *extremely* important to rewind the animation before you play it back each time. If you don't, Maya will become confused about its calculations, and you will see very strange results!

6. To make our ship stop going up and up, we need to turn off our impulse. Go to frame 104 (with the rocket still selected), select the channel for Impulse Y, and RM choose Key Selected. Move to frame 105, and type 0 in the Impulse Y number field (setting the impulse to 0 from this point on). When you play back the animation, the rocket should rise out of sight, and then, around frame 450, crash back down into the ground, bouncing around until it comes to rest.

TIP   To see the animation better, try zooming your camera back (press Alt with the left and middle mouse buttons, and drag left)—this is called *scaling* the view. Also, if you don't like the way the rocket bounces off the ground, you can set the ground's bounciness setting to lower (or higher), and you can change the rocket's impulse setting from 5000 at the start to some other very similar number (like 5001). This small change will make the bounces go in very different directions.

You should now have a complete rocket animation, using keyframes for part of it, and making Maya do the calculations for the rest. Next, we'll discuss how to make a new camera, and have it aim at the ship at all times; then we'll talk about how to render the whole animation out.

TIP   Save your work and take a break. Good work!

Creating a Follow Camera

As you may have noticed, the default perspective camera's view of this animation leaves something to be desired. What we need is a camera that follows the rocket into the air and back again—we need to aim our camera at the ship, just as we did with the lights.

NOTE   Aiming a camera at an object is not a good idea for realistic animation; it is generally better to keyframe the camera to follow the object's motion, as this introduces "human" errors into the camera tracking (making the motion look like a person operating a camera instead of a computer operating one). For our cartoonish animation, having a camera follow the rocket is all right; however, if you wish, you are welcome to keyframe the motion instead.

1. Create a new camera (Create ➤ Camera) and name it **followCamera**. Using the four view panes, move the camera down the X axis (to the right in the top view), and then move it up a bit off the ground plane—do *not* rotate the camera at this point!

2. Select the rocket, and then Shift-select the new camera. In the animation menu set, choose Constrain ➤ Aim to force the camera to point at the rocket.

3. To look through your new view, choose a panel (the top view, say), and choose Panels ➤ Look Through Selected. Make this your sole viewing pane (press the spacebar), and then play back the animation. You should see the camera follow the rocket up into the air, and then back down again.

4. Save your work.

 T I P   If the camera is too close to the action, or too far away, just zoom your view (Alt+LM and RM buttons and drag) to get a better view.

Rendering the Animation

While watching the animation play in your scene window is great, it's probably a bit bumpy (especially if you have a slower machine). There are two ways to render a cleaner view of your animation: playblasting and final rendering (batch rendering). While a final rendering gives very high-quality results, it takes a great deal of time to produce its results. Playblasting, on the other hand, produces a rougher (flat shaded) look, but goes as fast as your video card can spit out images. Thus, for a quick look at the animation, playblasting is a far better choice than a final rendering.

Playblasting the animation is one step: Choose Window ➣ Playblast and watch as Maya creates an animation for you, using the basic shading mode of your computer. Once the animation is complete, you will be able to view it in its own little movie window. You'll learn more about playblasting in Chapter 11.

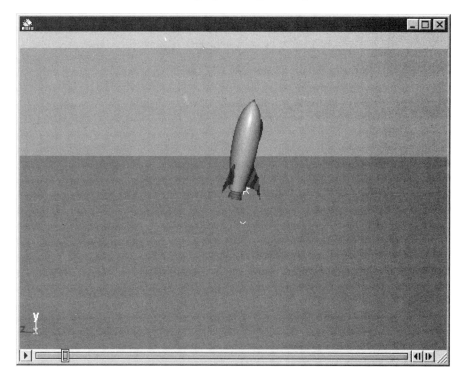

Rendering the final product is a bit more complex and takes much longer. Essentially, a final (batch) rendering creates a high-quality "snapshot" of each frame of the animation, using all the lighting, material, and animation information your scene can provide. The results of a final rendering can be excellent, but it is a fairly slow process, as your computer has to do many calculations for every pixel of every image. Thus, you will only want to proceed with these steps when you're sure you're happy with your animation.

1. Choose Window ➤ Render Globals to open the Render Globals option window. In the Image File Output section, set the Frame/Animation Extension to **name.ext.#**, set the end frame to about 700 (you want to be sure it's a large enough number that the rocket has come to rest first), set the Frame Padding to 4 (this adds zeroes before your frame number, so the frame will be numbered render.001, render.002, and so forth, instead of render.1, render.2, etc.), and set the active Camera to followCamera (otherwise Maya will use the default persp camera, and you will waste your rendering time).

2. Twirl down the Resolution arrow, and set the Render Resolution to 320×240.

3. Twirl down the Anti-aliasing Quality arrow, and set the Presets field to Intermediate Quality (this makes for faster rendering, but with decent quality).

4. When you have finished your settings, close the Render Globals window, and open the Rendering menu set (the top-left pop-up menu). Choose Render ➤ (Save) Batch Render. Type in a name (like **rocketRender**) in the File box, and click Save/Render.

5. Maya will render out all 700 frames of the animation (which will take some time). You can view the progress of each frame in the Feedback line (at the bottom-right of the screen), or, to view the current frame that is rendering, choose Render ➤ Show Batch Render. To cancel the render at any time, choose Render ➤ Cancel Batch Render.

6. When the rendering job is finished, you can view it using the fcheck utility. In IRIX, type **fcheck** in a shell window; in NT, choose Run (from the Start menu), and type **fcheck** in the text field. A window will open, letting you navigate to your images directory (it should find this for you automatically). Choose the first frame of your animation and hit OK. Fcheck will cycle all frames into memory and then play back the animation at full speed.

Congratulations! You have modeled, textured, lit, animated and rendered an animation in Maya. If patting yourself on the back isn't your style, you can move on to the "advanced" section (next), where you will learn how to create a particle exhaust trail for the rocket. If this was enough practice for a start, just skip right on to Chapter 2 and learn about the Maya interface.

Advanced Topic: Adding Exhaust

If you've worked extensively with other animation packages, what we've done so far may seem fairly straightforward. In that case, you're probably ready to explore another area of Maya dynamics, namely particles. We'll use a particle emitter to create a shower of particles, and then texture them to look like smoke and flames. To make it appear that the "exhaust" is powering the rocket, we'll turn the emitter on and off (via keyframes) at the appropriate moments.

1. First, we need to create our emitter. Select the nozzle on the rocket—this will be the emitter's "parent," forcing the emitter to go along for the ride when the rocket launches. In the Dynamics menu set (the top-left pop-up menu), choose Particles ➤ Add Emitter ❏. In the options window, make the name of the emitter **exhaustEmitter**, set the emitter type to Directional, set the Rate to 0, and the Spread to 0.3. Twirl down the Emission Direction arrow, and set the DirectionY to –1 (so the emitter points downward). Twirl down the Emission Speed arrow and set the Speed to 60. Finally, click Add and Close. You now have a particle emitter attached to the nozzle of the rocket.

2. Right now (if you play back the animation), the particle emitter will shoot out no particles, because its rate is set to 0 particles per second. Just before the rocket takes off (frame 63) we need to turn on the "engine"—our particles. Go to frame 59, select the Rate channel text for the emitter in the Channel box , and RM choose Key Selected to set a keyframe at 0 for this frame.

3. Now go to frame 60 and set a rate of 200 so there are suddenly many particles shooting out from the ship. If you play back the animation now, a shower of particles (points by default; we'll fix that in a moment) will shoot out from the exhaust nozzle.

4. Now we need to turn off our rocket. Go to frame 104 and set a keyframe for the Rate at 200 (select the Rate text, and RM choose Key Selected). Now, at frame 105 (where the impulse turns off as well), set a new keyframe for Rate at 0. When you now play back the animation, the particles will stop coming out of the rocket at frame 105—however, the particles hang around forever (they never die). We need to give our particles a life span so they will die off like good flames should.

5. With the emitter still selected, press Ctrl+A to toggle on the Attribute Editor. Once in the Attribute Editor, click on the particleShape1 tab at the top; then, in the Add Dynamic Attributes section, click the Lifespan button. In the resulting window, choose Add Per Object Attribute, and click the Add Attribute button.

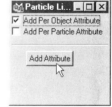

6. If you now scroll back up to the Render Attributes section, you will see that a new attribute, Lifespan, has been added with a default value of 1 (for one second). As this value is fine for our purposes, we can leave it at 1 second. When you now play back the animation, you should see the particles die out a second after they are created (thus the trail of particles follows the rocket up as it takes off). Save your work.

7. Now that we have a good trail of particles to work with, let's change the rendering type from points to something more interesting. In the Attribute Editor (with the particleShape1 node still selected), under the Render Attributes section, set the Render Type to Cloud (s/w—for software rendered). Next, click the Current Render Type button to add the attributes that belong with the cloud render type.

8. In the new fields, make the radius 1, the Surface Shading 1, and the Threshold 0.5. When you play back the animation (which will now run significantly slower), you should see that the exhaust particles are now spheres. To see what they would look like in a real rendering, choose Render ➤ Render into New Window (from the Rendering menu set).

9. Now we're closing in on a good exhaust cloud. The last piece of the puzzle is to create a texture for the particles. Play the animation to a frame where the particles are showing, then open the hypershade (Window ➤ Hypershade). To create a cloud texture, we need to create a volumetric texture. To do so, scroll down the left-hand window until you reach Create: Materials, and click the + sign to the left of the Materials folder. A Volume folder will appear below the materials swatches, and clicking on it will open the volume materials. MM drag the particleCloud material (the light blue ball) onto the right-hand window of the hypershade, and then rename the material **exhaustVM**.

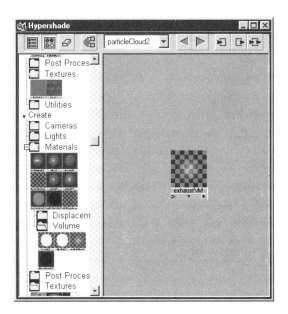

10. MM drag the material onto the exhaust particles, move over to the Attribute Editor, and set the color of the material to a bright yellow. Set the Transparency to a light gray (by moving the slider to the right), and set the Glow Intensity to 0.5. Test render your current frame—the exhaust should now glow a bright yellow as it is emitted from the nozzle. If you're not satisfied with the look of the exhaust, try adjusting some of the material settings or the render attributes of the particleShape1 node. Save your work again.

When you are satisfied with the look of your exhaust, you can render out the entire animation sequence (see the rendering section, above) to see how things look with your exhaust plume. To compare your work with mine, you can take a look at 01rocket.mov on the CD-ROM.

Summary

Congratulations! You have completed a real-world animation project your first time out. If your work is not up to the way you would like it, that's all right: it can take quite a while to get an animation package producing just what you had in mind. No matter how you did, you can always return to this project as you continue through this book.

You may find that after a few more chapters, you'd like to give this project another try. My suggestion in that case is to use this chapter as a reference, not a guide. In other words, try to do the work by yourself, and read the directions here only when you get stuck. In this way, you'll make the project your own, and you'll learn even more from it.

Whether you tried this rocket animation with years of digital 3D experience under your belt or it was your first foray into the wonderful world of 3D, you should see by now how powerful the Maya environment can be. Now that you have an idea of what Maya can do, it's time to learn why and how Maya does what it does. Throughout this book, we'll give you a great deal more explanation about what we're doing than we did in this chapter, but you'll also still be working on "real world" projects, refining both your understanding of and skill with Maya. You've taken your first step into the world of Maya—now use this book as your guide to a journey through your new and exciting world.

chapter 2

THE MAYA
INTERFACE

Featuring

THE MAYA INTERFACE

f you did the modeling and animation work in Chapter 1, you have certainly seen the power Maya can bring to your work. You may, however, have been a bit overwhelmed by the program's vast range and depth, especially if you are new to Maya. But as you'll see, Maya's user interface has been carefully and intelligently designed to make all this power easily accessible to new users—and to allow experienced users to customize it to meet the needs of particular projects. In this and the following two chapters, we will back off for a bit from specific projects and explore in more depth some of the interface and tools Maya has and how to make these elements work for you. If you are already very familiar with the Maya interface, you may wish to skip these chapters; however, we will cover several aspects of the program that have changed significantly in version 2, so you should at least skim through to find out about these new features. If you are new to Maya, reading these three chapters should get you up to speed to handle the rest of this book.

What's New in Maya 2

While the Maya interface may at first glance appear much as it did in version 1, there are many significant changes—too many, in fact, to detail here. Here are some highlights of the revised interface:

- A new Create menu that contains all object-creation items (except lights), and replaces the more awkward Primitives menu.
- The Hypershade, a Hypergraph-like window for the creation, modification, and connection of materials and textures.
- The Visor, a sub-window of the Hypershade, which allows you to create, view, and manage images, textures, and materials.
- A new, spreadsheet-type Component Editor.
- A new Relationship editor, which allows you to manage the relationship of sets, partitions, light linking, and other matters from just one window.
- All Maya buttons, fields, icons, and sliders now have pop-up text that describes the function.
- Maya Complete adds Artisan and F/X tools, built-in, while Maya Unlimited also provides Cloth, Fur, and Maya Live.

What's Behind the Maya Interface?

Maya (from the Sanskrit word for "world of illusion") is a program designed to produce groundbreaking, photorealistic models and animations. Built into this program are an abundance of tools and "subtools" that can overwhelm even the most wizened old 3D artist. To make all of Maya's tools work together in a logical, consistent, and intuitive manner is a monumental task. In fact, it is still ongoing, as witnessed by the changes to version 2 of the program. Still, the basic structure of the Maya interface is not only solid enough for most users to quickly learn and use, it is so revolutionary and intuitive that several other 3D software manufacturers are copying much of Maya's look.

What makes Maya different? First, interacting with it is very intuitive, for several reasons. All scene windows, plus the Hypershade and Hypergraph windows, are easily navigated via the same keyboard and mouse combinations for zooming, tracking, and rotation (in perspective camera views only). Because navigating all these windows is the same, you only have to learn one set of commands to get around Maya's world. Moving objects around a Maya scene window is similarly intuitive: Select the move, scale, or rotation (or any other) tool, grab a manipulator handle (or the center box, to

PART 1

manipulate on all axes simultaneously), and alter the object. To try out an example, you can create a new scene in Maya, add a ball (by clicking the sphere object in the toolbar, or by choosing Create ≻ NURBS Primitives ≻ Sphere). Now rotate around the ball by holding the Alt key down and pressing the left mouse button. This type of rotation is known as *camera*, or *scene* rotation. To rotate the ball itself, choose the rotate tool from the toolbar (or simply press the E key on the keyboard), then choose any of the manipulator rings around the ball and rotate it by dragging with the left mouse button. To move an object, choose the move tool (or press the W key). To scale, choose the scale tool (or press the R key).

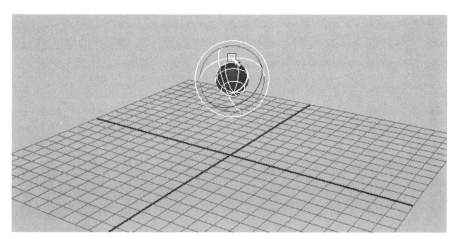

Three-Button Mouse Conventions in Maya

Maya makes extensive use of all three mouse buttons. This book—like the Maya manuals—uses a shorthand notation to describe the basic mouse operations.

Click, or **LM click**, means to click (press and release) with the left mouse button.

Drag, or **LM drag**, means to click the left mouse button, hold it down, and drag.

Shift+click means to LM click, then hold down the Shift key, and click another item.

Choose means to either click or hold the left mouse button down and choose an item from a menu.

MM drag means to click and drag with the middle mouse button.

RM choose means to hold the right mouse button down (in a specified area) and choose an item from the pop-up contextual menu.

Continued on next page

Rotate view means to rotate the (perspective) camera; that is, hold the Alt key and the left mouse button down, and then drag in the perspective window to rotate the view.

Move view means to move (any) camera; that is, hold the Alt key and the middle mouse button down, and then drag in any scene window to move the view.

Scale view means to scale—or zoom—(any) camera; that is, hold the Alt key and the left and middle mouse buttons down, and then drag in any scene window to scale (or zoom) the view in or out.

Another powerful difference between Maya and other packages lies in how you interact with Maya's GUI (its graphical user interface). There are nearly always two or more ways to accomplish a task—called *workflows*—in Maya. For example, if you prefer not to use menus on top of the screen, you can use Maya's hotbox (which is itself customizable) to access all menus, or any grouping therein, by merely pressing and holding the spacebar.

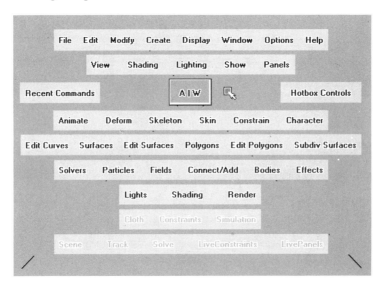

You can also, as noted before, create items via the toolbar or, equivalently, via menu commands. Most impressive, however, is that Maya will let *you* decide how you interact with it. If you are not satisfied with Maya's interface, you have many ways you can alter it, including creating marking menus, toolbar buttons, and hot keys. All of these can be created fairly quickly (especially the toolbar buttons) but can contain extremely complex instructions.

N O T E   For more on how to tune Maya's GUI for your own work, see Chapter 3, "Techniques for Speeding up Workflow," or Chapter 16, "MEL Basics."

Finally, Maya's plug-in architecture (or API) and especially its built-in scripting language, MEL, are very open and comprehensive. Because of Maya's API, plug-ins (like the built-in Artisan and FX) fit seamlessly into the program, so much so that it is often difficult to determine where the main program stops and the plug-in begins. While the API is fairly complex and is best left to knowledgeable programmers, MEL (or *Maya Embedded Language*) is a reasonably simple scripting language that gives just about anyone with a bit of programming experience access to nearly all of Maya's very powerful features in a program environment. Not only can you create specialized, time-saving scripts with MEL, you can also create entire windows, or even a whole new GUI for the program (because Maya's entire GUI is built on MEL scripts in the first place). This feature can allow, for example, a technical director to create a custom interface for her artists, allowing them to deal with character animation without their having to know anything about the low-level details of the construction and "stringing" (or animation setup) of the character.

As should be obvious from these features, Maya provides a very modern, intuitive, and customizable environment for you. Whether you are a shop of one person or one hundred, Maya's adjustable interface will get you building complex animations far more quickly than other—even more expensive—packages. Let's now take a more thorough tour through the Maya interface, looking at several important areas of the GUI.

Interface Elements

Although there are many elements to Maya, they can be grouped into about nine categories. We will work through each category in turn.

Scene Windows

The scene windows are your primary interface with the objects (and lights and cameras) you create. When you open a new Maya scene, it opens the default configuration, which is one large scene window (the default perspective camera), alongside either the Channel box (or the Attribute Editor if your preferences are set to toggle between the Attribute Editor and the Channel box).

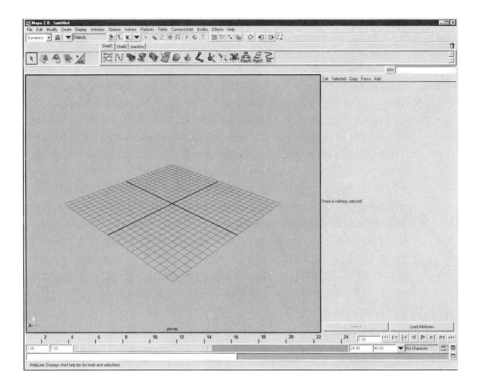

TIP   New to Maya 2 is that you can set the Attribute Editor to be a window adjacent to the perspective window (replacing the Channel box), rather than a floating window. You can then toggle between the Attribute Editor and the Channel box by pressing Alt+A. Should you wish to force the Attribute Editor to toggle with the Channel box, choose Options ➢ UI Preferences and select the Open Attribute Editor In Main Maya Window radio button.

Once the default window is open, you can select the perspective view by clicking anywhere inside the window. When this (or any) window is selected, its borders turn blue. At this point, you can rotate, scale, or translate the view to adjust what you see in this window (for specifics on how to do this, please see the earlier sidebar on mouse conventions). The default scene window is called the *Persp* (for perspective) view and is just the view from the default perspective camera that Maya builds upon opening a new scene.

TIP You can build other perspective cameras by choosing Create ➢ Camera. To view the scene through this new camera, select the camera (click on it in the scene window or choose it in the Hypergraph or Outliner), and choose Panels ➢ Look Through Selected, or, equivalently, choose Panels ➢ Perspective ➢ camera1.

In addition to the default perspective camera, Maya also creates three orthographic views—Top, Side, and Front—that you can also see (in what's called a "four view" layout) by selecting the perspective window and then quickly pressing and releasing the spacebar.

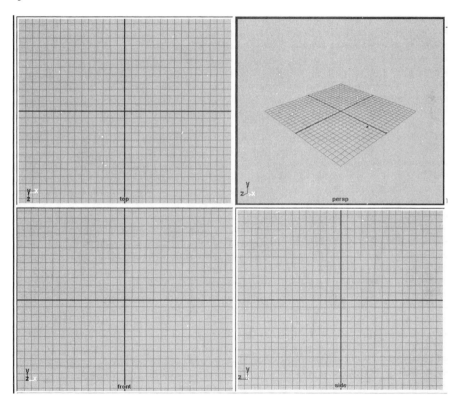

To make one of the orthographic views fill the screen, click in it (to select this window), and press and release the spacebar again. Being able to switch quickly between different view layouts and window sizes greatly speeds up your workflow in Maya, as no extensive menu selection process is required to rapidly change views.

TIP To switch views in Maya without losing your current selection, *MM* click in the view you wish to activate (e.g., the front view), then press the space bar.

Orthographic and Perspective Views

An orthographic view is a nonperspective view from a 90 degree (or orthogonal) angle. Because these are not perspective views, they do not reduce the size of objects as they move away from the camera. A perspective view of a row of columns, for example, would show the back column as smaller than the one nearest the camera, as the further an object gets from a camera, the smaller it appears. An orthographic view, on the other hand, will show all columns as the same size, as there is no scale reduction (perspective) in this view. An orthographic view may be thought of as similar to a blueprint drawing, while a perspective view is like a camera picture.

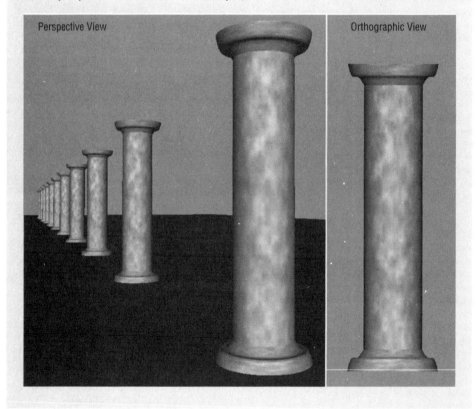

Perspective View

Orthographic View

Moving in Scene Windows

Moving around scene windows is fairly straightforward, once you learn the key and mouse combinations for doing so. Additionally, because you move in all scene windows (plus the Hypergraph and Hypershade) using these same commands, once you learn how to move in one window, you can move in all. As the perspective window has the most options (you can rotate as well as zoom and translate), let's quickly look at how to maneuver around the default perspective window.

Open a new scene in Maya; then hold down the Alt key and the left mouse button and drag the mouse around. The scene should spin around as you drag the mouse.

T I P   If the scene does not rotate as you drag (you may see the cursor become a circle with a line through it), you may be in an orthographic view, which does not allow rotations. To move to a perspective view, hit the spacebar to show the four-view layout; then click in the perspective window (top right) and hit the spacebar again.

To translate a scene (move up/down or left/right), hold the Alt key down once again, hold down the middle mouse button (MMB), and drag the mouse around. You will see the scene move around with the mouse movements (note that the camera is actually moving opposite to your mouse movements: as you drag right, the camera moves left, so the objects appear to move right. You can see this clearly if you make cameras visible and look at the camera in a different view as you drag).

To scale your view (zoom the camera in and out), hold down the Alt key once again, hold down both the left and middle mouse buttons, and drag. As you drag right, the scene grows larger (you're zooming in); as you drag left, the scene grows smaller (you're zooming out). If you wish to quickly zoom into a specific area of your scene, hold down the Alt and Ctrl keys, and then drag (with the left mouse button only) a box around the area of the scene you are interested in, starting on the left side. When you release the mouse, the scene will zoom in, covering the area you outlined. If you drag the mouse from right to left, the scene will zoom out so that the entire scene window you start with fits into the box you drag (the smaller your box, the further out you zoom). If you now open the Hypergraph or Hypershade (Window ➢ Hypergraph or Window ➢ Hypershade), you can use the same key/mouse combinations to scale or move around either of these windows. You will note, however, that you cannot rotate either of these views, as this would accomplish nothing useful.

N O T E   You can think of the Alt key as the "movement key." Whenever you hold down the Alt key, you are in move mode, rather than in object manipulation (or some other) mode. The consistent use of the Alt key for movement is just one more example of the thought that has gone into the Maya interface.

Scene Objects

Scene *objects* (geometry, curves, cameras, and lights) are the fundamental building blocks from which you create a Maya scene or animation. The procedure for creating and manipulating any object is generally the same: Create the object (most often in the Create menu), choose a manipulation tool (like Translate or Rotate), and alter the object. You can also adjust the pivot point (or "center") of an object, and you can manipulate the individual components of geometric objects.

Creating Scene Objects

Because most scene objects are created in very much the same fashion, we'll go through a few representative examples here, rather than a thorough examination of how to create all possible objects in Maya. Should you have specific questions about creating a type of object that is not covered here, you can always check Maya's online documentation (accessed via the Help menu).

T I P   Maya's built-in help files are a great (and easy) resource. To access them, just use the Help menu, and choose Maya Library (or the specific aspect of the program you are inter- ested in) from the Help menu. Within the startup window (which will open in a Web browser, as it is an HTML document), you will be able to search for a term, browse through a complete index of all Maya documents (the index alone is about 1.7MB of data!), or read any of the Maya manuals in electronic form.

To create a piece of geometry (a sphere or cone, for example), you choose the type of geometry you wish to create from the Create menu. For a three-dimensional object (like a torus or a cube), you can choose from either polygonal or NURBS primitives. Using the NURBS option, you can also select a two-dimensional (non-surface) square or circle. When you create an object, you can either use the last saved settings or open the Creation Options window and adjust the object's settings to what you desire before creating it.

N O T E   NURBS (or Non-Uniform Rational B-Spline) objects are created via a series of curves (or *isoparms*) that are mathematically derived from several points (control vertices, or CVs). NURBS surfaces are more complex to calculate, but they can be warped and twisted more before they show excessive unnatural creasing. Polygonal surfaces, on the other hand, are created by placing many small triangular or rectangular surfaces together. Polys are simpler to calculate—at least for simple surfaces—but tend to show their con- stituent blocks if they are bent or distorted too much—especially if the surfaces are cre- ated with a minimal number of polygons, or facets. NURBS surfaces tend to be better suited to organic forms (like bodies), while polygonal surfaces generally work better for more mechanical objects (like space ships); but this is by no means a hard-and-fast rule.

As an example, let's create a default polygonal sphere, and then use the options box to create a NURBS cylinder. To create the poly sphere, simply choose Create ➤ Polygon Primitives ➤ Sphere. On releasing the mouse, you should see a sphere appear at the center of Maya's default grid. If you look closely, you will note that the sphere consists of many rectangular objects (more accurately called quadrilaterals) that butt up against each other, forming the sphere. Now move the sphere aside (press the W key and move the sphere away from the center of the grid) and create a NURBS cylinder with nondefault options. To access the options window of the NURBS cylinder, choose Create ➤ NURBS Primitives ➤ Cylinder ❏ (choosing the ❏ symbol—the *option box*—in a Maya menu item always brings up an option window). Upon releasing the mouse button, you should see the following window.

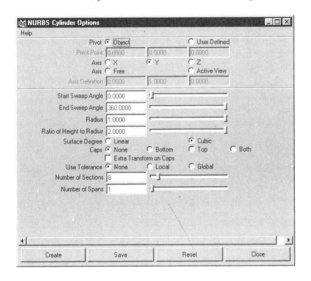

This window provides a great number of options. You can define any of the following:

- the pivot point
- the axis the cylinder will use as its long axis
- the start and end angles of the cylinder
- the radius
- the height-to-radius ratio (a higher number will make a taller cylinder)
- the number of spans (vertical pieces) and sections (horizontal pieces) that make up the cylinder

For the purposes of this little example, try setting the End Sweep Angle to 270 (this will create a three-quarters cylinder), the Height to Radius to 4 (making the cylinder taller), and the Caps option to Both (creating a cap on both the top and bottom of the cylinder). When you click the Create button at the bottom, you should get an object like this:

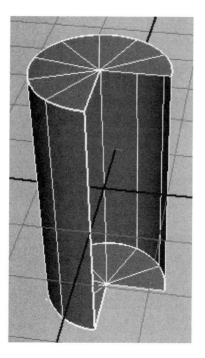

 T I P   You can almost always reset an object to its default settings by using the Reset button in the options window.

 T I P   To get a smoothly shaded object (instead of a wireframe), press the 6 key on your keyboard (not the numeric keypad). To view an object at a higher resolution, press the 3 key. The image above uses these settings to display the cylinder.

Creating a camera object is as simple as creating a geometry object. Choose Create ➢ Camera and a new perspective camera (initially called camera1, camera2, etc., until you save it with a more specific name) is created. To adjust the camera's options as you create it, choose the option box (❏), and change the camera's settings. While all the settings in the camera options box are a bit much for an introductory chapter, most are fairly self-explanatory to anyone familiar with photography or 3D animation.

N O T E   For more on camera options and other rendering basics, please see Chapter 18.

Some notable options are that you can make any new camera orthographic (as opposed to perspective), you have control over near and far clipping planes (where the camera stops "seeing" objects that are too far away or too close), and you can choose to have two or three nodes on the camera (allowing you to manipulate where the camera is looking, for example, via a manipulator handle outside the camera itself). Try creating a camera with two nodes (under Animation options). When you create this camera, it will automatically have a second manipulator handle you can move (by pressing the W key and dragging the handle around), and the camera follows where the manipulator handle goes.

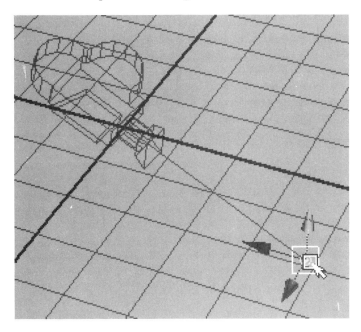

To create lights, use the Lights menu (under the Rendering menu set, or via the hotbox).

N O T E   Maya has four menu sets: Animation, Modeling, Dynamics, and Rendering. To switch between them, use the pop-up menu on the left of the toolbar to select the appropriate set. Optionally, you can choose Hotbox Controls ➣ Show All (brought up by pressing the spacebar); the hotbox will then show all menu sets.

PART 1

Maya Fundamentals

When creating lights, you can choose from Ambient (a light which fills all space evenly, like indirect sunlight in a room), Directional (parallel light rays from one source, mimicking direct sunlight), Point (radial light like that from a bare light bulb), and Spot (light as from a theatrical spot light). For example, create a spot light (Lights ➤ Create Spot Light ❏) with the following options: Intensity 1.5, Cone Angle 50, Penumbra 10, and Color a light blue (click the default white color chip to bring up the color picker; then choose a light blue color). The penumbra controls how

quickly your spotlight "fades out" around its edges: a value of 0 means that the spotlight goes from full intensity to 0 at its edges (not a very natural look); a value of 10 or 20 degrees makes the spotlight fade out from full intensity to 0 over that number of degrees. If your spotlight were aimed at a simple plane, the rendered image would look something like the light on the right (on the left is a spotlight with a penumbra of 0).

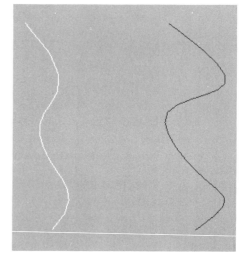

You can also create either CV (control vertex) or EP (Edit Point) curves via the Create menu (Create ➤ EP Curve Tool or CV Curve Tool). The CV Curve Tool creates a CV with each click of the mouse. The EP Curve Tool creates Edit Points as you click the mouse button. Control vertices lie off the curve they control, while Edit Points lie on the curve. Each type of curve tool is useful under certain circumstances—the basic rule of thumb is that for smoother curves, use the CV curve tool, while for more tightly controlled curves, use the EP curve tool. In the following image, matching a CV curve and an EP curve created with identical mouse clicks, note that the CV curve (on the left) is smoother, its extremes much less pronounced than the EP curve (on the right), as the CV curve is not forced to pass through each point you define, whereas the EP curve must.

N O T E   After an EP curve is created, it is automatically converted into a CV curve. You can see this by switching to component mode and noting that the edit points have changed into CVs, and that their position is no longer the same.

To create, say, a CV curve, choose Create ➤ CV Curve Tool (or click the CV Curve Tool button on Shelf 1), and then click several times in the scene window with the mouse. You can also drag the points around as you create them, or even erase points by hitting the Delete or Backspace key, or by pressing the Z key to undo the last action. When you are satisfied with the curve, hit the Enter key, and the curve is constructed.

Moving Scene Objects

Once you have created an object, you will probably wish to move, rotate, and/or scale it. Because the procedures are the same for all objects (and lights, cameras, and curves), let's just use a cylinder as an example here. Create a new cylinder with default options (Create ➤ NURBS Primitives ➤ Cylinder ❏; then hit the Reset button, followed by the Create and Close buttons). To move this cylinder, press the W key on the keyboard—you should now see a *move tool manipulator handle* that allows you to move the cylinder on any or all axes.

 T I P   If you do not see the manipulator handle, be sure the cylinder is highlighted by clicking (or click+dragging) on it.

To move the cylinder on the X axis only, click and drag on the red arrow; to move on the Y axis, click and drag on the green arrow; to move on the Z axis, click and drag on the blue arrow. To move the object freely in all directions, click and drag on the yellow box at the center of the manipulator handles. Try moving the object up a little on the Y axis and to the right on the X axis.

 N O T E   All manipulator handle colors are consistent with the axis marker, on the bottom-left of a scene window—X is red, Y is green, and Z is blue. This consistency lets you know what axis you are adjusting, no matter from what angle you are viewing the scene.

To scale the cylinder, press the R key, and then scale the object on the X (red), Y (green), or Z (blue) axis—or click and drag on the yellow box at the center of the manipulator to scale on all axes simultaneously. Try scaling the cylinder up on the Y axis and then out in all directions, as shown on the left below.

To rotate the cylinder, press the E key, and then rotate around the X (red), Y (green), or Z (blue) axes—or click the yellow circle on the outside to rotate on all axes at once (rotating on all axes at once is difficult to control and therefore not advisable). Try rotating clockwise on the Z axis and then counter-clockwise on the X axis, as shown on the right below.

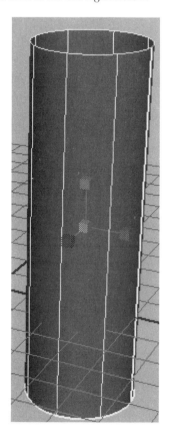
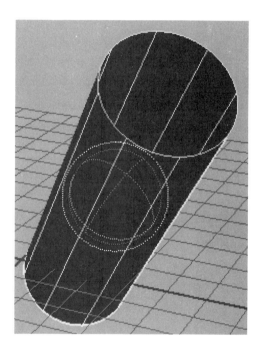

N O T E   Manipulator controls have their shortcut keys arranged so that they follow the top row of a QWERTY keyboard—Q for select, W for move, E for rotate, R for scale, T for the Manipulator tool, and Y for the Last Used Tool (like the CV curve tool, for example). This layout makes the manipulator tools very easy to access, and it's easy to remember their shortcut keys.

Finally, it is possible to move the pivot point of your cylinder (or any object) so that it is not in the object's center. To move the pivot point, press the Insert key on your keyboard (turning the manipulator handle into the pivot-point handle); then move the handle to where you want the object's center of rotation, movement, or scaling to be. Try moving the pivot point of the cylinder to its bottom, so that any further rotation will occur from that point.

T I P   Once you have moved the pivot point, you must return the manipulator to its "normal" state by pressing the Insert key once again.

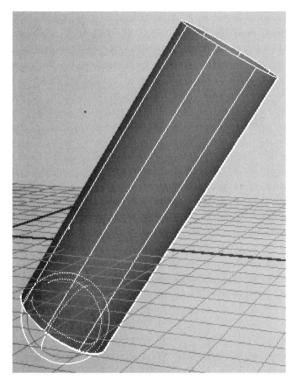

Objects versus Components

All geometric objects are made up of component elements. When you are in object mode, clicking or dragging on any part of an object selects the entire object. In component mode, however, you can choose only some pieces of an object to manipulate. Using the cylinder from the last section as an example (just create a default cylinder if you've deleted it), select the object (so it turns green) while in object mode and choose the Select By Component Type button (or just press the F8 key) to change to component mode. You will now see the CVs that make up the cylinder—if you had created a polygonal cylinder, you would see the points defining the edges of the polygonal facets.

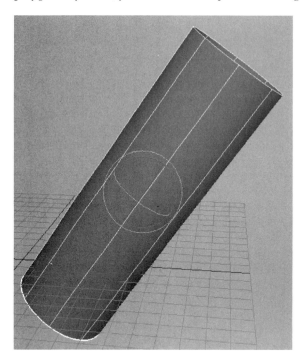

As shown below, the Select By Component Type button is on the Status line, just to the right of the word *Objects* (or *Components*, if that is selected). The leftmost of these three buttons is Select by Hierarchy; the middle button is Select by Object; the right button is Select by Component Type.

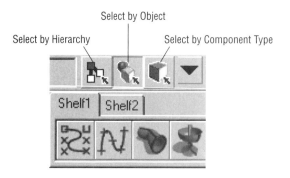

You can adjust components of an object just as you would an object itself by using the move, rotate, and scale tools. Try selecting the top row of CVs on the cylinder (drag a square around them), then moving them up some, scaling them out on the X and Z axes, and rotating them around a bit.

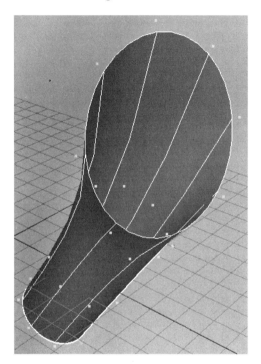

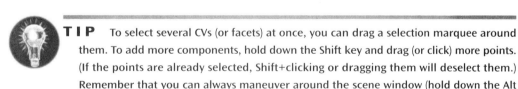

T I P   To select several CVs (or facets) at once, you can drag a selection marquee around them. To add more components, hold down the Shift key and drag (or click) more points. (If the points are already selected, Shift+clicking or dragging them will deselect them.) Remember that you can always maneuver around the scene window (hold down the Alt key as you drag the mouse) to make the selection easier.

If you now switch back to object mode, you will once again be able to choose and manipulate the entire object. Modeling (and even animation) is often a dance between object-mode and component-mode manipulation of your objects, and remembering that the F8 key switches between these two modes can be a real time saver.

Selecting by Component Type

One of the trickier aspects of Maya (at least for me) is picking the proper component of an object when in component mode. There are many types of components you can select, including CVs, surfaces, curves, dynamic objects, and so forth (and there are usually several options in each of these choices), but there are only two ways to make these selections. One method is more thorough; the other is better suited to quick selections of the most common component types.

The quicker, easier method for selecting specific component types is to use a contextual menu while your mouse is over an object. To try this, create a sphere in an empty scene and then, with your mouse over the sphere, hold down the right mouse button. You will be presented with several options for component masking, plus a menu of actions you can perform on the object (such as templating or untemplating it).

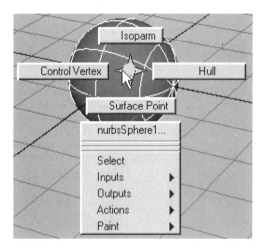

By selecting Control Vertex (for example) from this pop-up menu, you can easily move into component selection mode for CVs, and begin manipulating your CVs as you wish. To return to object mode, press the F8 key twice.

While the contextual menu method is quick and easy, it does not give you access to all the component types you might wish to choose from. To choose a component type not listed in the pop-up menu, you need to use the Status line. To the right of the Object/Component text field and Hierarchy/Object/Component icons is a set of eight blue icons, each representing a class of components you can enable or disable in your selection process. To the left of these icons is a black triangle; this allows you to enable or disable all objects for selection. The component types you enable here will then be available when you drag your mouse over an object in component mode.

WARNING If you turn off all components, you will not be able to select anything in the scene window—including objects in object mode! This is a good place to look first if you discover you cannot choose any objects in a scene.

If you hold down the right mouse button on any of the blue icons, you will see a menu of subtypes you can either enable (check) or disable (uncheck) for component selection. Enabling or disabling component types is known as *selection masking*, and it's a great way to simplify the task of picking a specific object or component in a complex scene. If you are not familiar with components or selection masking, try playing around with these options in Maya before going on.

Window Layouts

In addition to the default window layout (the perspective view plus either the Channel box or the Attribute Editor), there are many other built-in layouts Maya provides, and—as is consistent with the Maya interface philosophy—if you wish, you can create your own.

Built-in Layouts

Maya offers two types of built-in layouts: generic layouts and prebuilt, or saved ones. Generic layouts are just basic layouts elements (like a four-view layout), while saved layouts are useful combinations of the basic elements prebuilt into layouts for different purposes. To begin with, let's look at how to access a generic layout. Under the Panels ➤ Layouts menu (accessed either via the Panels menu in the scene panel, or, as shown below, the hotbox) are several layout choices for your scene windows.

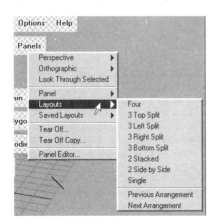

Choosing the Four layout (the first choice) will place the view you currently have active (often the perspective view) in the upper-left quadrant of a four-view layout. (Note that this is different from the layout you get by pressing the spacebar, as the perspective view—or whichever view you have active—ends up in the top-left quadrant, instead of the usual top-right.) The 3 Top/Left/Right/Bottom Split views place the active window on the top (or left/right/bottom) half of the screen, then split this view into two; the other half of the screen has a single view window. The 2 Stacked or Side by Side layouts are similar, except that they don't split the active view in half (thus the active view and one other view share the screen space evenly, either top-and-bottom or left-and-right). There is also a single view, which is the same as selecting a view and pressing the spacebar to make it fill the entire screen.

While the generic views can be useful (especially for building your own layouts—discussed below), the prebuilt layouts are more commonly used because they fulfil specific needs. To access the saved layouts, choose Panels ➤ Saved Layouts and then select a saved layout to use.

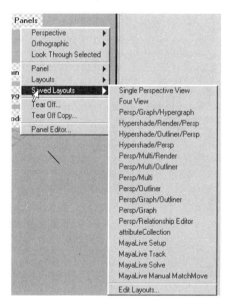

Single Perspective View and Four View are the views you are already familiar with. Rather than look at each saved layout in a list, let's examine just a few—once you understand a couple of the saved layouts, the rest are fairly self-explanatory. The Persp/Graph/Hypergraph is a generic three view (as described above) with the top half

split between the perspective view and the Hypergraph, while the bottom half of the screen is occupied by the Graph Editor. This view was created from the generic 3 Top Split view by changing each panel to the Perspective/Hypergraph/Graph Editor view and then saving it. New in version 2 of Maya are several layouts involving the Hypershade. The Hypershade/Outliner/Persp view is a generic 3 Bottom Split, with the Hypershade occupying the top half of the screen and the Outliner and perspective view splitting the bottom half. Also new in version 2 is the Persp/Relationship Editor layout, which stacks the perspective view on top of the Relationship Editor. Toward the bottom of the menu are several layouts specifically for use with Maya Live, including Maya Live Setup, Track, Solve, and Manual MatchMove.

Building Your Own Layout

If the prebuilt Maya layouts don't quite fit your needs, never fear: the final choice in the Saved Layouts menu (Edit Layouts) lets you create and save your own layout for later use. You can even erase any or all of the prebuilt layouts from the menu.

WARNING   If you decide to erase a saved layout, be sure that you (or anyone else working on your machine) is not interested in using it any further. To get the layout back, you'll either have to reconstruct it manually or reinstall Maya.

As an example of how to create your own layout for later use, let's create a layout with the perspective view filling half the screen on the top, and the bottom being split between the Hypergraph and the Hypershade. (This can be a useful layout if you need to connect several materials to several objects at a time, as selecting the objects in the perspective window can become tedious.) As with most things in Maya, you have a choice about how to create your new layout: you can either start from a generic layout or modify one of the prebuilt ones. Although starting from a prebuilt layout is often simpler, we will start from a generic layout in order to describe the whole procedure.

1. Choose Panels ➣ Layouts ➣ 3 Bottom Split.

2. Make sure the top half of the window is occupied by the perspective view (if not, select the top half, then choose Panels ➣ Perspective ➣ Persp).

3. Now select the lower left quadrant and choose Panels ➣ Panel ➣ Hypergraph. This should turn the lower left window into a view of the Hypergraph.

4. Finally, select the lower right quadrant and choose Panels ➤ Panel ➤ Hypershade, turning this corner into a view of the Hypershade.

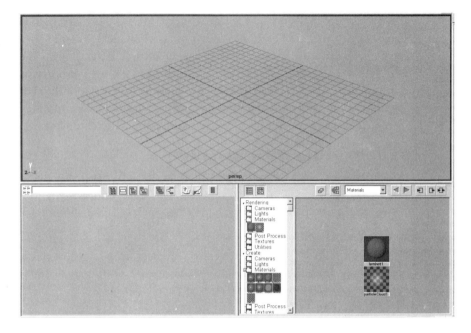

5. To save our new layout, choose Panels ➤ Saved Layouts ➤ Edit Layouts, which brings up a window with several tabs.

6. The Layouts tab should be selected (if not, choose it).

7. In the layouts tab, choose New Layout, then rename the layout from its default name (Panel Configuration 20) to something more memorable, like Persp/Hypergraph/Hypershade, and hit the Enter key to change the name.

On closing the window, your new layout will be placed at the bottom of the Saved Layouts menu. If you later choose to discard this new layout, return to the Edit Layouts menu, select the new layout, and click the Delete button.

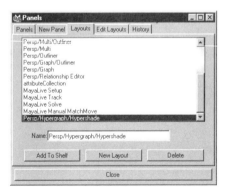

N O T E You can actually build a custom configuration directly inside the Edit Layouts menu, by using the Panels and Edit Layouts tabs. This method is more difficult than the one outlined above, however, so my recommendation is to stick with the above method.

The Hotbox

The *hotbox* in Maya is a tool for displaying all of the menus relevant to your work at a given moment, without taking up any screen real estate when it's not in use. While you can do everything you wish in Maya without ever using the hotbox, once you get used to the way the hotbox conserves space and puts nearly all of Maya's tools in easy reach, you'll wonder how you ever got along without it. The hotbox is so universally useful that one member of this author team has created a default setup with no menus showing at all, allowing that much more room for the scene windows. If you haven't ever used the hotbox before, it is accessed merely by pressing (and holding) the spacebar. In its default configuration, you will see something like the following.

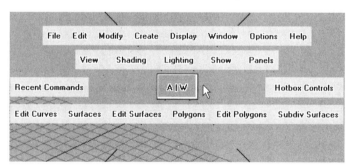

The top row of the hotbox always shows the general menus (the menus that are available in all menu sets), like the Window, Options, Create, and Modify menus. The second row replicates the menu set of the active panel (in this case, the perspective view), with menu items such as View, Lighting, and Panels. The third row has a Recent Commands menu (showing the last 15 commands you performed) and a Hotbox Controls menu, which allows you to fine-tune how the hotbox (and general menus) displays its information. The bottom row of menus is, in this case, the Modeling menu set, with specialized menus for editing curves, surfaces and polygons. In the very center of the hotbox (where the A|W logo sits) is a quick way to change views from perspective to front to side to top, as well as an options menu for how the hotbox displays. Access to all these menus is the same: press (and hold—the hotbox menus will not remain open when you release the mouse button) the left mouse button over the menu, then drag inside the nested menu to select the item you wish, releasing the mouse when it is over your selection.

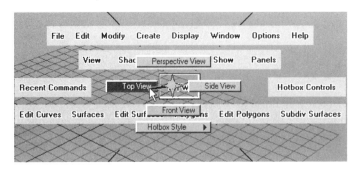

In addition to the menus you can see, there are four regions, called zones (defined by the four lines proceeding out from the hotbox at 45-degree angles), which have special functions. The top zone allows you to quickly select from several saved layouts. The right zone allows you to toggle elements of Maya's GUI on or off (we will discuss customizing your workspace in the following chapter). The bottom zone lets you change the selected window to any of several useful views (like the Hypergraph or the Hypershade). The left zone lets you toggle between object and component mode (mimicking the F8 key), and it also lets you toggle on and off several masking modes.

While you can use the hotbox in its default configuration, it is more useful (if a bit more cluttered) when you turn on all menu sets (Modeling, Rendering, and so on) at once. In the Hotbox Controls menu, choose Show All, which displays all menu sets at once.

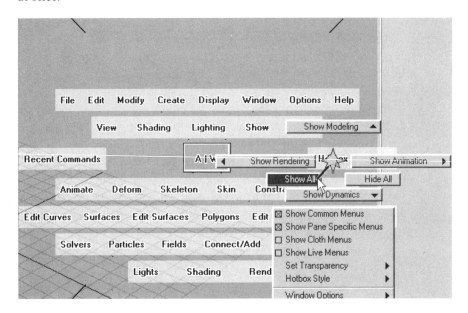

In this configuration, you have access to nearly all of Maya's tools in one place, and it's all available at the press of the spacebar. If you are not familiar with using the hotbox, try forcing yourself to use it for all your menu choices for a couple of hours of work; you will soon find out how powerfully useful the hotbox is, and you'll probably use it for most of your future work.

Menus

While we have discussed menu sets on and off throughout this chapter, let's take a moment to look at how Maya's menus are organized. The top row of menus (or the top row in the hotbox) is split into two parts: the menus that are always present (the constant menus) and those that change according to the mode the program is in (the mode menus, like the Animation menu set, for example). Always present are File, Edit, Modify, Create, Display, Window, and Options. To change the variable menus, choose the menu set you want from the Status line (just below the menus—or under Hotbox Controls in the hotbox). The sets you can choose from are Modeling, Animation, Dynamics, and Rendering. The elements listed in these menus are fairly obvious, for the most part; the only real curveball is that in order to create a light, you must be in the Rendering menu set (lights cannot be created via the Create menu).

In addition to the general menus, nearly every view window in Maya has a built-in menu. The perspective view, for example, has the following menus: View, Shading, Lighting, Show, and Panels (the Show menu allows you to show and hide different types of objects). The Hypergraph view contains these menus: Edit, View, Bookmarks, Graph, Rendering, Options, Show, and Help. For perspective and orthographic views, you can either access these menus from the top of the window pane or use the second row of menus in the hotbox. For views like the Hypergraph or Hypershade, pressing and holding the right mouse button will bring up the menus (or you can use the menu across the top of the window). There are also menus for the Channel box and Attribute Editor.

Generally speaking, most windows in Maya have their own menu set, which explains why Maya doesn't just use one menu bar across the top of the screen: there are at least one hundred individual menus, and there would be no space to place all these menus across one screen. Attempting to nest all these menus, on the other hand, might have taken 10 or more levels of nesting to fit all the menus into one menu bar, making the task of picking any individual menu item both laborious and baffling. Given the complexity of the task, organizing Maya's windows into contextual subsets was both a necessity and a more elegant solution to the problem.

Shelves

While we have not touched on shelves much in this chapter, they offer a convenient way of grouping your most frequently used commands and tools together in one place. The shelf bar is one of the most noticeable features of Maya's GUI. It appears just below the Status line. Labeled with Shelf1, Shelf2, and so on, the left side of the Shelf line contains the manipulation tools that we have discussed above. Additionally, there are several buttons, organized into a tab called Shelf1 (and Shelf2, etc.) that perform useful commands. For example, to create a NURBS sphere, you merely click on the blue sphere button; to create a spotlight, click the spotlight button; to create a CV curve, click the CV curve button (the leftmost button on the right side of the shelf).

N O T E   You can customize these shelf buttons to suit your needs. For more on how to do this, see Chapter 3 or Chapter 16.

Having these buttons available on a shelf makes the process of creating each item much more straightforward than having to find them in a hierarchical menu set.

The Outliner and Hypergraph

While we will cover the inner workings of the Outliner and the Hypergraph later in this book (Chapter 4 is devoted entirely to the Hypergraph), let's take a quick look at these two scene management windows. The basic purpose of the Outliner and the Hypergraph is the same: to allow you to see an abstract (or outline) of the scene. The way the two display a scene's outline, however, is very different.

If you have used a 3D animation program in the past, you will probably be familiar with a scene management tool like the Outliner. From top to bottom, the Outliner (Window ➤ Outliner) lists all objects in your scene, including cameras (note that the orthographic views—top, side and front—are just cameras listed in the Outliner), lights, curves, and geometric objects. If you have objects that are parented to one another (a leg, for example, is parented to a body so that they move together), the Outliner will indicate this by a twirl-down arrow to the left of the parent object (the body in this case). Clicking the arrow will show the child object (the leg) which, because it is the child object, is tabbed in under the parent. The Outliner menu contains several options, which will be discussed further in the following chapter.

The Hypergraph, by contrast, is probably like nothing you've seen before. It is, essentially, a linked (or hyperlinked) outline of your scene, showing not only your scene elements, but how they are connected. While the Hypergraph may at first appear bewildering, its fashion of laying out a scene can prove invaluable. The following image shows how the scene shown in the Outliner, above, would look in the Hypergraph.

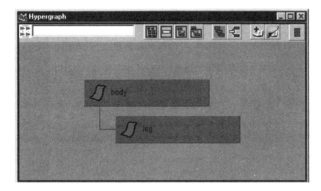

Again, you'll learn much more about the Hypergraph in Chapter 4.

The Channel Box/Attribute Editor

New to version 2, the Channel box and Attribute Editor can be set to toggle back and forth, filling the right-hand portion of your screen (to make the Attribute Editor and Channel box toggle, choose Options ➤ UI Preferences ➤ Open Attribute Editor in Main Maya Window). The Attribute Editor gives you access to all an object's attributes, while the Channel box gives a more simplified view of only the object's *keyable* (or animatable) attributes. As these two panels are counterparts, it makes sense for them to be grouped together, and this is the layout we use.

N O T E   The Channel box is so named because elements that can be animated in a 3D program have often been termed "channels." To animate a ball going up and down, you would animate its Y-axis channel (by setting several keyframes over time). While Maya uses the term *attribute* for anything that could potentially be keyable in a scene, those which have actually been set to keyable are placed in the Channel box.

As you'll see throughout this book, the Attribute Editor and Channel box are your keys to controlling all of an object's attributes, including numerical inputs for translation, rotation, scale, and visibility, as well as its construction history, like spans of CVs and the radius of a circular object. The Attribute Editor, in addition (via its tabbed windows) allows you to access materials, tessellation criteria, and other features. To toggle between the Channel box and Attribute Editor, or to bring up the Attribute Editor in a separate window, just press Ctrl+A.

N O T E   Materials? Tessellation? If you're new to 3D animation, don't worry about absorbing all the jargon right away. The following chapters introduce all the essential concepts in a logical and straightforward way.

If you click on the name of an attribute in the Channel box and then MM drag in the scene window, you will get a "virtual slider" that controls the number next to the channel name. This is a very powerful, time-saving feature in Maya.

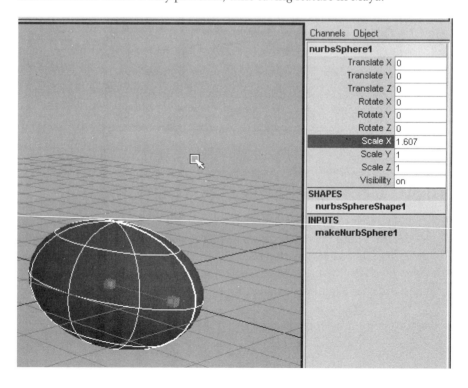

The Timeline

The timeline, just below the main scene window(s), is the key to animation in Maya.

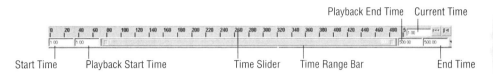

Start Time   Playback Start Time   Time Slider   Time Range Bar   End Time

Playback End Time   Current Time

The numbers on the timeline by default are set to frames (and by default, frames per second is set to film rate—24—so 24 frames equals one second of animation). To the right of the time slider is the current time marker (probably set to 1.00)—see the image above for where the current time (and other timeline items) is. To change the current time in your animation, you can either drag the time marker in the time slider or double-click in the current time field and enter a number (like 5)—you will then see the time marker move to that frame—larger numbers (like frame 20) are, of course, later in the animation. Below the time slider is a range marker (the gray bar with a 1 on one end and a 24 on the other) that lets you control the range of the time slider within a larger animation. To change the position of the time slider while maintaining the same range (24 frames by default), just drag the range bar by its middle. To change the starting point of the range, drag the left square left or right. To change the ending point, drag the right square to the left or right.

To the left of the time range bar are two numeric fields. The left-most field sets the animation start frame (often people will set this number to 0 for the first frame instead of 1). The field to its right sets the starting frame of the time range (changing this number is equivalent to dragging the left square of the time range slider). To the right of the time range bar are two more fields; the left one sets the ending time of the animation range (equivalent to dragging the right square on the time range bar), while the right field controls the end point of the animation (set to 48 frames as a default).

To change the settings for the time slider, open the animation preferences window (either click the Animation Preferences button, to the right of the key icon at the bottom right of the screen) or choose Options ➢ General Preferences ➢ Animation. In this tab, you can control how the units are displayed on the timeline and numeric fields, set playback to normal or free (required for playback of dynamics), and even adjust animation beginning and end points and so forth. Under the Units tab, you can change from the default film (24fps) to (25fps), (30fps), seconds, minutes, or even hours for your slider units.

TIP   To play back an animation, you can either use the VCR-like controls to the right of the time line, or press Ctrl+V to start and stop the animation, and Ctrl+Shift+V to reset the animation to its starting frame.

The Command Line, Feedback Line, and Script Editor

At the bottom of the Maya screen are the Command and Feedback lines. These two lines function in tandem, and are simply the last lines of the Script Editor's Input and History windows, respectively. Therefore, let's first take a quick look at Maya's Script Editor. As most of your interaction with Maya is via the GUI, most of what you actually tell Maya to do is passed to it via MEL (the Maya Embedded Language). The selections and other actions you make in the GUI are recorded as MEL commands. Creating a NURBS sphere, for example, is simply the command sphere followed by several optional flags. To access the Script Editor, either click on the Script Editor icon just to the right of the feedback line (at the bottom right of the screen), or use the menu (Window ➤ General Editors ➤ Script Editor). The Script Editor is split into two halves. The top, which is the History window, probably has several lines of code in it (these would be the last commands you have issued to Maya). The Input window at the bottom awaits any MEL commands you might wish to give to Maya.

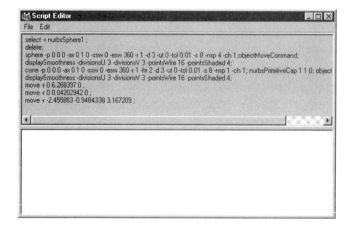

NOTE   For information on how to use MEL commands with the Script Editor, please see Chapter 16, "MEL Basics."

To see how the Script Editor works, type **sphere** (in lowercase letters) into the input window and press the Enter key on the *numeric keypad* (not the alpha keyboard). You should see the line

```
// Result: nurbsSphere1 makeNurbsSphere1 //
```

appear in the history window (telling you what Maya has done to complete your command), and a sphere will appear at the origin of your scene.

Because the Command line is just the last input line in the Script Editor, you don't have to open the Script Editor for a simple command. Try closing the Script Editor and then, in the Command line, type in **cone** (all small letters), and press either Enter key. A cone should appear in your scene, and the Feedback line (to the right of the Command line) should now read

```
Result: nurbsCone1 makeNurbsCone1
```

letting you know what actions Maya has taken to complete your command.

T I P   To "focus" on the Command line when you are in a scene window (so you don't have to click in the Command line field with your mouse), just press the ` key at the top-left of your keyboard.

Summary

You've seen in this quick tour that while Maya is a very deep and complex program, a great deal of thought has gone into making the interface as intuitive as possible. Consistent interface elements (like using the Alt key and mouse drags to move around many different windows), grouping tools together, and even placing clues about your orientation in space and the type of tool you're using directly in the scene windows—all of these features work together to ease the new user's entrance into this complex environment.

More importantly, the interface is completely customizable, from its smallest to its largest detail, so that you can tailor the program to meet your needs. As you grow more comfortable with using Maya, you will want to optimize its interface to allow you to work more quickly with less clutter. In the following chapter, we will explore exactly this issue, looking into built-in options, creating buttons and menus of your own, and making the best use of some of Maya's organizational windows (like the Outliner and Hypergraph). If you are very new to Maya, spend a bit of time playing with the interface after reading this chapter. If you are an advanced beginner—or beyond—read through the next chapter to see how you can make Maya work even better for you.

chapter 3

TECHNIQUES FOR SPEEDING UP WORKFLOW

Featuring

- *Adjusting interface options*

- *Using the hotbox instead of menu sets*

- *Shelves*

- *Hotkeys*

- *Marking menus*

- *Working in layers*

- *The Outliner*

- *The Hypergraph*

- *The Hypershade*

- *A workflow example: building an arm*

CHAPTER

3

TECHNIQUES FOR SPEEDING UP WORKFLOW

In Chapter 2, we examined many of Maya's interface features. Here, we will look at ways in which the default Maya interface can be adjusted to optimize the ways you interact with the program. From adjusting basic interface options to using hotkeys, shelves, and marking menus, and on to proper use of the Outliner and other windows, this chapter will show you how to customize Maya to do what you want quickly and easily. Finally, we will end with a quick demonstration of how to use Maya's tools to perform a modeling task with a minimum of pain and effort.

What's New in Maya 2

In addition to several subtle improvements that make the interface more consistent and easier to use, the new Hypershade is a striking improvement in the way Maya handles textures, materials, and the like. Because the Hypershade works much like the Hypergraph, working with materials and textures now feels similar to working with geometry in the Hypergraph, and navigating the complexities of a shading network is simplified greatly. This reworking of the Maya interface for version 2 (plus a little effort on your part to get to know the Hypershade) can greatly improve workflow in Maya, speeding up complex tasks, and making simpler ones ... well, simpler.

Adjusting Interface Options

The first and most obvious place to start customizing Maya's interface to optimize your work is via the general interface options. Changing these options can make the interface cleaner—allowing you to work with fewer distractions—and also give over more space to the main scene view.

Most interface options are, fittingly enough, under the Options ➢ UI Preferences menu. On selecting this choice from the menu, you will see a multi-tabbed window that allows you to adjust many of Maya's UI settings.

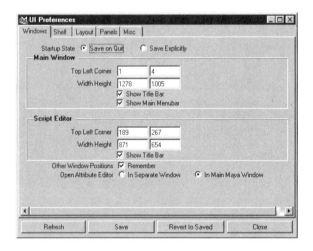

For each tab, you have the option of saving your preferences automatically (on quitting) for use in you next Maya session, or saving them explicitly (by clicking the Save button)—by saving explicitly, you can alter your preferences for one session without affecting the interface when you restart Maya. If you are unsure how to return to a default set of options, try using the Save Explicitly option until you are sure you like the interface changes you make. Under the Windows tab, you can adjust top and bottom dimensions for both the main window and Script Editor, though it is probably easier to do this interactively in the Maya window itself. You can also turn off the title bar and main menu bar—doing so removes the blue border at the top of the screen (which contains the title of the scene) and the menu set at the top of the main window, saving about 30 or 40 pixels of space for your scene window, and cleaning up the interface look a bit. You can also tell Maya to either remember or forget where you position your windows, and whether the Attribute Editor appears in a separate, floating window (as in version 1) or replaces the Channel box when Ctrl+A is pressed.

 TIP   You can also turn off the main menu bar and/or pane menus under the Hotbox Controls menu in the hotbox: display the hotbox and choose Controls ➢ Window Options ➢ Show Main (or Panel) Menu Bar.

Under the Shelf tab, you can adjust how the shelf icons are presented, and you can tell Maya whether to save shelf contents automatically or only when you explicitly tell it to save (generally it is better to have Maya save the contents automatically, unless you are experimenting with a new look). The Layout tab allows you to turn all components of the window (except the main scene window) on or off. If, for example, you are only modeling for a time, you could turn off the time and range sliders, freeing up more space for your scene. The Panels tab allows you to turn panel menus on or off, and also lets you specify how the main scene window will first appear when you open a new Maya scene (it defaults to Single Perspective view).

T I P You can also quickly turn panel menus on or off directly in the Options menu (Options ➢ Layer Bar, for example). Being able to turn panels on and off quickly makes it easy to switch from, say, a modeling user interface (UI) set to an animation UI set.

The Miscellaneous tab lets you choose how your Web browser (usually Netscape Communicator or Microsoft Internet Explorer) will be activated upon a request for online help. You can also choose which menu set Maya defaults to on opening, and whether the focus (the cursor) will stay on the command line after you execute a MEL command from it.

Using the Hotbox Instead of Menu Sets

As we discussed in the previous chapter, using the hotbox instead of dealing with all of the different Maya menu sets can really speed up your work, as well as clean up your Maya environment. In general, most professionals turn off menu bars (main and panel), and use the hotbox to choose menu functions. To turn off menus, either use the UI Options menu or uncheck the main and panel menus under the Hotbox Controls menu (Hotbox Controls ➢ Window Options ➢ Show Main (Panel) Menu Bar). Once the menus are off, just press and hold the spacebar to bring up the hotbox. Any or all menu sets can be displayed in the hotbox, depending on your choices under the Hotbox Controls menu. Again, generally speaking, most advanced users tend to display all menu sets (Animation, Modeling, Dynamics, Rendering, Maya Live, Cloth and Fur) at once, making the hotbox fairly complex to look at, but, once you find where all the different menus are, it's only a one-step procedure to access any menu from that point on.

N O T E For more on how to use the hotbox and how to set its options, see Chapter 2.

N O T E   This discussion of customizing shelves, hotkeys, and marking menus is very basic. Because MEL scripts are the most efficient tool for customizing these interface elements, you'll find a much more thorough discussion of these topics in Chapter 16.

Shelves

While we briefly discussed shelves in the previous chapter, they might have appeared only marginally useful. What makes shelves really useful is not what appears on them by default, but the fact that you can easily add new buttons to any shelf. You can, for example, make any menu item a shelf button, or even place MEL scripts on the shelf, allowing you to perform complex tasks at the click of your mouse. Additionally, as you can create and use multiple shelves (to create a new shelf, choose Options ➢ Customize UI ➢ Shelves, select the Shelves tab, and click the New Shelf button), you can make a shelf specific to a task. For example, a shelf could be devoted to just MEL scripts, and another could be given over to common tasks for a specific project you're working on.

To switch to a new shelf (shelf2, for example), simply click its tab on the shelf bar. To create a new shelf button from a menu item, hold down the Ctrl, Alt, and Shift keys (all together), and choose the menu item from the menu bar (*not* the hotbox). A new button will appear on the active shelf, and clicking this button will be the same as selecting the menu item you had chosen.

W A R N I N G   You must create shelf buttons from the main (or panel) menu bar, not the hotbox. As many users turn off these menu bars, it is a bit of a pain to create new shelf buttons—you first have to reactivate the menu bar, then create the button, and finally turn the menu bar off again.

To delete any shelf button, just MM drag it onto the trash can at the top right of the shelf bar. To move an item to a different place on the shelf, simply MM drag it to the place you wish it to be. Other shelf items will adjust themselves to the new placement.

As an example, let's create a button that automatically creates a NURBS cylinder, and place it just next to the NURBS sphere button on shelf 1. First, be sure you have shelf 1 selected by making sure its tab is frontmost. Next, hold down the Ctrl, Alt, and Shift keys and, from the main menu bar, select Create ➢ Nurbs Primitives ➢ Cylinder. A new button should appear at the far right of shelf 1. Finally, just MM drag the new button between the sphere and cone icons on the shelf. Voilà, one more primitive you can now create without resorting to the menu bar!

TIP You could also create a NURBS cylinder button that automatically brings up the options window. Just hold down the Ctrl, Alt, and Shift keys and choose Create ➤ Nurbs Primitives ➤ Cylinder ❑.

You can create as many of these buttons as you wish (though you might have to scroll through the list if you create too many on one shelf), and/or delete any of the default buttons Maya provides for you, thus customizing your shelves to contain buttons that are the most useful to you (buttons for items like the Hypergraph and Hypershade are very nice to place on shelf 1 for easy access). You can also create new shelves by opening the Shelves Options window (Options ➤ Customize UI ➤ Shelves). Under the Shelves tab, click the New Shelf button, give it a name, click Save All Shelves, and close the window.

You can also turn MEL scripts into shelf buttons. To see how this works, let's create a very simple example. Open the Script Editor (click the Script Editor icon at the bottom right of the screen, or choose Window ➤ General Editors ➤ Script Editor). In the input (bottom) section of the window, type in the following:

```
sphere -n ball -r 2;
```

Highlight this text (drag over it, or triple-click the line), MM drag the text up to the shelf, and a new button will appear. Now, whenever you click this new button, a new NURBS sphere named ball, with a radius of 2, will appear at the origin of your scene. Even this simple example makes it clear how powerful a little MEL scripting can be; clicking one button not only creates a sphere, but names it and gives it the radius you wish. You could even build a whole shelf for geometric primitives, with a group of buttons for each primitive type, each button having a different option set.

TIP You can also highlight any text in the history (top) section of the Script Editor, "recording" your actions into a macro. You could therefore perform several complex steps in the Maya interface (that you wish to repeat later), and turn all these steps into a button by highlighting all the text in the history window and MM dragging it to a shelf. Thus, with no MEL programming knowledge, you can create buttons that do very complex actions. For specific examples, see Chapter 16.

Hotkeys

If you have used Maya for any time, you are already familiar with many of its hotkeys, which are simply shortcuts to commands (or command modifiers) that are accessible by a keystroke. Accessing the Move tool, for example, is a simple matter of pressing the W key. As with most of Maya's interface, you are not limited to the hotkeys Maya has built in: You can create your own hotkeys, or even change or delete the hotkeys Maya has built in.

NOTE   Again, you'll find a more thorough discussion of customizing hotkeys in Chapter 16.

As an example of how to create a hotkey, let's make a keyboard shortcut to bring up the Hypergraph. First, open the hotkeys options window (Options ➢ Customize UI ➢ Hotkeys). In this window, scroll down until you reach the Window Menu set, then find Window–>Hypergraph and highlight it.

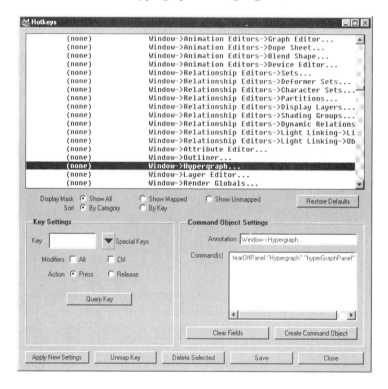

First, we need to find a key that is not currently mapped to any other hotkey. Under Key Settings, in the Key text field, type a lowercase **h** (H is different from h for hotkeys!), be sure the Press radio button is enabled, and check the Alt box (which means the hotkey will be Alt+h, not just h). Now click the Query Key button to see if any hotkey currently uses this combination. You should see a dialog telling you no command is currently mapped to this key (if not, try another key/modifier combination). To enable the new hotkey, click the Apply New Settings button; you should now see (in the text window at the top) that Alt h Press has been assigned to the Hypergraph command. Press the Save button to save your changes. To test the new button out,

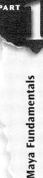

close the hotkeys options window, then press Alt+h in the scene window. The Hyper-graph should pop right up for you!

T I P   You can also create your own commands and assign them to hotkeys. This is covered briefly in the next section, and more thoroughly in Chapter 16.

Marking Menus

In addition to shelves and hotkeys, you can also create entire contextual menus (called *marking menus*) that appear either in the hotbox or when you press a hotkey combination.

N O T E   You'll find a more thorough discussion of creating and using marking menus in Chapter 16.

Let's create a marking menu that will create a sphere using one of four options: radius = 1, radius = 2, radius = 3, radius = 4. First, open the Marking Menus options window (Options ➢ Customize UI ➢ Marking Menus). In this window, you will see listed several marking menus that have already been created for Maya, including the region menus that appear to the north, east, south, and west in the hotbox (for more on this, see Chapter 2).

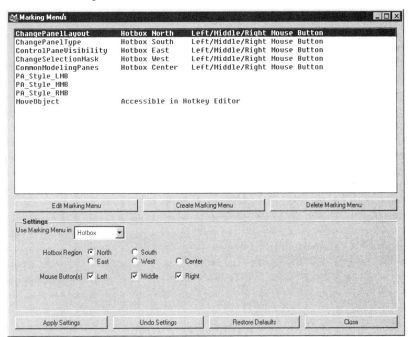

For our purposes, we want to create a new marking menu, so click the Create Marking Menu button. This brings up the Create Marking Menu window, with several blank boxes that we will use to create our own marking menu.

First, give the marking menu a name, such as CreateSpheres. Because we will create a marking menu with four options, it is logical to use the top, right, bottom, and left boxes as our menu positions. There are a couple of ways to assign a command to a menu item: you can MM drag a shelf button that you have made (or one of the default buttons, like the cone button) onto a menu box, you can MM drag MEL scripts or lines to the menu item, or you can RM click on a menu item and choose Edit Menu Item (the option we will use here). Starting at the top center box, RM choose Edit Menu Item, and in the window that pops up, type **Sphere radius 1** in the Label field, and type **sphere –r 1**; in the Command(s) field (be sure the sphere command is in lower case!). Finally, click Save and Close to save your changes.

Now, move over to the right center (east) box, RM choose Edit Menu Item, and repeat the steps from above, but this time label the button **Sphere radius 2**, and make the MEL command **sphere –r 2;**. Move to the south and west boxes, and repeat the steps, making the south box create a sphere of radius 3 and the west box create one of radius 4. When you are finished, your Create Marking Menu window should look as follows.

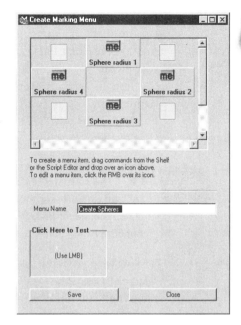

To test the buttons, click in the Click Here to Test box. You should see all your menu options appear, and if you choose an option, an appropriately sized sphere should appear in your scene window.

Once you have your menu working as you want, click Save and then Close to return you to the Marking Menus Options window. Your new CreateSpheres menu should now appear at the bottom of the list, highlighted (if it's not highlighted, do so). We now have our menu, but we can't access it from the scene window. To do so, we need to choose whether we want the menu to be part of the hotbox or accessible via a keystroke. This time, let's create a marking menu that will appear when we press a special key: under Settings, choose Hotkey Editor

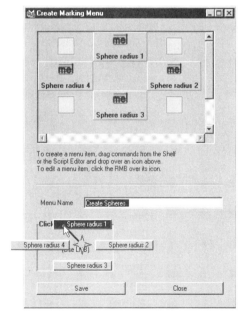

from the pop-up menu and then click the Apply Settings button. To the right of the CreateSpheres item in the list at the top of the window, there should now be the message *Accessible in Hotkey Editor,* meaning that we can now make a hotkey for our new menu.

Close the Marking Menu Options window and open the Hotkeys Options window (Options ➤ Customize UI ➤ Hotkeys). Scroll all the way to the bottom of the hotkey list, and, in the User Defined section, you should see CreateSpheres (Press) and CreateSpheres (Release).

T I P   The press and release states are important to a marking menu. When the hotkey is pressed (the press state), the menu will appear; when the key is released (the release state), the menu disappears. If you forget to define a release state for your menu, it will not disappear when you release the hotkey!

Now we just follow the steps we used in the last section to define a hotkey. First, select the CreateSphere (Press) item; then query a key—Ctrl+r should be open for your use. When you have found an open key combination, be sure your Action radio button is set to Press; then click the Apply New Settings button. You should see that CreateSphere (Press) is now set to Ctrl r Press in the top list. To define the release state, select the CreateSphere (Release) item, type **r** and the control modifier in the Key Settings, and be sure the Action is set to Release (*not* Press). Then click the Apply New Settings button, and the release state should be mapped. Finally, press the Save and Close buttons in the Hotkeys Options window. (Whew!)

To test your new marking menu, hold down Ctrl+r, and press the left mouse button. You should see your marking menu, ready for use!

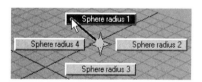

Although there are many steps involved in creating a marking menu (so you probably wouldn't create one for a quick, simple task), consider the power a marking menu gives you: a complete new menu with multiple items (and even subitems) that you can access anywhere in the scene window at the click of a key. Marking menus are relatively easy to create, and a great idea for tasks you repeat often—especially if they have multiple options.

Working in Layers

Working in layers can be particularly useful when you are modeling a multiple-part, complex object (the inner workings of a mechanical clock, for example, or a complex creature like a human or dog). By placing groups of objects in layers (fingers in one layer, hand in another, arm in another), you can easily hide, display, template or otherwise adjust large groups of objects all at once, rather than tediously selecting each object and then changing it—or, worse yet, being unable to select one object that is hidden behind another.

The Layer bar is a quick visual reference for working in layers, so if you have it turned off, turn it back on again (Options ➤ Layer Bar). The Layer bar should appear just above your scene window, with the Default layer already selected (the Default layer is where all objects that have not been assigned to other layers are stored). To create a new layer, just click the layer icon (the icon to the far left of the Layer bar that looks like three sheets of paper). If you double-click on the default layer name (layer1), a dialog box will open, allowing you to rename the layer to whatever you wish. Once you have made and named a layer, create a couple of simple objects (like a sphere and a cylinder), select them, and, from the triangle button to the left of the layer name, choose Assign Selected. The objects you had selected are now part of your new layer. Return to the scene window, deselect all objects, and (again from the Layer pop-up menu), choose Select All in Layer. You will see your objects selected once again, as they are a part of this new layer.

To get a better view of your new layer, choose Edit Membership from the layer pop-up menu. This brings up the Relationship Editor, with all layers on the left side, and all objects on the right side.

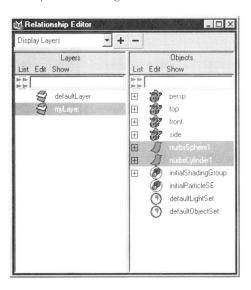

When you click on a layer name, all objects in that layer become highlighted on the right. You can then click on any object on the right side, toggling its inclusion in the layer (highlighted means it is included; not highlighted means it is not). You can quickly change which layer you are working with, and which objects are included in each layer by using this window. Try placing one object in your layer, another in the default layer.

N O T E   Each object can only belong to one layer. Therefore, if you highlight your sphere in the default layer (for example), it will be unselected from your other layer.

T I P   You can also adjust each layer's attributes by choosing Layer Attributes from the Layer pop-up menu.

To quickly hide or show all objects in a layer, check the Visible box in the Layer pop-up menu. This menu can also change the state of each layer individually. The Standard state is your normal working state. The Template state turns the objects into templates (they cannot be selected or moved, and they turn a pinkish orange). The Reference state makes the layer a reference layer, once again making all objects in it unselectable, but keeping their display properties.

While working in layers for a simple scene like our example may seem a waste of time, as we move on to more ambitious projects you'll see how useful being able to select, hide, template or otherwise alter several objects in a complex scene can be. If you have not used layers before in Maya or any other program, try modeling an intricate object that has many overlapping pieces and you'll quickly appreciate how useful layers can be.

The Outliner

There are two basic ways to look at all of the information in your scene: the Outliner and the Hypergraph. While the Hypergraph is the more flexible and powerful of the two, the Outliner is usually easier for a new Maya user, and it performs several tasks in a more straightforward fashion than does the Hypergraph. Conceptually, the Outliner is exactly what its name implies: it is an outline of the scene you are working on.

To open the Outliner, choose Window ➤ Outliner from the main menu set (or hotbox). If you had created a default sphere, and it was selected, the Outliner window would look as shown on the facing page.

The first four items in the Outliner are the four default cameras (plus any other cameras you might have created). Next are listed geometric objects (like the sphere). Finally, sets (groupings of objects, like the default light and object sets) are listed. Any highlighted objects (in gray) are selected in the scene, and vice versa. You can rename any object listed in the Outliner by double-clicking its name. You can also bring up the Attribute Editor and focus it on any object in the Outliner by double-clicking on its icon.

There are several viewing options available in the Outliner, accessed either via the Outliner's menu or by holding down the right mouse button anywhere inside the Outliner window. Some options you have are to show only specific types of objects, like geometry (Show ➤ Objects ➤ Geometry), to show shape nodes for objects (more on this in Chapter 4), or to show all objects, rather than just the DAG (Directed Acyclic Graph—a technical term for the common objects you see in the scene) objects. If, for example, you turn on Show Shapes, a plus sign appears to the left of any object in the scene that has a shape node (as a sphere or other geometric object would have). By clicking on the plus sign, you can expand the outline to see the shape node; in the case of our sphere, this would reveal the nurbsSphereShape1 node.

The Outliner can be used in several ways, but there are two that are probably the most appropriate: to get a quick look at the scene as a whole, and to access objects in a complex scene in a more convenient manner than having to pick the object. The first use for the Outliner—getting an overview of the scene—is the function of any good outline (from the outline of a term paper to the schematic outline of an electrical circuit). Because you can show or hide any type of object in the Outliner, you could, for example, look only at the lights in a scene; this would allow you to see quickly how many lights there are, and, by double-clicking on the light icons, you could just as quickly bring up the Attribute Editor to examine or adjust their options.

The second main use for the Outliner—allowing quick selection—flows from the first. As the Outliner provides easy access to any or all objects in the scene, you can rapidly choose, alter (via the Attribute Editor), or rename objects in a convenient list form, rather than having to hunt through a scene to find them, never knowing for sure if you have forgotten an object. In complex scenes, the ability to choose objects becomes even more important. Consider an object like a Christmas tree with a hundred ornamental lights on it. The tree itself might consist of two or three dozen objects (branches, base, and so on), and the hundred lights would be intertwined in the tree, making them very difficult to select for modification. In the Outliner, however, this job would be easy. First you would choose to show only light objects (Show ➢ Objects ➢ Lights) and then move down the outline of the scene, selecting and adjusting lights at will. As should be apparent, this method of interacting with your scene can be a real lifesaver.

The Hypergraph

The Hypergraph performs many of the same functions as the Outliner, but it uses a completely new interface design. The whole of the next chapter is devoted to the Hypergraph, so we will only mention it briefly here. This tool is worth noting in a chapter on interface optimization, as it can radically reduce the time you spend hunting through the scene and other windows, and it can really speed up your workflow.

To bring up the Hypergraph, choose Window ➢ Hypergraph from the main menu set. For a scene with a single sphere, the Hypergraph would look as follows when you first bring it up.

In its simplest incarnation (with many options turned off), the Hypergraph is actually simpler to understand than the Outliner. There is only one object apparent in the Hypergraph for the scene—in this case, the NURBS sphere. When an object is selected in a scene, the corresponding box in the Hypergraph turns yellow; if the object is not selected, the object remains gray (similar to the default shading color of all objects in Maya). Clicking on a box in the Hypergraph is the same as selecting the object in the scene window: the box turns yellow (indicating it is selected) and the object in the scene is highlighted in green. You can select multiple objects in the Hypergraph by either Shift+clicking on them or simply dragging a selection marquee around them. To deselect a single item, Shift+click on it in the Hypergraph. To deselect everything, just click in the empty space in the Hypergraph window. The Hypergraph contains many menus, and while a complete discussion of them must wait until the next chapter, it is worth noting that you can choose to display only certain objects in the Hypergraph (Show ➢ Objects ➢ NurbsObjects, for example), or show object components like shape nodes (Options ➢ Display ➢ Shape Nodes).

Where the Hypergraph really shines is in its ability to act like any other scene window. You can scale and track through the Hypergraph just as you would in any scene window, allowing you to see the entire sweep of a complex scene, or any part thereof, very easily. You can also focus on a selected object very quickly (say, for example, the object is selected in a scene window) by pressing the F key on the keyboard; or you can expand the view to contain all elements of a scene by pressing the A key. For simple scenes, the Outliner is a very useful tool, but for complex ones, the Hypergraph can be a much faster interface, as it allows such tracking and focusing across hundreds of scene elements. Which scene outline interface you want to use is, of course, your choice, but you should become familiar with both; one author, in fact, often uses both the Outliner and the Hypergraph in tandem on very complex scenes, allowing him to work in both views at once.

The Hypershade

While the multilister from Maya 1 was a useful interface for working with textures, materials, and utility nodes, it was not intuitive, and its interface did not fit in with the rest of Maya's interface conventions. Version 2 provides the Hypershade to remedy that problem (though you can still, of course, use the multilister). Using a similar convention to the Hypergraph, the Hypershade not only shows you interactive previews of what a material or texture will look like, it shows how the elements of a shader network are connected, giving you more information in a more intuitive interface than the multilister. Also, as with the Hypergraph, you can zoom and track the Hypershade like any Maya scene window, and use the F key (frame selected) and A key (frame all) to quickly focus on any element(s) you wish, making it easier to navigate scenes with large numbers of shading groups.

To open the Hypershade, choose Window ➤ Hypershade.

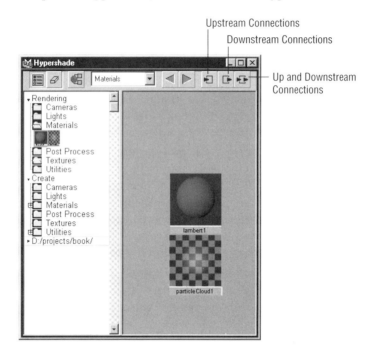

On the left is the Visor window, which is similar to the Outliner but contains graphic icons of textures and allows you to create, as well as view, any material node you wish. On the right is a Hypergraph-like window, known as the graphing window, with all materials listed—in a new scene, there will only be two materials listed, the lambert1 shader (the default shader for geometry) and the particleCloud1 shader (the default shader for particles).

T I P   The three buttons at the top left control your view of the Hypershade window. Click the left button to turn off the visor, so that the graphing window fills the Hypershade, or click the right button to turn off the graphing window and view only the visor. (Click either button a second time to restore the view.) Click the middle button to clear the view.

To select a material, simply click on it (it highlights in yellow to show that it is selected). You can then view that material's upstream connections, its downstream connections, or both by clicking the appropriate button at the top right of the Hypershade window—or by choosing Graph and the connection type from the Hypershade menu. The particle cloud, for example, has several inputs and outputs that appear as shown next if you click the Show Up and Downstream connection button. To get back to a general view of materials, choose Materials from the pop-up menu at the top of the Hypershade window.

NOTE An upstream connection is any Hypershade node that "feeds into" the selected node (its output is fed into the currently selected node—or it is upstream in the data flow). A downstream connection is any node that the currently selected node feeds data into—thus it is downstream from the selected node in the data flow.

TIP You can also view shading groups, utilities, lights, cameras, and so on, by choosing the item from the pop-up menu.

In addition to looking at materials, textures, and such, you can also create these items directly in the Hypershade in one of two ways. To create a material graphically, find the Create subsection of the visor (below the Rendering section), click on the Materials folder to open it (unless it is already open), and MM drag a material ball into the Hypershade side—try the phongE material, for example. After dragging, you will get a new phongE material in the Hypershade, ready for you to adjust. To assign this new material, you can just MM drag it on top of any object in your scene window. (Or you can click on the triangle below the phongE name and choose Assign Material to Selected; this is a good method of assigning the material to several objects at once.) To change the material's attributes (color or transparency, for example), double-click on the material ball to bring up the Attribute Editor, and then make any changes you wish to the material. The ball in the Hypershade, as well as any objects that have this material assigned to them, will be automatically updated with your changes. The other method for creating a new material is simply to choose Create Material from the menu in the Hypershade—Create ➤ Materials ➤ phongE, for example. This produces a new material in the Hypershade window, just as MM dragging the material icon from the visor does.

To assign a texture to your new material, you can again choose to create the material via menu commands (Create ➤ Textures ➤ 2D ➤ Fractal, for example), or just MM drag a swatch from the Create: Textures folder in the visor on top of your material.

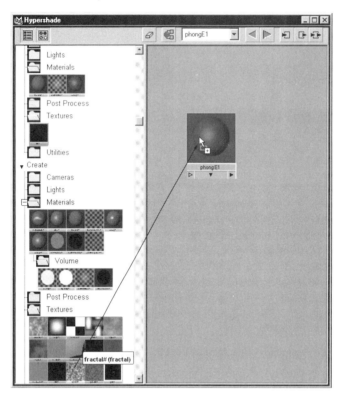

MM dragging a fractal texture onto the PhongE material

Once you complete the drag, a menu will open, letting you select which element of the material (which input) you wish to assign the fractal (or other) texture to. The most common choice is simply Color, so choose that. The Hypershade window will be updated to show that there is a texture input connection (coming from the left is input; going to the right is output) of a fractal texture, and the phongE material ball, plus any objects with the phongE material in your scene, will update to show the new texture.

While there are many other functions the Hypershade can perform besides the basics we have covered here, the centralized power of being able to create, modify, connect and disconnect materials, textures, and so forth, should be obvious from the quick tour we have taken. It is worth the effort to get to know the Hypershade, as it will save you a great deal of time and effort later on in your work with Maya's shader networks.

TIP   For more on rendering with the Hypershade, see Chapter 18.

A Workflow Example: Building an Arm

Let's take all the interface/optimization information we've gathered over the past two chapters and put it to use in a practical example. Over the next few pages, we'll model an arm, and then "string" it to bend at the elbow, using an Inverse Kinematics (IK) chain. Throughout this example, we'll put our understanding of Maya's interface to good use, making our modeling task that much easier.

Open a new scene in Maya. Either sketch out a top and side view of an arm and then scan it into your computer, or use the sketches included on the CD-ROM (ArmTop.tif and ArmSide.tif).

TIP   Sketching your image before you model is *always* a good idea—even if you have no skill at drawing. It is much easier to see what you're creating by quickly drawing it on paper than it is to try to create an object in 3D space out of your head. You will find that sketching an object before modeling it, far from taking extra time, will save you a great deal of time, and give you better-looking results as well.

NOTE   When you sketch an object for use as a background image for modeling, it is important that your two views (top and side here) are exactly the same size. We generally use graph paper in these circumstances, as it is easy to see how large the image is on this type of paper.

As we will use these sketches to make our model, they need to be loaded into Maya's top and side views so we can reference them as we build our arm. First, open the Outliner and select the top camera icon, double-clicking it to open the Attribute Editor. In the Attribute Editor, click the Environment triangle, and then click the Image Plane: Create button to create an image plane for the top view camera. When you click this button, the Attribute Editor will focus on the image plane (imagePlane1), but you still need to assign your arm image to the plane. To do so, scroll down to the Image Name line and click the Browse button. Find your top arm image (or use the ArmTop.tif image on the CD) and choose it. Repeat this process for the side view, using the side arm view image instead. When you are finished, your four view (press the space bar quickly to get this) should look as follows.

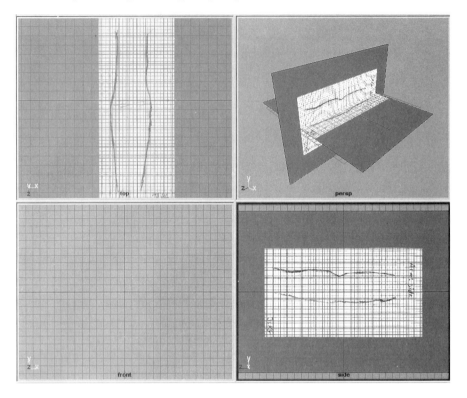

In order to keep from accidentally selecting one of these planes as we continue to work, let's put them on their own layer and make that layer a reference (unselectable) layer. From the layer bar, click the Create a New Layer button, rename this layer **Image-Planes**, select both image planes, and choose Assign Selected from the layer menu. To make the layer a reference layer, choose Reference from the layer menu.

There are several good modeling techniques to use from this point on, but we will use a common, fairly painless, method that produces good results quickly: lofting a series of circles into a shape.

N O T E   *Lofting* creates a shape in something like the way a wooden ship hull is laid (or lofted) over a skeleton of wood that defines the shape the hull will have once the lofting process is complete. (The metaphor of shipbuilding and hulls will become quite familiar, as it underlies much of the terminology of 3D modeling.)

First, create a new layer (click the New Layer button in the Layer bar) and name it Circles—we will assign our circles to this layer so they are separate from our eventual lofted surface. Next, expand one of the views (the top, say) to fill the screen (click in that pane, and then press the spacebar quickly). We could create our circles by going to the menu each time, but let's speed up our workflow by quickly making a button on the shelf to make our circles. Hold down the Ctrl, Alt and Shift keys and, from the main menu bar (this won't work from the hotbox!), choose Create ➤ Nurbs Primitives ➤ Circle; a new button should appear on your shelf, and clicking that button will create a circle.

If you now click the Circle button, the circle will probably be flush with the plane, which means we would have to turn it perpendicular to the plane each time. Rather than do this every time we create a circle, let's change the options once and save them, so that each new circle will be oriented correctly. Choose Create ➤ Nurbs Primitives ➤ Circle ❏, and in the options window, change the Normal Axis setting to the Z axis. (From our angle, the circle will now appear as a line.) Click the Save button (to save the settings) and close the window. The old Circle button on the shelf will remember its original settings (when you created it), so you will need to MM drag this button to the trash can on the shelf bar, then recreate the button (or, if you have read this far before starting the process, just change the circle settings first!).

Now we're ready to build our arm. In the top view (don't worry about the side view yet), Click the Circle button, move the new circle down to the bottom of the arm, and scale it to the same size as the bottom of the sketched arm. Remember that you can zoom your view in to see how accurately you're placing the circles.

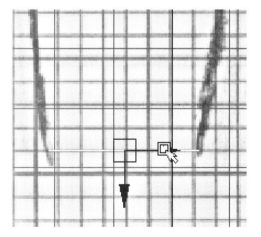

T I P   If you find the background image too distracting, select the camera (top here), open the Attribute Editor, click the imagePlane1 tab, and reduce the alpha gain to about 0.5. This will fade the image back a bit, giving you a clearer view of the circles you are creating.

To create the arm, create several circles, and position and scale them to fit the sketch of the arm in the top view. Be sure to place more circles around the elbow area, as that area will eventually bend (as any good elbow should), and therefore needs more definition. When you are finished, your "arm" should look similar to the following image.

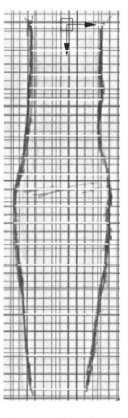

When you have finished with the top view, you will now need to switch to the side view, this time scaling and moving the circles so they fit from this view as well. (Don't move them along the X axis, however!) Your completed side view should look similar to this.

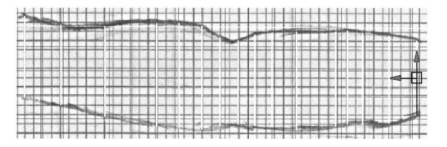

T I P   If you find you need a new circle to help build the shape in the side view, add one—just be sure to go back to the top view and adjust it there!

We now have the outline of our arm finished—it's time to create the arm itself! We need to select all the circles that will make up our arm and then loft them. But don't just drag a selection marquee around the circles; the loft tool depends on the order in which you select your circles, so we need to be careful about the order we select them. Starting at either end (the top or bottom of the arm), Shift+click on each circle in order, until all are selected. Before we loft these circles, first assign them to the Circles layer for later use (choose Assign Selected from the Circles layer menu). Now let's see how we did: Loft the circles into a surface (Surfaces ➤ Loft). You should see an arm-like tube appear in your perspective window.

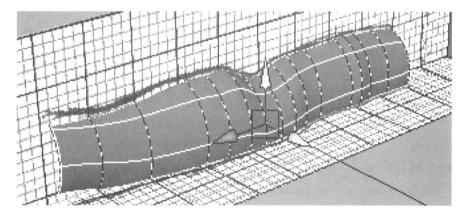

Because of the image planes, it's a bit difficult to see our arm. From the imagePlane layer menu, uncheck the Visible box to make the planes disappear.

You will probably find that the arm doesn't look quite realistic. Fortunately, because Maya remembers construction history, you can go back and tweak the position, scale, and rotation of the circles (using the same techniques we used to create the circles, above) to get the arm to look the way you want it. When you like your arm, turn off the circle layer's visibility so you can see the surface more clearly.

T I P   Templating the lofted surface (Display ➤ Object Components ➤ Templates) so you can't accidentally select it is a real time saver. To "untemplate" the object when you are finished with adjustments, select the lofted surface in the Outliner or Hypergraph, and choose Display ➤ Object Components ➤ Templates again.

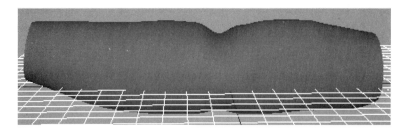

Now we need to string our arm with an IK chain so we can move it around like a natural arm. Make the side view fill your workspace, and then choose the IK Joint tool from the shelf (or choose Skeleton ➤ Joint Tool). Starting at the top (shoulder), click (or drag) the tool where the shoulder joint should be, then click again where the elbow should be, and finally, click where the wrist would be. If you don't like where your joint is, undo the last click (press the Z key) and try again. When you are satisfied with the look of the joints, press the Enter key to confirm the new skeleton.

 WARNING   Be sure not to make all three joints follow a straight line. Maya's IK solver uses the direction of the joint's initial bend to determine which direction it will bend later. If you make the joints straight, Maya won't know which direction to bend the arm, and you will get bizarre results.

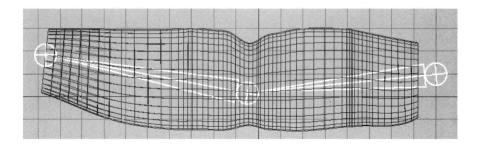

We could now manipulate the joints using the rotate tool, but it is generally easier to create an IK chain to make the moving process simpler. To do so, choose the IK Handle tool on the shelf (or choose Skeleton ➤ IK Handle Tool) and click first on the shoulder joint and then on the wrist joint. (Skip the elbow joint so that the kinematics chain will go through the elbow, allowing it to bend with the wrist movements). You should now see a green line connecting the shoulder and wrist joints. If you wish, you can now move the joint around by drag selecting the wrist IK handle and moving the arm—however only the joint moves at present; we need to attach the arm to our new joint.

T I P   If you move the joint around before attaching the arm to it, be sure to undo (press Z) back to the original position before attaching the arm.

The final step, attaching the arm surface to the arm joint, is a process of selecting the joint and surface and binding them together. First, select the root joint of the arm skeleton (the shoulder joint), then Shift-select the arm surface. Finally, choose Skin ➢ Bind Skin ➢ Smooth Bind to bind the two together. To see your beautiful new arm at work, drag-select the wrist joint and use the move tool to move the wrist around. The skeleton (and arm surface) should follow the wrist where you drag it.

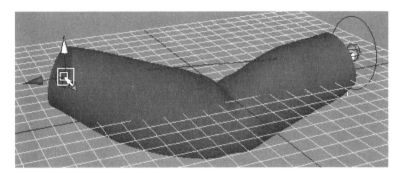

 N O T E   You may notice that the elbow doesn't bend properly (it folds too much). You can use the Artisan tool to adjust the joint goal weights of the arm to make the bend far more realistic looking. For more on how to do this, see Chapter 9.

Summary

In this chapter, we went over many elements in Maya that you can either adjust or use as-is to get the most out of your work. Looking at general options, shortcuts, organizational windows like the Hypergraph, the Hypershade, and the Outliner, and working in layers, we saw how much one can adjust Maya's default interface to improve your workflow. The final working example—building a moveable arm—took many of the workflow lessons we learned in this and the last chapter and put them to real-world use. We created a shortcut button, worked in layers, and used hotkeys to choose the scale, move, and rotate tools, all of which increased the speed with which we completed a reasonably complex task. In the next chapter, devoted to the Hypergraph, we will see how a thorough knowledge of this interface element can improve your workflow on complex tasks even more.

Even if much of what you have read in this chapter is a bit confusing to you now, try to remember, as you continue working on your projects, the little tricks and short-cuts we have discussed here. With a bit of practice, many of the techniques discussed in this chapter will become second nature to you, and your Maya skills and products will reflect this.

chapter 4

THE HYPERGRAPH: YOUR ROADMAP TO A SCENE

Featuring

THE HYPERGRAPH: YOUR ROADMAP TO A SCENE

I f you come to Maya from another 3D package (as many of us do), you are probably familiar with a window like Maya's Outliner, which helps you keep track of objects in your scene. On the other hand, it is unlikely that you have run across anything quite like Maya's Hypergraph. For this reason, even many seasoned Maya users steer clear of the Hypergraph (using the Outliner instead), as they can't make heads or tails of its interface. The goal of this chapter is to clear up any confusion you may have about the Hypergraph—whether you're a new Maya user or a long-time user who just doesn't use the Hypergraph—and reveal how powerful an ally the Hypergraph can be when you are working on anything from simple to very complex scenes. While the Hypergraph may seem confusing on its surface, once you see that its interface was designed to parallel Maya's scene window interface—and once you see the many different ways in which the Hypergraph can function—you will wonder how you ever got along without it. Even if you are an experienced Hypergraph user, you may find some useful tidbits in this chapter.

What Is the Hypergraph?

The Hypergraph is, in its essence, a hypertext-like view of your scene (thus the name). If you have worked with an HTML authoring tool, you will recognize the web-like appearance of linked objects in the Hypergraph. Every element visible in a scene is represented by a text box, and any linked objects have a line that connects them together, showing their connection in the scene. Passing your cursor over the line, you'll see which elements of each object are connected. Besides displaying the relationships between objects and elements in a scene, the Hypergraph also lets you create or modify those relationships—for example, you can parent two objects together or break an input connection directly in the Hypergraph, rather than having to go to the scene window or Relationship Editor. In essence, the Hypergraph *is* your scene— you can do pretty much everything you can do in a scene window, and more, only it's represented as text boxes instead of the objects you would see in the scene windows.

N O T E   The types of objects visible in a scene depend on the filtering choices you've made using the Hypergraph's Options ➤ Display menu.

Why Use the Hypergraph instead of the Outliner?

The Outliner is exactly what its name implies: an outline of your scene. While you can perform many useful functions in the Outliner, almost all of these can be performed as easily (or more so) in the Hypergraph, and the Hypergraph allows you to do many tasks that are impossible in the Outliner. While the Outliner is, for most people, easier to understand at first, the Hypergraph is actually much more aligned with the way Maya works, as it is organized around navigation and connection conventions used throughout Maya. Thus, once you get accustomed to using the Hypergraph, it will seem much more natural than the Outliner as a means of getting around your scene.

Getting to Know the Hypergraph

Because the Hypergraph offers so much information, it takes a bit of effort for most people to feel comfortable with it. We will therefore work through the Hypergraph piece by piece in the following pages, using examples to clarify certain concepts, but mostly just showing how the interface works. By the time you finish this section, you should feel comfortable enough with the Hypergraph to begin using it in your work (if you don't already)—and once you use it a while, it's likely you won't know how you got along without it.

Navigating the Hypergraph

Open a new scene in Maya, and create two objects—say a sphere and a cone. Now open the Hypergraph by choosing Window ➢ Hypergraph from the main menu set. In the Hypergraph window, you should see icons for the objects you created:

TIP   Because you will probably access the Hypergraph many times while working in Maya, it is a good idea to create a button on your shelf for it. From the menu bar (not the hotbox), choose Window ➢ Hypergraph while holding down the Ctrl, Alt, and Shift keys. A new button will appear on the shelf for the Hypergraph. You can also create a hotkey for the Hypergraph if you prefer (see Chapter 3 for more on how to do this).

If you compare this view to a view of the same scene in the Outliner, you can see that the Hypergraph is actually less complex (as it doesn't show the cameras or default sets), but it is organized in a side-to-side manner, rather than top-to-bottom.

You will also notice that the Hypergraph indicates a selected object by coloring it yellow (the cone in this case), while the Outliner highlights the object in a gray bar.

Zooming and tracking in the Hypergraph use the same techniques as in the scene windows. To zoom, hold down the Alt key and the left and middle mouse buttons—dragging to the left zooms out, while dragging to the right zooms in. To track across (or up and down) the Hypergraph window, hold down the Alt key and the middle mouse button, and then drag the mouse around to track through the window. By tracking and zooming, you can quickly move through even a large scene, finding the nodes you're interested in. Additionally, you can use two hotkeys to frame the Hypergraph around a selected object or around all objects in the Hypergraph. To focus the window on one or more selected objects (highlighted in green or white in the scene window), press the F key. To expand the view to fit all displayed objects, press the A key. If you try this with our example scene (with the cone selected), pressing F will fill the Hypergraph window with the cone node, while pressing A will expand the view to fit both the sphere and the cone.

T I P   The A and F keys also work in any scene window—pressing F will focus the window on the selected object(s), while pressing A will make the entire scene fit in the window. This is another way in which the Hypergraph and scene windows behave in the same manner.

If your scene is complex, and you find yourself consistently hunting for a particular object (or group of objects) in the Hypergraph, you can save yourself a great deal of time by bookmarking any or all views you are likely to need at a later point. Although our example scene is too simple to warrant using bookmarks, let's see how the process works by creating three bookmarks: one focusing on the sphere, one focusing on the cone, and the third showing both objects. First, highlight the cone and press the F key (or just zoom and track until the cone box fills the Hypergraph window). Then choose Bookmarks ➤ Create Bookmark ❏ from the Hypergraph menu set. Choosing the option box will open a window that lets you name the bookmark (if you don't open the option box, Maya will choose a default name for you). In this case, type **cone** and click the OK button. You now have a bookmark for this view arrangement, which you can return to at any time. Next, select the sphere object and press the F key, then create a bookmark for it (name it **sphere**). Finally, create a bookmark for the complete view of the scene (press the A key to jump to a complete view of the scene) and name it **all**.

To test your bookmarks, zoom and track the window to a completely different view, and then choose Bookmarks ➤ Cone (or Sphere or All) from the Hypergraph menu set. The view should jump back to the one you defined for that bookmark. To edit your bookmarks (add a new one, delete a bookmark, or rename one), choose

Bookmarks ➤ Bookmark Editor, select the bookmark you wish to edit, and choose the appropriate choice from the Bookmark Editor Edit menu. Again, using bookmarks in a scene as simple as our example is not very useful—however, in a scene with hundreds of objects, using bookmarks can save a great deal of time and frustration.

T I P   You can also create bookmarks for different types of views (with the Hypergraph in different modes—as discussed later in this chapter). This functionality can really save time, as you can avoid having to continually reset the Hypergraph's view modes as you switch between different aspects of your project.

One other nice feature of the Hypergraph is that it shows you when an object is keyframed, by changing its box shape in the window from a rectangle to a parallelogram. If you keyframe the ball shape, for example, its Hypergraph representation will change to give you a visual indication that it is now a keyframed node.

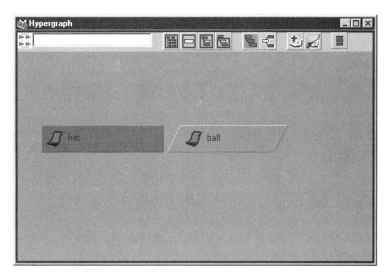

Doing Work in the Hypergraph

Besides viewing selected objects in the Hypergraph, you can also select any object in the Hypergraph window simply by clicking on its box. To select the sphere in our example, click on its box, turning it yellow (and selecting it in the scene window as well). To select multiple objects, you can either Shift-select them or drag a selection marquee around the boxes representing all the objects you wish to select. To deselect one selected object, Shift+click on it. To deselect all objects in the scene, click anywhere in the Hypergraph window outside a text box. To rename an object in the Hypergraph, Ctrl+double-click on the name in the box, and then type in the new name and press Enter. For example, we could rename the sphere **ball** and the cone **hat** in our practice scene.

Parenting one object to another (the child object will then follow its parent's movements, rotations, and scaling) is just a matter of MM dragging the child object on top of its parent-to-be. In our example, MM drag the ball (sphere) onto the hat (cone). The ball will now appear beneath the hat—with a line connecting the two—showing that it is now the child of the hat.

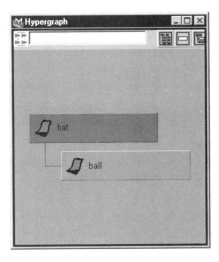

If you now select the hat, you will notice that the ball also becomes highlighted (in the scene window), and that any transformation you apply to the hat is automatically applied to the ball. To unparent (disconnect) the two objects, MM drag the ball into an empty space in the Hypergraph window. The objects will once again be side by side (with no interconnecting line), indicating that they are independent of each other.

Nodes and the Hypergraph

The underlying structure of a Maya scene is based on nodes and attributes. A node is the fundamental element of a scene, and often an object in a Maya scene window (or in a shader network or the like) has several nodes. An attribute is a behavior (or attribute) of a node, and each node can have many attributes, including custom attributes that you create yourself. Nodes are connected together, either by default when you create, say, a geometry object (which has a shape and a transform node connected together), or when you manually connect two objects (for example, by parenting one object to another, or by attaching a new texture to a material group). Most attributes that are of the same data type (for example, floats or vectors) can be attached to each other across two nodes.

If you are not used to working with Maya, the entire concept of nodes may seem pretty frightening. The theory may seem difficult, but in practice, nodes and attributes are fairly easy to understand: Nodes are anything that can be shown in the Hypergraph, while attributes are what appears in the channel box or Attribute Editor when a node is selected. (Actually, nodes appear in the Channel box and Attribute Editor as well: They are the boldface items you can click on to rename or to open their attribute groups in the Channel box, or the tabs in the Attribute Editor.) Thus, for the Hypergraph at least, all you see are nodes, and changing Hypergraph display modes just changes which nodes you are looking at for your scene.

To see how changing display modes changes the nodes you see in a scene, let's again look at our simple example scene (the ball and hat). From the Hypergraph menu set (or by holding down the right mouse button inside the Hypergraph window), choose Options ➢ Display ➢ Shape Nodes. Now that shape nodes can be seen in the Hypergraph, you will see the ballShape and hatShape nodes, which are separate from the ball and hat nodes. (The ball and hat nodes are called *transform* nodes, and are in control of where the object is, its rotation, and its scaling, while the shape nodes are in charge of what the object looks like.)

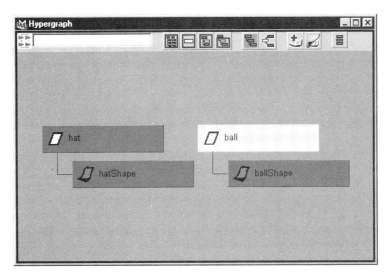

PART

1

Maya Fundamentals

You can also show all nodes (many of which are normally invisible) that lead into and out of an object node, revealing the hidden depths of what Maya is doing when you create a "simple" object. Select the ball node and choose Graph ➤ Up and Downstream Connections from the Hypergraph menu set. You will then see all of the input and output nodes connected to your ball.

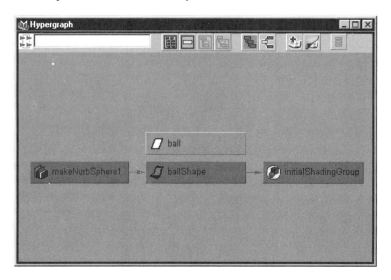

In this layout, the ball transform node sits atop the others, while the bottom three nodes show the flow of information for this object: the makeNurbsSphere1 node (where you control radius, U and V isoparms, and so forth) outputs to the ballShape node, which then outputs to the initialShadingGroup node, where the ball is given a texture and made visible.

N O T E   No objects in Maya are visible unless they are attached to a shading group. While the underlying structure of an object is contained in its shape and transform nodes, it is only in the shading group that the object is given a color and texture—therefore, without its connection to a shading group, you could not see the object.

If you wish to dig even deeper, choose the initialShadingGroup node, and display the up and downstream connections again. This time, you will see the shapes (plus a lambert shader—the default one) that feed into the initial shading group, plus the shading group's output to the renderer and lights, as shown next. To return to your original view, just choose Graph ➤ Scene Hierarchy—or choose one of the bookmarks you had previously saved: a nice time-saver!

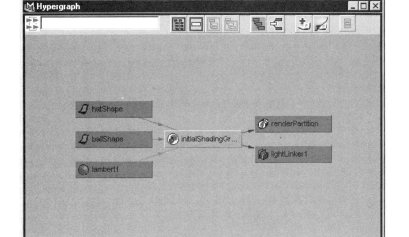

Because Maya is constructed on nodes, and the Hypergraph can show just about any node grouping (based on your filtering choices), you should begin to see how valuable a tool the Hypergraph can be as you work through the different stages of your animation process. From modeling to texturing to lighting to animation, the Hypergraph is flexible enough that it can display the data you need—and even *only* the data you need, should you wish—for each stage of your work. Just keep in mind that the Hypergraph shows nodes, and Maya is built on nodes, so all you have to do is figure out which nodes you want to see for any given stage of your animation process, and you can get the Hypergraph to display them for you.

Know Your Nodes

While there are a great number of nodes in Maya, they tend to fall under one of these general categories:

- Transform nodes (containing items like Translate X or Rotate Y)
- Shape nodes (containing items like the makeObject inputs)
- Invisible nodes (like default cameras)
- Underworld nodes (nodes that are created, for example, when a curve is drawn on a surface)
- Material nodes (like lambert or phongE)

Continued on next page

- Texture nodes (colors, procedural textures, or image files used to alter the behavior of a material node)
- Texture placement nodes (used to place textures on objects)
- Light nodes (lights, like a spotlight)
- Utility nodes (which provide a utility to a shader network, such as the multiply/divide node)

Menus and Buttons: Where the Action Is

While the Hypergraph's default view is very useful, it is just a first step to viewing your scene in the Hypergraph. By using the Hypergraph's menu choices (the most common of which are repeated in buttons across the top of the Hypergraph), you can make the Hypergraph show you just what you need in an organized, concise manner. To see what the Hypergraph can do, let's take a quick tour through its menus, highlighting several items that might prove especially useful in your later work.

The Edit Menu

The Edit menu contains several ways to control the display of selected items (or edit those items). First, you can rename an object—this is the same as Ctrl+double-clicking on the object's name. You can also collapse or expand a hierarchy; for example, if the ball has its shape node showing, you can collapse the shape node, hiding it beneath the ball's transform node. A red triangle reminds you that there are collapsed nodes beneath the visible one. To expand the nodes again, just choose Edit ➤ Expand.

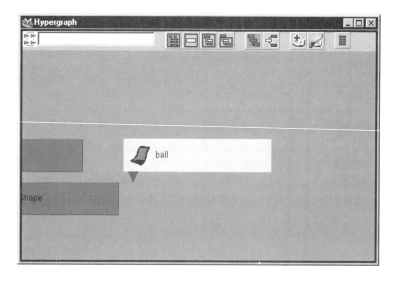

T I P   You can also collapse and expand nodes by simply double-clicking on the top node of the group you wish to hide or reveal.

If you have several groups of collapsed nodes beneath a parent node (for example, if you have several child objects, all of which have collapsed subnodes), you can expand all nodes at once by choosing Edit ➤ Expand All. The option Show Selected displays items that are selected in the scene window (or Outliner) but have been filtered out of the Hypergraph display. For example, if you have turned off display of NURBS objects in the Hypergraph, but choose a NURBS sphere in the scene window, you can force the Hypergraph to show it by choosing the Show Selected menu item. The Attributes menu item brings up the Attribute Editor for the selected item (the same as selecting the item and pressing Ctrl+A).

 N O T E   There are also a couple of options in the Edit menu (and elsewhere) for use with the freeform layout, but we will discuss this type of layout below.

The View Menu

Under the View menu, you can choose to change the Hypergraph to the last view you used—or the next, if you have moved backward and forward in views. This command can be useful if you move a great distance through the Hypergraph in a complex scene and wish to return to where you were previously. The Previous and Next View commands function in a similar manner to bookmarks but change according to the Hypergraph view. You can also frame your selection (this has the same effect as the F key), frame all (the same as the A key), frame the hierarchy, or frame a branch of the hierarchy.

These four framing options (Frame All, Selection, Hierarchy, and Branch) can be accessed by the four leftmost buttons in the Hypergraph toolbar, which is located atop the Hypergraph window.

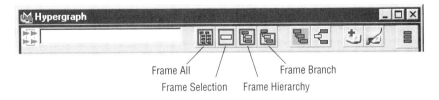

Framing a hierarchy frames the selected object plus any other objects in that hierarchy. Framing a branch frames the selected object plus any objects *below* it in the hierarchy. If the ball is the child of the hat in our example scene, selecting the ball and then framing the hierarchy would focus the window on the hat and ball nodes; framing the branch would focus the window only on the ball (and any child nodes it might have).

The Bookmark Menu

The Bookmark menu lets you create and edit bookmarks for any layout or view you wish to save in the Hypergraph. We discussed bookmarks earlier in the chapter, so here we need only note that two buttons on the Hypergraph toolbar are related to the Bookmark menu: the Add Bookmark button (a book with a red plus on it) and the Edit Bookmark button (a lifted leaf with a book below it). The Add Bookmark button simply adds a bookmark for the current view, while the Edit Bookmark button opens the Bookmark Editor window, allowing you to rename, delete, or add bookmarks.

The Graph Menu

The Graph menu controls the general parameters of what the Hypergraph shows. You can graph the upstream connections for an object (all nodes that feed into the selected object), the downstream connections for an object (all nodes that the selected object feeds information into), and both the up and downstream connections for that object. Because choosing one of these options changes the view from the default scene hierarchy, once you have chosen an upstream/downstream graph, you can also choose the Scene Hierarchy view to return to the scene hierarchy.

The graph Up and Downstream Connections and Scene Hierarchy menu items are also available as buttons on the Hypergraph toolbar:

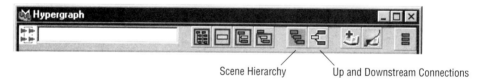

Scene Hierarchy   Up and Downstream Connections

Should your graph get behind your scene window (an unlikely event, but possible), you can force the Hypergraph to rebuild itself by choosing Graph ➤ Rebuild. By using this command, you can be sure the Hypergraph is up to date if you ever suspect it is not. Finally, the Layout command in the Graph menu lets you change (or reset) the arrangement of items when you are looking at upstream or downstream connections. Arranging these nodes may allow you to make more sense of them or to move unwanted nodes off screen while you work.

N O T E   When you graph the up and/or downstream connections in the Hypergraph, you are creating what is known as a *dependency graph*. Put simply, a dependency graph shows the connections between nodes (like shading network elements) in a Maya scene, allowing you to see the flow of information from one node to another—in other words, how each node *depends* on the others to which it is connected.

The Rendering Menu

The Rendering menu lets you focus the Hypergraph on materials, textures, shading groups, lights, and images. You can also use the Rendering ➤ Create Render Node command to create a render node directly in the Hypergraph, rather than having to use the Hypershade or the Multilister to do so.

NOTE With the advent of the Hypershade, the Rendering menu set in the Hypergraph is no longer as useful as it once was. It is still very convenient, however, to have all shading information accessible in the same window as the scene hierarchy, especially when you just want to take a quick peek at a shading item rather than work with it extensively.

The Options Menu

The Options menu gives you control over how the Hypergraph displays nonstandard (invisible, shape, or underworld) nodes, and also how the Hypergraph as a whole is laid out. Of the Options submenus (Display, Orientation, Layout, Transitions, and Update), the one you will probably use the most is the Display submenu. The Display submenu lets you choose which types of nodes and connections will be displayed in the Hypergraph window. As we have already seen, you can show shape nodes (which control the structural options of an object); you can also display invisible nodes (such as the cameras or any objects you have hidden) and underworld nodes (these are nodes generated by objects such as surface curves, which have their transform nodes in a local rather than a global space). You can also turn on (or off) the display of expression, constraint, or deformer connections. For example, if you aim-constrain the ball to the hat in our example scene (Constrain ➤ Aim), you can display the connections Maya makes between the ball, the hat, and the new aimConstraint node.

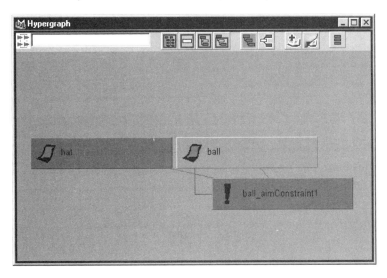

NOTE   You can also display a background image for the Hypergraph window if you are in freeform layout mode (see below) by choosing Options ➤ Display ➤ Background Image (in freeform) from the Display submenu.

The Orientation submenu of the Display menu lets you toggle between horizontal (the default layout) and vertical layout modes. If you like working in an Outliner-like fashion (with nodes stacked on top of each other), you may prefer the vertical orientation mode. The Layout submenu allows you to choose automatic (default) or freeform layout mode—the freeform layout mode lets you move nodes around into any shape you wish, while the automatic mode places the nodes in a predetermined order next to one another. The Transitions submenu enables you to create an animated transition between views when you choose View ➤ Previous or Next View. By default, the view changes instantaneously, but by checking the Animate Transitions box (and then choosing how many frames the transitions will be), you can force the Hypergraph window to scroll from one view to the other. While they are cute, transitions are more of a time waster than anything useful—unless you need to figure out where one view is in relation to another. The Update submenu lets you choose when to update the Hypergraph window; you can choose to update on a selection, on a node creation, on both (the default), or on neither.

The Show Menu

The Show menu lets you make very specific choices about the objects you wish to see in the Hypergraph window. Under Show ➤ Objects, you can show (or hide) geometry, lights, sets, and cameras, to name just a few. You can display all objects by choosing Show ➤ Show All. You can select several objects (in the scene window or the Hypergraph), and then show only other objects with the same type as your selected objects (Show ➤ Show Selected Type(s)). You can also invert the types of objects you display (Show ➤ Invert Shown). If, for example, you were working on a scene with 10 lights and 20 geometry objects, you could display only the lights while you worked on lighting the scene and then invert the selection filter to show all your other objects while you tweaked your models or animated the scene.

Making and Breaking Connections in the Hypergraph

One of the most interesting features of the Hypergraph is its ability to make and break data connections between nodes. To see how this works, take our example scene (the ball and hat), and add a lattice deformer to the ball (select the ball node, then choose Deform ➤ Create Lattice). Select the ball node again, and choose Graph ➤ Up and

Downstream Connections. In this new view, you will see connecting arrows between the nodes that make up the lattice-ball group. By passing your cursor over one of these arrows, you can see the output/input data connections between nodes.

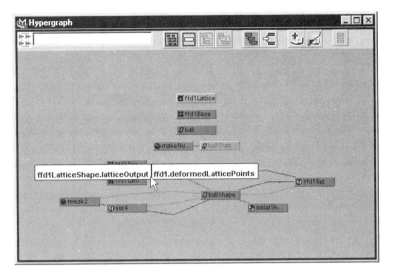

To break one of these connections, just click on one of the arrows (highlighting it yellow) and hit the Delete key. You can, for example, break the deformer connection between the lattice and the ball if you highlight the arrow that shows the ffd1LatticeShape.latticeOutput to ffd1.deformedLatticePoints connection (the one shown in the image above). If you alter the deformer (scale it, say), you will immediately see the ball return to its original shape when you delete the connection.

 TIP As should be obvious, it is dangerous to go around deleting connections between nodes—especially if you don't know what you're doing. This is not to say you shouldn't experiment; just save your file before you do start deleting connections, so in case you can't get what you want, you can at least return to a good version of your project.

To make a connection between nodes, just MM drag one node on top of another (the node that will output a value will be the one you drag; the one that will accept an input value will be the node you drag onto). Once you have completed the drag operation, the Connection Editor will open, allowing you to choose which attributes to connect. If, for example, you MM drag ffd1Lattice onto ball, you might connect the lattice's visibility attribute to the ball's visibility (click on each of these attributes on the right and left of the Connection Editor to connect them). Then, when you hide the lattice, the ball will hide as well. To confirm that the connection has been made, you will see a new arrow in the Hypergraph showing the connected attributes.

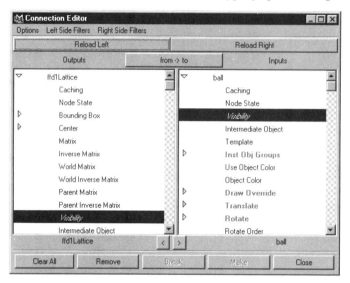

In general, most people use the Hypergraph (and now the Hypershade as well) primarily to make and break connections between shader nodes in a shader network, such as the luminance output of a texture being fed into the transparency of a material node. While the connected attributes are different, however, the method of making and breaking connections is the same as described above.

The Ins and Outs of the Connection Editor

The Connection Editor is an extremely useful Maya feature. Essentially, it lets you connect any output of one node to any matching (that is, of the same data type) input of another node. The Connection Editor can do some amazing things, connecting even the most bizarre attributes (as long as their data types match). This base-level control over connections gives you creative control over anything from ramp texture colors to object rotation order based on another object's position (or that of another node on the same object), visibility, node state, or whatever else you can dream up. In shader networks, the output color of one node (like a fractal map) is often automatically input into the input color of another node (like a phongE texture) when you create a texture map. With the Connection Editor, you can also plug the output color of one node into the bump map node—a node that controls how "bumpy" a surface looks—of a texture (which is the same as MM dragging the node onto the bump map channel of the texture), or even control the intensity (or height) of a different bump map based on the output of this node.

Continued on next page

While the number of attributes available to connect via the Connection Editor can be a bit overwhelming, the window's controls are fairly straightforward. Let's take a look at how the Connection Editor works.

Using the Connection Editor

To make a connection, first load the left and right sides of the Connection Editor with the two nodes you wish to connect (or, alternatively, MM drag one node onto another in the Attribute Editor to automatically open and load the Connection Editor). Then click on the output attribute you wish to use and, from the list of attributes with matching data types (not grayed out), choose the input node.

Some data types, like color, have arrows next to them, allowing you to access their component attributes—in the case of color, it would be the red, green, and blue components of the color. Thus, while color (a vector) may not be a match (and is thus grayed out) for the X scale of an object, you *can* connect the red component of color to the object's X scale; depending on the direction of this connection, the object's redness would be controlled by its X scale, or the object's scale would be controlled by its redness.

The Connection Editor Controls

The controls in the Connection Editor's window are easy to use. The buttons at the top enable you to reload the left or right side of the window (thus changing which node is loaded on each side of the window). By clicking the "from -> to" button, you can change the direction of the input/output of the two nodes (making it "to <- from").

The Right and Left Side Filters menus let you display (in the windows below) only those attributes you are interested in—this can be a great way to reduce the clutter of available attributes to a more manageable number.

Under the Options menu, you can change the default behavior of the Connection Editor—which is to make and break connections automatically as you click on the attributes in the left and right windows—to a manual mode. If manual mode is selected, you must press the (now enabled) Make and Break buttons at the bottom of the window to create (or disconnect) the connection between two attributes.

The Clear All button removes all connections, and the Remove button removes the loaded nodes.

Finally, the two arrow keys just below the left and right windows allow you to step through all nodes on an object (for example, the shape to the transform node of a geometric object), saving you a trip back to the Hypergraph to highlight a new node, and then reload it into the Connection Editor. To disconnect two attributes, just click on a connected attribute on one side of the window to unhighlight it.

Continued on next page

The possibilities for using the Connection Editor are so many and varied that the best advice is just to open a new project, create some objects and shader networks, and play with different connections, so you can get a feel for the different ways you can control one node via another. This way, when you are faced with what might appear a difficult problem in a "real world" situation, you may see that some clever use of the Connection Editor will do the trick nicely.

Freeform Layout Mode

There is one last way you can modify the Hypergraph to make the data in it even more understandable: the freeform layout. This layout mode allows you to place your nodes anywhere you wish in relation to each other (above, beside, around, and so forth). This can be a real help when you build a complex character like a human, as you can arrange the nodes for the hands, say, where the hands of a figure would be. You can even import an image as a background plate for the Hypergraph window (perhaps a sketch of your figure) to serve as a reference in the freeform layout mode.

To enter freeform layout mode, either choose Options ➤ Layout ➤ Freeform Layout, or click the Freeform Layout toggle button on the toolbar in the Hypergraph (the button farthest to the right). Once you are in freeform layout mode, you can drag nodes anywhere in the Hypergraph window that you wish, including into shapes or figures. To load a background image for your new layout, choose View ➤ Load Background Image and browse to find your image. You can also reset your freeform layout to its default arrangement by choosing Edit ➤ Reset Freeform Layout. Thus, no matter how much mess you make of your node arrangement, you can always return to a clean view at the touch of a button.

As an example of using the freeform layout, let's build a human figure in the Hypergraph (we won't actually build a character in the scene window, but if you have one you've already built, feel free to use that figure instead of our random assortment of primitives). First create 20 or 30 scene primitives (they can all lie on top of each other, as we won't use them in the scene window). If you wish, you can lay them out in the scene window in the form of a person, or you can just arrange them in the Hypergraph. In the Hypergraph, be sure you are in freeform layout mode, then drag nodes up to the head region (renaming them things like "skull," "nose," "right eye," and so on), the body, the arms, and the legs. When you're finished, you should have a graph that looks something like a person, where every node is intuitively related to its (supposed) function in the scene window. Obviously, arranging nodes like this in a complex

scene can save you a great deal of time when it comes to finding a particular node (the right eye, for example) that you wish to manipulate.

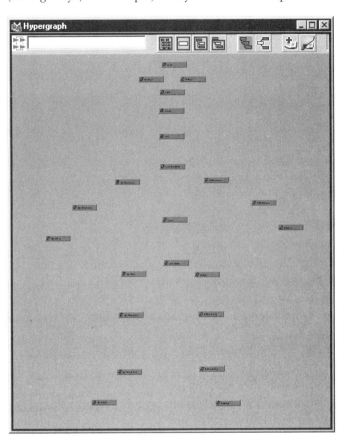

Summary

In this chapter, we have taken a fairly thorough tour of the Hypergraph, exploring its navigation features, the scene-related actions you can perform in the Hypergraph window, the different options for viewing and layout the Hypergraph gives you, and even how to see, make, and break attribute connections from the Hypergraph. You should feel more comfortable using the Hypergraph now, as you now understand how to use it and what options are available to you to aid in laying out the Hypergraph in an intuitive manner. As you proceed in this book (or in your own animation adventures), be sure to continue using the Hypergraph with your scenes. Soon, you will find this tool not only familiar, but indispensable for all your work in Maya.

PART II

MODELING

Use the basic modeling tools

Perform NURBS modeling

Perform polygon modeling

Perform organic modeling

Use the Artisan add-in

chapter 5

MODELING BASICS

Featuring

- *What is modeling?*
- *What makes a model good or bad?*
- *Maya's modeling aids*

MODELING BASICS

This chapter introduces the basics of modeling. The first section of the chapter will be devoted to the concepts you will need to become familiar with before plunging fully into the modeling tools and actions in Maya 2. A good understanding of the general principles of modeling will enable you to use your time wisely and efficiently as you work.

In the following pages you will have an opportunity to try out some of Maya's modeling aids as you learn some modeling fundamentals, and then you will create a living room scene using Maya's primitives.

What Is Modeling?

Before we delve into modeling specifically in Maya, we need to go through a few concepts of modeling in general. Let us begin with a working definition of what modeling is in computer animation. Here is one that would seem acceptable to most people: 3D modeling is the process of creating three-dimensional surfaces using a computer for the purpose of rendering them into a picture or a sequence of pictures.

But let's think about this for a moment. In fields such as the automobile industry, architecture, or engineering, the digital models are actually built with specific products in mind—their purpose is the creation of a physical model or prototype, and ultimately a working automobile, or building, or whatever. For such models, rendering is only a stage they go through in order to get to their ultimate destination. For the 3D artist working in computer animation, however, the ultimate destination for the models they build is pictures that only exist in TV, videos, or movies—all 2D environments.

This difference gives rise to a very important principle, which determines how we should build models for computer animation. Here is the principle: *The only thing that really matters in modeling in computer animation is the picture(s) people will see.* Modeling anything that will not be seen, therefore, is (generally speaking) a waste of time.

It's All an Illusion

Digital animation, then, is a world of facades. If you will only see the back and right walls of a room (as in the image below), it makes no sense to build the front or the left side. Modeling for the computer animator is all about creating illusions for the eye to feast on—build only what the eye (the camera) will see. We will certainly have more to say about this later on, but suffice it to say for now that this is the reason why careful preproduction planning is so crucial, and why well-organized production teams will always create very detailed storyboards before they commit to building anything.

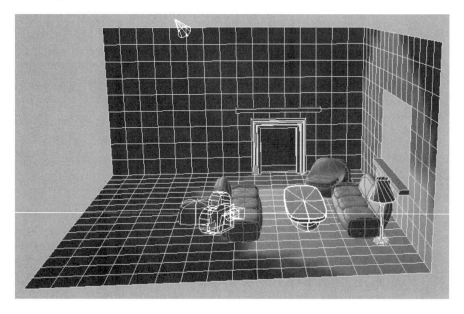

Are You a Modeler?

Let's face it, a professional sculptor or an architect will usually have a much easier time with modeling on the computer than a person with no such background, just as a painter or a photographer will find it easier to do texturing or lighting in a digital environment. Many of the skills that are used in these fields transfer immediately into the computer environment, and other skills soon follow, as the artist becomes familiar with their surroundings.

But don't be too discouraged if you want to become a modeler but have no such background. There are other things to keep in mind. Not all artists are able to transfer their traditional skills fully into the digital environment; and more importantly, there are other skills, specific to digital modeling, that also must be learned. Computer animation is a different world, and the computer, a different tool. Digital modeling should be viewed as a separate and independent artistic medium—as different as painting is to sculpting, for example, each with its own sets of rules and technical skills. One must feel as comfortable with the computer as a painter would with a brush, or a sculptor with clay. And just as some painters know nothing about sculpting but still are great painters, so can one be a great 3D modeler without being a sculptor, or an architect, or a painter.

Good Models and Bad Models

Good models look good when rendered, and bad models look bad—it's that simple. You may think that is stating the obvious, but the catch, of course, is that it takes a lot of time and care to produce models that look good, and always a lot of sweat and effort to produce great-looking models. Tight schedules and deadlines often make this a very difficult—if not impossible—task.

Having said these things, however, there are other, less obvious, factors in the production environment that determine whether a model is good or bad, and these are just as important. The two criteria most frequently used in animation are how *heavy* or *light* a model is and how well it can be set up for animation.

Improperly built models often end up being computationally heavy, meaning they are built with too much geometry and can cause numerous problems for the animators, or lose precious production time in rendering. A light model, in contrast, does not have a lot of geometry and thus allows the animator to act more interactively with it, producing better animation in shorter time. It generally renders faster, too.

If a model is going to be deformed in a certain way—in other words, to bend and stretch as it acts a certain way—the modeler needs to build the model with that in mind, putting the necessary points where they will deform properly. In some cases, not having points in certain areas is actually better. One reason why modelers build NURBS faces (the next chapter is an in-depth look at NURBS modeling) and not polygon faces (Chapter 7 covers polygon modeling) for facial animation is that a well-built NURBS face (on the left below) is a lot easier to set up for animation than a Polygon face, even though the latter is easier to build. Notice the extra lines in the Polygon model (on the right).

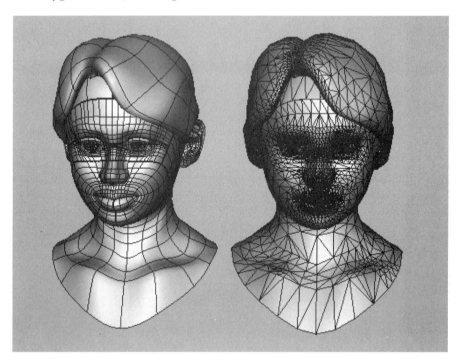

Modeling Tools

Later in this chapter you'll get a taste of the process of modeling in Maya. First, however, let's look at the Maya interface features available to us. Maya has a vast array of tools that can aid us in modeling. Here are some of the more basic and useful functions we will be covering in this chapter:

- Templates
- Layers
- Pick-masking
- Snapping
- Freezing transformations
- Construction history

Templates

Objects that become templates remain visible but cannot be selected like other objects. The standard way to turn an object into a template is to select the object and then select Display ➤ Object Components ➤ Templates. You can also open the Attribute Editor (Ctrl+A), choose Display, and toggle on Template.

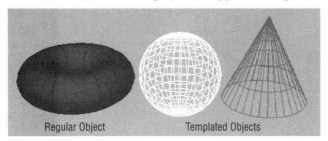

Regular Object   Templated Objects

Because the templated object cannot be selected in the usual way by dragging, in order to untemplate it, you have to select it either in the Outliner or the Hypergraph editor, or use a selection mask (see "Pick-Masking" later in the chapter), and then toggle it back with the same command.

There is another way to template objects, and that is by using the Layer Bar (discussed in the next section). A layer also has templating capability, and it is generally the more efficient way to template objects because it can handle groups.

T I P   Templating using layers is a bit different from templating using the method just described. A regular template can be picked using Selection Mask for templates, but not the ones templated using layers—they can only be selected from the Layer menu.

The Layer Bar

The Layer Bar is an extremely useful tool. It was originally created for Alias Power Animator, and now, with the release of Maya 2, the Layer Bar is back in its original form. A layer creates an exclusive collection of objects that can be selected, hidden, or templated together. Essentially, it acts as a directory or a folder for objects to aid in organization and work efficiency.

The Layer Bar is on by default, but if you don't see it, select Options ➤ UI Preferences and turn it on. You can also see the Layers using Windows ➤ Layer Editor. To create a new layer, you can click on New Layer in the Layer Editor, or click the New Layer button on the Layer Bar—it's the button left of the Default layer.

New Layer

To add an object or a group of objects, first select them. Then click on the layer to which you want to add the objects, display the Layers menu, and select Assign Selected. To move an object from one layer to another, simply select the object and assign it to the other layer. You can also use the Relationship Editor to do the same thing: display the Layers menu, select Edit Membership to open the Relationship Editor, and connect the objects and the layers the way you would normally do. You can hide the layer objects, template them, or reference them.

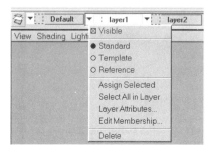

Referenced objects of a layer are just like templated objects, except that they can be used for snapping (see the section "Snapping" below) and they can appear as shaded surfaces. Removing a layer does not delete its member objects, but only the layer itself.

 T I P   Use the Layer Colors palette to identify different groups of objects as belonging to a layer. Double-click on the *color box* in the Layer Bar to pop open the Layer Colors palette and assign a color, or use the Layer Editor to do the same. Using different colors can not only make things much easier to work with for very complex scenes; it can also make the scene a bit more interesting to look at, as you can see below (and in the Color Gallery on the CD).

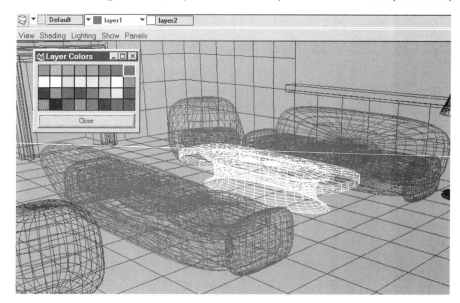

Pick-Masking

One of the most elegant features of the Maya interface is its ability to limit selection to specific types of objects, components, or hierarchical elements. This function is also known as creating a *pick mask* or *selection mask*. (Maya uses the terms interchangeably.) You can RM choose an object to pick-mask elements which specifically apply to that object, or you can use the buttons on the Status Line to pick only the elements you want to select.

When you RM choose an object you are working on, Maya automatically figures out which selections should become available for that specific object type and gives you the appropriate choices. For a curve, you get a different set of marking menu items from the one used for a NURBS surface, as you can see here.

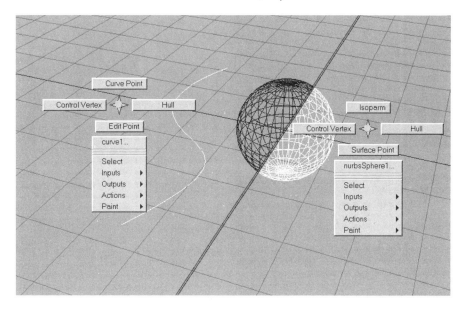

The really cool thing about this feature is that depending on the pick mask you choose, Maya adjusts the display of control vertices, edit points, and hulls accordingly so that you will only select what you want to select, and hides the rest. For example, if you pick-mask Control Vertex, Maya will automatically go into the component selection mode and display only the CVs for you to select. Or if you pick-mask Hull, it will only show hulls.

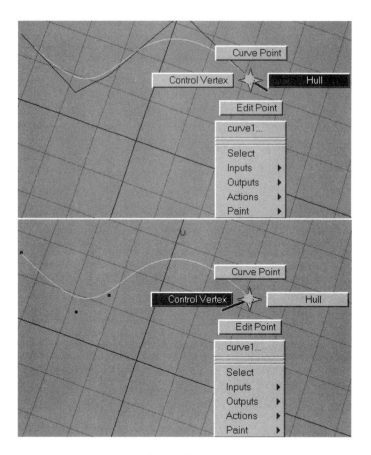

Various selection masks can be created using the Status Line in three different levels. You can limit your selection by *component types* such as CVs, Edit Points, Faces, Edges, and so on.

You can also create selection masks to pick only *object types* such as Curves, Surfaces, Joints, and so on.

And finally, you can limit selection by *hierarchy types*, such as pick-masking only the root or leaf level of a hierarchy. When you are in the hierarchy mode, you can also create a pick mask to select only templated objects as well.

N O T E   When you are limiting selection by hierarchy types, the marking menu's component selection masks do not work, because Maya is only allowing root or leaf nodes to be selected.

Note that when several elements are active in the selection mask, Maya has a *priority list* that causes certain elements to be selected before others. Maya's default selection mask is set to select by object type with all the different object types turned on, so when you drag over a NURBS surface and a joint at the same time, it should select both objects. But because Maya's default priority list has "joints" before "NURBS surfaces," it will select the joint and leave the NURBS surface unselected. If you want to see the priority list, go to Options ➤ General Preferences ➤ Select.

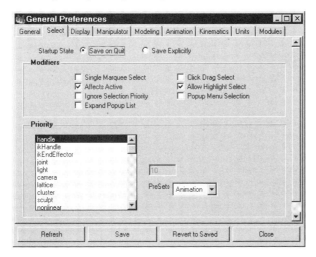

 W A R N I N G   Do not change the default priority list or turn it off unless you have a good reason to. The priority list was defined with careful deliberation, and you will find as you work your way through the various stages of a production in Maya that the default priorities make a lot of sense and are very efficient.

Snapping

The snapping tools allow you to transform an object or a component to snap to grids, curves, points, view planes, or a surface. These elements become targets, or magnets, when activated. You can access these tools, in the order just listed as buttons in the Status Line:

You also can use Maya's default hotkeys for snapping to grids, curves, or points. This is a more efficient way of using the snapping tools. These are the hotkeys:

- Press X and click or drag to snap to grid
- Press C and click or drag to snap to curve
- Press V and click or drag to snap to a point

Let's briefly try out these tools. Create two curves as shown below. Select Create ➤ CV Curve Tool and X+click on the grid. Click six times and press Enter to complete the first curve. Type **y** to access the CV Curve tool again and draw the second curve.

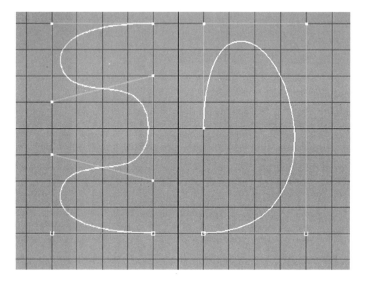

RM choose to pick-mask CVs over the first curve. Then select the bottom CV, select the Move Tool by typing **w**, and V+drag to the first CV of the second curve. It should snap to the CV as shown on the facing page. Now try to C+drag the last CV of the first curve to the second curve. It's not snapping because snapping to a curve is distance sensitive. Drag the selected CV over the second curve, making sure it's right over the curve. Now C+drag the CV again back and forth. It should stay on and along the curve. Snap-to-curve also snaps to curves on surface and surface isoparm curves as well.

TIP   You can also snap the manipulator to stay locked on one of the manipulator handles when you are in the perspective view, restricting the manipulator's movements to XY, XZ, or YZ handles, just as if you were in an orthographic window. Just Ctrl+click on the manipulator handle where you want the snap to happen, and the square plane at the center of the manipulator facing the camera will rotate to face the manipulator handle. Note that the constraint only applies when you drag the manipulator center, not one of the axis handles. To release the constraint, Ctrl+click the center of the manipulator (this actually snaps the manipulator to move along the camera view plane).

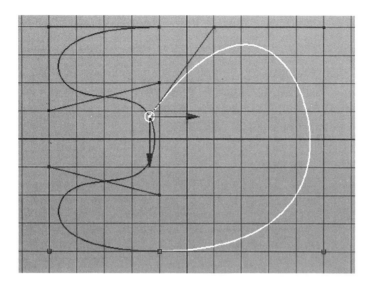

Making an Object Live

Yet another way to snap objects or components is to make an object *live*. This very useful modeling aid can be applied to any single object. To do this, choose Create ➢ NURBS Primitives ➢ Sphere, and then select Modify ➢ Make Live, or click the Make Live button, (with the magnet icon) on the Status Line.

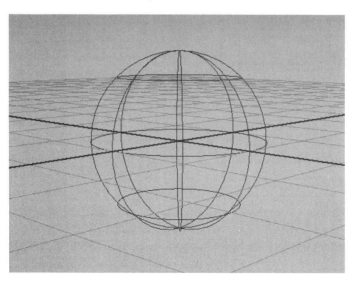

PART 2

Modeling

Trying this on your own computer, you'll see that the sphere has turned green, and if you are in shaded mode, the sphere is no longer shaded. It has become *live*, a magnet for other elements, and while it is in that mode it cannot be selected. Select Create ➤ EP Curve Tool and try clicking a few times in the perspective window. All the Edit Points snap to the sphere surface. Hit Enter to complete the curve and try translating it. The manipulator now shows only X and Y handles, which are actually U and V handles that move the curve along the parameters of the sphere surface. Toggle the Make Live button off, and the curve should translate in the XYZ 3D space again.

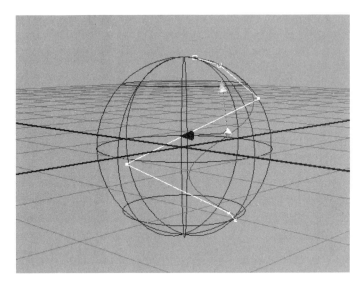

Using the Construction Plane

Maya has a special *construction plane,* available from the Create menu. It does not render and, with the default setting, is displayed as a 24-unit plane in the XY axis, but it's actually infinite in size, like the ground plane in the perspective window. It exists primarily to be made live and aid in the construction of curves as an alternate ground plane. To appreciate how the construction plane differs from a regular NURBS plane in the way it behaves as a *live* object, try the following short exercise.

Start a new scene. Select Create ➤ CV Curve Tool, and X+click to snap the CVs on the ground plane as shown below. Do not press Enter yet. Choose Create ➤ Construction Plane ❏, click Apply with everything at default, then set the Pole Axis to YZ and click Apply again. Close the option box. You should see the planes intersecting, as shown here.

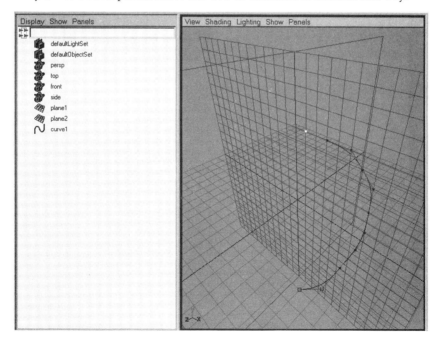

Select the hotbox (space bar) ≻ North Zone ≻ Persp/Outliner. In the Outliner,
select plane1 and then select Modify ≻ Make Live. Continue to X+click the CVs on the
plane1 as shown next, until it comes to the grid next to the intersection point of the
two construction planes. Since plane1 is now live, the CVs snap to the plane's grid.
Only construction planes allow the CVs to continue to build in this way.

In the Outliner, select plane2 and then select Modify ➤ Make Live. Start X+clicking the CVs on plane2 until it comes to the grid above the ground plane. Toggle off the Modify ➤ Make Live option and finish X+clicking the CVs once again on the ground plane, as shown below. Press Enter to complete the curve!

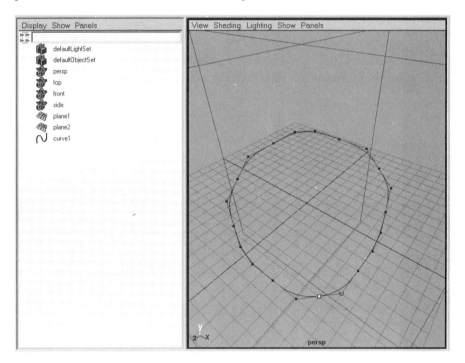

 TIP   If you are transforming an existing object to a live plane, you have to move the manipulator's center, not one of its axis handles, to make it snap to the plane.

Freeze Transformations

When you create any object, it is initially placed at the origin, or (0,0,0) in the world space. As you work with the object, transforming it in various ways through translation, rotation, and scaling, there may be times when you want the point where you've placed the object to become its local origin, or (0,0,0), even though it is not the world space origin. To do this, select the object, and then select Modify ➤ Freeze Transformations.

How Maya Handles Construction History

Maya 2's handling of construction history is much more powerful than in its predecessors (Alias Power Animator and Studio). Its procedural structure allows construction history to be maintained much longer in the model-building process than was previously possible, which means you have more control and greater freedom to explore alternative modeling possibilities. Because it makes the scene complex, however, in certain situations you may want to have the construction history turned off. You can do this by toggling the History button off in the Status Line.

You can also delete a specific object's construction history by selecting Edit ➤ Delete by Type ➤ History. You will see more examples of construction history in the next chapter's tutorial.

Modeling with Primitives

Finally, we are ready to begin modeling! Although Maya provides us with many different and interesting ways to do whatever we need to do, in many cases the fastest and easiest way to get the job done is to use *primitives*—ready-to-use basic shapes like those shown below (and in the Color Gallery on the CD). Maya has a wealth of NURBS and polygon primitives: spheres, cubes, cylinders, cones, planes, and, new in version 2, toruses. Maya also has a NURBS circle and square (another new addition), which are made of curves.

Although they are all different in form, many of these primitives are created involving similar variables, an example of which we will see a bit later. By starting with the primitives, you can immediately create simple objects, which then can be manipulated in various ways to produce more complex surfaces easily and quickly.

Building a Staircase

Let's begin exploring primitives by building a spiral staircase. In this example, we will start with a cube to represent an individual step in the staircase, and then copy it many times.

Start a new scene, and select Create ➢ Polygon Primitives ➢ Cube.

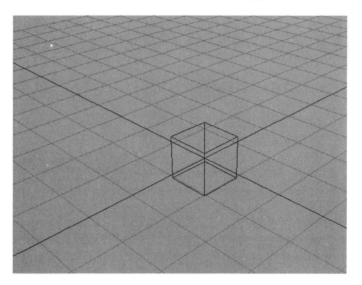

Manipulate it as follows: in the Channel box, type **–6**, **0**, and **0.5** for Translate X, Y, and Z respectively, and **5**, **0.5**, **1** for Scale X, Y, and Z. You should now see the cube placed as follows:

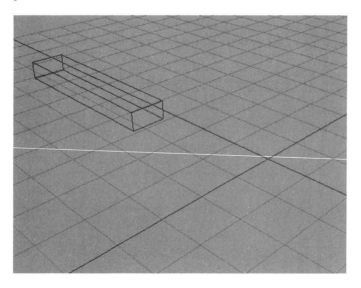

TIP In the Channel box, the default naming convention is set to "Nice." For example, you read "Translate X" in the first line of the Channel box. If you are a beginner, this is very helpful, because everything is clearly stated. But you can also change this to "Short" format by pressing RM choose ➤ Channel Names ➤ Short. The first line should now read "tx", which looks cleaner, and gives a bit more space for the modeling windows.

Keeping the cube selected, go to Edit ➤ Duplicate Option box. Set the numbers in the dialog box as follows: Translate **0,0.5,–1**; Rotate **0**, **–10**, **0**; Number of Copies, **35**; Geometry Type, **Instance**.

Click the Duplicate button, and voila! You should now have a spiral staircase. Note that the duplicates here are *instances*, which means any manipulation to the shape of the original cube will be applied to the duplicates as well. Go to the top view, RM choose Vertex over the original cube, select the four vertices at the top side of the cube, and then rotate and translate them until they overlap the duplicated cube at the bottom side, as shown below.

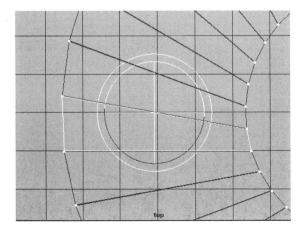

Modeling

PART 2

You can also, by selecting all the vertices of the original cube and translating them in X and Z, get different shapes for the spiral staircase, as shown here.

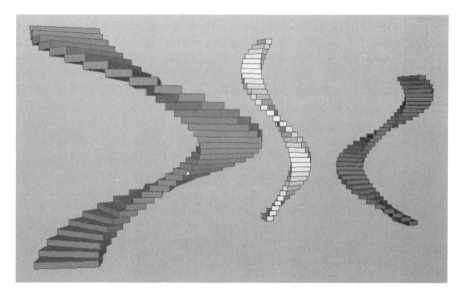

T I P   In situations like the example given here, you will find that it is better to use instances rather than make actual copies of the original geometry as they are much lighter (computationally less taxing on the CPU) than copied duplicates, and you can manipulate the shape of the instanced duplicates with the original geometry.

A Look Inside a Primitive: Torus

Since the torus primitive is a new addition in Maya 2, let us look at its properties in detail as an example of Maya's primitives. A torus is basically a revolved circle, a donut-shaped surface that is closed on both U and V parameters.

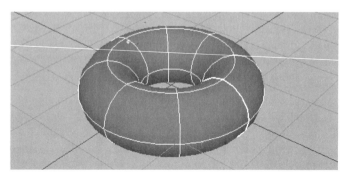

Choose Create ➤ NURBS Primitives ➤ Torus, and in the Channel box, under INPUTS, click makeNurbTorus1. You will see the various variables that form the shape of the torus.

SHAPES	
nurbsTorusShape1	
INPUTS	
makeNurbTorus1	
Radius	1
Start Sweep	0
End Sweep	360
Degree	Cubic
Sections	8
Spans	4
Height Ratio	0.5
Minor Sweep	360

NOTE You can also get to these same variables before you create the object via the Torus ❑ dialog box, or after you create the object via the Attribute Editor.

Try doing the same with some other primitives, like the cylinder and the sphere. Note that many of the torus primitive's properties have exactly the same counterparts in the other primitives—you should go over those variables with the other primitives as well in order to see the various possible shapes they can form with different settings.

TIP When dealing with these settings for the primitives, sometimes you just have to "play with it" and see what comes out as you experiment with the input variables. The results may surprise you.

Now let's experiment with some torus settings. Click on Radius; then, inside the modeling window, MM drag slowly and see what happens to the torus.

The radius measures the distance from the center of the geometry to its circumference. In the case of a torus, this measures the center of the circle revolving around it, which effectively means the Radius setting controls the size of the torus.

Start Sweep and End Sweep determine in degrees where the torus starts and where it stops revolving along V.

For the Degree section, click on Cubic and you will see a pull-down menu with Linear as the other degree choice—this setting will give sharp edges to the torus, as shown on the next page. Sections subdivide the torus along V, and Spans subdivide it along U.

WARNING The subdivisions should all be finalized before any CVs are pulled, as changing the sections or spans of the torus afterward will produce unpredictable results.

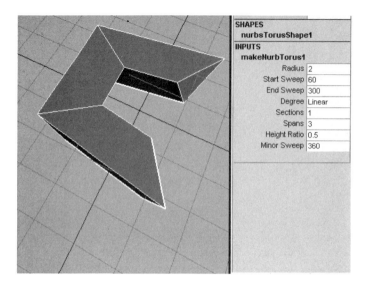

Height Ratio is the ratio between height and radius; this effectively determines the thickness of the torus.

And finally, Minor Sweep determines in degrees the amount of surface (along U) the circle revolving around the torus will have.

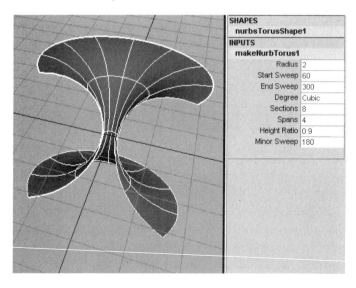

Now, before you say, "OK, so it's a donut," the facing page shows some example models that were created on the fly with the torus primitive. Though all are simple models, there probably are some examples in the collection that you did not expect to see, which illustrates the point: The primitives are very useful objects, not because of what they are, but because of what they are capable of becoming, and because they can help us create the final surfaces we want.

Sections =1
Spans = 6
Height Ratio =2
Minor Sweep = 240

CVs tweaked
Sections = 12
Spans = 6

Degree = Linear
Sections = 34
Spans = 1
Height Ratio = 4
Minor Sweep = 333

Degree = Linear
Sections = 1
Spans = 3
Height Ratio = 1

Height Ratio = 0.9
Minor Sweep = 218

5 Toruses
Degree = Linear
Sections = 8.4
Spans = 4
Height Ratio = 0.05

Hands-On Modeling: Creating a Living Room Scene with Primitives

In this tutorial, we will start building a living room scene with the primitives. Remember our principle, "build only what the camera will see"? The first thing we need to do, then, is to visualize what you want to see at the end. Picture the camera capturing a living room at an angle, with a sofa set, a table, a lamp, and a dog by the window! (You'll find the rendered image in the Color Gallery on the CD.)

We will get to the lamp and the dog by the window in the later chapters, but for now, we can build the rest with three simple primitives that Maya provides us with.

1. Create a new scene. Drop a sphere into the scene: either click on the sphere icon in Shelf1 or select Create ➤ NURBS Primitives ➤ Sphere. Go into side view, pick-mask Control Vertex, and drag to select the top two rows of CVs. Type **w** to use the Move tool.

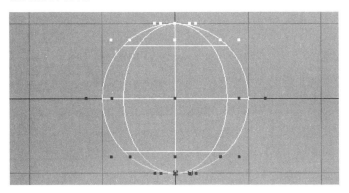

2. Snap the CVs to the first grid above the ground level by X+dragging the Y handle to the first grid above the ground level. Make sure you are not dragging the center of the manipulator, or all the CVs will snap to one point. If the grid isn't displayed, select Display ➤ Grid to make it visible. Repeat the same action with the two bottom rows of CVs to the grid below ground level, as below.

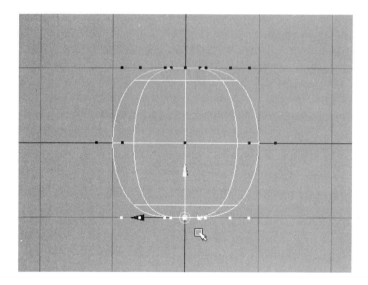

3. Go to the top view, and again snap the edge rows of CVs to the unit grids on each side of the sphere, as below.

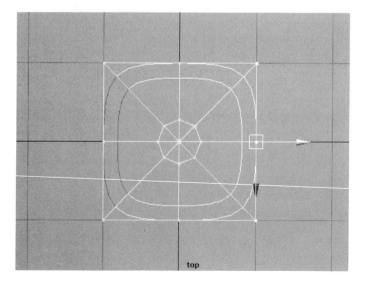

4. Take the sphere, which now looks more like a cube with round edges, and duplicate it several times (Edit ➤ Duplicate), scaling, translating, and rotating it to make the sofa, as shown here.

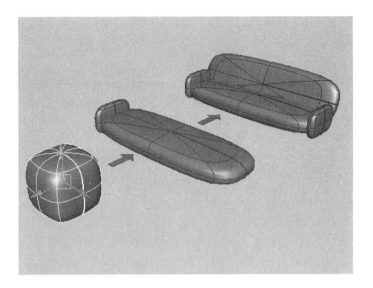

TIP When you are building several objects, it is good form to build each object at the origin and then move it out of the center when it is finished. As long as you do not freeze its transformation or change the pivot, you can always transform it back to its original position for further modifications.

5. For the cushions, copy the sphere, pull the top row of CVs (which looks like a single point) down just a bit, scale and translate it to be on the sofa, and make two more copies to cover the whole sofa. When the sofa is done, select all of its elements and select Edit ➤ Group. This makes it a lot easier for us to work with the sofa as one entity. We can hide the sofa for now while we move on to the table and the chair. Select Display ➤ Hide ➤ Hide Selection.

6. For the table, select Create ➤ NURBS Primitives ➤ Cylinder ❏, set Caps to Top and click Create. This will become the table top. Move it to a side for now. For the table stump, select Create ➤ NURBS Primitives ➤ Torus, and set the Height Ratio to 0.2 and Minor Sweep to 190 degrees. Translate the cylinder to the top of the torus, and scale and translate each object to form the table shape you see below. Group the cylinder and the torus; then translate them to the ground level.

PART **2**

Modeling

Select Display ➤ Show ➤ Show Last Hidden to make the sofa visible again. Place the sofa and the table roughly in the positions shown here.

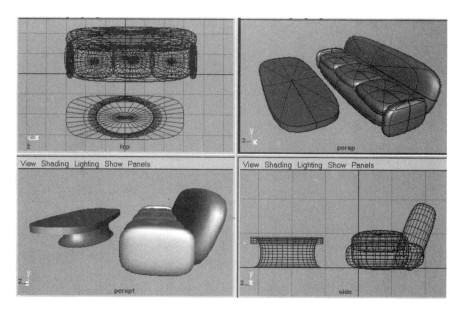

To select the whole hierarchy in the modeling window, select one object in the hierarchy and press the ↑ (Up Arrow) key. If there are branches in the hierarchy, press the ↑ key until you reach the root level.

7. The chair is a bit trickier. Copy the sphere, and hide all the rest. Translate the sphere to (0.5, 0, 0.5) using the Channel box. Switch to top view, and snap the middle CVs to the grid for each side of the sphere as shown:

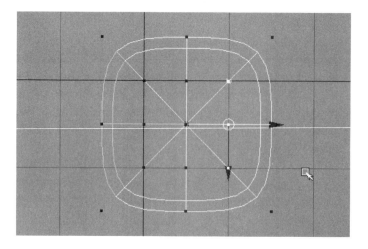

8. In the side view, grab the two rows of CVs at the right bottom corner and snap them to the Y axis. Grab the rows of CVs at the left side and snap them to the second grid to the left. Grab the CVs at the top-left corner and drag them down as shown below:

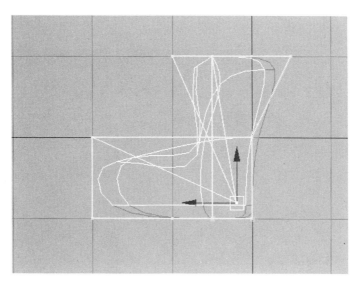

9. In the perspective view, select the CVs as shown and push them back in Z a little. You can also select the CVs at the chair's side and scale them out to make the chair look rounder. If you are having a hard time seeing the right CVs, toggle the hulls to be visible, by choosing Display ➤ NURBS Components ➤ Hulls.

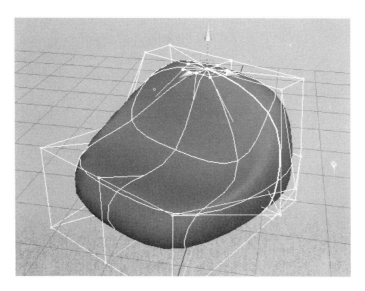

PART

2

Modeling

10. To finish, copy one of the cushions from the sofa and put it on the chair. Group the chair and the cushion. Select Display ➤ Show ➤ All. Create three planes by selecting Create ➤ NURBS Primitives ➤ Planes for the floor and the two walls, then arrange the "furniture" as you see fit. Shown below is the final textured and lit living room. We will come back to this scene later to add more interesting pieces.

Summary

This chapter introduced the basic concepts of modeling and the tools that Maya provides to aid you in creating and editing surfaces. You also learned how to use primitives to build more complex objects such as a staircase or pieces of furniture.

In the next two chapters, we will delve further into two major types of modeling: NURBS modeling and polygon modeling. NURBS modeling is often used in high-end productions that demand photorealistic models, while polygon modeling is still the preferred choice for gaming companies.

chapter 6

NURBS MODELING

Featuring

- *Curve and surface concepts*
- *Creating curves*
- *Editing curves*
- *Hands-on Maya: aftershave bottle, part 1*
- *Creating surfaces*
- *Editing surfaces*
- *Hands-on Maya: aftershave bottle, part 2*
- *Hands-on Maya: building a face (advanced)*

NURBS Modeling

This chapter covers modeling with NURBS curves and surfaces. It begins with an explanation of the basic theory and concepts involved in modeling curves. We won't get too technical; the goal is simply to give you a basic understanding of what you are doing as you work with Maya. If you are familiar with these concepts, you may wish to skim through this section.

The chapter then introduces the tools that Maya provides for working with curves and demonstrates them in the first of three hands-on tutorials, creating the curves for an aftershave bottle. The second half of the chapter moves on to Maya's tools for creating and editing surfaces and concludes with two more hands-on exercises: one that completes the aftershave bottle and one that creates a human face.

The last of these tutorials is quite advanced, in the sense that the operations are more involved and the instructions are not as detailed as in the basic tutorials. It assumes that the reader has more working familiarity with Maya's interface and basic techniques than the earlier tutorials. If you find you are having problems following the advanced tutorial, it may be wise to skip it and come back to it after you've got more Maya experience under your belt.

Curve and Surface Concepts

Part of the genius of Maya is that it makes the highly complex mathematics of modeling and animation almost completely transparent to the user. You don't need to know much about what Maya is doing behind the scenes when you use its tools, but it's very useful to know a little about it. Of course, not everyone wants to know what words like *NURBS*, *B-splines*, and *parameterization* mean. When you are striving for artistic expression, mathematical concepts may not be something you'd want to delve into deeply. These concepts may seem to you like unwelcome relatives to a hip party—you invite them in and exchange pleasantries ("How are you? How are the kids?") but want nothing to do with them afterwards!

Nevertheless, these and other "techno-words" are built into the very fabric of what computer animation is. Maya is, after all, computer software—the better grounded you become in these "esoteric" concepts, the deeper and further you will be able to go in mastering your art. At the same time, be assured that as dry (or exciting!) as things may get in the following sections, nothing overly technical will be thrown at you.

T I P   If you find you do not understand many of the concepts being presented in the next few sections, just skip them for now. You can come back later when those topics have become a bit more relevant to you.

Curves Are Equations

The curve you draw in the computer is actually a curve segment or a continuous series of segments. One segment is called a *span*. A curve span is a digital representation on the screen of a mathematical concept called a *parametric equation*. Because the equation is describing a position in 3D space, it always has three variables (x, y, z), and the power of the variable with the highest degree in the equation determines the classification of the curve. Hence, a first-degree curve is a linear equation, which is a straight line. A second-degree curve is a quadratic equation, or an arc. A third-degree curve is a cubic equation, which can actually twist in 3D space. There are two higher-degree curves: fifth- and seventh-degree curves, which can actually twist twice in one span. Maya has all these degree options in its curve-creation tools, but for most practical purposes, the cubic curve is almost always used. In Maya, the default curve is cubic.

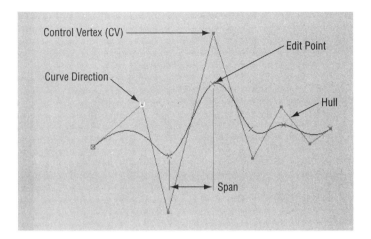

Curves Are Splines

A Control Vertex (CV) is a point in 3D space that determines the shape of the curve it is attached to by defining and influencing its equation. The CVs and the curve segments they control are collectively known as *splines*.

NOTE Historically, a spline was a plank of wood bent to form part of a ship's hull by forcing it between pairs of posts, known as "ducks." The placement of these ducks determined the shape of the plank's curve, just as the placement of CVs determines the shape of a curve in computer graphics.

There are different ways to calculate how the CV positions are interpreted into curve shapes, and these different methods—types of equations or formulas—distinguish the splines further into Bezier curves, B-splines, or NURBS. NURBS, the focus of our attention in this chapter, stands for *Non-Uniform Rational B-Splines*.

NOTE Unless you're a mathematician, don't worry about all the components of this daunting acronym. The important thing to understand is how a NURBS curve behaves.

The advantage a NURBS curve has over the other types of splines lies essentially in the way it can be cut and joined. Regular splines cannot be cut and joined at arbitrary points along the curve, only where their control points are. A NURBS curve, however, can be cut and joined anywhere, because any point on the curve can be calculated and located. This advantage carries over into surfaces as well. NURBS surfaces can be attached to other NURBS surfaces with different numbers of spans, or *isoparms*, for this reason.

PART 2

Modeling

Edit Points (EPs) are points where curve segments join to form one continuous line. They are also called *knots*. Maya has a CV Curve tool and an EP Curve tool for creating curves. But make no mistake—the two tools may create curves a bit differently, but in the end, both create the same NURBS curve.

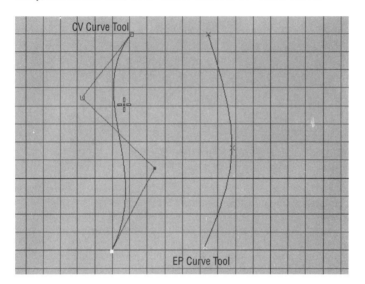

Surfaces and Parameterization

Curves cannot be rendered, only surfaces can. In modeling, curves are always created to help in the creation of surfaces. This means that at the end of the day, no matter how many curves you create, only surfaces matter. Any discussion about surfaces, however, needs to discuss *parameterization*—Oh yes, here comes another unwelcome relative.

To best understand parameterization, let's go back to curves. Parameterization of a curve is the calculation of where knots (edit points) are placed along the curve, enabling any point on the curve to be assigned a parameter value. The variable representing this value is defined as U, and the curve is given a direction as a result.

To see this at work, create a default curve made of two spans: either five clicks of CVs or three clicks of EPs. Now pick-mask Curve Point and try dragging along the curve. At the top of the Maya window you should see the curve parameter value changing as you drag. The start of the curve is assigned a parameter value, U[0]. The second edit point of the curve is assigned the value U[1], and the end of the curve, U[2]. The halfway point between the start of the curve and the second edit point is assigned a value of U[0.5]. Any point on the curve can be similarly assigned a parameter value this way. Easy enough. This method of calculating the point values along the curve is called *uniform parameterization*.

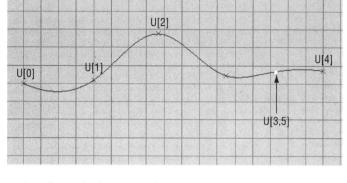

Another calculation method in Maya is called *chord length*·parameterization, and the way it assigns the *U* value to a point on the curve is more complicated. We need not go into discussions of exactly how the calculation is done, but the value assignment is dependent on the distances between successive edit points of the curve, not the number of edit points. So two curves with the same number of edit points but drawn differently will end up with different parameter values at those edit points.

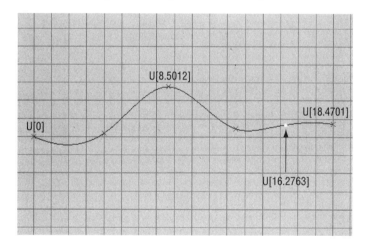

How does all this relate to surfaces? A surface is basically an area in 3D space defined by the parameterization of two variables, *U* and *V*. The surface is calculated in such way that at any point inside the area, a *UV* coordinate can be given, and the area is given *UV* directions. This is exactly the same situation as with the curves, except now you have the *V* parameterization of the surface as well.

Uniform parameterization produces more predictable values for the curves and surfaces than chord length and is therefore the preferred choice for modeling in general. Uniform is the default setting in Maya. The advantage of chord length parameterization is in texturing: it allows more evenly distributed textures on uneven surfaces than the uniform method. The bottles shown here are revolved from curves that have exactly the same CV placements, except that the one on the left uses chord length and the other is uniform:

Surface Normals

A surface also has a front side and a back side, and it has *normals*. A normal is essentially a vector shooting out perpendicularly from a point on the front side of a surface. In other words, it is the direction that surface point is directly facing. The concept of surface normals is very important for using certain modeling tools, as well as for texturing and rendering, and it is important that you become comfortable with the concept.

You can use the "right-hand rule" to determine which side of a surface is front, or which way the normals are pointing. If the thumb points to the increasing *U* direction, and the index finger points to the increasing *V* direction, then the middle finger bent perpendicularly to these two fingers is the direction of the surface normals.

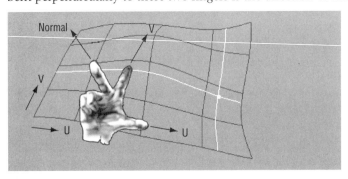

TIP   You can see the surface normals of an object while in shaded mode by selecting the object and then selecting Display ➤ NURBS Components ➤ Normals.

Surfaces, like curves, are made up of spans, or rather they span a given number of span areas. The area covered by one *UV* span is called a patch. The flowing lines separating the patches are called isoparms. These are the surface equivalents of knots, or edit points. Pick-masking the Isoparm element allows you to select any flowing *isoparametric* curve either with a *U* value or *V* value on the surface, just like selecting a curve point on a curve. With surfaces, you can also pick-mask Surface Point, which enables you to select any point on the surface with a *UV* parameter value.

 TIP   When you select a surface point and choose Edit Surfaces ➤ Insert Isoparms, both *U* and *V* isoparms are inserted.

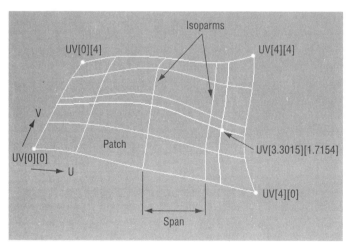

Creating Curves

Whew, that's about enough with those relatives! Let's move on to creating curves. Maya has several tools for creating curves, and also a Text tool. As mentioned already, Maya can create curves either with edit points or with CVs.

Generally, if the curve needs to pass through a specific point, then the EP Curve tool would be a better choice, as the edit points actually lie on the curve. The CV Curve tool should be preferred in most other situations because it is better at controlling the curve shape.

Using the CV Curve Tool

Go to front view and select Create ➤ CV Curve Tool ❑. Notice the default setting is at Cubic and Uniform. Leave everything at the default and X+click near the origin. Draw the curve on the left shown below. Oops! The last CV placement was a mistake. No problem. Just MM click and you can X+drag the CV back to where it should be placed like the curve on the right:

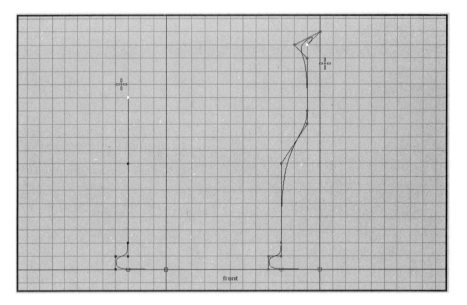

 TIP   You can also edit CVs or EPs while you are creating a curve by pressing the Insert key. With this method, you can select multiple points for repositioning. To continue creating the curve, just press the Insert key again.

Pencil Curve Tool

Pencil is another great curve-creation tool in the Create menu, especially if you have access to a digitizing tablet. It may look like it is producing a thousand edit points when you are using it, but with a simple rebuild command, Edit Curves ➤ Rebuild Curve, you can get an elegantly simple curve. Rebuild Curve ❑ has a Number of Spans setting for Uniform Rebuild Type that you can adjust.

Because when you release the mouse the Pencil tool completes building the curve, you will often end up with several separate curves when the drawing is done. Again, you can easily attach these curves using Edit Curves ➤ Attach Curves. The raw curves on the left here have been rebuilt and attached to create the curve on the right.

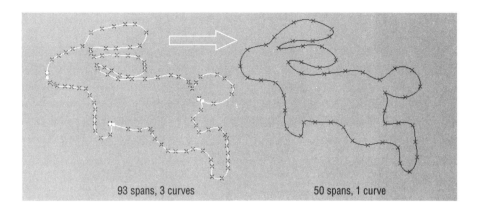

93 spans, 3 curves   50 spans, 1 curve

TIP   It's far better to end up with several separate curves that better represent what you wanted to draw than to trying to draw everything as one curve.

Arc Tools

In contrast to the free form of the Pencil tool, the Arc tools enable you to create circular arcs of various angles. There are two types: the simple two-point circular arc, and the three-point circular arc, which has one more control point than the other tool.

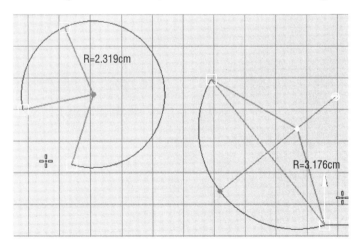

R=2.319cm

R=3.176cm

TIP   Once you've created, for example, a three-point circular arc, you can still manipulate the arc edit points. First select Modify ➤ Transformation Tools ➤ Show Manipulator Tool (or press the **T** hotkey) and then, in the Channel box, under Inputs, choose makeThreePointCircularArc. The three points should be visible now.

PART 2

Modeling

Duplicate Surface Curves

Yet another curve creation method is Duplicate Surface Curves, which is actually not part of the Create menu but appears on the Edit Curves menu. It can be a very efficient and powerful curve generator, especially now that in Maya 2 it has the ability to duplicate all the isoparms of a surface. Create a default cylinder, pick-mask Isoparm, select an isoparm anywhere on the surface, and select Edit Curves ➢ Duplicate Surface Curves. A curve with the same number of spans as the cylinder has been duplicated.

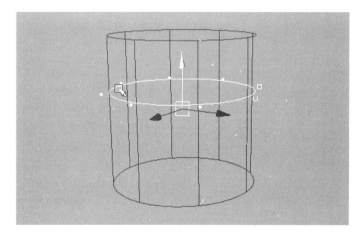

Translate the duplicated curve out of the cylinder. Select cylinder as object, and repeat Edit Curves ➢ Duplicate Surface Curves. This time, all the isoparms of the cylinder duplicated. You can set the options so that only *U* or *V* will duplicate. The default is both.

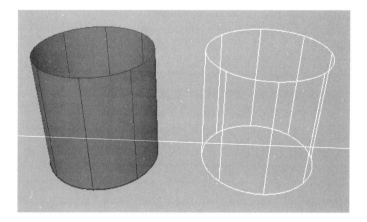

Editing Curves

Once you have created the curves you need, Maya provides various actions and tools to edit them. In this section, we'll talk about attaching and detaching curves, aligning curves and surfaces, rebuilding curves, inserting knots, adding points to a curve, cutting and filleting curves, and offsetting curves.

Attaching and Detaching Curves

The Attach Curves option requires that you pick either two curves or curve points. For most situations, Maya can automatically figure out which ends of the curves are being attached, and you only need to select curves as objects. In situations where the ends being attached are not correct, you can select curve points to force the proper ends to attach. To pick curve points, pick-mask Curve Point, and then drag the curve point to the curve end you want.

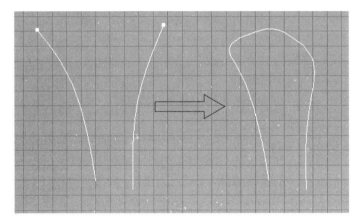

TIP When selecting curve points on two or more curves, first select the curve point on one curve, then pick-mask Curve Point on the other curve, and Shift+click the second curve point. The first selection stays selected.

When both proper end curve points are selected, select Edit Curves ➤ Attach Curves. Blend is the default attachment method, and Blend Bias 0.5 means both curves will meet halfway. This is the ideal setting when you need to maintain symmetry. When the Blend Bias is set to 0, the first selected curve will attach itself to the second curve.

If you find the curve shapes are changing too much when you attach them, try clicking Insert Knot in the option box. For situations where you absolutely need to have the curves maintain their original shape, you can change the Attach Method to

Connect. For this to work properly, however, the curve ends have to be touching already.

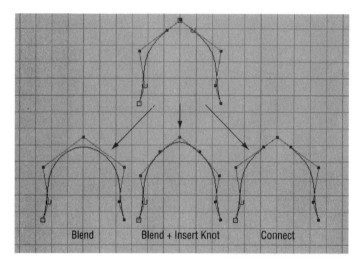

 WARNING   When attaching curves or surfaces, if the construction history is on, make sure the Keep Original option (the default setting) is toggled on as well. Odd behavior may occur if it is toggled off and the attached object is modified later.

Detach Curves is simple to use. It works by either selecting curve points, or edit points, or both, then selecting Edit Curves ➤ Detach Curves. It also works on multiple curves as well.

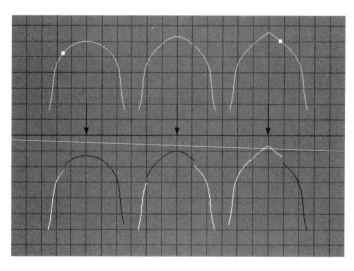

Curve and Surface Alignment and Continuity

When two separate curves or surface ends are not touching, they are said to be *discontinuous*. Once they are touching, there are three possible levels of continuity between the two: *position continuity, tangent continuity,* or *curvature continuity.* In creating a smooth continuous surface out of patches, you need at least tangent continuity between the connected patches. In this section, you'll work with two example curves to get an understanding of the concept of these degrees of continuity.

To set up the example curves, create two CV curves, as below, using X+click to snap them to the grid. Make copies and translate them aside:

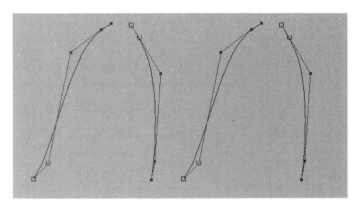

Position continuity, also called zero-order continuity (C0), occurs when the two end CVs are placed in the same 3D space. Select the two copied curves and select Edit Curves ➤ Align Curves ❑. Set Continuity to Position, and modify Boundary to Both. Click Align to see the result shown here:

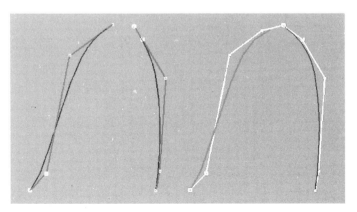

Tangent continuity, also called first-order continuity (C1), occurs when the tangents at the ends of the two curves have the same slope in addition to position continuity. Practically speaking, this occurs when the two end CVs of the curves all line up. Type **Z** to undo. Select the two original curves, change Continuity to Tangent in the option box, and click Align to see the result shown here:

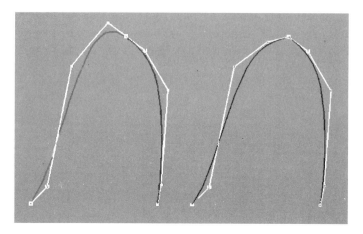

Curvature continuity, also called second-order continuity (C2), occurs when, in addition to having tangent continuity, the curves "curve" away from their end points in the same way. Another way of saying this is that the radii of the curvatures of the two curves are the same. Practically speaking, this means that in the curve being modified, the third CV from the end point, in addition to the second CV, is also translated to accommodate the curvature change. Type **Z** to undo your last change, then select the curves again, and change Continuity to Curvature. Click Align again. Notice the change in position of the third CV from the end.

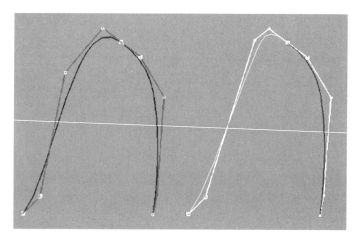

NOTE   There are few tools in Maya that give options for curvature continuity: Align is one, and the other is Project Tangent, which is not covered in this book.

The default setting for Align Curves and Surfaces (they are the same action) is Modify Position First, which means the first curve selected will move in its entirety to align itself. After you have performed the Align, try playing with the various optional settings in Channel box ➣ Inputs to get a better idea of the options.

Rebuilding Curves

Rebuild Curves allows you to rebuild curves in various ways. Rebuilding curves is important for creating good surfaces. When you work with curves for a while, they can end up with unnecessary CVs, or CVs bunched up unevenly. They can be cleaned with the Rebuild Curves tool, and from cleanly built (or rebuilt) curves come clean surfaces. Create a curve using the Pencil Curve tool. With the curve still selected, select Edit Curves ➣ Rebuild Curve ❏.

When the Rebuild Type is set to Uniform, which is the default setting, you have to manually state how many spans the curve should have. The default is set at four spans, but the number will vary greatly depending on the complexity of the required shape.

The Reduce setting simplifies the curve according to the set Global or Local Tolerance level. The Match Knots setting requires two curves to be selected: it reparameterizes the first curve to match the number of knots in the second curve. The No Multiple Knots setting gets rid of multiple knots which are sometimes created when curves are attached or knots inserted. A multiple knot occurs when more than one knot, or edit point, occupies the same position on a curve. The Curvature setting redistributes and inserts more edit points in areas of higher curvature according to a Tolerance level just like the Reduce setting.

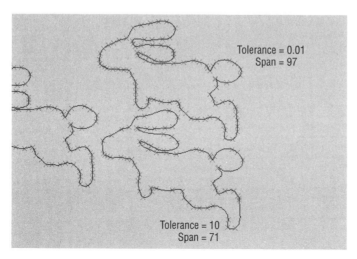

N O T E   To change the Global Tolerance setting for the Reduce or Curvature options, go to Options ➣ General Preferences ➣ Modeling.

Let's cover one more option. The Keep CV option allows you to rebuild the parameter of the curve while keeping the CVs in their original position. When you insert knots, the span of the curve increases, along with creation of more CVs, but the parameterized values of points along the curve stay the same as before the insertion. The Keep CV option recalculates the curve parameters to include the inserted knot, while keeping the CVs in the same position.

Inserting Knots

Insert Knot allows you to add more edit points or CVs to further edit a curve. To use Insert Knot, you select a curve point on the curve where you want the extra edit point to be created and then choose Insert Knot. Note that another CV is created as well. A new option for Insert Knot in Maya 2, also available for Insert Isoparms for surfaces, is the Between Selections option. Select two edit points; then select Edit Curves ➣ Insert Knot ❑, click the Between Selections option, and click Insert. Another edit point is added exactly halfway between the two selected edit points.

W A R N I N G   If you select two curve points with this option, these two curve points will also turn into edit points, along with the new edit point you've inserted in the middle. This may not be the result you desire.

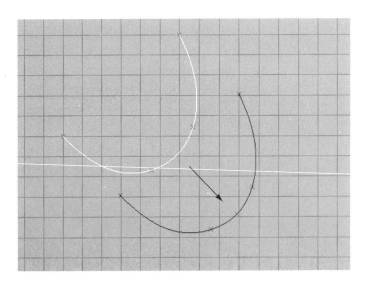

Adding Points to a Curve

Once the curve has been created and you want to add more curve to it, you can use Edit Curves ➤ Add Points Tool. If you want to add points not from the last CV but from the start of the curve, then select the curve and select Edit Curves ➤ Reverse Curve Direction. If you want to add additional edit points instead of CVs, just RM choose over the curve and pick-mask Edit Point. Then, when you select Add Points Tool, it will be set to add edit points and not CVs. Note the difference between Insert Knot and Add Points: the former adds more points inside an existing curve, whereas the latter actually creates more curve segments.

Using the Curve Editing Tool

Usually you can manipulate a curve by translating the CVs. But at times, you may want an edit point to stay in position while the CVs around it move to change the curve shape. The curve editor is especially useful in such a situation.

Create a curve, and then select Edit Curves ➤ Curve Editing Tool. Grab the Parameter position handle (see below) and move it along the curve while keeping V pressed to snap the editor to edit points. Once it's on the edit point you want, you can modify the curve tangent direction and scale around the edit point without moving the edit point itself.

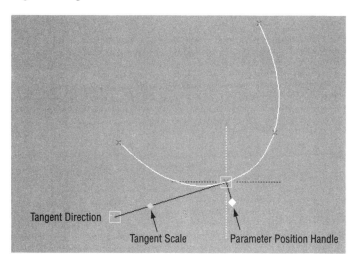

Cutting Curves

Edit Curves ➤ Cut Curve is another very useful curve editing function. It takes multiple curves and detaches them where they intersect. The default option setting for Find Intersections is In 2D and 3D, which finds the intersections for the curves even if they are not actually touching in 3D space, but only seem to touch in one of the active (2D) views.

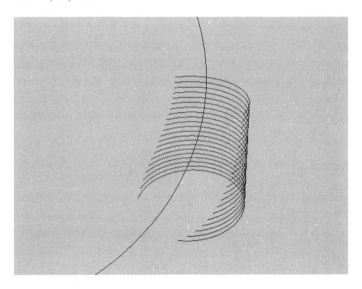

Filleting Curves

Curve Fillet takes two curves that intersect and creates a fillet. Unlike Cut Curve, which can be projected from a 2D view, the fillet curves actually have to be touching. The default setting creates a circular fillet from the two curves. Where the lines are intersecting, sometimes the fillet occurs at the wrong corner. In such cases, you need to cut the curves first, and then select the curves you want to fillet. The Trim and Join settings in the option box can also save you a lot of time by trimming the curves and attaching the segments into one curve.

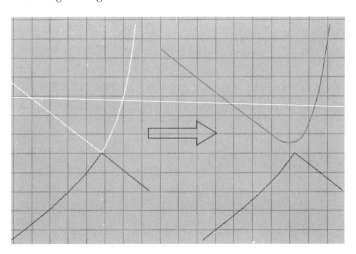

Offsetting Curves

Offset Curve duplicates a curve with an offset distance that you set in the option box. There is an important difference between offsetting a curve and copying and scaling a curve. When a curve is duplicated and uniformly scaled, it maintains the curve shape, whereas a curve created from the offset maintains the distance between it and the original curve, though not necessarily the original shape.

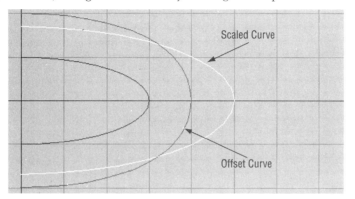

Hands-On Maya: Aftershave Bottle, Part 1

Let's try building an aftershave bottle. In part 1 of this exercise, we will create and edit curves using the actions and tools we've already covered. These curves will then be used to create the aftershave bottle surfaces in part 2.

1. Start with edit points building straight lines. Make sure you are in top view, and X+click the edit points as shown here:

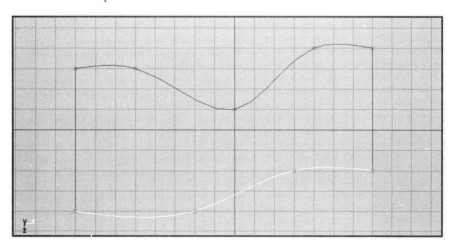

2. Select the two curves at the top-right corner, and fillet the curves with just the Trim option turned on. Do the same for the other three corners. Now you should have eight curve segments. Attach the curves, starting from the top-right corner, with the options set to Connect Attach Method and Remove Multiple Knots. You should have no problems with the corners until the last corner curve:

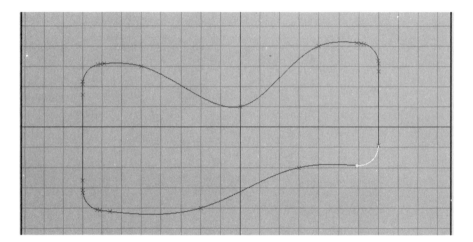

3. With the last corner, use Pick Mask Curve Point to force the curves to attach at the bottom right. With the curve still selected, select Edit Curves ➤ Open/Close Curves to close the curve, making it *periodic* (closed). Rebuild the curve with the options set to Uniform and Keep CVs. The curve should now have a parameter range of 32 spans. Snap the CV at the top middle to the origin as shown here:

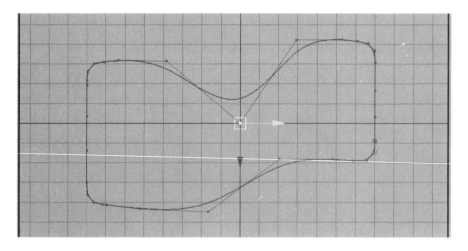

4. Using the marking menu, get into the Persp/Outliner view. Although there is now only one curve, you will notice there are a lot of invisible nodes because of the *construction history*. Since we no longer need the fillet and the attach history, we can delete these: select curve, then Edit ➤ Delete By Type ➤ History.

5. Select the curve, select Edit Curve ➤ Offset ➤ Offset Curve ❑, set the Offset Distance to 0.5, and reduce the Max Subdivision Density to 0. This is important in keeping the same number of curve spans for the offset. Click Offset, and check the Attribute Editor (Ctrl+A) to make sure the offset curve created has 32 spans like the original curve. Translate the curve up in Y to 1. Now duplicate the offset curve: Edit ➤ Duplicate ❑, set Translate to (0, 2, 0) and Number of Copies to 3. Click the Duplicate button to create three more curves. Close the option box. You should see three curves on top of the offset curve as shown here:

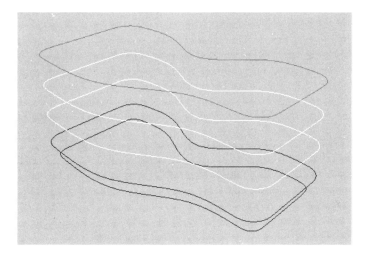

Modeling

TIP Clicking Reset before closing the option box is good practice after actions like Duplicate, especially when you often use the box with a hotkey. Resetting saves the effort of having to go into the Options again, unless of course, you know you will be using the nondefault setting next time as well.

6. Translate the first duplicated curve down in Y to 2, and translate the second one up to 6. Select the third one at the top and Offset it with Offset Distance –0.5. Note that the new offset curve's translation values are at (0, 0, 0). Move it up in Y to 1. Offset the curve again with Offset Distance 0.5. Duplicate the offset curve with the same settings. You should now see ten curves in total, as shown on the next page.

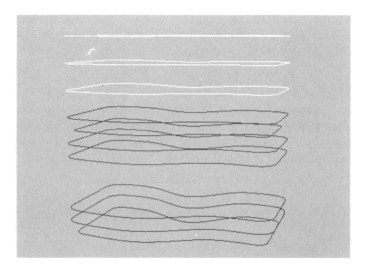

7. Delete the top curve. In the Surface section, we will use these curves further to create an aftershave bottle. Save the scene as Aftershave_1.

T I P   When you build curves for lofting, it is a good idea to build the curves in the order in which they will be lofted. In our tutorial, we built the curves in order so that we only have to marquee the curves and loft. If they are not built in order, you have to select them one by one sequentially in order for lofting to work properly. Having to select individual curves each time you are lofting, when there are a lot of curves to select, can be frustrating.

Creating Surfaces

Once the curves are all prepared, Maya provides us with various ways of creating surfaces from them. We will now cover these surface creation actions and tools in Maya's Surfaces menu. We will look at the Text tool under the Create menu as well, as it is closely related to the Bevel tool.

Revolve

Revolve takes selected curves and revolves them around a designated axis, which you set in the option box. The default revolve axis is vertical, which is Y. The other settings are X, Z, and Free. The last option makes available the Axis boxes, which use the translation values of the Show Manipulator axis handle (see Show Manipulator tool). This means you can interactively change the revolve axis after creating a surface by manipulating the Show Manipulator tool.

For a simple example, let's build a lamp to go into the living room we built in the previous chapter. Start a new scene and select CV Curve Tool. Draw curves in the front view as below.

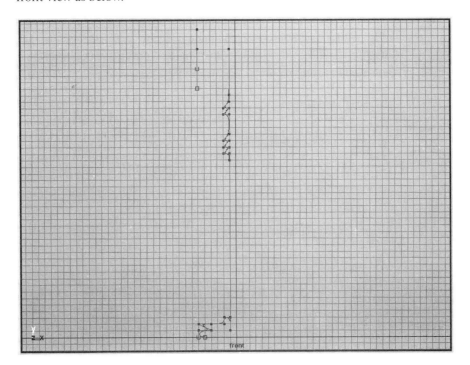

With the curves selected, select Surfaces ➤ Revolve. The default setting works fine for our purpose, and we see a revolved lamp. But wait, the lamp cover seems a bit lacking in design. Let's see if we can make it look a bit more stylish. Select the lamp cover, go to Channel Box Input, and click on revolve2. Change Degree to Linear, and Sections to 12. Now select the profile curve for the lamp cover and, again in Channel Box, translate it (1, 2, –2), rotate it (–25, –25, –25), and scale it (1, 2, 1). The Chapter 6 Color Gallery on the CD shows the finished version. We can add this lamp to the living room later on, so save the file as Lamp for future use.

Lofting

Lofting is without a doubt the most often used function in surface creation, and hence, the most important. The Loft command creates a surface using the selected curves, isoparms, or trimmed edges as spans and edges. The settings for Maya's Loft command are simple, and the default setting need not be changed for most occasions.

You can loft any combination of curves, isoparms, and even trimmed edges. One thing you must always be careful about, however, is the order of the curves you pick for lofting. Make sure you are picking all the curves in order and in the direction you want the *U* to be going. The first curve picked will set the *U* parameter in the direction of the second curve.

TIP   If the curves being lofted are uniform curves and have the same number of spans, then the resulting lofted surface will retain the same uniform parameterization and number of spans as the curves.

An excellent example to use for learning about lofting is the torus primitive. Create the default torus, and while it's still selected, open Edit Curve ➤ Duplicate Surface Curves ❑, click on *V*, and click Duplicate. Select just the torus and delete it. You are left with eight circles to loft. Select all of them and loft with the default setting by selecting Surfaces ➤ Loft. You end up with seven-eighths of a torus, as shown below. Select the surface and check the Attribute Editor. Note that it has seven spans in *U*, its Form U is Open, and from the top view, its span direction for U is clockwise.

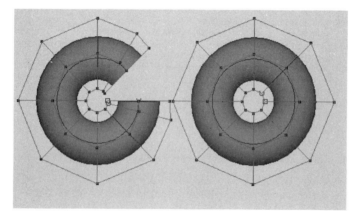

Undo with Z until you have only the curves again. This time, select the circles individually counterclockwise, and in the Loft option box, click on the Close setting. Loft, and you should get a complete torus as in the illustration. Note that now the *U* span is 8, its Form U is Periodic, or closed, and its span direction for U is counterclockwise.

Extrude

The Extrude command extrudes a surface from selected curves, or curves on surface, or isoparms. Extruding isn't complicated, but it can get confusing because there are so many buttons you can click in the Extrude option box.

Extruding usually involves two or more curves, or curves on a surface, or even isoparms. The first curve is the Profile that will be extruded, and the last one is the Path that will guide the extrusion.

The Extrude command provides several settings that control the shape of the surface being extruded:

- The Tube setting in the option box makes the profile curve turn with the path.

- The Flat setting lets the profile curve maintain its own orientation as it moves along the path.

- The Distance setting only requires one curve, and it activates the Extrude Length slider. With Distance, you can determine the direction of the extrusion with either the Specify setting, in which different axis choices are listed, or the Profile normal, in which the extrusion goes along the direction of the profile curve's normal.

- The Result Position option lets you either make the path come to the profile curve, which is the At Profile setting, or make the profile go to the path, which is the At Path setting.

The following example illustrates a general method that should work well as a way to create extrusions. Let's say you wanted to build a frame for the fireplace in the living room from Chapter 5. Start a new scene. With the EP Curve tool set to Linear, create the fireplace frame path using a construction plane as shown below. Then, in the top view, create the profile curve for the frame.

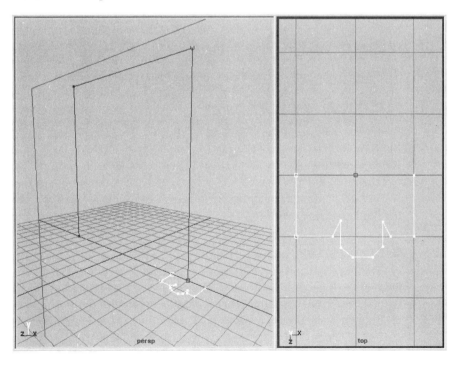

Now select the profile, move its center to one of the ends of the path curve and select Surfaces ➤ Extrude with everything at the default setting. We should now have a frame shape like the one below. Note that you can adjust the shape of the surface by manipulating the curves.

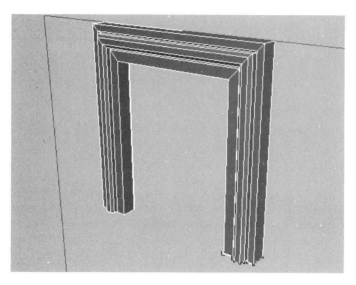

Working with Planars, Text, and Bevel

An object is *planar* if can be wholly mapped to a plane; that is, if it is a 2D object in 3D space. It has length and width, but doesn't have depth. A true planar object, then, cannot be twisted in three directions. As soon as it does, it ceases to be planar. A planar surface is an efficient way to create trimmed surfaces from closed curves. But, again, these curves themselves have to be planar curves. Planars are especially useful when it comes to creating text in Maya; in fact, there is actually a Planar option setting for creating text.

For a quick example of a planar, get a circle and apply a default planar on it by selecting the circle, then selecting Surfaces ➤ Planar to get a trimmed surface. Pick-mask on the circle and try moving a CV up and down. The trimmed circle surface will disappear and come into existence only when the CV is perfectly on the ground plane.

To get a good understanding of working with planar objects, let's create a simple letter M. Start a new scene, select Create ➤ Text ❑, and type **M** inside the Text field (we are being very economical here). Although the Trim option is available here for creating a planar surface, we will create it another way later. Leave everything at its default and click Create. A planar curve outline of the letter M is created. Go to the

Perspective window to see the planar curve letter in 3D. You should see the picture a) below.

Beveling is almost the opposite of planar in that it usually creates depth in flat things. It is a very flexible and powerful function that can take a curve, an isoparm, or even a trimmed edge and create bevels, or sloping edges.

Let's bevel the planar outline of the letter M you created in the previous section. Select the M curve and select Surface ➤ Bevel ❑. The options here are not complicated, but they can be a bit confusing because of the orientation: Top Side bevels the back of the letter, Bottom Side bevels the front, and Both bevels front and back.

T I P   When the text is created in Maya, it is facing front. If you have trouble relating Top to back, Bottom to front, and Height to extrusion depth, just imagine the letters lying face down on the ground.

You can make the bevel corners Straight or Circular, and you can have the bevel edges straight, arc in (Concave) with sharp definitions, or arc out (Convex) smoothly. You can leave the Bevel Width, Depth, and Height at default settings—we'll be interactively adjusting them afterwards. Click Bevel, and you should see the picture b) below.

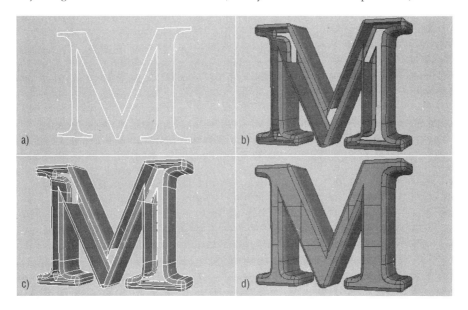

But first, if you want to change the default settings for corners and edges, go to Channel box ➤ Input and click on bevel1 to get at those settings. Press **T** to activate Show Manipulator for Bevel history. You should see three blue dots connected with lines. If you don't see these, go to Channel box ➤ Input and click bevel1 again, and they should appear.

These blue dots are handles with which you can manipulate Bevel Width, Depth (the depth of the bevels, or the sloping edges), or Height (which is the depth of the actual extrusion of the text curve). Manipulate them until you are satisfied with the shape of the letter M, then pick-mask Isoparm and select the front edge of the bevel surface, as in the picture c) above. Select Surface ➤ Planar and you should see the front side of the M now covered. You can use the letter to decorate the living room later. Save the file. You can see a rendered version of the letter in the Color Gallery on the CD.

Boundary

The boundary function is most easily described when compared to lofted curves. When two curves are lofted, the result is a four-sided surface, two of whose opposing edges are defined by the curves. The other two edges are automatically calculated to be straight lines going from one curve to the other. When more than two curves are being lofted, the other two edges can become curved, but these, too are interpolations between the curves being lofted. A boundary function, in contrast, enables the four sides of a surface to be created from four curves, thus giving the artist more control over precisely how the surface edges should be defined.

Let's take a closer look at boundaries. Start a new scene. Create four different curves with two or three spans each. Place them in such way as to have their ends intersect. You can select the curves in any order you want, or drag-select them all together, but the first curve picked determines the *UV* parameterization of the boundary surface, as the surface *U* parameters are determined by the curve's own *U* parameters. So if the *UV* direction for the boundary is important, you should keep that in mind when you are building the first curve.

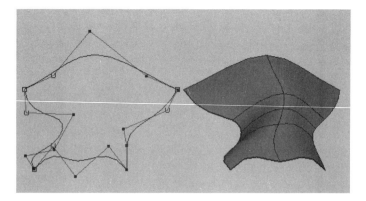

Once the curves are all selected, select Surfaces ➤ Boundary with the default settings. You should end up with a surface that has three or four *UV* spans. Save this file, as you can use the same curves for working with birails in the next section.

The Boundary function can also create surfaces with only three curves. This type of surface created with the boundary is not really a surface with three edges, but rather a surface with one zero-length edge. The order of picking is significant in this case because the pinched zero-length edge (also called the *degenerate surface*) occurs between the first two curves picked. This is important in situations where the surface patch needs to be attached to another surface patch.

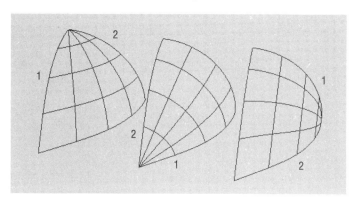

N O T E   Square works much like Boundary in that it takes three or four curves and produces a surface patch. The way it creates tangency, however, is more complex, and it is considered an advanced tool.

Birails

Birails are functions much like boundaries in that they work to determine the four sides of a surface. Essentially, birails extrude one or more profile curves along two rail curves, or paths. The parameters of the profile curve(s) define the *V* parameters of the birailed surface, and the two rail curves define the *U* parameters of the surface.

Let's see how birailing works. Get the curves you built for testing the boundary function. Select Surface ➤ Birail ➤ Birail 1 Tool. (We will delve into the options a bit later.) Maya asks you to select the profile curve; select one of the curves. Now you are instructed to select the two rail curves; select the two curves adjacent to the first picked curve. The birail surface is created.

You can try this again with different order of selections and see how the surface differs in each case, and how it also differs from the boundary surface. The fourth curve of the boundary is basically ignored, being replaced by the profile curve. Let's look at the other birail tools.

Choose Birail 2 Tool, and again leave all the settings at their defaults. You are instructed to select two profile curves now. Select the two parallel curves. Then pick the two rail curves. A birail is created. Notice how this surface looks much like the boundary surface? That is because the same four curves are used to create the surface.

For the Birail 3+ Tool, we need another curve to act as a profile curve. It would be good to build a curve with two or three spans like the other curves, and you should make sure the newly added profile curve is touching the rail curves. You should have something like the curves shown here:

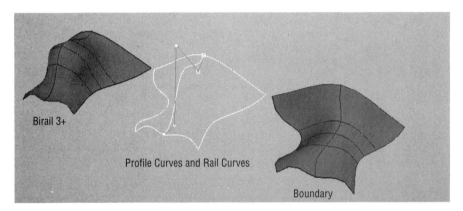

The Birail 3+ tool works a bit differently—you select all the profile curves first, hit Enter, and then pick the two rail curves. The birailed surface appears. Birail 3+ is basically a high-level loft, with the *U* parameter surface edges following the rail curves, and you can have control of the inner areas of a surface with the Birail 3+ tool that you cannot get with boundary or the other birail tools.

Let's look briefly at a few option settings. All three types of Birails have Nonproportional or Proportional settings under Transform Control. The first setting modifies only the parts of the profile curve that change when it birails, whereas the Proportional setting maintains the shape of the profile curve—thus the name. So if the rail curves grow wider, the Nonproportional setting will only stretch the profile sideways, but the Proportional setting will enlarge the entire profile.

The Rebuild option also allows the curves for the birail to have their own rebuild options, which may in some situations give us much lighter surfaces. For the rebuild settings, refer to Rebuilding Curves above.

Editing Surfaces

Once a surface is created, you will often need to manipulate it to produce its final form. Maya's many surface editing tools and actions behave exactly the same way as their curve counterparts, which we have already covered. We will be going through those pretty quickly, while some others we will be spending more time on, such as the Trim tool. We will also focus more on modeling techniques using these tools.

Attach and Detach Surfaces

These actions work exactly the same as their curve counterparts. With curves, you were pick-masking curve points, whereas with these surface actions, you pick-mask isoparms.

Working with Construction History

Start a new scene. Select Create ➤ NURBS Primitives ➤ Cone. Focus in on it by pressing F, and select its isoparm about halfway up. Now choose Detach Surfaces with the default settings. Select the top half, move it up a bit, apply Attach Surfaces, and translate it to the side. You should see something like picture a) shown below. Now grab the top part of the cone again and try transforming it in various ways while observing the effect it has on the new surface. Below are more examples of the various effects produced on the new surface.

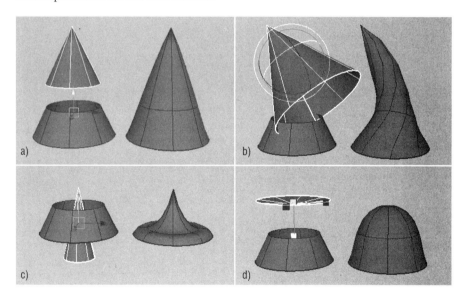

Inserting Isoparms and Aligning Surfaces

The Insert Isoparms command is the surface equivalent of Insert Knots for curves. When the option box is set for Between Selections, selecting isoparms (unlike selecting edit points) can be a bit tricky. (Make sure you are not click-dragging, but just clicking, or you may end up highlighting an isoparametric curve between the isoparms, in which case they will be inserted as isoparms as well.)

TIP   You can also check the Feedback Line just above the Layer Bar to see if what is highlighted has a neatly rounded parameter value (assuming it is a uniform surface). If it does, it usually means you have selected an isoparm.

Align Surfaces is the surface equivalent of Align Curves. They actually use the same option box. In most situations, simply attaching or stitching (see Chapter 8) creates the continuity we desire, but in those cases where you specifically want surface curvature continuity, you would want to use Align Surface first.

Extend and Offset Surfaces

Extend Surfaces extends a surface's edge(s) according to a set distance. It can either extrapolate the direction to the way the surface was curving at the edge, or simply go off in a tangential direction.

Create a torus. Go to the Inputs, click makeNurbTorus1, set its variables as follows, and you should see a quarter-formed torus:

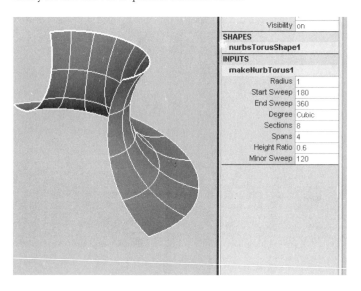

With the torus still selected, select Edit Surfaces ➤ Extend Surfaces. Open the Attribute Editor, select the extendSurface tab, and set Extend Side to Both and Extend Direction to V.

The Offset Surfaces option is the surface equivalent of Offset Curves, with simpler settings. In its option box, the Surface Fit setting calculates the distance of the offset from the surface, whereas the CV Fit setting calculates the distance of the offset from the CVs. Select the extended torus, and apply Offset Surface. Go into the Inputs window, click on Distance, then in the modeling window, MM drag to interactively adjust the distance of the offset. It seems –0.2 is a good distance. You should see something like the picture below.

T I P   It's often better to use editing functions at default settings, and then interactively change the settings by using the Attribute Editor or the Channel box with Show Manipulator.

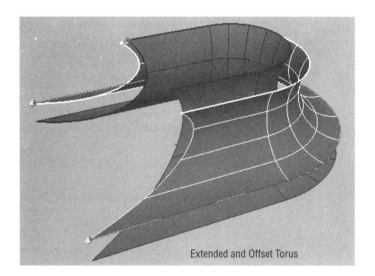

Extended and Offset Torus

Try offsetting a curve from one of the top edges, lower it a bit, and use it with the two surface edge isoparms to create a loft between the two surfaces. Repeat for the bottom edges, and you should see something like this:

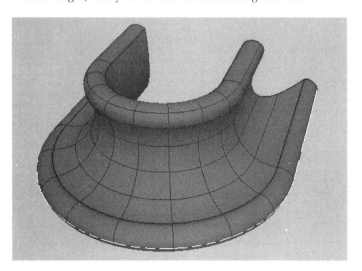

Trim and Round

Trimming is a way to cut surfaces into desired surface shapes using curves on surfaces (see below). Trimming indiscriminately can produce heavy models because it can create a lot of unnecessary isoparms, and that is always a factor to keep in mind when using the Trim functions; but at the same time, a well-applied trim can save a lot of work and produce better models

Projecting Curves On Surface

In order to trim a surface, you need "curves on surface" first. This is Maya's term for curves that are mapped to the UV parameters of the surface they are on, rather than to the XYZ coordinates of world space. Maya 2 can let us project curves, curves on surface, isoparms, or trimmed edges to a designated surface and create curves on that surface. Let's look at this with an extended example.

Let's try building a spherical opening protruding from a wall. We will use projections, trimming, and filleting to do this. Create a NURBS sphere, scale it uniformly to 2 and rotate it 90 degrees in X. Create a NURBS circle, which should appear right inside the sphere. Go to top view, select both, and select Edit Surface ➢ Project Curve On Surface, with the default setting. Go back to the Perspective window, and you should see two curves on surface on the sphere (as in the image on the left below).

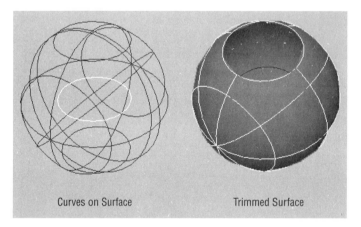

Curves on Surface   Trimmed Surface

The Trim Tool

Select the bottom curve on surface (you should be able to select it like a regular object) and delete it. Select Edit Surface ➢ Trim Tool. Select the sphere, and it should turn white. Click on the middle of the sphere to designate that as the part of the sphere you wish to keep. Hit Enter. You should see a trimmed hole as in the image on the right above.

Select the sphere and scale it up to (3, 3, 3). Notice that the hole on sphere is keeping its size. When you move the circle, the hole follows it. Select the sphere and apply

Edit ➤ Delete By Type ➤ History to erase the procedural relationship between the circle and the curve on surface.

Untrimming Surfaces

Oops! We made a mistake, we wanted to make a hole at the front of the sphere, not at the top—since we deleted the history, we can't move the hole. Now we have a bit of a problem. Curves on surface can be deleted like objects, but not trimmed edges. There is a command specifically designed for untrimming surfaces, which is Edit Surfaces ➤ Untrim Surfaces. You can choose to delete only the last trim or use the default setting, Untrim All. Select the sphere and apply Untrim Surfaces.

Projecting with Surface Normal

Let's try Project Curve on Surface again. Open its option box. The default setting is Active View, which means the curve is projected onto the surface from the camera of whatever view is active. The other option is Surface Normal, which determines the projection of the curve by the normals projecting from the surface. Here the projection is actually done the opposite way. Click on Surface Normal, keep the option box open, select the circle and move it to (0, 0, 4), rotate it (–60, 0, 0), and scale it (3, 3, 7). With the circle still selected, select the sphere and click Project button in the option box. Notice that you only see one curve on surface created near the circle and not on the other side. That is because the normals on the other side are not seeing the circle. Trim the sphere and delete the circle.

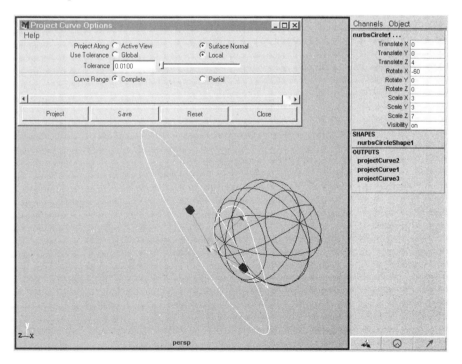

Intersect Surfaces

As well as projecting curves and isoparms, Maya can also create curves on surfaces when NURBS surfaces intersect. The Edit Surfaces ➤ Intersect Surfaces with default settings creates curves on surfaces on both intersecting surfaces. Create a NURBS plane, rotate it 90 degrees in X, translate it –1 in Z, and scale it uniformly to 30. This will be the wall. Drag-select both the sphere and the plane, and select Edit Surfaces ➤ Intersect Surfaces. You should see curves on surface on both surfaces. Select the plane and trim out the circle. Trim the sphere as well, and you should see something like below.

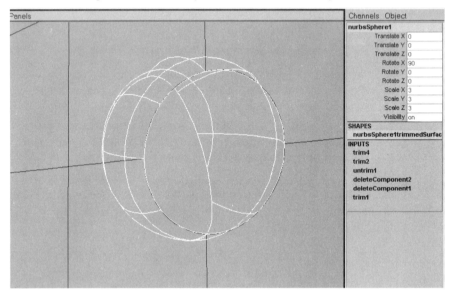

Round and Fillet

Fillet and Round are similar functions, but Round is considered a more advanced tool. Let's try both, starting with Fillet. Drag-select the plane and the sphere. Select Edit Surfaces ➤ Surface Fillet ➤ Circular Fillet. The default setting works well here. In other situations, you may have to go into Input and fiddle around with Primary or Secondary Radius to get the fillet to curve the right way. The option box also has a Create Curve on Surface setting for further trimming.

Now, to try out Round, undo the fillet action. To use Round, we must have two edges. Select Edit Surfaces ➤ Round Tool, and select the trimmed edges. You should see the yellow Round radius manipulator indicating the fillet radius. You can interactively change the radius by grabbing the end handles of the manipulator. The default is 1, which is fine for this example. Press Enter, and you'll see the fillet created once again. But with Round, the surfaces are also trimmed so that the fillet actually joins the trimmed edges of the surfaces. To finish up, you would want to offset the sphere and loft their trimmed edges to get some thickness, and create a tunnel into the wall, as in the picture on the right next.

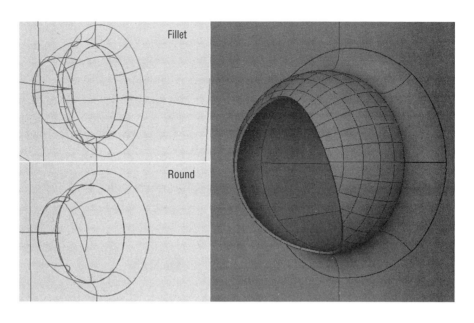

Fillet

Round

PART **2**

Modeling

Hands-On Maya: Aftershave Bottle, Part 2

Now we're ready to return to the aftershave bottle we began creating earlier in the chapter.

1. Open the Aftershave_1 file from the previous exercise. Marquee-select the nine curves (they should be in proper order) and apply Edit Surfaces ➤ Loft. Delete all the curves. Duplicate the lofted surface, and enter –1 for Scale Y in the Channel box. Translate it up, and you should see something like image a) below.

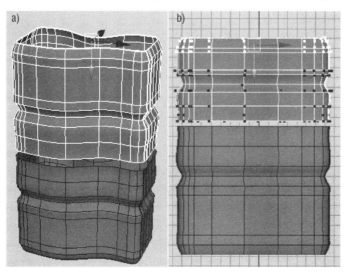

a)

b)

2. Pick-mask Control Vertex over the top surface and, in the front view, translate the points down in Y and closer together. You should have something like image b) above.

3. Select the edge isoparms and select Edit Surfaces ➢ Attach ❑, check off Keep Originals, and click Attach. We now have the body of the aftershave bottle. Select the top edge isoparm of the surface, select Edit Curves ➢ Offset ➢ Offset Curve ❑, set Offset Distance to –0.5, Max Subdivision Density to 0, and click Offset. An offset curve is created as below. Loft between the surface edge isoparm and the offset curve. Then select the offset curve again, and apply Surfaces ➢ Planar with the default settings. You should have the surface's top covered as below.

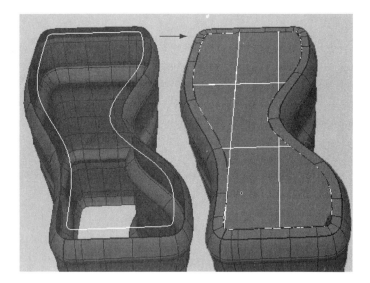

4. Attach the lofted surfaces together. Put a cylinder and a sphere to the top as the bottle cap. You may want to squash the bottom of the sphere a bit. The modeling part is done. Again, you can find the finished version in the Chapter 6 Color Gallery on the CD.

Hands-On Maya: Building a Face (Advanced)

This is an advanced exercise. The steps are complex and presented only in outline form, and you will have to infer a great many little details. There are many different ways to build a human face. The method being used here, generally referred to as the radial method, may not necessarily the best one, but it is one of the most efficient ways to create detailed, ready-to-animate faces.

The face we'll create appears in the Chapter 6 Color Gallery on the CD.

1. Start out with a sphere. Cut out the front and the back parts—the front will be the mouth, and the back will be the neck. Shape the sphere into a very rough figure of a human head as below.

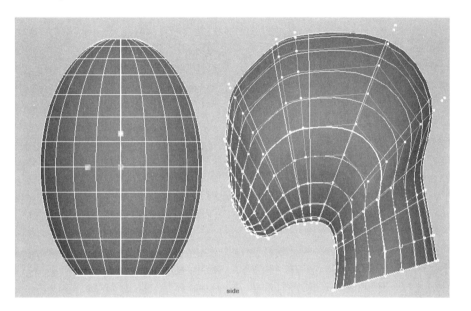

side

NOTE   A person's face was used for this model, but it is not shown here for reasons of privacy. When you are modeling a face, make sure you have a picture or a sketch to import as image plane.

2. Cut the head in half in the middle. Refine the head more, pulling out the chin, nose, and cheek. When you are moving the boundary edge CVs in the middle, make sure you are moving the CVs beside them as well. You also want to keep the X values of the edge CVs at zero, and only move them in Y and Z. The isoparms should be tightly gathering at the beginning of the neck area as shown on the next page. Insert isoparms where you need them, and delete rows of CVs where you do not need them.

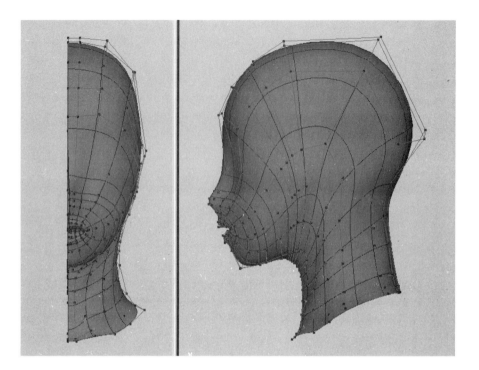

TIP   When you are inserting isoparms, make sure you are using the Between Selections option whenever you can.

Note the number of isoparms at this stage. We have enough to have a simple head and neck, if not the face. The number of *U* isoparms isn't so important right now, but there are eight *V* isoparms radiating from the mouth for half a face, which is about right at this stage. Rebuild the surface with the Keep CVs setting checked, and everything else at default.

3. The mouth should be built first. As a rule, for a simple half face, you want three isoparms for the mouth bottom, three for the mouth corner, and three for the mouth top. This would be listed in the Attribute Editor as eight spans of *V* isoparms, the first isoparm having the value of zero. Cut the face just around the forehead area. Hide the head. Duplicate the half face, then make its Scale X value –1. This becomes the half face on the right. Open the Connection Editor. Select the first face's shape node and load it into the Output window. Load the second face's shape node into the Input window. Connect World Space to

Create as shown in the next illustration. Now the second face on the right deforms when the CVs of the first face on the left are moved.

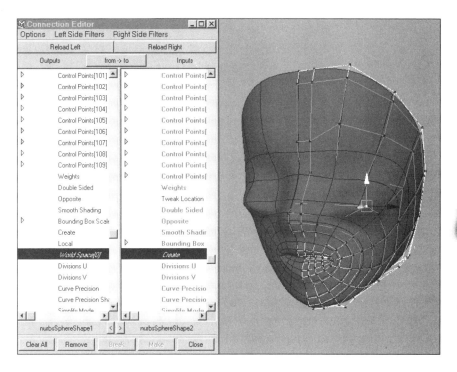

PART 2

Modeling

4. Don't create the oral cavity. The surface edge should be right at the end of the inner lip. Concentrate instead on forming a clean mouth, with the CVs all placed properly and not bunched up chaotically, especially in the mouth corner area. You can add *U* isoparms to make the nose more defined, but do not add *V* isoparms at this point. Once the mouth looks acceptable, rebuild the surface. The *V* isoparm count should still be eight spans.

5. Duplicate curves from *U* isoparms of the face. Unhide the head, and do the same. Delete the surfaces. You are left with only the curves, as in a) shown next. Loft, and tweak the curve CVs to refine the head further, as in b).

6. Cut the face from the head as before, and add *U* and *V* isoparms to define the nostril area, as in c). Make sure to insert the isoparms gradually as you are sculpting; otherwise you are unnecessarily challenging yourself. Although the face and the head are detached, they are still procedurally connected to the curves. If you want to make changes involving both surfaces, you can still do so by moving the curves' CVs. Their tangency is maintained.

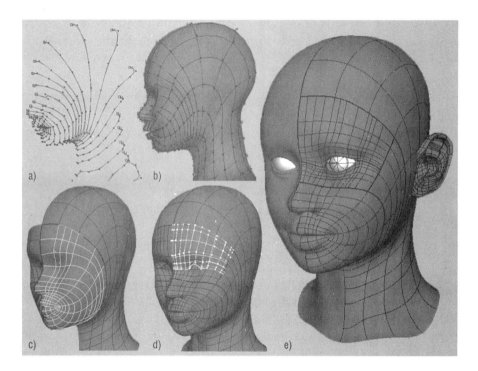

7. Once the nose is finished, you can move on to the eyes. What we are going to do is cut the face into four patches. The mouth and the nose are basically done, and there is no reason to add anymore isoparms to it. The eye area requires a lot of isoparm insertions, and we'd like to localize the density as much as we can. And cutting the eye area into two patches along the eyeline allows you to create holes for the eyes.

8. Cut the mouth area from the face, selecting the isoparm a bit below the eye sockets. Cut the jaw area from the face, again, along the isoparm just beside the eye sockets.

9. Only the eye area remains to be sculpted—and it is probably the most difficult. Before cutting the eye area into eye_top and eye_bot patches, insert all the V isoparms you'll need. You need two isoparms close together to clamp the eye's corner, two on each side, at least three or four isoparms for the eye itself, and at least one isoparm between the eye area and the edge. Once the V isoparms are inserted as in e) above, you can cut the U isoparm along the eyeline. You need to insert the U isoparms in the two eye patches as you are sculpting the eye area, but they should roughly look like e) after a while.

The picture d) above is an example of what can go wrong at this stage. The *U* isoparm was cut prematurely. You can still insert isoparms in the two resulting patches carefully so that they will match, but it isn't efficient. Also, the cut was made without putting in eyeballs to see exactly where the eyeline is. As a result, the cut was made a bit lower than it should have been.

10. The ear is basically a deformed sphere with holes. If there is a trick to building it, it's not much of a trick—build the front half first, and then the back half. The ear below has been cut in half to show this. The rest is sculpting, pushing and pulling CVs into the shape you see. The eyes can be as simple as a plain sphere, or as complicated as the one here. There are two spheres, the inner one deformed for realistic pupils, and the outer one transparent and used for specularity only.

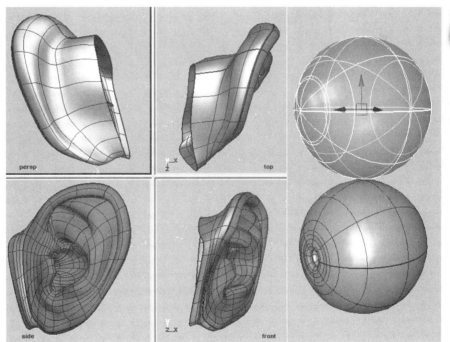

11. You need to insert two more isoparms in order to fold the eyelids. Since we're building a child, the eyes should become a bit larger and the nose a bit rounder. Once the shapes look OK, attach the left and the right side geometries. Use the Blend with Insert Knot setting. You should end up with eye_top patch, eye_bot patch, mouth patch, and the jaw patch as shown below. If the edges no longer

meet perfectly, it is not a problem, as long as they are not too far apart. For the space that gets created between the eyes and the face patches at the corners, stick in a simple polygon face to fill the hole, as shown here. The eye area should be built in such way that the patches will close the eyes without any problem.

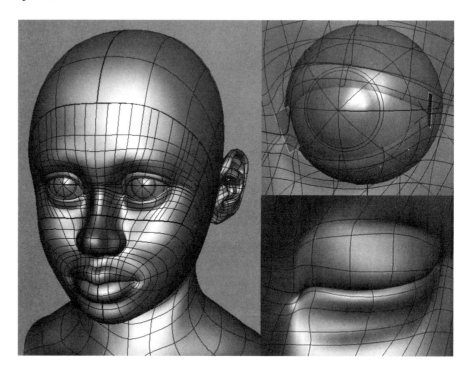

12. Use the Global Stitch with Tangency option. Select everything, including the head geometry. If any seams were noticeable, this should get rid of them. Make a copy of the face. You can delete the curves, the original face patches, and other unnecessary nodes. We did not build an oral cavity for this model, but if you wanted to build one, you would start by offsetting the inner mouth edge isoparm, and duplicating the offset curves. You should build it when you are building targets for Blend Shapes. The hair is built from a plane, which starts out from the back and wraps around the head like a towel.

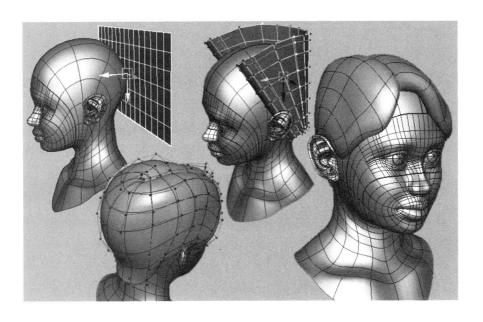

Summary

This was a long chapter, covering a lot of material. You learned to create and manipulate NURBS curves and surfaces, and saw examples of building things with them. We also went through an advanced tutorial on building a human face, which takes a lot of practice to become good at. The next chapter will also be quite substantial, introducing the world of polygons. Then we will come back to modeling with NURBS again in Chapter 8, where we will proceed to build a puppy dog in patches.

PART 2

Modeling

chapter 7

POLYGON
MODELING

Featuring

- *Polygon faces, solids, and shells*

- *Techniques for creating and displaying polygons*

- *Polygon selection and editing tools*

- *Texture mapping in Texture view*

7

POLYGON MODELING

P olygons are the preferred modeling choice for many gaming companies. If you are interested in going into that field, you should be particularly interested in this chapter. Of course, this chapter also is of interest to anyone who uses Maya for modeling.

We begin by introducing some terms and concepts related to polygons. Then we describe how to create and edit polygons using the Maya tools. Finally, we discuss the more advanced topic of mapping textures. To demonstrate all the concepts, the tutorial at the end of this chapter provides instructions for building a hand using polygons.

Polygon Concepts and Terms

The word *polygon* is derived from a Greek word meaning "many angled". In mathematics, a polygon is defined as a closed figure formed by a finite number of coplanar segments that are not parallel and intersect exactly two other segments only at their endpoints.

As far as we (and Maya) are concerned, polygons are triangles, rectangles, pentagons, and other many-sided line drawings. The endpoint is called the *vertex*, the line is called the *edge*, and the area inside is called the *face*.

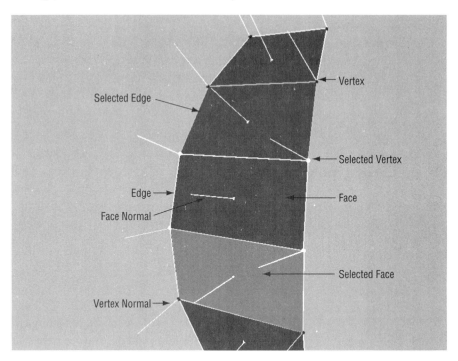

Polygon Faces

Faces have a front side and a back side. When you are building the face, the front side is determined by the direction of the vertices creating the edges (see the "Creating Faces" section later in this chapter).

The most basic polygon surface is the triangular face. The front side of a triangular face has only one normal vector, because triangles are, by definition, planar. Quadrangular polygons (quads) are four-sided faces, which may or may not be planar. You also can create faces that have five or more sides, called *n*-sided faces. However, as a general rule, you should try to keep your polygon surfaces as triangles or quads.

N O T E   We could say that a triangular face is the building block of all modeling. Every type of surface geometry is converted into triangular faces (a process known as *tessellation*) before it is rendered.

Faces in a polygon surface are usually connected (attached to each other), sharing common vertices and edges. They can be *extracted* with their own unshared edges and vertices while still being part of the polygon surface, but then they will not become *soft edges,* which means they will not be smoothed in the tessellation process. (Extracting faces is discussed later in this chapter, in the "Editing Polygons" section.)

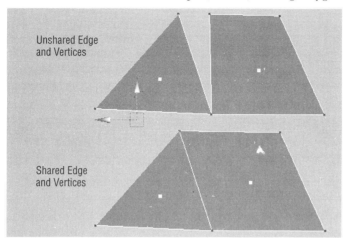

Polygon Solids, Shells, and UV Values

Polygons are classified as either solids or shells. A polygon *solid* is made up of connected faces that form an enclosed volume, where each edge is shared by two faces. A polygon *shell* is a collection of connected faces that leave some of its edges open as border edges. A polygon object can have more than one shell, as in the example shown below.

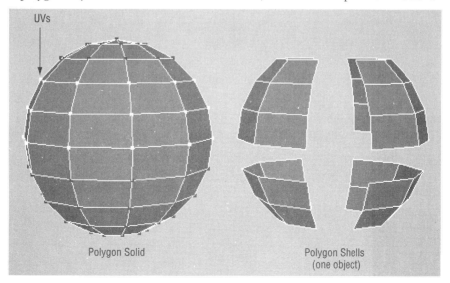

Polygon Solid

Polygon Shells (one object)

By default, faces have UV values assigned to them when they are created. As explained in Chapter 6, a surface in 3D space is defined by the parameterization of the variables *U* and *V*. A UV coordinate can be given at any point inside the area, and the area is given *UV* directions. UVs are needed for texturing purposes. UVs are difficult to distinguish from the regular vertex points, but they turn bright green when they are selected.

N O T E   You may find polygons that do not have UV values, especially when the surface is a model imported from another program. If the UV values are missing from the polygon surface, you need to assign them manually, as described in the "Mapping Textures" section later in this chapter.

Valid and Invalid Polygon Surfaces

When working with polygons, you will often end up creating surfaces with a lot of vertices that you need to tweak, or you may have high-resolution imported or converted models that need to be cleaned up. We will discuss ways to make the process easier in this chapter. However, there are certain rules you should always keep in mind:

- You should not create a dangling edge, which is an edge without a face.
- You should not have one edge of a face shared by three or more faces.
- Adjacent normal vectors should not be pointing in opposite directions.
- Vertices and edges should match up neatly, and they should not be placed without somehow contributing to the shape of deformation of the surface.

Some invalid polygon surfaces are illustrated below.

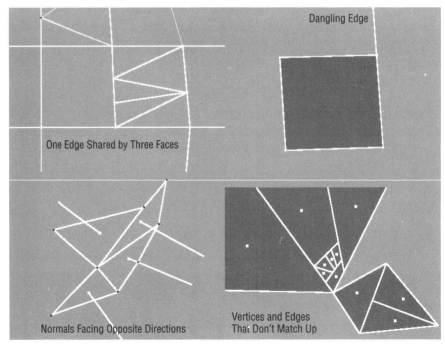

Creating Polygons

Polygons are usually created by clicking on vertices, much like creating curves, to generate edges. Two or more edges create a face, which contains face normals and vertex normals. You can also create polygon primitives or convert NURBS into polygons.

Using Polygon Primitives

As with NURBS, Maya provides several default polygon primitives you can use as starting points for creating more complex polygonal surfaces. When you select Create ➢ Polygon Primitives, you'll see the choices Sphere, Cube, Cylinder, Cone, Plane, and Torus.

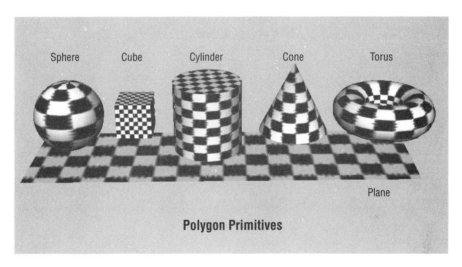

Polygon Primitives

N O T E   Notice that the polygon cube, cylinder, and cone surfaces are all one-piece solids, unlike their NURBS counterparts, which are made up of several pieces.

As an example, select Create ➢ Polygon Primitives ➢ Sphere ❑. The Subdivisions Around Axis attribute is equivalent to the Sections attribute of the NURBS sphere, and Subdivisions Along Height is the same as the Spans attribute of a NURBS sphere. You also can choose the axis for the sphere's up direction. The Texture setting, which is turned on by default, maps UV values to the sphere being created. We will talk more about textures toward the end of this chapter. To create the sphere, click Create.

You can try editing the sphere's radius and subdivision attributes in the Channel box's Input section or in the Attribute Editor's polySphere tab. In the latter, you can also edit the Axis setting to change the sphere's orientation. The examples below show spheres with different settings.

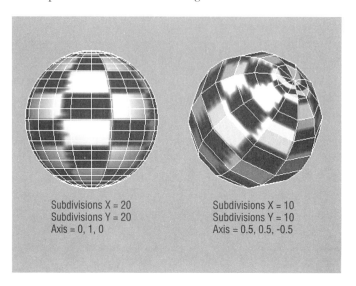

Subdivisions X = 20
Subdivisions Y = 20
Axis = 0, 1, 0

Subdivisions X = 10
Subdivisions Y = 10
Axis = 0.5, 0.5, -0.5

Displaying Polygons

Maya provides many different ways of modifying the display of polygons (perhaps too many, in fact):

- From Display ➢ Polygon Components, which is an easily accessible submenu
- From Display ➢ Custom Polygon Display ❏, which provides more details and the ability to control the display of more than one polygon
- From Options ➢ General Preferences (in the Display Polygons section), which is a detailed display that lets you control multiple polygons, similar to the Custom Polygon Display dialog box
- From the Attribute Editor's Shape tab (in the Mesh Component Display section), which focuses on one polygon, as shown next

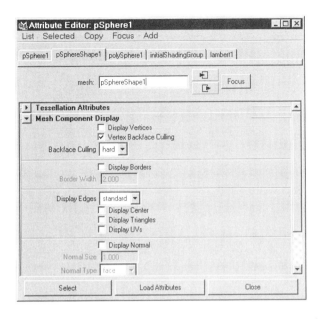

The following sections describe the display options for the polygon surfaces that are available through these dialog boxes.

Displaying Vertices

You can set vertices so that they are visible when the polygon is not selected. Vertex normals also can be made visible. The Backface Culling option for vertices is turned on by default in the Custom Polygon Display Options dialog box (shown below), but it doesn't have any effect if the Backface Culling option is set to Off.

There are three degrees of backface culling, and they can be very useful when you need to select only the front side of a surface (the Attribute Editor and the Custom Polygon Display Options dialog box have slightly different wording for these options):

- Wire (or Keep Wire) mode blocks you from picking vertices and faces of the back surface, while still enabling you to select edges. Wire mode displays the back faces.

- Hard (Keep Hard Edges) mode works like Wire mode, except that it doesn't display the back faces.

- Full (or On) mode does not display the back side at all, and you can't select anything at the back of the shape.

These three modes are illustrated below.

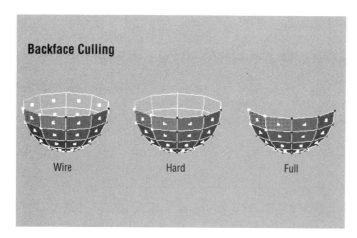

Displaying Edges and Borders

Edges can be displayed in three ways:

- The Standard setting displays all the edges.
- The Soft/Hard setting displays the soft edges as dotted lines.
- The Only Hard setting displays only hard edges.

The Border Edges setting is off by default. When you turn on this setting, you can see the border edges in thicker lines. The default width for border edges is 2, but you can increase the thickness. The Custom Polygon Display Options dialog box also offers a Texture Borders option, which represents the starting point and endpoint for the texture UV placement. These display options for edges and borders are illustrated below.

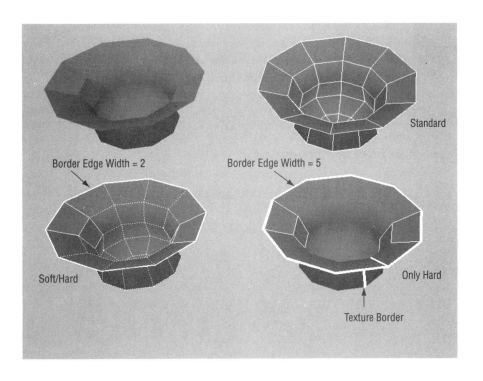

Border Edge Width = 2

Border Edge Width = 5

Standard

Soft/Hard

Only Hard

Texture Border

Displaying Faces

The choices for displaying faces are Centers, Normals, Triangles, and Warp. The Triangles option is available if the faces are not triangular, and it displays the faces in triangles made up of dotted lines. When Warp is turned on, it detects any face that is warped, or nonplanar. The different settings for displaying faces are shown below.

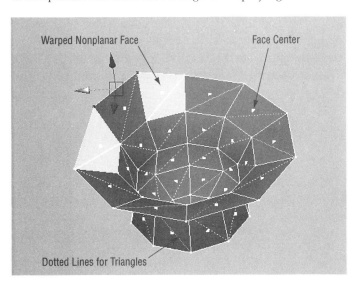

Warped Nonplanar Face

Face Center

Dotted Lines for Triangles

N O T E   The Triangles option for face display is different from the Triangulate function, which actually adds the edges to the faces. With the Triangles option, the surface itself does not change; it only *displays* triangles.

You can choose to display face normals, as well as vertex normals, and set different line lengths to represent them.

Displaying Numbers

Through the Custom Polygon Display Options dialog box, you can display numbers for vertices, edges, faces, and UVs of polygon surfaces in the order of their creation. Examples of item numbering for vertices, edges, and faces are shown below. UV topics are covered later in the chapter.

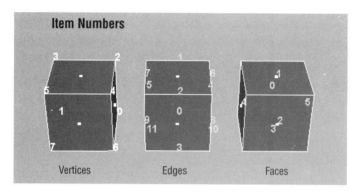

Coloring Vertices

You can color vertices in Shaded mode by checking the Color In Shaded Display option in the Custom Polygon Display Options dialog box. To apply color to vertex, select the appropriate vertices and select Edit Polygons ➤ Colors ➤ Apply Color ❑. In the option box, you can create the color you want for the vertices, and then click the Apply Color button. (See the Color Gallery on the CD for the full effect.)

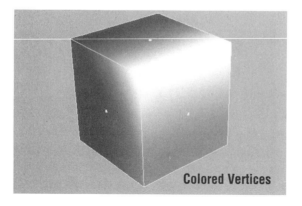

Displaying the Polygon Count

Another display function that is indispensable in working with polygons is accessed by selecting Polygons ➣ Display Poly Count. In many game productions, keeping a model's poly count below a certain number is crucial in maintaining real-time inter-activity of the game.

Display Poly Count shows the following statistics:

- The numbers in green on the left side of the window show the total polygon count in vertices, edges, faces, and UVs for all the visible polygon surfaces inside the window.

- The numbers in white on the left side of the window show the numbers of the specific selected components.

- The numbers in white on the right side of the window show the total polygon count for the selected object.

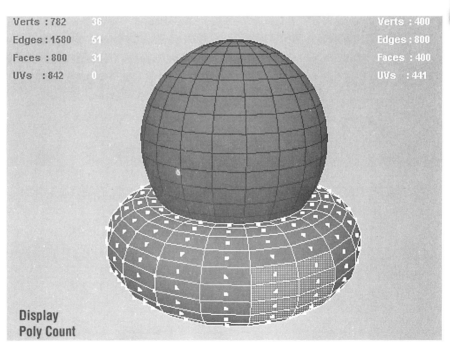

Display
Poly Count

Creating Faces

Let's use the Create Polygon tool to draw two faces:

1. In the side view, select Polygons ➣ Create Polygon Tool ❏.

2. Set all the options to their default values by clicking the Reset Tool button, and then change the Limit Points setting to 3.

3. Click in the modeling window in a counterclockwise direction as shown below. On the third click, a triangular face is created.

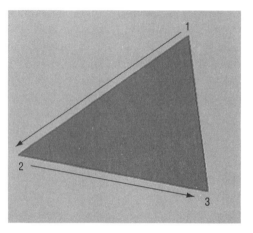

4. Change the Limit Points setting to –1 (the default). Then click again, as shown below. Press Enter after the fourth click to create a quadrangular face.

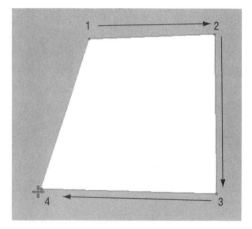

N O T E   If you leave the Limit Points setting at its default of –1, then after you've entered the desired number of vertices, you just press Enter to complete the action.

5. Choose Display ➢ Custom Polygon Display ❑. Click the All button at the top of the dialog box to set the display for both faces. Then check the Normals check box next to Vertices and the Vertices check box next to Show Item Numbers.

Switch to perspective view, and you will see that the normal directions for the faces are opposite, as shown below.

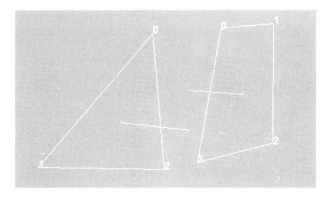

The direction of the vertex creation determines the direction of the normal. This means that the front side of a face is created by vertices going counterclockwise.

NOTE   Faces that are not triangular may or may not be planar. If you want to make sure the faces you are building remain planar, you can select the Ensure Planarity option for the Create Polygon and Append To Polygon tools. This option forces the face being built to remain planar.

Adding Faces

The Append To Polygon tool is the same as the Create Polygon tool, except that it adds faces to existing faces rather than creating new ones. Let's add some faces to our triangular face:

1. Switch to side view and select Polygons ➣ Append To Polygon Tool.

2. Click on the triangular face to select it. You can tell it's selected because the border edges appear thicker.

TIP   By default, to select a face, you need to click or marquee its center. If you want to be able to just click anywhere inside the face and select it, choose Options ➣ General Preferences ➣ Modeling, and change the Polygon setting from Center to Whole Face.

3. Select the edge on the left side, and you will see pink arrows going clockwise around the triangular face. Also, a bright green dot appears at the zero vertex. That is where the appending begins. (Because the arrows go in the opposite direction from the way the face is created, this process can be rather confusing if you are not careful.)

4. Click two more times, as shown below. Then press Enter. You now have a quadrangular face attached to the original face. Note the vertex numbers are 3 and 4. You can continue to add faces this way.

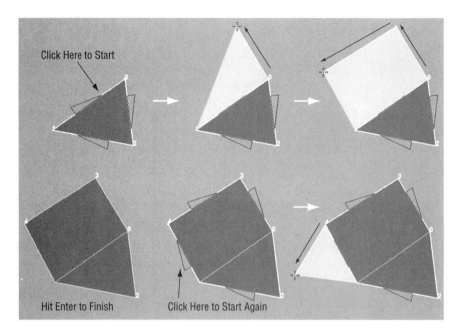

You can set the Append To Polygon tool to continue adding faces by setting the Limit Points option to 4. You can try this with the quadrangular face. After the second click, another quadrangular face is created, and you are still in the Append mode. You can build polygonal strips in one round of clicking this way, as illustrated below. You also can create a triangular face by pressing Enter after the first vertex placement, but that will exit Append mode. Another technique is to click on one edge, then click on another adjoining edge to create a face that is attached to those two faces, and continue to attach the face to more edges as you go.

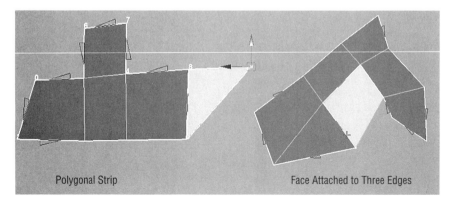

TIP You can reposition a vertex while you are creating it, just as you can with curves (see Chapter 6). Just MM click or press the Insert key.

Creating Faces with Holes

With the Create Polygon or Append To Polygon tool, you can easily create faces with holes. After you've positioned the desired number of vertices with the default tool settings, do not press Enter. Instead, press the Ctrl key, and then place a vertex inside the surface area. This becomes the first vertex of a hole inside the surface. If you want to create another hole, Ctrl+click to start again. When you're finished placing holes, press Enter to complete the action. Note that the resulting surface, when triangulated, is pretty messy, so you'll want to clean it up.

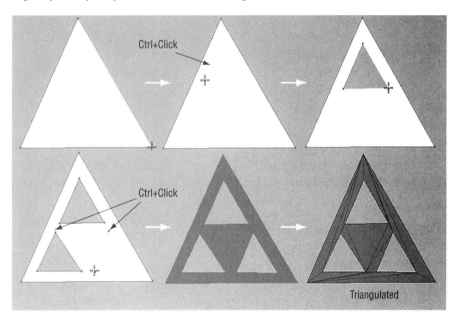

Converting NURBS to Polygons

Maya has an efficient NURBS-to-polygon conversion function. The default is set to triangles and the tessellation method, with a standard fit. You can change the settings to suit your needs.

Quadrangles usually convert more cleanly than the triangles. However, after the conversion process, you may prefer to work with triangles or a quadrangulated version, as shown in the center illustration on the next page.

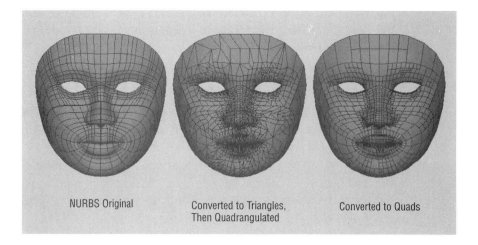

| NURBS Original | Converted to Triangles, Then Quadrangulated | Converted to Quads |

The Count setting forces the converted polygon to try to match a set number of face counts. The Control Points setting creates vertices in place of CVs. After the conversion, you can edit the conversion settings in the Attribute Editor or the Channel box.

Selecting Polygons

Before you can edit and manipulate your polygons, you need to select them. As usual, Maya offers several techniques for accomplishing this task. You will most often select components using the selection mask, by RM choosing over the surface you're working on. Alternatively, you can use hotkeys and the tools on the Polygons ➤ Selection menu.

Selecting with Hotkeys

You can use the following hotkeys for selecting components of polygons:

F8	Toggles between object and component selection
F9	Selects vertices
F10	Selects edges
F11	Selects faces
F12	Selects UVs
Ctrl+F9	Selects vertices and faces

To select more than one component, select a component, pick-mask to another selection mode, and then Shift+select the other component. The illustration below shows the marking menu list for the various polygon components.

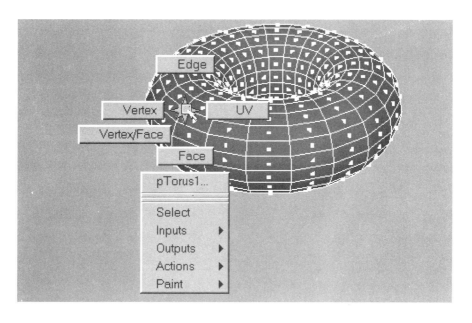

Using the Selection Tools

Maya also provides some tools to aid you in selecting components. Select Polygons ➤ Selection to see a submenu with selection tools. The Grow Selection Region function increases any selected component elements by one unit. Shrink Selection Region does the opposite. Select Selection Boundary leaves only the boundary of the selected component elements still active and deselects the rest.

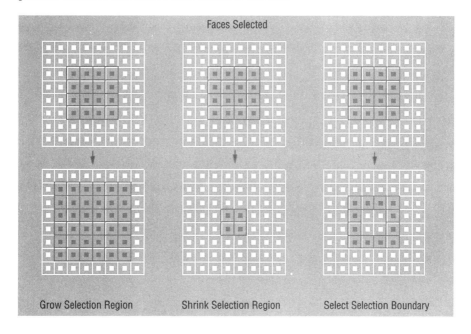

Faces Selected

Grow Selection Region   Shrink Selection Region   Select Selection Boundary

You can also convert any selected component elements to another by using the Convert functions on the Selection submenu. As you can see in the illustration below, conversion is not cyclical—converting the selected vertices to UVs will give a larger region of UVs than the one you started with.

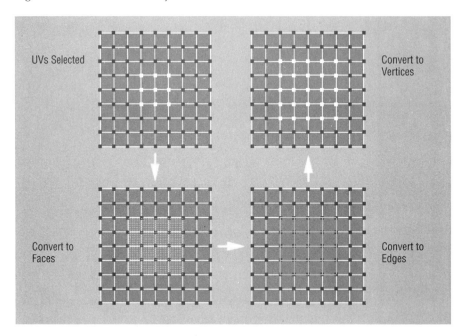

Constraining Selections

At the bottom of the Selection submenu is an advanced tool called Selection Constraints. Here are some examples of what you can do with this tool:

- You can constrain the selection to specific locations, such as border components or inside components.
- You can have only hard edges selected or only soft edges selected.
- You can select only triangular faces, only quads, or only faces with more than four sides.
- You can select components with a set amount of randomness.
- You can expand or shrink a selected region, or select the selection's boundary.

Some examples of polygon selection constraints are shown below. You may notice that the *n*-sided faces look like they are quads. It's easy to confuse the two, but when you count the vertices or the edges, the selected *n*-sided faces have more than four. All the *n*-sided faces have smaller adjacent faces that divide their sides into two edges and three vertices. Another way to tell if a face is *n*-sided is to turn on the Triangles option in the Custom Polygon Display Options dialog box.

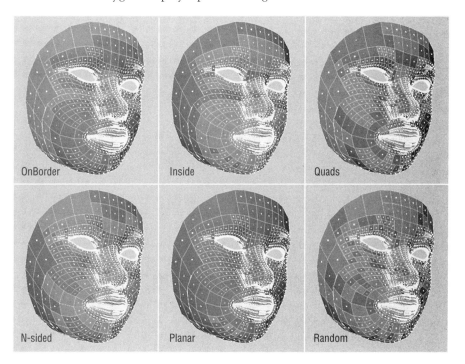

OnBorder   Inside   Quads

N-sided   Planar   Random

Modeling

T I P   The contents of the Selection Constraint dialog box depend on the types of components being constrained. A good practice is to pick-mask the component you wish to select, and then open the dialog box. Another is to make sure to click the Constrain Nothing button before you close this dialog box.

Editing Polygons

This section focuses on the tools for working with polygons. You have many options, ranging from moving polygon components to manually softening or hardening a polygon's edges. You can find the editing tools on various menus, including the Edit Polygons menu, the Tool Options submenu, the Booleans submenu, and the Normals submenu.

N O T E   The number of Polygon tools available has expanded considerably in Maya 2. Here, we cover the option settings for the functions you are likely to use most often. For information about the other functions' option settings, consult the Maya documentation.

Moving Polygon Components

You can move, rotate, and scale polygon components using the tools introduced in Part 1. Additionally, you can use the Move Component function on the Edit Polygons menu to translate, rotate, and scale the components.

The Move Component function has a local mode and global mode. You can switch between these modes by clicking on the toggle handle, as shown below. In local mode, the Z axis is always pointing in the direction of the surface normal.

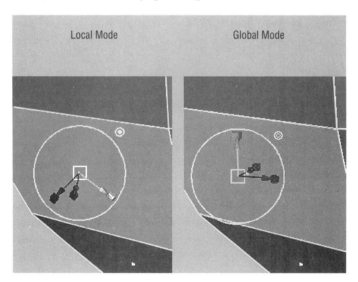

Extruding and Duplicating Faces

When working with faces, you can use the Duplicate Face and Extrude functions on the Polygons menu. The example below shows a sphere that has been extruded and smoothed (smoothing is discussed a bit later in this chapter).

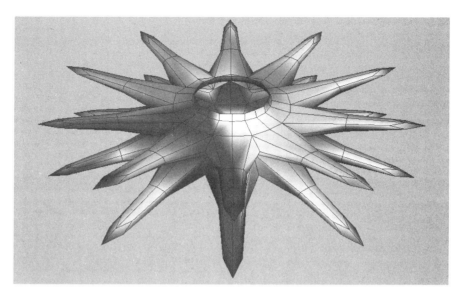

With the Duplicate Face and Extrude functions, you can either keep the resulting faces together or have them remain separate by toggling Polygons ➤ Tool Options ➤ Keep Faces Together. Note that although the duplicated faces are discontinuous from the original faces, they are still components of one polygon object.

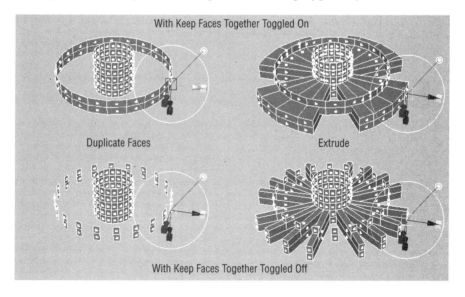

Making and Filling Holes

You can use a face to create a hole in another face. The examples below were created by duplicating the face, then selecting Polygons ➤ Make Hole Tool. With the default settings, the Make Hole tool creates an extrusion with the second face becoming a hole for the first. Alternatively, you can produce holed surfaces by selecting Merge settings in the option box. If you do not want to disturb the position of the original surface, set Merge to First.

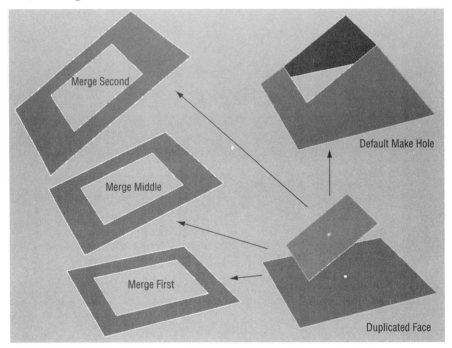

To fill surfaces with unwanted holes, use the Fill Hole function on the Polygons menu. You must select edges around the hole before it can be filled.

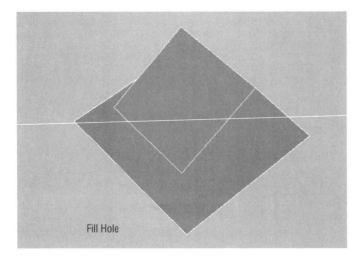

Performing Boolean Operations

You can perform simple Boolean operations—such as union, difference, and intersection—on polygons at the object level. These functions are on the Polygons ➤ Booleans submenu. They are simple functions that can aid you tremendously in working with polygons.

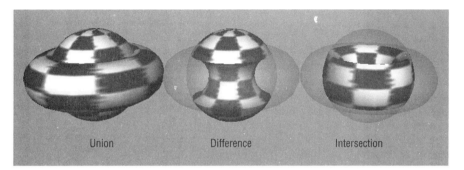

Union   Difference   Intersection

After a Boolean operation, the vertices may end up not matching well, requiring some cleanup. For example, in the Difference operation, the first picked object remains, minus the intersecting part. In the operation shown below, the torus ends up with some messy face topology at the intersection point, which will need to be cleaned up.

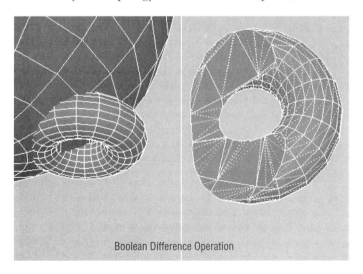

Boolean Difference Operation

Modeling

Combining, Extracting, and Separating Polygons

The Combine function on the Edit Polygons menu is similar to the Boolean union operation, but there are differences. The Combine function takes any collection of polygonal surfaces and turns them into one object, as the Boolean union does, but it does not trim away the unnecessary parts. As you also can see in the example shown below, the union surface seems to have more triangles than the combined surface. This is because the Boolean operation actually attaches the edges and vertices of the objects being unioned together, whereas the Combine operation leaves them unshared, or extracted.

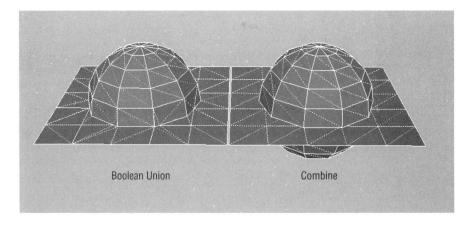

Boolean Union   Combine

Combining polygon objects is simple, but dividing one polygon object into separate objects is a bit more involved. Before any of the faces of the polygon object can become separate objects, they must be extracted to become different shells.

 N O T E   An object that was created through the Combine operation already has extracted pieces. Thus, you can simply apply the Edit Polygons ➢ Separate operation to undo the Combine action; you don't need to use Extract first.

The Extract function, also on the Edit Polygons menu, does exactly what it says: It extracts the selected faces from their neighbors so that the edges and vertices of the extracted faces are no longer shared. Once a face is extracted, it becomes a separate shell inside the object, and the Edit Polygons ➢ Separate operation can be applied.

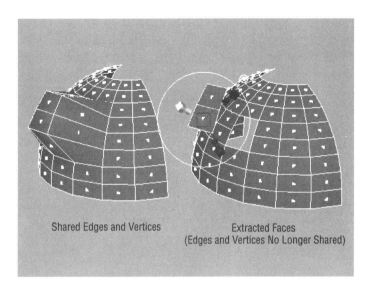

Shared Edges and Vertices   Extracted Faces
(Edges and Vertices No Longer Shared)

Merging Vertices and Edges

Merging is the opposite of extracting. Whereas the Extract function separates vertices and edges so that they are no longer shared, the Merge function makes them shared by faces.

The Edit Polygons ➤ Merge Vertices function merges vertices so that instead of there being several overlapping vertices at one point, only one vertex is shared by the edges. Often, you will not see any difference until you try moving the edges or faces, as shown below.

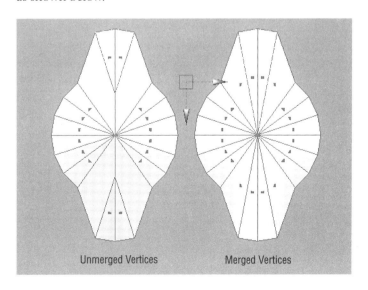

Unmerged Vertices   Merged Vertices

The Edit Polygons ➤ Merge Edge function merges border edges. When you select the tool, the border edges become thicker. Click on the first edge, and then the second edge. Both edges turn orange. When you click again, the two edges merge. There are three Merge modes:

- With Middle, the default mode, the first and the second edge merge at the halfway point.
- With the Merge mode set to First, the second edge snaps to the first edge.
- With the Merge mode set to Second, the first edge snaps to the second edge.

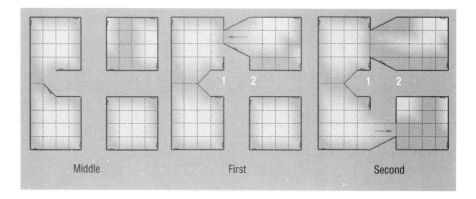

After the merge, you are still in the Merge mode, and the tool asks for another first edge to be picked.

You can also merge adjacent edges to clean up messy polygons or simplify edges. The Edit Polygons ➤ Merge Multiple Edges function takes multiple edges and *sews* them together, as shown below. After you use Merge Multiple Edges, you can polish the results by using the Merge Edge tool.

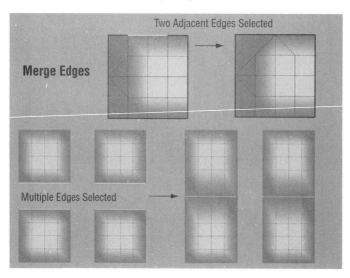

Deleting and Collapsing Polygon Components

Although deleting polygon parts is straightforward, there are a few things to keep in mind when deleting components:

- You can delete only corner vertices, or vertices that are joined by only two edges (called *winged* vertices).

- You cannot delete border edges.

- You can always delete faces.

WARNING   When you delete an edge inside a surface, be sure the vertex of adjoining edges is not a winged vertex. If it is a winged vertex, then you should not delete it.

The Edit Polygons ➤ Collapse function does not work like Delete. In contrast, Collapse allows you to collapse faces and edges so that the remaining vertices are shared, as illustrated below.

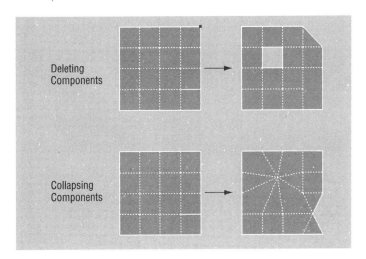

Deleting Components

Collapsing Components

Subdividing and Splitting Polygons

The Subdivide tool on the Edit Polygons menu allows you to automatically and evenly divide an edge or a face into equal parts. The default setting is Subdivision 1, which divides an edge into two edges or divides a face into four quads or triangles. If you are about to refine a rough polygon shape, subdivision provides you with a quick way of gaining more control elements.

You can't subdivide faces with holes. In those cases, use Edit Polygons ➤ Split Polygon Tool. In fact, the Split Polygon tool is probably one of the tools you'll use most frequently. With this tool, you can divide faces into smaller pieces.

 N O T E   Do not confuse the Split Polygon tool with the Append To Polygon tool on the Polygons menu. The Append To Polygon tool creates faces at the outer edges of a surface, whereas the Split Polygon tool edits faces by dividing them into smaller pieces.

You can insert vertices on edges, thereby splitting an edge into two, and insert edges on faces, thereby splitting the face. Let's see how this works:

1. Create a plane, zoom in from the top view, and select Edit Polygons ➤ Split Polygon Tool. The surface is highlighted in green.

2. Click on one of the inner edges, as shown below. A bright green dot appears on the edge.

3. Press Enter, pick-mask Vertex, and you'll see that a vertex has been added, splitting the edge into two.

4. Select the tool again, click on the opposite side, and click-drag to the point you first created. Press Enter, and the face splits into two.

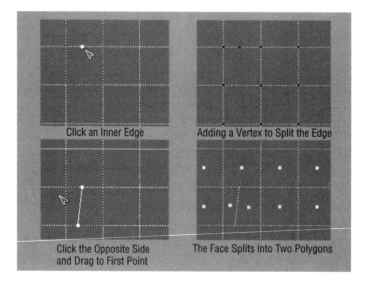

Click an Inner Edge   Adding a Vertex to Split the Edge

Click the Opposite Side   The Face Splits into Two Polygons
and Drag to First Point

You can set the Subdivision option for the Split Polygon tool so that with each click, it creates any number of vertices. This option is especially useful in situations where you want to create evenly distributed vertices, as shown in the lower image below. However, the Subdivision setting will not work if your second click is inside the face and not on another edge, as shown in the upper image below.

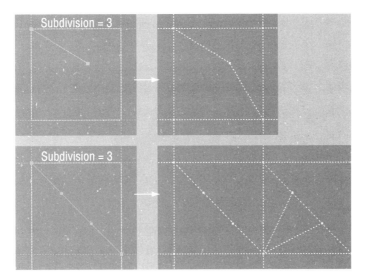

 WARNING   When you want to place a vertex at the end of an edge, don't click on the endpoints of that edge. You may select the wrong edge that way. Instead, click on the middle of the edge you want and drag to the endpoint.

Smoothing and Sculpting Polygons

Smoothing is a simple but indispensable function that you will use over and over again. The Smooth tool on the Edit Polygons menu subdivides a surface, or selected faces of a surface, according to the division setting in the option box (the default setting is 1) to create as smooth a surface as its division setting will allow. It always produces quads, and you should generally leave the subdivision setting at the default. If you are going to apply Smooth more than once, you usually want to tweak the surface before applying it again.

The Sculpt Polygons tool, or Artisan, on the Edit Polygons menu is also especially useful in polygonal modeling. It can save you hours of pulling and pushing vertices on dense surfaces with just several brush strokes. See Chapter 9 for more information about using the Artisan tools.

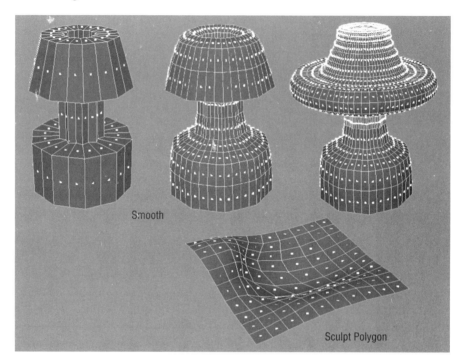

Smooth

Sculpt Polygon

Reverse and Soften/Harden

A surface needs to have all its normals on the same side. When you're working with various polygons, separating and attaching them, you may find that normals on a surface have become inconsistent. The Reverse function, found on the Edit Polygons ➤ Normals submenu, reverses the front and back sides of the selected faces, reversing their normal direction as well. The Reverse and Propagate function is the same as the Reverse function, except that it not only reverses the normal of a selected face, it also "propagates" to other faces, reversing their normals as well if they are facing the same side of the surface as the first selected face.

Soften/Harden, another function found on the Normals submenu, can manually determine if a polygon's edge is to be hard (edgy and sharp) or soft (smooth and rounded). Let's try out this tool:

1. Create a polygon sphere and set its subdivisions to 10.

2. Select Display ➢ Custom Polygon Display ❏. In its dialog box, turn on both Vertex Normal and Face Normal.

3. Zoom in to look closely at the vertices of the sphere in Shaded mode. You should see normals, as shown below.

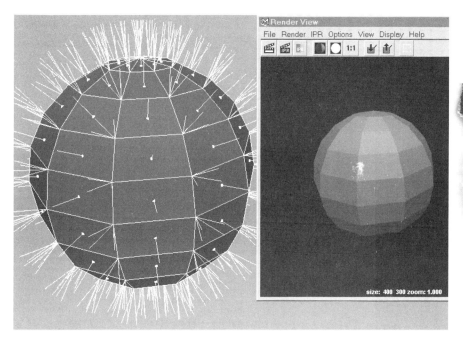

4. It may appear messy, but if you look carefully, you can see that each vertex has four normals coming out of it, with each vertex normal in parallel to its corresponding face normal. Pick-mask Edge and select the upper half of the sphere.

5. With the upper sphere's edges still selected, select Edit Polygon ➢ Normals ➢ Soften/Harden ❏.

6. Click the All Soft (180) button, then the Soft/Hard button. The upper half of the sphere now has only one vertex normal coming out, which is not parallel to any of the face normals, as shown below. The other vertex normals are deleted because the edges are now soft edges. Note that the upper half of the sphere is rendered smoothly as well.

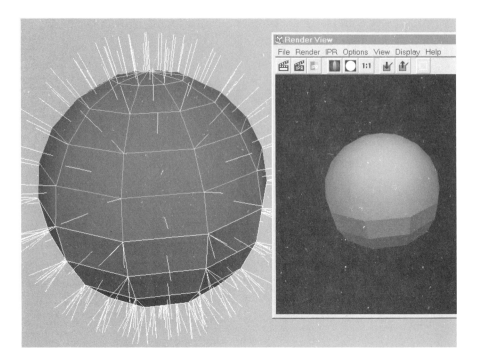

7. Open the Attribute Editor for the sphere and go to the tab called polySoftEdge1.

8. Open the Poly Soft Edge History. You'll see the Angle slider set at 180. Try moving the Angle slider down. From around 35 degrees and lower, you should see the deleted vertex normals popping back in, and the edges becoming hard edges again.

Mapping Textures

As with NURBS surfaces, textures are mapped to polygon surfaces *parametrically,* with UV values. But UVs are not an intrinsic part of a polygonal surface. They must be mapped. A polygonal surface can acquire UV values through various types of projection mapping, normalization, or unitization. The best way to explain all this and the other tools you need to use for texturing is to step through some examples, which is what we'll do here.

N O T E   This section requires some familiarity with Hypershade. You may want to read through "Using Hypershade" in Chapter 19 first.

Working in Texture View

The Texture View window allows you to view how UVs are mapped to a polygonal surface. The bright green selected UV dots in the modeling window become yellow dots in texture view, and the shapes shown are flat 2D representations of UVs being mapped to faces. You can copy and paste UVs, as well as access the texture-editing functions in the Texture submenu. You can also pick-mask to select vertices, edges, faces, and UVs of the polygon represented in the view.

First, let's create a polygon to work with in the Texture View window.

1. Start a new scene and select Edit Polygons ➤ Texture ➤ Texture View.

2. Select Polygons ➤ Create Polygon Tool ❏. Make sure that the Texture option is set to Normalize.

3. Go to top view and create a triangle, as shown below. Press Enter to complete the action, and you will see the triangle appear in the Texture View window.

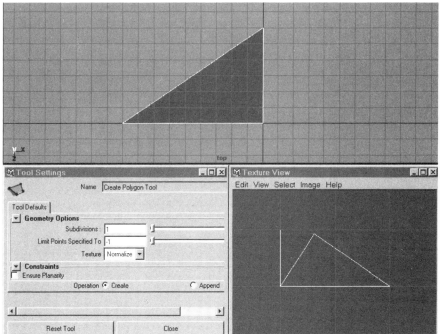

4. Create a blinn shader in Hypershade, assign a diagonal ramp to it, and assign the shader to the triangle.

5. Press number 6 to get into Textured Display mode and select the triangle again. Your display should look something like the one shown below. Note that the tri-

angle fits the texture horizontally, which represents *U* parameterization from 0 to 1. Normalized texture maps to the surface in this manner.

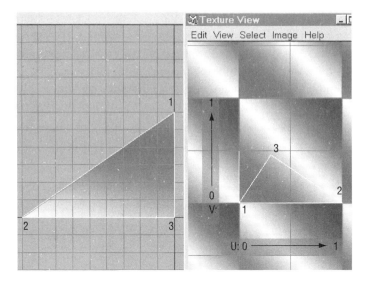

 NOTE   You'll find the image above and the following series of images in the Color Gallery on the CD.

 TIP   It's a good idea to keep the Texture View window open when you are working with polygon textures. Most of the Texture submenu options can be accessed from inside this view, and we will be using it constantly in this section.

In the Texture View window, the texture image repeats according to the settings in Image Range; the default is 10 repetitions. You may find the repetitions a bit disorienting at first, but it's better to have it repeat than to have it show just once. If you find the default grid setting distracting, you can turn it off or change its display setting. You can transform UVs in the Texture View window in the same way that you transform regular vertices. If the selected faces have a projection mapping, you can edit the Mapping manipulator as well.

Transforming UVs

We'll continue and transform the UVs.

1. In the Texture View window, select the UVs and select the Move tool. A 2D Move manipulator appears. Move the manipulator, and you will see the texture in the triangular face update.

2. Select the Rotate tool, and a 2D Rotate manipulator appears. Rotate the UVs, and the texture inside the triangle updates accordingly.

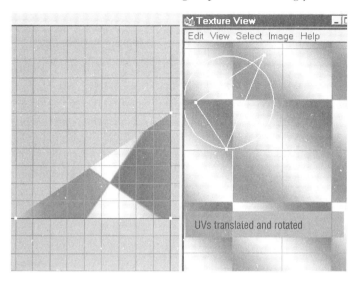

3. Append a quad to the triangle.

4. Open the Append To Polygon Tool option box, turn off Ensure Planarity, and set Texture to Normalize.

5. Select the right edge, then switch to side view and click the vertices up so that you end up with a diagonal face, as shown below.

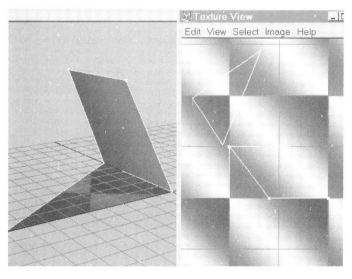

When it becomes part of the surface, the ramp texture is automatically assigned. As the texture map is normalized, it is mapped to the diagonal face horizontally, from 0 to 1.

Sewing Textures

In our example, although the faces are attached to each other with shared edges and vertices, the UVs are mapped separately. If you want to have the two faces share the texture mapping, you can *sew* the textures. But first, let's position the textures properly.

1. In the modeling window, select the UVs on the edge that joins the faces.

2. In the Texture View window, take note of which two UVs of the triangle and the diagonal face are selected. Select all the UVs of the diagonal face, then rotate and translate them so that the two UVs of the triangle and the diagonal face are next to each other, as shown below.

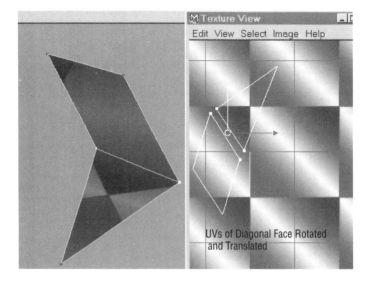

3. Select the common edge of the two faces. Then in the Texture View window, select Edit ➤ Sew Texture. The UVs of the triangle and the diagonal face snap to each other and become shared UVs.

NOTE   The Edit ➤ Cut Texture option performs the opposite function. It takes shared UVs and separates them, creating two new UVs per edge.

Unitizing UVs

Now let's see what happens when we unitize our polygonal surface.

1. Open the Append To Polygon Tool option box. Set Texture to Unitize and turn on Ensure Planarity.

2. In perspective view, select the longest edge of the triangle. When you see pink arrows, click on the nearest edge of the diagonal face.

3. In front view, click a vertex straight up to the diagonal face's height. The new face is planar, and it should look something like the image shown below. The Unitized setting stretches the UVs for the new face to fit the texture UV unit.

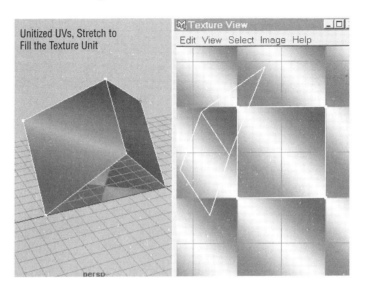

4. Repeat the sewing procedure: Rotate and translate the unitized UVs to line up to the triangle and sew it. You should see something like the image shown under step 2 in the next section. Notice that now there is a smooth texture transition from the triangle to the unitized face.

Assigning UVs

From time to time, you will encounter models imported from other programs that carry no UV information with them. You will need to assign UV values to these surfaces, following a procedure like the one outlined here.

1. Open the Append To Polygon Tool option box again if you've closed it. Set Texture to None.

2. Select the top edge of the unitized face. When you see the arrows, select the top edge of the diagonal face. Press Enter to create a triangle, as shown next. Although it is part of the polygonal surface, this new triangle has no UV information, and therefore no texture is displayed. Note that nothing new appears in the Texture View window.

Modeling

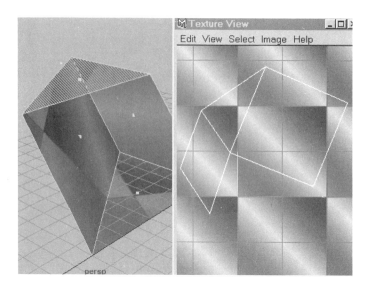

3. Select the face of the new triangle. Open the Normalize UVs option box from the Texture submenu or the Edit menu in the Texture View window. The default setting will make the triangle stretch from 0 to 1 in both U and V, which is not what we want.

4. Select Preserve Aspect Ratio, and it will normalize only one of the two values, in this case, U. Click on Apply, and texture appears on the new triangle as well as in its normalized UV points in the Texture View window.

5. Sew the new texture to the diagonal face by rotating and translating the new triangle. You should see the UVs connected, as shown below.

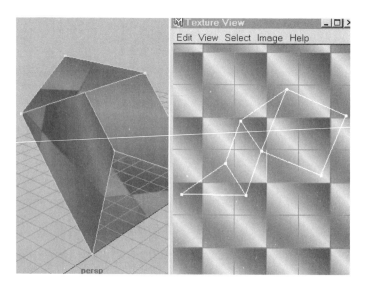

Projection Mapping

Maya has three types of projection mapping functions available from the Texture submenu: Planar, Cylindrical, and Spherical Mapping. There is also a Create UVs Based on Camera function, which creates UV values of a planar mapping projected from the camera view.

Let's try out the planar mapping.

1. Start a new scene and create a polygonal cube. With the cube still selected, open the Texture View window. You should see the cube UVs laid out as shown below. The default setting for the cube normalizes UVs so that they are all connected for the whole object.

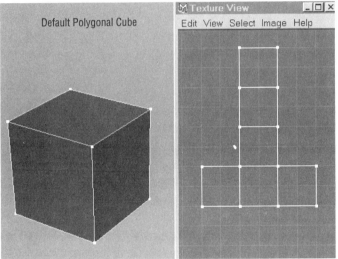

2. Rotate the cube in the Z axis 45 degrees. Then select its front face. Make sure that the Assign Shader to Each Projection function on the Texture submenu is checked, and apply Planar Mapping with the default settings. The Assign Shader to Each Projection setting automatically creates a default polygon shader with a checker texture and assigns it to the selected polygon. The default planar projection fits the texture to the bounding box of the selected object or face, and projects the map along the Z axis.

3. The black and white checker colors are too intense for viewing in the Texture View window. In Hypershade, select the checker texture and assign dull blue to one color and green to the other. Note how the UV points are mapped as a square rotated 45 degrees in the Texture View window.

4. Select the cube. If you don't see the texture showing in the Texture View window, as shown below, select Image ➤ Selected Images ➤ texturedFacets pCube1.

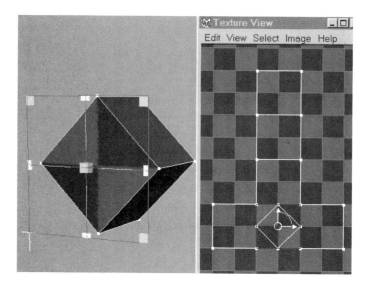

WARNING   Do not confuse projection mappings for polygons with the projections for NURBS. When creating textures for polygons in Hypershade, use the Normal setting. If you need to create a texture as a projection, the Interactive Placement button should be used only for NURBS, not polygons.

An example of a situation where mapping would be a bit harder is if we selected the face at the top and rotated it in the Y and X axes to make it near vertical and diagonal, as shown next. If we apply the default planar mapping, we get stretched UVs (as in the top-left image). Note how the UVs are stretched in the Texture View window as well. If we set the option to Y-axis projection, again the result is not what we want (as in the top-right image). We could grab the manipulator handle and rotate and scale until the texture fits the surface straight, but that takes effort. Instead, we can set the option to Fit to Best Plane. The projection will project in the direction of the surface normal, and as a result, we get a perfect fit (as in the bottom-left image). Another option is to apply planar mapping with camera direction (as in bottom-right image). For this example, the cube was selected as object, so all the UVs are mapped exactly as the UVs you see through the camera in the modeling window.

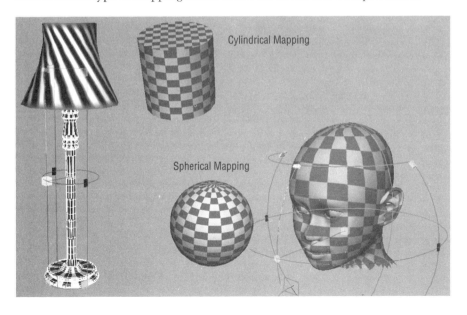

The Cylindrical and Spherical Mapping options are similar in principle to planar mapping, and they are simpler to apply. Often, the shape of the polygonal object will dictate which type of mapping is best suited for it. See the examples below.

Hands-on Maya: Building a Hand

It's time to practice using the tools and actions we've covered in this chapter. Let's build a polygon hand. Hands are usually built as polygons because it's difficult to create a NURBS hand that is not heavy and at the same time deforms well.

N O T E   In this tutorial, we will use some tools that haven't been covered yet in this book. You are encouraged to look ahead for more information about those tools, as well as to infer things from looking at the pictures.

Building the Rough Hand

We begin by building the rough hand, starting with a poly cube.

1. Start a new scene. Create a poly cube. Select a face on the X axis and extrude it four times. Scale it until you see something like the image shown below. Delete the faces at the back side.

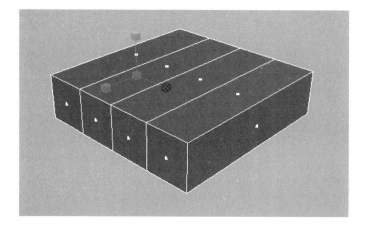

2. Select Polygons ➤ Tool Options and turn off Keep Faces Together. Select the four front faces and extrude them three times, as shown next. These will be the fingers. As you are extruding, scale the faces down a bit each time to taper them. At every point, you should be tweaking the vertices to try to form a rough hand shape. For example, try to roughly round the wrist area at the back.

TIP   Turn on the Backface Culling options' Keep Wire setting. This will help you to avoid accidentally selecting vertices or faces at the back side of the hand.

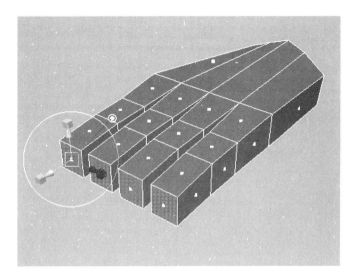

3. Push back the pinky finger, pulling it away from the ring finger to the side, and pull the middle finger out a bit. You can select faces to do this; however, in this situation, moving vertices seems to work best. Push up the two vertices where the knuckles should be.

Creating the Thumb

Building the thumb is one of the trickiest things you'll do in this tutorial. We'll use the Split Polygon tool to create the shape.

1. On the left side of the hand, draw two edges using Edit Polygons ➤ Split Polygon Tool. Next, at the bottom (the palm of the hand), draw four more edges. Pull out the vertex at the side and the one at the bottom beside it, then pull them down. Select the face that sticks out with the vertices, and extrude it twice, turning and scaling it as you do. See the next graphic for guidance. This is going to be the thumb. Save the file as hand_one. (Maya will append a .mb extension automatically.)

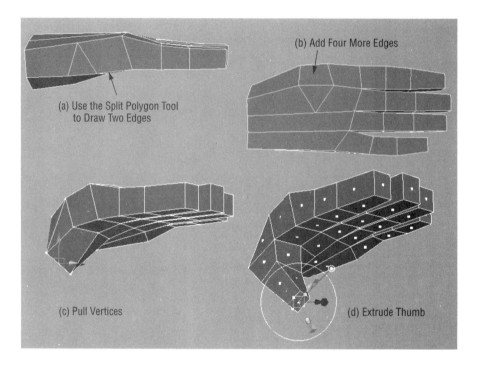

(a) Use the Split Polygon Tool to Draw Two Edges

(b) Add Four More Edges

(c) Pull Vertices

(d) Extrude Thumb

2. Add two lines of edges going around the hand using the Split Polygon tool. Use the tool to place extra faces around where the thumb bends into the hand, and move the triangular face further into the palm.

3. For the wrist, select the border edges, apply Polygons ➢ Fill Hole to create an *n*-sided face, select it, and then extrude the face at the back, as shown next. After you extrude it, delete the face again.

TIP　Keep the faces you are creating limited to quads and triangles. They should also run smoothly along set lines and not be placed haphazardly.

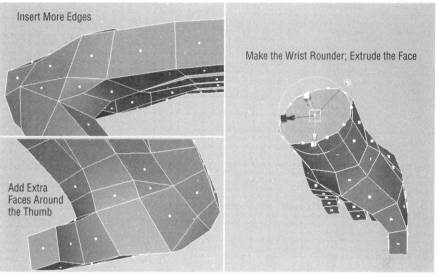

Insert More Edges

Make the Wrist Rounder; Extrude the Face

Add Extra Faces Around the Thumb

4. Scale out the hand to make it wider. Bend the fingers straight down, and bend the thumb into the palm at an angle, as shown below.

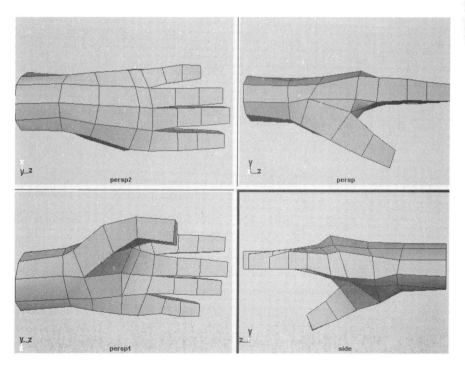

persp2

persp

persp1

side

5. A lot of history has accumulated on the hand by now. Delete the history from the object and save the scene as hand_two.mb.

Creating a Procedural Connection

The rough hand is now ready for smoothing. Once smoothing is applied, however, the hand becomes more difficult to shape because there are a lot more vertices to deal with. To make things easier, we'll use the rough hand as a lattice around the smoothed hand.

1. Make a copy of the hand and scale it up a bit. We'll call this the rough hand and call the original one the smooth hand (it isn't yet, but it soon will be).

2. Using Hypershade, assign a material to the rough hand, and make it totally transparent. In the Shaded mode, the rough hand should still display as a wireframe, as shown below.

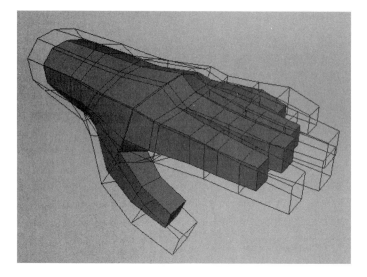

3. Select Window ➤ Connection Editor. Select the rough hand, press the down arrow key to select its Shape node, and load it to the Outputs window by clicking the Reload Left button. Load the smooth hand's Shape node to the Inputs window the same way.

4. Scroll down in the left window until you find World Mesh[0] and select it. Scroll down in the right window until you find In Mesh and select it. Both attributes become italicized, as shown next. When you select the rough hand, the smooth hand turns pink to show that the hands are procedurally connected.

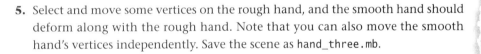

5. Select and move some vertices on the rough hand, and the smooth hand should deform along with the rough hand. Note that you can also move the smooth hand's vertices independently. Save the scene as hand_three.mb.

Smoothing, Layering, and Rough Tweaking

Now we need to smooth and tweak the hand. We will need to do this in two stages, beginning with applying Smooth and fixing some problems.

1. Select the smooth hand and apply Edit Polygons ➤ Smooth to it with the default setting. Some things immediately stand out as needing improvement, such as consistency in the width and the direction of the fingers. We need to fix these problems before we can apply Smooth again.

2. Before we start to tweak, let's put the smooth hand and the rough hand on different layers. Once the smooth hand is in a layer, select the Reference setting for the layer. The Template setting will only display the hand as a wireframe, but the Reference setting will display the hand in Shaded mode, while still disabling it from being selected.

3. Tweak the rough hand until you are comfortable with the shape it has created in the smooth hand, as shown next. You can hide the rough hand for now, and move back to the smooth hand by switching from Reference to Standard in the Layer menu.

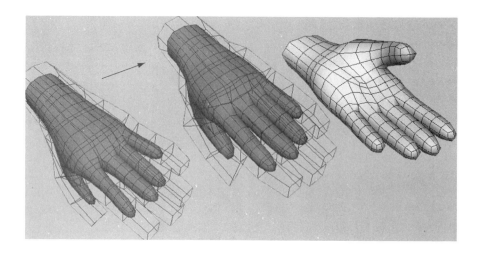

Fine Tweaking, Smoothing, and Applying Artisan

Now we will do some tweaking to prepare the hand for another smoothing. We will also be using the Sculpt Polygons tool to get more surface definition and smooth out any unwanted creases.

1. Place vertices around the fingers and the thumb where the joints will bend. Think ahead to how another edge line will be placed in between every line with the second Smooth. The area between the fingers needs to have a bit more space, and the knuckles should stick out more as well. (Don't worry too much about creating hard edges or creases at this point.)

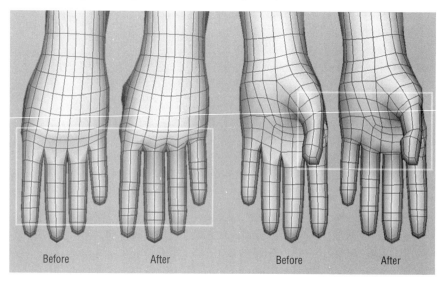

Before   After   Before   After

2. The thumb area needs special attention. Get rid of the extra edges, as shown below. Make sure that there are no winged vertices left behind. If you need to make adjustments that require moving a whole area, use the rough hand. Save the scene as hand_four.mb.

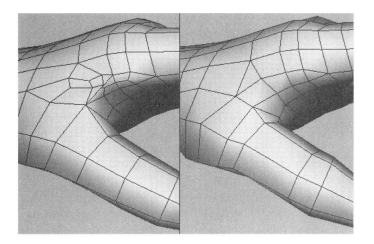

3. Apply Smooth one more time. At this point, the density of the surface calls out for the Sculpt Polygon tool. But such areas as the finger joints and fingernails should still be modified by selecting vertices. Notice the vertex placements around the finger joint areas and fingernails shown below.

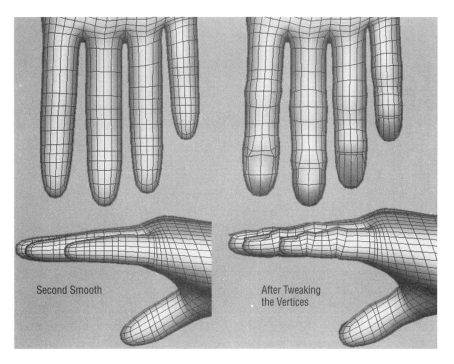

Second Smooth

After Tweaking the Vertices

4. Using Edit Polygons ≻ Sculpt Polygon Tool, start pushing and pulling to get more definition for the hand, especially the palm, the knuckles, and the wrist area. Smooth out where the thumb joins the hand as well. If you want to build a more mature-looking hand, you can try making the bones protrude along the back of the hand, and put more space between the fingers.

T I P   Change the Radius setting according to the specific area you are sculpting, and always set the Opacity low. It may be frustrating to need to click many times, but retaining control of the tool you are using is important.

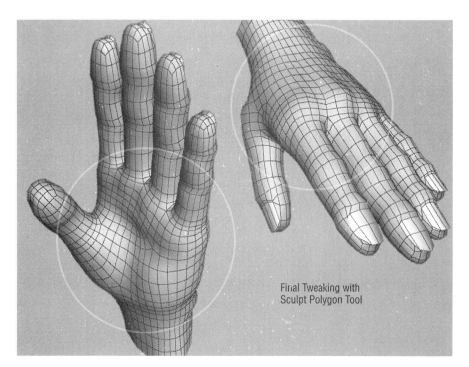

Final Tweaking with Sculpt Polygon Tool

The hand model is pretty much finished at this point. The hand will be used in the child model we will be building in upcoming chapters, so save the file as child_hand.mb.

Summary

In this chapter, you learned what polygons are, how to create them, and work with them in Maya, and how to texture-map them using the Texture View window. We went through an advanced tutorial, building a polygon hand, which we will use for the child model later in the book.

In the next chapter, we will explore NURBS (*patch modeling*). We will build a dog model in NURBS patches, covering some advanced modeling concepts as we go.

chapter 8

ORGANIC
MODELING

Featuring

- *Isoparm selection and insertion*
- *Surface division into patches*
- *Stitching preparations*
- *Parameter rebuilding*
- *Stitching tools*
- *Mirroring and attaching techniques*

ORGANIC MODELING

This is a fun chapter. Rather than making you read through discussions of the various organic modeling procedures, we will work through a project. This is a real-life project in which we will build a dog from scratch to finish. A hands-on exercise is the best way to get down to the nitty-gritty details of organic modeling.

At the same time, this is a difficult chapter. The time required to build this model will vary depending on your skill level and familiarity with organic modeling, but you probably won't be able to build the whole dog in one session. It is also important to keep in mind that you are not producing a work of art at this point. Spend time learning the tools and techniques of organic modeling, but don't dwell too long on tweaking CVs! (And you can always use the prepared model found on the accompanying CD instead of building it from scratch.)

One last reminder. As with any real-life projects, things can get pretty messy as you work your way through this chapter. It is important for you to practice good work habits. Save your work often. Name things carefully. Take regular breaks to clear your head. Always ask why you are doing what you are doing, instead of blindly working through the steps of the project. You will learn much more that way.

Laying the Groundwork—Start with a Sketch

One of the worst ways to start your modeling process is to plunge in without having any idea of how you want your model to look. Such an approach will make your work sloppy and waste a lot of valuable time. Usually, the resulting model will not look as good as if it had good 2D references.

The best way to start is to actually sketch your model if you can. This approach encourages you to be aware of the parts you need to create and to think of ways to build them.

For this example, we need to know what the dog will look like. We'll start with a sketch of a puppy, which is based on several pictures of various dogs. As long as the body proportions and the bone structures remain similar, the sketch should be sufficient for our purposes. For our project, we will use this sketch as a background image.

The next thing we need to know is what this dog is going to be doing. Let's say the dog will be walking or running, so we only need to concern ourselves with the movements of the dog related to those specific actions (walking and running are fairly easy to set up). If the dog were to move in other, more complicated ways, such as sitting or rolling on the ground, then we would need to test the dog to account for those movements as well.

NOTE   In studio productions, the models are not considered complete until they have gone through many extreme poses to test their suitability for animation. The designer may need to modify the model if it fails to hold its shape under certain extreme poses at the testing stage. In some cases, different versions of the model may be required for different animation situations.

Building the Head and Body

Let's start at the top, with the head and body. To keep things a bit simpler, we will not build eyelids or a mouth for our puppy.

1. Create a new scene and go to side view. To bring in the image of the dog from the accompanying CD, select View ➤ Camera Attribute Editor ➤ Environment and click the Image Plane Create button. You can use the Image Name field to browse for the image puppy_sketch.tif on the CD.

2. Create a sphere, rotate it 90 degrees in the X axis, and scale it out. Go to the Channel box, open makeNurbSphere1, and set Sections to 10 and Spans to 20. Translate the sphere to about where the puppy's body is, as shown below.

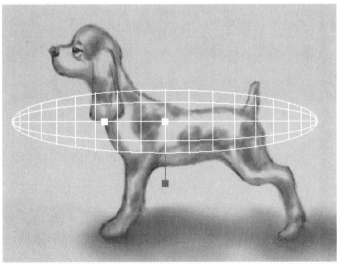

TIP   If you find the image plane too bright, you can darken the picture by lowering the Color Gain setting in the Image Plane Attributes section of the Attribute Editor.

3. Pick-mask the sphere's CVs or hulls and transform them using translate, rotate, and scale procedures to get the same profile form as the dog in the picture. Space the isoparms as shown and explained below.

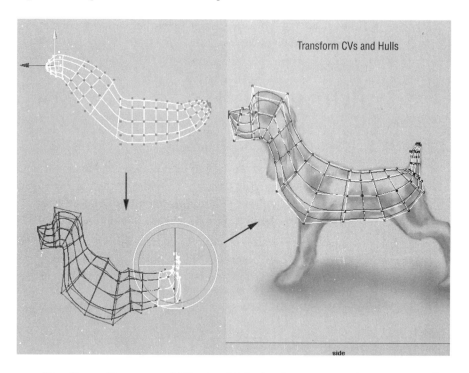

The Face   Two rows of CVs should do for the nose area, because we will place a sphere for the nose later. Also, since we are not including eyelids or a mouth, we can use a minimum number of isoparms for the face—three rows of CVs will do.

The Body   Use three rows of CVs for the back of the head and the neck, and three more for the chest area. Use one row for the stomach area, and three rows for the back leg area. Note that the stomach shape is actually created by three rows of CVs; the row for the stomach area works together with the last row of the chest area and the beginning row of the back leg area.

The Tail   Two rows "tie" the tail to the back of the torso, and two more make the tail curve tightly towards the end. The last three rows shape the endpoint of the tail—one more than we need. Select the third row of CVs from the end of the tail and press the Delete key to remove it. Scale the last two rows out to fit the profile of the tail.

4. Switch to a two-view layout by selecting Window ➤ View Arrangement ➤ 2 Side by Side (you can also use the marking menu and select Panels ➤ Layouts ➤ 2 Side by Side). Make one window perspective view and the other top view.

5. Select hulls again, and scale the CVs in the X axis to make the shape look more like a puppy. You can scale in the Y or Z axis as well, to fine tune the profile shape. You can hide the camera for the perspective view by turning off Show ➤ Cameras. You should end with something like the shape shown below.

T I P　Use the arrow keys to go up and down the UV parameters with the selection of CVs. This technique is especially useful when you are selecting hulls.

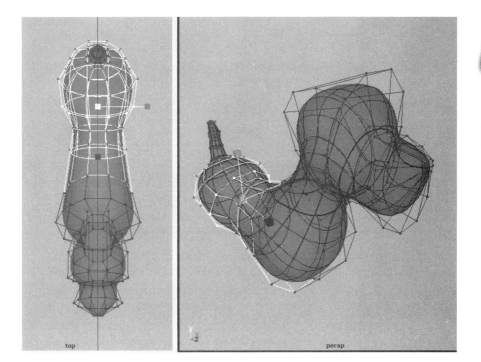

How Many CVs Do You Need?

As you are building your model, you should always be asking yourself how many CVs you need to get the shape you want. In answering that question, there is one simple rule: It takes three CVs to curve a line. It follows that only three rows of CVs are needed to curve a surface. When you study models with this rule in mind, it may surprise you to see how often unnecessary isoparms are placed for simple curvatures on surfaces.

Continued on next page

You might want to add one more row to "tie" the curve, making it very tight and edgy. Another way to tighten a curve is to increase the CV weights, instead of adding more CVs. The only drawback to this technique is that sometimes the weight information gets lost when models are transferred to other programs.

Be a minimalist when you are starting out. The fewer CVs you have, the easier it is to control the surface area. You can easily insert more isoparms later to refine your model, but it is more difficult to get rid of them without disturbing what you've already built. Having fewer CVs also lets you concentrate on the big blocks of the model you are creating and ignore the details, which is considered good form in drawing and sculpting.

Cutting Up the Body

Things are going to get a bit more complicated from here on. We need to make holes for the legs, which means we need to cut the body into pieces. But first, we need to put in more isoparms in select places for smoother stitching later on.

Selecting and Inserting Isoparms

To insert isoparms, you need to select existing isoparms and specify where you want to put the new ones.

1. In perspective view, select the Select tool from the Minibar. Pick-mask Isoparm and click on the first vertical isoparm going around the nose area. In the Feedback line (above the Layer bar), you should read "U Isoparm 19.000." When you select the next isoparm, it should say "U Isoparm 18.000," and so on.

2. Click on the horizontal isoparm around the eye level. You should see "V Isoparm 9.000" in the Feedback line. The isoparm around the mouth level should be "V Isoparm 1.000," and so on. If your isoparms show opposite numbers, such as 1.000 in place of 19.000, you can reverse the parameter values by selecting Edit Surfaces ➤ Reverse Surface Direction ❏, setting the Surface Direction to V, and then clicking the Reverse button.

TIP   When selecting isoparms, if the number ends neatly, such as 1.000 or 1.25, it usually means you have selected the proper isoparm. If the number ends not so neatly, such as 9.01 or 15.476, it usually means you've missed the isoparm. One way to be sure is to select any U or V isoparm near the isoparm you want, then enter the exact value for the isoparm in the numeric input field in the right corner of the Feedback line section.

3. Shift+click U isoparms 13, 12, and 11. Then choose Edit Surfaces ➤ Insert Isoparms ❏, select Between Selections, and click Insert. You should see two U isoparms inserted: 12.5 and 11.5.

4. Repeat the procedure for V isoparms 7 and 8 to insert an isoparm 7.5.

5. Insert three isoparms between V isoparms 2 and 3 to get 2.25, 2.5, and 2.75. The inserted isoparms should be placed as shown below.

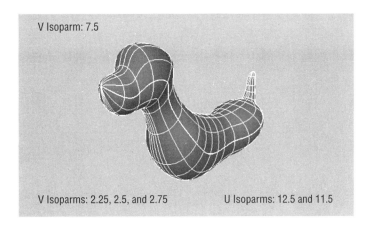

Dividing the Surface into Patch Regions

Now we're going to cut the puppy into pieces. Yes, this seems cruel, but it will help us a great deal in reducing the amount of work we need to do.

1. Select the V isoparms 2.5 and 7.5, then choose Edit Surfaces ➤ Detach Surfaces. Delete the right half. The image should look like the one shown below.

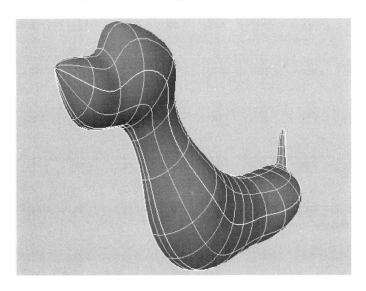

2. Select V isoparms 2.375 (or it may be 3.375 depending on the way you cut your surface) and 1.875 and choose Edit Surfaces ➤ Detach Surfaces again to detach those areas. Now there are three pieces. We need to divide these into 15 separate regions.

3. Select the U isoparms 12.5, 11.5, 9, and 7 along the three pieces and detach them. You may want to do this in several steps. Get rid of the patches where the legs will be. We end up with two holes and 13 patches.

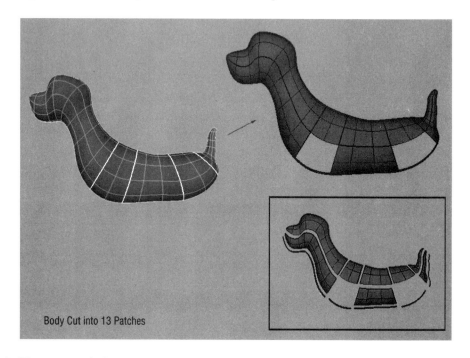

Body Cut into 13 Patches

4. This is a good place to pause and clean up. Group the 13 pieces and name them if you wish. If you haven't saved the file yet, do so now. While you are in the middle of building a model, the naming of objects and their groupings are simply for your own convenience, and they don't need to be organized too carefully. The scene name, however, should be indicative of what you've done, such as Dog_13pieces, or of where you are in the modeling stage, such as Dog_model_1.

TIP It is simplest to rename objects in the Outliner. Just double-click the node and type in the name. When you are naming a series of nodes, such as obj1, obj2, obj3, and so on, you can also copy one name and paste it repeatedly—the numbers will be updated automatically.

After you've cut up the surface, the smaller patches retain the parameter values they had before they were detached. They must be parameterized again using Rebuild Surfaces before you can apply stitching. If you don't do this, the results will be unpredictable. We will take care of this a little later in the chapter, in the "Rebuilding the Parameters" section.

Building the Legs

Because we are dealing with only half of the puppy's body, we need to come up with just one front leg and one back leg. Later, we'll duplicate these to add the other two legs. Note that we're deliberately keeping the paws simple.

1. Create a layer, name it something like Dog Body, and assign the 13 patches to it. We can hide them or turn them into templated objects later when we are working with the legs.

2. Create a sphere and set its spans to 20. Detach it in the middle to get a half sphere with 10 spans. Delete the top half. Use move, rotate, and scale procedures to transform the bottom half to the position shown below.

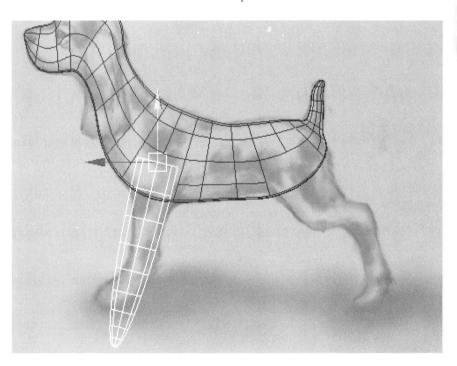

3. Select hulls and build the leg in side view (in the same way that we built the profile of the dog's body). Note the way that the rows of CVs are distributed in the side view shown below. Then scale the leg to the proper size in the X axis in the perspective view or the front view.

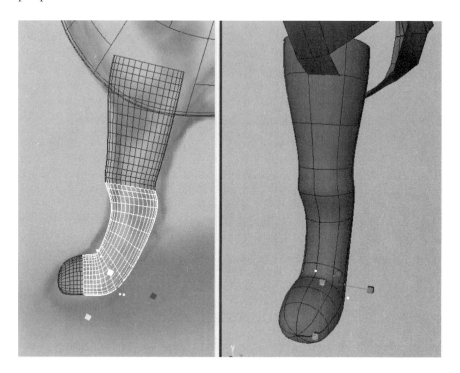

4. Move the leg to where it should be on the dog, a bit to the side, and tweak the CVs to place the top opening of the leg near where the hole is on the dog's body, as shown on the next page. It is important to try to place the two spans of the leg geometry next to the two spans of the hole on each side. This may be frustrating, but you actually must guess how well the leg is being positioned for stitching with the body pieces. Keep in mind that after you gain some experience, your guesses will become more accurate.

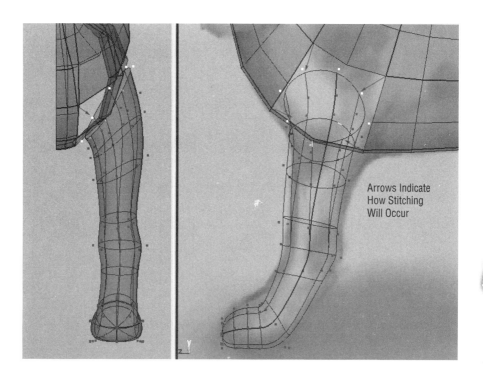

Arrows Indicate
How Stitching
Will Occur

T I P   By now, you should be aware that typing in numbers to position items is often not possible when you are building models. Organic modeling is fun and frustrating at the same time because you need to trust your artistic senses more and start "guesstimating," as opposed to being precise. Guessing is not being sloppy. It is doing things roughly now, knowing that you will tweak later.

5. Create a layer and name it Dog Legs. Assign the front leg to it and turn off its visibility.

6. Build the back leg the same way you created the front leg. Ten spans of isoparms are enough. You now should have something similar to the illustration shown at the top of the next page. Notice how the isoparms are placed around the joints as you are moving the hulls and the CVs. Also, the top end of the back leg is a bit higher and to the back than the hole on the body. This was done intentionally in preparation for stitching.

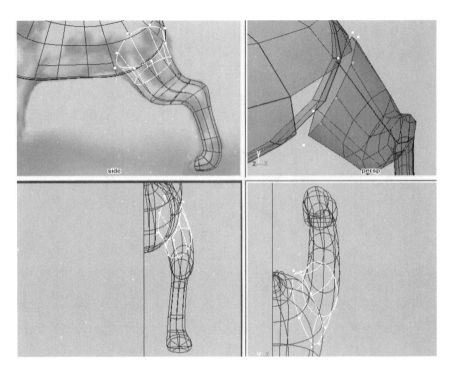

7. As a final step, we need to cut the legs into four pieces. Select V isoparms 1, 3, 5, and 7 and detach them. For both the front and the back legs, the isoparm values should be the same. Group them accordingly, name them, and assign them to the Dog_Legs layer.

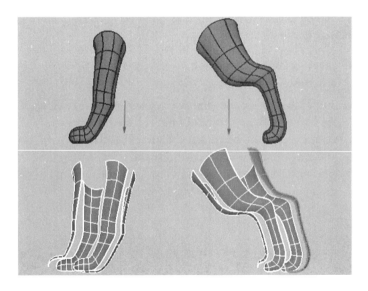

Rebuilding the Parameters

Now that we have the patches all built, we are almost ready to stitch them together. However, first we need to rebuild the parameters. Currently, the smaller patches still have the same parameter values they had before they were detached. We need to reparameterize so that we can have the proper calculations between the patches for stitching.

1. Select Edit Surfaces ➤ Rebuild Surfaces and make sure the setting is as below. The Keep CVs box should be checked. Don't close this dialog box.

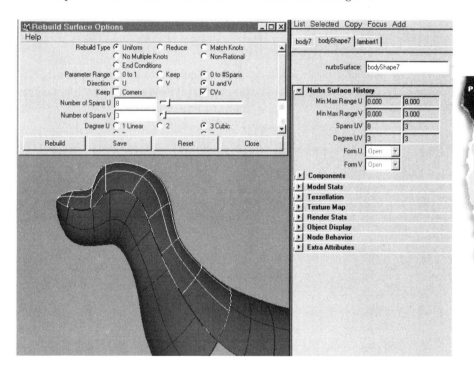

2. In the modeling window, press Ctrl+A to open the Attribute Editor. Select the top patch of the dog's head, and look at the Nurbs Surface History of the geometry. In the Spans UV fields, the values are 8 and 3, but the Min Max Range for U and V have different numbers. We need to reparameterize the patch to get the Max Range numbers to match the Span values (or go from 0 to 1, which is another optional setting in the Rebuild Surface Options dialog box).

3. Select all the geometry pieces in the modeling window and click Rebuild. You should see very slight changes in the isoparm placements. Although the changes may seems insignificant, they are necessary for proper calculations between the patches to take place. Select the dog's top head patch again. The Max numbers for UV should now match the corresponding Span values.

Stitching the Puppy

Now we're ready to stitch the puppy. However, before we continue, let's take a brief break from building the model and see how stitching works in Maya.

Stitching Basics

Maya has three different types of stitching available from the Edit Surfaces ➤ Stitches submenu: Stitch Surface Points, Stitch Edges Tool, and Global Stitch. We will use the Stitch Edges tool to put together the different parts of the dog and continue to shape its body, and then use the Global Stitch function to keep the patches seamless.

Stitching Surface Points

Stitch Surface Points is a simple tool used to join CV points from different surfaces. To use this type of stitching, select one CV you want to stitch from each of the surfaces and apply Stitch Surface Points. The points should snap together, meeting each other halfway as shown on the left side of the picture below.

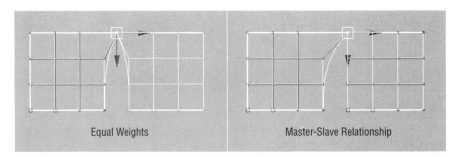

Equal Weights   Master-Slave Relationship

Another way to use Stitch Surface Points is to open its option box and turn off the Assign Equal Weights setting. Then when you select CVs and apply the stitching, the first point will stay where it is, and the other points will snap to the first point, as on the right side of the picture above. The points in this setting are said to be in a *master-slave relationship*. The point that does not move is the master, and the points that move are the slaves.

Stitching Edges

The Stitch Edges tool is used to join two surface edges together. The default setting joins the edges in a master-slave relationship. When you open the option box for this tool, you will see that Weighting Factor On Edge1 is set to 1 and Weighting Factor On Edge2 is set to 0. This means the first edge isoparm you picked will not move, and the second edge isoparm you picked will snap to the first edge, as on the top right of the picture shown on the next page. If you want to apply equal weighting for both edges so that they will both move to meet in the middle, adjust the Weighting Factor settings

to 0.5 for both edges. The edges will then meet halfway, as in the picture below on
the bottom right.

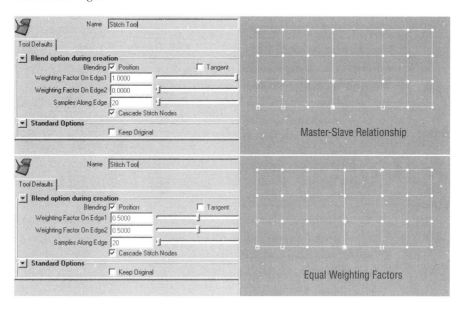

Master-Slave Relationship

Equal Weighting Factors

Global Stitching

Global Stitch is a new addition in Maya 2. This function can stitch all of the edges of
adjacent surfaces together. It automatically gives all the surface edges being stitched
equal weights.

N O T E   For both the Stitch Edges tool and the Global Stitch function, you have the option
of maintaining C0 continuity or C1 continuity, also known as tangent continuity, between
the stitched edges. See Chapter 6 for more information about the degrees of continuity.

Stitching between Two Edges

Now it's time to put the pieces of the dog together into a seamless whole. For the following procedures, you may want to get into the wireframe or the x-ray viewing mode,
because either of these modes makes it easier to pick isoparms. To switch to the x-ray
viewing mode, go to the modeling window and select Shading ➤ Shade Options ➤
X-Ray.

First, we'll attach the legs to the dog's body by stitching the leg edges.

1. In perspective view, select the front leg and press the F key to center the geometry so that you can rotate around it. Select Edit Surfaces ➤ Stitch ➤ Stitch Edges
   Tool ❑ and click the Reset Tool button to make sure you're using the default settings. Then check the Tangent setting and close the option box.

2. Select the top-edge isoparm (it's also called a *surface boundary* isoparm) of the leg patch. Then select the patch edge located at the top side of the hole. The patch edge should snap to the leg patch, and the two patches should turn bright green. (You don't need to press Enter to complete the stitching process at this point.)

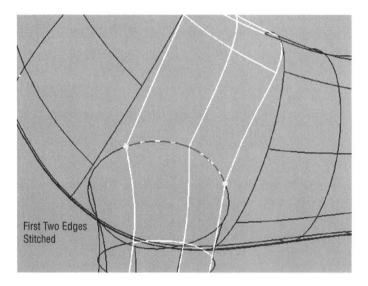

First Two Edges Stitched

3. Go to the next boundary isoparm of the leg and repeat the stitching with the side edge of the hole.

4. Repeat the process with the next two edges. You should have a cross shape of green patches coming out from the body to the leg patches, as shown below.

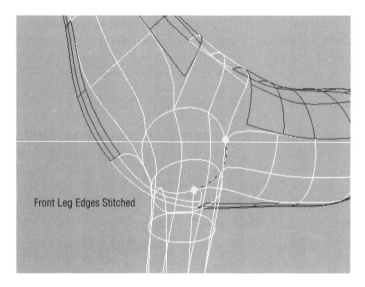

Front Leg Edges Stitched

5. Press Enter to complete the action.

T I P   In addition to pressing Enter to complete the stitching action, you can press any of the tool hotkeys, such as the Q key for the selection mode. To repeat the stitch action, press the Y key.

6. Repeat the procedure with the back leg, as shown below. Make sure to select the leg boundary isoparm first and the body boundary isoparm second because the order of selection determines the master-slave relationship. The slave edge snaps to the master edge, and it is important that the leg patches function as master edges.

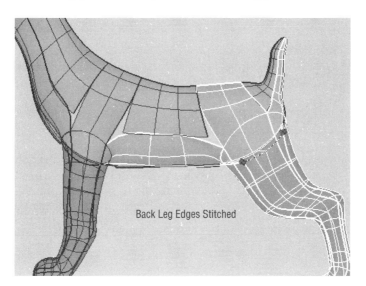

Back Leg Edges Stitched

Stitching the Corners

So far, we've stitched seven body patches to the legs. There are still six corner patches that need to be stitched. Let's try stitching one of the head patches as an example.

1. To stitch the top patch of the dog's head to the adjacent patches, select Edit Surfaces ➤ Stitch ➤ Stitch Edges Tool (leave the default settings). Select the boundary edge of one of the adjacent patches, and then select the edge of the head patch, as shown on the left side of the image on the next page. Complete the action by pressing Enter. Then repeat the procedure with the other adjoining patch as shown on the right. Even though the head patch may look like it is lined up after the first stitching, you still need to stitch it to the second adjacent patch to make sure that the patches are lined up properly.

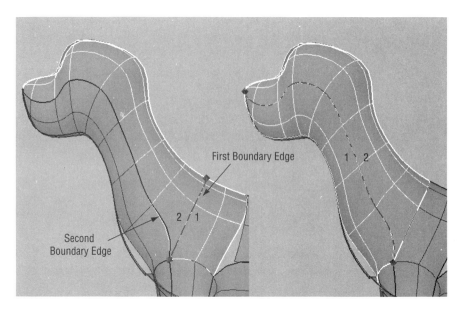

2. Repeat the procedure to stitch the corners on the other five patches. Below is an example of one of the patches that must be stitched three times. The patch represented as number 2 needs to be stitched to three other number 1 patches. Pick the number 1 patch boundary isoparms first each time, and then select the boundary isoparm of the number 2 patch being stitched.

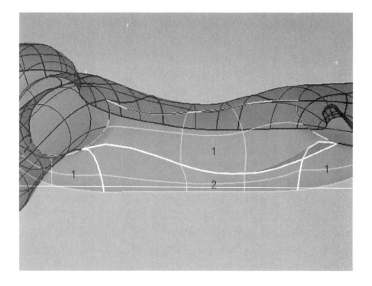

Tweaking the Stitched Surfaces

When you look at the final stitched surface in shaded mode, you will probably notice creases. The places where the creases occur and their severity will vary with how you've built your own model. The one we've built so far should look similar to the model shown below. Unfortunately, there is no easy way to get rid of these creases.

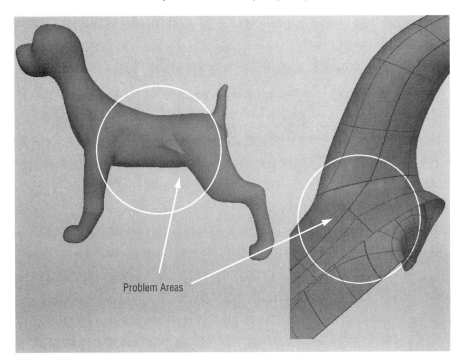

Problem Areas

In the case of where the stomach meets the back leg, the isoparm has actually folded (as shown on the right side above). In such situations, you need to tweak the CVs of the master edges (the leg patches in our example) to get rid of the creases. Shown on the next page are some of the ways CVs have been pulled and rotated to correct the problems. Note that where the two edges are being joined as in the top-left picture, you must move the four CVs on each of the patches, eight CVs in all, together in order to maintain their tangency. When you move the CVs on the master edges, the slave edges will follow to keep the tangent continuity between the surfaces.

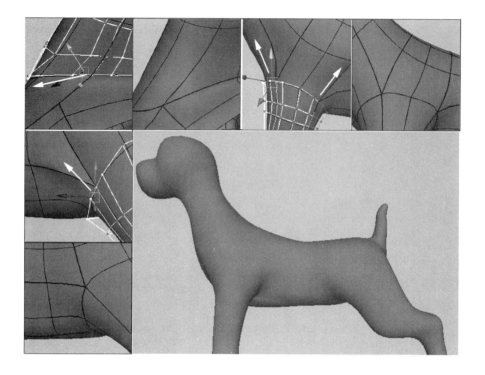

Building the Face

In contrast to the elaborate modeling that went into building the body, we'll keep the dog's face simple. Use spheres for the eyes, nose, and ears, as shown below.

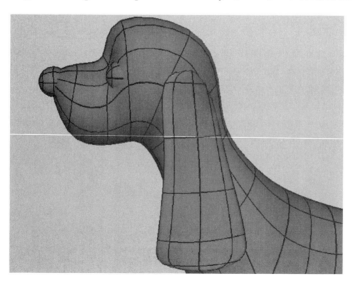

Place the eye and the nose in the appropriate positions, and pull in a couple of the CVs on the head to make room for the eye (but don't touch the two end CVs along the boundaries). You can create the ear by deforming the hulls of another sphere with six spans.

Mirroring and Attaching the Model

Mirroring is a common modeling technique. As its name implies, mirroring duplicates the selected items as a mirror image of the original items along a selected axis. We will use mirroring to duplicate the right half of the puppy.

1. Select all the objects in the modeling window except for the nose. Group them. Select Edit ➤ Duplicate ❑, set Scale X to –1, and click Duplicate. You should have a mirrored group of objects.

2. You now see the whole model of the dog. Before you attach the middle patches, make sure you like what you see. Are the body parts proportional? Are the legs too close or too far apart? If you want to modify any parts of the dog, undo the duplication and make the necessary changes before continuing.

3. When you are satisfied with the way everything is, select the edge isoparms of all the patches that meet at the middle, or the Y axis, and attach them using the default settings. You should end up with ten attached pieces making up the profile of the puppy.

In the picture of the final model of the puppy, shown below, notice that the left side patches are still stitched together, while the right side patches are not. This is fine, because we no longer need the stitches.

PART 2

Modeling

Cleaning Up the Model

Now we can clean up our model by deleting the history and the transformation information. We can also group the model parts.

1. Select all the patches in the modeling window and select Edit ➤ Delete By Type ➤ History.

2. Select Modify ➤ Freeze Transformations.

 N O T E   In our particular project, the history and the transformation information of the patches are no longer needed, so we can delete them. However, in other situations, this information may be important. Of course, this depends on the application of whatever command was used to create the history or the transformation information. So, you'll need to decide whether to delete or retain this information on a case-by-case basis.

3. Group the legs and name them. Give the group nodes sensible names, such as Front_Legs, or L_frontleg. You may not feel you need to name the leaf nodes; however, it is a good idea to rename everything, rather than leaving a node named something like leg33detachedSurface2detachedSurface2.

4. Group the body and the face, renaming them appropriately.

5. Put the face and body pieces into the Dog_Body layer. Put the leg pieces into the Dog_Legs layer.

Global Stitching

Finally, there's the matter of global stitching, a new surface-editing feature in Maya 2. Unlike regular stitching, global stitching doesn't have master-slave distinction; all the pieces are held together with equal weight. When we were building the model, we didn't use this stitching method because we needed the control provided by the regular stitch, namely the master-slave relationship of the edges being stitched. Now that the model is put together seamlessly with first-order continuity (C1) among the patches, we can easily stitch all the pieces together with one command.

1. Select all the pieces except for the face objects, then select Edit Surfaces ➤ Stitch ➤ Global Stitch ❑.

2. Click Reset to set everything to the default settings. Then click Global Stitch. Now if you move any of the patches, you will notice that they behave like rubber, stretching to keep themselves together.

3. The model is now ready to be set up for animation. Save the final scene as Dog_Final.mb. You can find this finished version in the working files and a rendered image in the Chapter 8 Color Gallery on the CD.

Summary

In this chapter, we stepped through building a complicated patch model of a dog, from scratch to finish. In addition to learning one specific method of building a dog in patches, we also covered the concepts and techniques for building complex models in general. These techniques included rebuilding surfaces, mirroring and attaching parts, and stitching to create seamlessness.

We will return to the dog model to fit it with skeletons in Chapter 11, then set it up for animation in Chapter 13.

One special tool we did not use in this chapter is Artisan, which is revolutionizing the way that computer animators do their work. The next chapter is devoted to the topic of Artisan.

PART 2

Modeling

WORKING WITH ARTISAN

Featuring

- *The tools: a quick overview*
  ....

- *Sculpting polygons: deforming a sphere*
  ....

- *Sculpting NURBS surfaces: sculpting across seams*
  ....

- *Creating sets with Artisan*
  ....

- *Painting selections*
  ....

- *Painting weights*
  ....

- *Painting scripts: hair on a head*
  ....

- *Painting vertex colors*
  ....

- *Painting attributes: painting goal weights*
  ....

- *Painting skin weights*
  ....

CHAPTER

9

WORKING WITH
ARTISAN

N ew in Maya 2 Complete (and Unlimited) is a set of
plug-ins called Artisan. Available previously as a separate package, the functionality of Artisan is now
yours for Maya's base price. Artisan is a set of nine
tools available within standard Maya menus ranging
from Deform to Edit Surfaces to Modify (the fact that they are not all grouped together
is one big cause for confusion for anyone trying to figure out what Artisan is). These
tools are generally used for modeling purposes, but the primary feature that links
them is that they all act like virtual paintbrushes, "painting" on everything from
shape to color. In an analogous way to the paint or airbrush tools in Adobe PhotoShop,
Artisan paints attributes onto any model you select—but Artisan does this in three
dimensions! Taken together, the tools that make up Artisan provide one of the easiest
and most intuitive ways to model, select, and edit geometry available in any graphics
software today—and it's all built seamlessly into Maya!

TIP Because they work as paintbrushes, Artisan tools are most efficiently used with a
graphics tablet. In this book, however, we're assuming a "plain vanilla" configuration that
doesn't include a tablet, so the instructions in this chapter show how to use Artisan with a
mouse and keyboard as the only input devices. If you do have a tablet, it should be con-
figured, for the most part, automatically when you launch Maya. For more information on
how to use your tablet with Artisan, see the online documentation under Basics: Artisan.

What's New in Maya 2

A great deal has changed in Artisan for version 2 of Maya, including the much-needed new polygonal sculpting tool (which lets you sculpt polygons as well as NURBS surfaces). Other new tools have been added, including the extremely versatile Attribute Paint tool, which lets you choose to paint any (paintable) attribute on your geometry—say goal weights for soft bodies or polygon facet colors on your model. Other enhancements to Artisan include a more streamlined options window (with more options, grouped in a more logical order) and better control while painting on complex surfaces like multi-surfaces that have been stitched together. Artisan has gone, in its present incarnation, from a cool but underdeveloped plug-in to a robust, easy to use, and incredibly powerful set of tools—what's more, these better tools are now built right into Maya Complete!

The Tools: a Quick Overview

Here is a quick run-down of the nine tools in Maya Artisan, with a brief description of what they do and how to open them.

Sculpt Polygons   This tool allows you to sculpt polygonal shapes as if they were virtual clay. To open this tool, choose (from the Modeling menu set) Edit Polygons ➢ Sculpt Polygons Tool.

Sculpt Surfaces   This tool allows you to sculpt NURBS surfaces as if they were virtual clay. To open this tool, choose (from the Modeling menu set) Edit Surfaces ➢ Sculpt Surfaces Tool.

Paint Set Membership   This tool allows you to paint on membership in sets, rather than having to pick each point and assign it. To open this tool, choose (from the Animation menu set) Deform ➢ Paint Set Membership Tool.

Paint Selection   This tool allows you to select vertices on a NURBS or polygonal surface by painting on the surface rather than selecting points individually. To open this tool, choose Modify ➢ Paint Selection Tool.

Paint Weights   This tool allows you to set the weights of clusters of vertices by simply painting on a surface. To open this tool, choose (from the Animation menu set) Deform ➢ Paint Weights Tool.

Script Paint   With this tool, you can paint onto an object the output of a MEL script using your mouse or graphics tablet, instead of manually running the script at each point. To open this tool, choose Modify ➢ Script Paint Tool.

Attribute Paint   This tool allows you to paint any (paintable) attribute onto your selected model. You can paint on colors, goal weights, or other attributes that you assign to be "paintable." To open this tool, choose Modify ➤ Attribute Paint Tool.

Paint Skin Weights   After binding skin to bones, you can use this tool to modify the weights of the bound points to each joint in your bone chain, resulting in smoother, more natural skin motion. To open this tool, choose (from the Animation menu set) Skin ➤ Edit Smooth Skin ➤ Paint Skin Weights Tool.

Paint Vertex Color   This tool lets you paint colors directly onto individual polygons on a surface. To open this tool, choose (from the Modeling menu set) Edit Polygons ➤ Colors ➤ Paint Vertex Color Tool.

T I P   If you don't see the Artisan tools in the menus listed above, Artisan may not be auto-loading. To get Artisan to load when Maya launches, choose Options ➤ General Preferences. Click the Modules tab, check the Artisan check box, and then restart Maya.

Sculpting Polygons: Deforming a Sphere

Let's begin our work with Artisan by using one of its most anticipated new tools: the Sculpt Polygons tool. Open a new scene in Maya and create a polygon sphere (Create ➤ Polygon Primitives ➤ Sphere)—don't just click the sphere button on the shelf, or you'll get a NURBS sphere and the Sculpt Polygons Tool won't be very effective! In the Channel box, under Inputs: polySphere1, set the subdivisions X and Y to 40.

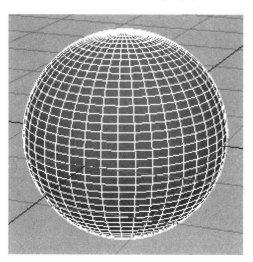

N O T E   When using Artisan sculpting tools, it is always important to have a large number of points to work with—either vertices (for NURBS surfaces) or facets (for polygon surfaces). If you do not provide enough points for Artisan to work with, it will not push and pull the object's surface in ways you expect.

With the sphere selected, choose Edit Polygons ➣ Sculpt Polygons Tool ❏ (from the Modeling menu set). This brings up the following window, which is generally the same for every Artisan tool.

N O T E   As most settings are the same from one tool to another, we will introduce them here and refer back to them in later sections of this chapter.

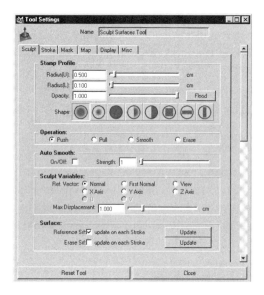

In this window (be sure you're in the Sculpt tab), set Radius U and L to about 0.3, set the Operation mode to Push, and set the Maximum Displacement to around 0.5. When you move your mouse over the sphere now (don't click anything just yet), you will see a red circle with an arrow pointing inward (toward the center of the sphere) and the label *Ps*. The circle tells you your brush's radius of influence, the arrow is the direction of the effect, plus the amount of influence it will have (longer arrows mean bigger pushes and pulls), and the *Ps* stands for "push," the current mode of the brush. To see how this feedback works, try changing the radius of the brush to a smaller value; the red circle will diminish to match. You can also change the direction of the effect; under Sculpt Variables, choose the X axis radio button. As you now move the mouse around, you will see that the arrow always stays pointing down the X axis. You can try the other settings here as well—when you're done, set it back to Normal.

Now that you have a feeling for some of Artisan's settings, try clicking and dragging the mouse over the surface. You should see the sphere dent inward as you drag your mouse across its surface, the dent always pointing inward toward the center of the sphere (because the brush option is set to Normal). If you make a few drags across the sphere, you will end up with something like the following.

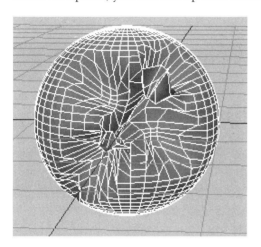

If you don't like what you have (or just to see how this works), you can erase your work. Click the Erase radio button (under Operation), then paint over the parts you don't like. If you want to reset the entire sphere, click the Flood button near the top right of the window. This will "flood" the entire sphere with the Erase command, thus resetting the sphere back to its original shape.

TIP   The Flood button can be used with any operation, such as push and pull, to apply a certain value to an entire object. You can then fine-tune specific parts of your surface by painting on them as normal.

You may notice that, as you make several strokes on top of one another, the polygon facets will tend to get very jagged looking (as if the sphere were made up of crinkly paper instead of clay). To smooth out your strokes, there are two options: the Smooth operation or the Auto Smooth option. Let's start with the Smooth operation. Once you have several strokes deforming your sphere (try pulling the points out this time), switch over to the Smooth operation by selecting its radio button on the Sculpt tab. Now brush over the sphere, concentrating on the sharpest edges. You'll see these edges move back toward their original positions on the (undeformed) sphere, and the strokes you have made will smooth out.

N O T E   The Smooth operation "relaxes" whatever you paint over, making it tend to return back to its original position, and thus smoothing the shape back out.

Now erase your sphere back to normal, check the Auto Smooth option, and set the Strength slider to about 5. As you paint strokes over the surface of the sphere (be sure you're in push or pull mode!), you will notice that the polygons don't become as jagged as they did when the Auto Smooth option was off. To create smoothly organic shapes, always use a combination of the Auto Smooth option and the Smooth operation mode.

Aside from adjusting radius, modes, and other options, you can also change brush shapes, using the row of buttons near the top labeled Shape—the icon on each button shows its stamp shape. Erase the sphere back to neutral, and then try stamping the sphere with each of the brush shapes to see how they compare.

N O T E   *Stamping* is simply clicking and releasing your mouse button (without dragging). The brush creates a "stamp" of its shape right on you object's surface. When you drag over the surface, you are laying down a series of stamps. You can see this effect if you drag very quickly over your object's surface: If the mouse is moving quickly, each stamp will be noticeably separate from the others, rather than all running together.

As the Sculpt tool is set up right now, every time you make one stroke on top of another, the sphere will deform more and more (as if the effect were layering on top of itself) because you have the Surface: Update on Each Stroke option turned on.

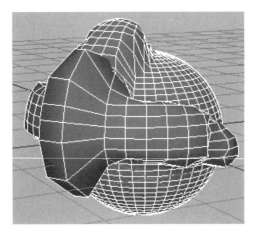

If you wish to set a maximum amount by which your strokes can deform the sphere, just uncheck the Update on each stroke option. The same strokes will then produce something like this:

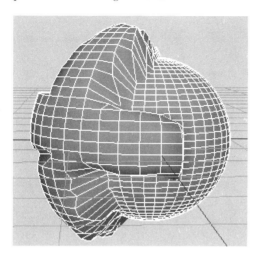

As you have probably noticed, you can also set the *opacity* of your brush. Opacity refers to the percentage of a tool's total effect that each application of it will have on your object. As an analogy, consider a real-world paintbrush: If the paint you're applying is highly opaque, one coat may be enough to cover your wall, whereas a semi-transparent paint would take several coats. In Artisan, if you have your brush set to Push with a maximum displacement ("push in") set to 1, and your opacity is 0.5 (or 50%), when you click on the surface of your sphere, it will only push in about 0.5 units, instead of 1. You can use the opacity setting to reduce the effect of your strokes, making each one subtler, thus allowing you to deform your objects in smaller increments than we have done so far.

Before we leave this introductory section, you should note that you can bring up a marking menu with several Artisan options by simply pressing the U key and clicking the mouse button. In addition to the settings available in the marking menu, there are hotkeys defined for several of the most common tasks, and you can create your own hotkeys for most Artisan settings.

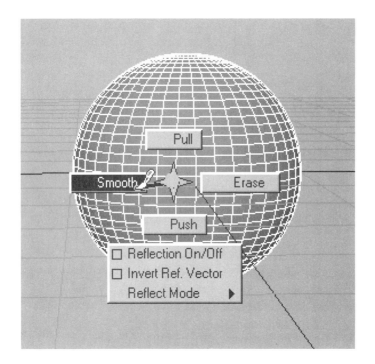

 TIP   In version 1 of Maya, altering the radius of the brush was mapped to the **Ctrl+right-** and left-arrow keystrokes. In version 2, modifying the *upper* brush radius is now mapped to B plus mouse-dragging right or left (the new lower radius setting is not yet mapped). Max displacement is now mapped to M plus mouse-dragging right and left. **To find out how to map other tool settings to hotkeys, see the Maya help files, or Chapters 3 and 16 in this book.**

 TIP   If you have a graphics tablet, you can set the pressure of the stylus to map to brush radius or displacement amount. **See the Maya help files for more on how to do this.**

If you are familiar with Artisan's marking menu and hotkeys, you do not need to keep the options window open for most operations. If you are starting out, however, it is a good idea to keep the window open. Throughout this chapter, we will access all Artisan options via the option window, though experienced users will find it more efficient to access them through the marking menu or hotkeys.

TIP For a complete list of Artisan's hotkey functions (and those that are not yet mapped), choose Options ➤ Customize UI ➤ Hotkeys, and scroll down to the Artisan section of the list (it's near the bottom). If you map any new hotkeys, be sure to save your preferences for future use (Options ➤ Save Preferences).

Sculpting NURBS Surfaces: Sculpting across Seams

We're now going to look at Maya's Sculpt NURBS Surfaces Tool, and use the head you created in Chapter 6 to see how Artisan works with complex issues like surface seams.

TIP If you do not have (or don't like) the head from Chapter 6, use the file headStarter.ma on the CD-ROM.

First things first: we don't want to alter the shape of the person's ears or eyes, so hide them from view (select each, and then choose Display ➤ Hide ➤ Hide Selection).

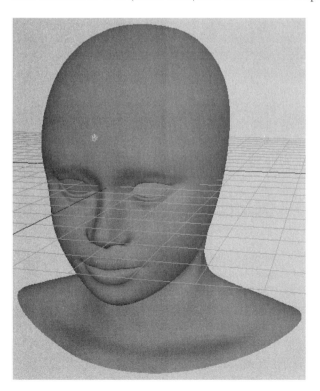

PART 2

Modeling

Drag-select the remains of the head, and then open the Sculpt Surfaces Tool (Edit Surfaces ➤ Sculpt Surfaces Tool ❑). The entire surface of the head will now be available for sculpting (if you had only selected one portion of the head, it would have been the only part available for sculpting). You will see yellow bands where each surface is stitched to the others—if you see all the surfaces' isoparms, go to the Display tab and uncheck Show Active Lines. Because there are stitched seams in this model, it will be bit more challenging to sculpt this surface without pulling apart the seams.

N O T E   Seams are a highly complex surface structure, and, while Artisan does a great job treating the object as a whole, you have to know how to adjust the Sculpt Surfaces Tool settings to get it to work as well as possible.

In the Sculpt Surfaces Tool window, select the Seam tab and adjust the Seam Tolerance and Min Length to 1. Setting these a bit higher than their defaults allows Artisan to "see" the common edges more easily as you work with the tool.

T I P   Before you start deforming the face shape, it is a good idea to save a temporary version the project file. If your settings get too messed up, it's easier to go back to that file than to have to go back to the original and hide the eyes and ears again.

One problem you will run into (if you let your brush stray too far) is that the upper head will not deform correctly—it has too few isoparms to deform well with Artisan. If we were planning to model the upper head next, we would need to insert more isoparms. But since we are not, we can just leave it alone for now (you can even deselect it if you want to be safer).

Let's create a heavier pair of eyebrows, using the Pull mode. We don't need to pull out each one, because Artisan has a Reflect mode that will allow us to do both sides simultaneously. Click the Stroke tab, turn the Reflection option on (check the box), and set the reflection mode to V Dir (Horizontal). When you now pass your mouse over the head, you will see two brushes, mirrored around the centerline of the head. Now turn back to the Sculpt tab, set the Operation mode to Pull, and adjust the radius of the brush(es) to something that looks appropriate for eyebrow size, turn the opacity down to about 0.5, and set Max Displacement to about 0.5 as well.

T I P   By holding down the B key and moving the mouse left and right, you can interactively adjust the brush size and see the changes in the brush right on the face (the range of sizes the brush can take on—min to max size—is determined by the brush minimum and maximum settings in the Sculpt Surfaces options window). This is a much faster way to adjust brush size to a desired radius.

Starting close to the center, pull a stroke along the top of the eyes (where the brows are), and pull out a heavier eyebrow. You'll notice both sides pull out with just one stroke—a great time-saver! If you don't like your work, remember that you can erase your model back to its original state again with the Erase function.

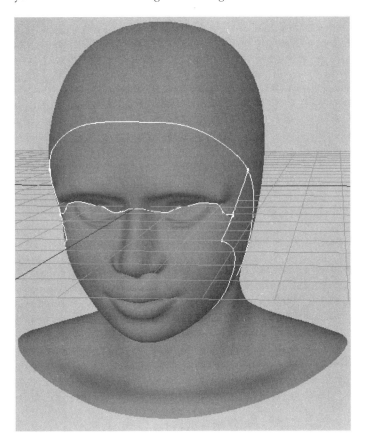

Once you have eyebrows you're pleased with, let's try creating an indentation below the cheeks that goes back toward the ears—specifically, across the seam boundary between the face and cheek patches of the face.

TIP   This is a well-modeled face: the stitches occur in places that would normally get no "tweaking" by tools such as Artisan (even though we're going to do that here). Placing seams in areas that won't move is very good practice: even though Artisan works well with stitches, it is not perfect. Whenever possible, it is better if you don't have to tweak stitched surfaces in the first place.

You will probably get unsatisfactory results at this point (and you may have to reopen your saved temp file; even erasing sometimes fails to set the stitches back to normal). The two surfaces are obviously not working as one, each one deforming a different amount under the brush's pressure.

The solution here is to increase the number of surfaces the tool looks for as it works. (Be sure to get a clean copy of your head to start from first!) Click the Miscellaneous tab and set the number of surfaces to two or more (or just click the Infinite radio button), and turn on the Use Common Edge Info option. With these new settings (and a bit of practice—try starting with the brush completely on one surface, then moving it to the other), you should get a nice "sunken cheek" look. Save this project for use later in this chapter.

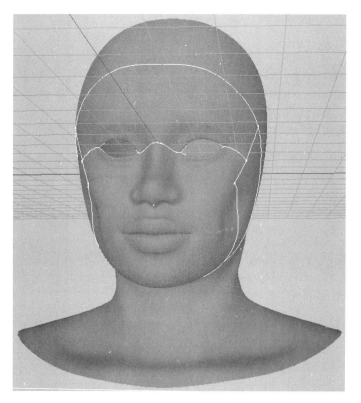

Although this was a fast and simple introduction to real-world modeling using Artisan, it should give you a good idea of just how powerful the tool can be for making subtle adjustments to your models. All it takes is a bit of practice and some knowledge of what the Sculpt Surfaces Tool can do.

N O T E   You can actually stitch surfaces using the Sculpt Surfaces Tool. For more information on how to do this, see Maya's online help (Basics: Chapter 7).

Creating Sets with Artisan

Another sometimes useful tool Artisan now includes is the Paint Set Membership tool. With this tool, you can edit the set membership of points—for grouping with bones, for example—without having to pick individual points. (And if you've ever had to do that, you know why this is a useful tool!)

Let's use our base head from the last section, and create a few sets of points on it (or you can use the 9headStarter.ma project on the CD-ROM). First drag-select the entire head, then open the Paint Set Membership tool (Deform ≻ Paint Set Membership Tool ❑). With the Paint Set Membership tool open, the head should now be made up of several colors, each representing one of the sets that has been created for the head. (See the Chapter 9 Color Gallery on the CD for the full effect.)

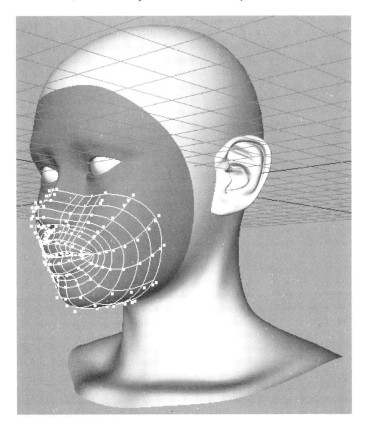

TIP If you do not see a colored face, click the Display tab and be sure the Color Feedback option is on. While here, you can also (if you prefer) turn off Active Display Vertices, which hides the isoparms and CVs on the head.

The Paint Set Membership tool works in three modes: Add, Transfer, and Remove. Add adds the painted points to the selected set, Remove deletes points from the selected set, and Transfer transfers points to the selected set. You will notice that there is no opacity setting: all points are either in a set or not—there is no in-between.

T I P   It is important to understand the difference between Add and Transfer. Add places the painted points into the selected set, but does *not* remove them from membership in any other sets. Transfer both adds points to the selected set and removes them from membership in any other sets.

To begin, let's add some points from the top of the head to the shapesSet that has all face points in it (in the Set Membership tab, select shapesSet under Set to Modify). With your brush mode set to Add (you can adjust the radius just as you did previously), paint some points on the top of the head into the shapesSet. The newly added points will change color as they are added to the set. (See in the Chapter 9 Color Gallery on the CD for the full effect.)

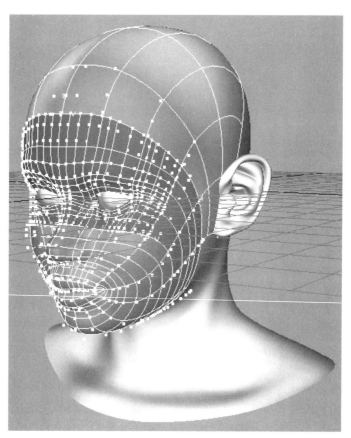

Now let's remove some points from set3 (the set around the jaws). Set your Paint Set Membership tool to Remove and paint out some of the points. As the CVs are removed, they disappear from view. (See the Chapter 9 Color Gallery on the CD for the full effect.)

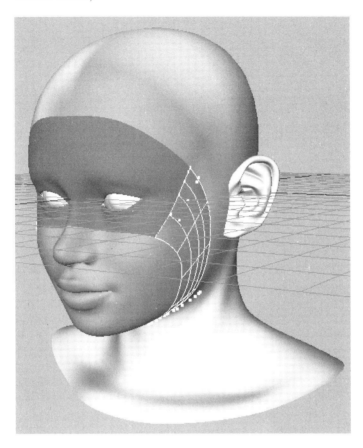

Finally, let's transfer some points from one set to another. With the Paint Set Membership tool set to Transfer, select set2 (the set of CVs around the mouth), and then paint over the area below the eyes. You will notice that the points change color as they are transferred from their old set to set2. (See the Chapter 9 Color Gallery on the CD for the full effect.)

N O T E   The set you select in the Paint Set Membership Tool window is the set the points will transfer *to*. Points from any other set will be moved into your selected set.

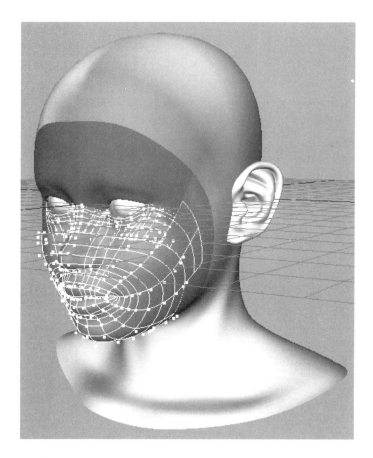

The Paint Set Membership tool can be very useful if you have several objects (such as this head) and you wish to form selection (or deform) sets across object boundaries for use in later deform processes, or just for ease of selection. Rather than have to carefully pick out points—and be sure you don't accidentally pick points on the back side of the object!—you can intuitively paint these points into your sets with a brush.

Painting Selections

Akin to the Paint Set Membership tool, the Paint Selection tool allows you to pick vertices (or polygon facets) that you can then manipulate in standard ways. Open a new scene, create a NURBS plane, scale it out a bit, and set its U and V patches to around 50 each (to give Artisan enough points to work with). Now open the Paint Selection tool (Modify ➤ Paint Selection Tool ❏).

The selection types here are Select, Unselect, and Toggle (which selects unselected points and vice versa). There are also global Select, Unselect and Toggle buttons. To quickly see how this works, pick out a brush shape and paint over part of the plane to select its points. You can now use the Move, Rotate, or Scale tools to alter just these points.

The advantage of being able to paint on selections may not be obvious with a simple plane, where you could just drag out selections with the Marquee tool. But on something more complex, like our head, the Paint Selection tool can be a great asset. Once again, open your neutral head project (or use the 9starterHead.ma project on the CD-ROM). Now, using the Paint Selection tool, select points around the mouth and make the face smile, using the Move tool and the Scale tool—you will probably have to move back and forth between the Paint Selection tool (changing the points selected) and the Move and Scale tools.

T I P   Remember that the Reflect mode allows you to select points on both sides of the head simultaneously—cutting your selection time in half.

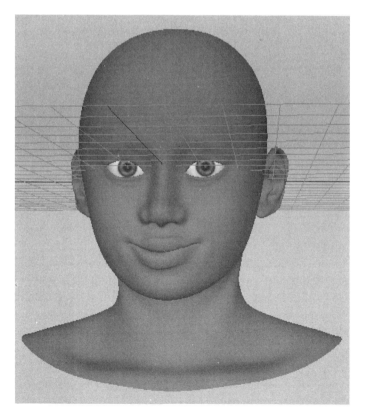

PART

2

Modeling

Painting Weights

If selecting CVs via painting doesn't give you enough control over the points you're manipulating, you can use the Paint Weights tool to set the goal weight (the amount of effect a manipulation will have on a given vertex or facet) of each CV in an intuitive manner.

N O T E   There are several other ways to set CV weights, but the Paint Weights tool is so easy to use, it's not often necessary to go beyond this tool.

To see how this tool works, let's create an Aztec (stair-stepped) pyramid just by painting different weights on a simple NURBS plane. Open a new scene, create a NURBS plane with about 50 U and V patches, and scale it out to about the size of the scene grid (for easier viewing). There is one step we must do before we can use the Paint Weights tool—we must first make the plane's CVs into a cluster so their weights can be manipulated (select the plane, then choose Deform ➢ Create Cluster). If you forget this step (which is very easy to do), you will be extremely confused by the lack of responsiveness the tool has!

Now that you have a cluster, drag-select both it and the plane the cluster is mapped to, and open the Paint Weights tool (choose Deform ➢ Paint Weights Tool in the Animation menu set).

T I P   You should see the plane turn white, indicating that its goal weights are all set to a value of 1. If this doesn't happen, be sure you created a cluster from the plane, and then check to see if color feedback is on (it's under the Display tab of the tool). It may be hard to see the color with the plane's isoparms showing, so turn off Show Active Lines as well.

First, we need to flood the entire plane/cluster with a goal weight of 0, or no influence (CVs with a 0 weight won't react to any manipulation). Set the operation mode to Replace (which replaces the old goal weight with your selection), set the Value (of the goal weight) to 0, and click the Flood button. The entire plane should turn black, indicating it now has a goal weight of 0. This is the base of our pyramid, which will not move. Now we need to paint our "stairs." Choose the square brush option (the button that looks like a blue square), and change the value to 0.1 instead of 0. This next part is a neat trick: Instead of having to manually increase the goal weight value each time, we can place the Paint Weights Tool into Add mode (by clicking the appropriate radio button), and each brush stamp will increase the goal weight by 0.1. Thus, the more times you click on a spot, the higher the goal weight goes, and the lighter the area's shade of gray will become.

T I P   This tool also has Smooth and Scale operation modes. The Smooth mode smooths transitions between areas of different goal weights. The Scale mode scales (or multiplies) the object's goal weight by the number in the Value box.

With the square brush chosen, set the radius of the brush larger than the edges of the plane, center the brush around the origin, and stamp a higher goal weight onto a large square area of the plane (you will probably find this easier to do in the top orthographic view).

N O T E   You can set the orientation of any brush that's not round. In the Stroke tab, you can choose from Up Vector (default), U and V Tangent (horizontal and vertical aligned), and Path Direction (which changes the orientation depending on your stroke).

You should see a large square portion of the plane become a slightly lighter gray than before. Make the brush radius a bit smaller and repeat the stamp—now a smaller portion of the plane should get just a bit lighter. Continue this process until you are at the center with a very small radius. Your plane should look as follows.

Modeling

To make your pyramid, switch to the Move tool, select the cluster weight *only* (not the plane—you may need to do this in the hypergraph or outliner), and then move it straight up the Y axis. You should see something that looks like a stair-stepped pyramid.

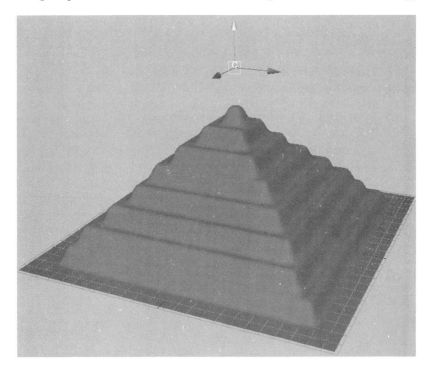

As a further exercise, try making a hilly terrain by using a simple plane, a cluster, and painted goal weights.

Let's now return to our favorite head—either open your own file or use `9head-Starter.ma` from the companion CD—and examine how to weight the mouth clusters to allow for better manipulation of facial expressions. With the head showing, select only the lower face section (with the mouth) and create a cluster out of it. Shift-select the cluster and mouth, then open the Paint Weights tool (you should see the area turn white, indicating a goal weight of 1 for all points). As before, first flood the area with a goal weight of 0 (so the areas we don't want to move won't). Using the Add (or Replace) and Smooth modes, paint the areas around the lips, giving the corners of the mouth, and the cheeks above them, the highest weighting. Try to imagine where the skin bends and stretches the most as you smile and frown (or look in the mirror), and then paint these creases onto the mouth. You may find it necessary to move the mouth and then repaint the goal weights to get the effect you want.

T I P   Remember that turning on Reflection will cut your work in half.

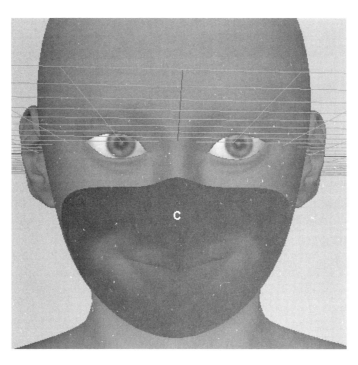

When you are finished, try making the face purse its lips and then frown. You should find that this method of creating facial animations can—after a bit of practice—become a very powerful tool in your character animation bag.

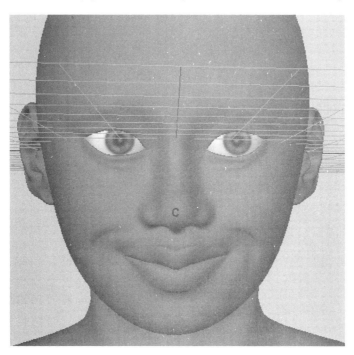

PART 2

Modeling

Painting Scripts: Hair on a Head

The Paint Scripts Tool lets you paint a MEL script onto your selected surface. Maya provides several predefined scripts in the C:\WinNT\Profiles\<UserName>\maya\ 2.0\scripts (or ~Maya/2.0/scripts for IRIX) directory, or you can create your own for use in a project.

N O T E   To learn how to create your own scripts, see Chapters 16 and 17.

The predefined scripts include painting on geometry, particle emitters, and soft body goal weights. For our purposes—putting a fuzzy haircut on our head—we'll use the geometry paint script.

Open your head project (or use 9headStarter.ma on the CD-ROM). In an empty space in the scene, create a short, very narrow cylinder (be sure to cap it in the cylinder creation options, so it's not hollow). As the hairs will be very thin, and we will paint on lots of them, reduce the number of sections to four and be sure there is only one span. In relation to the head, the hair should look something like the small tube to the right of the ear.

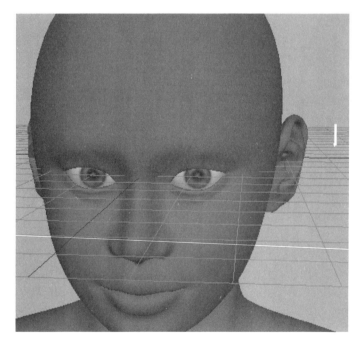

Now open the Script Paint tool (Modify ➣ Script Paint Tool ❑), click the Setup tab, and, in the Tool Setup Command text field, type **geometryPaint**, and hit the Enter key. This will bring up a window with options for the geometryPaint.mel script. In the Geometry text field, type in **nurbsCylinder1** (or whatever you name your hair shape).

Geometry Paint Settings

Geometry:	
Identifier:	Geom
Operation:	⦿ Create/Modify ○ Modify ○ Remove
	☑ Grid ☑ Jitter Grid
U Grid Size:	20
V Grid Size:	20
Control:	☑ X Scale ☑ Y Scale ☑ Z Scale
	☐ X Rot ☐ Y Rot ☐ Z Rot
	☐ X Trans ☐ Y Trans ☐ Z Trans
Options:	☐ Proportional ☑ Attach ☑ Duplicate
	☑ Group ☑ Isolate ☐ Align
Jitter Value:	0.00

TIP If you would like a more random look (as hair isn't usually all the same length!), you can create a second (or third) hair strand. Then, in the geometry field, type in the names of all geometry you wish to use for the hair, with a space between each name.

For Operation Mode, select Create/Modify, set the grid to about 100 by 100 (this determines how densely the hair will be placed), be sure the Align checkbox is enabled (so the hair will point out from each point on the head), and set the jitter to 0.3 or greater (this controls how randomly each hair is placed).

If you try to use the paint brush now, you will probably see the hair being built all around the head, but not attached to it—there is an offset to your geometry (its distance from the origin) that is causing this problem. To correct this problem, move all your hair objects back to 0, 0, 0 on the grid. Back in the Script Paint Tools Settings window, be sure your brush mode is set to Replace, pick a good radius for your brush, and paint some hair on your head!

TIP With all the geometry you create building hair, your system response time may become very slow. In a situation like this, you'll need to find a compromise between the amount of hair your head needs and the time (and patience) you have, or feel free to use the hair brushes in Paint Effects (see Chapter 25).

You may notice that you have difficulty getting the hair to paint on the head properly. As painting shapes on a complex surface (the head) involves difficult calculations on Maya's part, you may need to adjust several of the settings in the Script Paint settings window to get the right look.

PART 2

Modeling

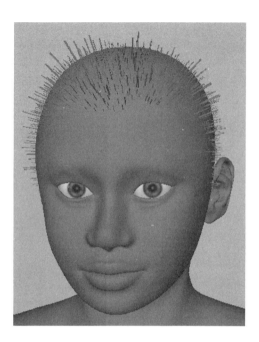

Painting Vertex Colors

Another of Artisan's tools—which has a more limited use—is the Paint Vertex Colors tool. This tool allows you to paint colors directly onto any polygonal surface using the by now familiar Artisan brush. Create a polygon cone, say, with about 40 divisions in each direction (so there are plenty of facets for Artisan to work with). With the cone selected, open the Paint Vertex Colors tool (choose Edit Polygons ➤ Colors ➤ Paint Vertices Tool). Set your brush radius to whatever you wish, and then click the color swatch next to Color Value and select a color. All that's left to do is paint on some color! (See the Chapter 9 Color Gallery on the CD for the full effect.)

N O T E   The Paint Vertex Colors tool is a simply series of presets of the **Attribute Paint** tool, which we will use next.

PART 2

Modeling

Painting Attributes: Painting Goal Weights

The Attribute Paint tool is very useful, as you can use it to paint any "paintable" attribute onto a surface. For our work, we're going to use this tool to paint on the particle goal weight of a soft body, making a simple cylinder into a bendable fishing rod.

TIP   We could also use the Script Paint tool to do this; it has a predefined script, paintGoalPP, which will do the same thing.

NOTE   For information on how to create soft bodies, see Chapter 24.

N O T E   For information about how to make an attribute paintable, see Appendix C of Maya Basics in the online help documents.

Open the file 9rodSB.ma, on your CD-ROM (or build a skinny cylinder, animate it, and make it a soft body). If you play back the animation, you will see that the entire "fishing rod" moves back and forth as one solid piece—we're going to change that by reducing the goal weights at the top of the rod. Select the rod and open the Attribute Paint tool (Modify ➢ Attribute Paint Tool ❏). Click the Attr (attribute) tab and then, under Paintable Object Type, expand the particle selection (click the + sign) until you see goalPP and highlight it. The goalPP attribute will now be placed in the Paintable Object list beneath; highlight this text, then click the right arrow, moving the goalPP over to the Selected side. Finally, click the Save Selection checkbox, so you don't have to repeat these steps if you change tools.

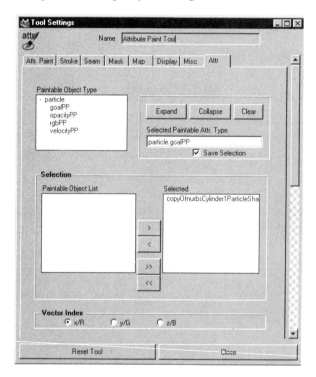

Move back to the Attr. Paint tab, set the operation mode to Replace and the Value (goal weight) to 0, and click the Flood button. This sets all goal weights to 0, meaning that the soft body will not move with its (invisible) animated parent anymore—you can play back the animation to test this, if you wish. Once you see how the goal weight attribute works, flood the entire rod with a value of 0.5, so there will be some connection between the rod and its animated parent.

Once you have the entire rod set to 0.5, set your mode to Add, and set your value to 0.1—we're going to increase the goal weight as we go down the rod by simply painting on a lighter color. Set your brush radius fairly large, so it wraps around the whole cylinder—you can also change the brush shape to square if you prefer. To get a smooth transition from dark to light, you will probably need to use the Smooth mode as well as the Add mode. Run a couple of frames of the animation frequently to see how you are progressing.

TIP A very good method for getting smooth transitions on an object like this is to start at the bottom and make a series of upward brush strokes, each one going up a bit further.

WARNING You must rewind animations using soft bodies before playing them back. If you don't rewind, the animation will give you bizarre results.

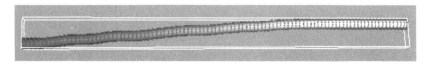

While it can take a bit of practice to paint goal weights onto objects effectively, learning how to do so can really improve the control you have over soft body animations, allowing you to create much subtler variations of motion than would be feasible without such a paint method for applying goal weights.

Painting Skin Weights

If you are working with skinned, jointed characters, the Paint Skin Weight tool is just what you need for precise control over how your character's skin bends in relation to joint movement. We will use a simple "character" setup of a cylindrical arm and an elbow joint to examine how to use this tool. You can either create this scene on your own, or use the 9armStarter.ma file on your CD-ROM.

With your project open, try moving the joint up and down (drag-select the bottom joint and then use the Move tool to move it—and the arm—up and down). You will notice that, while the bound skin moves with the joints, the elbow area doesn't respond correctly: it needs to crinkle just a bit more.

Select the cylinder and open the Paint Skin Weights tool (in the Animation menu set, choose Skin ➤ Edit Smooth Skin ➤ Paint Skin Weights Tool ❑). You should see a grayscale image of the cylinder and, in the Skin Paint tab, you will have a choice of your three joints (joint1 at the shoulder, joint2 at the elbow, and joint3 at the wrist). If you select joint1, for example, the color of the cylinder will show what the bind weight of each point is for this joint. Again, white represents a bind weight of 1, fully affected by any joint motion, and black is a bind weight of 0, not affected at all.

 T I P   If your cylinder is not colored, be sure Color feedback is on (under the Display tab), and also be sure your scene is set to shaded mode (press the 5 or 6 key on the keyboard).

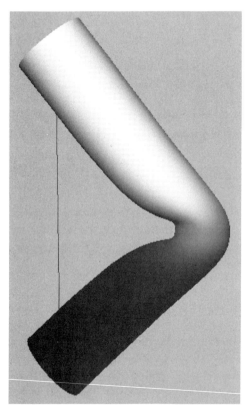

You can see by looking at the color feedback (in the Chapter 9 Color Gallery on the CD) that the inside of the elbow is very dark when either joint1 or joint2 is selected, indicating it is not being influenced by either joint very much. Let's paint slightly higher values into this area. First, bend the arm some (as above) so you can see your results as you work. Set your brush mode to Add, set the value to about 0.1, and set your opacity fairly low (like 0.1 or 0.2). Next, set your brush to a fairly small radius, zoom in on the elbow area, and start painting higher goal weights on, switching between joints 1 and 2, and watching what happens. Your goal is to get a nicer crease between the upper and lower arm here, and setting higher goal weights at and just above the elbow for the top toint (or just below the elbow for the bottom joint). The elbow will increase the joint's influence, making it pull the elbow area into more of a crease.

TIP   If your strokes make the elbow area too lumpy, use the Smooth mode to smooth the lumps out—you may not want to smooth out all the lumps, however, as skin does wrinkle as it bends!

Once you have worked a while, you should end up with something like the following (also see the Chapter 9 Color Gallery on the CD).

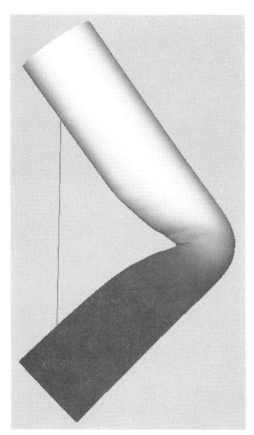

Modeling

The effect here is subtle, but subtlety is what this tool is all about. The difference between the two images above is not great, but the second is far more appealing and "realistic" than the first—and getting this elbow bend without the Paint Skin Weights tool would be very difficult and time-consuming. Once again, Artisan makes a difficult, painstaking task a lot easier.

Summary

This chapter has presented all the Artisan tools and, while the review was fairly brisk, you should have a very good feel for how Artisan works by now. Keep in mind that all the tools operate in a similar manner, just with different options. You may be thinking at this point that virtual painting is something of an "art" to master (hence the name "Artisan"), but don't be intimidated. Consider this: How would you accomplish any of the tasks we have done in this chapter without Artisan tools? Only when you imagine working without these tools is their power really evident. Artisan's tools take highly complex tasks that used to require custom programming and/or hours of dull, painstaking work and place all of these tasks in easy reach. Artisan is also highly intuitive: after all, just about anyone understands paintbrushes. Because Artisan is now built into Maya Complete (and Unlimited), and with all the new improvements of the tool set in version 2, you can save yourself hours of time and frustration if, the next time a job seems too difficult, you first consider using Artisan.

PART III

ANIMATION

ANIMATING IN MAYA

Featuring

- *Keyframe animation defined*
  ....

- *The time slider and range slider controls*
  ....

- *Techniques for creating keyframes*
  ....

- *Techniques for editing keyframes*
  ....

- *The Set Driven Key feature*
  ....

ANIMATING IN MAYA

T his chapter introduces you to animating in Maya. We will go over the fundamental concepts of keyframing, the various interface controls, and the tools for creating and editing keyframes in Maya. The tutorial in this chapter also demonstrates how to use Maya's Set Driven Key tool. The techniques you'll learn in later chapters are quite challenging, so gaining a firm grasp of the basic tools will help you to get through those upcoming chapters more smoothly.

Keyframe Animation

Animation, at its most basic level, is *change over an interval of time*. In Maya, almost anything can be changed over time; in other words, almost anything you create in Maya can be animated.

You've learned how Maya has a node-based structure. Any attribute within the node that has a numeric value is *keyable*. Keying, or *keyframing*, in Maya is the act of assigning a numeric value to a node attribute at a specific time frame. As the frames change, so can the attribute value. For example, the basic attribute Visibility actually has a numeric value of either 1 (for on) or 0 (for off), so it can be keyframed and animated.

Keyframing is a concept taken from classic 2D animation. Senior animators draw important "key" poses of characters being animated at certain frame intervals, called *keyframes*. Then the junior animators take over and draw all the frames between the keyframes, which are called *in-betweens*. The same thing happens when you are animating in Maya. You are the senior animator who establishes the key poses of whatever it is you are animating, and the computer is the whole department of junior animators drawing the in-betweens for you.

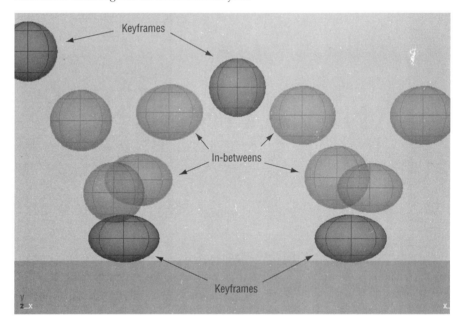

N O T E   Other kinds of animation include rotoscoping, which is actually a kind of keyframe animation, and motion capture, a way of creating function curves from live actors' performances. Motion capture is a complicated procedure, and although the technology is improving quickly, it is still difficult to use it to produce high-quality animation without needing to do manual cleanups.

Are You an Animator?

There are different levels of animating. At the most basic level, you are moving things from A to B, which almost anyone can do. The next level of animating involves learning and intelligently using certain animation principles, such as squash and stretch, anticipation, key posing, and so on. The 2D cell-animation schools are still the best places to learn these things, although computer animation schools are beginning to offer classes in this area. If you want to be an animator, there is no way around it—you must learn these principles.

Continued on next page

The ability to bring life to a character, however, requires more than just following animation principles. A successful animator also has a good sense of timing, which belongs to the realm of performance. Timing is a skill you are born with as much as it is a learned thing, and certain individuals are naturally better at animating than others, just as some people are naturally better dancers or singers than others. In fact, the ability to create authentic emotions and pathos in animated characters requires great acting skills.

A good way to discover if you are an animator or not is to go through a whole animation project, and ask yourself which parts of the project you enjoy spending time on the most. An animator's focus will generally be different from that of the other 3D artists. Modeler and texture artists, for example, are usually interested in how things look; they want to create beautiful images, evoking certain feelings. Animators are usually interested in telling a good story.

Animation Controls

Before we get more deeply into keyframing, let's look at some animation control tools: the time slider and the range slider. These and the other tools discussed in this chapter are in Maya's Animation module.

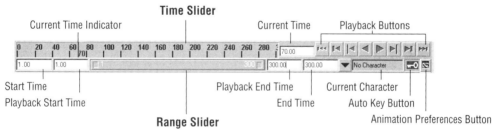

Playing Back and Updating Animations with the Time Slider

The time slider comes with playback buttons, which look like those on a video player control panel. You can also use the following hotkeys to control the playback:

Alt+V	Toggles between play and stop
Esc	Stops the playback
. (period)	Moves to the next keyframe
, (comma)	Moves to the previous keyframe
Alt+. (period)	Moves to the next frame
Alt+, (comma)	Moves to the previous frame

You can click or drag in the time slider to do various things. When you click on a frame number, that frame becomes the current time. If you drag the mouse, the animation updates interactively, which is called *scrubbing*.

When you MM click or drag, the current time indicator moves to where the mouse is without updating the animation. This is a valuable function when you want to quickly keyframe the values of one frame to other frames. MM dragging is also used for scrubbing only the audio, as opposed to scrubbing the whole scene.

The time slider can also become a virtual time slider inside the modeling window, the Graph Editor, or the Dope Sheet. This happens when you press the K key on the keyboard at the same time that you press the mouse buttons. By K+dragging in any window, you can scrub the animation. By K+MM dragging, you can move the current time without updating the scene, and scrub only the audio. This technique can be especially useful when you are editing function curves in the Graph Editor. The Graph Editor and Dope Sheet are discussed later in this chapter, when we get to the topic of editing keyframes.

RM choosing inside the time slider opens the Key Edit menu. This menu offers the standard key-editing functions, which we will discuss later in the chapter in the "Editing Keyframes" section. It also provides access to several useful submenus:

- With the Set Range To submenu, you can control the playback range in various ways. One option here is the Sound Length setting, which you can also use to discover the length of an audio file.

- With the Sound submenu, you can show, hide, or rename any of the audio files that have been imported.

- With the Playblast function, you can preview your animation as real-time movie clips (the Playblast function is discussed in Chapter 11).

 TIP   In order to actually play the audio file, you need to set the Playback Speed setting to Normal in Animation Preferences, found under Options ➢ General Preferences.

Controlling the Playback Range with the Range Slider

The range slider is a simple tool used to control the playback range of the time slider. You can set where the time slider starts and ends by sliding, shortening or lengthening the range slider.

The Auto Key button on the range slider (the next-to-last item on the slider) lets you set keys automatically as you transform the selected object in the modeling window. Using Auto Key for keyframing is explained in the "Creating Keyframes" section of this chapter.

The Animation Preferences button on the right end of the range slider lets you view the animation settings in the General Preferences dialog box. The animation settings include options that let you adjust the time slider. For example, setting the Height to 2x or 4x, as shown below, can help you see the audio waves more clearly, which is helpful when you are scrubbing audio files.

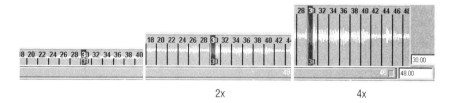

2x   4x

You can also select the Units tab of the General Preferences dialog box and adjust the Time setting. The default Time setting is 24 fps (frames per second).

Creating Keyframes

There are many ways of creating keyframes in Maya. You can use the hotkeys, the Set Key or Set Breakdown function in the Animate menu, the Channel box, the Graph Editor, or the Attribute Editor. All of these methods are described in the following sections.

Using Hotkeys for Keyframing

Several hotkeys are useful for keyframing:

S	Keyframes a selected object at a specified frame (same as Animate ➣ Set Key, discussed in the next section)
Shift+W	Keys the translations
Shift+E	Keys the rotations
Shift+R	Keys the scales

Keyframing with Set Key

The standard way to keyframe a selected object at a specified frame is to select Animate ➣ Set Key. The default setting is to Set Keys on All Keyable Attributes. With this setting, when you click the Set Key button in the Set Keys Options dialog box (or press the S hotkey), all the attributes displayed in the Channel box are keyed. This setting may not be practical for many situations.

PART 3

Animation

Set Key Settings

When you change the Set Keys setting to All Manipulator Handles, all the manipulator values are keyed. When the setting is Current Manipulator Handle, as shown below, only the active manipulator handle is keyed. This is a useful setting if you want to restrict the keying to only the attribute values you are changing, such as the Y-axis translation.

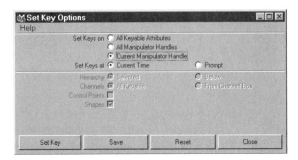

The Prompt setting lets you set keyframes at multiple frames. If you select Prompt, when you click on the Set Key button (or press the S hotkey), you are prompted for the frames to keyframe. Enter the frame numbers you want keyframed and click OK.

Keyable Attributes

All keyable attributes are displayed in the Channel box. The default attributes are Translation, Rotation, Scale, and Visibility.

In Maya, each object can have its own keyable attribute settings. You can add or remove the keyable attributes of an object by using the Channel Control. Select an object, then choose Window ➤ General Editors ➤ Channel Control.

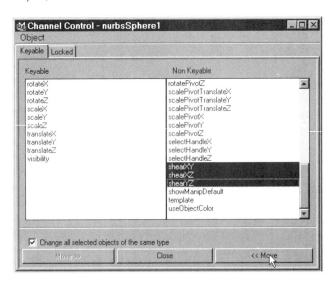

The Channel Control shows a long list of nonkeyable attributes on the right, and a list of ten default keyable attributes on the left. When you select an attribute in either list, the Move >> or the <<Move button becomes active, and you can move the selected attribute to make it keyable or nonkeyable. Any changes you make in the Channel Control are reflected in the Channel box. The Channel Control also has a tab for Locked attributes. When an attribute becomes locked, its value becomes static and nonkeyable. The fields for the attribute also become gray.

TIP Some people find it easier to use the Channel box to lock attributes. Creating keyframes with the Channel box is discussed after the following section on the Set Breakdown function.

Keyframing with Set Breakdown

Set Breakdown, a new feature in Maya 2, works the same way as Set Key, except that instead of setting keys, it sets *breakdowns*. What distinguishes breakdown frames from keyframes is that when regular keys are inserted into a breakdown curve, the breakdown frames become "bound" by the regular keys, and the breakdowns maintain a proportional time relationship to those keys.

To get a better idea of how breakdowns differ from keys, try the simple exercise in the "Working with Breakdowns" section later in this chapter.

Keying Attributes in the Channel Box

You can key different attributes in the Channel box. Select an object, open the Channel box, select any attribute(s), and RM choose over the attribute names. A long menu pops up, as shown here, offering many key-editing functions.

The Key Selected option keyframes the attributes that are selected in the Channel box. The Key All option keyframes all the keyable attributes for the selected object. The Breakdown Selected and Breakdown All options work the same way for breakdowns. The Lock and Unlock options work on selected attributes.

TIP You can create a user-defined hotkey for Key Selected in the Channel box. Shift+S is a good choice. You may find that selecting attributes in the Channel box and hotkeying them is a very convenient method of keyframing.

Keying Attributes in the Attribute Editor

You can also set keys in the Attribute Editor the way you do in the Channel box. A difference is that when you RM choose over the keyable attributes in the Attribute Editor, you don't get as many functions in the menu that pops up.

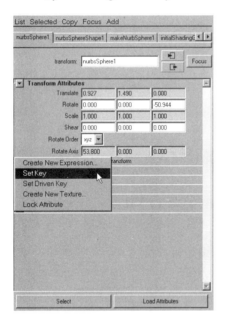

You can lock attributes and set keys, but the keys are set for all X, Y, Z values of translation, rotation, or scale attributes. One advantage of using the Attribute Editor is that you can easily access nonkeyable attributes and keyframe them using the editor.

Keyframing with Auto Key

Auto key is probably the most efficient way to keyframe for a lot of situations. When you click the Auto Key button on the right side of the range slider, the key icon turns white and the background turns red. With Auto Key turned on, any change you make to the attributes of selected objects at any frame are automatically keyframed. The only precondition is that a keyframe must already exist for an attribute before that attribute can be auto keyed. The Auto Key button is a toggle; click it again to turn the function off.

As an example of using Auto Key, follow these steps:

1. Create a Sphere and set keys for its translation attributes at frame 1.

2. Click the Auto Key button to turn on the function.

3. Move to frame 10, and translate the sphere to a different position. The change is automatically keyframed.

4. Move to frame 20 and try rotating the sphere. Nothing is keyed because there are no initial keyframes for the rotation attributes.

WARNING   If you use Auto Key, make sure you toggle it off when you are finished. If you don't, you may unknowingly keyframe objects and end up with a lot of undesirable and unnecessary animation.

Editing Keyframes

After you've created the keys or breakdowns, you can edit them using the Edit ➤ Keys submenu, Channel box, Graph Editor, Dope Sheet, or time slider. We will cover the Graph Editor first because it is the most important keyframe-editing tool, and you will use it most often.

Working with Animation Curves in the Graph Editor

When you create a series of keyframes, these keyframes can be represented as function curves, or animation curves, inside the Graph Editor. The Graph Editor works like a regular orthographic window in that you can use hotkeys like A and F for viewing the function curves, the Alt+MM drag technique to track, and the Ctrl+Alt+LM or MM marquee method for zooming. However, the settings for the Move and Scale tools change in important ways when the Graph Editor is the active window.

TIP   If you are not familiar with animation curves, the Graph Editor may look complicated to you. It is more complex than most other editors in Maya, but it is very important that you learn to work with the Graph Editor and the animation curves. Animators should know how to "read" animation curves, visualizing how an object will move differently when the curves are edited a certain way. This alone often separates good animators from bad ones.

To see how the Graph Editor works, let's create some animation curves:

1. Create a sphere. Key translation and rotation animation to it over 30 frames.
2. Using the marking menu hotbox, select Persp/Graph View. The top window should now show perspective view, and the bottom should display the Graph Editor.
3. Press A to fit all the curves to the window. You should see six animation curves, one for each channel of the six attributes.

PART 3

Animation

4. Marquee-select a few keyframes near the current time indicator. Notice that the graph outliner to the left shows which curve keys were selected. Move them, and you will see the sphere update interactively.

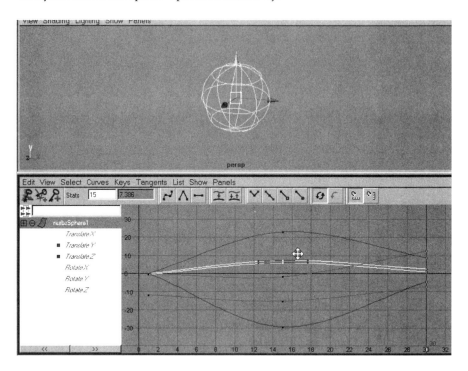

5. You can also work with only the curves you want by selecting those curves in the graph outliner. Select the translate curves, and only those curves are displayed.

6. Make sure the Graph Editor is the active window by clicking inside it, then double-click the Move tool to open the option box. As shown below, listed under MoveKey Options are moveOnly and moveOver. The default moveOver setting lets you move selected keyframes over other keyframes. The moveOnly setting allows you to move the keyframes only between other keyframes.

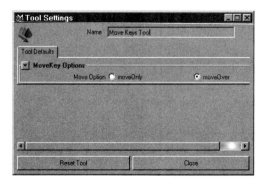

7. Open the Scale tool option box. Again, you'll see settings that are different in the Graph Editor. The default Gestural setting sets the pivot point for scaling the selected keys to where you place the mouse. The Manipulator setting lets you create a box to move and scale, as shown below. This may be the better setting for many situations.

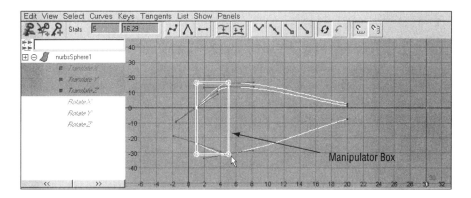

Using the Graph Editor Tools

The Graph Editor provides many toolbar tools to help you edit curves.

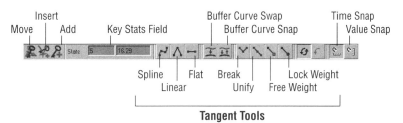

The Time Snap and Value Snap Tools The Time Snap tool, which makes the keyframes snap to frames, should always be turned on, because it makes editing keyframes easier. You will have fewer occasions to use the Value Snap tool, which snaps the keyframes to the nearest integer values. Before moving on to the other tools, turn on the Time Snap tool. Instead of working without the snap function, then needing to snap the keyframes later, it is much better to have the Time Snap tool on from the beginning.

The Move Tool   As you saw earlier, the Move tool in the Graph Editor is actually the Move Nearest Picked Key tool, and it works differently from the Move tool you pick from the Minibar. The Move tool moves only one key at a time. It will move anything that is closest to the mouse arrow on an active curve, whether that item is a keyframe or a tangent handle. It will not move curves. You can constrain the tool using the Shift key for horizontal or vertical movements, just as you can constrain the regular Move tool.

The Insert Key and Add Key Tools   The Insert Key and Add Key tools are similar. Insert Key inserts a key on the curve at the selected frame. Add Key adds a key to whatever value and frame you are clicking, changing the curve shape accordingly.

The Tangent Tools   The tangent tools let you change the shape of the curve around the keyframes. The Spline (the default shape), Linear, and Flat tools let you pick those shapes. You can see other types on the Tangents menu. Select a few keyframes and play with the types to see how they behave.

In situations where you want to break the tangent or increase the roundness of the curve at specific keyframes, you can use the Unify or Break tool (also available from the Keys menu).

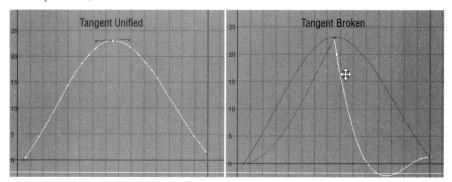

Before you can free a keyframe's tangent weight and change it, the tangent of the keyframe must become weighted. Select the keyframe (you can also select the entire curve) and select Curves ➤ Weighted Tangents. The tangent handles change, as shown on the next page. You can then unlock the weights, using the Free Weight tool, and change the curve shape. After you are finished adjusting the curve shape, you can use the Lock Weight tool to lock the tangent weights of the keyframes.

Weighted Tangents

Free Tangent Weight

Buffer Curve

The Buffer Curve Snap and Swap Tools   The Buffer Curve Snap and Swap tools are new features in Maya 2. When you edit a curve, changing its shape, the original shape remains as a buffer (as shown above in the example of the free tangent weight). The Buffer Curve Swap tool snaps the changed curve to the buffer. The Buffer Curve Snap Tool snaps the buffer to the changed curve.

The Key Stats Fields Tool   The Key Stats Fields tool lets you enter precise values for keyframes. It is especially handy when you need to assign the same values for multiple keyframes.

Using the Graph Editor Menus

The Graph Editor menus provide some of the same tools as the toolbar, as well as some other useful functions.

Cut, Copy, and Paste Functions   Using Edit menu functions, you can cut, copy, and paste selected keyframes. Before you paste, however, make sure to set the proper option settings, or unexpected results could occur. Go to Edit ➤ Paste ❏ and look over the different settings.

The curves shown on the next page were copied from the original curve (shown as a white curve), then pasted with different option settings back to the original curve. The first example shows a curve inserted into the current time with the Connect setting checked. Notice that the curve being pasted has moved up in such a way that the starting point of the curve connects to the original curve at the current time indicator. If you turn off the Connect setting, you get the second example shown on the top right. The pasted curve is still inserted into the original curve, but it is not translated vertically to connect with the original curve. The Merge setting produces the third example, where the curve being pasted merges with the original curve. Note that the last keyframe of the resulting curve is the same as the pasted curve. The fourth example is pasted with the Time Range set to Start and Time Offset set to 30. Note that, in this case, you would get the same result if you set the Time Range to Clipboard and Time Offset to 29, because the copied curve on the Clipboard starts from frame 1.

PART **3**

Animation

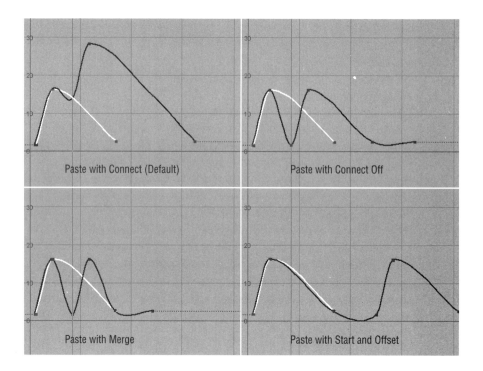

Paste with Connect (Default)   Paste with Connect Off

Paste with Merge   Paste with Start and Offset

 N O T E   When using functions with numerous optional settings, you will often have different ways of achieving the same result. Different situations will make different settings optimal for those situations. In order to know which are optimal for a particular setting, you need to have a clear understanding of what the settings do. It's frustrating to discover that a function that works for one situation will not work for another because different settings are required, and you don't know what those setting changes should be.

Pre and Post Infinity Cycles and Extrapolations   View ➣ Infinity displays the curve values before and after the first and last keyframes, to infinity. Under the Curves menu, you can select Pre and/or Post Infinity cycles or extrapolations, as shown in the images on the next page.

- The default setting is Constant, which means the values for the first and last keyframes are maintained.

- The Linear setting takes the slope of the tangent.

- The Post Infinity Cycle with Offset takes the last keyframe value as the starting point for the next cycle.

- The Post Infinity Oscillate setting mirrors the cycle before it.

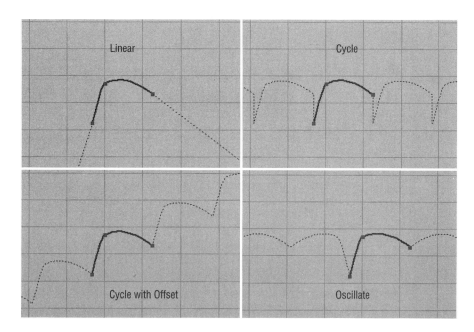

Add and Remove Inbetween Functions   Two other nifty functions are Add Inbetween and Remove Inbetween, found on the Keys menu. These are simple functions that either add or remove a frame into the current time, causing all the keyframes after the current time to move one frame forward or backward.

The Auto Load Option   In some situations, you may want to deselect an object and select another, but still maintain the keyframes of the first object. In such a situation, you can turn off the Auto Load function on the List menu.

Editing Key Times with the Dope Sheet

The Dope Sheet has many of the same editing functions that are available in the Graph Editor. To open the Dope Sheet, select Window ➢ Animation Editors ➢ Dope Sheet. Because the Dope Sheet edits only key times, it is designed to allow you to easily move around keyframes, curves, and whole groups of curves.

The Dope Sheet also has a Dopesheet Summary line, which selects all the keyframes of the selected objects for editing. Alternatively, you can open the summary to select all of the specific keyable attributes of the selected objects for editing. For example, you can select the Move tool, select all objects in the modeling window, select the Dopesheet Summary in the Dope Sheet, and move all the keyframes for the entire scene. You can also open the Dopesheet Summary, select Rotate, and then move only the rotation keyframes of all the selected objects in the scene.

PART 3

Animation

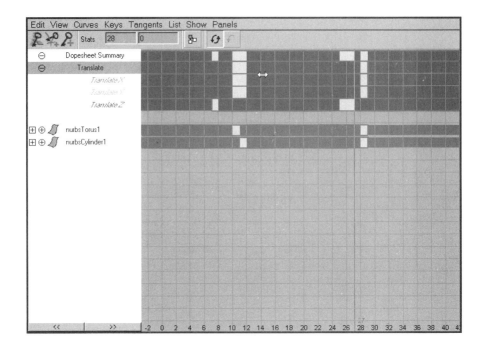

Editing Keys in the Channel Box

Key editing in the Channel box works the same as in the Graph Editor or the Dope Sheet, except that you don't have access to the option boxes. The Cut, Copy, Paste, and Delete functions, when they are RM chosen inside the Channel box, are performed with the default settings.

NOTE The difference between Delete and Cut is usually not significant, but it is worth knowing. Cut puts the keyframes into the Clipboard. Delete simply deletes. If you have keyframes in the Clipboard that you want to keep, use Delete to remove animation from the selected attributes so that you don't replace the Clipboard items.

Using the Keys Submenu

You can access several key-editing functions by selecting Edit ➤ Keys. The functions on this submenu work differently from those with the same name in the Graph Editor, and it's important not to confuse these functions. The functions in the Keys submenu edit keyframe curves at the object level. They are used mainly to transfer animation curves between objects.

Cut Keys and Copy Keys have the same option settings. Select Edit ➣ Keys ➣ Copy ❑ to open the Copy Keys Options dialog box. The Hierarchy setting Selected copies only the animation curves of the selected object. The Below setting copies all the curves of the object plus all the objects below the hierarchy of the selected object. You can also control the time range of the curves being copied by clicking Start/End and typing values in the Start Time and End Time boxes.

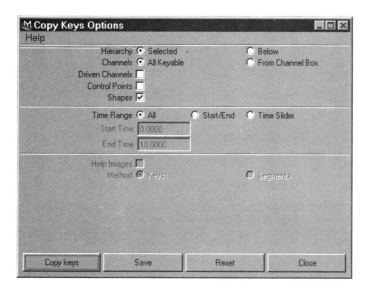

The Paste options are the same as the Graph Editor's Paste options. If you copy animation curves from a hierarchy, you can paste them into the same hierarchy as well as into other hierarchies.

TIP You can cut or copy curves from multiple objects. The objects' selection order is important in this case because the curves are copied in the same sequence. Also, when you are pasting to multiple objects, their selection order needs to be the same as the order in which the objects were selected for the Copy Keys function.

Working with the Time Slider

The time slider has several key-editing functions, which you can access by RM choosing them. When you select an object that has keyframes, the time slider displays key

ticks—red vertical lines showing where keyframes are in the time slider. (Breakdowns are displayed as green ticks.)

By Shift+clicking and dragging, you can select a frame, or a range of frames, which is displayed in a red block with arrows at the start, in the middle, and at the end of the block. You can then move the frame or frame range by dragging the arrows in the middle of the block, scale it by dragging the arrows at the side, or edit it by selecting the functions with RM choose.

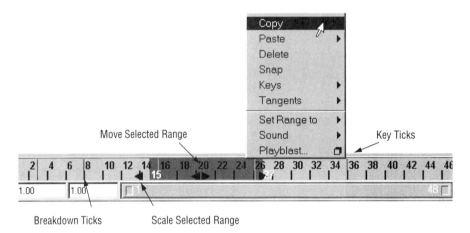

The Cut, Copy, Paste, and Delete functions are the same as those in the Graph Editor, without the options. The Paste function has Connect set to Off. The Paste Connect function works like the Graph Editor's Paste with the default settings.

Working with Breakdowns

Here is a short exercise to clarify how breakdowns work in Maya 2.

1. Create a sphere and keyframe it in the X axis at frame 1.

2. Translate it in the X axis to 5 at frame 20, and 0 again at frame 30, setting breakdowns. You can set breakdowns by RM choosing in the Channel box or by selecting Animate ➢ Set Breakdown. Everything should be the same as if keyframes were used, except that the ticks in time slider are red at frame 1 and green at frames 20 and 30, as shown in the next image.

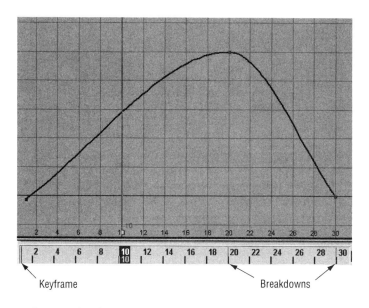

Keyframe   Breakdowns

3. Set a keyframe at frame 10 with the X-axis translation value of 10.

4. Open the Graph Editor, select the keyframe at frame 10, and try moving it to frame 15. Note that the breakdowns at frames 20 and 30 move as well, maintaining their curve shape with respect to the keyframe being moved. This is what is meant by breakdowns being "bound" by keyframes.

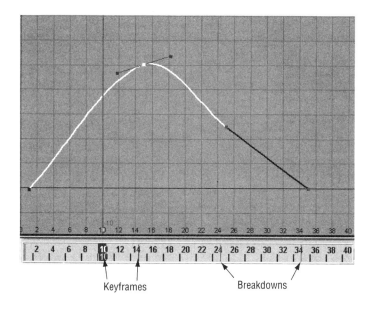

Keyframes   Breakdowns

PART **3**

Animation

Hands-on Maya: Setting a Driven Finger

In some cases, when one object's attributes change, another object is affected accordingly. For example, consider the way that fingers fold: Whenever the second joint of a finger folds, the third joint generally folds as well. Or whenever a button is pressed, a light may be turned on or a door may open. It would be nice if you could make such processes automatic. The Set Driven Key tool enables you to do this kind of thing.

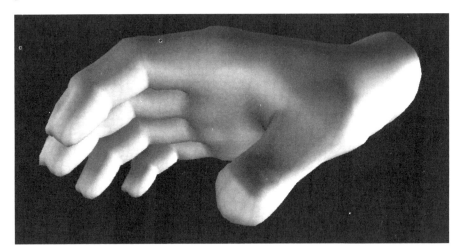

You can open the Set Driven Key window from the Channel box, Attribute Editor, or Animate menu (select Animate ➤ Set Driven Key ➤ Set ❑). Its function is to link attributes to each other in a master-slave relationship. The attributes that influence the other attributes are called *driver* attributes; the ones that are influenced are called *driven* attributes.

Using One Driver Attribute

Let's try a simple tutorial to see how this works. For this example, we'll use three spheres to represent finger joints and have one of the sphere's rotation drive the other two spheres' rotation (whenever nurbsSphere1 rotates in the X axis, nurbsSphere2 and nurbsSphere3 also will rotate in the X axis).

1. Create a torus. Set its values as follows:

Translate	(0, 3, 0)
Scale	(1, 4, 1)
Sections	1
Spans	1
Minor Sweep	180

2. Select Move, then press Insert to get into the pivot mode. X+drag the pivot to the origin. Your torus should look something like the one shown below.

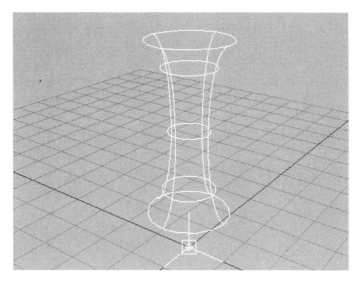

3. Duplicate the torus twice. Move one copy to (0, 9, 0), and the other to (0, 15, 0).

4. Create three spheres. Place them at (0, 0, 0), (0, 6, 0), and (0, 12, 0). We'll pretend this is actually a finger, with the spheres being the finger joints.

5. Select All in the modeling window, then select Modify ➤ Freeze Transformations. In the Hypergraph window, group the objects into the hierarchy shown below (note that the torus's pivots match the spheres' pivots).

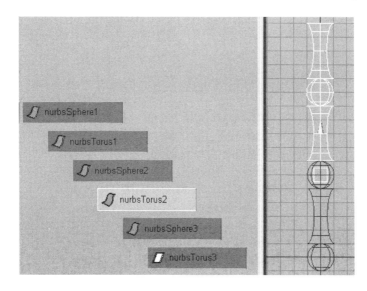

PART 3

Animation

6. Drag to select all the objects in the modeling window. Then, in the Channel box, select any attribute and RM choose to open the Set Driven Key window.

7. Click Load Driver and Load Driven. All the toruses and spheres are loaded in both the Driver and the Driven lists. We want nurbsSphere1 to be the driver, so select that in the Driver list. You see the default keyable attributes appear in the box on the right.

8. Ctrl+click nurbsSphere2 and nurbsSphere3 in the Driven list to be the driven objects. The default attributes representing both spheres appear in the box on the right.

9. Select rotateX in the Driver and the Driven lists, as shown below, then click Key.

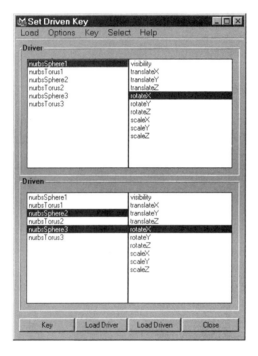

Notice that the nodes for the two driven spheres are now diagonal shaped, indicating they have animation. But there are no red ticks showing in the time slider, because there are no explicit keyframes. If you select either one, you will see in the Channel box that Rotate X field has become shaded as well.

10. Select nurbsSphere1 and rotate it in X 90 degrees. Rotate nurbsSphere2 100 degrees in X. Rotate nurbsSphere3 90 degrees in X. Click Key in the Set Driven Key window again. Now select nurbsSphere1 and try rotating it in X. You will see the other two spheres rotating as well.

11. Select nurbsSphere2 and nurbsSphere3 and open the Graph Editor. You will see curves representing the way nurbsSphere1 drives the other two spheres, as shown below. Because the values before the first key and after the last key are constant by default (as explained earlier in the chapter, in the section about using the Graph Editor), when you rotate nurbsSphere1 to a negative value or a value greater than 90 degrees, the other two spheres will remain at zero, or at 100 and 90 degrees, respectively.

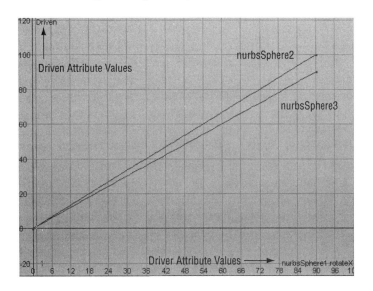

12. If you want the driven sphere values to keep changing when the driver sphere values become less than zero or greater than 90, select the curves in the Graph Editor and select Curves ➤ Pre Infinity ➤ Linear. Then select the curves and select Curves ➤ Post Infinity ➤ Linear. Now when you rotate nurbsSphere1 in the X axis to any value, the driven spheres will update accordingly.

As you can see from this tutorial, using Maya's Set Driven Keys feature is not difficult at all. In our example, one driver sphere was driving two spheres.

Using Multiple Driver Attributes

You can also have one attribute be driven by two or more driver attributes. For example, suppose that we want the second joint of our finger to bend with the first joint while the third joint remains straight or even bends the other way (such as what happens when you snap your fingers). Let's try using multiple driver attributes.

1. Continuing with the scene we were working on in the previous section, select nurbsSphere1 and set the rotations to (0, 0, 0).

PART

3

Animation

2. Create another sphere and translate it to (0, 18, 0). Its name should be nurbsSphere4. Group it under nurbsTorus3 in the Hypergraph window, as shown below. Keep it selected, and select nurbsSphere3 as well.

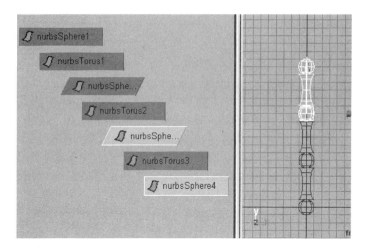

3. Open the Set Driven Keys window. Click Load Driver and Load Driven. Select nurbsSphere4 in the Driver list and nurbsSphere3 in the Driven list. Select rotateX for both. Click Key.

4. Select nurbsSphere in the modeling window and rotate it –90 degrees in X. Do the same with nurbsSphere3. In the Set Driven Key window, click Key again.

5. With nurbsSphere3 still selected, go to the Graph Editor. You can see two curves under the nurbsSphere3 attribute for Rotate X. These are the two driver attributes from nurbsSphere1 and nurbsSphere4. Select the nurbsSphere4.rotateX curve and assign linear extrapolation for the pre-infinity and post-infinity curves.

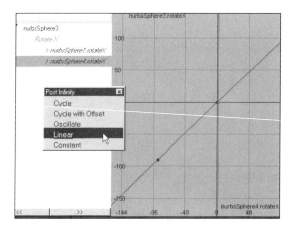

6. Select nurbsSphere1 and rotate it in X 50 degrees. Then select nurbsSphere4 and rotate it to –100 degrees. Notice how the rotation value of nurbsSphere3 changes as it averages its two driven values and rests at –50 degrees in X. The finger is ready for snapping.

Summary

In this chapter, we covered the basic concepts of keyframe animation and the tools Maya offers for creating and editing keyframes. Some of the interfaces are more challenging than others, especially the Graph Editor if you are not familiar with function curves. It is the Graph Editor, however, that you will come to love using as you become more familiar with animating in Maya. The next few chapters are going to be quite challenging, so take a break before you continue.

PART 3

Animation

chapter 11

PATHS AND BONES

Featuring

- *Path animation*
- *Skeletons with bones and joints*
- *Forward and inverse kinematics*
- *Constraints*
- *A hierarchy for animation*

PATHS AND BONES

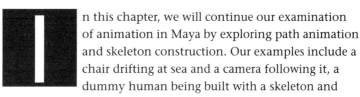

In this chapter, we will continue our examination of animation in Maya by exploring path animation and skeleton construction. Our examples include a chair drifting at sea and a camera following it, a dummy human being built with a skeleton and spheres, and a hierarchy of nodes to set up the dog model (built in Chapter 8) for binding and animation.

Path Animation

Path animation is essentially animating objects along a designated path such as a curve. This type of animation is ideal for animating things like roller coasters, ships, and moving cameras.

Attaching an Object to a Path

For path animation, you attach an object to a path. To see how this works, let's try creating a simple path animation.

1. Create a curve and a cone, as shown below. Make sure that the time slider range is at 48 frames.

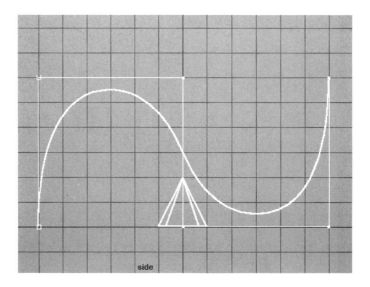

2. With the cone still selected, select the curve as well, then select Animate ➤ Paths ➤ Attach to Path ❑. Click Reset to make sure you're using the default settings, then click Attach. You should see the cone snap to the beginning of the curve. Try scrubbing through the frames (by dragging the mouse across frames in the time slider) and watch how the cone moves.

3. Under Inputs, you will see motionPath1. Click it, and you will see the U value, which is 0 at frame 1 and 1 at frame 48.

4. Go to frame 15 and check that the U value is 0.298. MM drag the current time indicator back to frame 1. The U value should still be reading 0.298. Click the U value, then RM choose and use Key Selected to keyframe that value at frame 1. Now the starting point has changed to U value 0.298, and the cone travels only about 70 percent of the curve from frame 1 to 48.

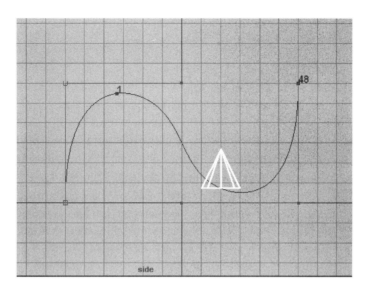

5. Open the Attribute Editor and click the motionPath1 tab. Change the settings to Follow and World Up. Make sure that X is set as Front Axis and Y is set as Up Axis. Scrub the timeline on the time slider and see how the cone moves differently. Change Front Axis to Y and Up Axis to Z and see how this affects the cone's movement.

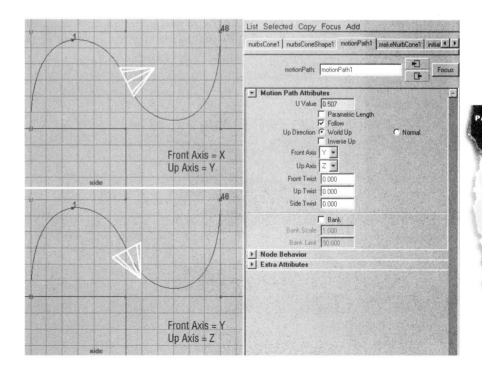

Now that you have an idea how path animation works, we'll try a more complex exercise next.

Making an Object Float

In this tutorial, we will create a short animation of a chair floating at sea. (You can find a finished version on the accompanying CD; it's named cam_anim.mov.) In addition to exploring further how to use path animation, we will also introduce using cameras and previewing in Maya.

1. Open the living room scene you created in Chapter 5, and select the chair group node. Rename it to Chair. Make sure that the cushion is at the bottom of the hierarchy, then select File ➤ Export Selection and save the file as Chair.mb. (You can also find this file on the CD.) You've just exported only the chair hierarchy into a new file.

T I P　Maya's default Export function exports everything associated with the model(s) being exported, including its history, expressions, and animation. If you want to export only the model, turn the other settings off in the option box.

2. Start a new scene, create a NURBS plane, scale it to 100 uniformly, and increase the Patch UV spans to 30.

3. Switch to the Modeling module. Select Edit Surfaces ➤ Sculpt Surfaces Tool ❑ and click Reset Tool. Switch to the Map tab and load in the Wave.tif file from the CD-ROM. You will see the plane become wavy, but it's not wavy enough. Click the Reload button three more times. Each time you will see the waves become more pronounced, as the displacement is compounded.

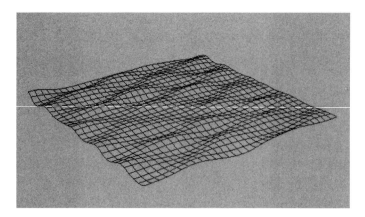

NOTE   If you want to create the Wave.tif file yourself, create a plane and open the Hypershade window. Assign a blinn material with the water texture, and manipulate the variables until you see something like the **Wave.tif** file. Use the Edit ➤ Convert Material to File Texture command, then convert the .iff file to .tif format using Fcheck. See the discussion of Hypershade in Chapter 19 for details on shading and texturing surfaces.

4. Go to the top view and create a simple curve near the middle of the wavy plane. Select both objects and create a curve on the surface by selecting Edit Surfaces ➤ Project Curve on Surface, as shown below.

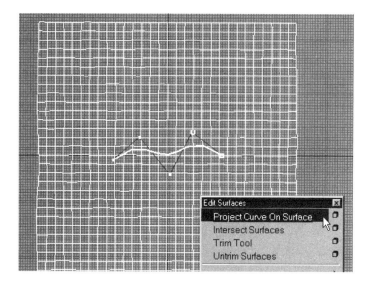

5. Hide the curve (make it invisible). It's better not to delete anything until you are sure you no longer need it; in this case, you may want to adjust the curve on surface later when animating the camera. Import the Chair.mb file into the scene.

6. Set the time slider range to 240 frames. Select the top hierarchy of the chair, then select the curve on surface. Switch to the Animation module and select Animate ➤ Paths ➤ Attach to Path, with the default settings.

7. Open the Attribute Editor and go to the motionPath1 tab. Click Follow and set Up Direction to Normal. Try different settings for Front Axis and Up Axis until the chair is sitting upright. (It should be X for Front Axis and Y for Up Axis, but you may end up with different results.) Your scene should look something like the one shown next.

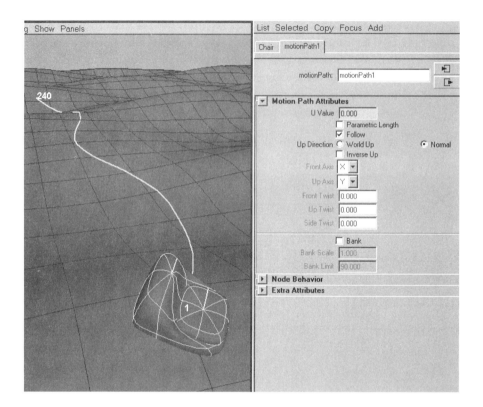

 WARNING   When you're using curves on surface as the path, using the Normal for Up Direction setting works well, because it makes the attached object's Up direction the surface's normal. However, when you're using regular curves as the path, the Normal setting does not work as well, because a curve's normal will reverse if the curve's path goes from convex to concave. The attached object, therefore, may end up flipping as it animates along the curve.

Moving the Chair

The chair is a bit too low in the water, but if you try to move it, it will snap back when you scrub the time slider because it's attached to the path. You can move the node below the top hierarchy to move the chair up, which would actually be the best solution, because the node below the top hierarchy isn't constrained to the path. However, for this tutorial, we will try to move the top node up.

1. Select the top Chair node, and press Insert to show the pivot manipulator. Drag the Y-axis handle down, and you will see the chair go up. This is because the pivot is constrained to the path.

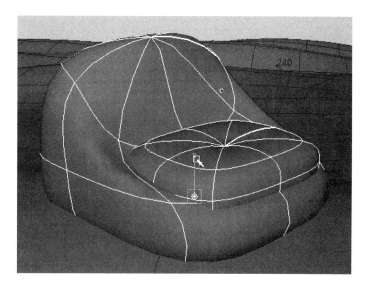

2. Press Insert again to turn off the pivot manipulator. Select the node that is one below the top Chair node and check to make sure its Y rotation value is 0 in the Channel box. Then use Key Select at frame 1. Move to frame 240, enter 360 for Y rotation, and keyframe it.

3. Now as you scrub the animation, the chair should slowly rotate as it floats along the curve on surface. Preview the animation to see how the chair moves.

Animating the Camera

The chair seems to be floating, but the water isn't moving. We can make it seem like it is by animating the camera.

1. In the Perspective window, select Panels ➢ Perspective ➢ New to create the Persp1 view. This will be our animated camera.

2. With the Persp1 camera still selected, zoom in to the curve on the surface and Shift+select it. Select Animate ➢ Paths ➢ Attach to Path ❏. Check Follow, X for Front Axis, Y for Up Axis, and Normal for Up Direction. Click Attach.

3. Switch to perspective view and press F to center in on the Persp1 camera. You should see the camera positioned as on the next page.

PART

3

Animation

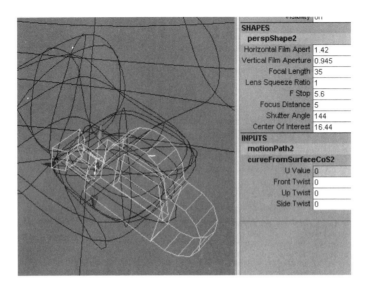

4. As you can see, the camera isn't looking exactly where it should be, and it should also be a bit behind the chair. Click motionPath2 in the Channel box, and you will see the Front Twist, Up Twist, and Side Twist input variables. Select them one at a time and try MM dragging in the modeling window to see what effect each has on the camera.

TIP   If the Twist attributes are grayed out, you probably attached the camera to the curve on surface a bit differently. This isn't a problem. Just select the grayed out areas, RM choose, and select Unlock Selected to unlock the attributes and make them keyable.

5. Return the Front Twist and Side Twist values to 0, and set the Up Twist value to –90. The camera should now be looking along the curve.

6. Select the curve on the surface. In the Channel box, select motionPath1. This is the path animation for the chair. Go to frame 60, then MM drag the current time indicator back to frame 1. Select the U value, which should be at 0.247, and keyframe it. If you scrub the timeline now, the chair should start in front of the camera, as shown in the top picture of the next illustration.

Start at Frame 1

Finish at Frame 240

7. Select motionPath2. This is the path animation for the Persp1 camera. Go to frame 200, then MM drag to frame 240. Select the U value again, which should be at 0.8333, and keyframe it. Now the camera should finish behind the chair at the end of the animation, as shown in the bottom picture above.

8. The only thing that remains for us to do is to adjust the height of the Persp1 camera. It's sitting too low on the surface plane. Go to Four Views layout, and make one window Persp1 camera view and another one the perspective view.

9. Select the Persp1 camera in the perspective view, select the Move tool, and press Insert to display the pivot manipulator. Grab the Y-axis handle and push it down to make the camera move up. You should scrub the timeline back and forth to come up with the ideal height for the camera. You may even want to move the chair farther away from the camera.

10. When you are satisfied with the camera view, use Playblast, as described in the next section, to see how everything looks. Save the scene as Wave.mb. You may want to use it again later to try texturing the water and the sky.

Previewing and Playblasting

When you are previewing an animation, before you click the Play button, you should make the active viewing window as small as you can without losing important details. Select the Four View window setting, then drag the active window to a smaller size. If

PART **3**

Animation

you can see the animation well in wireframe, then by all means, preview it in wireframe. In the Shaded mode, make the NURBS display Rough (Display ➤ NURBS Smoothness), or in the modeling window, select Shading ➤ Flat Shade All. Check whether you can still preview the animation clearly. Press Alt+V to play. Press Alt+V again to stop.

For most of your animation projects, viewing the animation in real-time or near real-time will not be possible with the Play Control buttons because the scene will be too heavy (built with too much geometry) for that. Maya provides a quick way for you to view these scenes as movie clips or picture sequences. Select Window ➤ Playblast ❑, click Reset, adjust your time slider range to about 30 frames for testing purposes, then click Playblast. Maya quickly captures the active window view for the duration of the timeline and makes an .avi movie clip in your C:\Temp directory. This movie clip will be deleted automatically when you exit Maya.

Many of the Playblast options are self-explanatory, but a few are not so straightforward:

- The default compressor for the movie player is the standard Microsoft Video 1, which you can change to suit your computer's own capacity by clicking the Compression button.

- Instead of using the From Window setting for Display Size, you can have a Custom setting set to 320×240 or something similar in ratio, with Scale set to 1.0, to gain more control over the area of your active window that is captured.

- If you check Fcheck, picture sequences are created instead of a movie clip. The Fcheck setting enables you to acquire wireframe renders for your model turnarounds in minutes. You can save the .iff picture sequences into any directory by using the Save to File setting, or convert them to other image formats using Fcheck's Save Animation option.

Making the Camera Move

In this next brief tutorial, we will set up a moving camera attached to a path that can still remain focused on an object. We will continue working with our floating chair.

Animating Waves

Open the scene you've just finished. The surface plane is wavy, but is not moving. Let's create some animated waves on it.

1. Select the plane and choose Deform ➤ Nonlinear ➤ Wave to apply Wave deformation to it (see Chapter 12 for more information about Maya's deformers).

2. Translate the waveHandle node to (–100, 0, 100) and scale it to 300 uniformly.

3. Set the Amplitude wave property to 0.005 and the Wavelength property to 0.1. Leave the other properties at their default values.

4. Keyframe translate X at frame 1. Keyframe again at frame 240 with the X value at –60.

The waves look more realistic now. The surface still needs smaller ripples, but that's a texturing matter (see Chapter 19 for details on texturing techniques).

Adding a Three-Node Camera

Now we can use path animation with a three-node camera to get the proper effect. The default camera Maya creates is a single-node camera, which is what the perspective view is. A two-node camera also has a camera_view node, which determines the camera's center of interest. A three-node camera has an additional camera_up node as well.

1. Create another simple single span curve above the surface to act as the camera path, as shown below. Observe carefully where the CVs are placed in relation to the floating chair. The CVs have been positioned so that the camera will be able to follow the chair from behind and up at an angle.

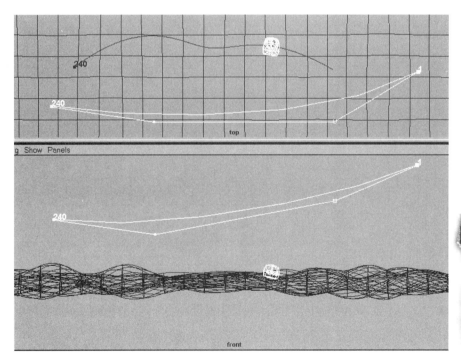

2. Select Create ➤ Camera ❏. At the bottom of the option box, click the Three for Nodes setting. Click Create.

3. Select the camera_group node and then select the curve. Use the Attach to Path function with the Follow and World Up settings checked.

4. Select the chair, then Shift+select the camera_view node, and select Constraint ➤ Point. The camera_view should now be constrained to the chair (constraints are discussed in detail later in this chapter).

5. Scrub through the animation in camera view. You may find that the upper-right edge of the surface plane is visible for a few frames. You can fix this by going into the motionPath2 properties and rotating the Front Twist setting.

6. Use the Playblast function to see how the curve moves. You may need to tweak the curve to make the camera view stay inside the surface plane.

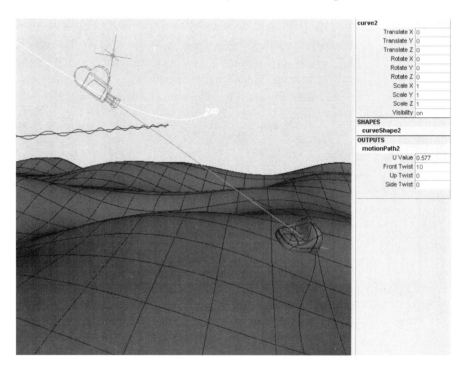

As you've seen in these "floating chair" examples, path animation is relatively easy and can be useful when you want your animation to follow a particular route. Now we will turn to the more complex techniques of skeletons and kinematics.

Skeletons and Kinematics

With skeletons, we are entering the realm of advanced character animation. Using skeletons at a basic level is very easy in Maya, but it can also become very complex.

Skeleton Concepts

As in the song that goes "The knee bone is connected to the hip bone…," everyone knows that bones are connected and that together they make up a skeleton. A skeleton is a protective structure that houses the vital organs of animals, maintains their shape, and enables them to move about. There are no vital organs in a digital character to protect (not yet anyway), but Maya does provide joints, which enable us to animate characters efficiently and maintain or deform their shapes properly.

Skeletons are built with bones and joints. Using the Skeleton ➤ Joint Tool, you click to place joints in the modeling window, much as you would edit points for a curve, and the joints are connected by bones. In building skeletons, it's good to know the kinds of joints you can create:

- A Ball joint can rotate in all three axes, like the neck bone. This is the default Joint tool setting.
- A Universal joint can rotate in two axes, like the wrist bone.
- A Hinge joint can rotate in only one axis, like the knee bone.

PART 3

Animation

It's better to limit the joints you create according to their functions, because it means more efficiency in your animation and fewer calculations for Maya to perform.

Forward Kinematics

Forward Kinematics works well for free rotational motions such as a character's arms swinging when she walks or her spine rotating when she turns. Your main concern with Forward Kinematics is setting up the joints correctly for animation. Let's use the Joint tool to build a human skeleton (a very simple one, of course).

Building a Leg

We will begin by building our skeleton's leg. We need to place leg, knee, and foot joints.

1. Select Skeleton ➤ Joint Tool ❑. Click Reset Tool to set all the options to their defaults, then check Auto Joint Limits.

2. Go to side view and X+click the joints, as shown below. At any time during the creation of these joints, you can MM drag to adjust the position of the last joint you created, or you can use the Up arrow key to go back to other joints as well. (Note that if you go back up a few joints and click with the left mouse button, you will get another bone branching out of the joint.) When you've created all the joints, press Enter to complete the action.

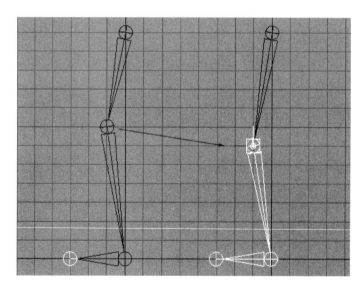

N O T E   You can use the Move tool to move joints you've created. If you select a joint and move it using the Move tool, the joints below its hierarchy will move with it. If you select the Move tool and then press Insert to show the pivot manipulator and move the pivot, only the selected joint will move. You can also use Maya's other tools to edit the joints you've created (or are in the process of creating) to Insert, remove, connect, and disconnect joints, and even to reroot a skeleton. These are all straightforward, easy-to-use functions on the Skeleton menu.

3. Name the joints as Lleg, Lknee, and Lfoot (*L* is for left). We don't need to worry about the last joint in the chain.

4. Go to the perspective view, select the knee joint, and try rotating it. You'll see that you can only rotate it in the Z axis, and that there is a limit to the Z rotation. The Auto Joint Limit setting creates a Hinge joint, which will not rotate past its parent joint or bend away from it more than 180 degrees. It works well here with the knee.

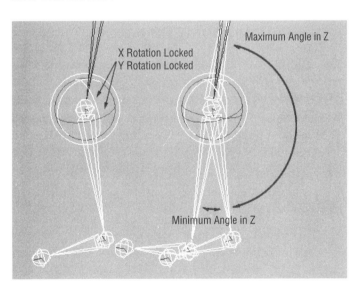

There are a couple of important things to observe here. The bones were *created at an angle*, not in a straight line, because the angles between the bones determine which way the bones will bend. Also, the default joint orientation in Maya is XYZ. This means that when a joint is created, its local X axis points into the bone, the Y axis points toward the bending direction, and the Z axis is perpendicular to the bending direction. You can display a joint's local rotational axes, as shown on the next page, by selecting Display ➤ Object Components ➤ Local Rotation Axes.

PART

3

Animation

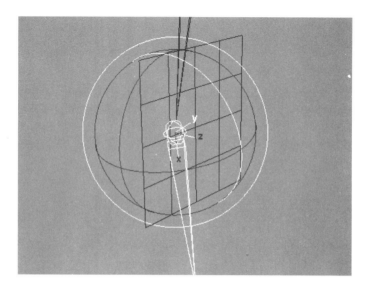

When joints are created with the default setting, Z-axis rotation will always bend the bones, and Y-axis rotation will rotate them from side to side. A corollary of this is that the window in which you decide to build the joints is important. You should figure out how you want the bones to bend, then build them accordingly in the proper window.

Mirroring Joints

Now we can use mirroring to create the other leg. Because joints behave differently from regular object nodes, we need to use the Mirror Joint function to duplicate the right leg symmetrically.

1. Select the foot joint and open the Attribute Editor. The foot, unlike the knee, can rotate in the X axis as well as the Z axis. Under the Joint section, for the Degrees of Freedom setting, click X.

2. Move the leg hierarchy to (2, 0, 0). Then select Skeleton ➤ Mirror Joint ❑, select YZ as the setting, and click Mirror.

N O T E   The rotational limit information should copy into the mirrored joints as well, but you may find that they are not activated. If this happens, go into the Attribute Editor and activate them—the numerical information is already there. If some of the Rotate fields are grayed out but the joint is still rotating, click twice on the Degree of Freedom boxes to activate the lock. Also, if you find that the joints are not being mirrored properly, you can group them under another joint, mirror them, and then ungroup them.

3. Try rotating the left and right knee together. They should be rotating like mirror images of each other, as shown next.

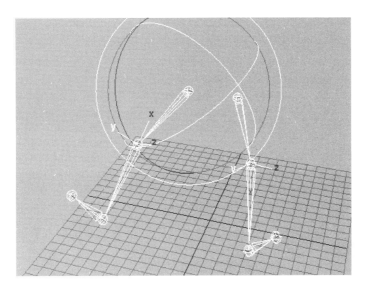

4. Name the mirrored joints as Rleg, Rknee, and Rfoot.

Building the Rest of Human Skeleton

We'll quickly go through the steps for adding the spine and shoulder hierarchy of joints.

1. Go to the side view and create the spine chain with the default Joint Tool option settings, as shown below. The spine joints need to be Ball joints.

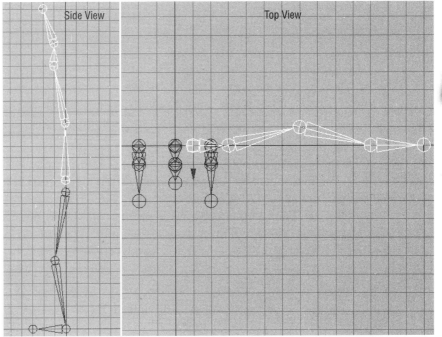

2. From the top view, create the left shoulder chain, as shown above. (Remember that we're creating a very simple skeleton.)

3. Name the spine hierarchy as waist, chest, neck, and head. Name the shoulder hierarchy as Lshoulder, Larm, Lforearm, and Lhand. We don't need to worry about the last joint in the chains.

4. In the front view, translate the shoulder chain up until it's a little below the neck bone.

5. In Hypergraph or the Outliner, group the legs under waist, and the Lshoulder chain under chest. You should see something like the hierarchy and picture shown below.

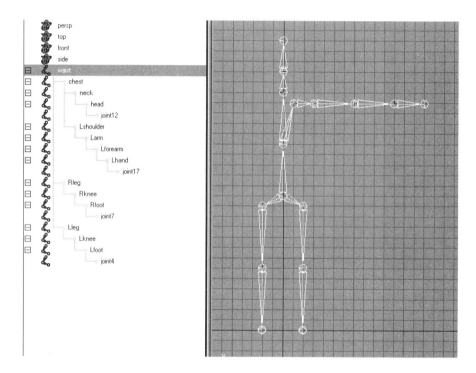

6. To put rotation limits on the shoulder joints, open the Attribute Editor and select the Lshoulder joint. The shoulder does not need to rotate in the X axis, so turn off X in the Degrees of Freedom setting. We want the Larm to rotate like a Ball joint, so don't change its settings. The Lforearm is a Universal joint that cannot rotate in the Y axis, so turn off Y. The Lhand is also a Universal joint that can't rotate in the X axis, so turn off X.

7. For these joints and others, you can also set specific minimum and maximum rotational limits. Let's do this for the Lforearm as an example. Select the Lforearm. In the Attribute Editor, open the Limit Information, Rotate attribute.

You'll see three Rot Limit fields, with Y rotation grayed out. Put checks in the four Rot Limit X and Z boxes, and the Min and Max fields become unlocked.

8. In the top view, try rotating the Lforearm in the Z axis. When it's straight, the current degree reads about –28, so put in –30 for the Min value. When it starts overlapping Larm, the degree is around 137, so put in 130 for the Max value.

9. For the X rotation, let's assume the palm is facing straight down. In this case, Lforearm should be able to rotate about –90 degrees to make the palm face front, and about 45 degrees the other way. Enter those values for the Min and Max fields.

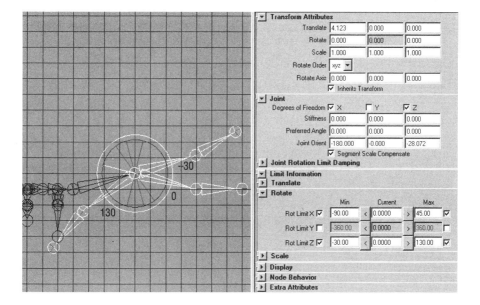

 T I P There are limits for Translate and Scale as well, which you may sometimes want to use. Maya also has Rotation Limit Damping settings, which allow the joints to ease in and ease out of the rotation limits.

10. Select the Lshoulder joint and mirror it. You should now have a complete, albeit very simple, human skeleton.

11. Scale, rotate, and translate the spheres to their positions and group them to their respective joints in the Outliner or Hypergraph. It's not all that important exactly how the spheres are shaped or where they are placed, as long as they roughly represent the body parts being controlled by the individual joints. The final dummy human is shown on the next page. Save this scene as `Dummy_human.mb`. You can try skinning and animating it later.

PART 3

Animation

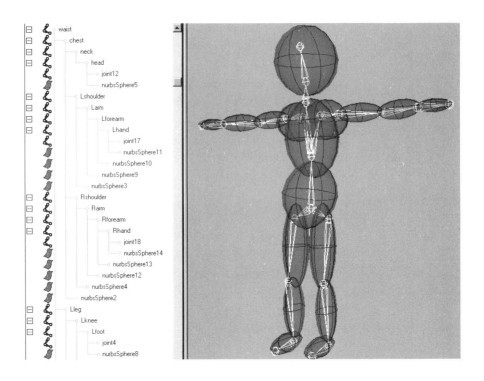

Reorienting Local Axes of Joints

To gain precise control over how the joints rotate, you need to know how to reorient joints. In the skeleton you've just created, let's say you've translated the shoulder joint down one unit using the pivot manipulator. If you display the local rotation axes, you will see that the X axis is no longer pointing directly into the bone's center. It's off about –24 degrees.

To reorient the X axis, select the Rotate tool and switch to the component mode. RM choose the question mark button (Miscellaneous) and check Local Rotation Axes, then select the shoulder joint. You can rotate the Y-axis handle in the front view until you see the X axis pointing directly into the shoulder joint. You can also enter precise rotational values by typing in a MEL command in the Command Line field; for example, type `rotate -r -os 0 -24 0` to relatively rotate the local axes –24 degrees around the Y axis.

For those interested in MEL commands, there is also the `joint -e -oj xyz -zso` command, which reorients the local axes of a joint automatically. But be careful how you use this command, because it may destroy the mirror properties of symmetrical hierarchies.

Animating the Dummy Human

As noted earlier, using Forward Kinematics mainly involves setting up the joints the right way. Now that we've created and grouped the joints and applied the proper limits to them, all we need to do is transform the joints and keyframe them. Work on the top hierarchy first, then move down to the lower joints until you achieve the poses you desire.

Inverse Kinematics

For goal-oriented motions, such as having a character plant her feet on the ground or reach out her hands and open a door, you need to animate using Inverse Kinematics (IK).

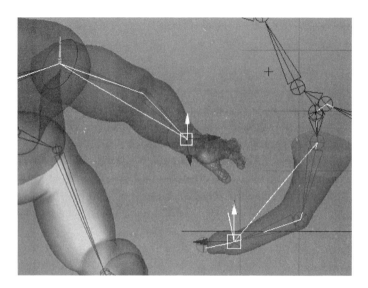

Inverse Kinematics involves *IK handles* and *IK solvers*. An IK handle runs through the joints being affected. The joints being affected are called the *IK chain*, and a handle wire runs through them. A *handle vector* starts from the start joint and finishes at the end joint, where the IK handle's *end effector* is located.

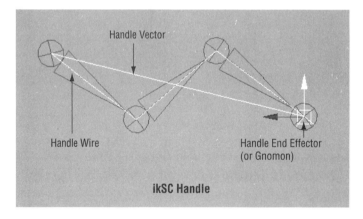

An IK solver looks at the position of the end effector of an IK chain and performs the necessary calculations to make the joints rotate properly, from the start joint to the end joint of the IK chain, in such a way that the end joint will be where the end effector is. When the end effector moves, the IK solver converts the translation values of the end effector to the rotation values for the joints, and the joints update accordingly.

Maya's interface has three kinds of IK solvers: the ikRP (Rotate Plane) solver, the ikSC (Single Chain) solver, and the IK Spline solver. Each type of IK solver has its own type of IK handle.

Using the ikRP Handle

Since the ikRP solver is the default setting for the IK Handle tool, let's see how that works first. In the side view, draw a simple joint chain (as in the inset on the upper left shown below). Select Skeleton ➤ IK Handle Tool ❑, and reset the tool to its default settings. Click on the first joint, then click on the last joint. You should see that an IK handle has been created. The circle at the top looks complicated (as in the inset below), but it's actually a fairly simple setup, once you've learned what its components are.

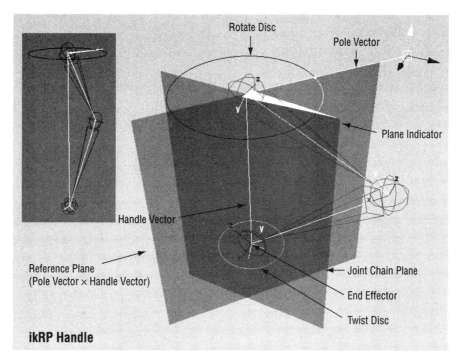

ikRP Handle

The ikRP solver calculates only the positional value of the end effector, which means it ignores the rotational values of the end effector. The joints are rotated by the ikRP solver in such way that their Y axes are planar, their X axes are pointing to the center of the bones, and their Z axes are perpendicular to the bending direction. This is the default local orientation set up for joints. If you do not see the rotate disc, select the end effector and press the T key to display the Show Manipulator tool.

The plane along which the joints are bending is represented by the plane indicator. The plane itself is called the *joint chain plane*. You can rotate this plane about the handle vector using the twist disc, which rotates the IK chain. The Twist degree is measured relative to a reference plane created by the handle vector and the pole vector, which can be translated and keyframed.

WARNING   At times, the way you want the arm to bend will cause the IK chain to flip with the default reference plane setting. To avoid this flipping, adjust or animate the pole vector.

Open the Attribute Editor for the ikRP handle. The Snap, Stickiness, and Solver Enable settings are discussed in the "Switching between Inverse and Forward Kinematics" section, following the discussion of the ikSC handle.

The advantage of using the ikRP handle over the ikSC handle, discussed next, is that you can get more precise control over the rotation of the IK chain. The disadvantage is that it necessarily has more components to deal with.

Using the ikSC Handle

The ikSC handle is simpler than the ikRP handle. To experiment with it, go to the side view and draw another simple joint chain. Select Skeleton ➤ IK Handle Tool ❏ as before, but this time, select the ikSC solver setting, then close the option box. Click on the first joint, then click on the last joint, and you will see the ikSC handle.

If you press T to display the Show Manipulator tool, you will see nothing, because there are no extra manipulators for the ikSC handle— everything is controlled by the end effector.

Select Rotate and try rotating the end effector. You will notice that only the local X and Y rotate handles seem to have any effect, and that they snap back to certain angles after you release the handles. The ikSC solver calculates the rotational values of the end effector and rotates the IK chain in such way that all the joints in the chain will have the default local orientation for joints. The joint chain plane exists in the ikSC solver, although you do not see any representation of it in the handle.

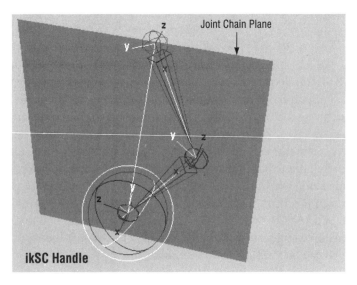

Open the Attribute Editor for the ikSC handle. The ikSC handles can have a Priority assignment when there are two or more chains overlapping. The handle with the Priority 1 setting will rotate the joints in its chain first, next the handle with the Priority 2 setting will rotate its joints, and so on. The Po Weight setting determines the handle's position/orientation weight. If the weight is 1, then the end effector will try to reach only the handle's position; if the weight is 0, the end effector will try to reach only the handle's orientation. You should leave this setting at the default value of 1. The Snap, Stickiness, and Solver Enable settings are discussed in the next section.

The advantage of using the ikSC handle is that you only need to use the end effector to control the IK chain. For situations where you do not need a great amount of IK chain rotations, this would be the more economical method of animating.

T I P   When you are using the ikSC handle to rotate IK chains, use the Graph Editor to interactively adjust the rotational values. It produces most predictable results. See Chapter 10 for more information about the Graph Editor.

Switching between Inverse and Forward Kinematics

Maya allows you to switch back and forth between using ikRP or ikSC handles and rotating joints (forward kinetics). It's easy to do, and you may find it useful. Let's go through the technique using the ikSC handle we created in the previous section.

1. Go to frame 1 and turn on Auto Key. Without this setting, the process becomes cumbersome.

2. Keyframe the end effector, move to frame 10, and translate the end effector. You should have another keyframe automatically set.

3. In the Attribute Editor, turn off Solver Enable to locally turn off the ikSC solver for this handle.

4. Select the two joints in the IK chain and keyframe them. Go to frame 20 and rotate the joints. Go to frame 30 and repeat the action.

5. Select the ikSC handle again. In the Attribute Editor, turn on Solver Enable to turn on the ikSC solver. You will find that the end effector acquired the keyframes for frame 20 and 30 in the same positions where the joints were keyframed.

In order for this switch to be possible, you need to have the end effector's Snap setting on and Stickiness off in the Attribute Editor. If Snap is off or Stickiness is on, then the end effector will not snap to the end joint when the joints are rotated.

PART **3**

Animation

One more thing to be aware of in switching back and forth between inverse and forward kinetics is that the movements generated by the rotation of the joints and the corresponding keyframes of the end effector will not always match. They will roughly be the same, but you may need to tweak the end effector's animation.

Using the IK Spline Handle

While the ikRP and ikSC handles are similar in their attributes, the IK Spline handle is quite different in the way that it functions. The IK Spline solver takes a NURBS curve as part of its handle and rotates the IK chain to follow the shape of the curve. The CVs of the NURBS curve, rather than the end effector of the handle, are animated. The IK Spline handle is ideal for animating curvy or twisty shapes, such as tails, spines, snakes, or tentacles. Let's try out this last type of IK handle.

1. In the side view, build a joint chain, as shown below. For IK Spline handles, the joints need not be built at an angle, but the bones should be short to ensure the chain will move smoothly.

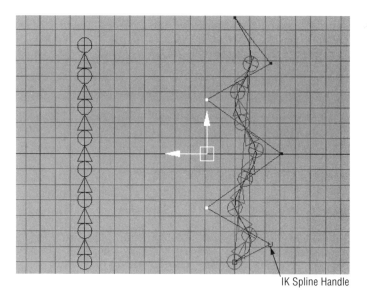

IK Spline Handle

2. Select Skeleton ➤ IK Spline Handle Tool ❑ and check Number of Spans 4. Leave the other options set to their defaults and close the option box.

3. Click on the top joint, then click on the last joint, and you will see the IK Spline handle.

4. In the Outliner, select the joint chain or the IK handle and try moving the joints. The joints have become attached to the curve, and the IK handle doesn't show a manipulator.

5. Display the CVs and move them around, as shown below.

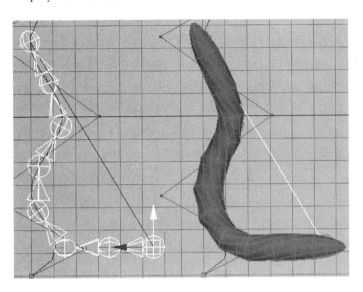

N O T E   You can also create your own NURBS curve and have the IK Spline handle use that curve. Turn off the Auto Create Curve setting in the IK Spline Handle option box. Click on the root joint, the end joint, and then the curve to create the IK Spline handle.

6. Open the Attribute Editor for the IK handle. You'll see the regular attributes and some specifically for the IK Spline handle. Try typing in numbers for the Offset, Roll, and Twist settings.

Offset translates the joint chain along the curve, with 0.0 as the start of the curve and 1.0 as its end. Roll rotates the whole joint chain. Twist gradually twists the chain from the second joint on. If the Root Twist Mode is turned on, then the twist begins from the root joint. The Root on Curve setting constrains the root joint to the start of the curve. Turn it off, and you can move the root joint off the curve, but note that it is still constrained to the curve.

As we have seen, skeletons can be moved and rotated with Forward Kinematics or Inverse Kinematics to animate various parts of a character. In addition to the IK tools, Maya provides the Constrain menu in the Animation module. The functions in this menu are often used in conjunction with the IK tools to set up a character for animation.

PART **3**

Animation

Constraints

Objects in real life are "constrained" in many different ways. For example, if you are holding a baseball, when your hand moves and rotates, the ball moves and rotates with it, because the ball is constrained by your hand movements. As another example, consider a tennis player, whose eyes are always looking at the tennis ball. If you wanted to imitate these actions in Maya, it would be difficult and time-consuming to try to reproduce the motions of the baseball or the eyes by keyframing them. Instead, you can use constraints to automate such animation tasks.

Let's briefly go over the constraints in Maya. Under the Constrain menu, Maya has the standard Point, Aim, Orient, and Scale constraints. In addition, it also has Geometry, Normal, Tangent, and Pole Vector constraints. All the constraints work in the same way. You select two or more objects, then select the constraints you want to apply. The first objects you select act as the targets that constrain, and the last one is the object being constrained. When you select more than one constraint target, the constrained object is shared between the targets according to their weights.

Point Constraint

The Point constraint makes the center of the constrained object stick to the center of the target object. When there is more than one target, the Point constraint places the object being constrained at a point between the targets' pivot points, with the placement determined by the average value of the weights of the targets.

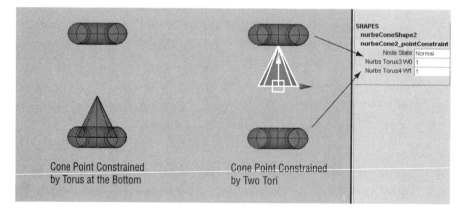

Cone Point Constrained by Torus at the Bottom

Cone Point Constrained by Two Tori

T I P   Maya also has a Point on Curve Locator constraint (Deform ≻ Point on Curve Locator), which creates a locator at a selected point on curve or an edit point. This constraint makes the locator position constrain the curve at that point, without breaking the curve's tangency.

Aim, Orient, and Scale Constraints

The difference between the Aim and the Orient constraints can be a bit confusing. The Aim constraint creates an Aim vector (the default setting is the X axis of the object), which points the object being constrained to the *position* of the Aim target, as shown below. In the example on the right, with two tori, notice the tilt toward the torus on the right. This is because that torus's weight input is 1, while the other torus's weight input is 0.7.

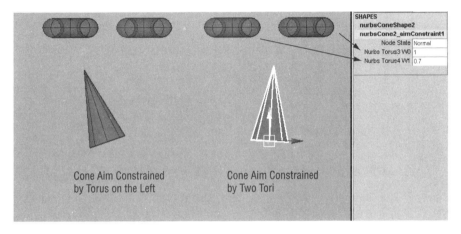

The Orient constraint causes the rotation values of the object being constrained to be the same as the *rotation* of the Orient target. In the example on the right below, the cone has the average rotation value of the tori.

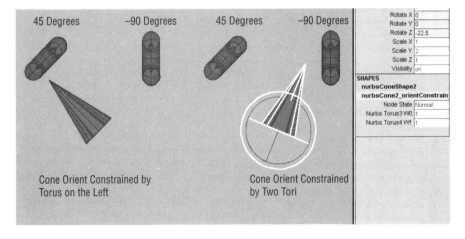

Aim constraints are especially useful for quickly making a character look at, or focus on, different objects. Orient constraints are great for controlling joints.

The Scale constraint functions the same way as the Orient constraint. The object being Scale constrained has the same scale values as the target object, or the average scale values of the target objects.

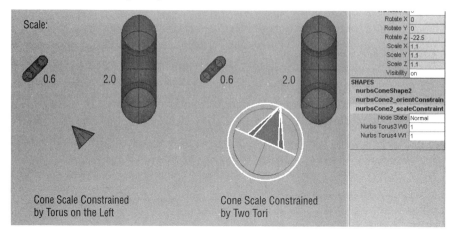

Cone Scale Constrained
by Torus on the Left

Cone Scale Constrained
by Two Tori

Geometry and Normal Constraints

The Geometry constraint makes the center of the constrained object stay on the surface of the target object. It doesn't lock the attributes of the constrained object, allowing it to slide along the target surface.

The Normal constraint acts much like the Aim constraint. The difference is that the aim vector of the object being constrained aligns itself with the normal vector of the surface that passes through the constrained object's center.

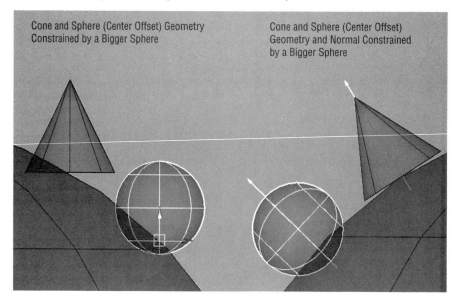

Cone and Sphere (Center Offset) Geometry
Constrained by a Bigger Sphere

Cone and Sphere (Center Offset)
Geometry and Normal Constrained
by a Bigger Sphere

Tangent and Pole Vector Constraints

The Tangent constraint aligns an object's aim vector to the tangency of the target curve, and works in much the same way as the Aim constraint and the Normal constraint.

The Pole Vector constraint is a Point constraint specifically designed to constrain the Pole Vector of an ikRP handle (discussed earlier in this chapter).

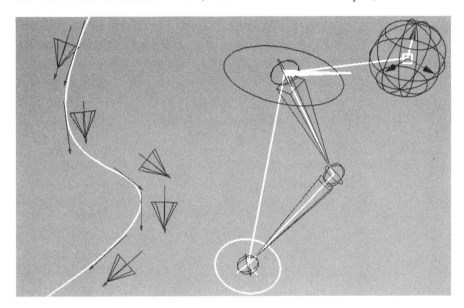

Hands-on Maya: Setting Up the Puppy for Animation

Before we finish this chapter, let's build the skeleton for the dog that we created in Chapter 8. We'll also put some IK handles and constraints on it, and organize the hierarchy to get it ready for animation.

Creating the Skeleton

We'll begin by using the Skeleton ➣ Joint Tool to give the puppy bones and joints.

1. Bring in the file dog_final_model.mb, the final global stitched model of the dog.

2. In the side view, draw the backbone as shown below, starting from the hip area and finishing at the nose. Draw the tail. Draw the front leg and the back leg

with Auto Joint Limits turned on. Note where the wrist is—that is where the IK end effector will be placed.

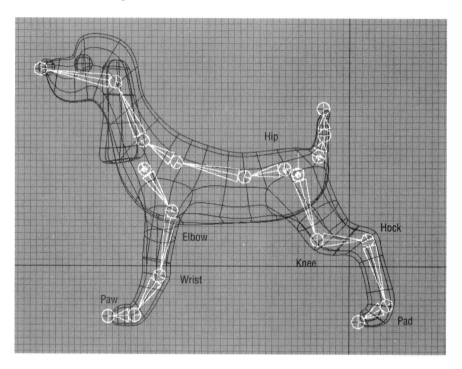

3. To make the back leg the proper shape, increase the grid division and use X+click. This is important because we will be using IK with the three joints of the leg. If the bones are not built symmetrically as in the picture below, they will not bend the way we want them to.

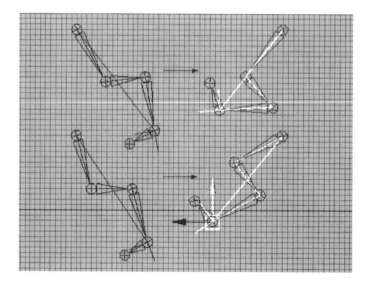

4. Name the joints. The backbone chain should be hip, back, chest, neck, and head. The tailbone chain should be tail1 and tail2. The front leg chain should be named Larm, Lelbow, Lwrist, and Lpaw. Finally, the back leg chain should be Lleg, Lknee, Lhock, and Lpad.

Adding IK Handles

Now we're ready to apply inverse kinetics to the puppy, using the Skeleton ➤ IK Handle Tool.

1. In the perspective view, move the leg joints to the left side so that they are placed properly as shown below. Put ikSC handles on them to test how they bend. For the back leg, try to keep the three bones that will use IK coplanar. Think also of how the skin is going to stretch with the skeleton as the joints are moving.

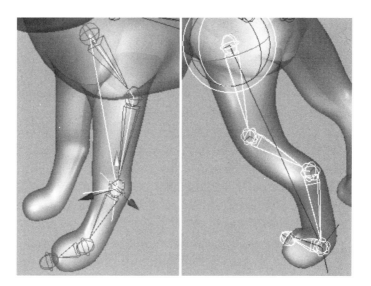

2. Mirror the front and back legs on the YZ axis. The ikSC handles should copy as well. Check to make sure the joint limits are working (see "Mirroring Joints," earlier in this chapter).

PART

3

Animation

3. Group the front legs to chest. Group the back legs and the tail to hip. You should have the joints placed somewhat like below. Name the joints properly, such as Rarm and Relbow. Name the IK handles Lfront, Rfront, Lbackleg, and Rbackleg.

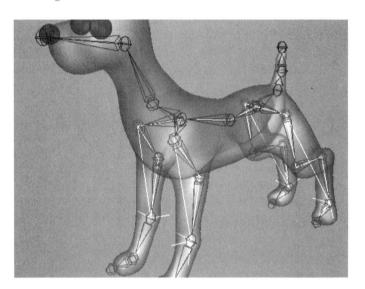

Constraining the Legs

We have a problem with the puppy's front legs. We would like to have the paws planted on the ground when the dog walks, but because the IK chain is to the wrist, the rotation center is the wrist, not the paw. We'll solve this problem by using locators and the Orient constraint. The steps below can be a bit tricky, so follow the instructions carefully.

1. Select Create ➤ Locator and scale it down to 0.5 uniformly. Select Lpaw, then select locator1, and select Constrain ➤ Point. The locator should snap to the Lpaw joint.

2. Select Lwrist (make sure you select this joint and not the Lpaw joint), then locator1, and select Constrain ➤ Orient. The locator should rotate to match the rotation values of Lwrist. Name the locator Lfrontleg.

3. Repeat step 2 for the right side of the leg. Name the locator Rfrontleg. You should see the locators positioned as shown next.

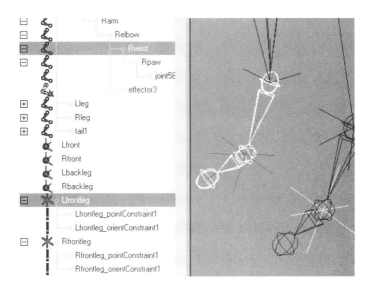

4. Open the Attribute Editor for the Lwrist joint. Click the X and Y Degrees of Freedom settings. They need to be activated before the joint can be constrained. Repeat this process for Rwrist.

5. In the Outliner, delete the constraint nodes under the locators. In the modeling window, select the Lfrontleg locator first, then Lwrist, and select Constrain ➤ Orient. Do the same for Rfrontleg and Rwrist. The rotation attributes of the wrist joints are now constrained to the locators.

6. In the Outliner, group the Lfront ikSC handle to the Lfrontleg locator by MM dragging it to the locator node. Do the same for the Rfront ikSC handle and the Rfrontleg locator. Now if you try moving or rotating the locators Lfrontleg and Rfrontleg, the legs should follow pivoting around the paws.

7. Select the hip joint and group it to itself by selecting Edit ➤ Group with the default setting. This produces a parent node. Name the node Puppy, and group the ikSC handles and the locators under it. The Puppy node is the top node, which will move the whole dog. In the Outliner, you should see a hierarchy like the one shown below. Save the scene as puppy_skeleton.

PART 3

Animation

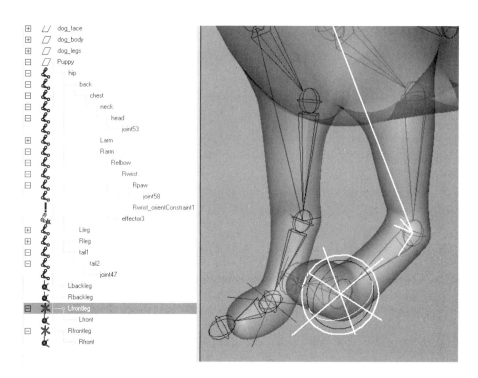

In your own work, it's important to remember that there is no one proper way to build skeletons or place constraints to set up a character for animation. In each case, you need to consider what the character will be doing, how the body should deform, how the limbs should rotate. Different situations call for different solutions. A properly prepared character will move well, have the necessary range of movements, and be easy to animate.

Summary

In this chapter, you learned how to animate objects and cameras along paths, build skeletons properly, and create different kinds of IK handles on joints. You were also introduced to using constraints. Finally, you built a hierarchy of nodes involving joints, IK handles. and constraints to prepare the dog modeled in Chapter 8 for animation.

In the next chapter, we will cover how to bind the dog to the skeleton, weight it properly, and test it for animation.

chapter 12

DEFORMERS

Featuring

- *Lattice deformation*
- *Cluster deformation*
- *Nonlinear deformation*
- *Sculpt deformation*
- *Wire deformation*
- *Blend Shape deformation*
- *General deformation controls*
- *Advanced facial animation techniques*

CHAPTER 12

DEFORMERS

I f the only way to model and animate were by pushing and pulling points, it would make life very difficult for modelers and be the bane of many animators' existence. Thankfully, Maya provides *deformers*, which let you bypass most of the menial work. With Maya's deformers, you can quickly build and animate deformed surfaces with a high level of control.

In this chapter, we will go through several deformers that are indispensable for modeling and animating in Maya. We will also focus on facial animation, including an in-depth discussion of advanced facial animation techniques at the end of the chapter.

Creating Deformers

Maya provides many types of deformers, which work in different ways. All of the deformers can deform anything with control points, including CVs on curves and surfaces, vertices on polygons, and lattice points. Many deformers can also deform multiple surfaces, maintaining their tangency during the deformation process.

All deformers also work as sets, called *deformation sets*. You can edit the points being influenced by a deformation by changing their membership in the set using the Relationship Editor, the Edit Membership tool, or the Paint Set Membership tool (discussed later in the chapter, in the "Editing Deformations" section).

All the deformers and editing tools we will be covering in this chapter can be found on the Deform menu in the Animation module.

Using Lattice Deformation

Lattice is one of the most frequently used deformers. When you apply Lattice to an object, Maya creates an influence lattice and a base lattice around the object. When you transform the influence lattice, or its points, the object inside the lattice transforms with it, or gets deformed by it, according to the degree of difference between the influence lattice and the base lattice.

Lattice allows you to control the deformation of complicated objects with fewer control points than you would need if you were deforming the objects directly. Because of this, the deformation is easier to create and the results are smoother.

Creating Lattices

You can apply Lattice to a group of objects, only some points of an object, or points of a group of objects. You can even apply Lattice to points of a lattice, as shown below on the right. In the examples below, the lattice on the left is made up of points from four objects. The shape in the middle is two tori, with the top torus latticed at the object level and the bottom torus latticed at its two top rows of CVs.

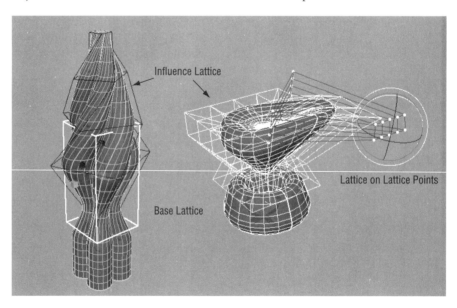

To apply Lattice, simply select the points or object(s) you want deformed, then select Deform ➤ Create Lattice. You see the influence lattice. The base lattice has also been created, but it is hidden.

If you are animating the object being deformed, you want the lattice to translate with the object. For this type of translation, group the lattice and its base lattice under the deformed object. Grouping is available as an option setting when you are creating the lattice, or you can do it after you create the lattice.

Lattice has its own local space, which parallels the XYZ coordinate system, called STU space. When you create or edit a lattice, you can adjust the STU divisions of the lattice, giving it more or fewer lattice points than the default setting.

NOTE Lattice also can be used for skinning, which we will do with the puppy in the next chapter. Skinning an object indirectly with Lattice can be a great way to animate because Maya's lattice is so efficient, but sometimes you may run into a situation where an object is being transformed twice from the lattice and skinning. See the discussion of the Relationship Editor later in this chapter for an example of how to deal with double transformation problems.

Another way to adjust a lattice is through the Local Divisions setting, which is activated with Local Mode. When Local Mode is turned on, each point exerts influence according to the Local Divisions setting, as shown below. The default is 2, 2, 2, which means each point exerts influence up to two points away in STU space. When Local Mode is turned off, each point in the lattice exerts influence on the whole area. You usually want to leave Local Mode turned on.

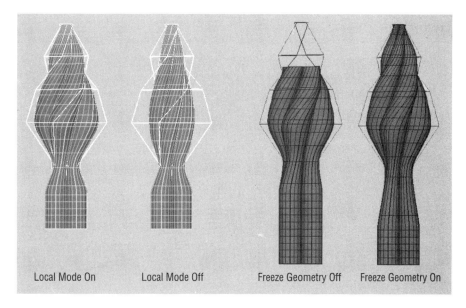

Local Mode On   Local Mode Off   Freeze Geometry Off   Freeze Geometry On

The Freeze Geometry setting locks the object where it is being influenced. With this setting, when the object transforms, the deformed part of it stays fixed, as shown above. You can activate Freeze Geometry in the Attribute Editor after lattice creation. You can also move the deformed object partially first, then turn on Freeze Geometry, and the object will lock where it is.

Tweaking Lattices

To tweak a lattice, pick-mask Lattice Point over it, and you can manipulate its points in the same way as regular CVs.

You can also manipulate the lattice to fit around an object better by transforming both the influence lattice and the base lattice. You can select the hidden base lattice in the Outliner. As long as the two lattices are being transformed together, no deformation occurs. When you are doing this, make sure that all the control points of the object being deformed remain inside the lattice, or they will not deform with the lattice.

 TIP   The lattice is created to fit an object's bounding box. If you find that some points are not deforming along with the lattice, try scaling up the lattice and the base lattice a bit to make sure no points will stray outside the deformation.

If you've been tweaking the lattice points and you decide to start over from the original shape or to add more STU subdivisions, select Edit Lattice ➢ Remove Lattice Tweaks. If you want to undo the transformations you've applied to the lattice at the object level as well, select Edit Lattice ➢ Reset Lattice.

Cluster Deformation

Unlike the other deformers, Cluster produces a weighted deformation. When you apply cluster to an object, it creates weighted points in the cluster set. This is probably the most useful thing about using clusters.

The default weight of the clustered points is 1.0, but you can adjust their weights by using the Component Editor or the Paint Weights tool (Artisan). Let's try a simple exercise to see how to create clusters and adjust their weights:

1. Create a plane. Set it to span 10 patches in U and V.

2. Drag to select 25 CVs at the center of the plane. Select Deform ➢ Create Cluster and accept the default settings.

3. A cluster handle appears as the small letter *c*. Select the Move tool and pull the *c* up. You should see something like the picture shown on the left.

4. Select the surface, and start the Paint Weights tool (from the Deform menu). Apply a bit of smoothing with low settings around the edges of the clustered

points. You should be able to get a more rounded shape, as in the picture on the right. (See Chapter 9 for more information about using Artisan.)

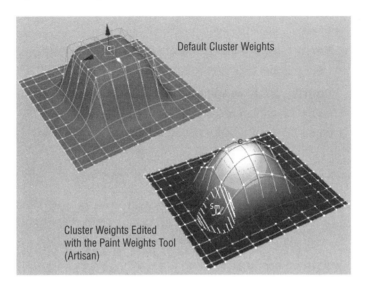

5. Select the clustered points and choose Window ➣ General Editors ➣ Component Editor. Click the Weighted Deformers tab. Here, you can type in lower weight values to round the cluster edges.

In general, when you want to have precise control over the percentage of the weighted points and the points are easy to pick in groups, the Component Editor is a good tool to use. When you want a more organic look, or if the surface is very dense, the Paint Weights tool (Artisan) is more efficient.

T I P When you are working with clusters, the cluster handle *c* has a default Select Priority Level of 2, which means that it is selected along with the surface it's deforming. You can open the General Preferences dialog box and change the Select Priority Level for the cluster handle, or you can open the Attribute Editor and check Display Handle in the Cluster Handle Display section. A handle with the highest Select Priority Level will appear, which will allow you to select only the cluster.

When you move an object that is clustered, you would expect the cluster handle to move with the object, but it doesn't. If you want the cluster to stay on the surface as it moves, group it under the object. First, open the Attribute Editor, click the Cluster tab, and make sure the Relative setting is on for Cluster Attributes. Next, if the object is at the origin, you can simply group the cluster under the object in the Outliner or Hypergraph. If not, group the cluster to itself once to move the center to the origin, then group that node under the object. (Edit ➣ Parent will produce the same result.)

PART 3

Animation

Nonlinear Deformations

The six deformers in the Nonlinear submenu all deform in, yes, nonlinear fashion:

Bend   Bends an object along a circular arc.

Flare   Flares out and tapers off an object.

Sine   Curves an object into sine waves.

Squash   Stretches and squashes an object.

Twist   Twists an object.

Wave   Creates circular ripples on an object.

These are all simple functions, but they are remarkably effective in creating their intended results, as illustrated below.

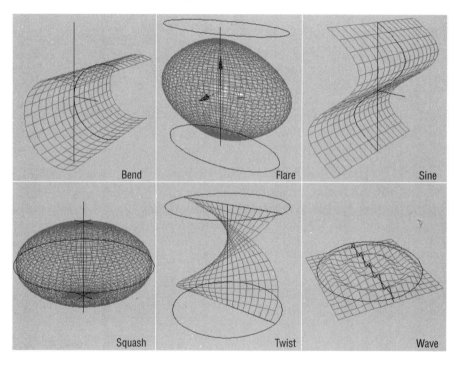

Each of the nonlinear functions can deform just the selected points of objects, just like lattices or clusters. They can also deform multiple objects and maintain tangency between patches. The deformations start and finish along an axis line, by default, the –1 and 1 of the local Y axis of the object being deformed. You can use the manipulator handles to interactively adjust the deformation attributes (select the deformer in the Channel box Input section to display the Show Manipulator option).

You can combine any number of deformers. It's easy to create complex shapes by manipulating the deformer attributes of the different deformers. Note that when you use multiple deformers, their order of creation is important (see the "Changing the Deformation Order" section later in this chapter). You can animate the deformers, and you can also animate the deformed objects.

Let's try some examples with the nonlinear deformers. First, we'll use Bend and Sine to twist an object.

1. Create a plane. Increase its subdivisions.

2. Apply Bend to it (select Deform ≻ Nonlinear ≻ Bend), with Curvature set to 3. Then rotate the plane about 15 degrees in the X axis. The plane twists.

3. Add Sine to it (select Deform ≻ Nonlinear ≻ Sine), with Amplitude set to 0.5. Transform the plane back and forth in Z. The twisting now seems more random.

4. Group the deformers and the plane. Now you can transform the deformers and the plane together as well.

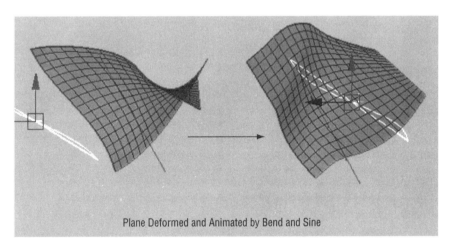

Plane Deformed and Animated by Bend and Sine

You can quickly create a rough jet engine by applying Wave to a sphere (as in the inset picture after the following exercise; notice the dots for manipulator handle settings). You can also try creating something as organic as a tree, as follows.

1. Create a cylinder. Increase its sections and spans, and scale it up in Y into a pillar shape.

2. Apply Flare to it. Flare out the bottom and taper the top.

3. Apply Sine to the object. Make the cylinder form about two waves.

4. Apply Sine again with a different wave length and rotate it to make the cylinder wave more randomly.

Animation

5. Apply Wave, setting the Amplitude and Wave Length to about 0.1. Rotate the wave until the cylinder becomes gnarled like a tree, as shown below.

6. Copy and scale the cylinder to make smaller branches.

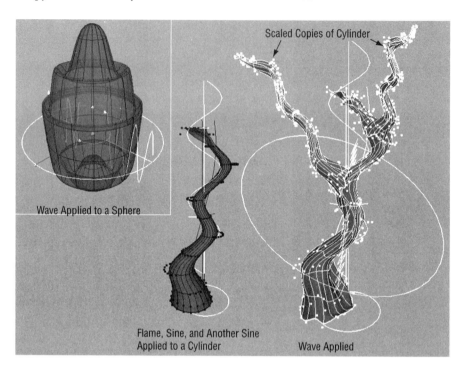

Wave Applied to a Sphere

Scaled Copies of Cylinder

Flame, Sine, and Another Sine
Applied to a Cylinder

Wave Applied

Sculpt Deformation

Sculpt deformation uses a sphere as a sculpting tool to make round or flat ring-shaped deformations. It can deform objects in three different modes: Flip, Project, and Stretch.

N O T E   The Max Displacement and Dropoff Distance settings may seem similar, but they're not. The Max Displacement value determines the amount of strength with which the sphere can push or pull a deforming point. The Dropoff Distance setting determines the area of points that can be influenced.

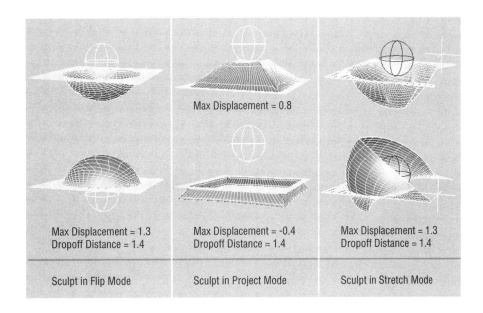

Max Displacement = 0.8

Max Displacement = 1.3
Dropoff Distance = 1.4

Max Displacement = -0.4
Dropoff Distance = 1.4

Max Displacement = 1.3
Dropoff Distance = 1.4

Sculpt in Flip Mode

Sculpt in Project Mode

Sculpt in Stretch Mode

Using Sculpt in Flip Mode

When Sculpt is in Flip mode, the sphere acts as if it has a force field, pushing points away from its center in the direction of the sphere's normal vector. If the sphere's center crosses a point, there is a "flip," because the point being pushed is suddenly pushed in the opposite direction.

Using Sculpt in Project Mode

The Project mode is the opposite of the Flip mode. In Project mode, the sphere acts as a magnet, causing the influenced points to snap to it. A Max Displacement value of 1 causes the points to snap to the sphere's surface; values between 0 and 1 cause the points to travel a percentage between their original position and the sphere's surface. Note that the deformation shapes produced by Flip and Project are quite different.

Using Sculpt in Stretch Mode

In Stretch mode, the sphere calculates its position relative to a Sculpt stretch origin locator, which is created with the sphere and stretches the affected points away from the locator. With the Stretch mode, you can group the stretch origin locator and the

PART 3

Animation

sphere and animate them together, as in the example shown. You can also change the Inside Mode setting to Ring or Even, as shown on the top right.

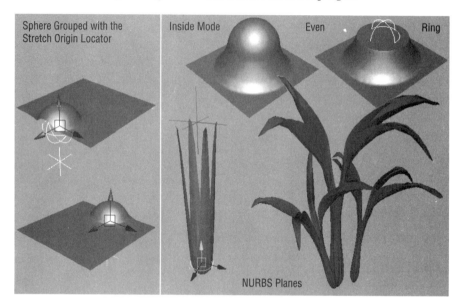

As with the Nonlinear deformers, Sculpt can be used in many creative ways. Just by sculpting a NURBS plane, you can easily fashion plant leaves, as shown on the right. Once you've stretched the plane, scale out the CVs at the top, tighten the CVs in the middle, and tweak the CVs a bit to make the leaves asymmetrical.

Wire Deformation

Wire deformation works with an influence wire and a base wire, somewhat like Lattice deformation. The deformation occurs according to the relative distance between the two wires. Wire deformation is most useful for creating facial expressions, as you will soon see.

Applying Wire Deformation

First, let's try out Wire deformation with a simple shape.

1. Create a NURBS plane. Scale it out to 3, and make its patches U and V 16.

2. Place a circle on the plane, and draw a curve with one span inside, as shown below on the left.

3. Select Deform ➤ Wire Tool and accept the default settings. Maya asks you to select shape(s) to deform. Select the plane and press Enter. Maya then asks you to select wire curve(s). Select the curve inside the circle and press Enter. If the deformer has successfully been created, the plane should turn pink.

4. The curve is now called a *wire*. Note that a hidden duplicate of the wire, called the base wire, has been created as well. Translate up the wire as shown below on the right. Then try moving up the base wire. As the distance between the two curves decreases, so does the intensity of the Wire deformation.

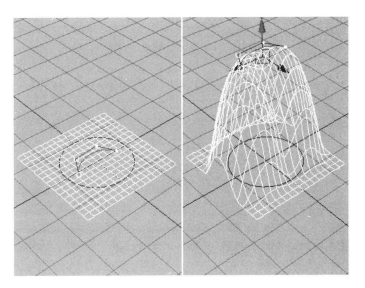

5. Place the wires to their original position, select the plane, and delete history. The Wire deformer node disappears, but the base wire remains.

Using Holders

Let's repeat the process, but this time, we'll use the Holders option. Holders generally function to restrict Wire deformation by limiting the influence of the wires.

1. Select Deform ➤ Wire Tool ❑ and click Holders. As before, select the plane and press Enter. Then select the curve and press Enter.

2. Maya asks you to select a holder shape or clear selection. Select the circle and press Enter. Maya now asks you to either select another wire (for more influence wires) or clear the selection. Clear the selection by deselecting all objects and press Enter to complete the wire creation. Notice that another invisible base wire is created.

PART

3

Animation

3. Try moving the wire again and note the difference. In the following example, on the left, the wire influence is overshooting the circle holder area.

4. In the Channel box, select wire1 under Outputs and decrease the Dropoff Distance setting to 0.3. The wire influence is now restricted inside the circle holder, as shown in the middle picture below. Try moving the circle up to see the difference between having a holder and not having one.

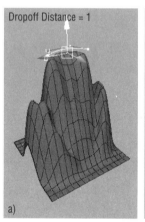
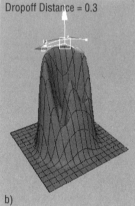
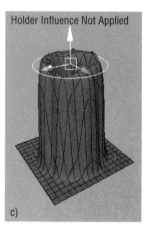

T I P   Group all the wires—the influence wire, the base wire, and the holder wire—under the object being deformed so that they will move with the object.

Using Dropoff Locators

Wire deformers have an additional control tool called Dropoff Locators, which can give you very subtle localized control over the Wire deformation. Let's continue with our plane example to see how this tool works.

1. Move the wire down nearer to the plane surface. RM choose over the wire and pick-mask Curve Point.

2. Select a point near the second CV, then Shift+select another point near the third CV.

3. Select Deform ➤ Wire Dropoff Locator with the default settings, and you should see something like the next top-left picture.

4. Open the wire's Attribute Editor. There is now a Locators section, where you'll find sliders to control the locators' positions, their influence percentages, and their twist. The Twist setting simply twists the deformed points around the curve at the locator point.

5. Change the Locators settings as follows: Percent[1] to 2, Twist[1] to 163, Percent[2] to 2.5, and Twist[2] to 140. You should see something like the bottom-left picture in the following example.

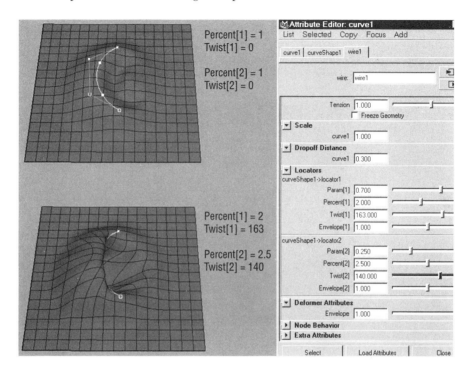

Controlling Deformer Effects with Envelopes

For all the deformers, there is a general attribute channel called the Envelope. Some deformers such as Blend Shape and Cluster actually have it as part of their option box. On all deformers, it can be accessed through the Attribute Editor, under the Deformer Attributes tab, or through the Channel box Inputs section.

The default value is always 1, but you can change it from –2 to 2. When the value is at 0, the deformer has no effect. At –1, the deformer produces the opposite effect. At 2, the deformer's effect is doubled. Such capacity is especially useful for Blend Shape, because its default sliders in the Attribute Editor or the Blend Shape Editor go from 0 to 1 only. When you increase the Envelope value to 2, the sliders' range essentially increases from 0 to 2.

PART 3

Animation

Forming Facial Expressions

Now that we've experimented with a basic shape, let's look at how Wire deformation works on a face.

1. Open the file `Child_face.mb` from the CD, or if you created one yourself in Chapter 6, open that file. Pick-mask over the mouth patch and select the edge isoparm, the isoparm at the nose tip, and the one around the lip area, as shown below.

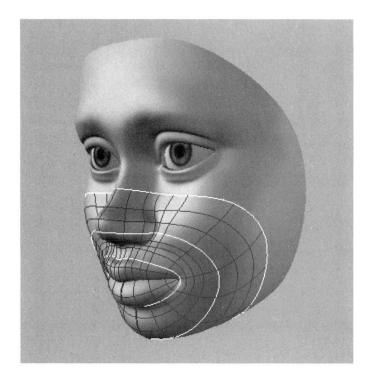

2. In the Modeling module, select Edit Curves ➤ Duplicate Surface Curves. With the curves still selected, choose Edit Curves ➤ Rebuild Curve ❑, set the Number of Spans to 16, and click Rebuild.

3. The curve near the nose tip will be a holder, and the other two will be wires. Delete history from the curves.

4. Switch to the Animation module, and select Deform ➤ Wire Tool ❑ and click Holders. Select the four patches of the face and press Enter. Select the curve at the mouth patch edge for wire, and press Enter again. Select the curve near the nose as holder and press Enter. Clear the selection and press Enter again to complete the wire creation.

5. Repeat the process for the third curve, using the middle curve as a holder curve again. This time, you only need to select the mouth patch as the object to be deformed.

6. Try moving around a few wire CVs. You'll find that you probably need to lower the Dropoff Distance for the curves. Once the settings are done, it's quite easy to create subtle expressions by pulling the wire CVs. You can proceed to animate the CVs, as well as the curves. You would also want to add at least one more wire to control the eyebrows (as shown below), and group the wires (including the base wires) to the head.

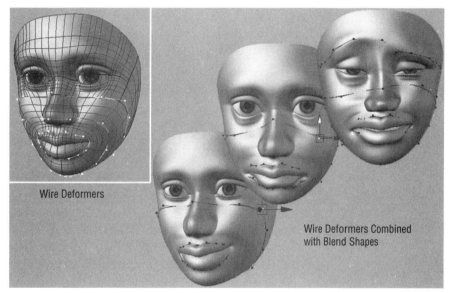

Wire Deformers

Wire Deformers Combined with Blend Shapes

Blend Shape Deformation

Blend Shape is different from other deformers. It is specifically designed to perform morphing tasks, and it has a separate slider editor. You can also access those sliders in the Attribute Editor, or through the channels in the Channel box.

Blend Shape is especially useful for facial animation. In this type of animation, a group of set shapes such as certain phonemes or facial expressions need to be readily accessible, editable, and, as the name suggests, blendable.

Applying Blend Shape Deformation

Blending works best when the *target object* and the *base object* have the same *topology*, meaning they have the same number of CVs and their order is the same. Although

Maya allows you to blend objects with different topology, you may not always get the results you want.

To see what we mean, let's go through some examples.

1. Create two spheres. Change the first sphere's shape by pulling points, as in (a) in the following example.

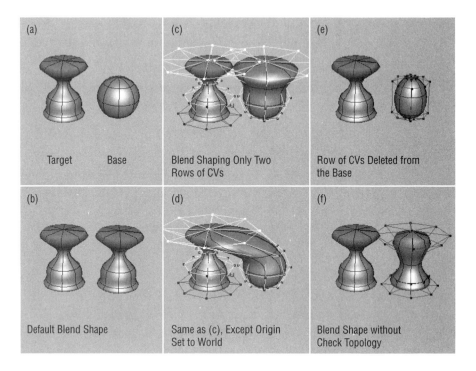

(a) Target   Base

(c) Blend Shaping Only Two Rows of CVs

(e) Row of CVs Deleted from the Base

(b) Default Blend Shape

(d) Same as (c), Except Origin Set to World

(f) Blend Shape without Check Topology

2. Select the first sphere, which will be the target, then Shift+select the second, which will become the base. Then select Deform ➣ Create Blend Shape and accept the default settings.

3. Select Window ➣ Animation Editors ➣ Blend Shape. An editor opens with a target slider. A blendShape node is created, and the target slider is an attribute of that node. Slide it to 1, and the second sphere should morph into an exact replica of the first sphere, as in (b).

4. You can also Blend Shape points. Select the first two rows of the first sphere (target) and the same for the second (base), then apply Blend Shape. You get something like (c).

5. Notice that there is now another slider in the editor. Repeat step 4, but set the Origin setting to World in the option box. The blending calculates not only the

relative translation of the target points, but their world space coordinates as well, as in (d). The morphing points of the base object translate exactly to where the target points are, no matter how the base object is transformed.

6. Select the middle CVs of the second sphere and delete them, as in (e). The topology of the second sphere has changed; it now has eight fewer CVs than the first sphere.

7. Apply Blend Shape to the spheres again, Maya replies with the message, "Error: No deformable objects selected." This is because the default Blend Shape setting checks to make sure the topology of the target object matches that of the base object's. Turn off the Check Topology setting in the option box. Maya proceeds to morph the base object the best it can. The result is as shown in (f).

Blend-Shaping Hierarchies and Adding Shapes

When you are morphing a group of objects, you must make sure that the hierarchy of the target objects is the same as the base objects' hierarchy, or the morphing will not work properly.

In the picture shown below, the head on the left is the base, and the one on the right is the target. Notice that the hierarchies in the Outliner are all in the same order. Selecting the top Smile node, then the top Face node, and then applying the default Blend Shape produces a slider named Smile.

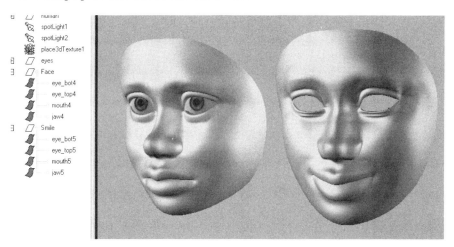

To add more shapes, simply create more shapes, select them, select the base object, and apply Edit Blend Shape ➤ Add. If you get an error message saying you must specify a blendShape node, click Add in the option box, check Specify Node, and enter the name of the existing blendShape node, which should be something like blendShape1. Some examples of shapes are shown below.

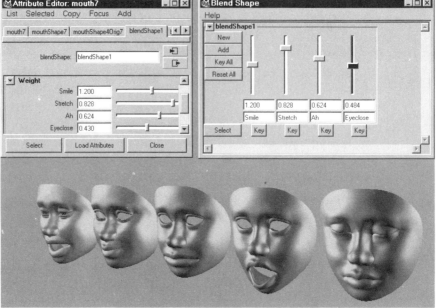

You also can edit the target values in the Channel box or in the Attribute Editor, where the targets appear as sliders under the Weight section of the blendShape tab. You can remove the targets from the blendShape the same way you added them. Select the target objects in order, select the base, then apply Edit Blend Shape ➤ Remove.

 TIP   Once you are satisfied with all the blendShape targets, you can delete the target objects to lighten the scene. The blending information remains with the base object, so you can always recreate a target geometry by copying it from the blended base object.

Editing Deformations

Deformations depend on the relationships among points and their groupings. The controls you can use for your deformations include the Relationship Editor, Edit Membership tool, Paint Set Membership tool, and the Prune Membership function. You can also edit the deformation order.

Editing Deformation Sets

Whenever you create a deformer, Maya creates a deformer set of the same name. This set shows up in the Deformer Set Editing module of the Relationship Editor. You can use this editor to edit the membership of points in the deformer sets. The editor's Edit menu allows you to select any point in a set, add points to a set, and remove points from a set. It also lets you select or delete deformers. Let's go through a simple example.

1. Start a new scene. Create a cylinder.

2. Select the top two rows of its CVs and apply Lattice deformation with the default settings to the points.

3. Select both the cylinder and the lattice in the modeling window, and apply Cluster deformation with the default settings.

4. Try moving the cluster. You will see that you have a problem commonly known as *double transformation*, which is illustrated below. The points inside the lattice are being moved twice—once by the lattice deformer, and again by the Cluster deformer. To solve this problem, the cluster should stop moving the points inside the lattice, because you want the lattice to still be able to affect the points on the cylinder.

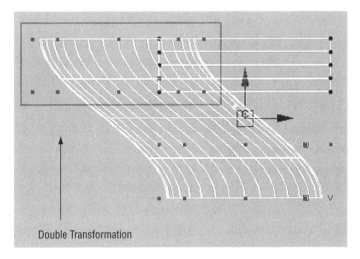

Double Transformation

5. Select Window ➤ Relationship Editors ➤ Deformer Sets. You should see the editor with two deformer sets on the left side: ffd1Set and cluster1Set. Click the plus signs to their left, and you see a list of all the points that are being deformed by the lattice and the cluster.

6. Highlight ffd1Set and select Edit ➤ Select Set Members. You also can highlight the points inside the set and select Edit ➤ Select Highlighted. In the modeling window, the points become selected.

7. Highlight cluster1Set, and either click the minus sign button at the top of the window or select Edit ➤ Remove Selected Items. The selected points are no longer part of the cluster set, and they are not transformed twice.

PART **3**

Animation

TIP   When you are in the Relationship Editor, you can unclutter the right window by RM choosing over it and clicking Show DAG Objects Only. (DAG stands for Directed Acyclic Graph.)

Using Tools to Edit Membership

Maya provides a quick way to do what we just did in the previous section without using the Relationship Editor. You can use the Edit Membership tools to solve the double transformation and other deformation problems. Let's try it.

1. Use Undo to create the double transformation situation again (or repeat steps 1 through 3 in the previous section to recreate it).

2. Select Deform ➤ Edit Membership Tool. Maya asks you to select a set or a deformer. Our goal is to remove points from the cluster, so select it. All the points belonging to the cluster become selected.

3. Ctrl+click or marquee the points you want to remove. (If you want to add points to a deformer, you can Shift+click or marquee the points.)

The Paint Set Membership tool works in the same way as the Edit Membership tool. To use it in our example, you would select the cylinder, select Deform ➤ Paint Set Membership Tool ❏, select cluster1Set as the set to modify, and choose the Remove operation. The advantage of the Paint Set Membership tool is not readily seen in this instance. However, because it gives you a color feedback telling you which points belong to which deformer, it can be very useful when you are editing rigid skinned objects (see Chapter 13 for more information about skinning techniques).

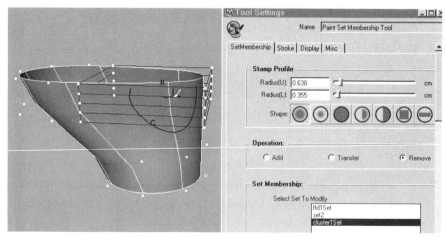

Pruning Membership

With Lattice, Cluster, Sculpt, and Wire deformers, Maya provides a quick pruning function. The Deform ➤ Prune Membership function removes all the points of a deformer set that, at the time of the pruning, have not been moved from their unde-formed positions.

While pruning can lighten a scene by reducing deformer calculations, you may remove points that seem unnecessary from sets, but later find that they need to be deformed after all. In such cases, you can always add those points to the deformer set again, using the editing tools described in the previous sections.

Changing the Deformation Order

Deformation order, or the deformation chain, refers to how multiple deformers affect a surface in order. Their order is usually determined by their order of creation, but you can use the advanced option settings to change their placement in the chain. You can also use the Complete List window for a selected object to edit the order. The best way to understand how deformation order works is to go through a simple example.

1. Create a NURBS cylinder. Scale it up to 5 in Y, and increase its spans to 4.

2. Copy the cylinder. Translate it out and deform it to look something like the one in (a) below.

3. Apply Blend Shape to the original cylinder, as in (b) below. Set the Blend value to 0, and delete or hide the copied cylinder.

4. Apply Sine to the original cylinder, with an Amplitude setting of 1. You should see something like (c) below.

5. Increase the cylinder's Blend value to 1. You no longer see (b) but rather some-thing like (d). If you want to see the cylinder morph into a shape like (b) again, you need to change the deformation order assigned to Sine and Blend Shape.

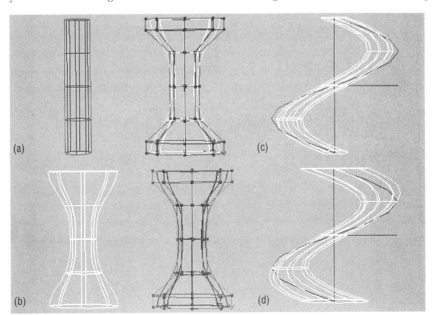

6. With the cylinder still selected, click the List of Operations button (adjacent to the Make Live button) and choose Complete List. You can also RM choose over the cylinder and select Inputs ➤ Complete List.

7. In the Complete List window, notice that history of the node chain starts from the bottom. MM drag the Non Linear node down to the Blend Shape node until you see a box appear around it, then release the mouse button. The nodes' placements have switched. Now when you increase the cylinder's Blend value, it overrides the Sine shape, as shown below.

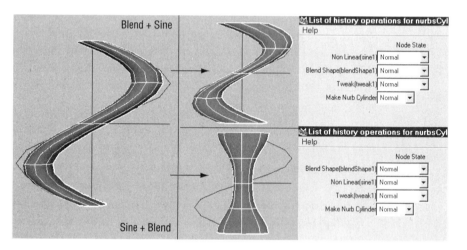

Advanced Facial Animation

Facial animation is a big field on its own. Here, we will deal with only several relevant points. At the simplest level, you can have a character talk with two shapes: open_ mouth and close_mouth. Consider any muppet character and you will see what we mean. For facial expressions at the simplest level, you need only close_eyes, and open_eyes (and perhaps not even those). For a more realistic setup, however, the number of facial shapes, or targets, can quickly grow to dozens.

Creating the Teeth, Tongue, and Oral Cavity

Before you can work on facial shapes, you need to create the teeth and gums, as shown in (a) below. The upper teeth do not move because they are fixed to the skull; the lower teeth should rotate with the jaw. You should use Set Driven Key to have the lower teeth driven by open mouth shapes such as *ah* and *oh*. Make sure the rotation pivot for the lower teeth is similar to the jaw bone's, around the ear area. (See Chapter 10 for details on the Set Driven Key feature.)

You may also want a tongue, its tip clustered, to strike the back of the upper teeth for what the linguists, if not the dental experts, call the *alveolars* (*s*, *z*, *t*, *d*, *n*, *l*), or to the bottom of the upper teeth for the *th* sounds. An example is shown in (b) below.

Another necessity is the oral cavity. A good way to proceed is to offset two or three curves from the boundary isoparms of the lips so you can maintain a procedural connection with the mouth shapes, create copies of those offset curves, translate them into the throat area, and loft (see Chapter 6 for more information about lofting). This is illustrated in (c) below. You may want to wait until you have finished building the face before creating the oral cavity. It should become a morphing part of all the mouth targets.

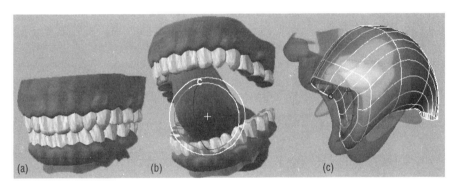

(a)   (b)   (c)

TIP   Creating the inner mouth parts can be tricky and time-consuming. If you are not going to have close-up shots of a character's mouth, it may not be worth the effort. As an alternative, you can create a textured plane, curve it, and position it inside the mouth.

Creating Mouth Shapes

There is no fixed list of facial shapes you should create, nor is there a standard guide for how to set them up for facial animation. Specific projects call for specialized solutions, and animators will always experiment with different methods. But the idea of using Blend Shapes for lipsyncing makes a lot of sense.

Setting up well-thought-out mouth targets may take longer, but it will save you much more time in the long run, especially if you will be using the character repeatedly. Using Blend Shape for lipsyncing and Wire deformation for fine tweaking and

PART 3

Animation

facial expressions probably will offer the best results. Below is a sample list of blend shapes for lipsyncing.

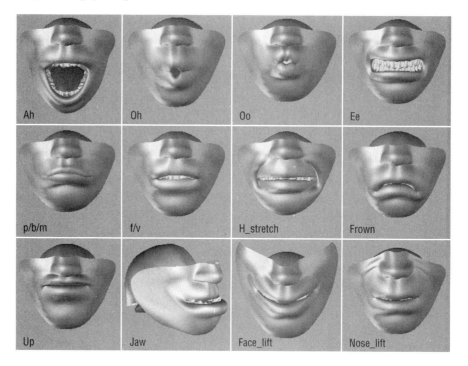

The *ah* and *oo* shapes are absolute necessities—*ah* because it opens the mouth and lowers the jaw, and *oo* because it can also be the shape for sounds such as *ch*, *sh*, and *w*, not to mention kissing and whistling.

You can get by using one shape for oo and oh, but they really are different shapes. The jaw drops for *oh*, creating a hollow space inside the mouth, whereas for *oo*, everything pushes up. The *ee* shape shown above is an extremely strong shape, which can double as an expression of anger or, combined with *ah*, screaming. For unaccented *ee* shapes, you may want to use the H(horizontal)_stretch instead.

For H_stretch, Frown, and Face_lift, you could separate them further into Left and Right targets. If you do, then be careful not to disturb the few middle CVs of the face, or you will get the double-transformation effect (described earlier in the "Editing Deformations" section).

For many of these shapes, if you build the targets carefully, you can also use their negatives. Below are the negatives of some of the shapes.

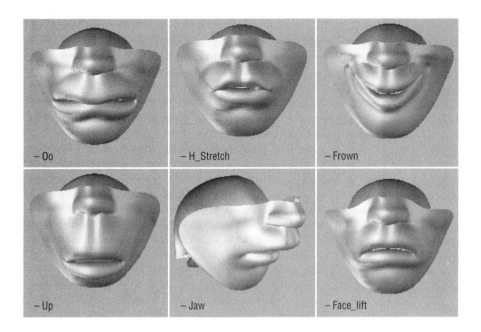

- Oo — H_Stretch — Frown

- Up — Jaw — Face_lift

NOTE The sounds are not accurately-spelled phonetic sounds. They've been spelled out like regular words here. For proper phonetic spelling, you should follow the IPA (International Phonetic Alphabet). Different dictionaries use slightly different spelling methods, but *ah* would generally be listed as [a:], *oo* as [u:], *ee* as [i:], and so on. Letters such as *c* are represented differently depending on how they are used. A soft *c* is [s], whereas a hard *c* is [k]. For more information about phonetic spelling, refer to a linguistics book.

Setting Up Multiple Blend Shapes

When you are setting up your blending targets for the face, separating mouth shapes from facial expressions is more economical and efficient than throwing everything in together. For this technique, you create two groups of blendShapes. The mouth and the jaw patches can hold mouth shapes such as those described in the previous section. The eye patches can hold facial expressions such as eyes closing and showing emotions—happy, sad, and angry. Setting things up this way is a bit more complex, however, and requires the use of the Set Driven Key feature.

In the example shown below, Blend Shape was applied not to the top Face node, but to the Eye_area and Mouth_area nodes. There are also two blendShape groups: one for the mouth area and another for the eye area. The two targets, Ah and Eyeclose, are working well with the base object. The two shapes are independent of each other,

PART **3**

Animation

so that when the eyes close, the mouth area is not affected, and vice versa. The third shape, smile, is actually a combination of two target shapes: the Sm_eyes and Sm_mouth shapes. In the bottom-right picture below, both shapes are at their maximum target value.

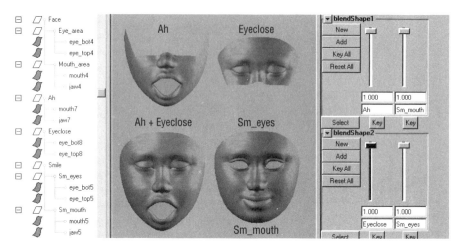

However, there is a problem with the smile shapes in the example below. When the Sm_mouth slider is moved, creasing occurs as shown below. This is because the Sm_eyes slider did not move with the Sm_mouth slider. We can solve this problem by making the Sm_mouth slider a driver for the Sm_eyes slider.

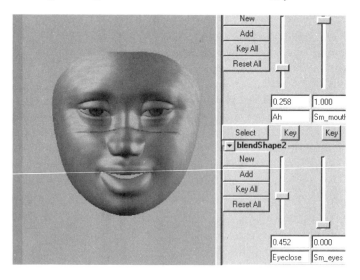

RM choose over a numeric input field in the Blend Shape Editor to pop up a menu. Select Set Driven Key. You can select the blendShape node in the Blend Shape Editor by clicking the Select button. Specify Sm_mouth as the driver and Sm_eyes as the driven. Key them at 0 and 1. Sm_mouth should now drive Sm_eyes, as shown below.

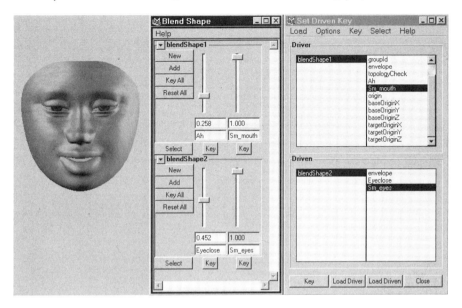

Discerning Spoken Sounds

When you are lipsyncing, one of the worst mistakes you can make is to try to figure out the mouth shapes by going through the alphabet, spelling out what is been spoken. It is better to reference a list of phonemes if you can, but better still to just follow the mouth shapes as the sounds are made. Here are a few rules that can help you to get started.

- Consonants are greatly affected by the sounds that surround them, which is a phonetic phenomenon called *assimilation*. For example, the consonant *d* in "how *do* you do?" and "how *did* you do?" forms two different mouth shapes, because the vowels that follow the *d* are different. A good rule to follow is to go through the vowels first, because they will often dictate how the neighboring consonants will be shaped. Once you figure out the vowels, the consonants will often naturally fall into place.

- There is also a rule called vowel reduction or omission, which is a specific type of assimilation. For example, a phrase like "how did you do?" is often spoken "how ju do?". In a case like this, it helps to "unlearn" your reading skills; instead of trying to find sounds from the words, just listen.

- English is an intonational language. It's rhythmic, with regular beats of accented and unaccented syllables, and a few strong emphases punctuating different parts of sentences. You should listen to these emphases and figure out where the beats are falling. You can then skim through the unaccented segments and concentrate on nailing the accented syllables.

PART 3

Animation

- For animation, you should be concerned only with what will be seen. If a character's back is toward you, for goodness sake, don't animate her face! If that seems obvious, then in the same way, you don't need to animate what goes on inside the mouth. Consonants such as *s*, *z*, *t*, *d*, *n*, and *j*, among others, can often be shown as just a slight up and down movement of the mouth. Consonants such as *k*, *g*, *ng*, and *h* matter only in that they fill time between vowel shapes. The *th* sounds (as in "*th*ing" and "*th*ey"), too, are indistinguishable in terms of shapes, and should be treated as one sound.

 T I P   For many animators, lipsynching is not such an important part of facial animation. Far more important is creating proper facial expressions, especially in the eye area.

Keyframing and Tweaking Mouth Shapes

There are various methods of keyframing mouth shapes. You can use the Channel box, the Attribute Editor, or the Blend Shape Editor. It is generally not a good idea to keyframe individual shapes, because the shapes that are not keyframed may end up "floating" between their keyframes. A much more efficient method is to keyframe all the shapes, then tweak them individually in the Graph Editor.

 T I P   You can lock certain targets to exclude them from being keyframed if you know you won't be using them for a specific scene. For example, you might lock a smile target in a scene where you know the character isn't going to smile.

Keyframing with the Channel Box or Attribute Editor

In many ways, the Channel box and Attribute Editor provide a better setup for facial animation than the Blend Shape Editor. Although the Blend Shape Editor offers more functions, it can get a bit awkward when there are a lot of targets to consider.

In order to use the Channel box, you need to have the mouth selected. The Attribute Editor has the Copy ➤ Tear Off Copy function, which creates a copy window that still remains when the object is deselected. Another advantage of the Attribute Editor's torn-off copy is that it has sliders. The Channel box's targets are restricted to a value range of 0 to 1 for the targets, but you can set the sliders to have a wider range of target values. Just type in numbers like **–1** or **2** into the numeric input field, and the slider range will adjust accordingly.

You can Key All in the Blend Shape Editor and in the Channel box, but not in the Attribute Editor. One way to get around this is to use the hotkey for setting keys. You may need to adjust the Set Key options to All Keyable Attributes in order to keyframe blended shapes.

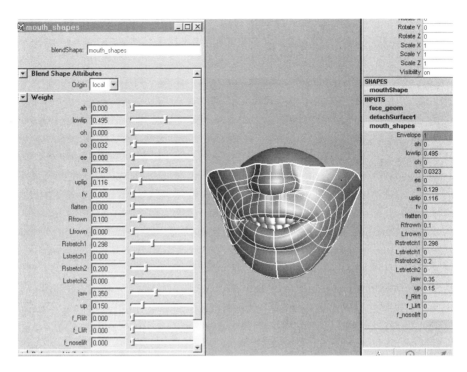

Tweaking with the Graph Editor

Once you've roughly animated the mouth shapes, you can use the Graph Editor to tweak the animation curves. You can also tweak using the Channel box or the sliders (turning on the Auto Key function will help), but only the function curves can give you a sense of how the shapes are moving through time.

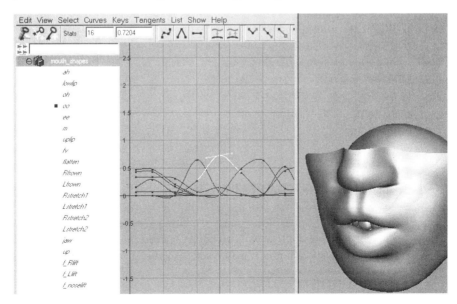

PART 3

Animation

You would usually want to select either one or just a few different targets inside the Graph Editor and focus on tweaking only those curves at one time. You may also want to turn off Curve in the Select menu if you are editing only keyframes.

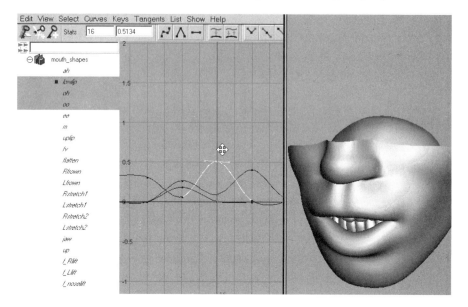

Summary

In this chapter, you have learned how to apply various kinds of deformers to objects, or parts of objects. One of the wonderful things about deformers is that they can be combined in different orders to produce some remarkable effects. In particular, Wire and Blend Shape deformations allow you to produce high-level facial animation. Lattice can also be a very useful tool for both smooth and rigid skinning. In the next chapter, we will be covering skinning, as well as building and setting up a complete human character.

SKINNING AND CHARACTER SETUP

Featuring

- *Rigid skinning*

- *Flexors and Artisan tools*

- *Smooth skinning*

- *Surfacing the puppy*

- *Advanced character setup*

SKINNING AND CHARACTER SETUP

I n this chapter we will learn how to attach surfaces to skeletons and make them deform appropriately for animation. In the attaching process, called *binding*, the bound geometry becomes the skeleton's *skin*; and the skin's deformation is affected by a process known as *weighting*. All of this terminology will soon become familiar as you go through the examples and exercises below. We will also go through setting up the puppy dog for animation, and then devote the remainder of the chapter to building the child model and setting him up for animation as well.

Skinning

We've already talked about how skeletons can bind objects and deform them properly as they move. The process through which skeletons do this is called *skinning*, and the objects that become bound to skeletons this way are called *skins*, or *skin objects*.

Like other deformers, skeletons can skin anything that has control points, such as CVs, NURBS curves, surfaces, polygonal vertices and objects, and lattices. Although you will most often skin whole objects, it is worthwhile knowing that you can bind only a selection of points as well.

There are two kinds of skinning: *rigid* and *smooth*. Rigid skinning creates a joint cluster for every joint binding the objects. These clusters can contain points of multiple objects, and you generally use flexors to smooth the bends. Smooth skinning creates a skin cluster for every object being bound; this cluster is shared by a set number of joints with different influence percentages. You can use influence objects, discussed later in this chapter, to manipulate the deformation of smooth skins. For both kinds of skinning, you can use the Artisan tools to edit set membership and weights of the skinned points. When you are working with dense organic models, the difference between using Artisan and using the regular tools can be quite noticeable.

Rigid Skinning

Rigid skinning is called "rigid" because only one joint can influence a CV. There is no sharing of CVs as in smooth skinning, and the joint clusters that are created have a default influence value of 100%, which results in a rather rigid deformation when joints are bent. You can edit rigid skins by using flexors (a special type of deformer) or other deformers, or by changing skin point weights. All the tools we'll be using, unless stated otherwise, are available in the Skin menu in the Animation module.

Creating Rigid Skin

Let's start out with a simple example. Create a cylinder and increase its sections to 10, its spans to 6, and its Height Ratio to 10. In the side view, create a skeleton chain as shown below. Select the cylinder and the skeleton—the order of selection here doesn't matter—and apply Animation ➢ Skin Bind Skin ➢ Rigid Bind with the default settings. The cylinder turns pink to show that is bound, or skinned, by the skeleton chain. Try rotating the second joint in Z 90 degrees; you'll see that all the points bound by it rotate fully, or "rigidly" as below.

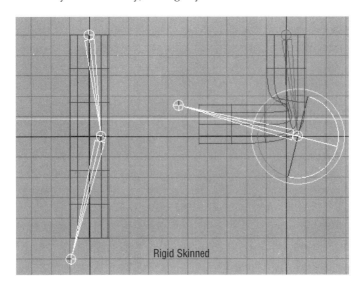

Rigid Skinned

T I P   You can also skin selected joints in the same way you would complete skeletons, but you would do this with different geometries, such as skinning the hand, then the arm, and so forth. Trying to skin one object separately to two joints brings up some tricky partitioning problems, and fixing them is usually not worth the effort. Instead, if you have to do something like that, try creating lattices with the object's control points instead and skin them to the selected joints.

Rigid Skin Editors

Open Window ➤ Relationship Editors ➤ Deformer Sets, and you will see two jointSets, one for each joint. The two sets contain all the points of the cylinder, and if you remove any of the points from the sets, those points will cease to be bound by the skeletons. Open Window ➤ General Editors ➤ Component Editor, and select the Joint Clusters tab. There are now two columns for the jointClusters. Select all the CVs of the cylinder and click Load Components in the Component Editor. You will see the points weighted under the joints they belong to. You can manipulate the weights here to make the bending smoother if you want to. For most situations, however, there are more elegant ways to make the bending smoother.

T I P   If you have trouble selecting CVs with a pick mask because the skeleton gets selected over the CVs, switch to component mode and select them. Skeletons are not selected in the component mode.

Flexors

The easiest way to make joints bend smoothly is to use a flexor, a special type of deformer that works with rigid skinned joints. There are three types of flexors: lattice, sculpt, and cluster. You will usually want to use the lattice.

Joint Lattice   Select the skeleton, and apply Go To Bind Pose. The cylinder is no longer deformed. Select the second joint and, from the Skin menu, apply Edit Rigid Skin ➤ Create Flexor. Leave everything at the default setting and click Create. A joint lattice (or flexor) is created, with its orientation the same as the joint's local axes. Rotate the joint 90 degrees again, and you'll see that the bending is smoother—the flexor deforms the cylinder around the joint. You can further change the way the flexor is deforming by selecting it and then editing its attributes in the Channel box. The next illustration shows how each attribute changes the way the flexor deforms the cylinder.

PART **3**

Animation

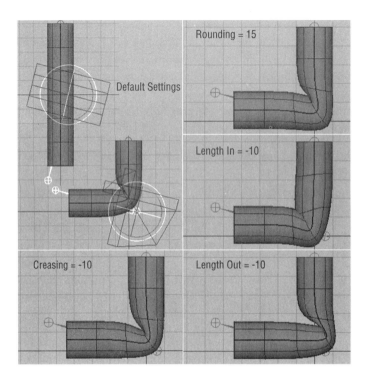

Bone Lattice   You can also apply flexors to bones, but bone flexors are applied a bit differently. Their deformation is affected by the rotation of their child joint. Think of biceps and triceps bulging when you rotate your forearm. To try a bone flexor, select the first joint and apply Create Flexor. In the Create Flexor option box, turn off Joints and check At Selected Bones. Click Create, and a lattice is created around the first bone. Rotate the second joint 90 degrees, select the flexor, and, in the Channel box, change the values for the boneFlexor attributes. Notice that, instead of Creasing and Rounding, boneFlexor has Bicep and Tricep as the first two variables. You can easily get something like a) in the next illustration.

You can move, rotate and scale the flexors to adjust the way they are affecting the skin. In the Outliner, select the lattice group, which selects both the flexor and its latticeBase, and transform it. You can see the way the skin deformation changes while you are transforming the lattice group: b) is the result of the lattice group being moved and rotated.

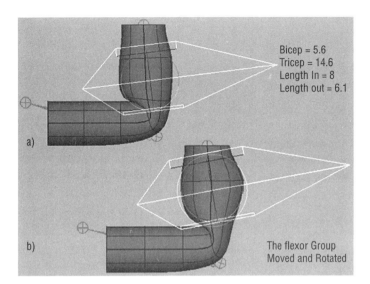

Bicep = 5.6
Tricep = 14.6
Length In = 8
Length out = 6.1

a)

b)

The flexor Group
Moved and Rotated

Sculpt Flexor   You can also use a sculpt sphere as a flexor. It works just like a regular sculpt deformer, and there are no automated attribute controls as with lattice flexors. To have those controls, you need to use Set Driven Key. You can use the sculpt flexor as a bulging upper arm if you want, or as other parts of the body that regularly stretch with joint rotations, such as chest muscles. It can be applied as a joint flexor as well, although it is generally used as a bone flexor.

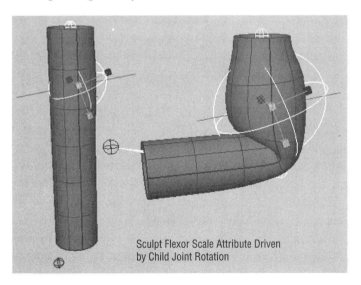

Sculpt Flexor Scale Attribute Driven
by Child Joint Rotation

PART 3

Animation

Cluster Flexor   Cluster flexors have no options attached to them, and they exist only within joints. You can manipulate the smoothness of the joint's deformation, as well as the distribution of the parent and child joints' deforming influences. Select the joint with the cluster flexor and press T to activate the manipulator handle. It shows two rings: one for the child joint, and another for the parent joint. The center of the rings slide up and down the bones, changing the joints' Upper or Lower Bound values, and the radius of the rings changes the Upper or Lower Value values. Below are some of the ways you can change the bending with a cluster flexor.

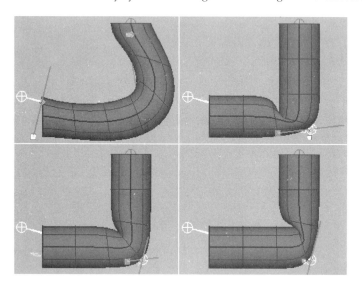

Go To Bind Pose

Do not confuse the Skin ➤ Go to Bind Pose command with Skeleton ➤ Assume Preferred Angle. The latter rotates the joints back to their creation positions, which can be changed with the Set Preferred Angle command. Bind Pose instead keeps track of not just the rotation but all the transformation values of the joints when the object was skinned.

If you decide to detach and reattach skinned objects, you would want to reposition the skeletons to their Bind Pose again. In order for Go To Bind Pose to work properly, the joints must not be locked. Often, however, some of the joints will become locked, because of constraints, expressions, or keyed IK handles. In such case, you can temporarily disable these nodes by going to Modify ➤ Disable Nodes and selecting the nodes causing the blockage.

Copy Flexor Copy Flexor function allows you to copy flexors to other joints. This is useful for creating flexors on the mirrored joints, or creating flexors on finger joints. Simply select the flexor you want to copy, then select the joint you want it copied to, and apply Edit Rigid Skin ➤ Copy Flexor. If you have many copies of the same flexors deforming something like finger joints, and you are comfortable using the Hypergraph, you can try setting up the connections so that one flexor node can drive all the lattice nodes. This would be especially helpful if you had to animate the attributes for all the flexors.

Edit Membership and the Artisan Tools

We've already been introduced to the Edit Membership, Paint Weights, and Paint Set Membership tools under the Deform menu. Rigid skin works with all of these tools.

NOTE Smooth skin does not work with these tools, because it has only one cluster set. It uses the Paint Skin Weights tool instead for weighting points.

We are back with the cylinder and the two joints. Delete all the flexors, go to Bind Pose, and apply Detach Skin. Select the skeleton and the cylinder, select Bind Skin ➤ Rigid Bind ❏, turn on Color Joints, and click Bind. Note that the joints are now colored. Rotate the second joint 90 degrees as before. Select Deform ➤ Edit Membership Tool, and the mouse arrow changes shape. Select the first joint, and all the points belonging to it are highlighted, as below. Shift + click on the points at the bend to include them to the first joint, until you see something like the picture on the right side below.

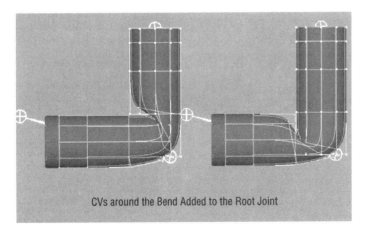

CVs around the Bend Added to the Root Joint

Select the cylinder, and select Deform ➤ Paint Set Membership Tool ❏. In the shaded mode, the cylinder shows two colors, representing the points that belong to the two joints. You can see here (and in the Color Gallery on the CD) that because the joints themselves are colored, you can easily identify which part of the surface is being bound by which joint. Select the second joint, and you can add points to it with the paintbrush.

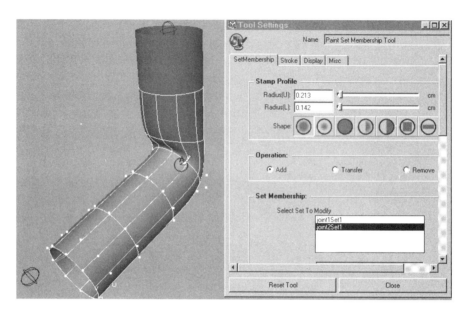

With the cylinder still active, select Deform ➤ Paint Weights Tool ❑. Set the Operation setting to Smooth, and select the second joint for the Clusters setting. Now the cylinder's color has changed again. The cylinder is black, except for the section bound by the second joint. (You can also see this image in the Color Gallery on the CD.) The smoothing operation actually reweights the points in the second joint. You should always keep the brush at low settings, and it may take some practice, but once you get used to smoothing the weights, you can very efficiently smooth out the bend. Using these Artisan tools (introduced in Chapter 9) is definitely faster than using the Component Editor.

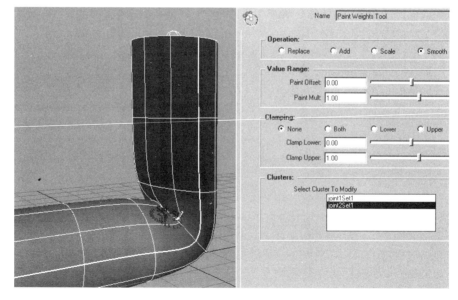

For fine control over deformations such as bending and bulging, you still need to use flexors and other deformers, but for simple smoothing tasks, or creating organic weighting around a surface, Artisan should be used. It creates a lighter scene, without the extra deformer nodes.

Smooth Skinning

For each object being skinned, smooth skinning creates one cluster set of points, which can be influenced by more than one joint. You can set the number of joints that can actually influence the points in the Smooth Bind option box, but all the joints in the skeleton can potentially influence the smooth skin.

The advantage of smooth skinning is that it creates a simpler and (computationally) lighter scene than rigid skinning. You do not need flexors or the Edit Membership tool to edit points in the cluster set. If you need that kind of deliberate control over the bends, you can always use deformers or influence objects, which are deformers specifically set up to work with smooth skinning. Artisan's Paint Skin Weights tool (Chapter 9) is especially useful with smooth skin. Because there are often many joints influencing a skin point, weighting dense smooth skins could be quite a challenge otherwise.

Creating Smooth Skin

Let's get back to our cylinder. First use Go to Bind Pose, and then detach the skin. Select the cylinder and the skeleton, select Bind Skin ➢ Smooth Bind ❏, click Reset, and then slide Max Influences down to 2. The default Max Influences is 5, but you'd rarely need anything higher than 2 or 3. The default Bind Method is Closest Joint, meaning joint influence priority is based on joint hierarchy. If you choose Closest Distance, joint hierarchy is ignored and whatever joint is closest to the skin point will have the greatest influence. Unless you specifically want it to be this way, this is not how a hierarchically structured character deforms. You should generally leave this setting at default. Click Bind, and the cylinder is smooth-skinned. Rotate the second joint 90 degrees, and notice the difference in the way it bends as in the first cylinder below: the skin deforms a lot more smoothly. Too smoothly, in fact. We want a bit more rigidity around the bending area than the default setting, something like the second cylinder in the next picture.

PART **3**

Animation

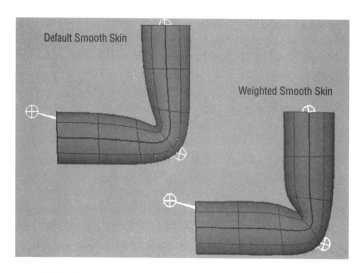

Weighting Skin Points

Before we address the lack of rigidity, however, let's see the differences in the smooth skinned cylinder from the rigid skinned one. Go to the Relationship Editor and choose the Deformer Set Editor, and notice that there is only one set. In the Component Editor, under the Skin Clusters tab, you will notice three columns of joints, including the very end one, and they all share in influencing the skin points. All the numbers in a row always add up to 1, meaning 100% influence. Select the cylinder, and select Edit Smooth Skin ➢ Paint Skin Weights Tool. Set the brush values low, set Operation to Add, and select the second joint to work on. The cylinder is black except for the area that is being influenced by the second joint. You can easily make the bend more rigid on the second joint, as below (this image also appears in the Color Gallery on the CD). Repeat the process for the first joint. If you make a mistake, you can always undo it, and if you want to restart from the beginning, just select the object and apply Edit Smooth Skin ➢ Reset Weights To Default. When you are in the Paint Skin Weights mode, you can also select different joints for weighting by RM choosing Paint Weights over the joint you want.

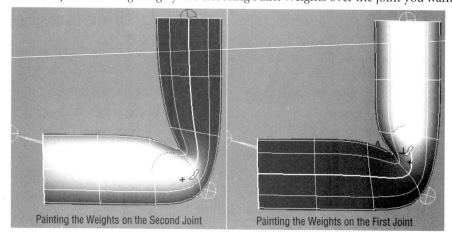

Painting the Weights on the Second Joint   Painting the Weights on the First Joint

Influence Objects

Let's say we want the biceps and triceps to bulge. We can use an influence object to accomplish this. Create a sphere and scale it to fit in side the upper arm. Select the cylinder skin, then the sphere, and apply Edit Smooth Skin ➤ Add Influence with the default settings. The sphere becomes an influence object, like a lattice deformer, with a hidden sphereBase object also created. You will generally leave the Base object alone, although you can optionally pull points of the Base object to change the deformation effect of the sphere. You can use Set Driven Key to automate the bulging by scaling up the sphere when the second joint rotates, as below. The influence sphere and the sphereBase should be grouped under the first joint.

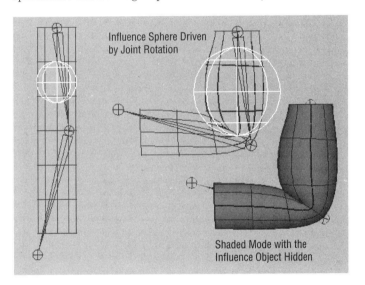

Influence Sphere Driven
by Joint Rotation

Shaded Mode with the
Influence Object Hidden

WARNING   Do not delete an influence object the regular way, as it will mess up the smooth skin weighting. Select first the skin and then the influence object, and apply Edit Smooth Skin ➤ Remove Influences.

We used a sphere, but we could have used any object with control points. The biceps and the triceps above look shapeless. Let's try the Influence object again, this time deforming a torus to get more definition for the biceps and triceps. Set up a torus as an Influence object with Minor Sweep at –180 and everything else at the default setting, as below. Select the skin and, in the Channel box, open the skinCluster and set Use Components to On. An easy way to do this is to enter 1 in the field. When this is turned on, component-level deformation of the influence object influences the skin as well. Sculpt the torus until the upper arm takes on the shapes for biceps and triceps as on the left below. Keyframe the CVs, and move to a different timeline. Rotate the second joint, and sculpt the torus again until you see bulging biceps and triceps as on the right below. Copy the bulging torus.

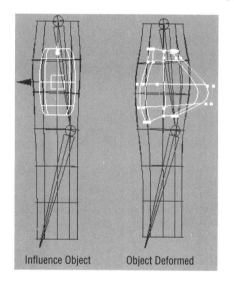

Influence Object   Object Deformed

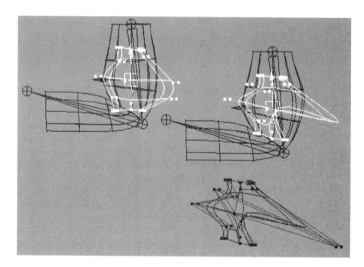

Move back to the frame where the torus CVs were keyframed. You can now delete the keyframe. Apply Blend Shape to the torus, making the copied torus its target. In the Channel box, open the blendShape channels, highlight the nurbsTorus target, and RM choose Set Driven Key. Make the blend shape driven by the joint rotation, as shown here:

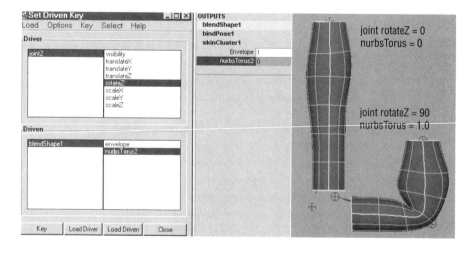

Binding the Puppy

Now let's return to the puppy from the last chapter. We are first going to create two lattices, one for the puppy's head, another for the body. Then we'll bind the two lattices plus the tail and the legs to the skeleton as smooth skin. The skeleton will deform the lattices, which will then deform the puppy's head and body. This method of indirectly moving the puppy using lattices is easier to weight, and it produces smoother deformation. We'll first have to solve a double-transformation situation (discussed under "General Deformation Controls" in Chapter 12), and then we can weight the skin objects as we test the dog's movements.

1. Open the file you saved as Puppy_skeleton. Create a skeleton layer to control the visibility of the skeleton, IKs, and constraints. Hide the layer for now. Select the head patches, eyes, ears, and nose; then go into component mode and select all the CVs, except the last two rows of the neck area, as shown below. Create a default lattice, and increase its STU divisions to (4, 5, 5).

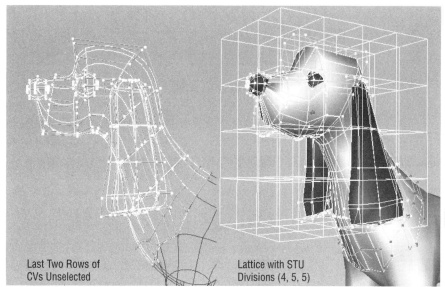

Last Two Rows of
CVs Unselected

Lattice with STU
Divisions (4, 5, 5)

2. Creating the body lattice is a bit more involved. You have to select rows of CVs from different patches, and it may help to create a temporary set in the Relationship Editor to contain all the points for selection purposes. Select all the CVs of the body patches. Select the two rows of CVs from the neck area. Select the top three rows of the front leg patches. Select the top two rows of the back leg patches. Finally, select the bottom three rows of CVs of the tail patches. The following pictures should help.

PART 3

Animation

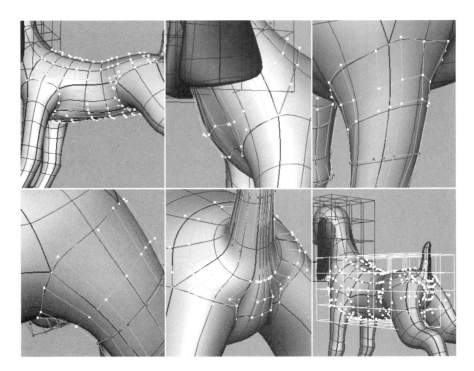

3. Try moving the lattices to see that none of the points that should be included have been left out. Select the lattices, the leg patches, and the tail patches. Unhide the skeleton, and include it in the selection as well. Apply Skin ➤ Bind Skin ➤ Smooth Bind ❑, click Reset, reduce Max Influences to 2, and click Bind. Maya starts to create a skin cluster for each of the patches and the lattices. Open the Relationship Editor and go to the Deformer Set Editing module. You should see 24 sets altogether. There are two lattice sets and 22 skin cluster sets: 16 for the leg patches, 4 for the tail patches, and 2 for the lattices. Remember, they are smooth-skinned objects now as well.

4. We have a double transformation with the lattices. Grab the top skeleton and move it up—some of the leg CVs and the tail CVs are translating further than they should. There is a simple way to fix this problem. Highlight the body lattice set, apply Edit ➤ Select Set Members, and you should see the CVs for the body lattice get selected as shown next.

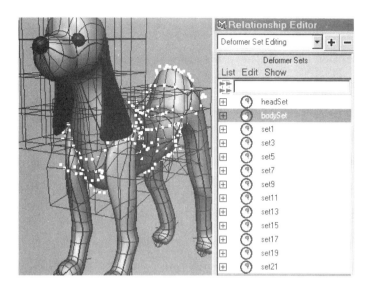

Highlight all the skin cluster sets (not the lattice sets) and click on the minus button at the top, or choose Edit ➢ Remove to get rid of the selected items. The offending CVs are removed from the skin cluster set, and the dog should look normal again. Move the dog down to its original position.

5. Start weighting from the head. With lattices, you have to use the Component Editor to weight the lattice points. Rotate the head joints and see how the integrity of the head shape holds up. The head area should mostly be fine with the default setting. You will probably want to set the lattice points around the face all to 1 in the Component Editor.

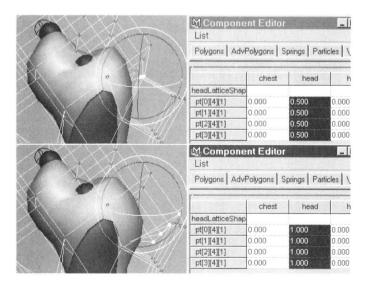

PART 3

Animation

6. Create a cluster on the ears. Select the CVs as below, and apply Create Cluster with Relative mode on. Weight the points so that the bottom of each ear gets deformed the most. Group and parent it to the head joint. The ears should mostly deform well enough within the lattice, but in cases where they are going through the head geometry, you can use the cluster to adjust the ears.

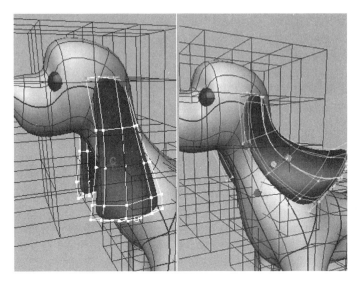

7. As you are weighting the different parts of the body and rotating the joints, you can always use Go to Bind Pose. But if you move the IK handles or the constraints, the Bind Pose will not work. One way to handle this is to keyframe those nodes. After you've tested them, you can return them to their original positions, after which the Bind Pose should work again.

8. We can't go through all the lattice weight tweaking here, as it is a time-consuming process. To give you an idea of what's involved, let's go through a simple example of lattice tweaking at the chest area. The four points below are being influenced by Rarm, Relbow, Larm and Lelbow. The elbows, however, shouldn't be influencing the chest area, so punch in zero in the elbow columns. The arms are each assigned the value of 1 for two points. But the chest bone should be influencing the chest as well, so assign 0.5 in the chest joint. The value for the arm joints drops to 0.5 accordingly. As you can see, a lot of weighting actually consists of getting rid of unnecessary influences and thinking about which joints should be influencing the points, rather than punching in numbers.

	Larm	Lelbow	Lhock	Lknee	Lleg	Lpad	Lpawe	Lwrist	Rarm	Relbow	Rhock	
bodyLatticeShap												
pt[0][1][6]	0.000	0.000	0.000	0.000	0.000	0.000	0.000	0.000	0.716	0.284	0.000	0.00
pt[1][1][6]	0.000	0.000	0.000	0.000	0.000	0.000	0.000	0.000	0.759	0.241	0.000	0.00
pt[2][1][6]	0.759	0.241	0.000	0.000	0.000	0.000	0.000	0.000	0.000	0.000	0.000	0.00
pt[3][1][6]	0.716	0.284	0.000	0.000	0.000	0.000	0.000	0.000	0.000	0.000	0.000	0.00

Polygons | AdvPolygons | Springs | Particles | Weighted Deformers | Joint Clusters | SkinClusters

Load Components   Close

9. You can use the Paint Skin Weights tool for the legs and the tail if you want, but apply them only if you see the need. In our case, the default skinning has done a fairly decent job of weighting. Once you are done with weight tweaking, save the file as Puppy_ready. You can try a four-legged walk cycle with it.

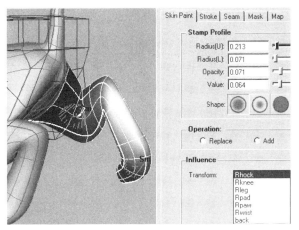

Advanced Character Setup

In Chapter 6 we built a human child's face, and in Chapter 7 we built his polygon hand. In this section, we will go through how the child's body is built—the torso, the arms, the legs, and the shoes. We will then import the hand, build a skeleton for him, put IKs on the joints, put in set-driven keys and constraints, build a proper hierarchy suitable for animation, lattice his torso, rigid-skin the geometry, apply flexors, and weight the points. All this in half a chapter? Well, this is an advanced tutorial; we'll

Animation

cover most of the steps in accelerated outline form. Check the illustrations carefully to infer the many little details we are necessarily leaving out.

Building the Body

In completing the child model, we will first create a sleeveless shirt in NURBS, which will then be converted to polygons. Arms will be created to connect smoothly with the shirt, and hands built in Chapter 7 will be connected to the arms; then we'll create the shorts, legs, and then the shoes.

Torso and Arms

Open the file Child_head from the CD, or the one you've built. We'll build the torso as a sleeveless shirt, because doing that conveniently bypasses the tricky problem of creating a seamless shoulder. We start out with a torus, with Minor Sweep set to –180. Sculpt it to resemble the image below, tucking it at the top and at the bottom, with a cylinder for the arm. You should pull the neck area down so that it seems to disappear into the shirt. Cut the torso in half, and intersect it with a plane. Position the plane so that it makes an acceptable shirt opening. The plane here is straight, but you can curve it as you see fit. Increase the span of the cylinder and roughly shape it like an arm.

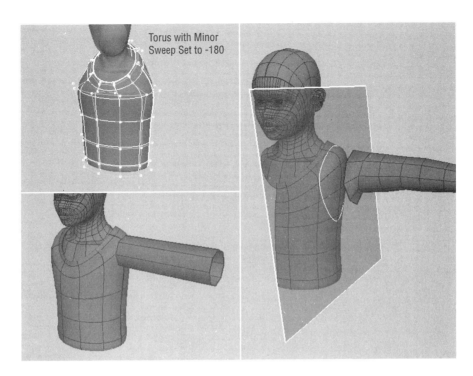

Create curves on surface with the torso and the plane by using Intersect Surfaces and then Trim. Duplicate curves from the cylinder, and offset and duplicate curves from the trim edge of the torso, or a shirt, as in image a) below. Rebuild the curves into uniform 8-span curves and then loft them. Use the curves to sculpt the arm a bit more, and then you can delete them. Duplicate the geometries with scale –1, and you will see something like image b).

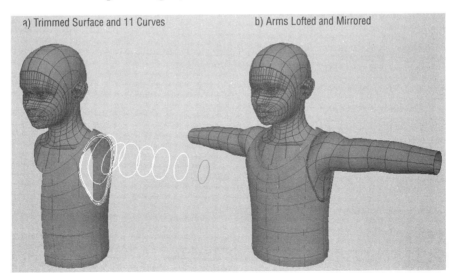

a) Trimmed Surface and 11 Curves   b) Arms Lofted and Mirrored

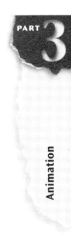

PART 3

Animation

TIP   This has been emphasized already, but build models as simply as you can. You can always increase isoparms; it's hard to do the opposite. With the arms, you'll probably insert more isoparms later when we are at the skinning stage; but when you're modeling, one less isoparm is one less thing to worry about.

The trimmed shirt is converted into polygons, its two halves combined, and separate edges merged (note the soft edges in image a) next) except for the side opening. The lofted edge surfaces (b) are converted and combined, but not merged. The thickness comes with a cost, however; the shirt's geometry becomes heavier (c). If you wanted still a better-looking shirt, you would also add thickness to the neck opening as well. The shirt was touched up with Artisan at the end.

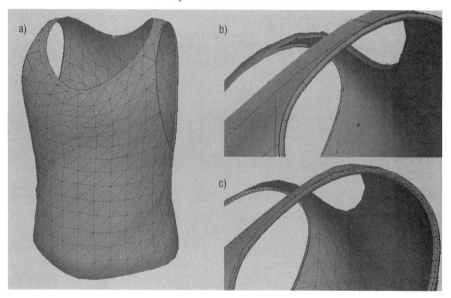

Pants and Legs (and Shoes)

The pants are built from a cylinder. It becomes one side of the pants and is sculpted using Artisan and pulling CVs. Attach and sculpt a bit more, creasing the crotch area as shown next.

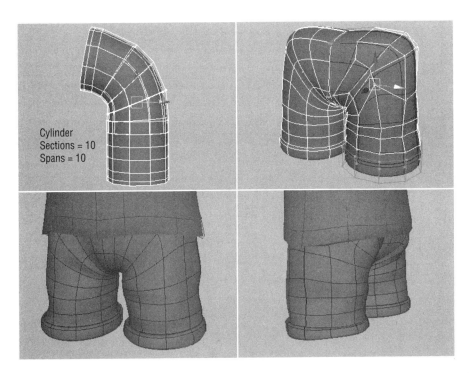

Another cylinder is used for the leg, is mirrored for the other leg. Note the bunching of CVs at the knee area. The shoe is created from a sphere. Several sections are bunched up at the sides to make the bottom flat, and it is perhaps too simple a shoe, but it'll deform well enough.

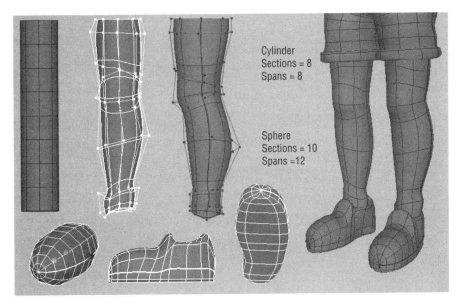

PART 3

Animation

Hands

Open the file `Child_hand` from the CD or the one you've built. It's a bit big and long for the child, so scale it down appropriately. There are different ways of attaching hands to arms. You can build them as seamless NURBS objects, or hide the seams by overlapping their surfaces as shown below. You can also give the character wristbands, or a watch, or gloves to wear.

Finally, check to see that all the normals and UVs are going in the right direction. Checking this now will save a lot of hassle when texturing the surfaces later.

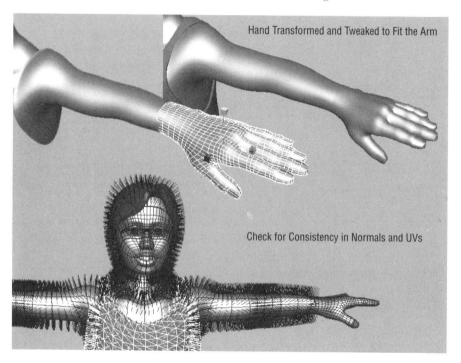

Hand Transformed and Tweaked to Fit the Arm

Check for Consistency in Normals and UVs

IK Setup

We've already gone through much of the skeleton setup process in Chapter 11. Again, there are some general rules to follow:

- Choose the window where you will create the joints carefully—the bending should always occur as Z rotations.
- The local rotational X axis should be pointing directly into the child bone.

- Limit degrees of freedom when they apply.
- Test to make sure the mirrored joints are rotating properly.

Also, this is the last stage where you can readily make changes to your model. In particular, check for proportions and see whether you need to increase isoparm numbers. When you have the shoulder chain made, for example, skin just the arm and the hand and try bending them different ways. You may find that the arms are too short or that more isoparms need to be inserted.

Spine

The spine joints will be moved by the IK Spline tool, which allows us to build it more like the human spine, as shown below. The joints must have no limitations; otherwise, the spline won't work. Note the start joint is one above the root joint. The curve is four spans, which means it has seven CVs. Create three clusters—the first one containing six CVs, the second containing four, and the third containing the top two—and display their handles. They will serve as three spline control handles. Parent the clusters to the Root joint, and note that extra group nodes are created for them.

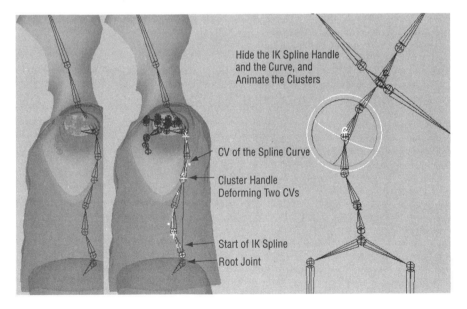

Hide the IK Spline Handle
and the Curve, and
Animate the Clusters

CV of the Spline Curve

Cluster Handle
Deforming Two CVs

Start of IK Spline

Root Joint

Shoulder and Leg Chains

We want the shoulder joint to primarily bend up and down, so create it in the Front view, as in a) next. Create the arm chain in the top view, because you want the chain to be bending forward, as in b). Take note of the extra joint at the end of the chain. Name the second-to-last joint **wrist** and the last joint **hand**. We'll be using the extra joint to set up a special orientation constraint. Group the arm chain under the shoulder joint, and then group the shoulder chain to the joint where the IK Spline ends, as in c). Note the difference in the local rotational Z axis for the joints. The hand joints should be created so that Z rotation bends the fingers down, whereas the thumb bends sideways at an angle, as in d).

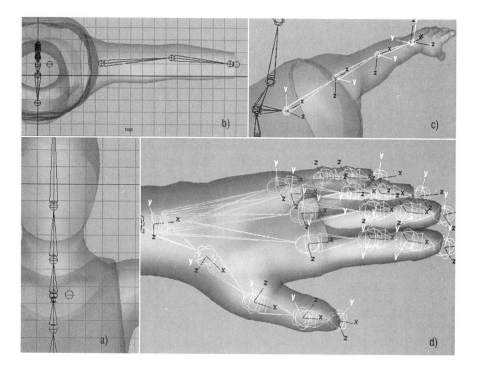

The leg chain should be created from the Side view, since we want the legs to bend back and forth. Build the joints as in a) next. Once that's done, group the chain under the root joint, and mirror the leg chain and the shoulder chain. You should see something like b). If you have set limitations to any of the joints' Degrees of Freedom setting, check to make sure they are active on the mirrored joints.

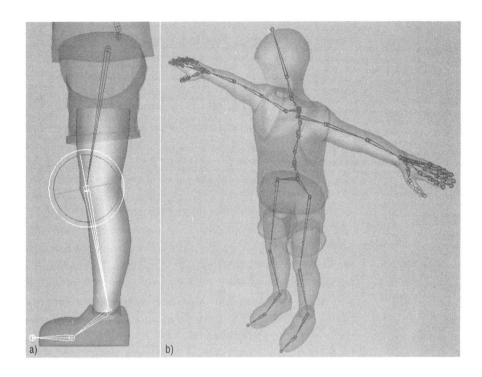

a)   b)

IKs, Constraints, and Hierarchy Setup

Once the joints are all built, we can put IK handles on the arms and the legs. The IK handles will then be constrained to the cubes. The cubes will give us better visual feedback in selecting and transforming the arms and the legs than using just the IK end effectors.

Hand Cubes   We'll use the ikRP Handles option setting, because you can get more rotational control with it. Start an IK handle at the left arm joint, and end at the wrist joint. Create a polygon cube, scale it as you see below, V+drag it to the wrist joint, and point-constrain the IK handle to the cube.

What we will do now is a bit complicated. We want the hand to have an orientation constraint to the cube so that we'll only need to animate the cube for translating the arm and rotating the hand. This setup is especially useful when you need to have the character's hands stay planted not only positionally but also rotationally—pushing against a wall while the body is moving, for example. But we also want to make the wrist joint rotate only in X and the hand joint rotate only in Y and Z. That way, we can make the wrist joint influence the forearm deformation, while restricting the hand joint's influence to the wrist area for bending in Y and Z.

PART 3

Animation

Select the cube and then the wrist joint, and select Constraints ≻ Orient. If the wrist joint rotates or flips, go into its Attribute Editor, and adjust its Rotate Axis value for X (the other two don't matter) under the Transform Attributes section to offset the rotation and get it back to the initial position. Go into the dependency graph or the Connection Editor and disconnect the rotate Y and Z constraint from the wrist joint. Apply an orientation constraint again to the hand joint; but this time, disconnect the rotate X constraint from the hand joint. Check the Color Gallery on the CD to see how things should look afterwards; the joints that appear in pink there are the arm, the elbow, the wrist, the hand, and the fingers.

You can proceed to lock all the channels for the wrist and hand joints, except for wrist X rotation and joint Y and Z rotations. Repeat the same steps for the right arm.

Foot Cubes   Setting up the legs for animation isn't as involved as the arms. The problem with the foot is that it has three pivotal spots: the ankle, the heel, and the ball of the foot. Trying to account for these pivot points can get very complicated, and for the sake of efficiency you may not want to bother. The simplest setup will only use one pivot point for the foot, generally the heel, and work around the other two pivots. We'll try for two here.

First, create an ikRP handle from the leg joint to the ankle joint. Then create another handle from the ankle joint to the ball joint, as shown next. Snap a cube to the ankle joint, and slide it straight down to the ground level. The cube represents the heel. Press Insert, and snap the cube's pivot to the ball of the foot. Group the ankle IK handle under the cube, and the ball of the foot IK handle under the ankle IK handle. When you translate the cube, the whole leg moves, and when you rotate the cube, the leg rotates around the ball of the foot.

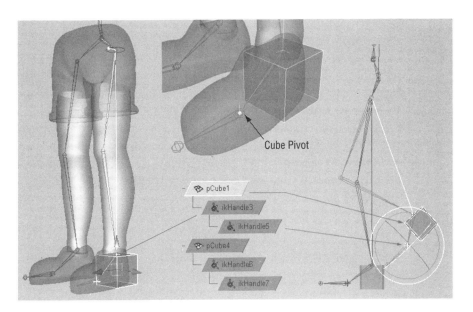

Cube Pivot

When you want to rotate just the foot, rotate the ankle end effector as shown below. When you want to rotate the leg around the ankle, use the ankle ikRP handle's Twist channel. Make the Z rotation of the ball of the foot joint driven by the X rotation channel of the end effector at the ball of the foot (also shown below). You should lock the translation channels for the IK handles and the Y and Z rotations for the ball of the foot IK handle as well. Pivoting around the heel would have to be simulated by rotating and translating the ankle IK handle.

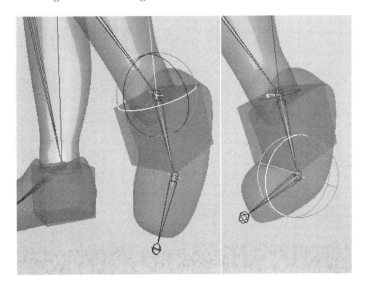

Hierarchy Setup   Group the cubes together and name the top node **Child**. This will be the node you will use to translate the entire character, and its pivot should be placed somewhere around the child's belly area. Group the root skeleton under this node as well, and the skeleton setup is complete. If you want to, you can also set up set-driven keys for the finger Z rotations. The geometry should be organized as the following: Under the Face node, you should have all the face patches, hair, eyes, ears, and teeth (if you created them); and under the Body node, you should have the head, hands, arms, torso, pants, legs, and feet. The Face hierarchy will be grouped under the head joint, whereas the Body hierarchy will be skinned. Here you can see the finished skeleton, with IKs added and constrained, and the Outliner shows the hierarchy you will be using for animation.

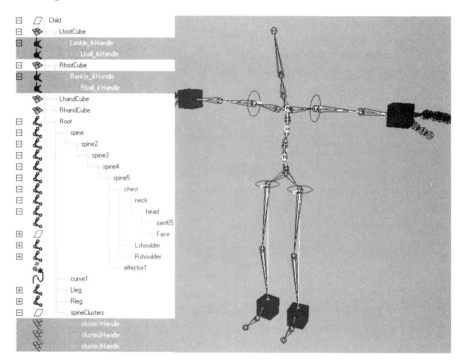

Skinning and Weighting

Our final steps in setting up the child for animation are to create a lattice for the torso, add a rigid skin, and apply flexors and weights. In the process, we'll see how the Preserve Skin Groups option enables us to correct skinning errors without extensive reworking.

Latticing the Torso

We proceed in the same way that we skinned the dog. Create a set and add the polygon shirt, two bottom CV rows of the head, four edge rows of the arms, and top CVs of the pants, as shown next. Create a default lattice and increase the STU divisions to (4, 8, 3). If the shirt were denser and we wanted more detailed control, we could increase the STU divisions, but for what we have, it isn't necessary.

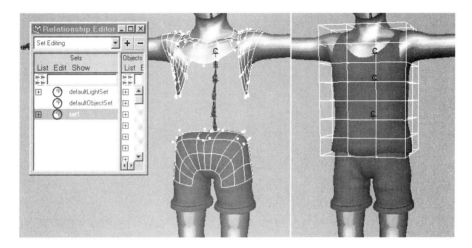

Rigid Skinning and Membership Editing

Select the Body node, which should contain all the geometry to be skinned, and the root joint; then apply rigid skinning with Coloring on. Move the Child node, and you will see points shooting out. Use the Edit Membership tool or the Paint Set Membership tool to go through all the joints that are double-transforming and remove the offending CVs, as shown below (and in the Color Gallery on the CD). Hide the surfaces and meshes, and reassign the lattice points to the spine chain in the following way. There are eight rows of lattice points, but the bottom row should be influenced by the legs, so leave them alone. Assign the second row to the spine joint, the third row to spine2, and so on. The chest joint gets the two middle CVs of the seventh row and the top two middle points at the front and the back. The forearm CVs are assigned to the wrist joint, so they will twist with the cube. When you are doing the legs, if there are many incorrectly assigned points, it may help to spread the legs out a bit. Go through other parts of the body roughly because you will find when you are weighting the surfaces that you'll need to reassign some points. Weighting points and editing their membership is necessarily an iterative process.

PART 3

Animation

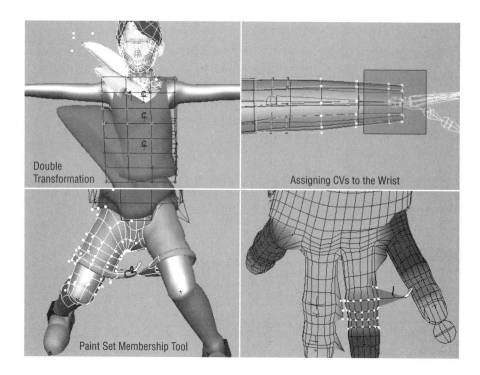

Double Transformation

Assigning CVs to the Wrist

Paint Set Membership Tool

Preserve Skin Groups and Correcting Errors   Oops! We've made a horrible mistake, as so often happens in real life. We discover when we test the arms that they are too short, and that the hand joints should be placed closer to the hand. But we've already skinned the geometry to the skeleton, and the skeleton has the cube constraints already in place. What do you do? Maya's Preserve Skin Groups to the rescue.

Let's correct our terrifying mistake at once. Select the skeleton group and apply Skin ➢ Edit Rigid Skin ➢ Preserve Skin Groups ➢ Detach Skeleton. Select the arm IK handles and in the Attribute Editor disable the IK Solver. If you've locked the translation attributes for the joints, you also need to unlock them. You can now translate the elbow and the wrist joints to lengthen the arm. To place the hand joint closer to the hand, use the Insert key to move only the hand joint, as shown below. Move the wrist joint as well. Before you reactivate the IK Solver, you'd also want to snap the cube to the new wrist joint position. Select the CVs of the arm and the hand and lengthen the arm, keeping the proportion of the CV positions. Make sure the fingers match the finger joint positions. Select the skeleton group and apply Reattach Skeleton.

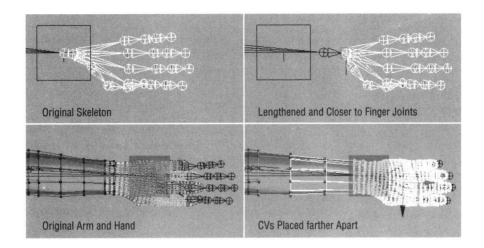

Original Skeleton | Lengthened and Closer to Finger Joints

Original Arm and Hand | CVs Placed farther Apart

Maya may warn you that the bind position has changed for a number of joints. Detaching and reattaching skinned objects may necessitate some reassignment of point membership. In our case, because the wrist and hand joints have moved closer to the hand, we need to update the previous set of membership of those joints and perhaps that of the thumb joint. Everything else should work just as before.

This was an easy example of correcting a mistake in the setting up stage. In a production situation, one of the most frustrating things is to discover too late that there's a problem with the character you've built. So right now would be a good time to check again what you have done so far for any potential problems. Once you've gone through weighting a character, you will not want to weight it again.

Flexors and Point Weights

Weighting is a major endeavor, and it can be quite frustrating. You can go bonkers trying to set up a character to move in all kinds of ways, but it is simply impossible (so far) to make a digital model move in all the ways a human being can. You should set specific limits to your character instead, like constraining the knees not to go above the waist, for example. By doing that, you've simplified your weighting task a thousandfold.

Once you have roughly gone through reassigning the points, you can create flexors to the fingers, wrist, elbow, and legs. It's a good idea to weight the points as you are creating the flexors. The finger, for example, has three joints, the second and the third of which take flexors; but the first joint, which connects the finger to the hand, is not an ideal flexor recipient. Apply the Artisan tool to the first finger joint, as shown next (and in the Color Gallery on the CD). It's more difficult to properly

PART 3

Animation

weight the palm than the back of the hand when the fingers curl. Fortunately, the palm is usually not visible when that happens! You would want also to use Artisan or the Component Editor to weight the forearm so it will twist smoothly. Also weight the shoulder area and the neck. For the shoulder, you need to test the shoulder joints as well as the arms. For the neck, make sure the head area is weighted at 100% so that it will stay with the face when the neck joint rotates.

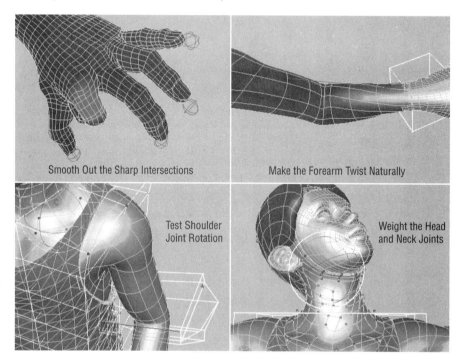

Smooth Out the Sharp Intersections

Make the Forearm Twist Naturally

Test Shoulder Joint Rotation

Weight the Head and Neck Joints

The crotch area is another difficult area to weight. You need to lift the leg up to the front and to the back to see how the pants stretch and fold, and also how it takes the ikRP handle twisting (shown below and in the Color Gallery on the CD). The joints at the ankle and the ball of the foot are other bending areas you should weight. As you go through these and other areas, it's crucial that you move the joints to get the character into different poses. What seems to be deforming smoothly in one pose may go berserk in another one.

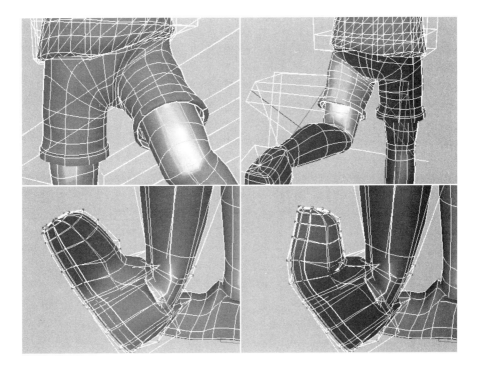

Cleaning Up

Assuming that the model's been textured as well, which we'll get to soon enough (in Chapter 19), there are little things you can do to aid you in animating efficiently. Have the Child hierarchy set up in a Hypergraph window you can access while animating. Use layers to convert the geometry into reference objects now that you don't need to select them. You can hide the geometry if you'd like and work only with the skeleton. Display selection handles for the root joint and the cubes so you can pick them in the window. The selection handles can easily be offset in the Attribute window. You can also create eye constraints if you want (so you won't have to rotate the eyes), by using Aim constraints. Delete anything that you no longer need, whether it's geometry, curves, history, or empty nodes. Save the file as Child_ready.

PART 3

Animation

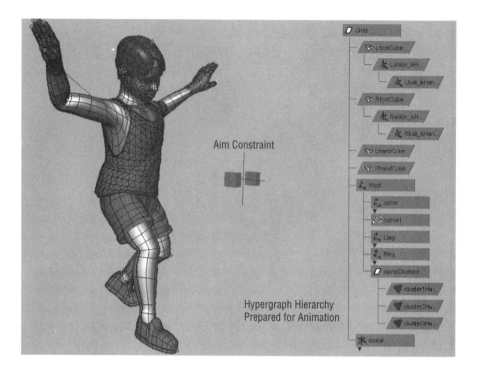

Aim Constraint

Hypergraph Hierarchy
Prepared for Animation

Summary

In this chapter we've covered rigid skinning and smooth skinning, using the puppy as an example of the latter. We learned how to edit point set membership and weight the points. The chapter also went through an advanced-level character setup, during which we tried to create a production-quality character and ready him for animation, covering a lot of important topics along the way. And that's it. No more tweaking CVs, applying IKs, or constraining. We are now ready to animate the child, and that is what we will do in the next chapter.

chapter 14

CHARACTER ANIMATION: A WALK CYCLE AND MORE

Featuring

- *Creating a walk cycle*
- *Creating more interesting walks*
- *Creating a run cycle*
- *Performing a somersault*
- *Catching and throwing a ball*

14

CHARACTER ANIMATION: A WALK CYCLE AND MORE

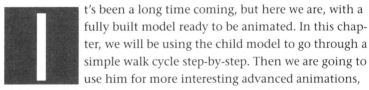t's been a long time coming, but here we are, with a fully built model ready to be animated. In this chapter, we will be using the child model to go through a simple walk cycle step-by-step. Then we are going to use him for more interesting advanced animations, such as running, grabbing and throwing a ball, and, yes, somersaulting. Along the way, there will be selective presentations of a few of the more important classical animation principles. For a fuller treatment of classical animation and its mysterious ways, you should try perusing *The Illusion of Life: Disney Animation* by Frank Thomas and Ollie Johnston, which is still the most enlightening, entertaining, and inspiring reference book for aspiring animators. For studies in how people and animals actually move in real life, Eadweard Muybridge's photo books are still the definitive source for many artists.

Creating a Walk Cycle

Walk cycles are used very often as animation lessons because there's probably nothing more familiar than walking; just about anyone can go through the motions (or watch others walk). At the same time, a walk cycle requires you to be aware of and properly apply many fundamental animation principles. If you already have an animation background, this chapter may help you to get some needed sleep, but if you are still fresh from having entered the animation world, this chapter may turn out to be quite educational. You should take time to read through the explanations and understand them fully.

When creating a walk cycle, you should be aware that there are two different types. The first type is a stationary walk where the ground seems to be moving under the character; this is the simplest kind of walk cycle. The second type is a more realistic walk in that the character actually moves forward. This second type is a bit more complex than a stationary walk but involves the same principles. We will be doing the simpler stationary walk. (You can see an example in the Color Gallery on the accompanying CD.)

Setting Up the Character

To begin setting up a character, create a ground plane and stretch it out. Select File ➤ Import, and open the Child.mb file from the CD. Translate the Child node up or the ground plane down until you see his feet just on the ground. Select the child geometry and press the 1 key to get into the rough display mode, as you want to concentrate on quickly creating rough poses. You can work with only the skeleton if you wish (and some animators do). Working with cubes is very helpful in such a case as they give you better visual feedback on how the arms and feet are rotating.

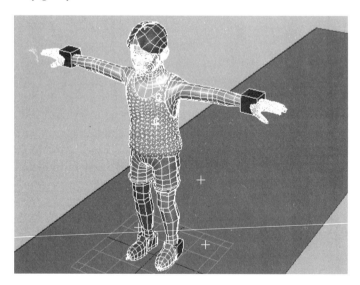

Animation is a very iterative procedure. You can try to animate everything at once, right from the beginning, and some people do work like this. But usually you end up working at a much slower pace, and then you can easily lose sight of the forest for the trees—lose your perspective on how the character is animating overall because you are bogged down on translating and rotating so many control nodes.

It's much better to key in rough poses one or two nodes at a time, working on different parts of the character in stages, much like painting or sculpting. For the walk cycle, the workflow will be as follows. Animate the left leg first; then transfer and offset the animation to the right leg. Then animate the root and the spine joints, including the head. Animate the arms last. Once the rough animation is done, you can tweak and refine the function curves and change subtle details of the walk to give it more personality. At every stage, you would want to do simple playblasts to see how the keyframes move in real time.

Animating the Left Leg

This is how you would usually start the walk cycle and it sets the framework for all the rest of the walk in terms of time and distance covered. You need to decide how many frames the cycle should be. Bigger and heavier characters tend to walk slower, whereas lighter characters walk faster, but you can infer more than just that. For instance, a slow walk done well can convey seriousness, dignity, and grace in a character such as a king or a queen at a coronation, whereas a fast, bouncy walk can convey the lightheartedness of a clown or the intense energy of a soldier. Long steps can imply confidence or urgency, whereas small steps can imply shyness, or leisure. Different walks can reveal many things about a character.

To begin animating the left leg, set the animation speed to 30 fps (frames per second) by going into Options ≻ General Preferences ≻ Units, and changing Time to NTSC (30 fps). We'll do a fairly brisk walk and make the cycle 24 frames. This is an easy number to deal with, as it gives us 12 frame halves and 6 frame quarters. In the modeling window, translate the LfootCube (left foot cube) in X to 1.5, and animate the LfootCube and the Lball_ikHandle (which rotates the toe area of the foot) together. Start out with an extreme pose, where the legs are widest apart at frame 1. The heel is just touching the ground, and the toes are curled as in the figure below. Copy the keyframe at frame 25 by MM dragging the current time indicator. Go to frame 13, and translate and rotate the cube and the toes to the back.

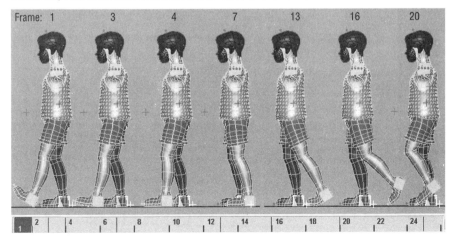

At frame 16, the foot is actually farther back than at frame 13 because it takes time for the ball of the foot to press down to the ground and kick up. But it covers more distance between frame 16 and frame 20 as a result. This kind of delay and recovery in the foot's motion creates the appearance of weight. It also makes the movement snappy. If there was no keyframe 16, and you keyframed only 13 and 20, it wouldn't make a lot of difference, but that subtle extra "kick" would be missing. Try playblasting both, and see if you can notice the difference. If you were to ignore keyframe 20 as well, the leg might appear to be floating more than walking, a common mistake a lot of beginners make. Floating usually happens when a keyframe is missing from where it should be and the computer automatically calculates the in-betweens.

It's important to achieve realistic motion here. When a client or audience criticizes an animation, lack of weight or snap is a common complaint; and the reaction that a character "just floats" is usually the death knell for the animation.

Copying the Animation

Now we need to copy the animation from the left leg to the right. With the cube still active, select Edit ➤ Keys ➤ Copy Keys ❑, click on the Below setting, and then click Copy Keys. Select the RfootCube. Select Edit ➤ Keys ➤ Paste Keys ❑, type 12 in the Time Offset field, and click the Paste Keys button. Select both cubes, open the Graph Editor, and apply View ➤ Infinity, then Curves Pre Infinity ➤ Cycle, and then Post Infinity ➤ Cycle. Select the Translate X curve for the RfootCube, and change its value from 1.5 to –1.5. You should also change the Rotate Y to its negative value as well. Now the legs walk together and cycle indefinitely, with the right leg's animation trailing the left leg's by 12 frames. You can also see this view of the Graph Editor in the Color Gallery on the CD.

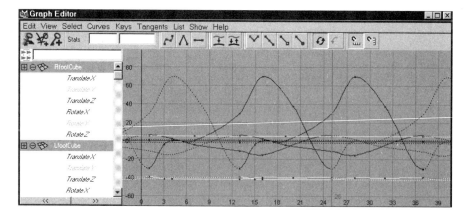

Animating the Hips and the Upper Body

The next step in the walk cycle is animating the hips and the upper body of the child. The pelvic area, or the root joint, must be animated first, and then the upper body, because the upper body rotation values are dependent on the pelvic movements.

The Root Joint

The pelvic area moves in many different ways in a walk cycle: you need to translate the root joint up and down, but it also has to rotate in X and Y. (For the root joint created in the side view, the X axis is going up the spine, Z rotation is bending forward and back, and Y rotation is rotating sideways.) You could rotate the joint in X just a bit and translate it in X as well, if you want. A female walk usually has greater X translation, making her hips sway, whereas a male walk generally doesn't have any. Rotate the root joint first; at frame 1, when the left leg is forward, the joint should be rotated in the direction of the right leg about –10 degrees in X. Repeat the keyframe at frame 25. At frame 13, it should be 10 degrees. (This is not a set rule; you can rotate the joint 20 or 30 degrees if that's the kind of walk cycle you're going for.) At frame 7, rotate the joint 5 degrees in Y, and at frame 19, rotate it –5 degrees. (Again, a female walk would generally have at least twice that amount of rotation in Y to make her hips sway more noticeably.) You also need to have the body rotated in Z about 5 degrees because the body needs to be leaning forward.

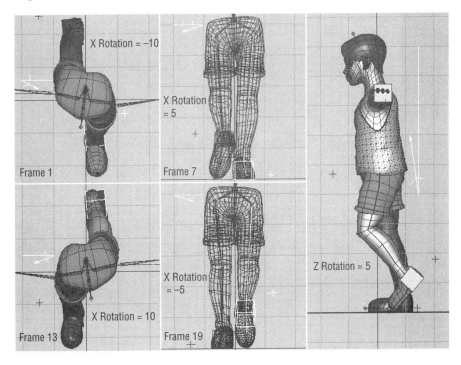

TIP   Walking is often referred to as a continuous falling. When you walk, your body is pushed by the leg in the back position, and then the body leans and falls forward. If it weren't for the back leg speeding ahead of the body to break the fall, your body would actually fall to the ground.

For the up-and-down movement, there are a couple of things you need to keep in mind. First, contrary to what you might think, frame 1 is not when the body is the lowest; that occurs around frames 3 or 4. At frame 1, the front foot touches the ground, preventing the body's fall, but the weight of the body still makes it sink before it can spring back up. The heavier the body, the longer this recoiling will take. Then, around frames 7 or 8, the body reaches its highest position. If the recoiling process takes longer, the steps become a heavy, serious walk. If the body hangs in its highest position a bit longer, then the steps become a light, bouncy walk. Try both styles, and playblast to see the difference.

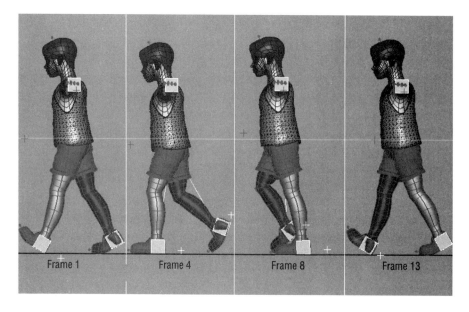

The Graph Editor here shows the root joint's Translate Y function curves for different walks. Just by looking at these curves, you should be able to tell that the first one is a fairly bouncy walk, the second is an extremely bouncy walk, and the third is a heavy walk. Notice how fast the body goes up in the extremely bouncy walk and how slowly the body goes up in the heavy walk.

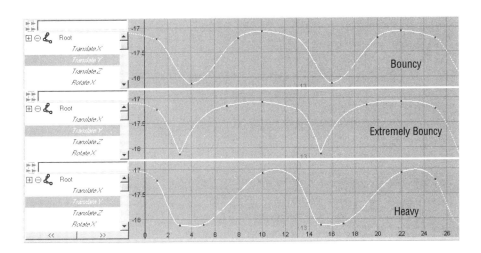

Understanding Squash and Stretch, Rigidity, and Volume

One of the corollaries of a character (or anything) having weight is a principle called *squash and stretch*. In classical animation, this is considered one of the cardinal principles. In our preceding example of the body sinking to its lowest recoil position around frames 3 or 4, the character is being "squashed" by the force of gravity and the resistance of the ground. When it bounces up, the body "stretches" to its highest point. What is a subtle movement in real life often becomes greatly exaggerated in animation. Especially in cartoonish animation, squash and stretch in characters can become extreme.

In order to use the squash-and-stretch principle properly, you have to always apply it as a consequence of weight. Weight is force times mass (remember high school physics?), so something that has more mass will squash more; it will also squash more if more force is applied. This principle, however, needs to be balanced with another factor called *rigidity*.

In real life, rigid bodies such as tables or chairs do not squash or stretch at all, or so little as to not be noticeable. In animation, especially in cartoonish animation, this physical reality is often overlooked, and you will see objects such as an anvil or a boulder being squashed and stretched as if they were made of rubber. But the fact is that the more rigid a thing is supposed to be, the less it should squash and stretch. Carelessly applying squash and stretch to what is supposed to be a rigid object (or character) can undermine its believability. A steel hammer, for example, even if it walks and talks, should stay mostly rigid if we are to believe that it is made up of steel, that it is a hard object. If it squashes and stretches like some soft, rubbery substance, then its characteristics as a hammer are undermined.

Continued on next page

PART **3**

Animation

When applying squash and stretch, another factor to keep in mind is consistency of *volume*. When a water-filled balloon is put on a hard surface, for instance, gravity causes the mass of the water to exert pressure on the rubber, meaning, of course, that the balloon squashes. But as it flattens, it also stretches out sideways because the volume of the water hasn't changed. Even cartoon characters need to have a sense of volume, and once a character's form becomes easily recognizable, that sense of volume must be maintained.

The IK Spline Handle, Clusters, and the Chest

Animating the upper body is mostly a matter of counter-rotating and counter-counter-rotating. When the root joint is rotating one way, the shoulder rotates in the opposite direction, moving to counterbalance the upper body against hip rotation. You can use the IK spline handle's Roll and Twist attributes to twist the spine; animate them as illustrated in the following graphic. At frame 1, the Roll and Twist values are 10 degrees; at frame 13, they are –10 degrees; and at frame 25, they return to their original values. The twisting causes the body to lean sideways a bit, which you can fix by rotating the bottom cluster that controls the CVs of the spline curve. Note the cluster1Handle's Rotate Z curve in the graphic below (and in the Color Gallery on the CD). The body should stay upright all the time.

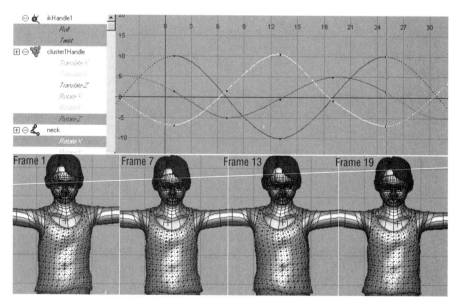

The face should always be facing forward as shown in the preceding graphic, which means that the neck bone should be rotated to counter the Roll and Twist of the Spline handle. Note the neck joint's Rotate X curve in the preceding graphic. You could change this later to add more personality to your character.

Animating the Arms

Arm movement follows the shoulder—specifically the shoulder rotation—transferring the translation motion like a wave starting from the shoulder and moving down to the fingers. First, you need to lower the shoulder joints about –10 degrees in Z. Because the shoulder-bind position is for outstretched arms, when they come down so should the shoulders. (Don't worry about the fingers for now.) Move and roughly rotate the LhandCube, as shown next.

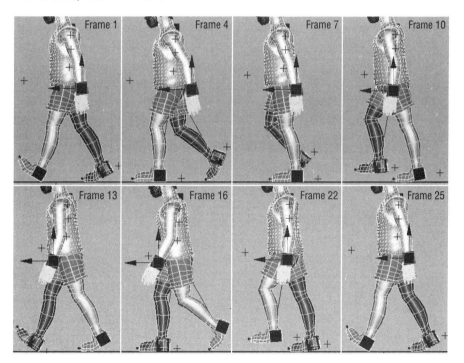

The cube follows the shoulder rotation about four frames behind; it reaches its extreme position at frame 4. This is called *follow-through* or *overlapping action* in classical animation. Loose limbs such as the arms do not stop when the object they are attached to comes to a stop but rather continue to move for a few more frames, perhaps dangling a bit, before stopping. So when the shoulder rotation changes direction, the arms follow through and alter their movements a few frames later. This is also called overlapping action because the change in the direction of the shoulders overlaps with the change in direction of the arms. The following curves illustrate this animation principle (you'll find a better view in the Color Gallery on the CD):

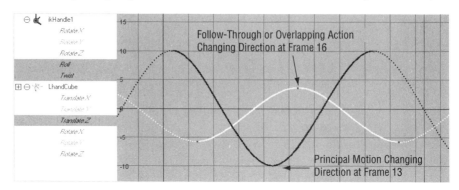

Once you are satisfied with the way the arms are moving back and forth, rotate the hand to make it follow through the arm movement about three frames behind. It may help to get rid of the rough rotations you had keyframed and start over from frame 7. The hand rotation in real life is usually nonexistent or very subtle. In animation, however, you may want to exaggerate the rotation to make it more noticeable. Examine the following poses and the overlapping curves (you'll also find this in the Color Gallery on the CD).

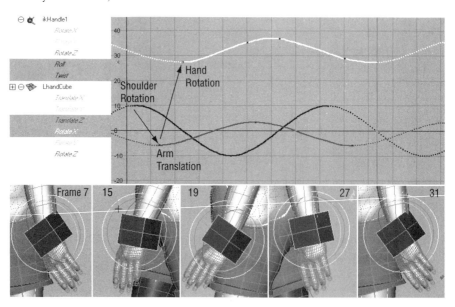

You may choose to animate the fingers as well, making them overlap the hand rotation by just a frame or two, but you'll probably want to just curl up the fingers a bit and keep them that way. Fingers generally do not move when you walk. Now we can transfer the animation we created on the left arm to the right arm by using the copy and paste functions in the Edit ➤ Keys submenu. Copy the animation from LhandCube to RhandCube with an offset of 12 frames, change the X translation to its negative value, and cycle both cubes. The hands will now sway correctly, but the rotation values of the right hand are wrong. To correct this, keep the same X rotation values but mirror (scale to –1) the Y and Z rotations. Go to the Graph Editor, and select the Rotate Y and Rotate Z curves. Select Edit ➤ Scale ❑, set the Value Scale to –1, and click Scale Keys. Now the hands should rotate correctly. Save this file as `Walk_regular`.

Creating More Interesting Walks

The walk the way it is now has all the characteristics of walking, but it's boring. And boring in animation is synonymous with *dead*. But you can easily tweak the curves, now that you have them to play with, to create much more interesting walk cycles.

The Happy Walk

The walk is already fast, so just increase the bounce to be a bit snappier, a bit higher, which is more characteristic of a happy walk. The front knee should be raised a bit more when the body is passing its highest point. Rotate the root joint forward, including the bottom cluster, and then rotate the second and third clusters back so the spine will arch back. Rotate the neck as well so the child's chin will be pointing up. Animate the shoulders to lift a bit when the attached arm is forward. Bend the arms and lift them up more when they are forward, and, by rotating the Twist attribute of the arms' IK handles about 20 degrees, make the elbow come out to the side. You may also want to rotate the Roll and Twist of the IK spline handle more as well. Of course, putting a smile on his face isn't a bad idea either.

The Sad Walk

A sad or dejected walk is usually much slower, so RM choose Select All, select Edit ➤ Keys ➤ Scale Keys ❑, set Time Scale to 2, and click Scale Keys. Now the walk is half the original speed. You will want to adjust some keyframes for the feet so they won't seem to be moving in slow motion. All the rotations are scaled down—the hip rotations, the shoulder rotations, and the arm rotations. The arms should generally be drooping at the front, and the spine should be hunching forward, head downcast. The bounce should disappear, and when the back leg is coming forward, the knee shouldn't go up as high. (The happy and sad walks are illustrated on the next page.)

PART 3

Animation

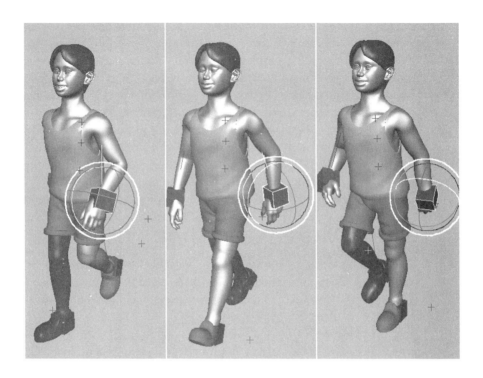

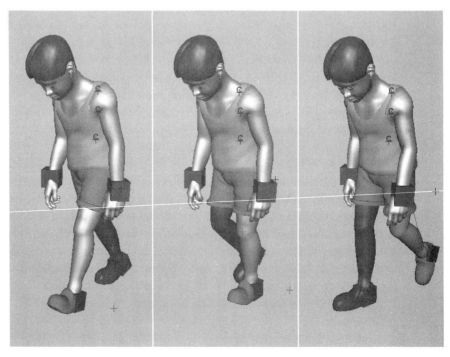

Advancing Beyond Walk Cycles

Clearly, it would be very difficult to present in this chapter all the techniques for animating a human character. Instead of attempting to undertake that nearly impossible task, we'll provide tidbits of information to help you develop your own sense of animating a bit more wisely and intuitively. We'll continue to use the child model for our examples.

Creating a Run Cycle

Running differs from walking in that when the body is at its highest position both feet are actually off the ground. A runner is constantly leaping or bouncing forward. Except for this one difference, a slow jog is almost exactly the same as a very bouncy walk. Also, as the run becomes faster, the body will lean forward more. Since we haven't done a forward-moving walk cycle, quickly going through the run cycle will also help to illustrate that type of forward motion.

Start out with the front foot just touching the ground, as frame 1 of the next image shows. The child here is in full pose, but if you are going through this yourself, remember the rule about working on one or two control nodes at a time; you should concentrate on the feet and the hips first and then move on to the rest of the upper body. The foot translation and rotation as well as the hip rotation generally have to be worked out together because the hip rotates more in a run, and it's hard to accurately extend the leg when the hip hasn't been properly rotated first. The arms are kept more bent, and the body generally rotates and leans forward more. At frame 1, the body is coming down for recoil (squash and stretch), but it's more efficient if we move on to frame 7 for the opposite pose first and then come back to deal with the recoil. Go to frame 7, select the hand cubes and the root joint, and then move them forward. The left leg should translate forward by a significant amount ahead of the left foot cube, as in frame 7 of the next image.

PART 3

Animation

Frame 1   Frame 7

Translate and rotate the foot cubes and the root joint until you have the same pose as in frame 1, except with the opposite leg, as shown in frame 7 below (and in the Color Gallery on the CD). You don't need to punch in exactly the same values for the cubes in frame 7 as for their counterparts in frame 1 because later on you will edit the function curves anyway, but also because you should get into the habit of trusting your eyes as well. You then need to select the root joint and open the Graph Editor. Select the Translate Z curve, and apply Cycle With Offset. We now have a fixed rate of distance being covered by the run. Go to frame 13 and the body should automatically move forward. Make the child get into the original pose he was in at frame 1 and keyframe the pose. Select the root joint again, and in the Graph Editor, select and cycle all the curves except the Translate Z curve (which is cycling with offset). If you see that some of the curves are not cycling properly, move the keyframes to make them cycle smoothly. You should see curves like the ones below. Repeat this cycling procedure for the other control nodes as well.

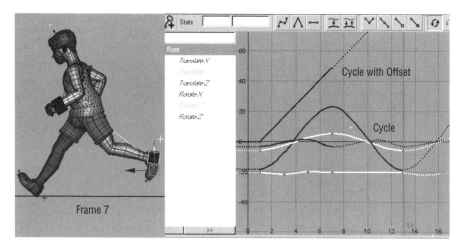

Go back to frame 3, where the body is at the lowest position and is being squashed. For a regular run, the front foot will be flat, as seen in Frame 3 of the next picture; for a sprint, the weight of the body should be on the ball of the foot. Frame 5 shows the stretch; the body is lunging forward and is at its highest point, with back arched, the back leg stretched, and the front knee raised and bent. You also should raise the shoulders a bit at this point.

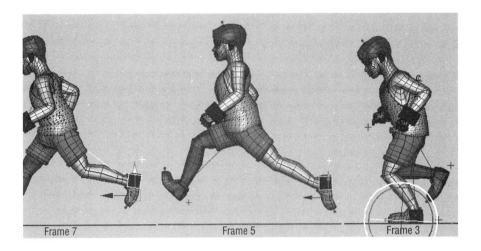

Frame 7   Frame 5   Frame 3

Repeat the squash and stretch for frames 9 and 11. When you are done with the footsteps and the arms, cycle all the joints except the Z translation. The Translate Z function curves are cycled with offset. Afterwards, select the LfootCube and the root joint, and look at their Translate Z function curves. If you see them branching out like those in the top two lines in the next picture, it means the Lfoot Cube translate node should be modified. The correct cycle should keep the Z translation values between them roughly parallel, like those in the lower two lines in the picture. Do the same for the hand cubes as well.

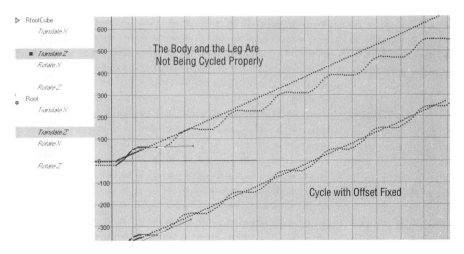

PART 3

Animation

Looking at Arcs and Staging

Arcing is another important classical animation principle; in order to imitate life, you need to show motion as arcs, or waves. Nothing in this world moves in a totally straight line. Nature is comprised of arcs and waves, including all motion that occurs within it, as Tai Chi practitioners like to point out. We are told that even something as apparently straight as a ray of light is not perfectly straight. A run cycle, such as the one we just covered, is all wave motions, as you can readily see in the Graph Editor.

But it's one thing to create wavy function curves and quite another to show them as wavy motions. Consider the often-used example of head-turning. Although the motion itself is an arc, depending on the angle from which you are looking at the head, the head-turning can appear as a straight-line motion. In order to show it as an arc movement, you need to either change the view or dip the head as it turns and then bring it back up. When you have roughly animated your character, get into the habit of going to the camera view and checking the lines the character's motions are creating. If you see a lot of straight lines even though the motions themselves are arcs, perhaps the camera view needs to be changed.

This brings up yet another important animation principle called *staging*. No matter how great the action in a scene is, it has to be seen clearly in the first place. Staging a character involves making sure the character's actions are being accurately transmitted to the viewers. The run steps above, for instance, were shown in the side view because it best staged the motions of the body. If the same steps were captured in the front view, you would have a much harder time grasping what is going on. Classical animators will often only look at the silhouette of a character to determine whether the character's actions are being staged properly.

Staging also involves making sure that only one principal action is being presented at one time. If you want to show a character getting up from a chair and also flashing a smile, it would be poor staging to have her do both at the same time; it would be much better to have her stand up first and then flash a smile, or vice versa.

Performing a Somersault

The way the hierarchy has been set up for the child model's joints, IK handles, and control cubes, you should only use the Child node for translating the whole character, the root joint for the body, and the four cubes for arms and legs. But there are situations where you may want to change the hierarchy of the set-up to fit your animation purpose. Let's say you want a character to somersault over a table. If you rotate the top hierarchy node, the legs rotate with the body, which is what you want, but the arms rotate with the body as well, which is not what you want. You want the hands to stay fixed on the table while the body is somersaulting. You can do this by restructuring the hierarchy.

Remove the hand cubes from the Child node by dragging them in the Outliner or Hypergraph. (You could also create another group node to include all the other nodes under Child, but, for our purposes, taking out the hand cubes is simpler.) Place the hand cubes on the table (cube), as illustrated below. Move and rotate the Child node to move both the body and the foot cubes, and rotate the root joint to bend the body. When the arms are going over the shoulders as in this case, you need to rotate the shoulder joints up and forward. Also, use the IK handle's Twist attribute to prevent the arms from twisting, and rotate the cubes so the hand will be ready to hit the table with palms down.

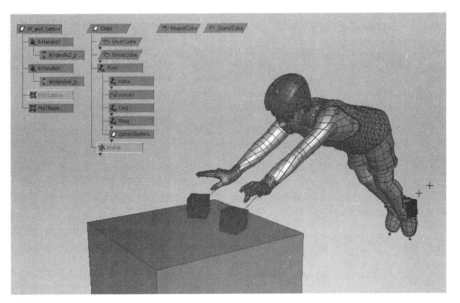

It's always a tricky business to have a character's arms do things over their head, especially if you have to keep their hands planted in a fixed position, because the joints tend to twist and cause unnatural deformations in the shoulder area. It's important, therefore, to rotate the shoulders and the IK handle's Twist attributes properly at the right moments. The elbows should be pointing outward during the somersault as well.

Placing the hands on the table and making them stay there would be a difficult endeavor if they weren't orient-constrained to the cubes. When the wrists get rotated as extremely as in our case, it's easy for the hands to flip. Adjusting the IK handle's Twist values usually gets rid of the problem. If you find that the hands are still flipping even after you've adjusted the IK handle's Twist value, try placing the palms in such a way that the fingers are pointing inward.

When the child hits the table, there is a squash (see below), a bending of his arms for recoil, and then a push-off (stretch) about four frames later. His forward momentum

(Z translation in this case) shouldn't be slowed down if you can help it. Because the foot cubes are under the Child node, when you move and rotate the Child node, the feet move and rotate with it. You should animate the Child node first to get a rough sense of the somersault, and then you can animate the feet separately for folding and stretching. You should also rotate the root joint and the IK Spline clusters to make the child bend his waist and arch his back. You can find a complete version of this animation on the accompanying CD.

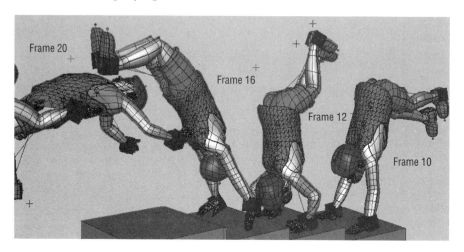

Catching and Throwing a Ball

Animating a character interacting with things or other characters is always more challenging than working with a solitary character. Fortunately, it is more rewarding as well because you can develop a character much more fully when it is acting and reacting in a more complex setting. But what may be an easy task in real life, such as two people shaking hands, can cause severe headaches for the person trying to animate such a scene. Also consider the perils of animating something as detailed as a battle between two sword fighters. How do you make them grasp their swords with both hands, clash blades, briefly stick the swords together, and then merrily continue in their deadly ways? It's not for this book to figure out such things; you can tackle that one at a later date. Instead, we will only put you through the simpler task of grabbing and throwing a ball by animating constraints, which is essentially the way you would solve the more complex problems just described as well.

Grabbing the Ball

Create a ball (sphere) scaled to 1.5 uniformly, and group it unto itself, creating a parent node. Apply Modify ➤ Center Pivot to make sure the parent node's pivot point coincides with the ball's. Place the child's hand on a table (cube), as demonstrated below. Create a locator, scaled to 3 uniformly, group it under the RhandCube, and place it somewhere near the hand (see the left picture below). Position and Orient-constrain the ball's parent node to the locator, and the ball should snap to the locator positionally and orientationally, as in the middle picture below. Move the locator closer to the hand, and rotate the fingers to make it look as if the hand is holding the ball. Keyframe the finger joints and the cube at frame 15, as in the right picture below. This is how the hand will be seen as grabbing the ball.

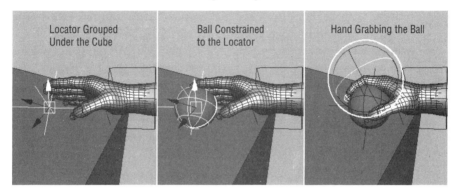

Select the ball's parent node and you will see pointConstraint and orientConstraint attributes in the Channel box. Select the Node State, where it should say Normal for each attribute, and keyframe them at frame 15. In the Graph Editor, you can see that a value of 0 is created. Go to frame 14, in the Channel box click in the Node State field to open the submenu, and select Block; keyframe that for both attributes. You should then see a value of 2 created in the Graph Editor. (Note that the curve created is a stepped curve.) Try moving the cube and you will see at frame 14 that the ball is not constrained to the locator. Keyframe the ball where it is (at frame 15) just to make sure the ball will be at that spot when the hand grabs it. Now you can animate the cube and the finger joints, starting from a distance at frame 1 and then swooping in to scoop the ball at frame 15, as shown next. (You can find a complete version of this animation on the accompanying CD.)

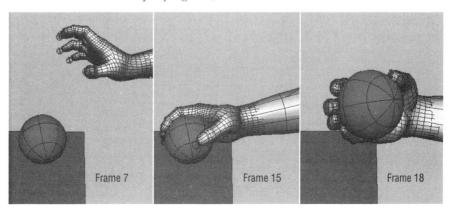

Frame 7   Frame 15   Frame 18

Throwing the Ball

Throwing a ball is essentially the same thing as grabbing a ball except that you are working backward. Start out at frame 25 with the ball constrained to the hand. Swing the child's arm as if he were throwing the ball, and reach the point of release at frame 30. This means he should be flicking his wrist between frames 30 and 32. Finish the throw at frame 35. Once you are satisfied with the throwing motion, go back to frame 30 and keyframe the ball where it is. Go to frame 31, select the ball's parent node, and, in the Channel box, change the Node State setting to Block for the Position and Orient constraints. Then, at frame 35, translate the ball to the direction where the ball has been thrown, and keyframe. Now, when you move the time slider, the ball seems to be thrown from the hand at frame 31 and then shoots out from there, as shown below. (You can find a complete version of this animation on the accompanying CD.)

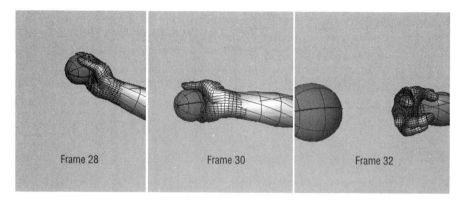

Frame 28   Frame 30   Frame 32

Summary

In this chapter on animation, we went through a simple walk cycle step-by-step, and then we examined a few advanced-level animations such as running, somersaulting, and grabbling and throwing a ball. We also discussed a few of the more important animation principles. In the next and later chapters, we'll be switching gears in a major way. So relax and take a break; we'll soon be getting physical.

WORKING WITH RIGID BODY DYNAMICS

Featuring

- *What are rigid body dynamics?*

- *Creating a simple rigid body*

- *Converting a body from passive to active mode*

- *Using fields to add effects to rigid bodies*

- *Using the Rigid Body Solver*

- *Using impulse and a Newton
  field to simulate orbital dynamics*

- *Converting (baking) a rigid
  body animation into keyframes*

- *Working with the Dynamics Simulator*

- *Adding constraints to a rigid body*

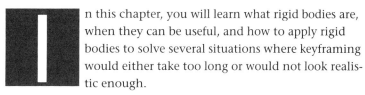

CHAPTER

15

WORKING WITH RIGID
BODY DYNAMICS

In this chapter, you will learn what rigid bodies are, when they can be useful, and how to apply rigid bodies to solve several situations where keyframing would either take too long or would not look realistic enough.

Before you begin this chapter, you should be familiar with Maya's basic interface (Chapter 2) and how to create and move objects around the scene (Chapters 1–4).

What Are Rigid Body Dynamics?

If you've done any animation (either computer or traditional), you're familiar with the concept of keyframes, introduced in Chapter 10. Rigid body animation, on the other hand, is essentially a physics simulator built into Maya that tries to mimic (or completely exaggerate, if you want) what happens to real-world objects as they move under the influence of forces (like gravity or wind) and collide with other objects. If you've ever tried to keyframe even the simple motion of a ball bouncing on the ground, you know how difficult it is to make a keyframed animation work in this scenario. If you try something more difficult, like bouncing a cube off a wall, it can get really frustrating trying to make the collisions look realistic.

Fortunately, Maya has the answer for you: rigid body dynamics, or simply rigid bodies. Using rigid bodies is pretty straightforward: you create one or more rigid bodies; create one or more fields that influence it, such as gravity (if you wish); give the rigid bodies an initial position, velocity, and impulse (if you wish); and play back the animation. Maya's *dynamics engine* does all the calculations to make the body behave realistically, based on your initial information; you don't need a degree in physics, just a bit of practice with the settings you have available.

N O T E   Maya also uses its dynamics engine to create particle effects. See Chapters 21 through 24 to find out how Maya works with particle dynamics.

Rigid bodies come in two flavors: passive and active. Passive rigid bodies are *not* affected by fields, and cannot be moved by collisions—though they can take part in collisions. Passive rigid bodies *are* keyframable (so you can move them around). Active rigid bodies *are* affected by fields, and will be moved by collisions. They are *not* keyframable (so you can't move them around on your own).

Generally, a passive rigid body would make up a floor, wall, or other object that is fixed to the world, while an active rigid body would be any kind of falling, moving, or colliding object (a basketball or a coin, for example). Although it would seem a great disadvantage that active rigid bodies cannot be keyframed, you can convert rigid bodies from passive to active at any time in an animation, allowing a rigid body to be passive for a time, and then to become active (we'll get to an example of this in a moment).

Let's begin with a simple example to see how rigid bodies work.

What's New with Rigid Bodies in Maya 2?

Rigid bodies are not significantly different (to the user, at least) in version 2 than they were in version 1—with one exception: A new Rigid Solver menu allows you to create multiple rigid body solvers, assigning different rigid bodies to different solvers. Assigning different (non-interacting) objects to different solvers allows Maya to solve rigid body equations more quickly and efficiently than it could in version 1.

Creating a Simple Rigid Body

In this example, you'll create a simple rigid body—a bouncing ball—and experiment with a few settings that will affect the motion of the ball.

Start by creating a new scene in Maya. Create a NURBS plane and scale it out to about the size of the Maya grid. Now make a NURBS sphere with a radius of 1 and move it above the plane.

Now select the plane and choose Bodies ➤ Create Passive Rigid Body from the Dynamics menu. The plane is now a passive rigid body.

Next, select the sphere, and choose Bodies ➤ Create Active Rigid Body from the Dynamics menu. The sphere is now an active rigid body.

To allow dynamics simulations to play back properly, the playback rate has to be set to Free, so that the physics engine can calculate what it needs to before going on to the next frame. Either select Options ➤ General Preferences and choose the Animation tab, or click the Animation Preferences button at the lower right of the screen to bring up the same window.

Animation Preferences

In the Animation Preferences window, choose Playback Speed: Free from the Playback area.

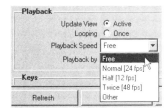

Close the window, rewind the animation, and play it back.

WARNING   You must rewind any animation that contains dynamics—otherwise, the animation will not play back properly! You also cannot "scrub" through an animation by sliding the time marker back and forth. All dynamics data is calculated frame by frame, so if any frame is skipped, the calculations break down and the animation goes berserk. If this happens, just rewind the animation and start over—all will be well again.

TIP   To rewind, either click the Back button on the playback controller (located in the lower-right corner of the screen; it looks like a VCR control) or press Ctrl+Shift+V on the keyboard. To play the animation, either click the Play button on the playback controller or press Ctrl+V on the keyboard.

Nothing very interesting happened, right? Even though you have made two rigid bodies, you have not created any animation yet because you have not added any fields or initial motion. Let's create a gravity field to make things a bit more interesting.

From the Dynamics menu, choose Fields ➤ Create Gravity. Now open the Dynamic Relationships window (Window ➤ Animation Editors ➤ Dynamic Relationships), choose the nurbsSphere name in the Outliner on the left side of the window, and make sure gravityField1 is highlighted in the selection window on the right—if not, be sure to click gravityField1 to highlight it.

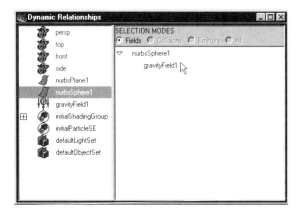

TIP   If you select the sphere before creating gravity, the two will automatically be connected. (If there are other active rigid bodies that you haven't selected, they will be unaffected by this force.)

Now rewind and play back the animation. You should see the ball fall toward the plane and bounce off it. If the animation is cut off too quickly to see this, increase the number of frames in the animation to 200 frames or more (type **200** in the text field under the time slider).

Now let's examine the rigid body settings for our objects. In the Channel box, you'll see rigidBody1 (or 2, or whatever) listed under the shape node for the object you pick. For now, pick the plane and then click the rigidBody1 text.

Several text fields will pop up, giving you more control over the rigid body than you probably want. For now, just look down to these items: mass, bounciness, damping, static friction, and dynamic friction. Change the bounciness to 0.9 and replay the animation (remember to rewind first!). On the first bounce, the ball should bounce nearly as high as the height from which it was dropped, and it should take longer to settle to rest as the animation plays on. Now try setting the bounciness to 1.5. What happens? The ball bounces further up each time, soon disappearing from view—talk about a super ball! In our virtual world, not only do we get to simulate reality, we get to break the rules if we want.

Try playing with some other settings, like friction and damping—and remember to play with the settings for both the ball and the plane. You can also play with the mass settings, but a passive rigid body is defined to have an infinite mass (so the setting won't matter). Changing the mass of the ball won't make much difference at this point because gravity is a universal force, affecting all objects in the same way. Later, we'll see where mass can be used more effectively.

N O T E   Playing with the numbers is a great way to learn how rigid bodies work. Don't be afraid to try different settings for each of the channels of each rigid body—try to guess what your changes will do before playing back the animation.

Catapult! Converting a Body from Passive to Active Mode

Now let's create a catapult and see how easy it is to turn the active key on and off for a rigid body. Again, start with a new scene. Create a NURBS plane scaled to about the grid size. Now create a cylinder, rotate it so it lies along the X axis, and squash it nearly flat.

Now move the insert point of the cylinder all the way to its right.

T I P   To move the insert point, select the Move tool, press the Insert key on your key-board (which will change the Move tool's handle from one with arrows to one without), and move the new handle around. Don't forget to press the Insert key again when you're done, or you'll stay in insert mode!

Once you have this set up correctly, add a sphere of radius 1 and place it on top of the left end of the cylinder:

Now select the plane *and* the sphere, and make them passive rigid bodies. In the Hypergraph or Outliner, MM drag the sphere onto the cylinder, making the sphere the "child" of the cylinder (so they will rotate together). Now set a keyframe at your first frame on the cylinder's rotation channels (select the rotation channel names and RM select Key Selected), move the time slider to about 15 frames, rotate the cylinder so it is close to upright, and keyframe this new setting.

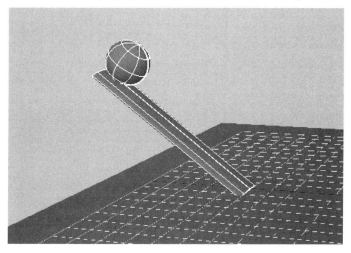

 TIP Setting the auto keyframe button to On will make Maya automatically set a new keyframe whenever some channel changes—after you manually set the first keyframe for that channel.

Play back the animation. You should see the cylinder (and its attendant ball) rotate up in a few frames, then stay still.

Now let's shove this ball out of the nest and let it fly! Select the sphere and, in the Channel box, find the Active channel (or attribute), located toward the bottom of the rigid body attributes. It should currently have a value of Off. Select the *name* of the channel (Active), set the time slider to around 12 frames, and RM select Key Selected while pressing on the Active name. This will set a key (with a value of off, or false, or 0) on the Active channel. Now move forward one or two frames, click in the text next to the Active name, and type **On** in the Channel box. If the Autokey function is on, you'll automatically generate a keyframe; otherwise select and manually keyframe this channel.

What you have done here is forced the sphere to become an active rigid body *just as the sphere is being pitched up in the air by the cylinder*. This timing allows us to take advantage of some clever programming by the Maya developers; the sphere will "inherit" speed and rotation from the movement of the cylinder, meaning it will fly away from the cylinder the moment it becomes an active rigid body.

To test this, rewind and play back the animation. The sphere should go flying off to infinity. Of course, to finish this simulation correctly, we need to add gravity once again. Select the sphere and then choose Fields ➢ Create Gravity (it should automatically connect to the sphere). Now play back the animation. The ball should (depending on

PART

3

Animation

how fast your cylinder rotates) either shoot or "plop" off the cylinder. If the ball flies off the catapult too slowly, try rotating the cylinder further at its last keyframe, or shorten the number of frames over which it rotates up. If the ball flies off too quickly, rotate the cylinder less at the last keyframe, or lengthen the number of frames over which it rotates up.

We've already played with the numbers on the rigid bodies in the last example. This time, let's play with gravity itself. (Be careful that you don't get motion sick!) In the Outliner or Hypergraph, select the gravity node you just created. In the Channel box, you'll see several settings for gravity, including Direction and Magnitude. Direction defaults to –1 in Y, or down, as gravity in the real world pulls down—a negative value—on the Y, or vertical axis. Magnitude defaults to 9.8 (that's 9.8 meters—or 32 feet—per second squared, the force of earth's gravity). Let's make things a bit heavier. Try setting gravity to, say, 200 or so. Now, when the ball comes off the cylinder, it should drop like a *very* heavy stone. Or try a value of 2—now we're on the moon!

Although the geometry in this scene is simple, the results are not: This same trick could be used as a character throws a ball at a can or bottle, creating a very nice mix of keyframed character animation and realistic physics.

Using Fields to Add Effects to Rigid Bodies

After you play with the gravity settings for a while, find a value for gravity that will give the ball a good long flight time, because now we're going to add some other fields to affect the ball's flight.

First, let's add some wind. Select the sphere, then select Fields ➤ Create Air ❑. The Options (Create) window opens, giving you several ways to adjust the air field.

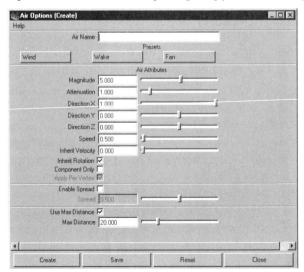

You'll see three buttons at the top (Wind, Wake, and Fan) that are simply preset options you can use to create the effect of wind, wake (like leaves moving in the wake of a car), or a fan. You can click all three buttons to see what settings are changed with each one, but in the end, click the Wind button, and then the Create button, and close the window. A new field, called airField1, will appear in your Outliner or Hypergraph.

Now play back the animation again. You should see the sphere get shoved right off the end of the plane (as the wind, by default, pushes in the positive X direction). Try changing the X component of the wind to 0 and the Y component to 1. Now the ball should fall more gently (like a beach ball). Next, increase the magnitude from 5 to a large number like 200. The ball will now "blow" up into the air, as the wind force is stronger than gravity. Set wind back down to a reasonable number like 5 or 10.

N O T E   As another experiment with fields, try turning the wind on and off by keyframing its magnitude.

Now let's add turbulence. Select the sphere and choose Fields ➤ Create Turbulence. Play back the animation. With the default magnitude of 5, the effects on the motion of the sphere will be very subtle. If you set the turbulence field's magnitude to 50, you will see the sphere move about in random ways as the turbulence field affects its motion. Try different numbers for the channels of the turbulence field and see what results from making these changes.

N O T E   You can also add fields to objects using the Fields ➤ Add Item menu options. All fields will travel with their parent object, and can therefore be used to create a wake or turbulence as the parent object passes rigid bodies or particles.

T I P   With rigid bodies, fields, and particle dynamics, it is a very good idea to take a simple animation and experiment with what each channel does by changing the numbers and watching the results in the animation. It is only by this kind of experience that you can see how Maya's physics engine really works.

We've seen how different fields can change a rather humdrum animation into something more interesting. Now let's make the simulation engine work a bit harder by creating more complex shapes.

Using the Rigid Body Solver

When you work with more complex shapes you may find that Maya's default settings don't get you the speed or accuracy that you are looking for out of your rigid body simulation. For such occasions, Maya allows you to adjust how it calculates rigid body

Animation

simulations through the *Rigid Body Solver*. With the Rigid Body Solver you can adjust how Maya calculates the simulation, giving you the ability to fine-tune your simulation for speed or accuracy.

Let's look at the solver in action. Create another empty scene, add a plane and a sphere (at some height above the plane), and make the plane a passive rigid body and the sphere an active one. Add gravity and test the animation to be sure the ball bounces on the plane as it should.

Now let's make the shape a bit more complex. First, increase the U and V isoparms to 16 or more each (on the makeNurbsSphere1 node). Then take the sphere and mold it into some bizarre, angular shape—something like this:

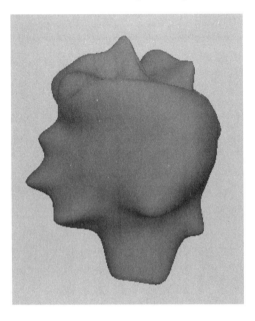

You can create this shape quite easily using Maya's Artisan utility (Edit Surfaces ➤ Sculpt Surfaces Tool ❑). If you are unfamiliar with Artisan, see Chapter 9, or just pull individual CVs out of the sphere.

When you play back the animation this time, Maya will probably go just a bit slower—this time, it has to keep track of a lot more surfaces! If you play back the frames one at a time (and look under the plane), you'll probably also be able to see a few points when some of the sphere's surfaces poke through the plane.

At full-speed playback, you probably won't notice these errors, but there are times when you might wish to correct these problems—or perhaps speed up playback for a particularly complex simulation. In these situations, you can use the Rigid Body Solver menu to adjust how Maya calculates its rigid body simulations. Essentially, the Rigid Body Solver gives you some control over the way Maya's dynamics engine handles the mathematics involved in the movement and interaction of rigid bodies. As you've just seen, complex shapes interact in complex ways, and adjusting calculation options via the solver is useful when the result of using Maya's default settings isn't accurate enough or fast enough to look realistic.

You can get access to the Rigid Body Solver in one of two ways: either choose Solvers ➣ Rigid Body Solvers, or select a rigid body and open the Attribute Editor (Ctrl+A) and select the Rigid Solver tab in the Attribute Editor window. Either way, you get a window that allows you to adjust the solver to meet your needs.

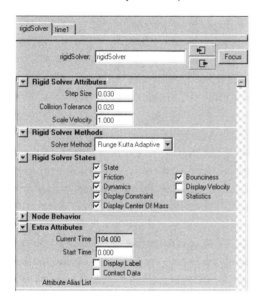

Notice the Rigid Solver States section of the window. Here you can turn most major functions on and off. For example, turn on the Display Velocity check box, and play back the animation. You will see an arrow that points in the direction of the sphere's velocity, with a length that represents the speed of the sphere. If you turn off the State check box, the animation will do nothing, because turning off this check box turns off the solver (this is a good way to quickly eliminate dynamics so you can concentrate on other elements of an animation). If you turn off the Dynamics check box, the sphere will fall, but it will no longer bounce, as dynamic interactions no longer work. Try turning off each of the check boxes in turn and see what effect this has on playback. When you're finished, reset the check boxes to their default state.

You'll also see a section of the window called Rigid Solver Methods. There are three choices here, though normally you would use the default method, Runge Kutta Adaptive. If you have a very complex simulation, however, and either wish to view it more quickly in interactive playback or don't care about the accuracy of the simulation for your final rendering, you can (temporarily) set the method to either Runge Kutta or to Midpoint. Midpoint is the least accurate but fastest. Runge Kutta is a compromise between the two extremes. For your dented ball, you probably won't see much difference between the three methods.

PART 3

Animation

N O T E   The Runge Kutta and Runge Kutta Adaptive options are named for the Runge Kutta solution, a mathematical method of solving an interlocking system of differential equations using first-order derivatives. In Maya, time is broken down into discrete steps (referenced through the Step Size field), and the integral of the equations is approximated at each step. Though the technique is mathematically complex, it is fast and accurate enough for most applications. (If you are interested in the subject, a number of books and articles are available on the Runge Kutta solution methods.)

The top—and most useful—section is called the Rigid Solver Attributes section. Using Step Size, Collision Tolerance, and Scale Velocity, you can alter the way in which the solver simulates rigid body dynamics. Let's look at each option:

> **Scale Velocity** is useful only if you have checked the Display Velocity check box in the section below—the Scale Velocity slider lets you scale the arrow that sticks out from the rigid body, making it fit within your window.

> **Step Size** defines the "chunk" of time (measured in fractions of a second) the solver divides the timeline into. A smaller step size means more calculations per second of animation, but it can also mean a more accurate simulation. If you have troubles with rigid body *interpenetration errors* (meaning that two bodies have "pierced" each other, as in our example), reducing the step size is a good place to start.

> **Collision Tolerance** tells Maya how carefully to evaluate frames where collisions take place. A large collision tolerance will speed up playback but can become very inaccurate.

Try making the collision tolerance 0.8 and playing back your animation. You will notice that the sphere doesn't bounce correctly on the plane. Now set the tolerance to 0.001 (the smallest possible value). If you saw frames at which the sphere's points stuck through the plane before, they should no longer appear.

Experiment with different step sizes and collision tolerances, and see how the changes affect the simulation. Often you can get away with making either the step size or collision tolerance very large, as long as you keep the other element small. Finding a compromise between speed and accuracy for a complex simulation is often the key to using rigid body dynamics effectively.

Speeding Up Calculations with Additional Solvers

Each additional object a rigid solver has to keep track of can geometrically increase the calculation time. To compensate for this, you can speed up calculations by isolating different parts of a simulation from one another and assigning additional solvers to each part.

Let's see how this works by making some changes in the deformed sphere scene you created in the previous section. (If you no longer have that scene, just create a ball and a plane, make the ball an active rigid body and the plane a passive rigid body, and then create gravity. Play back the animation to be sure the ball bounces off the plane.)

Now we're going to create a second Rigid Body Solver and assign the ball to it. Choose Solvers ➤ Create Rigid Body Solver. This creates a new solver, which will be called rigidSolver1 (or 2 or 3, depending on how many others you have created).

Set the new solver as the default (so that all new objects will be assigned to this solver): Solvers ➤ Current Rigid Solver ➤ SolverX, where SolverX is the solver you wish to establish as the default. Since we have already created both of our rigid bodies using the same solver, we need to assign one of the two bodies (the ball) to the new solver—rigidSolver1. Unfortunately, there is no button to do this, but you can do it with a quick bit of MEL (Maya Embedded Language) scripting.

In the scene window, select the sphere, then in the command line (accessed by pressing the ~ key while you're in a scene window), type the following:

```
rigidBody -edit -solver rigidSolver1;
```

This command tells Maya to edit the rigid solver for whatever objects are selected in the scene.

N O T E   For more on MEL scripting, see Chapters 16 and 17.

Now play back the animation again. This time, the ball should pass right through the plane. Although the plane and ball are both still affected by gravity, they no longer interact with each other, as they "live" in different solver states.

If you wish to edit the settings of your new rigid solver, be sure it is selected (in Solvers ➤ Current Rigid Solver), then select Solvers ➤ Rigid Body Solver. This will bring up the Attribute Editor with the rigidSolver1 selected.

Finally, with rigidSolver1 selected, you can create a new plane (or other object), make it a passive rigid body, and play back the animation. As both the ball and the new plane share the same solver, they will collide properly.

Using Impulse and a Newton Field to Simulate Orbital Dynamics

Let's now see how rigid bodies can be used to create a realistic simulation of a rocket ship going into orbit. We'll use a small cone for the rocket and a big sphere for the planet, but you can model just about anything you wish and substitute those objects in their places.

PART 3

Animation

First, create a sphere with a radius of 25 units and name it planet—scale your view out so you can see it clearly. Now, create a cone (named rocket) and scale it so it looks this size on the sphere:

It really doesn't matter how big the cone is, just so it looks good to you (I just left it at its default settings).

N O T E   Be sure you place the cone a little above the surface of the sphere, or you'll get rigid body interpenetration errors, like those we saw earlier.

Now make the sphere a passive rigid body (Bodies ➤ Create Passive Rigid Body) and make the cone an active rigid body (Bodies ➤ Create Active Rigid Body).

We could add a simple gravity field to these objects, but gravity pulls everything in the same direction. What we need here is a field that's centered on our planet; we'll use the Newton field (named after Sir Isaac). The Newton field creates a gravitational "well" in the planet that will attract all other rigid bodies to it, its force depending on how far from the planet the object is.

Select the planet and choose Fields ➤ Add Newton. In your Outliner or Hypergraph you will now see a Newton field parented to the planet. Choose the cone and open the Dynamic Relationships Editor (Windows ➤ Animation Editors ➤ Dynamic Relationships). In this window, click on the Newton field to highlight it—this connects the cone to the Newton field.

Set the frame length to 1000 or more, and play back the animation. The rocket should fall and land on the surface of the planet, bounce a bit, and stay there. If not, try turning the magnitude of the Newton field down to 5 or 6 and see if that helps.

Now we've got gravity; what we're missing is the thrust (or impulse) every rocket uses to escape the bounds of gravity. With the rocket selected, click the rigidBody2 tab in the Channel box and set the rocket's impulse Y to around 5. Play back the animation. Most likely, the rocket will go flipping around out of control as it rises, just like those ill-fated rockets in the early V-2 tests. The reason is that the impulse (or thrust) is coming from the bottom of the cone, so any slight error in thrust spins the rocket.

In reality, this is a serious and very difficult aspect of rocket science. But in our virtual world, we have a quick fix: set the ImpulsePositionY to around 4 or 5, making the thrust come from atop the cone, and thus making it much more stable in flight. When you now play back the animation, assuming the rocket has enough thrust, it will smoothly rise and disappear from the screen.

At present, our rocket has infinite fuel, so it just keeps going. To make a more realistic flight, let's create a ballistic trajectory, allowing the rocket to rise for a time and then fall back to the planet.

To do this, keyframe the thrust (impulse) on and off. Select the Y impulse name, set the time slider to the first frame, and RM select Key Selected. Now go out to about frame 15 and set the value of impulseY to 0 (the impulse will fall off from 5 to 0 over those 15 frames). When you play back the animation, the rocket should launch, rise, and then fall back to the planet.

N O T E   Getting this sequence to work right will take a bit of tweaking the numbers. It is very easy to get the rocket stuck on the ground, or flying off at an amazing speed. If you are completely stuck, try opening the premade project (15orbit.ma) on the CD that accompanies this book.

We've now gone suborbital; it's time to get into orbit! To do that, we need to add an in-flight correction, to make the rocket move sideways as well as up and down. Move the time indicator to frame 10, and key the impulseX (at 0) on this frame. Now move to frame 11 and key the impulseX to 2. Move the time to 39 and key impulseX back to 0 (again, you may need to change these numbers around to get good results). If all worked well, when you play back the animation, you will see the rocket orbit the planet (in a *very* scary-looking, squashed orbit, but an orbit nonetheless). If you didn't give the rocket enough thrust, it will crash back into the planet in a pretty spectacular manner.

In order to get our orbit a bit cleaner, we need to add yet another in-flight correction. At around frame 90, set another key on impulseY (at 0). At about frame 95, set a key on impulseY to –1 (so it pushes down on the rocket). At about frame 115, set another key on impulseY, this time back to 0 again. If these numbers work for you, you should see the rocket following a much cleaner orbital path.

PART 3

N O T E   As an exercise, how close can you get the orbit to circular? Can you keep the rocket from spinning around as it orbits the planet? With all the tweaking involved, you can see why they're called "rocket scientists"!

Animation

Converting (Baking) a Rigid Body Animation into Keyframes

Once you've got an orbital motion you like, you can "bake" the rigid body animation into keyframes so you can change the keyframes into other sorts of motion. *Baking* is the term Maya uses for creating a set of keyframes that mimic the dynamic motion of a rigid body simulation. As we will see below, baking an animation allows you to adjust motion paths and keyframes for what was once a dynamic simulation (and thus did not allow this kind of adjustment).

WARNING   If you may eventually wish to return to your rigid body simulation, save a *different* copy of your project before you bake the simulation. You can't go back once the simulation has been baked!

Select the rocket and choose Edit ➢ Keys ➢ Bake Simulation. The simulation will run, and when it's finished, you will have a baked animation (and a mess of keyframes in the time line!).

Let's put this baked animation to good use, getting rid of that nasty rotation around the Z axis that the rocket developed. With the rocket still selected, open the Graph Editor (Window ➢ Animation Editors ➢ Graph Editor). On the left side, highlight the rotateZ channel, and then press F on the keyboard (to frame the selection). You'll see a curve with hundreds of keyframes on it—a few more than we need for our animation!

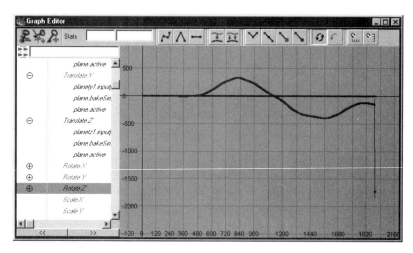

To get rid of the cone's Z rotation problems, we could first attempt to simplify the curve. Choose Curves ➢ Simplify Curves from the Graph Editor's menu (or RM select this). Maya will remove many keyframes it considers unimportant to the curve. Unfortunately, even if you run the Simplify Curves command several times, the curve is still very heavy—and we don't want any of that motion, anyway! Let's just kill the whole curve.

Select the entire curve and press the Delete key, and away it goes. Now when you play back the animation, the Z rotation is gone—all of it. To get some form of rotation, you'll need to first delete the rigid body from the rocket (so it doesn't interfere with your setting keyframes). In the Outliner or Hypergraph, choose Display ➤ Show Shape Nodes to reveal the rigid body nodes. Select the rigid body associated with the rocket and delete it. Now set a 0 keyframe on the Z rotation of the rocket at about frame 15 (just where it begins to tip over). Go to the end of the animation and set a keyframe of about –1080 for the Z rotation (this is about 3 revolutions, which matches how many times the rocket goes around in my 1500 frame animation). To get the rotateZ curve to look right, you'll have to adjust its shape in the Graph Editor. (See Chapter 10 for more information about the Graph Editor.)

N O T E   For a finished project, see 15orbitBaked.ma on the CD-ROM that accompanies this book.

Throwing Dice: Working with the Dynamics Simulator

On a quick trip to Vegas, you might play craps, a game in which you throw two dice into a horseshoe-shaped pit and watch them bounce around (hoping for lucky 7!). As you might guess, this is another great event to simulate in Maya using rigid bodies. Here, in a simplified version of the craps table, we will get to see how Maya's dynamics simulator handles a more complex, multiple-body collision.

First, build a NURBS plane and stretch it to the size of the grid. Now build a second plane and place it near the end of the first, at right angles to it.

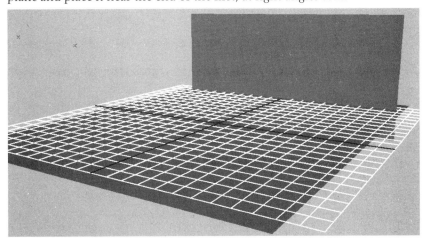

Now add a cube of about default size, or a little smaller, and name it something like die1.

T I P   A cube is actually six pieces, or faces, and it is easy to choose only one of these faces by accident. A way to avoid choosing only a face is to be sure to name the cube itself (the parent level) something that you can easily recognize (like die1, in this case).

Add a second cube and name it die2. You can add a checker 2D texture to the dice to make them stand out better if you wish. (See Chapter 19 for information about basic texturing and other rendering techniques.) When the dice are textured and placed at the front of the "table," it should look something like this:

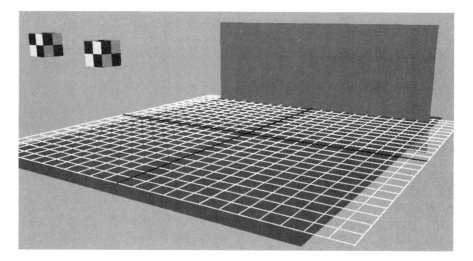

Select both of the planes and choose Bodies ➢ Create Passive Rigid Body. Next (in the Outliner or Hypergraph), choose the top level of each die (remember, this must be the top level, or you will get very strange results!) and choose Bodies ➢ Create Active Rigid Bodies. Be sure both dice are still selected (or select them again) and choose Fields ➢ Create Gravity.

When you play back the animation, you should see both dice fall and bounce off the table. If the dice break apart, you have created the rigid bodies on the sub-faces of the cubes, not their top levels, so you'll need to go back and try again. If you get stuck, try opening the file 15dice.ma on the CD.

To make life a bit more interesting, we need to give the dice some initial motion. Select one of the dice, click on the rigid body name in the Channel box, and set the initial velocity to, say, Z to –15 or so. Repeat with the other die, but give this one a slightly different velocity. When you play back the animation, both dice should travel down the table and bounce off the far wall (if they don't, increase their velocities).

You will notice, however, that they stay perfectly upright (that is, they don't rotate), which is a bit odd looking. Give them an initial spin in X, Y, and Z, or anything you like, and tweak the numbers until you get a nice-looking simulation. If the dice now bounce off the table, you can either scale the plane bigger, or increase the plane's dynamic friction, which will make the dice "stick" to it more.

Finally, add a positive X velocity (maybe 5) to the left die, and a negative X velocity to the right die, making them collide in mid-air before hitting the table. You will probably need to adjust their velocities in both X and Z to get them to collide. Because of the complexity of the collisions between the spinning dice, you will notice a slowdown when the two collide, making it a bit difficult to determine if the motion looks good. To get a better idea of how the scene really looks, you can *playblast* it, and watch it play back in real time (to playblast a scene, select Window ➤ Playblast). The Playblast tool will record the animation one frame at a time, and when it is finished, you will get a window with the completed animation in it.

 TIP A fully rendered version of the dice throw is available as a QuickTime movie (15diceFinished.mov) on the CD that accompanies this book.

Building a Chain: Adding Constraints to a Rigid Body

As a final example of rigid bodies, let's build something a bit more complex: a link of chains like a child's swing would have. Along the way, we'll learn how to add constraints and how to adjust the rigid solver to speed up some very difficult calculations.

Create a new scene, add a cylinder (named Bar), rotate it 90 degrees in X, and then scale it large on the Z axis.

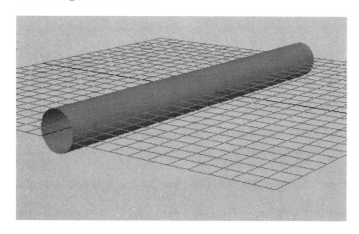

Animation

Now create a torus (named EmbeddedLink) and stretch it into the shape of your basic chain link. Rotate the torus into position below the bar.

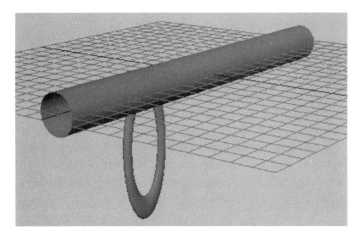

Once the first link is in place, duplicate it, rename it Link1, rotate it 90 degrees around Y, and move it into place. Do this three more times, until you get a link of chains that looks like this:

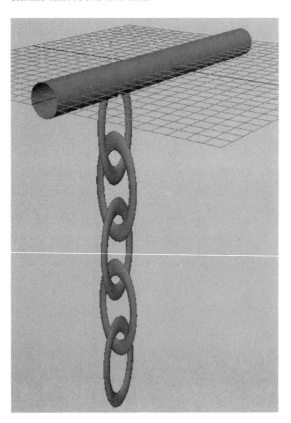

WARNING   Be sure there is a separation between each link (so they do not touch each other). Otherwise, when you create the rigid bodies, you will get an interpenetration error, and the simulation will break down.

TIP   After you make your first duplicate, move it, and rotate it, you can then use the Smart Transform option in the Duplicate options window to do the rest. Each duplicate will be rotated and moved into position automatically.

Now select the bar and the first link, and choose Bodies ➤ Create Passive Rigid Body. Next, choose all the other links and choose Bodies ➤ Create Active Rigid Body. With all the links still selected, add gravity to the scene (Fields ➤ Create Gravity). When you play back the animation, you should see all the links fall and then bounce off of one another, finally coming to rest after about 200 frames.

This is a good first step toward our chain link, but there are a couple of problems. First, the chains aren't in a "resting" position at the start of the animation, and second, they bounce all over the place when playback starts. Let's deal with problem two first.

Our chains really don't need to bounce very much (it's just slowing the simulation down), so we could either turn all the bounciness attributes down to 0, or take care of the whole thing in one fell swoop by turning off the bounce state attribute. Choose Solvers ➤ Rigid Body Solvers, and in the attribute window, uncheck the Bounciness check box. This globally turns off all bounciness calculations, and makes the remaining calculations run more quickly and smoothly. With the bounciness calculations off, the links should just drop nicely into position when you play back the animation, coming to rest by frame 20 or so.

To finish our swing, we're going to add a weight to the bottom of the chain links. Create a sphere with a radius of about 3 (named weightBall), and position it just below the bottom link in the chain (remember not to allow the sphere to touch the link!). Looks a bit medieval, huh? First select the bottom link, and then Shift-select the sphere. Now choose Bodies ➤ Create Constraint ❏. This brings up a window that allows you to create a constraint between the two selected objects. Choose the Pin type of constraint, and leave the other settings at their defaults. When you click Create, below, the sphere will be made into a rigid body, and a pin-type constraint will be added between it and the last link in the chain (as if the two were pinned together).

With the sphere selected, go to Window ➤ Animation Editors ➤ Dynamic Relationships, and highlight the gravity field (connecting it to the sphere). When you playback the animation, all the links plus the sphere should drop down (as before).

Now let's deal with the first problem noted above: getting our links and ball into a resting position at the start of the animation so they will not fall into place to start every animation. Play the animation forward until the chain comes to a complete

PART **3**

Animation

rest. Stop the playback, but don't rewind the animation. Choose Solvers ➤ Initial State ➤ Set For All Dynamics. This programs the current state of all dynamic objects into Maya as the initial state. When you rewind the animation now, it should remain in its current, rest position.

Great! We now have a completely lifeless simulation that does absolutely nothing! Let's make things a bit livelier. First, try adding an initial X velocity of around –10 to the weight. When you play back the animation, the ball (and the chain, following it) should swing out to the left, then pendulum back to the right, slowly settling back to stillness. You can try adding velocity in other directions, and even a rotation to the ball. When you have experimented a bit, reset all the initial velocities back to 0.

Instead of an initial velocity, let's now add an impulse of –4 or –5 in the X direction. When you play the animation back, the ball and chain will appear to be blowing in a wind from the right of the screen (you could actually achieve the same effect by connecting an air field to the ball). To allow the ball and chain to fall again, keyframe the impulseX back to 0 after 30 or 40 frames.

You may notice that the ball and chain get kinked up near the bar, and this slows the animation way down. To compensate for this, you might try adjusting the rigid solver settings. (I set step size to 0.1 and the solver to Runge Kutta—not Adaptive—and got acceptable results.) You might also get interpenetration errors, in which case you might wish to reduce the step size a bit.

Finally, you might notice that the ball doesn't look very weighty in the way it is thrashed around by the chain. Try increasing the ball's mass to 50 or 100 (and set the impulse higher to compensate), and see how it looks now.

N O T E   The only real drawback to adding mass to objects is that it drastically increases calculation times.

T I P   A rendered movie of a chain and ball is available on the CD (15ballAndChain.mov).

Summary

In this chapter, we saw how easy it is (relatively speaking) to get Maya to do the work for us when simulating real-world events like falling and colliding objects. We also found that rigid bodies can be changed from passive (keyframable and not affected by fields) to active (nonkeyframable and affected by fields), and that, when a passive rigid body is made active, it inherits the motion it had before. This allows rigid bodies to work within a keyframed animation and with keyframed characters. Finally, we created more complex interactions, and we adjusted the rigid solver to give us realistic, but faster, simulations.

PART IV

WORKING WITH MEL

MEL Basics
....

Programming with MEL
....

chapter 16

MEL BASICS

Featuring

- *MEL fundamentals*

- *The Script Editor*

- *Hands-on MEL: building lights automatically*

- *Hands-on MEL: creating, moving, and naming an object—with one keystroke*

- *Placing objects using a marking menu*

- *What's an attribute?*

- *Using expressions with MEL*

MEL BASICS

T his chapter introduces Maya's embedded scripting language, MEL. You will learn how Maya uses MEL, and you'll see how you can increase your productivity by automating repetitive tasks and getting Maya to do exactly what you want it to the first time. Along the way you'll have an opportunity to try out what you've learned in hands-on exercises that illustrate the power of MEL.

While MEL does require a bit of programming savvy, you really don't need to be a rocket scientist to use it—at least at the basic level. If you have had some programming background, MEL's basic syntax will seem pretty straightforward. If you know the C programming language, MEL's syntax will seem like second nature.

If you have never looked at a computer program before, MEL will at first seem baffling, but don't worry. Even if you never intend to do any real programming with MEL, you will find in this chapter and the next one many nuggets of information that will allow you to use Maya far more effectively than you may have thought possible.

Before reading this chapter, you should be familiar with basic Maya concepts, like interface conventions, how to create and animate objects, and how to move around Maya's windows and menus (see Chapter 2). If you have some knowledge of computer programming, that will also prove helpful, but it is not necessary.

MEL is Fundamental

MEL (Maya Embedded Language) is the foundation from which you interact with Maya. When you open Maya, the program first runs several scripts, which actually build all the windows you see—that's right: Maya itself has no interface whatsoever. You can even run Maya from your operating system command prompt by typing in **Maya –prompt**! Behind nearly everything you see in Maya is a MEL script.

What does this mean to the average Maya user? Simple: whatever the original programmers did, you also can do. You can write windows that have sliders, text fields, and buttons in them; you can create attributes in the Channel box; you can even add menu items to the main menu bar. The fact that Maya is built on MEL is one of the program's most powerful features.

What is a Scripting Language?

MEL is a scripting language, not a complete programming language (like Java or C++). A program written in a programming language is compiled and becomes an independent program (like the core program, Maya, which just runs off your computer's operating system). A scripting language, on the other hand, resides on top of another program (in this case, Maya) and is interpreted at every line rather than compiled. Because scripting languages are interpreted by the "mother" program, they are a bit slower than compiled programs; however, they require much less programming overhead than do compiled programs.

If you are a real "propeller head" and like to get into the guts of a program, Maya has its own API (Application Programming Interface)—appropriately enough named "Maya API"—in which you can create plug-ins for the program itself using the C++ programming language. MEL does just fine for 95% of the things most people want to do, however, and it isn't too difficult to learn.

 N O T E   Although the API is outside the scope of this book, you can contact Alias|Wavefront about developing plug-ins for Maya.

The Script Editor

One of the best features of Maya, as it relates to MEL, is the Script Editor. MEL is a huge language (with over 600 commands and about 75 functions), but the Script Editor will clue you in on how different commands are used, and allow you to "cut and paste" whole scripts together without the need to program a thing yourself. You don't even need to use the Command line to enter the MEL commands; operations you perform in the Maya interface are recorded as MEL commands in the Script Editor.

 N O T E   The Command line, which we discussed in Chapter 2, is just one input line in the Script Editor. Type a command in the Command line and you can see it appear in the Script Editor's History window.

You can bring up the Script Editor in two ways: either select Window ➤ General Editors ➤Script Editor, or click the button in the lower-right corner of the screen that looks like a square with lines in it.

 ⟵ Script Editor

When opened, the Script Editor will look as follows:

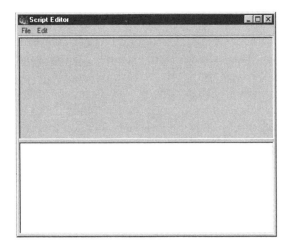

Notice that there are two windows in the editor. The top window is called the History window; the bottom, the Input window. With the Script Editor open, create a NURBS sphere (the easiest way to do this is to click the blue ball on the shelf tab at the top of the main window). Now look at the History window. The very last line of that window should read something like:

```
sphere -p 0 0 0 -ax 0 1 0 -ssw 0 -esw 360 -r 1 -d 3 -ut 0 -tol 0.01 -s 8
    -nsp 4 -ch 1;
```

What you see in the top window is the command you told Maya to perform when you clicked the ball on the shelf. Sphere is Maya's command to create a NURBS sphere; all the characters with dashes before them (-p, -ax, and so on) are "flags" that tell the Sphere command how to build the sphere. For example, -p stands for pivot, which is the pivot point of the sphere (since it's 0, 0, 0, the pivot of the sphere is at the origin); –r stands for radius (the sphere's radius, in this case, is 1 unit); and –ssw and –esw are the start and end sweep (in degrees here). Finally, the semicolon at the end of the line tells Maya the command is finished. (Nearly every line of MEL code needs a semicolon at the end.)

NOTE   As you can see, more characters will fit into the Input window than we can squeeze into the printed page, so the semicolon is also your guide to where one command actually ends and the next begins. (As a further guide, we've indented the "wrapped" portion of these longer lines by about six characters.) As you enter commands from this book into the Script Editor, you generally need to press the Enter key only after semicolons.

Create a few more objects (like lights, cones, curves, etc.) and look at what appears in the History window of the Script Editor. You can see that every command you perform in the interface is relayed to Maya's core program via MEL commands. For ease of reading, you can clear the top window. Go to the Script Editor menu and select Edit ➢ Clear History. The top window should now be cleared of all commands.

Now try opening one of Maya's windows (for example, the Hypergraph window: Window ➢ Hypergraph). What do you see in the History window? Probably nothing at all. To keep from cluttering the History window, Maya's programmers created a filter that blocks from view in the History Window many of the MEL commands programmers don't commonly need to see. Sometimes, however, it is very useful to see what's really going on in Maya. Close the Hypergraph, select Edit ➢Echo All Commands, and reopen the Hypergraph. Now you should see something like this:

```
hotBox;
tearOffPanel "Hypergraph" "hyperGraphPanel" true;
addHyperGraphPanel hyperGraphPanel1;
HyperGraphEdMenu hyperGraphPanel1HyperGraphEd;
createModelPanelMenu modelPanel1;
createModelPanelMenu modelPanel2;
createModelPanelMenu modelPanel3;
createModelPanelMenu modelPanel4;
buildPanelPopupMenu hyperGraphPanel1;
// Result: hyperGraphPanel1Window //
```

All these strange words represent the steps by which Maya builds the Hypergraph window for you. (Actually, nearly all the words above, like buildPanelPopupMenu, are calls to other MEL scripts in the Maya2.5/Scripts/Others directory. You can look through them to see how the window is actually constructed.) So you see, even the windows in Maya are created through MEL.

One other note worth mentioning about the lines above: the last line,

```
//Result: hyperGraphPanel1Window//
```

is called the *result line*. The two slashes at the beginning of the line are a comment marker that tells MEL to ignore the rest of that line (you'll see these comment lines in all well-made MEL scripts). MEL then prints out for you the result of the operation (in this case, that it created the window as you asked). If there had been a problem making the Hypergraph window, the result line would have contained an error message instead of a result message.

Now let's take a look at the Input window (the window on the bottom half of the Script Editor window). First empty the scene of all objects and clear the History window; then place your cursor in the bottom window and type in the following:

```
Sphere -radius 1 -pivot 0 0 0 -name myBall;
```

Press the Enter key on your numeric keypad (not the one on your main keyboard). You should see the text disappear from the Input window and appear in the History window (you will also see another result line, telling you that the command was successfully completed). At the same time, you should see a sphere appear at the origin of your scene, named myBall. Congratulations, you have just executed your first MEL command!

NOTE   If you're wondering why you have to use the numeric keypad's Enter key, it's because the alpha Enter key is reserved for in-line returns. In other words, pressing the alpha Enter key just creates a new line in the editor window. To force the contents of the editor window to be evaluated (executed), you must use the numeric pad's Enter key.

Now try this: delete the sphere from your scene; then triple-click the line in the History window that you typed earlier (Sphere -radius 1 -pivot 0 0 0 -name myBall). Once you have the entire line highlighted, copy that line into the Input window (in IRIX, simply MM click in the Input window; in NT, Ctrl+C (copy) the text, click in the Input window, and Ctrl+V (paste) the line there). Now hit the Enter key (on the numeric keypad, remember!). You should see the exact same sphere (called myBall) created at the origin of your scene, meaning that you have copied a command from the History window and made a mini-script (called a macro) out of it.

This was a very simple example, but consider the power this little cut-and-paste trick gives you: you can "record" anything you like from the History window and turn it into a MEL macro (or even a full-blown script). By storing this little script, you can return to it any time and, at the click of a button, make all those actions happen.

NOTE   As Chapter 3 details, you can create buttons for MEL commands simply by highlighting those commands, and then MM dragging the command lines up to a shelf.

Hands-On MEL: Building Lights Automatically

Let's put all this information to some use now. We're going to record several actions we perform to create a default lighting setup, copy those actions into a macro, and place that macro on a shelf. Once we've done that, we can automatically set up our scene lights for any scene we wish, at the click of a mouse.

1. Open Maya or begin a new scene.

2. Create a new NURBS plane object (Create ➤ Nurbs Primitives ➤ Plane), scale it to about the size of the Maya grid, and turn on hardware lighting (press the 7 key on the main keyboard). This plane will help you see how your lights are affecting the scene.

3. Open the Script Editor and clear the History window.

4. Now create and place one or more lights in your scene. You can also set color, intensity, and name for each of these lights.

 TIP   Refer to Chapter 20 for tips on best lighting setups. We tend to like a three-light setup: a key light, a fill light, and a back light (all spotlights).

5. Once you're happy with the lights' positions, colors, and other attributes, simply select everything in the History window and MM drag the highlighted text up to the shelf of your choosing. A new button will appear that looks as follows:

 — Button Added for New Script

Let's see if it worked.

6. Select all in your scene and hit Delete (or you can actually type in the Script Editor the following to do the same thing: select -all; delete;).

7. Once your scene is empty, go up to the shelf and click your newly made button. After a couple of seconds, you should see your lights magically appear in the scene, just as you had set them up.

Not bad for a couple minutes of work and no programming! If you like, you can create several more lighting setups, each of which creates a different lighting setup for your scene.

One problem you might notice right away is that the shelf buttons all look alike. Fortunately, Maya can handle this quite easily.

1. From the main menu, select Options ➤ Customize UI ➤ Shelves. A window will appear that has three tabs. Let's take a quick look at all three.

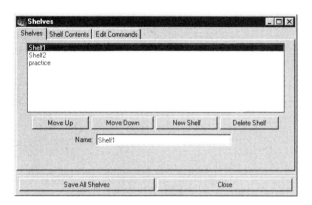

2. First, select the Shelves tab. In the window, you'll see listed all the shelves you currently have, along with buttons to add, delete, or move shelves up and down in the order they appear onscreen. Click the New Shelf button, and a new shelf appears, titled shelfLayout1. You can either rename this to create a shelf for you (like myShelf) or click the Delete Shelf button to remove the new shelf.

3. Now select Shelf1 from the list and click the Shelf Contents tab. In the window, you'll see all the buttons on the selected shelf listed below. Click the first item in the list (Curves With CVs) and look at the area below the top window. Here, you'll see the Move Up, Move Down, and Delete Item buttons, as well as other buttons and fields:

   • The Label button contains the text you see in the window above (the internal label for the button).

   • The Overlay Label contains the text you see under the button in the shelf window. (For the Curves With CVs button, this is blank, so there is no text on the shelf button. Try adding text and see what happens!)

    • The Change Image button allows you to find or create the bitmapped image that appears on the shelf—in the case of the Curves With CVs button, it's this image, stored in the Maya 2.5\Bitmaps folder.

You can also navigate to the Maya2.5\extras\icons directory and browse through many pre-built icons for your use in creating shelf buttons.

TIP   You can also create your own icons. In Windows NT, the icons can be in BMP, JPG, or XPM formats (BMP and JPG are supported by nearly all NT graphics editing packages). In IRIX, you must save the image in .xpm format (using Xpaint or another program). The icons are 32 × 32 pixels, and you should make your images that size. Note that if you wish to place text at the bottom of the image, you should leave a blank space to allow room for it.

4. Now go back to the Shelves tab and select the shelf that contains your new light button.

5. Return to the Shelf Contents tab. Add a label and an overlay label to your button. Now change the image of the button to one of the images in Maya2.0\extras\icons (if you want text on your button, a good choice of icons is the UserMenuIcon group in this directory—they have room for text at the bottom of the button).

The final tab, Edit Commands, is for more advanced users. This window actually allows you to rewrite the scripts for the menu buttons right inside the Customize Shelves window. The script for whatever item you had selected in the Shelf Contents tab will appear in the main window. You can then change any commands you wish, or add comments to the script.

To make these changes "stick," however, you *must* press the Enter key on your numeric keypad (not on your keyboard); otherwise, when you select another tab, all your changes will be lost! For practice, try adding a comment line like the following to your lights macro:

```
//This is my macro to make several lights in a scene.
```

Click another shelf button and then return to the Edit Commands tab. Did your changes hold? If not, try again, this time remembering to press the Enter key to make your changes stick.

Before leaving the Customize Shelves window, it is always a good idea to click the Save All Shelves button at the bottom of any of the tabs (assuming you want your changes to stick!). This button writes all the changes you just made to your Maya\Prefs\Shelves directory, so that the next time you start up Maya, your shelves will look just as they do now.

In this example of MEL, you have learned to quickly record your actions, save them as a macro, place them in your shelves, and finally, change the text and image of the button to customize its look. Next, we will create a small script that will execute when we press a keyboard key.

Hands-On MEL: Creating, Moving, and Naming an Object—with One Keystroke

Let's say you often make a NURBS sphere, rename it to **ball**, and move it some distance from the origin (you can modify this to be a light, a plane, or whatever; but for now, we'll just do it with a sphere). Even though Maya has a very efficient workflow, it's a waste of your time to do the same things over and over, so let's make Maya do it for you at the press of a key.

1. Open the Customize Hotkey menu by selecting Options ➤ CustomizeUI ➤ Hotkeys. This brings up a pretty scary looking window like the following:

Fortunately, we really don't have to worry about the top window for now; we only care about the stuff at the bottom.

N O T E   The window at the top of the Customize Hotkeys window lists all commands Maya has and whether or not they are mapped to a keyboard command. This means that you could (should you wish) change, remove, or add hotkeys for any of Maya's commands. See Chapter 3 for further information about how to do this.

2. Let's query a key to see if it's free for us to use. In the Key Settings box, type **N** in the Key field, and check the Alt box in the Modifiers group below. Click the Query key. You should get the following message:

```
Alt-n <press> is not mapped to any command object.
```

This means the key is available for your use (if it's not, try another key). Click OK to dismiss the dialog box.

3. Now, in the Command Object Settings box on the right, enter something like the following in the Annotation field (this is the text that will appear in the list above):

```
Make and move a sphere.
```

Then, in the Commands window, type the following (you could also paste commands from the Script Editor):

```
sphere -radius 4 -name ball -pivot 0 0 0 -ssw 0 -esw 360;
move -relative 0 5 0;
```

4. Click the Create Command Object button. The list window at the top of the screen will now update, and you'll see your command text listed at the bottom of the window. On the left, next to your new command, you'll see the word (None), telling you that the command has not yet been mapped to a key.

5. Return to the Key Settings section, type **N** in the Key field, select Alt and Press, and click Apply New Settings. The list window above will update again, reflecting that your command has now been turned into a hotkey:

```
Alt n          Release  make and move a sphere            ▼
```

6. Click the Save button and close this window.

7. Now hold down the Alt key and press N. If you did everything right, you should see a sphere sitting in your window called "ball" and resting 5 units up from the grid on the Y axis.

Congratulations! You have now written some MEL commands and made them work simply by pressing a key! As a further exercise, try to take the commands used in the "create lights" exercise we did above, and map them to a hotkey of your choosing.

NOTE   If you didn't get what you expected, check the Script Editor to see if there was an error. If so, go back to the Customize Hotkeys commands and edit the command to make it work. If the Script Editor doesn't show anything happening at all, check that you mapped the command to the Alt+N key combination. If you're still having trouble, try typing the sphere commands into the Script Editor and get them to work properly, then copy them into the Command window.

Placing Objects Using a Marking Menu

Working with MEL

So far we have seen how to record MEL commands and make them into a button on a shelf, and we've seen how to issue MEL commands in text form and turn them into a hotkey. Now we will learn just how easy it is to create a marking menu that performs any of several MEL commands.

Let's say that you wish to move a selected object (or objects) around in different directions simply by selecting an item from a GUI (Graphical User Interface) list. This is the perfect situation in which to use a Maya marking menu.

1. First, create a new NURBS sphere (or cone or whatever) at the origin of the grid. Now, in the Script Editor, type in the following:

```
move -r 0 5 0;
```

2. When you execute this command, the ball (or other object) should move 5 units up the Y axis (remember, -r stands for relative in this case, meaning that the object will move relative to its current position along the Y axis). To move the ball back to 0, type this:

```
move -r 0 -5 0;
```

The ball moves 5 units down, and goes back to 0.

3. Now open the Customize Marking Menus window by selecting Options ➢ CustomizeUI ➢ Marking Menus. The following window will appear:

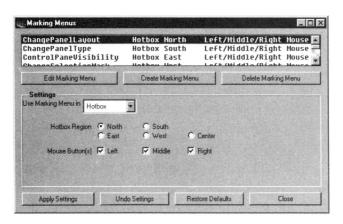

Once again, the top list shows marking menus built into Maya (part of the hot-box that appears when you hold down the spacebar). But of course you can build your own as well.

4. Simply click Create Marking Menu to bring up a window that will let you build a menu of your own.

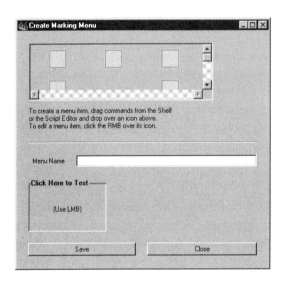

5. Under Menu Name, type in **MoveObject**. Now RM click the top center yellow-ish button in the internal window and select Edit Menu Item.

 N O T E   In addition to the eight main marking menu positions (North, Northeast, East, and so on), there is a ninth position, at the bottom left of the window, called the "over-flow" menu item. If you add a command to this item, another will be created just below it, allowing you to make the menu as large as you wish. Also, all menu items can have sub-menus, allowing you even greater flexibility in building a marking menu.

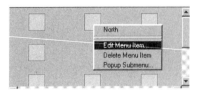

This brings up a window in which you add the commands for the button.

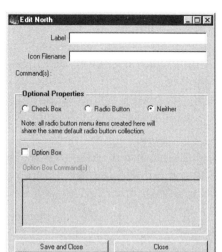

6. Under Label, type **Move Up**, and leave the Icon Filename field blank (you can specify a path for an image that will appear in this position when the marking menu is accessed). In the Commands field, type in

```
Move -r 0 5 0;
```

7. Leave Optional Properties set at Neither, leave the Option Box blank, and click Save and Close.What you have just done is to create a marking menu item that will move a selected object up by 5 units.

8. To test how this action works, press the LM button in the Click Here To Test window (select an object in your scene first!). Whatever you selected should move up by 5 units when you select the command.

9. Now, edit the East, West, and South marking menu buttons to the following, respectively:

```
Move -r 5 0 0;
Move -r -5 0 0;
Move -r 0 -5 0;
```

10. Give them appropriate titles and test that they work as they should.

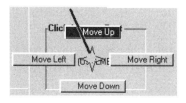

11. Once you're happy with how the menu buttons work, click the Save button and return to the Marking Menus window.

12. At the bottom of the list, you'll now see MoveObject listed. With this item selected, in the Settings window, select the Hotkey Editor option (this allows you to make a hotkey for the menu you just made). Click the Apply Settings button and close the window.

13. Now, in order to use our new marking menu, we have to go to Options ➤ CustomizeUI ➤ Hotkeys and make a hotkey for the menu.

14. Scroll to the bottom of the list window and you'll see two new items in the list: MoveObject (Press) and MoveObject (Release). By mapping these two items, we will create a hotkey that will bring up our new marking menu (the release key must be mapped for marking menus, or the menu will just stay up even after the hotkey has been released!).

15. First, let's find an unmapped key. Query the Alt+O key to see if it's mapped (if it is, try another one).

16. Now, select the MoveObject (Press) item in the list, type **O** in the Key field, check Alt, and be sure that the Press radio button is selected. Click Apply New Settings and the MoveObject item should be updated to show that Alt+O is its new hotkey.

17. Now let's map the Release item. Select MoveObject (Release) in the list, type **O**, and select Alt and the Release radio button, and click Apply New Settings. Once complete, the items should look as follows:

18. Click the Save button and close the Hotkey window.

19. Let's test our new marking menu: select an object in the scene window, press and hold the Alt and O keys, and press the mouse button down. You should now see your marking menu, ready for action!

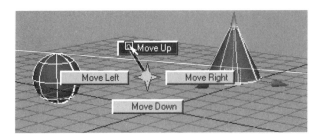

20. Move the object(s) you have selected around the screen to see how the new menu works.

You can take these simple steps and reuse them to create marking menus to do anything you like. For example, if you created several lighting setups in the work above, you could now create a marking menu to allow you to select any of these lighting setups very quickly and intuitively. We've seen how we can record or type simple commands, and place them on the shelf, in a hotkey, or even a marking menu. Now let's take a closer look at how MEL can work with the attributes of any object in your scene.

What's an Attribute?

An attribute (Attr) is any item that lives on a Maya node (a Maya node is anything you can see in the Hypergraph). This sounds a bit obscure, but it's really fairly straightforward: anything like rotateX, transformZ, or scaleY is an attribute of an object (more specifically, an object's transform node).

When you build, alter, or animate an object, you're changing one or more attributes on one or more nodes in the object—and of course, all of these changes are just MEL commands, so you can make Maya do the work for you.

 N O T E   In this chapter, we'll take a quick look at how MEL works with attributes; in the next chapter, we'll go into more detail about how to build complex scripts using attributes.

You may have noticed when you created the lights in the exercise earlier in this chapter that the Script Editor was filled with many statements that started with setAttr. The setAttr statement tells MEL to set a certain attribute to a certain value. Likewise, the getAttr statement gets (reads) the value of an attribute on a certain object so you can use that value in another MEL statement. The addAttr statement tells MEL to add a custom attribute to a certain item. Essentially, the setAttr statement is the same as going into the Attribute Editor window and changing a value in one of its fields (try changing a value in the Attribute Editor, and note that the Script Editor History window shows that a setAttr statement has been issued).

The syntax (the rules of what goes where) for an Attr statement are as follows:

```
setAttr [flags] objectName value;
```

Flags, as we've seen, are any special requests for MEL to complete; the object name is the name of the item to set the attribute on (like nurbsSphere1); and the value is the value to set the attribute to. The getAttr and addAttr commands have similar syntax. For example, we could move a sphere called "ball" to 10 on the X axis by typing the following in the Script Editor:

```
setAttr ball.translateX 10;
```

Once you execute this command, your ball will move from where it is to 10 on the X axis. (Of course, if you have no object called "ball," you will get an error message.)

This is pretty much like giving the move command: move 10 0 0. Unlike the move command, however, setting the attribute of translateX will not affect the other two attributes (the Y and Z translate attributes). Also, the setAttr statement is far more flexible than the move command, which can only translate an object.

As a quick example of how setAttr can work, let's make a ball and manually set several of its attributes. Type the following into the Script Editor's Input window:

```
sphere -n ball;
setAttr makeNurbSphere1.radius 4;
setAttr makeNurbSphere1.ssw 20;
setAttr makeNurbSphere1.esw 250;
setAttr ball.rotateY 90;
setAttr ball.translateX -5;
setAttr ball.scaleY 0.7;
```

Can you figure out what each command does on your own? Try highlighting each of these lines by itself and pressing the numeric Enter key to execute it.

TIP   Using the technique of highlighting one line at a time is a very useful way to figure out what's happening in a script—and to see where things go wrong!

The first line builds a sphere. The next six lines change many attributes, either on the shape node of the sphere (the makeNurbSphere node) or on the transform node (the ball node). The first three setAttr statements change the radius, the start sweep angle, and the end sweep angle, respectively. The last three change the position and scale of the sphere's transform node (named "ball"). The finished product should look as follows:

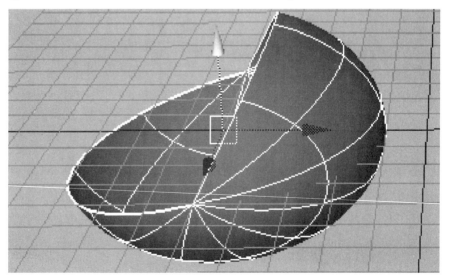

If, for some unknown reason, you needed to create a flattened half-ball over and over again in different scenes, you could just MM drag these commands to your shelf and you'd be able to make the object at the click of a button—quite a time saver!

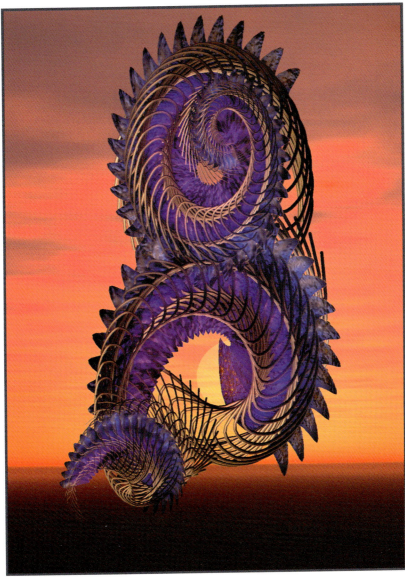

Chinese Dragon

Created by technical editor Mark Smith as a test animation for a video project called "Organix," this piece was our first attempt at using Paint Effects in conjunction with the iterative replication of geometry. The gold rib-like appendages are Paint Effects brush-strokes joined to volume-textured geometry. The animation sequence is quite hypnotic, as the dragon curls and convulses upon itself.

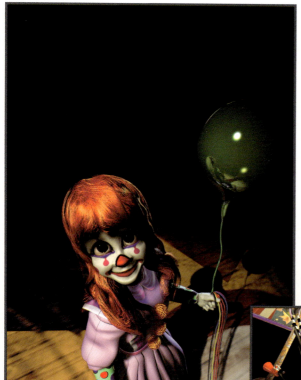

Image of BINGO, Chris Landreth, courtesy of Alias|Wavefront,
a division of Silicon Graphics Limited.

Image of BINGO, Chris Landreth, courtesy of Alias|Wavefront, a division of
Silicon Graphics Limited.

Image of BINGO, Chris Landreth, courtesy of Alias|Wavefront, a division of Silicon Graphics Limited.

Bingo

Created at Alias|Wavefront, a division of Silicon Graphics Limited, by Chris Landreth in conjunction with the development of Maya® software. The award-winning animated short *BINGO* was presented as the grand finale of the Electronic Theater at SIGGRAPH '98. As explained by Duncan Brinsmead in his conversation with Perry Harovas, included in the Appendix, the challenges involved in creating the hair for the Balloon Girl helped inspire Mr. Brinsmead to create Maya software's new Paint Effects™ tool. Although *BINGO* was developed partly to test and demonstrate Maya software's capabilities, *BINGO* is more than just a dazzling technical achievement; you can see from these stills that it is an artistic achievement as well.

Image of BINGO, Chris Landreth, courtesy of
Alias|Wavefront, a division of Silicon Graphics Limited.

Stingray

This image was created in Maya 2 by Michael Leone at Viewpoint Studios. The stingray was generated from a primitive NURBS sphere with the help of nonlinear deformers and by manually pushing and pulling the CVs. Nonlinear deformers were also used to create the lifelike motion of the stingray as it glides through the water. Complex layers of procedural shaders were used to generate the stingray's skin.

Negative Balance

This piece, also by Michael Leone, was created entirely in Maya 2. The artist's intention was to create an image that evoked concentration, frustration, and defeat—and we think you'll agree that he succeeded, at least with the first two. The resulting dynamic compositing was achieved by the careful placement of objects, detailed modeling, particle systems, and raytracing (to provide realistic reflection).

Hamlet

These four images, created by author Peter Lee, are from *To Be or Not to Be*, an animation short shown at the Animation Festival, SIGGRAPH 99. The character recites Hamlet's famous soliloquy in his own unique style. A short segment is included in the accompanying CD-ROM.

The Child

Created by author Peter Lee, this is a finished rendering of the boy built in stages beginning in Chapter 6. The head was built in several NURBS patches, the hands were created using polygon modeling, and the body was bound using Rigid Bind. The constrained and weighted model is included in the CD-ROM.

The Dog

Created by author Peter Lee, this is a finished version of the dog begun in Chapter 8 and completed in Chapter 13. This simple dog was built in NURBS patches, using the Stitch tool, and bound using the Smooth Bind. The constrained and weighted model is included in the CD-ROM.

The Living Room

Created by author Peter Lee, this is the complete living room scene built in stages beginning in Chapter 5 and completed in Chapter 19. It includes the furniture, the lamp, the letter M, and the dog. An Env Sky was used as the environment texture, and the glow was applied to selected shaders.

The Woman

Created by author Peter Lee in 1998 for Alias|Wavefront's Maya contest. All the textures, with the exception of the eyebrows, were created in Maya 1.

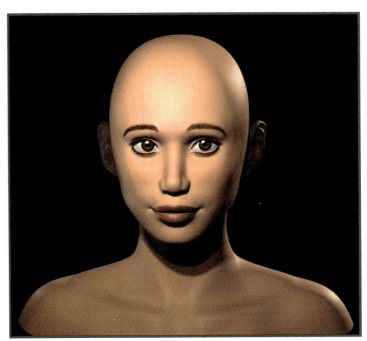

Eden

Created for a direct-to-video film, by author Perry Harovas. This was our first test of Paint Effects for film, used to give a storybook feel crossed with realism. Every blade of grass casts shadows. Running a Paint Effects pass at 1800×1350 resolution took only 5 minutes.

Go Play Outside

Created by author Perry Harovas for the cover of this book, with heavy use of Paint Effects. The tree is casting shadows on the house, and in the animation on the CD-ROM, it gives the impression of a nice breezy day.

Blinding

Created by author Perry Harovas for a direct-to-video film, this image makes heavy use of light fog, shader glow, and depth-of-field. You'll find the complete animation on the accompanying CD-ROM.

© 1999 Perry Harovas

Underwater Dance

Created by author Perry Harovas for a direct-to-video film. The caustic effect was created as a 2D animation, and then applied to a point light located underneath the water. The light was exclusively linked to the rocks, so that it wouldn't affect the water surface, which was displaced with the same 2D animation, to tie the effects together. You'll find the complete animation on the accompanying CD-ROM.

© 1999 Perry Harovas

Murk

Created by author Perry Harovas for a direct-to-video film. The cave was generated from a heavily subdivided cylinder, which was deformed with Artisan. The ground plane that makes up the water intersects a flattened side of the cylinder, which makes up the floor of the cave. Spotlights with Intensity Falloff were used to good effect for a realistic feel.

© 1999 Perry Harovas

© 1999 Perry Harovas

Childhood Memories

Created by author Perry Harovas, this stark room tries to evoke the weird memories that seep into our adult minds from childhood. The ball has a very plastic feel, easily achieved with a specularity map to break up the highlight.

Yiayia's

Created by author Perry Harovas to bring back memories of your grandmother's house. The walls are reflected in the table, but the ceiling was excluded because it created too many reflections, and was a distraction. The bleeding light on the walls mimics radiosity through the use of some point lights with intensity falloff.

Muffled Scream

Created by author Perry Harovas for a direct-to-video film; this image was used on the cover box. The beast was created with minimal geometry, evoking fear with the use of motion blur and letting the viewer's imagination fill in the missing details.

Water head

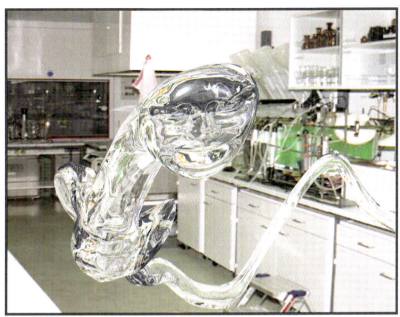

In this image created by author John Kundert-Gibbs, the pseudopod and head are an example of several concepts from this book, from facial modeling to blendshape animation to soft bodies and texturing. This is an enlarged still from the animation available on the accompanying CD-ROM.

©1999 John L. Kundert-Gibbs (head model by Peter Lee)

Fountain

The fountain, created by author John Kundert-Gibbs, is a marriage of modeling, dynamics, texturing, raytracing, Paint Effects, and a bit of tricky compositing. Because of the level of complexity in the scene, the three passes required to create this still image took over two hours of rendering on a dual 550MHz Pentium III machine. An animated version of this scene is available on the accompanying CD-ROM.

©1999 John L. Kundert-Gibbs

Fizzing Tablet

Created by author John Kundert-Gibbs, these are two views of the antacid tablet developed in Chapters 22 and 23. The tablet is a particle emitter, and the bubbles are spherical particles. An animated version of this scene is available on the accompanying CD-ROM.

©1999 John L. Kundert-Gibbs   ©1999 John L. Kundert-Gibbs

Composited Fountain

Created by author John Kundert-Gibbs, this is a still from the fountain animation developed in Chapters 22 and 23, also available on the CD-ROM. In this composited image, you can see the beginnings of a production-ready image.

©1999 John L. Kundert-Gibbs

Fire Man

This image, created by author John Kundert-Gibbs, is a still frame from a low-resolution "proof of concept" animation for an upcoming made-for-TV movie. In it, John used Paint Effects to paint fire onto geometry that was matched to the person in the background plate (originally, he had used particles, but these proved more difficult to control than Paint Effects brushes). The rest of the shot was done in a compositing package, where different layers of fire, geometry, and the background plate were combined, and colors were altered in the background plate to indicate the effects of the fire on the surroundings.

© 1999 Perry Harovas

Mary

The mood is meant to be quiet and introspective, like an unspoken prayer. Created from memories of the priests' room to the side of the altar, where the vestments were kept.

Using Expressions with MEL

Expressions are a specialized subset of the MEL scripting language which are designed to execute through time, not just when the command or script is called. While MEL is only evaluated when the script or macro is run (except in special cases), expressions are evaluated at every frame, or after each interaction on screen (like moving an object). Expressions deal primarily with changing an object's attributes based on time, the current frame, or another attribute. Thus, expressions are well suited to calculating particle properties (see Chapter 23) or to creating relationships between scene objects in Maya. Unlike MEL, expressions do not need you to specifically make a `setAttr` or `getAttr` statement, allowing their syntax to be somewhat simpler, and making them very powerful aids to creating complex behaviors in your Maya animations.

In this section you'll find three examples that give you an opportunity to try out the Expression Editor. In the first, you'll make a cone move up and down by moving a sphere back and forth. In the second you'll make a ball move back and forth in rhythm as time elapses. In the last example, you use an expression to devise a way to make a wheel "stick" to the pavement so it doesn't slip.

The expressions we'll deal with here are fairly simple; however, if this kind of thing appeals to you, and especially if you like to work with particles and dynamics, there is a more advanced discussion on the use of expressions with dynamics in Chapter 23.

Transforming a Cone

Let's begin with a simple example: we're going to make a cone move up and down by moving a sphere back and forth on the Z axis.

1. First, make a new scene and create a sphere and a cone (call the sphere "ball" and the cone "cone"). Select the cone, and open the Expression Editor (Window ➤ Expression Editor).

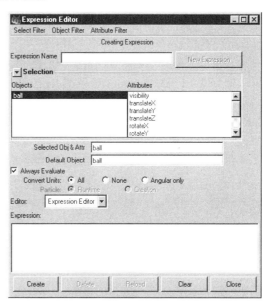

2. In the Expression Name field, type **moveCone**.

3. In the Expression field at the bottom, type the following:

```
translateY = ball.translateZ;
//to save time, you could also just type:
//ty = ball.tz;
```

Because the cone was selected, Maya knows to apply the `transateY` command to the cone (if the object is not selected, just type `cone.ty = ball.tz;`). Click the Create button. If you entered the information correctly, the feedback line (or the Script Editor's History window) will show

```
Result: expression1
```

If not, you will get an error message. (Note that paired forward slashes are comment markers in expressions as well as in scripts.)

4. Once the expression is accepted, move the ball back and forth in the Z axis, and watch the cone move up and down.

Though this is a very simple example, it should indicate how you could solve some very complex interactions between objects much more efficiently by using an expression than by keyframing.

Rock the Boat

Now we're going to dust off those ancient memories of high school math class, and put them to practical use—bet you thought you'd never hear that one! Using the Sine function, we're going to get our famous sphere to move back and forth over time.

1. Make a new scene in Maya, and add a NURBS sphere (called "ball").

2. Go to the Expression Editor and type in the following:

```
ball.tx = 5 * sin (time);
```

3. Set your time slider to about 400 frames and play the animation.

You should see the ball moving back and forth in rhythm as time (frames divided by frames-per-second) goes by. The Sine function takes an input number (the time of the animation) and converts it into a wave that goes back and forth between –1 and 1. Multiplying the Sine function by 5 just makes it bigger (increases the amplitude). Starting from 0, the Sine function itself looks as shown on the next page.

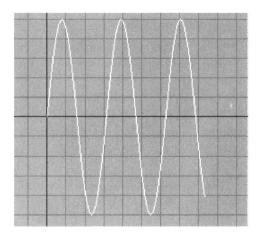

The X component of the sphere's motion just moves up and down (or back and forth) from –5 to 5 as time increases. We can also make the ball go back and forth more quickly by typing in the following (and clicking Edit in the Expression Editor):

```
ball.tx = 5 * sin (2 * time);
```

Here, the ball will go back and forth twice as fast, since time is being multiplied by 2. In general, you can alter the Sine function's amplitude and frequency as follows:

```
Amplitude × Sine (Frequency × Value)
```

The frequency component adjusts how fast the ball goes back and forth, while the amplitude adjusts how big the motion is.

You can also put the frame number into the expression as well as time:

```
ball.tx = 5 * sin (frame);
```

When you play back this expression, the ball will travel back and forth far more quickly than before, as the number of the current frame increases much more rapidly than does the time.

Now let's make the ball do something a bit more interesting, like move in a circle. Once again, edit the expression on the ball, this time to the following:

```
ball.tx = 5 * sin (time);
ball.tz = 5 * cos (time);
```

Here, the ball's X position is controlled by the Sine function, while the ball's Z position is controlled by the Cosine function. (Remember that the Cosine is perfectly "out of phase" with the Sine function. In other words, it begins at a value of 1 rather than 0.) When you play back the animation, the ball should move around in a perfect circle. How would you make the circle "squashed" (an ellipse)? Try changing one of the amplitude multipliers to 2 instead of 5. What happens when you increase the frequency of one of the positions? Try making ball.tz equal to 5 * cos (2 * time) and see what happens. What if the frequency number is 3 or 5? You can quickly see how you can make some very complex motion with relatively simple expressions.

As a further exercise in using expressions, try making the ball move around a three-dimensional circle instead of just on the X-Z plane.

Wheels That Stick

As a last example of simple expressions, let's make something that can really come in handy: a way to make a wheel (in this case, our famous ball) "stick" to the pavement so as not to slip. If you've ever tried to keyframe a non-slipping wheel, you know what a pain it is to do; but with a simple expression, Maya will do it for you!

1. In an empty scene, create a sphere with a radius of 1 unit and name it **tire**.

2. Create a plane and scale it big.

3. Now move the ball up by 1 on the Y axis so that it just rests on the plane (if you think you're good, try making the plane and sphere, and then moving the sphere, all using MEL commands in the Script Editor).

4. Select the tire ball and open the Expression Editor. Name the expression **stickyTires** and then, in the Expression window, type the following:

```
tire.rz = - (tire.tx * (360.0 / (2 * 3.1415)));
```

This expression takes the translateX component of **tire** and turns it into an angle for the rotateZ component. The negative sign ensures that the tire actually rotates the proper direction when the wheel is moved. The parenthetical expression just converts degrees to radians so that the two numbers will match up properly.

5. In the scene window, move the ball back and forth in the X direction and watch how the ball always rolls just the right amount to keep up with how far it moves.

In the next chapter, we'll briefly revisit this tire expression and make it more generally useful—and readable!

As a further exercise, can you make the ball roll properly as it's moved in the Z direction (be sure to set the X, Y and Z positions back to 0 before you do this)?

Finally, let's use a nice little built-in MEL function called noise to make the tire move back and forth in the X direction, as it sticks to the ground. The noise function creates random, but connected, motion paths (as opposed to the rand function, which goes all over the place!). Compare the following two motion paths.

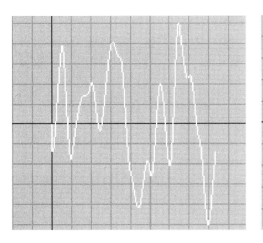 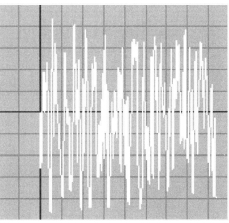

While the noise function, on the left, is a random motion, it moves from point to point in a smooth path. The rand function, on the right, however, is very chaotic. There are cases where each has an advantage; here, we need to use the noise function to make the tire move smoothly back and forth. In the Expression Editor, type in the following (to modify the expression you've already been working on):

```
tire.tx = 5 * noise (time);
tire.rz = - (tire.tx * (360.0 / (2 * 3.1415)));
```

As time increases, noise generates a new number for each new time, but each number is connected to the old one in such a way as to keep them relatively close together. When you play back the new tire animation, the wheel will move back and forth on the X axis, all the while "sticking" to the ground as it rolls. Considering how simple this expression is, it produces very complex motion that would be difficult to reproduce using keyframes.

Summary

In this chapter, you have learned what MEL is and how Maya is constructed on it, and you have gained hands-on experience with some basic (yet powerful) ways to take advantage of scripting. You also learned how to make your scripts quickly available as buttons, hotkeys, or marking menus. Finally, you learned the difference between MEL commands and expressions, and how to create some basic expressions that do neat things. (If you are interested in further exploring expressions and how they are used in dynamics, please see Chapter 23.)

In the following chapter, we will go into more depth about how to use MEL to create flexible procedures and complex scripts that can even have their own user interface. If this chapter was as far as you want to go with MEL right now, don't bother with the next chapter. If you're ready to learn how to really program the pants off Maya, just turn the page!

PROGRAMMING
WITH MEL

Featuring

- **How to get Maya's help with MEL**
- **Debugging MEL scripts**
- **Placeholders, circles, and trees (variables, loops, and branching)**
- **Creating a GUI**
- **Using procedures and scripts**
- **Commenting**
- **Studying the masters**

PROGRAMMING WITH MEL

The previous chapter introduced the Maya Embedded Language (MEL). You learned how to work with the Script Editor, create your own marking menus, and use expressions. This chapter takes you further into the language; it focuses on using MEL to maximize productivity, to create graphical user interfaces (GUIs, pronounced "gooeys"), and to create full-blown MEL scripts suitable for framing.

Although you can benefit from this chapter without any prior programming experience, it will be a big help if you already have some understanding of a programming or scripting language. If you'd like to try some programming first, you can avail yourself of a wealth of books, classes, and references for a dizzying array of programming languages. Otherwise, let's dig into the meat of MEL!

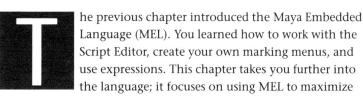

 TIP As Maya's syntax is very similar to that of the C programming language, a good primer on C is your best preparation for MEL. The publisher of this book offers numerous titles on C and C++, including *C++: No experience required,* by Paulo Franco (Sybex, 1998), and *Mastering Visual C++ 6,* by Michael J. Young (Sybex, 1998).

How To Get Help with MEL

Before we delve too far into the more complex aspects of MEL, let's take a moment to examine the powerful Help tools Maya has available—and how easy they are to use.

First, you have Maya's internal Help function. Because there are so many MEL commands and functions (about 700), the Help function is a very quick and useful feature (you can even type in **help help** to get a look at how the help command works).

Here's an example of the type of information available with Help. Open the Script Editor and type the name of the command you want help with into the Input window (or just type it into the Command line below the main window):

```
help setAttr;
```

Execute the command, and in the Script Editor's History window, you'll see the following result lines:

```
// Result:
Synopsis: setAttr [flags] Name[...]
Flags:
   -e -edit
   -q -query
   -av -alteredValue
   -k -keyable        on|off
   -l -lock           on|off
   -s -size           Index
 -typ -type           String
 //
```

These result lines give you a quick look at the setAttr command: a synopsis of its syntax (or how to use it) and a list of flags that you can use with the command.

If you're an experienced programmer, this information may be all you need in order to use the command. If you're just starting out, however, you'll probably want more guidance. In that case, try typing the following into the Input window:

```
help -doc setAttr;
```

When you execute this command, Maya will automatically bring up your browser of choice (usually Netscape Communicator or Microsoft Internet Explorer) and find the right HTML page in your online documents (contained on your hard drive) that contains the command you want help with. In the case of the setAttr statement, you get the following display:

Name

       setAttr

  Synopsis

       setAttr

           [flags] object.attribute value [value..]

ReturnValue

   None.

Description

   Sets the value of a dependency node attribute. No value for the attribute is needed when the -l/-k/-s flags are used. The -type flag is only required when setting a non-numeric attribute.

There is also a table of flags and what they do (notice that this table is far more complete than the smaller help text you get inside the Script Editor history window). Finally, you get what we consider the most useful aspect of the help files—several examples of how to use the command:

Examples

```
// Set a simple numeric value
setAttr transform1.translateX 5;
// Lock an attribute to prevent further modification
setAttr -lock on curve1.translateX;
// Make an attribute unkeyable
setAttr -keyable off curve1.translateZ;
// Set an entire list of multi-attribute values in one command
setAttr -size 6 "curveShape1.knots[1:6]" 0 0 0 1 1 1;
// Set an attribute with a compound numeric type
setAttr "revolve3.axis" -type "double3" 0 0 1;
// Set a multi-attribute with a compound numeric type
setAttr "madeUpNode.multiAxis[0:2]" -type "double3" 0 0 1 1 0 0 0 1 0;
```

As you can see, a few examples can do a lot to clarify how a command is used. Between the internal Help files and the online help on your hard drive, you can access excellent reference material very rapidly.

T I P   Examining other users' scripts as guides for what you wish to do is another great way to learn more about MEL—you can even copy and paste portions of scripts for your own use (just be sure that you have the author's permission).

Debugging MEL Scripts

If you were careful entering the commands in the last chapter, you may have gotten away without seeing a MEL error; in the work ahead, however (and certainly as you begin building MEL scripts of your own), you will encounter errors, the most common of which is the syntax error. Every command has a particular structure or form that needs to be followed in order to execute successfully. Otherwise, the script interpreter won't know what to do with your command and will most often return a syntax error.

While debugging a script is a bit of an art form, there are a couple of ways you can help yourself. First, check the History window when you execute a script: If the last line of your script is the last line of the History window, the commands executed without an error. If, however, you get a comment line like the following:

```
setAttr tire 5;
//Error:  line 1:  No attribute was specified. //
```

you know that there has been at least one error in parsing the script.

N O T E   *Parsing* is the programming term for the search the script interpreter does through the script to make sure all the commands are correct.

The Feedback line (at the bottom-right of the screen) will also turn orange-red to indicate that the MEL interpreter has discovered an error in your code. One way to help you quickly identify where these errors might lie is by turning on the Edit ≻ Show Line Numbers option in the Script Editor menu. Generally, it's a good idea to keep this option on at all times, as it does not slow Maya down in any way, and it provides useful information about where errors are occurring.

As you begin scripting, one error that will probably creep in is forgetting the final semicolon at the end of each line. This can be difficult to spot if you're not aware of the problem. If you are getting errors in your script that don't make sense, try looking at each line of code to be sure it finishes with a semicolon.

Finally, since MEL is an interpreted scripting language, you can execute a script one line at a time, rather than as a whole. This can be a very useful way to figure out where a problem is occurring in your program. A brief exercise will illustrate:

1. Type in the following, but don't execute it yet:

```
print "hello, world!";
print hello, world;
```

2. Now highlight the first line and execute it (by pressing the Enter key on your numeric keypad). You should see `hello, world!` printed out in the History window.

3. Now highlight and execute the second line. You should see something like the following:

```
// Error: print hello, world; //
// Error: Line 1.12: Syntax error //
```

The first line executed properly, but the second had an error in it—the `print` command needs a string to work with, and you need to include quote marks to identify the string. In a two-line script, spotting the error would be simple; in a longer script, this method of going through the script one line at a time can be a great way of uncovering problem spots.

Great. We know how to get help and debug a script—now let's get down to business!

Placeholders, Circles, and Trees (Variables, Loops, and Branching)

If you've done any programming at all, you've probably been waiting for this point: the main reasons to program are to (1) create flexibility and to (2) do repetitive tasks. Flexibility comes through variables (or placeholders), while repetition is made possible through looping and branching.

Variables

It's actually much easier to see what a variable is than to talk about it. Type the following in the Script Editor:

```
string $myVariable;
$myVariable = "hi there";
print $myVariable;
```

When you execute these commands, you'll see that "hi there" is printed in the last line of the History window, indicating that when you told Maya to print $myVariable, it printed "hi there." The first line of the script, above, is called a declaration of the variable: string is the variable's type (a string is just text contained in quotes), and $myVariable is its name.

Types of MEL Variables

The other types of variables we'll be dealing with are

int   An integer number—used to represent a whole number, like 3 or –45.

float   A decimal number—used to represent a "real" number, like –35.4725.

vector   Three decimal numbers that make a vector number—used to represent a point on a three-dimensional grid, like (26, 31.67, 5.724). A vector number is very useful for three-dimensional quantities like position (X, Y, Z coordinates) or color (red, green, blue colors).

array   A list of numbers—used to store lists of either integers or floats. Arrays are useful for storing data about many similar items, like the color of each of a group of particles.

We'll examine vectors and arrays more closely as they come up.

Every MEL variable needs to start with the $ symbol, so MEL knows it's a variable. (This is easy to forget, and it causes strange errors—so remember your $ symbol!) The second line is called the assignment line: the text string "hi there" is placed into the variable (or placeholder) for future use. The last line is simply a `print` statement, telling Maya to print out what's inside the variable, $myVariable (which, in this case, is "hi there"). If we wished, on the following line we could type in

```
$myVariable = "goodbye";
```

which would change the data in the variable $myVariable to the word goodbye. As you can see, variables can be extremely useful because they can store different data at different times in a program.

MEL has a convenience feature built into it: you can declare and assign a variable in the same line. In other words, the script above could be written as follows:

```
string $myVariable = "hi there";
print $myVariable;
```

There is no real difference between the two scripts, except for less typing and a bit easier readability—you are free to use whichever method appeals to you (though most seasoned programmers opt to save keystrokes!).

Looping

Next, let's examine looping. Say you wish to create five spheres in your scene using MEL commands. You could either do this by typing in `sphere -r 1 -n ball` five times, or have MEL do it for you using the `for` loop. To build our spheres, type in the following:

```
int $i = 0;
for ($i = 1;  $i<= 5;  $i++)
    {
    sphere -r 1 -n ball;
    }
```

Voilà, five spheres named ball 1 through 5. (However, you'll need to move them away from each other in order to see them as separate objects. We'll do that in a moment.)

NOTE   MEL supports implicit variable declaration, so the `int $i = 0` line is not necessary. However, in most cases, it is preferable to declare all variables explicitly to avoid possible complications in the script.

Note that there is no semicolon after the for statement: MEL expects there to be one or more commands (contained within the {} brackets) after the for statement, so it doesn't need a semicolon. Additionally, the closing bracket, }, functions as a semi-colon, so there is no need for a semicolon on the last line either. The syntax for the for loop is as follows:

```
for (initial value; test value; increment);
```

The *initial value* is what the counting variable is set to at the beginning. The *test value* is how high (or low) the number can go before it tests negative—and thus how many loops the counter goes through. The *increment* is how quickly the counter increases in value ($i++ is a simple way of saying "increase the value of $i by 1 each loop").

To make this loop do a bit more for us, let's have it move the spheres on top of each other on the Y axis as it creates them:

```
for ($i = 1; $i<= 5; $i++)
    {
    sphere -r 1 -n ball;
    move -r 0 (2 * $i) 0;
    }
```

Now as the spheres are created, each one is moved up by twice the value of $i, plac-ing them just atop one another.

Branching

The last basic program structure we'll look at is branching, a slightly more complex type of loop that allows MEL to ask a question and decide whether to do some further action given the answer (the for statement actually contains a branch in its *test value* statement). Let's use the same script as above, only this time let's put a conditional statement inside it:

```
for ($i = 1; $i<= 5; $i++)
    {
    sphere -r 1 -n ball;
    if ($i<=3)
        {
        move -r 0 (2 * $i) 0;
        }
    else
        {
        move -r (2 * $i) 0 0;
        }
    }
```

What happens when you execute these commands? The first three balls are stacked up on the Y axis (when $i is less than or equal to 3), and the last two are stacked along the X axis (when $i is 4 and 5, and therefore greater than 3). In abstract terms, the syntax for the if statement is as follows:

```
if (test)
    {
    commands;
    }
else if (test)
        {
        commands;
        }
else{commands;}
```

The elseif and else statements do *not* have to exist for the if statement to work. The else if statement, listed above, allows you to make as many tests as you like (there can be as many else if statements as you wish in your conditional statement), allowing you to test for multiple possibilities within one large conditional statement. The else statement must always be last in such examples and is the "default" answer if no other conditions are met. Note that all the commands for an if, else if, or else statement must be enclosed in {} brackets. If we wish, we could increase the complexity of our create-and-move-ball code with an else if statement:

```
for ($i = 1; $i<= 10; $i++)
    {
    sphere -r 1 -n ball;
    if ($i<=3)
        {
        move -r 0 (2 * $i) 0;
        }
    else if ($i>3 && $i<=6)
        {
        move -r 0 0 (2 * $i);
        }
    else
        {
        move -r (2 * $i) 0 0;
        }
    }
```

Here, the balls will stack along the Y axis if $i is less than or equal to 3, along the Z axis if $i is between 4 and 6, and along the X axis if $i is greater than 6.

T I P If there is only one line of commands below the `if` statement, you do not need the brackets—however, it's a good idea for readability to always include them anyway.

Now that we have all these time-saving functions at our fingertips, let's revisit a project from last chapter and make it a bit more useful.

Using Variables, Statements, and Loops in Expressions

Not only can you use variables, conditional statements, and loops in MEL scripts; they can also be used in expressions. Let's take a quick visit back to that sticking tire expression we worked on in the last chapter.

If you don't have the scene saved, open a new scene, create a sphere and name it **tire**, and make a plane under it (scaled to about the size of the default grid). We're going to take the expression we had before, add variables to it, and add a conditional statement to do different things if the ball is being moved up the Y axis.

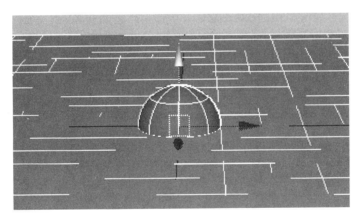

One thing we haven't yet discussed, yet is very important to our work, is the *reverse apostrophe*—the apostrophe that's above the Tab key on the keyboard and looks like this: `. Enclosing a statement in these apostrophes tells Maya to evaluate the statement inside them and pass the result on to the variable on the other side of the equation. The statement

```
float $myVariable = `getAttr tire.radius`;
```

returns the decimal (or floating point) number representing the radius of the sphere called **tire**. As you can probably tell, this ability to get the value of any attribute and read it into a variable is quite powerful. Just remember that this isn't the normal apostrophe that lives on the key with the double quote—type in that apostrophe and you'll get an error!

Now let's redo that expression:

```
float $radius = `getAttr makeNurbSphere1.radius`;
float $pi = 3.1415926;
float $deg = 360;
float $howHi = `getAttr tire.ty`;
if ($howHi != $radius)
    {
    tire.translateY = $radius;
    }
tire.rotateZ = - ( tire.translateX * ($deg / (2 * $pi * $radius)));
```

The first four statements declare and assign values to variables. $pi is the value of π. $deg is the number of degrees in a circle. Having these variables in the expression just makes reading the equation below easier. The two variables $radius and $howHi are assigned values by using reverse apostrophes to enclose getAttr statements. The reverse apostrophes "evaluate" the getAttr statements and then read the sphere's radius and Y position into the variables. (Note that the attribute for radius belongs to the makeNurbSphere node, not the transform node, which has been renamed tire.)

The conditional statement asks whether the Y position is different than the sphere's radius (!= is MEL's "not equal" operator). If so, it places the sphere directly on top of the plane (1 radius above 0). Also notice that the equation for Z rotation has been modified to take the sphere's radius into account now (the rotation angle being equal to 2πr, you'll recall from high school math classes). With this equation, no matter how big or small the sphere is, it will always sit right on the plane and will roll without slipping!

Using variables and a conditional statement, we have reworked the simple one-line expression into a flexible tool that can be used in varying situations.

We'll return to variables, looping, and branching as this chapter continues, but now let's turn to creating a GUI in Maya.

Creating a GUI

While typing commands into the Command line or Input window of the Script Editor is very useful for simple tasks, it is often much more elegant (not to mention user-friendly) to create a graphical user interface window in your script to give users access to all the script's commands in a familiar point-and-click environment. While creating these windows can be somewhat challenging, nearly all high-quality scripts use them, so it is good to learn at least the basics of GUI creation using MEL.

Windows in Maya can be very complex (just look at the Attribute Editor window for an example), but the basic way to create a window is fairly simple. At a minimum, you need three commands to make a window:

```
window -title "title" -wh 400 200 myWindow;
some kind of layout;
showWindow;
```

Executing the window command creates a window with a certain title that appears at its top (the -title flag), optionally a predefined width and height (the -widthHeight or -wh flag), and an optional name (the last item in the window command).

The showWindow command makes the window appear onscreen (it will never appear if you forget this line)—this command usually resides at the end of a "make window" series of commands.

The layout commands specify what sort of layout the window will have. Some common types are columnLayout, scrollLayout, rowColumnLayout, and formLayout. The column layout creates a column, the scroll layout makes the window a scrollable window, the row-and-column layout makes a grid of rows and columns (like a table), and the form layout creates a flexible space that can be laid out in many ways. These layouts can also contain other layouts nested within them, creating the ability to make very complex windows relatively easily (the form layout is often the parent layout, with many other layouts inside it).

Let's create a simple window with one button and one slider in it. Type the following into the Script Editor:

```
window -t "The Big Window!" -wh 400 200 myWindow;
columnLayout -cw 200;
button -l "Click this button" myButton;
text " ";
attrFieldSliderGrp -l "Slide this around" -min 0 -max 10 theSliderGroup;
showWindow myWindow;
```

These commands create a window (which Maya knows as myWindow, but which is titled "The Big Window!") with a width of 400 and a height of 200 pixels. A column layout is then set with a width of 200 pixels. Next, a button (labeled "Click this button" and known to Maya as myButton) is created; then a field-and-slider group is created (labeled "Slide this around" and known as theSliderGroup) with a minimum value of 0 and a maximum value of 10. The text command just puts a space in between the button and the slider group. Finally, we display the window via the showWindow command. Obviously it's not too difficult to create windows with buttons, sliders, or other objects in them.

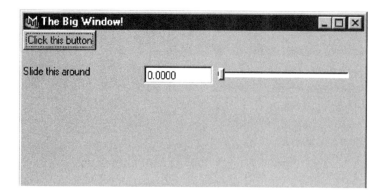

 TIP   If you make some errors typing in the MEL script, and then go back and try to run the script again, when you try to recreate the window, you may run into the following error: `Error:  Object's name is not unique: myWindow.` If you get this message, you need to delete the window myWindow: even though it doesn't appear onscreen, MEL has created a UI object named myWindow (note that the `showWindow` command is last, so an object can be created and not shown). Thus, while myWindow doesn't appear, it can exist in your scene, and it needs to be deleted. To do this, type `deleteUI myWindow`. This is a very useful command to remember as you create GUI windows, so commit it to memory.

Now let's make our buttons do something. Clear all objects in your scene and create a sphere called "ball." Edit your script to include the −command and −attribute flags, as follows:

```
window -t "The Big Window!" -wh 400 200 myWindow;
columnLayout -cw 200;
button -l "Press this button" -c "setAttr ball.ty  5" myButton;
text " ";
attrFieldSliderGrp -l "Slide this around" -min 0 -max 10 -at ("ball.tx")
    theSliderGroup;
showWindow myWindow;
```

The −c flag tells Maya to perform the quoted instruction each time the button is pressed. Thus, when this button is pressed, Maya sets the ball's Y position to 5 units. The −at flag in the slider group tells Maya to connect the slider and text field to the quoted attribute (in this case, the X position of the ball). When you click the button, the ball jumps up to 5 on the Y axis. When you slide the slider (or enter numbers in the text field), the ball moves back and forth between 0 and 10 on the X axis.

TIP You can set the slider and text field to have different minimum and maximum values. The –fmn and –fmx flags give the field's min and max values. The –smn and –smx flags give the slider's min and max values. This allows the user to enter numbers outside the slider's bounds, which can be useful.

You can also create radio buttons and check boxes that perform functions when pressed (see the MEL documentation for more information on these).

NOTE As an exercise, what command could you place on the button to make the ball move up 5 units every time the button is pressed?

Now that you've seen how quickly you can create a basic window as an interface to your scripts, let's make a script that automatically creates a useful window for you. Make a new scene, and then create several lights and aim them at an object in the scene (you could use the "create lights" shelf button you made in the last chapter to do this for you automatically—or you could open a scene you have already created that includes several lights in it). Now enter the following in your Script Editor window:

```
string $sel[] = `ls -lights`;
string $current;
string $winName = "lightWindow";
if (`window -exists $winName`)
    {
    deleteUI $winName;
    }
window -title "Lights" -wh 400 300 $winName;
scrollLayout;
rowColumnLayout -nc 2 -cw 1 150 -cw 2 400;
for ($current in $sel)
    {
    text -l $current;
    attrFieldSliderGrp -min (-1) -max 10 -at ($current + ".intensity");
    }
showWindow $winName;
```

When you execute this script, Maya will automatically create a "light board" for you, allowing you to control the intensity of all lights in the scene from one floating window.

The most interesting thing about this script is the first line:

```
string $sel[] = `ls -lights`;
```

This line assigns to the variable string array $sel[] the name of every light in the scene. The [] after the variable name tells Maya this variable is an array, or list of variables, starting with the number 0. If there were three elements in the list, they would be $sel[0], $sel[1], and $sel[2]. By declaring one array, then, you get three (or four, or however many you want) variables for the price of one! The ls command tells Maya to list the items that come after (in this case, -lights means "list all lights in the scene"); then the reverse apostrophes tell Maya to evaluate this command (which returns the name of each light) and read the result into the array, $sel[].

Next, other variables are declared to store the "current item" ($current) and the window name ($winName), and the script checks to see if the window already exists—if it does, the script kills the old window (using the deleteUI command) so it can write a new one. This little piece of code is good to include in all your GUI scripts, to ensure that you don't accidentally generate any errors if a window by that name already exists. Then a window is created with a scroll layout (so the window can scroll if it's too small) and a row/column layout (a table). Then the script performs a variation of the for loop, called the for...in loop. The for...in loop looks through an array (in this case, $sel[]) and does one loop for each item it finds, placing the value of $sel[number] in the variable $current.

N O T E   The type of $current must therefore match the type of $sel[] (in this case, they're both strings).

The loop then prints out the name of the light (in column 1) and makes a field slider group that's attached to the light's intensity setting (in column 2).

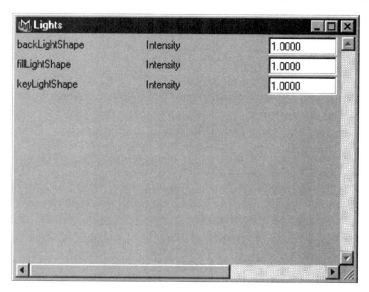

T I P   If you only wanted the lights you had previously selected in the scene to be in the window, you could add the flag `-selected` to the `-ls` command on the first line.

This little script should indicate how powerful a workflow enhancer MEL can be: in just a few lines of script, you have created a way to control potentially dozens of lights in a complex scene in a completely simple, intuitive manner. If you needed to create just the right light levels on twenty lights in a scene, it could take hours navigating to each light and adjusting it individually. This script could make the job a 10-minute effort instead!

N O T E   As an exercise, try creating sliders that let you adjust the light's colors as well as its intensity (hint: there are three attributes, `colorR`, `colorG`, and `colorB`, which control the red, green, and blue intensities). If you really want to get crazy, try placing each group of controls for each light in its own subwindow (so `intensity`, `colorR`, `colorG`, and `colorB` are all inside a window). You'll need to know about the `setParent` command, as well as how to make a frame layout with the flag `-cll` (collapsible) set to true (to make each window close by clicking its triangle). You could also add check boxes to turn off each light's visibility, so that you can see the effects of each light separately. You can find help for these commands in Maya's online reference documents, and if you get stuck, there is a finished MEL script listed at the end of this chapter and included on the CD.

Using Procedures and Scripts

In the past two chapters, we've touched on most of the basic elements of MEL. However, all the work we've done so far won't be very valuable if we try to give them to someone else or save them to our scripts directory. We haven't done anything to save the commands we've written in a format that Maya can read as a whole. Now we need to learn how to make these bits of code into full-fledged ("standalone") scripts that you can port from one place to another and trade with friends and relatives.

In this section, we'll look at procedures and scripts. A *procedure* is the basic building block of a MEL script. At its most fundamental level, it's simply another declaration line that tells Maya that all the contained lines form one named function. A *script* is just a collection of one or more procedures.

Procedures

In abstract, a procedure would look like this:

```
proc myProcedure ()
{
commands
}
```

Maya will execute all the commands contained in the curly braces every time you type **myProcedure** into the Command line or the Script Editor's Input window. MyProcedure is the name of the procedure, and the parentheses can contain any number of declared variables that can either be called from another procedure or entered by the user when executing the procedure. As a simple example, let's make a procedure that will create a user-defined number of—you guessed it—spheres.

```
global proc makeBall (int $num)
{
int $num;
for ($i=1; $i<=$num; $i++)
    {
    sphere -r 1 -name ("ball" + $i);
    }
}
```

Enter ("source") this text into the Script Editor. Then, whenever you type **makeBall** into the Command line or Input window, followed by an integer number, you'll get that many spheres (called ball1, ball2, etc.) in your scene. Typing **makeBall 5**, for example, would make five spheres named ball1 through ball5 in your scene. We've made this procedure "global" so that Maya can reference the procedure from within your \scripts directory (more on this in a moment).

You know that a procedure is just a bunch of MEL commands contained in braces and given a name; so how would you turn our series of light board commands into a procedure? If you need a hint, it would look something like this:

```
global proc lightBoard ()
{
string $sel[] = `ls -lights`;
string $current;
string $winName = "lightWindow";
if (`window -exists $winName`)
    {
    deleteUI $winName;
    }
```

```
window -title "Lights" -wh 400 300 $winName;
scrollLayout;
rowColumnLayout -nc 2 -cw 1 150 -cw 2 400;
for ($current in $sel)
    {
    text -l $current;
    attrFieldSliderGrp -min (-1) -max 10 -at ($current + ".intensity");
    }
showWindow $winName;
}
```

Once you source (enter) this procedure, each time you type **lightBoard** in the Command line, the procedure will run and you will get a light board for all your lights.

Scripts

What is the difference between a procedure and a script? A script is just a collection of one or more procedures. Thus, the lightBoard procedure we just wrote is actually a script as well. A true script is also saved as an external text file, and given a name, which must end in .mel, and the name of the script *must* be the same as the name of the last (global) procedure in the script (plus the .mel extension). For our lightboard example, we would save the script as lightBoard.mel, and store it in our AW*user name*\ Maya\scripts directory (when you choose Save Selected from the Script Editor's menu, this is the default directory that shows up, so just save it there).

Now let's make a simple script that contains two procedures, to see how that's done.

```
//Source this script, and then type "makeBall <number>"
//in the Command line or Script Editor.  The
//procedure will make the number of spheres you
//specify, and call them "ball1, ball2, etc.".
//Created by:  John Kundert-Gibbs.
//Last Modified:  May 31, 1999.
//Use at your own risk.


//makeIt creates the spheres and gives them names.
//This procedure is passed the number of balls
//you specify from the main procedure.
proc makeIt (int $theNum)
{
//$theNum must be redeclared internal to the
//procedure.
```

```
int $theNum;
for ($i=1; $i<=$theNum; $i++)
    {
    sphere -r 1 -name ("ball" + $i);
    }
}
//end, makeIt.

//makeBall is the main procedure you call.  It just
//calls the procedure makeIt with the number of
//spheres you specify.
global proc makeBall (int $num)
{
int $num;
makeIt ($num);
}
//end, makeBall.
```

All we've done with this script is to create a subprocedure that will actually make the spheres. The main (or global) procedure merely calls the subprocedure (this is often the case with very complex scripts—just look at the end of a script, and you'll often find a very small procedure that simply calls all the other ones in the script). Note that the *last* procedure is the one that you call by typing **makeBall 5** in the Command line. This is (and should be) the only global procedure in the script—the makeIt procedure being a local procedure (and therefore not visible outside the script).

A Comment on Commenting

Notice that we have commented the script in the previous section extensively (with all the // lines). At the very least, you should put in lines at the top of the script about what the script does, what arguments (inputs) it needs, who wrote (or modified) it, and when it was last modified. We also put in the "use at your own risk" line to indicate that some unforeseen problem could arise while using the script, and that we are not responsible for any mishaps because of the script's usage. It is also a very good idea to comment the beginning and end of every procedure (so it's easy to read where they start and stop), and to comment any particularly tricky portions of the script.

You may think these comments are of use only to others and not yourself, and you'd rather not bother with them if you don't plan to distribute the script. But remember that two months after you create the script, you may need to modify it, and if you can't figure out what you did or why, you'll waste a great deal of time hunting through the script instead of getting right to your modifications.

T I P   *Don't get lazy!* **Always comment your scripts well (even the simplest ones). It's a habit (and for once, a good one), so get into it!**

Studying the Masters

No matter how much you learn in these chapters, space and time simply aren't sufficient here to learn everything MEL has to offer. One of the best ways to continue learning MEL is, quite simply, to look at (and copy from) other people's scripts. If you can go through each line of a script and figure out what it does, you will learn a great deal. Better yet, if you can grab some code someone else wrote and modify it to do what you want it to, you can really start to put together some neat and useful scripts to solve your everyday work bottlenecks.

To begin your journey of discovery, let's take a quick peek at three scripts (they are all contained on the CD that comes with this book, so you don't have to type them in). So that you get used to reading commented scripts, we have made our comments about the scripts *inside* the scripts, rather than here. First is a reworking of the lightBoard script into a fairly robust tool for the user.

```
//Source this script; create and position one or more
//lights in your scene. Then type "lightBoard" in the
//Command line.
//The script will generate a set of collapsible
//windows (one for each light) that control each
//light's
//intensity, RGB colors, and visibility.
//Created by John Kundert-Gibbs
//jkundert@unca.edu
//Last Modified:  May 31, 1999.
//Use this script at your own risk.

//The check procedure just checks to see if the window
//already exists.  If so, it kills the old window.
proc check (string $theName)
{
string $theName;
if (`window -exists $theName`)
    {
```

```
        deleteUI $theName;
      }
  }
//end, check.


//beginning, lightBoard. This is the script's main (global) procedure.
global proc lightBoard ()
{
string $sel[] = `ls -lights`;
string $current;
string $winName = "lightWindow";
string $main = "mainWindow";
int $count = 0;


check ($winName);


window -title "Light Board" -wh 600 300 $winName;


scrollLayout;
rowColumnLayout -nc 1 -cw 1 500 ($main);


for ($current in $sel)
    {
    $count++;
    //the -cll flag in the frameLayout command means
    //that the window will collapse when the user
    //clicks the triangle next to the window.
    frameLayout -cll true -w 400 ($current);
    rowColumnLayout -nc 1 -cw 1 400;

    attrFieldSliderGrp -min (-1) -max 10 -at ($current + ".intensity");
    text " ";
    attrFieldSliderGrp -min 0 -max 1 -at ($current + ".colorR");
    text " ";
    attrFieldSliderGrp -min 0 -max 1 -at ($current + ".colorG");
    text " ";
    attrFieldSliderGrp -min 0 -max 1 -at ($current + ".colorB");
    text " ";

    //The visibility slider group was intended to be a
```

PART 4

Working with MEL

```
//check box for visibility.
//However, the checkbox group does not properly
//connect to attributes when
//it's created in a for loop, so a slider group was
//created instead.
//The -s flag set the step value to 1 (meaning an
//integer jump) so the
//group is either 1 or 0.
attrFieldSliderGrp -min 0 -max 1 -vis on -at ($current + ".visibility")
     -s 1;

//the setParent command sets the focus of the
//window back to the rowColumnLayout
//above. Thus, the windows are stacked below each
//other instead of inside each other.

setParent $main;
}
showWindow $winName;
}
//end, lightBoard.
```

The next script is a way to adjust all keyable attributes of a selected set of objects (for example, joints in an IK body), key each one individually, key all, record a "default" pose, and go back to that pose. Like the light-board script, this window can be a real time saver when it comes to keying complex motion.

```
//Source this script; select several objects, or
//joints in a character; type in "setPose" in the
//Command line.
//You will get a window that allows you to manipulate
//all keyable attributes
//on the selected objects.  Additionally, you can
//record a "default" pose
//and go back to that pose.  You can also keyframe any
//or all attributes.
//Created by John Kundert-Gibbs
//jkundert@unca.edu
//Last Modified, June 1, 1999.

//Procedure to perform a loop, keying all attributes
//in the window.
```

```
proc keyAll ()
{
global string $list[];
string $current;
string $Attr;

for ($current in $list)
    {
    string $attrLST[] = `listAttr -k $current`;
    for ($Attr in $attrLST)
        {
        setKeyframe ($current + "." + $Attr);
        }
    }
}//end, keyAll


//procedure to record the current value of all
//attributes in the window.
//This creates a 'default' pose one can return to.
proc recDefault ()
{
global float $gDefault2[];
global string $list[];
string $current;
string $Attr;
int $j = 0;
for ($current in $list)
    {
    string $attrLST[] = `listAttr -k $current`;
    for ($Attr in $attrLST)
        {
        $gDefault2[$j] = `getAttr ($current + "." + $Attr)`;
        print ($current + "." + $Attr +"\n");
        $j++;
        }
    }
} //end recDefault


//Procedure to return all attributes in the window to
//their default values,
```

PART 4

Working with MEL

```
//as recorded in the procedure above.
proc gotoDefault ()
{
global float $gDefault2[];
global string $list[];
string $current;
string $Attr;
int $j = 0;

for ($current in $list)
    {
    string $attrLST[] = `listAttr -k $current`;
    for ($Attr in $attrLST)
        {
        setAttr ($current + "." + $Attr) $gDefault2[$j];
        $j++;
        }
    }
} //end gotoDefault

//main procedure.
global proc setPose ()
{
global string $list[];
$list = `ls -sl`;
string $current;
string $Attr;
string $main = "mainWindow";
window -t "Set Pose";
scrollLayout;
columnLayout ($main);

text -l "Keyable Attributes";
text -l " ";

button -l "Record Default Pose" -w 200 -c "recDefault";
button -l "Go To Default Pose" -w 200 -c "gotoDefault";
text " ";
button -l "Key All" -w 100 -c "keyAll";
text -l " ";
```

```
for ($current in $list)
    {
    frameLayout -cll true  -h 380 -w 600 ($current);
    scrollLayout;
    gridLayout -nc 2 -cw 400;

    string $attrLST[] = `listAttr -k $current`;

    for ($Attr in $attrLST)
        {
        attrFieldSliderGrp -smn -100 -smx 100 -fmn -1000 -fmx 1000 -at
            ($current + "." + $Attr);
        button -l "Keyframe" -w 100 -c ("setKeyframe " + $current + "." +
            $Attr);
        }

    setParent $main;
    text " ";
    }

showWindow;
} //end setPose
```

The final script revisits the chain of rigid body links we made in Chapter 15. Here, instead of creating the links by coding MEL directly, we copied chunks of MEL output from the History window and reworked it into a flexible script that builds the links for you (with a heavy ball at the bottom). With all that goes on in this script, it appears pretty complex, but remember that we built this script up in pieces, mostly by modifying MEL output as we performed each command.

```
//Source this script; and then type "makeChain <number of
//links>" in the Command line.
//The script will generate a series of linked loops
//(like a swing chain) that are all connected and have
//gravity attached to them.
//It also creates a ball called weight, at the bottom
//of the chain, and makes the ball (and chain) swing.
//There may be some rigid body interpenetration
//warnings, depending on how many links you have.
//Created by John Kundert-Gibbs
//jkundert@unca.edu
```

PART 4

Working with MEL

```
//Last Modified:  May 31, 1999.
//Use this script at your own risk.
//Procedure that actually builds the chains
proc makeEm (int $num)
{
string $linkName = "linkNum";
float $moveNum = -5.160681;
float $offSetNum = 1.741263;
gravity -pos 0 0 0 -m 9.8 -dx 0 -dy -1 -dz 0 ;
cylinder -n mainBar -p 0 0 0 -ax 0 1 0 -ssw 0 -esw 360 -r 1 -hr 2 -d 3 -ut 0
     -tol 0.01 -s 8 -nsp 1 -ch 1; objectMoveCommand;
setAttr "mainBar.rotateX" 90;
scale -r 1 5.995727 1 ;
scale -r 1 1.530854 1 ;
torus -n embeddedLink -p 0 0 0 -ax 0 1 0 -ssw 0 -esw 360 -msw 360 -r 1 -hr
     0.2 -d 3 -ut 0 -tol 0.01 -s 8 -nsp 4 -ch 1; objectMoveCommand;
setAttr "embeddedLink.rotateX" 90;
scale -r 1 1 2.188674 ;
move -r 0 -1.910194 0 ;

select -cl;
select -r mainBar embeddedLink;
rigidBody -passive -m 1 -dp 0 -sf 0.2 -df 0.2 -b 0.6 -l 0 -tf 200 -iv 0 0 0
     -iav 0 0 0 -c 0 -pc 0 -i 0 0 0 -imp 0 0 0 -si 0 0 0 -sio none ;
for ($i=1; $i <= $num; $i++)
    {
    select -cl;

    torus -n ($linkName + $i) -p 0 0 0 -ax 0 1 0 -ssw 0 -esw 360 -msw 360 -r
      1 -hr 0.2 -d 3 -ut 0 -tol 0.01 -s 8 -nsp 4 -ch 1; objectMoveCommand;
    setAttr ($linkName + $i + ".rotateX") 90;
    setAttr ($linkName + $i + ".rotateY") (90 * $i);
    scale -r 1 1 2.210896 ;
    if ($i == 1)
        move -r 0 $moveNum 0 ;
    else
        move -r 0 ((($moveNum + $offSetNum) * $i) - $offSetNum) 0 ;
    rigidBody -active -m 1 -dp 0 -sf 0.2 -df 0.2 -b 0.6 -l 0 -tf 200 -iv 0 0
      0 -iav 0 0 0 -c 0 -pc 0 -i 0 0 0 -imp 0 0 0 -si 0 0 0 -sio none ;
    connectDynamic -f gravityField1 ($linkName + $i);
```

```
        }
} //end makeEm
//procedure to add the ball to the bottom of the
//chain.
proc addBall (int $num)
{
float $moveNum = -5.160681;
float $offSetNum = 1.741263;
string $linkName = "linkNum";

select -cl;
sphere -n weight -r 2;
move -r 0 ((($moveNum + $offSetNum) * $num - $offSetNum - 5)) 0 ;
select -cl  ;

//now select the last link and the "weight" ball, and
//make a pin constraint.
select -r ($linkName + $num) ;
select -tgl weight ;
constrain -pin -i 0 ;
select -cl  ;

//make the sphere's weight 50, connect gravity to it,
//and create an
//expression to drive the weight back and forth in X
//(impulseX).
select -r weight ;
setAttr ("rigidBody" + ($num + 3) + ".mass") 50;
connectDynamic -f gravityField1 weight;
//The next line actually adds an expression to the
//weight ball, driving it back and forth.
//How cool is that?!
expression -s "impulseX = 5 * sin (2 * time);" -o ("rigidBody" + ($num + 3))
      -ae 1 -uc all ;
} //end, makeBall
//Main procedure.

global proc makeChain (int $numLinks)
{
makeEm ($numLinks);
```

```
//comment out the following line if you don't want the
//ball at the bottom of the chain.
addBall ($numLinks);

select -cl;
select -all;
displaySmoothness -divisionsU 3 -divisionsV 3 -pointsWire 16 -pointsShaded
    4;
//Change some elements of the rigid solver so Maya
//doesn't choke on the data!
showEditor rigidSolver;
setAttr "rigidSolver.collisionTolerance" 0.0001;
setAttr "rigidSolver.bounciness" 0;
}  //end makeChain
```

If you got through these last three scripts, and have a good idea what's going on in them, you are ready to start making scripts of your own! Use the online reference documents, build on other people's work, and make something really useful for yourself. Even better, share it with others via a Web site (like www.highend3d.com) or an e-mail listserv.

Summary

In this chapter, we moved beyond the basics to discover just how powerful and complex MEL scripting can be. We worked with variables, loops, and conditional branches. We learned how to make custom GUIs for any purpose we wish. Finally, we created and examined full-blown MEL scripts.

Although big scripts look complex, the secret to writing them is to build them up from small pieces, and grab chunks of code (either from the Script Editor's History window or from other Maya users' scripts) and modify them for your own use.

Advanced MEL scripting is not for everyone, but if you like this sort of work, and get good at MEL, chances are you can land yourself a full-time job just scripting for Maya.

PART V

RENDERING

Use the Render Globals dialog box, Render View window, and other basic rendering tools

Use the Hypershade and work with Maya's texturing tools

Work with Maya's lighting tools and techniques

chapter 18

RENDERING BASICS

Featuring

- *Camera and resolution setup*
- *The Render Globals dialog box*
- *The Render View window*
- *Interactive photorealistic rendering*
- *Image planes*
- *Batch rendering*
- *Rendering techniques*

18

RENDERING BASICS

Rendering is a many-faceted process. First, you need a proper camera through which objects can be seen and captured into 2D images. You also need to decide on the quality and resolution of the image output. Then you can select how you want the surfaces to be lit—your choices include four different lights or incandescence. Next, you need to create materials and textures for the surfaces. You may also want to create an appropriate background, such as a stage set, an image plane with live footage, or an environmental texture. Alternatively, you could render the surfaces in layers with alpha channels and put them together with compositing software.

This chapter deals mainly with cameras, render settings, and using Maya's IPR (Interactive Photorealistic Rendering) tool. Shading and lighting will be covered more thoroughly in the following chapters.

Rendering an Object

As we've done in previous chapters, we will explore the process by plowing through an example from beginning to end. To demonstrate the rendering process, we will use a beveled text letter. We will light it, texture it, and animate it appearing and disappearing against a textured background. Then we will render the animation as a video-quality picture sequence.

Setting the Camera and the Resolution

First, we need to set the camera. As you've learned in earlier chapters, cameras are windows through which you look at things in Maya's world space. The default four views that you see when you start a new scene are actually four nondeletable cameras: one camera with a perspective view and three cameras with orthographic views, which we know as the front, side, and top views. Generally, the orthographic views are used for modeling, texturing, and animation purposes, and rendering is done only through the perspective views.

1. Create a beveled text letter *M* (using the Surface ➢ Bevel function), as we did in Chapter 6.

2. Create another perspective view by selecting Panels ➢ Perspective ➢ New. Persp1 camera is created.

3. In the Outliner, rename the view to Cam_1. Open its Attribute Editor and set Film Back ➢ Overscan to 1.1. Open Display Options and check Display Resolution. (You can also turn on Display Resolution by selecting View ➢ Camera Settings ➢ Resolution Gate.) The box shows you the exact area that will be rendered. Check the Display Film Gate setting (just above Display Resolution).

 N O T E   If you see another box overlapping the resolution gate, this means there is an imperfect match between the width × height ratio of the pictures to be rendered and the ratio of the medium in which the pictures will be presented.

4. Go to the Film Gate setting in the Film Back section and select different mediums, such as 70mm projection, to see how the resolution ratio changes. Change the preset to 35mm TV Projection, as shown below. This setting has the proper 1.33 width × height ratio for television. The Film Gate and the Resolution Gate settings should match perfectly.

NOTE You may want to render at a smaller size as a test render, but still maintain the correct (larger) aspect ratio, similar to the lock-aspect ratio feature available in Photoshop and other graphics software. Maya provides a setting for this in the Render Globals dialog box, discussed in the next section.

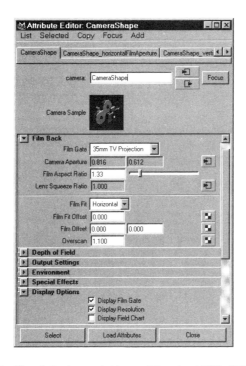

5. The default resolution setting is at 320×240, which you can see at the top of the resolution gate, but you probably will want to render the pictures at a higher resolution. Select Window ➤ Render Globals and open the Resolution section. For our example, set the Render Resolution to 640×480.

6. Adjust the Cam_1 view, dragging and rotating the camera until you have the proper composition for the letter *M*. Then keyframe the Cam_1 attributes. Now you will be able to switch back to the regular Perspective window and test render the Cam_1 view as you make changes to the lighting and textures.

As you saw in step 5, Maya provides many Render Resolution presets. If you are working with television and video productions, the most common resolution setting is CCIR 601, which is 720×486, Device Aspect Ratio 1.333, and Pixel Aspect Ratio 0.9. This means that the image will be 720 pixels wide and 486 pixels high, but it will be shown with a 4:3 width × height ratio because the pixel aspect ratio is not square. The 640×480 resolution that we are using has Device Aspect Ratio 1.333 and Pixel Aspect Ratio 1, and it is considered the minimum broadcast-quality resolution.

Broadcast Standards

There are different broadcast standards in existence in different parts of the world. The PAL (Phase Alternating Line) and SECAM (Sequential Color And Memory) systems are used in Britain and in Europe. The NTSC (National Television System Committee) system is used in North and South America and many Asian countries.

Unfortunately, these systems are incompatible in a number of ways. NTSC broadcasts 525 horizontal lines in a picture; PAL and SECAM broadcast 625 lines. NTSC transmits 30 fps (frames per second); the others transmit 25 fps. They also have different broadcast channel widths and types of signals. However, all of these standards broadcast pictures at a 4:3 image aspect ratio.

We render pictures at 640×480 resolution with square pixels, or 720×486 resolution with a pixel ratio of 0.9, in order to make them fit the 4:3 aspect ratio. Device Aspect Ratio of 1.333 is another way of stating that images are being displayed at a 4:3 width × height ratio.

With the coming of HDTV (high-definition TV), these standards are changing. Although there still isn't a universal standard for DTV (digital TV), the accepted image ratio for HDTV is 16:9, which is the same ratio as the wide-screen format used for films. This ratio translates to 1.777 Device Aspect Ratio. The minimum resolution for the HDTV is 1280×720. For film, 2:1 and 16:9 are currently the most commonly used image ratios.

Render Globals Settings

There are a few other things we need to set in the Render Globals dialog box. This dialog box offers many settings, but for now, we will set the quality, the output filename and format, and some frame rendering details.

1. Select Window ➤ Render Globals and open the Anti-aliasing Quality section. Set the Presets option to Intermediate Quality. You can change this setting to Production Quality when you are ready to render, but for test renders, the Preview or Intermediate Quality settings are usually good enough.

T I P   For production quality or higher quality anti-aliasing presets, Maya automatically turns on the Multipixel Filtering setting. Multipixel Filtering is good for situations where you see thin surface edges. If there are no thin edges to anti-alias, it's best to have this option turned off, because it can slow down the rendering process significantly.

2. Open the Image File Output section and type in a name for the picture sequence you will be rendering in the File Name Prefix field. If you don't enter a name, the rendered pictures will automatically be assigned the scene filename.

3. Set Frame/Animation Ext to name.#.ext. The animation settings become activated. If you leave the setting at name.ext, then only the current time frame will be rendered.

4. Set End Frame to 60, because we will be rendering two seconds of animation.

5. The default Image Format is Maya IFF (iff) picture format. Change it to something more widely acceptable, like the Targa (tga) format.

6. Set the Camera to Cam_1 to make it the renderable camera. Before closing the Render Globals dialog box, check to make sure you have the settings shown below.

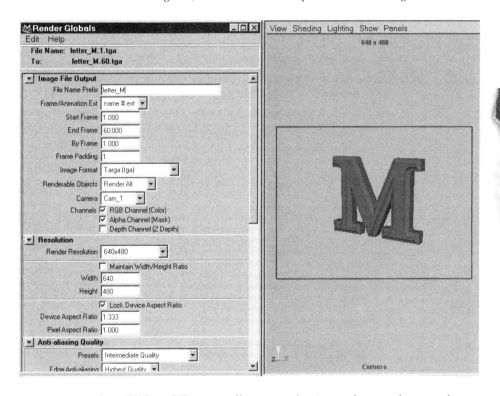

Formats such as JPEG or GIF are usually not used as image formats, because they do not carry alpha channel (mask) information, which is often needed for compositing purposes, and they compress the pixel information of the output, which may lower the picture quality.

N O T E Regular color pictures have 24 bits of color information for each pixel, stored in three RGB (red, green, blue) channels. A picture with an *alpha channel* has an extra 8-bit channel, which contains the masking information for each pixel of the picture. The information is stored in the form of a grayscale picture, which often turns out to be the outline of the objects being rendered.

By default, Maya renders the RGB channels and the alpha channel. You can also render the depth channel (Z-depth) by checking the Channels box. Z-depth is similar to the alpha channel in that it is represented as an 8-bit grayscale picture. As its name indicates, it stores the depth information of pixels to be rendered. As with the alpha channel, it is mainly used for compositing purposes. If the image format is the default .iff, then the Z-depth information is stored inside the image file being rendered, like other alpha channel information. If you are rendering in a format like .tga, Maya creates a separate Z-depth file for every image it renders.

The Renderable Objects setting is set to Render All by default, but you can switch it to Render Active if you want, which will only render what you've selected. Using the Render Active option is useful if you are rendering in layers.

T I P   In the Render Globals dialog box, you see Cam_1 as the camera available for rendering. If you want to render multiple cameras, Cam_1 and persp, for example, open the persp camera's Attribute Editor, go to the Output Settings section, and turn on Renderable. Now if you go to the Render Globals dialog box's Image File Output section and look at the Camera menu, you will see that both Cam_1 and persp are identified as Renderable.

Working in the Render View

Now we will set up some spotlights and take a look at our letter in the Render View window.

1. Create a default spotlight. Select Panels ➤ Look Through Selected, and move the spotLight1 view to something like (a) below.

2. Create another spotlight, and repeat the procedure to look something like (b) below. This is a very convenient and intuitive way to set lights. You do not need to fine-tune anything at this point—we will be doing that with the IPR tool soon.

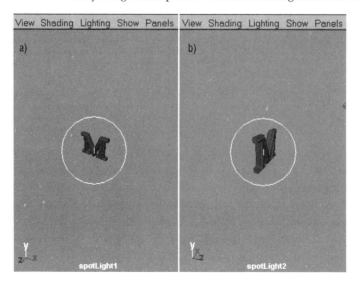

3. Select Window ≻ Rendering Editors ≻ Render View.

You can open any image in the Render View window, but you can only save an image in .iff file format. Here are some of the things you can do in the Render View window:

- Keep multiple images by selecting File ≻ Keep Image in Render View for each picture you want to keep.

- Take wireframe snapshots of different cameras available for rendering, or select a region to render only that area.

- Zoom in and out and drag the image in the Render View window by using hotkeys and mouse buttons, just as you can in a modeling view.

- Use the options on the View menu to change the view. Frame Image shows an entire image, Frame Region focuses on just the selected region, and Real Size shows an image without any zooming. You can also see a rendered image as separate color planes, luminance, or its alpha channel (Mask Plane).

N O T E The toolbar in the Render View window includes buttons for the most-often used functions. You can see what their functions are by placing the mouse arrow over the icons.

Using IPR (Interactive Photorealistic Rendering)

The IPR tool allows you to edit colors, materials, textures, lights, and shadows interactively. When you invoke IPR, Maya creates an IPR image file that stores both the shading and the visibility information of surfaces. The file size is considerably larger than a regular image file of the same resolution because it stores the extra visibility information. Then, when a tuning region is selected, Maya loads all the IPR information for the pixels in the region into memory. You can change the tuning region at any time, and the IPR will continue to load the pixel information for the new region.

Now we will use IPR on our letter *M*, but first we will get a snapshot. It's always a good idea to take snapshots before you do any rendering, because it provides a quick view of what you are about to render. Taking a snapshot also sets the camera you've chosen as the active camera, and you can later use the Redo Previous Render and Redo Previous IPR Render icons to render the same camera view.

1. From the Options menu, turn off Auto Resize and turn on Auto Render Region.

2. Select Render ≻ Snapshot ≻ Cam_1.

3. Click the IPR button to start the IPR process. Once the letter *M* has been rendered, select a region to start IPR tuning, as shown below.

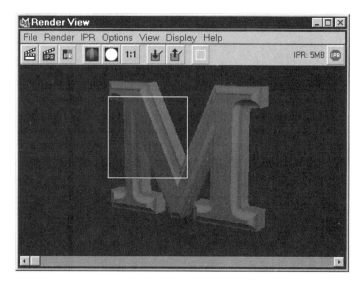

If the image is real size, the marquee box stays green. As soon as the image is zoomed in or out, the box turns red. Note that the IPR icon in the top-right corner has turned red as well, indicating that IPR is active. The indicator to the left of the icon shows how big the IPR file is. Now any change you make to the lighting or texture information relating to the letter *M* will be updated within the tuning region automatically.

There are some neat things you can do within the selected IPR tuning region. You can Shift+click over any pixels within the region to find out which shades and lights are affecting them, and select those nodes. You also can drag materials and textures onto the objects within the region, and they will update accordingly. Any modification in the shading information is updated in the region with speeds comparable to that of a Hypershade swatch update, because the visibility calculations have already been made. (We will use the Hypershade window in the next section and examine it in detail in Chapter 19.)

Having the visibility information already stored in the IPR file means that once the file is there, you can change the camera view and make changes in the surfaces without disturbing the IPR tuning region. Those changes are not recalculated until you start another IPR. While this allows you to get more mileage out of a single IPR file as you are editing lighting and shading, keep in mind that if the changes in the surfaces' visibility are significant enough, the IPR updates can go out of sync with how the surfaces actually look. If this happens, you should create another IPR file.

Shading the Object

Next, we'll use the Hypershade window to shade the letter *M*. As in the Render View window, you can zoom in and out and move around in Hypershade using the hotkeys and the mouse buttons. You can also zoom in and out of the Visor panel, a render-centric file browser. This may seem a bit weird at first, but it allows you to clearly see the swatches and the labels, which is a must when working with shaders. We will go through the steps to shade and texture our current example, without much explanation of the settings. You will get a proper introduction to Hypershade in the next chapter.

1. Keep the Render View window open, and adjust the spotlights until you are fairly satisfied with the way the letter *M* is being lit in the tuning region. After you've shaded the letter properly, you can come back to this view and fine tune the lighting.

2. Select Window ➤ Hypershade. Zoom in to the Visor panel that appears on the left side of Hypershade. Go to the Create directory, then the Materials folder under it (open the folder if it's closed), and MM drag the blinn# material onto the Hypershade, as shown below.

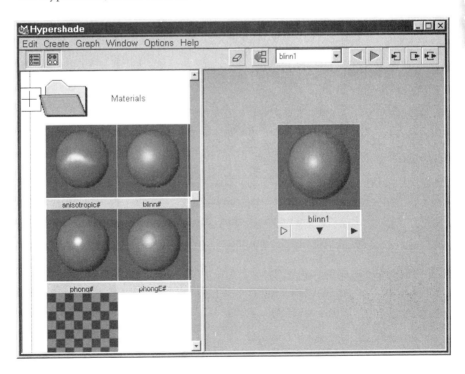

3. Go down to the Texture folder in the Visor panel and MM drag the brownian# texture into the layout and over the blinn material. A list of possible input connections pops up. Connect to color, and you will see the brownian texture come up on the blinn material swatch.

4. Drag the same brownian texture over the blinn material to see the list pop up again. This time, connect to bump, as shown below. You'll see the bump effect of the brownian texture on the blinn material, along with the creation of a bump node.

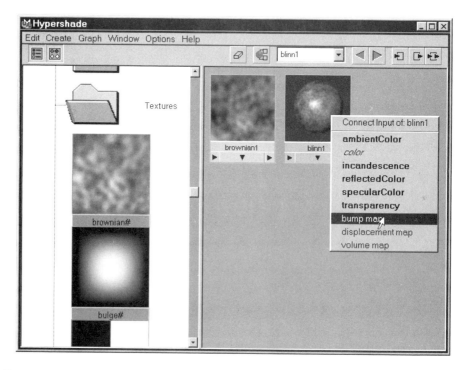

5. In Hypershade, RM choose Graph ≻ Rearrange Graph to sort the nodes, then click the icon in the top-left corner to hide the Visor panel.

6. With the Hypergraph and the Render View windows close to each other, drag the blinn material onto the letter *M* inside the tuning region of the IPR window. Since there are two surfaces comprising the letter *M*, you'll need to apply the material twice. The material, along with the brownian color and bump, should update on the letter *M* almost immediately, as shown on the next page.

TIP   There are many other ways to apply the blinn material to the letter *M*. One way is to drag the swatch onto the object inside the modeling window. Another way is to select the object, then move the mouse over the blinn swatch and RM choose Assign Material to Selection.

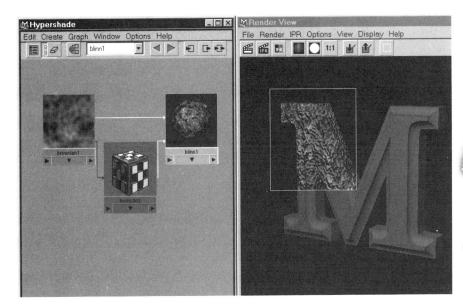

7. The default bump value is too high for our purposes. RM choose over the brownian texture to open its Attribute Editor, open Color Balance, and move the Alpha Gain slider down. You should see the bump on the letter *M* start to lessen in the IPR tuning region. Adjust the Alpha Gain value until you like what you see. To adjust the bumpiness in a different way, you can also try playing with the increment value slider in the Brownian Attributes section.

8. Work in the same way with brownian's Color Gain and Color Offset values to adjust the color of the texture.

9. Go to the blinn material and adjust Specular Shading by moving the Eccentricity, Specular Roll Off, and Color sliders. (Specular Shading has to do with how the light is reflected from an object.)

10. Return to the spotlights and fine tune the lighting, this time adjusting not only the angles, but also the Color, Intensity, and Dropoff values. You may also want to change the tuning region to different areas to make sure there are no hidden surprises. The updates we've made appear as shown here. (You can also see this image in the Color Gallery.)

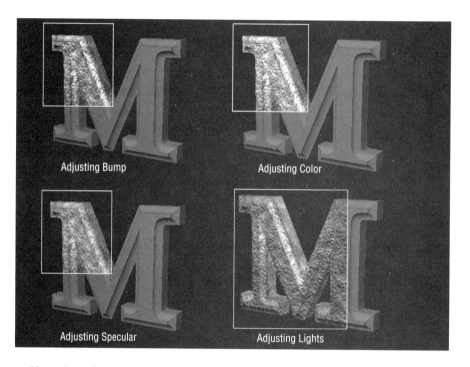

If you have been experimenting with the other sliders and fields, you've seen that some of them do not affect the letter *M* at all and that some others should be left alone. It's very easy to play with the texture, material, and the light attributes and get immediate feedback from the IPR tuning region. One of the best things about IPR is that it frees you to experiment with the attributes and think of other possibilities—there is less reason for number crunching and more room for artistic impressions.

If a single image were the goal in this exercise, once you were satisfied with the way everything looks, you might increase the Anti-aliasing to Production Quality setting, then click the top-left corner icon, Redo Previous Render, to render a final image. You could then save the letter *M* image and convert it to another format using the Fcheck utility. But our example is for a sequence of images, which requires us to do a bit more work.

Making an Object Disappear

We would like the letter *M* to appear and disappear against a textured background. First, we will work on the letter's appearance and disappearance. We can accomplish this by using the Transparency, Specular Color, and Set Key attributes.

1. In the blinn material Attribute Editor, slide up the Transparency value all the way to white. In the IPR region, the letter's surface disappears, but the specular highlights still remain. Notice that the alpha channel for the letter also becomes black, which you can check by clicking the Display Mask button.

2. To make the letter *M* become completely invisible, you need to turn down the Specular Color slider all the way to black. At frame 5, RM choose Set Key for Transparency and Specular Color.

3. Go to frame 15, turn down the Transparency value, raise the Specular Color value, and Set Key those attributes. The letter *M* now appears over a ten-frame time interval.

4. Repeat the process in the opposite direction between frames 50 and 60 to make the letter disappear. Notice that as you move the current time indicator in the time slider, the IPR tuning region updates the changing transparency and the specularity.

5. Select Window ➤ Animation Editors ➤ Graph Editor. Here, you can see the blinn material's keyframed attributes, as shown below. (See the Color Gallery on the CD for the Graph Editor's color coding.)

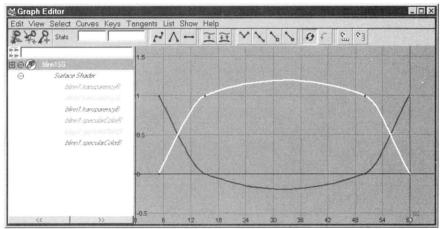

6. Select all the curves and apply Tangents ➤ Flat to make sure the Tranparency and Specularity attributes stay constant between frames 15 to 50. The ease-in/ease-out shape of the keyframes also ensures the smooth appearance and disappearance of the letter *M*.

Adding a Textured Background

Our work on the letter *M* is done. Now let's add a background for the letter. In the Environment section of the camera's Attribute Editor, the Create button lets you create an image plane. You can set the display to show the image only through the camera or have it displayed in all views. When you are modeling, you want to be able to see the image in different views. You can hide the image temporarily by setting the Display Mode to None. You can also load any image to use as the background by clicking the browser button beside Image Name, and place it anywhere in the modeling window using the Placement and Placement Extras attributes. For our example, we will create a texture to use as the background.

1. Select Cam_1 and open its Attribute Editor. Open the Environment section and click the Create button to create an image plane.

2. Click the Create button beside the Texture field to open Create Render Node and select a solid fractal texture.

3. Since background textures do not show up in the IPR, you need to render the region to test how the solid fractal matches up with the letter *M*. Adjust its Color Gain, Offset, and placement attributes to get it to look the way you want—something like the image shown below.

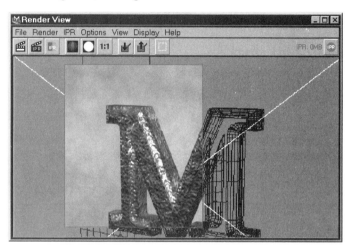

TIP   You can select the image plane in several different ways. One way is to first select the camera, then click the arrow beside the **Image Plane Create** button to get to it. Another way is to go into the component mode and click the question mark icon, which enables image plane selection. A third alternative is to open the **Outliner**, RM choose to toggle off **Show DAG Objects Only**, then scroll down to select the **Image Plane** node.

Batch Rendering

We are now ready to render. Before you save the scene, however, let's see where the rendered pictures will be placed.

1. Select File ➢ Project ➢ Edit Current. The Edit Project dialog box tells you the location of the current project. Go to Render File Locations section and look at the field beside Images. If this field's entry says Images, there is a default subdirectory in the current project called Images, and the rendered pictures will be placed into that directory by default. If nothing is in the field, the rendered images will be placed into the current project directory.

2. Save the scene as letter_M. You can exit Maya.

3. Open an MS-DOS Command Prompt window (if you are using SGI, open a Unix shell window). Go to the directory where you've saved your letter *M*, and you will see the file listed as `letter_M.mb`.

4. Type **Render** and press Enter. All the options that you can use with the Render command are listed.

5. For our example, enter the following command:

`Render -s 1 -e 60 -b 1 -rd D:\Sybex\Chapter18\Renders\ -n 2 letter_M.mb`

The Maya Rendering program will take the file `letter_M.mb`, render frames 1 to 60 using two available processors, and put the rendered pictures into the directory listed in the path.

In this example, we used the most common Render command options: -s for start frame, -e for end frame, -b for by frame or step, -rd for the directory path in which to store rendered images, and -n for number of processors to use. You also could leave out the -rd option, render the pictures into the default render directory, and move the pictures out of that directory later.

Other options, such as -mb for motion blur and -sa for shutter angle, can also be handy in certain situations. For example, let's say you've rendered a run cycle, and while checking the rendered pictures, you notice that frame 12 is looking very weird because of the motion blur. Rather than opening the file and fixing this, you can either render just that frame without the motion blur (-mb off) or reduce the motion blur by typing in a lower shutter angle value (-sa 70, for example).

Once the rendering is done, you can view the rendered pictures using the Fcheck utility. Fcheck allows you to view a single image or a sequence of images, check their alpha channels, view the different color planes, and see the Z-depth information. You can also save the images into many different picture formats. (If you are working with SGI machines, you can use the imgcvt command to convert images into different formats.)

NOTE   You can reduce the time it takes to render your scenes by using some optimizing techniques. See Chapter 20 for some render optimization tips.

Using Other Rendering Techniques

So far, we've gone through the process of lighting, shading, and rendering a sequence of images for a simple beveled letter *M*. We've tried to keep the options as simple as we could, but rendering, by nature, is a rather complex endeavor. For the rest of this chapter, we will cover some other areas of rendering that you may find useful for your own projects.

Layer Rendering, Compositing, and Editing

What we've done with the letter *M* rendering is actually pretty dumb. The 60 frames of rendering were not necessary; only the first 10 frames were. In studio environments where meeting deadlines and work efficiency are always paramount, this kind of rendering redundancy would have been frowned upon, to say the least.

With any editing software, or with some renaming and renumbering script commands, you can extend frame 1 forward to frame 5, reverse the animation from frames 5 to 15 to make them frames 50 to 60, and hold frame 15 until frame 49.

We also should have rendered the letter *M* separately from the fractal textured background. Since the background remains constant, only a single frame is necessary. Using compositing software, the letter *M* could have been composited onto the background.

In a production, the rendering pipeline is often set up to layer render anything that can be layered. Below is a partial example of how the letter *M* can be rendered as multiple-layered render passes. The floor has been added to illustrate the shadow passes. (You can also see this image in the Color Gallery on the CD.)

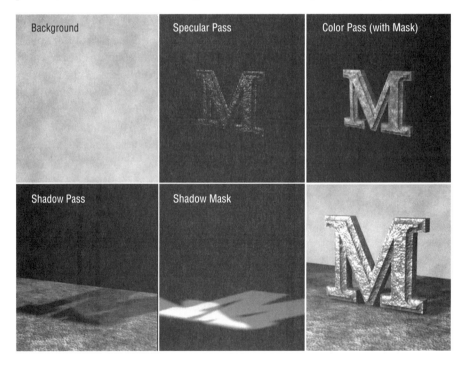

Although not included in the sample pictures, there also should be a separate render for the floor, with the accompanying alpha channel. To create just the shadows on the floor, select the letter *M* surfaces, go to the Attribute Editor's Render Stats section, and turn off Primary Visibility. To create the shadow mask, color the floor black, make the lights black as well, and turn their shadow color to white. Separating these elements may seem like extra work, but it allows you more control at the compositing stage, and can ultimately save you time in terms of making changes or corrections.

You can increase or decrease only the specularity or change the colors on the letter *M*. You can darken or lighten just the shadows, or sharpen them or blur them. If you have the proper compositing software, you can even transform and animate the different layer elements. If the render was being done in one pass, you would need to re-render the whole scene each time you wanted to make changes to any of these things. However, if you had rendered these items as separate elements, you would only need to re-render the elements you wanted to change. Whether these refinements are worth the extra effort depends on your specific production situation, but having more control at the compositing stage is usually the better way to go.

Adding Depth of Field

Maya cameras also have the ability to imitate the depth-of-field functionality of real-world cameras. To be able to use it in any practical way, however, requires a bit of a setup.

Open the letter_M file, select Cam_1, and open its Attribute Editor. Go to the Depth of Field section and check Depth of Field. Its attributes become active. The Focus Distance attribute does what it says—it sets the distance for the camera focus.

It would be useful to have a way of interactively controlling that distance in the modeling window, instead of punching in numbers. An easy way to do this is to open the Connection Editor with the Camera Shape loaded on both windows, and connect the Center of Interest output to the Focus Distance input. This constrains the focus distance to the camera's center of interest, which shows up as part of the Show Manipulator handle.

In the picture below (also available in the Color Gallery on the CD), the F Stop value may be a bit too low. Also, the blurring, a post effect, is expensive (meaning it takes longer to render). However, because it is a 3D blur, it adds much more realism to the rendered image than any post-effect 2D blur can. If you want more control, or just need to have the camera's center of interest and the focus distance to be separate entities, you can connect the focus distance to a locator instead.

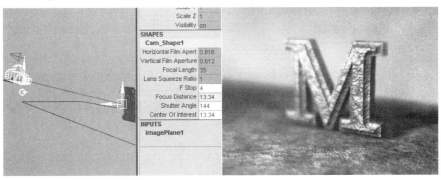

Importing Live Footage

If you want to match an animation with live footage, you need to animate the image plane. Let's assume we have ten frames of footage properly numbered and with proper extensions. In order to bring in the sequence of images, in the image plane's Attribute Editor, turn on the Use Frame Extension under the Image Plane Attributes section. Click the browse button beside the Image Name field to load the first frame of the footage. The result should look something like below.

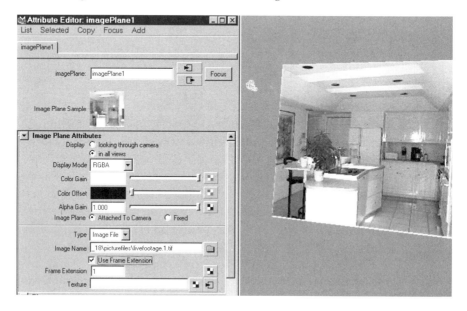

Go to frame 1, enter 1 in the Frame Extension field, and RM choose Set Key to keyframe it. At frame 10, enter 10 into the field and keyframe that. Now when you move the time slider, the frames update. If you open the Graph Editor for the image plane, you can see a linear curve for the Frame Extension, as shown on the next page.

Loading picture sequences is easy. Camera tracking the live footage, however, is a tedious and time-consuming affair—usually frame-by-frame matching work. Once the tracking is done, matching up lighting and shading to the live footage is yet another grim task. But as we will see in the next chapter, using IPR can make even that an enjoyable process.

T I P   Maya Live, which comes bundled with Maya Unlimited (the other Maya package that Alias sells), is tracking software. That program works wonderfully and can save you days of work. If you're interested, you can search the Alias Web page for more information.

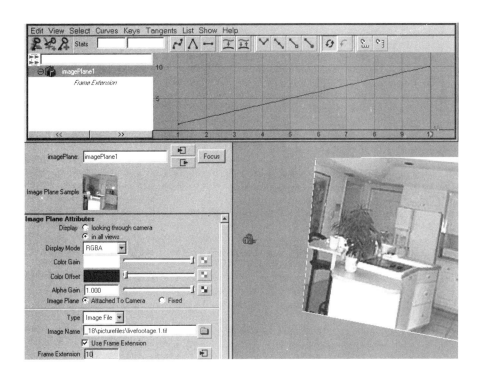

Summary

This chapter introduced you to the many varied parts of rendering. You learned how to create and set up a camera and how to set the resolution and the format of the output in the Render Globals dialog box.

We also covered the Render View window and IPR function, one of the more delightful new inclusions in Maya 2. Then we took a brief look at other topics, such as working with image planes and batch rendering.

Hypershade and lighting were also introduced. These topics are covered in depth in the next two chapters.

chapter 19

SHADING AND
TEXTURING SURFACES

Featuring

- *Hypershade operations*
- *Surface coloring*
- *Shininess and bumpiness control*
- *Transparency, incandescence, and glow*
- *Texturing techniques*

SHADING AND
TEXTURING
SURFACES

Objects look different because they are made up of different materials. We can distinguish materials generally by the way that they reflect light. A metal object shines more than a wooden object. The brightest spot where the light is reflecting from an object is called the object's *specular highlight*. In Maya, materials are generally classified according to the way that specular light is calculated to represent them.

We also identify objects by their color and texture. Maya has many default textures, such as wood, rock, leather, and so on. These allow you to quickly create easily identifiable everyday objects.

In this chapter, you will learn how to use these default materials and textures to create great-looking objects. For examples, we will use the dog, living room, and child models from the previous chapters. But first, you need to learn how to use Hypershade.

Using Hypershade

Just as you can view and edit nodes and node network connections using dependency graphs in Hypergraph, you can also work with them the same way in Hypershade. Hypershade differs from Hypergraph in that it uses swatches, which give a level of visual feedback that Hypergraph lacks. For viewing and editing render nodes such as textures and materials, Hypershade is indispensable.

Working in the Hypershade Window

When you select Window ➤ Hypershade, you see a render-centric file browser, called the Visor panel, on the left side of the window. As you learned in Chapter 18, from the Visor panel, you can zoom in and out and MM drag the various nodes (or folders in the Rendering directory) onto the layout area on the right side of the window. The top-leftmost button in the Hypershade window opens and closes the Visor panel. The next button opens and closes the Hypershade layout area. The button with the eraser clears the view.

Let's briefly go over some of the menu functions available in the Hypershade window. Then we will see how the nodes and networks work in Hypershade.

The Edit Menu

On the Edit menu, the Delete Unused Nodes function deletes all the nodes that are not assigned to geometry or particles. This is a great cleanup command that you will want to invoke at the end of your session.

The Duplicate command has three options. The blinn1 material with the checker texture in the picture below forms a simple network.

- Duplicate ➤ Shading Network produces the blinn2 node network.

- Duplicate ➤ Without Network produces just the blinn3 node, which copies all the properties of the blinn1 material, but not the network.

- Duplicate ➤ With Connections to Network produces blinn4, which inherits the same upstream node network connections as the original blinn1 node.

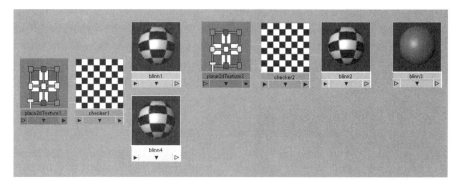

The Convert Material to File Texture function converts a material or texture into an image file, which then replaces the original as a File Texture with UV coordinates. You can adjust the image size and turn on Anti-aliasing in the option box. The image will be placed into your current project directory. You can select material nodes, 2D or 3D textures, or projections for the conversion. If you select the Shading Group node, the light information will be baked into the image as well.

The Create Menu and Create Directory

Under the Create directory in the Visor panel, you will find the following folders:

- The Camera folder contains the camera and image plane nodes.

- The Lights folder contains the four standard light types.

- The Materials folder contains nine material types. When you drag one of them into the layout area, a Shading Group is automatically created and linked to it.

- The Post Process folder holds the opticalFX, which creates light effects such as glow, halo, and lens flare.

- The Textures folder contains the 2D and 3D textures, in alphabetical order.

- The Utilities folder contains the Color, General, Particle, and Switch subfolders.

On the Create menu, the Create Render Node command opens a window with tabs. For volumetric materials such as Env Fog, you need to use the Create menu or the Create Render Node window, because these materials are not listed in the Materials folder. Also, if you want to apply a texture as a projection or a stencil, you should use the Create Render Node window to change the setting from Normal to As Projection or As Stencil.

PART

5

Rendering

For Users of Previous Versions of Maya

The Create menu is organized the way it was in previous versions of Maya. The Create Render Node command opens the tabbed window, which, for most users of earlier Maya versions, was the primary venue for creating render nodes.

The Visor panel's organization is a bit different, but the render nodes are all the same nodes. Under the Create directory, the camera and the image plane nodes are now in the Camera folder, not in the Utilities section. The opticalFX has also been moved from the Utilities section to its own Post Process folder. The material types can now be changed in the Attribute Editor, but their settings may get lost during the change.

The Graph Menu

The Graph menu has several useful functions. The Graph Materials on Selected Objects command allows you to work with a select group of render nodes according to the surfaces you select. By moving the materials, textures, and networks that have been applied to the selected objects into the layout area, this command provides an efficient way to isolate the render nodes you want to work with in complicated scenes. The Graph Materials on Selected Objects command also is available through the Hypershade window button next to the eraser button.

The Up and Downstream Connection command performs the same function as it does in Hypergraph, listing the nodes connected to the selected nodes in the layout area. The Upstream Connection and Downstream Connection commands can be useful when you know which stream you want to view and edit. They also reduce the clutter in the work area when you are working with a complex scene.

The Rearrange Graph command cleans up the layout area and reorganizes the nodes for better viewing.

Other Menus

The Window menu gives you access to the Attribute Editor, Attribute Spread Sheet, and Connection Editor.

The Options menu's Swatches ➤ Keep Fixed Size command keeps the swatch resolution to a fixed size, so that when you zoom in, the resolution doesn't update. This makes the swatches less accurate when closely zoomed in but increases their interactive speed.

The Layout menu enables you to switch the layout area to viewing only Shading Groups, Materials, Textures, Utilities, Cameras, or Lights. It also creates a new layer when you bring a new node into the layout area. Subsequent nodes that are brought in stay in the same layout area so you can view their input/output relationships.

TIP   If you want to create a separate layer for any node, select Graph ➤ Clear View and drag the node into the work area. A layer is created with the node's name. Subsequent nodes that are brought in will stay in that layer.

Working with Nodes and Networks

To see how you can work with nodes, MM grab a blinn node in the Materials folder and drag it into Hypershade, then try the following:

- RM choose over the left-bottom corner. You see a list of the attributes that can be connected with incoming information, as shown in (a) below.

- RM choose over the right-bottom corner. You see a list of the attributes that can go out to the other nodes, as in (b) below.

- MM drag a checker texture over the blinn material. The default connection box pops up. In the example below, labeled (c), this is the triple-channel connection. If the incoming information were a single-channel connection, a different box would pop up. Also, different nodes have different channels listed for their input/output connections.

• RM choose over the material node. A box pops up with a list of operations you can perform on the material node, as in (d) below. The Graph Shader Network function lists nodes that are connected to the material node. Assign Material to Selection assigns the material node to selected surfaces. Select Objects with Material selects all the surfaces that have the material node assigned to them. Frame Objects with Material selects and frames the surfaces with the material in the modeling window. You can also open the Attribute Editor for the material node or rename it.

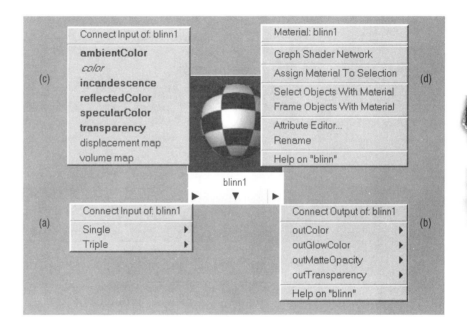

N O T E   You can assign different shading groups to different faces of a polygon object. For NURBS surfaces, only one shading group can be assigned to a surface.

Below is an example of a fairly simple network, which includes different swatches you will soon become very familiar with. (It's also in the Color Gallery on the CD.) Working backwards, the blinn1SG (Shading Group) is getting its shading information from the blinn1 material swatch and nurbsSphere node. The blinn node is getting its color information from the checker1 node, which is also outputting its alpha channel information to a reverse node. The reverse node, true to its name, is reversing the information it's getting and is passing it on to the 2D bump node, which is connecting to the blinn's bump channel input. The leather and brownian textures connect to the checker texture's color attributes, and there are placement nodes for each of the textures: a 2D

placement node for the checker texture and 3D placement nodes for the leather and
brownian textures.

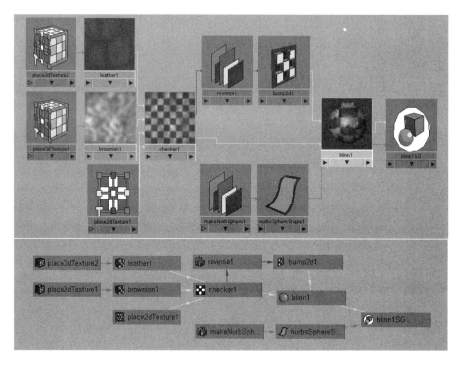

Note that everything is arranged exactly the same way as in the Hypergraph node
network. Like Hypergraph, Hypershade lets you move the mouse over the lines connecting the nodes to find out exactly what attributes are being connected:

- The green lines are triple attributes, such as the RGB color information or the
  world space (X, Y, Z) coordinates.

- The light-blue lines are double attributes, such as the UV coordinates of a geometry surface.

- The dark-blue lines are single attributes, such as the 8-bit grayscale masking values of the alpha information.

To check or change these and other color designations, select Options ➤
Customize UI ➤ Colors and open the Hypergraph/Hypershade section.

 TIP   MM dragging a node over another node opens the appropriate connection list.
Ctrl+MM dragging a node over another one lets Maya choose the default connection automatically. If you want to use the Connection Editor to connect the two nodes, Shift+MM
drag the node. You can also drag a node into another node's Attribute Editor.

The nodes and networks can also be imported or exported. To bring in a scene, use the File ➤ Import function or open your current project directory in the Visor panel and drag in the Maya scene you want. You can save specific nodes or node networks by selecting them and applying File ➤ Export Selection. The nodes will be saved as a Maya scene.

Using Shading and Texturing Attributes

Shading in Maya can be divided into the categories of color, shininess, bumpiness, transparency, and self-illumination. We will go through these "global" material properties first, and then proceed to cover some general texture properties.

Coloring Surfaces

When you create a material and open its Attribute Editor, you can find its default Color attribute in the Common Material Attributes section. The default is set as a gray color with zero saturation and 0.5 value in HSV, or 0.5 RGB. Maya provides many ways to adjust the color of the material:

- Use the Color Chooser. To access the Color Chooser, click the color box beside the Color attribute.

- Connect textures or file textures to the Color attribute, typically by dragging them to the Color attribute in the Attribute Editor. The Diffuse attribute acts as a scale factor to the color values, with 0.0 being black and 1.0 being the original color values. The default Diffuse setting is 0.8.

- Map 2D textures to a surface as normal UV textures or as one of many types of projections: planar, spherical, cylindrical, ball, cubic, triplanar, concentric, or perspective.

- Apply 2D textures as stencils image files are more often used as stencils).

- Map 3D textures as if they were solid objects occupying space in and around the surface.

- UV map images as file textures or project them on a surface. They can be single pictures or sequences of pictures (as you saw in the previous chapter).

- Use Surface Shader for coloring a material node. Although it is stored in the Materials folder, a Surface Shader has the information for only the color, transparency, glow, and matte opacity of a material. When you want to use the same color for many different materials or textures, Surface Shader enables you to have one node control the color information of many nodes.

- Use Shading Map to color a surface. Shading Map is typically used for non-photorealistic, or cartoonish, shading effects. It takes the colors sampled by a regular shader and replaces those colors with a simpler color scheme using the brightness and hue of the original colors.

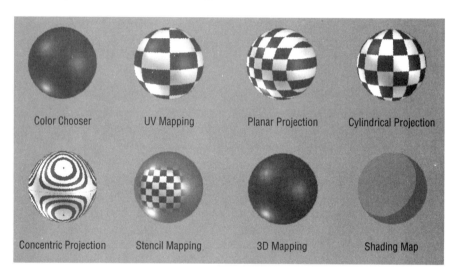

Controlling Shininess

Different materials reflect light differently on their surfaces. Lambert material does not have any specular highlight. Blinn, phong, and phongE materials have different variables for calculating specular highlight.

Blinn has the softest specular highlights among the three and is usually the material recommended for surfaces with bumps or displacements, because it tends to rope or flicker less than the phong materials. Blinn and phong are called *isotropic* materials, which means that they reflect specular light identically in all directions.

New in Maya 2 is the anisotropic material, which reflects specular light differently in different directions according to its Specular Shading settings. It more faithfully adheres to the way materials such as hair, satin cloth, feathers, or CDs reflect light unevenly.

Shading Map also calculates specular highlight, but in a non-photorealistic way, as mentioned in the previous section. The Use Background material's Specular and Reflectivity variables only work with raytracing. The layered shader does not have specular variables because it creates layered materials. See the "Applying Textures" section later in this chapter for more information about layered shaders.

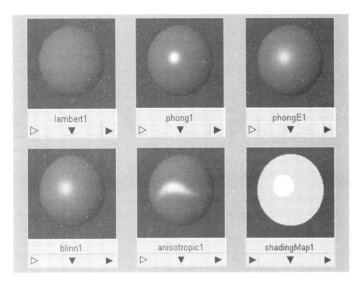

All the materials with specular highlight have Specular Color, Reflectivity, and Reflected Color attributes. You can use the Color Chooser to tint the specular color, or map textures or image files in the same way that you can with material color. In the picture labeled (a) below (also in the Chapter 19 Color Gallery on the CD), the Specular Color attribute in the sphere with the anisotropic shader has been tinted blue to match the blue color of the material. In (b), the sphere has a checker texture mapped to Specular Color. You can also do the same thing with Reflected Color, and fake reflection in this way, although true reflection only occurs with raytracing. In (c), the sphere has an Env Sky shader with the floor texture mapped to its Reflected Color. The sphere in (d) is raytraced; notice the reflection on the floor in that picture.

PART 5

Rendering

Raytracing

Raytracing lets you create refractions and shadows through transparent objects. Although raytracing may be desirable and necessary when you want to create photorealistic images, it is also more expensive than the regular rendering. When the settings are set high, the render time can increase very dramatically.

To raytrace, you need to turn on Raytracing under Raytracing Quality in the Render Globals dialog box. For refractions, you need to open the material Attribute Editor of the selected surface and turn on the Refractions setting in the Raytrace Options section. To have raytraced shadows, you also need to open the shadow casting light's Attribute Editor and check the Use Ray Trace Shadows setting in the Raytrace Shadow Attributes section. You also can control a surface's visibility in other surfaces' reflections by turning on or off its Visible in Reflections setting, which is in the Render Stats section of its Attribute Editor.

Creating Bumpiness

There are two ways to create bumpiness on a surface:

- Apply a bump map to a surface, which fools the camera into believing that there are bumps on a smooth surface.

- Apply a displacement map, which actually moves the geometry to create the bumps.

There are advantages and disadvantages to both methods. Bump mapping is much more efficient in terms of rendering, but it fails at the edges of a surface and cannot create the appearance of extreme bumpiness. Displacement mapping does a better job of creating bumpiness because it actually displaces the geometry of the surface, but it takes longer to render. Also, often the geometry's UV spans or its tessellation count must increase significantly before you see proper displacement, as shown below.

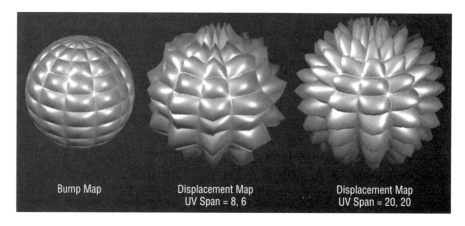

Bump Map   Displacement Map   Displacement Map
                  UV Span = 8, 6   UV Span = 20, 20

When you drag a texture over a material node and connect to its bump map, or drag to its Bump Mapping field in the Attribute Editor, a bump map node is created. If the texture is 2D, a bump2D node is created. If the texture is 3D, a bump3D node is created. Projection bumps also will create a bump3D node. The texture's alpha value, which is a single-channel attribute, connects to the bump node's Bump Value attribute. The bump node then outputs a triple-channel outNormal to the material's normal-Camera attribute, which creates the appearance of bumpiness on the material surface.

When you connect a texture to a material's Displacement attribute, two nodes are created: a regular bump node that connects to the material's normalCamera and a displacement node that connects not to the material, but directly to the material's Shader Group node. Even though a displacement map actually transforms the geometry it is applied to, you still need a bump map to be applied with it to give the surface the correct bumpy look. Try deleting the bump node from a material with a displacement mapping to see the difference.

You can also bump a bump map to add more detail to a bump mapped or displacement mapped surface. In the example below, we displacement-mapped a bulge texture to a blinn material, which we assigned to a sphere. We then created a leather texture and connected it to a 3D bump node (because leather is a 3D texture). Finally, we connected that bump node's outNormal value to the normalCamera attribute of the bulge's bump node, essentially bumping the bump node. The result is the picture of the sphere below. (It's also in the Color Gallery on the CD.)

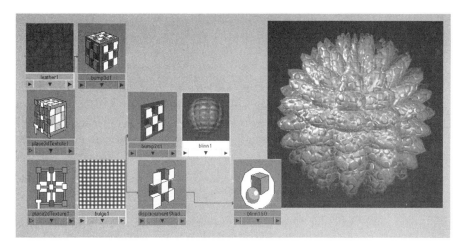

Adding Transparency

Transparency is a triple-channel color attribute, with black making the material opaque, and white making it transparent. As with color and specular attributes, you can map textures or image files for transparency, as shown below. Once a material becomes transparent, you can also turn on refraction for raytracing. The Refractive Index in the Raytrace Options section of the material's Attribute Editor controls how much the light bends as it passes through the transparent material. For the refraction to have any effect, there must be more than one layer of surface that the camera can see through. You can set up a simple example with two concentric spheres with a textured floor to test how they raytrace with different Refractive Index settings, as shown below (and in the Color Gallery on the CD).

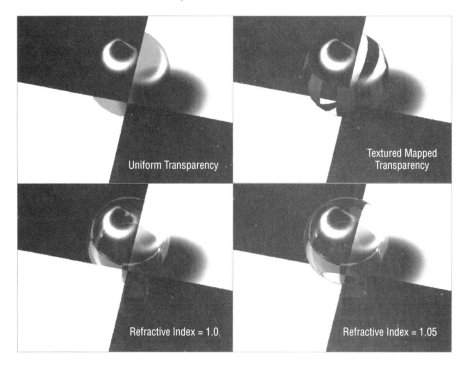

Uniform Transparency

Textured Mapped Transparency

Refractive Index = 1.0

Refractive Index = 1.05

For true refraction to happen to even a simple thing, such as a glass cup, you need to set the Refraction Limit to at least 9. The light must go through at least four surfaces just to get to the other side, bounce back, then travel through the cup to the camera for us to see the other side of the glass cup. The Refraction Limit setting is in the Raytrace Options section of the material's Attribute Editor, and it's also listed simply as the Refractions setting in the Raytracing Quality section of the Render Globals dialog box. Both settings need to be adjusted; the lower of the two values will act as the maximum refraction limit for the material.

You can also use transparency to layer different materials and textures on top of one another with a layered shader. For more information about using layered shaders, see the "Face Textures" section later in this chapter.

A related material attribute that needs brief mentioning here is Translucence. A translucent object isn't necessarily transparent, but it does transmit light through its surface. Objects such as sheets of paper, leaves, clouds, ice, and hair are examples of translucent materials, as shown next. (This image is also in the Color Gallery on the CD.)

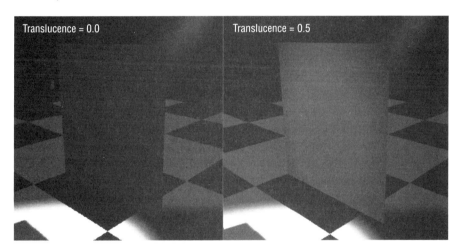

Adding Self-Illumination

You can add self-illumination attributes to materials through Incandescence, Glow Intensity, and Ambient Color settings.

Incandescence

Many materials have Incandescence under their Common Material Attributes. This attribute makes the surface with the material appear to give off light on its own. Red-hot metal and neon signs have a noticeable incandescence.

Incandescence can also be used more subtly in many other surfaces. With an almost unnoticeable amount of incandescence, a person's eyes seem much brighter, and flower petals and tree leaves look much more like living things. You also can map textures or image files to Incandescence, as shown below (and in the Color Gallery on the CD).

PART 5

Rendering

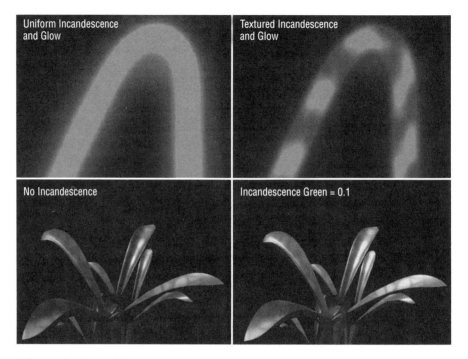

Glow Intensity

Materials can glow as well. Incandescence usually works better when it is combined with a bit of glow. Many materials have a Glow Intensity attribute under the Special Effects section in their Attribute Editor. When Glow Intensity is at zero, no glow is calculated; when the value is nonzero, materials start to glow (as shown next and in the Color Gallery on the CD). The Hide Source setting in the same section allows you to hide the surface with the material and show just the glow. Glow can be very effective in creating certain atmospheric effects with the surfaces, like a hazy moon, a warm sunset, or candlelight, as shown below. Halo Intensity works with Glow Intensity in the shaderGlow shader Attribute Editor to control the way the surfaces will glow in a scene.

You need to be careful when using glow effects because they can get tricky. Unlike the Incandescence attribute, glow is a post process. It bases its calculations on the amount of light the surface is receiving from the light sources, including other objects that are glowing. In extreme circumstances, an object's glow intensity will visibly change when other glowing objects enter the scene. In such a situation, you need to go to the Post Process folder in the Visor panel, open shaderGlow shader's Attribute Editor, and turn off its Auto Exposure. You then need to readjust the Glow Intensity and the Halo Intensity in the Attribute Editor to get the proper glow look for the surfaces in the scene.

Another thing to watch out for with glow effects is that their intensity can change with changes in the render resolution. This means when you are test rendering with glow effects, you need to test them with the same resolution as the final output.

Ambient Color

Materials also have Ambient Color. Ambient Color is similar to Incandescence in the way it actually lights the surface, but whereas Incandescence illuminates the material, Ambient Color illuminates the material's color, or its texture. Ambient Color is also different from Diffuse in that Diffuse brightens the material color in areas where the light is hitting the surface, whereas Ambient Color lights the whole surface. You could render a surface only with Ambient Color if you wished.

Applying Textures

Maya's Visor panel offers 26 textures: 9 2D textures, 11 3D textures, 5 environment textures, and a layered shader. The layered shader is included in the Textures folder because it creates layered textures as well as materials, and it can be used as a texture. With the exception of the layered shader, all the textures get a placement node when they are created. Most textures also have a Color Balance section and an Effects section.

Texture Placement

3D textures or 2D projections are placed much like real objects. You transform them in the world space, and you can shear them as well. They are more expensive to deal with in that rendering them will generally take longer than rendering 2D textures. You can convert 3D textures or projections to 2D file textures using the Edit ➤ Convert Material to File Texture command in the Hypershade window, but you may lose some quality in the process.

Because of the nature of 3D texture placements, when the surface with the texture deforms, the surface will seem to swim through the texture, as shown below. New in Maya 2 is a function called Reference Object, which enables the 3D textures or 2D projections to deform with the surface. After you have assigned a 3D texture to a surface, select the surface and select Shading ➤ Create Texture Reference Object in the Rendering module. Maya creates a reference object, translated 5 units in the X axis by default. If you want the same 3D texture placement, either translate the reference object back to zero in the X axis or translate the 3D texture placement node 5 units in the

X axis. Notice that the texture in the third plane in the graphic below is squashed and stretched with the surface.

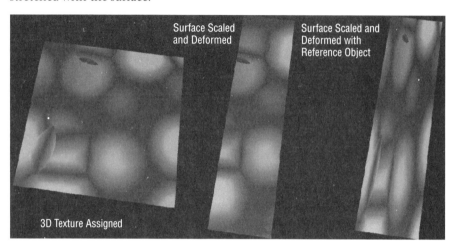

 NOTE   Reference objects must be created before any deformation or animation is applied to the original surfaces. A texture's placement is determined by its relationship to the reference object, not to the original surface.

A place2dTexture node covers whatever surface it is assigned to exactly 100 percent. The Coverage determines the percentage of the surface area the texture covers, and Translate Frame and Rotate Frame transform the texture over the surface in UV. These attributes should not be confused with the UV Repeat, Offset, and Rotate attributes, which determine the way the texture is mapped within the coverage area. The examples below show how the various attributes affect the texture placement.

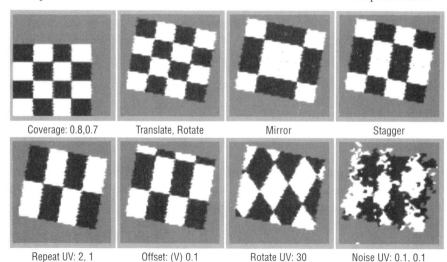

Coverage: 0.8,0.7   Translate, Rotate   Mirror   Stagger

Repeat UV: 2, 1   Offset: (V) 0.1   Rotate UV: 30   Noise UV: 0.1, 0.1

Color Balance and Effects

The Color Gain and Color Offset attributes of a texture are typically used to control the color and brightness of the texture. The Default Color attribute is the color of the surface area that is not covered by the texture. Usually, you wouldn't need to change this setting. However, if you are using the texture as a mask and the texture coverage is partial, you may need to turn the Default Color attribute to black or white.

The Alpha Gain attribute scales the alpha channel and is used for bump or displacement effects. The default value is at 1.0, which is usually a bit too much for most situations. Below is an example of the fractal texture, first with the default settings of gray for Default Color and 1.0 for Alpha Gain, then with Default Color turned to white and Alpha Gain turned down to 0.3 to tone down the extreme bumping. The fractal texture's Threshold value was also pushed up to 0.7.

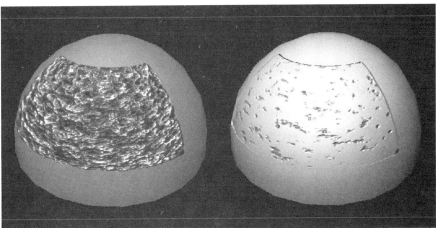

In the Effects section, many textures have Filter, Filter Offset, and Invert attributes. The Invert setting inverts the texture's colors and hue, changing white to black and vice versa. It also inverts the alpha channel, changing bumps into dents and vice versa.

The Filter and Filter Offset attributes blur textures, and they are useful for when the textures are too sharp or are aliasing. When a texture is too sharp, you may have shimmer or noise problems with the surface when the textured surface or the camera is animated. By blurring the texture, or smoothing it, you can usually make those problems disappear. Filter's default value is 1.0, but you can lower it to something close to zero. Filter Offset basically adds a constant value to the Filter attribute, and usually a tiny fractional value is sufficient to correct any excessive sharpness.

Below is the same example of the fractal texture as shown above, but with Invert turned on, Default Color set to neutral gray, and Alpha Gain moved back to the default value of 1.0. The first half-sphere has Filter set to 0.01, and it is a bit too sharp and may shimmer with a moving camera. The second half-sphere has Filter Offset set to 0.005, and the bumps have been noticeably blurred, perhaps even a bit too much. But that much blurring has made the second surface safe from any problematic shimmering.

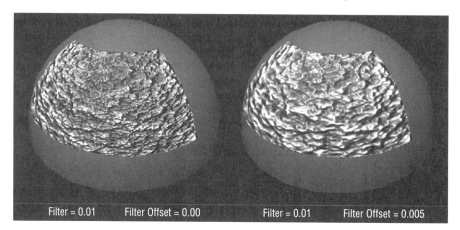

For 3D textures, the Effects section has three extra attributes: Wrap, Local, and Blend (illustrated below and in the Color Gallery on the CD). Because a 3D texture is placed as a solid cube around an object, if the object is partially moved outside the cube, that area is colored by the Default Color attribute, as shown below. Wrap, which is on by default, enables the texture to extend to cover the whole surface. The Blend attribute mixes the Default Color to the texture color. It only works when Wrap is turned off. 3D textures are also applied globally, meaning when a texture is assigned to three surfaces, those surfaces get different parts of the texture. When Local is turned on, the textures are applied locally, so that the three surfaces get the same texture placement.

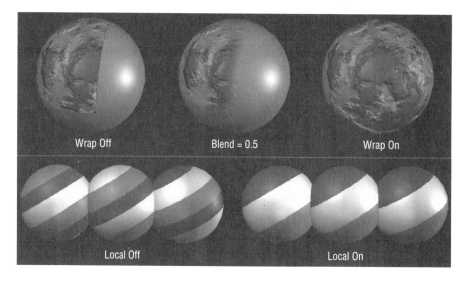

Using Shading and Texturing Techniques

Now we're ready to apply some of the shading and texturing techniques discussed in this chapter. We will work with the puppy, living room, and child models that we've developed in previous chapters.

Texturing the Puppy

In Chapter 8, we constructed a dog model using many small patches. If we had to texture each piece one by one, it would be an extremely complicated (and tedious) task. One way to get around this is to apply a 3D texture and create a reference object for the dog. Here are the general steps:

1. Select all the patches of the dog, except for the eyes and the nose, and assign a blinn shader. (You could also assign a lambert or an anisotropic shader, depending on the way you want the dog's fur to shine or not shine.) Adjust the specular settings until you are satisfied with the way the material looks.

2. Assign a leather texture as the color. You need to use a 3D texture because a 2D texture will map differently to the different patches. Adjust the settings and the placement node until your dog looks something like the one shown below (and in the Color Gallery on the CD). Connect a solid fractal to blinn's Bump attribute, and make it bump very subtly, as in the picture below. The Attribute Editor values on the left are only a rough guide. You will want to use the IPR tool to fine tune the texturing.

Rendering

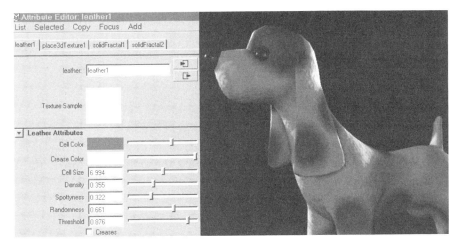

T I P   Leather is a remarkably useful texture. It can serve as basis for a great variety of surfaces, such as spots on dog fur, human skin, grunge, plant leaves, or a field of stars, just to name a few examples.

3. When you are satisfied with the colors and the placements of the spots and their sizes, select the patches and choose Shading ➤ Create Texture Reference Object. The reference duplicate of the dog is created five units away from the original dog. Translate them back to the origin, and the texture placement on the dog should be the same as before.

When you're finished, test the dog's legs or head to make sure the spots move and deform with the surface.

Adding Textures to the Living Room

We created the living room model in Chapter 5 and added a lamp to it in Chapter 6. Now we will add some texturing to make the floor and wall appear old, then refine the lamp with some texture and glow attributes.

The Floor and Wall Textures

Let's create a worn-out floor. It takes only a few more steps to go from a clean floor with a single texture to a more complicated dirty floor, but often the results (improvements?) can be startling.

1. Start with a blinn material for the floor, and assign a marble texture to it as its color. Turn down the specular quite a bit.

2. Create a fractal texture and a brownian texture. Connect them to the Vein Color and Filler Color of the marble texture, respectively, as shown on the next page (and in the Color Gallery on the CD). You can adjust the texture settings as you see fit. You may want to also connect the same fractal texture to marble as a bump map, and turn down the Alpha Gain setting to a very subtle level.

3. For an old wall, first we need an acceptable wall pattern. Start with a blinn material and apply a checker texture as color. The placement node for the first picture shown in the next graphic has a Repeat UV of 32 and 1. Connect a cloth texture to Color1 of the checker attribute, and make its Repeat UV, 64 and 32. You should see something like the top-right picture in the next illustration, and we have our wall pattern.

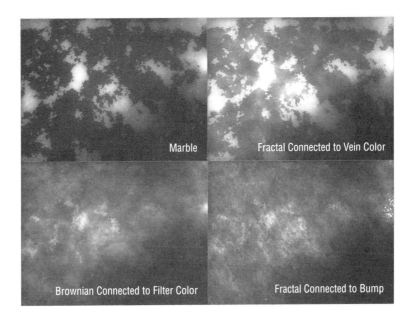

4. To create a worn-out look, you can use a handy technique called *smearing*. Take a brownian texture and connect its alpha channel to the Offset U and Offset V attributes of the placement node for the checker texture, as in the bottom-right picture (and in the Color Gallery on the CD). Reduce the Alpha Gain value to keep the smear effect from being too drastic. The bottom-left picture is a good example of a subtle smear.

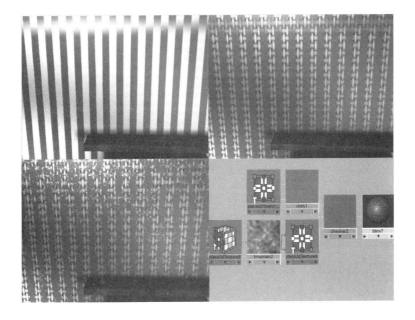

Rendering

At this point, the colors themselves are still pretty clean, but there are many ways you can make the colors dirtier. You can map the Ambient Color attribute of the blinn material, Color2 of the Checker attribute, tint the lights shining on the wall, or map their Color attributes. If you want to be able to dirty localized sections of the wall with total control, you can reassign a layer shader to the wall, make the blinn material part of the layer shader, and start adding more layers, or dirt.

The Lamp Textures

A simple deformed sphere has been added to the floor lamp for the lightbulb. The lamp stand, lamp shade, and lightbulb need shading and texturing. We will use a ramp texture for the lamp stand, but first we need to briefly go over what a ramp texture is.

Ramp is basically layers of colors, and it is probably one of the most often used textures. By default, the ramp texture has three layers of RGB colors, which are called color entries. You can create additional color entries by LM clicking in the ramp. The circles that appear at the left side of the ramp allow you to drag the color entries, or you can type in a precise position value in the Selected Position field. The square boxes at the right side delete the color entries.

As you can see in the examples below (and in the Color Gallery on the CD), you can apply the ramp along the V isoparms, U isoparms, diagonally, radially, circularly, and so on. The color entries mix according to a set Interpolation type; if you set Interpolation to None, the color entries will not mix. You also can distort the ramp with waves and noise, and you can map other textures into any of the color entries.

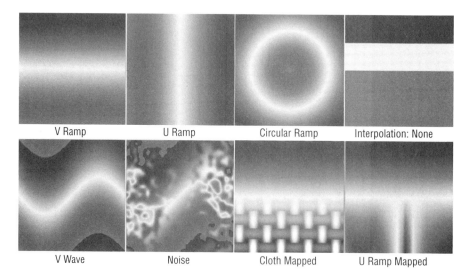

V Ramp   U Ramp   Circular Ramp   Interpolation: None

V Wave   Noise   Cloth Mapped   U Ramp Mapped

Now let's add texturing to the lamp.

1. Assign a blinn to the lamp stand. Add a ramp to its color. Delete one of the color entries in the ramp texture, and set Interpolation to None. Make the first color entry white and the second entry blue. Adjust the position of the blue entry until you see the white is covering only the lamp base and the blue is covering the lamp pole, as shown below.

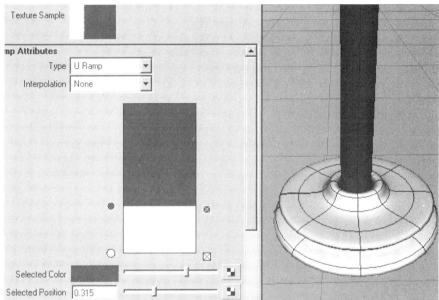

2. Apply a fractal texture to the ramp's white color entry, and apply a wood texture to the blue color entry. You could, for added effect, apply a subtle fractal bump on the blinn material. You can use the same fractal texture for the bump mapping, because you can control its Alpha Gain value without affecting its color values. Adjust the settings until you see something like the lamp stand in (a) below. (This image is also in the Color Gallery on the CD.) A little glow was also added to the blinn.

3. We want the lamp cover to be thin and a bit transparent. Assign a blinn, then a checker texture as Color. The checker texture for this example has a Repeat UV of 16 and 32. In the blinn Attribute Editor, increase the Transparency setting a bit, as well as the Ambient Color attribute; add a tiny bit of Translucence. Glow Intensity should be fairly strong, but not so strong as to wash out the texture. Play with the values in IPR until you see something like the lamp cover in (b) below.

4. For the lightbulb, assign a blinn to the bulb, make the color dark orange, and choose a darker orange for the Incandescence setting. Raise the Glow Intensity

setting and turn on Hide Source. Start an IPR process and adjust the settings until you see something like the lamp shown in (c) below.

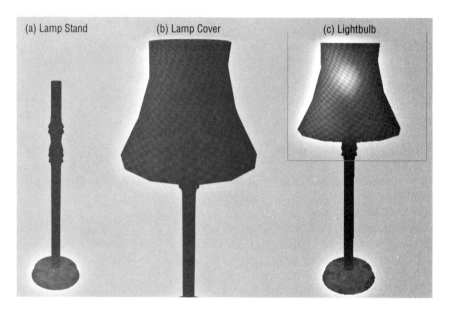

(a) Lamp Stand   (b) Lamp Cover   (c) Lightbulb

TIP   The glow on the materials will change slightly each time you introduce a new element into the scene, so don't spend too much time fine-tuning the glow until you have all the elements you want in the final render in the scene.

Texturing the Child Model

Now we can turn to the varied textures needed for the child model we've been working with throughout this book. We will apply texturing to the hair, shoes, face (mouth and eyes), and clothes.

The Hair Texture

Let's start with the easiest part of the model to texture—the hair.

1. Assign an anisotropic shader to hair, and connect a fractal as the color and bump.

2. Start IPR and set the fractal texture's Repeat UV to something like 32 and 0.8. Reduce its Amplitude and Alpha Gain, and darken Color Gain, until you see something like the middle picture shown below.

3. Go to the settings for the anisotropic material, and adjust the specular variables until you are satisfied with the way the hair is shining.

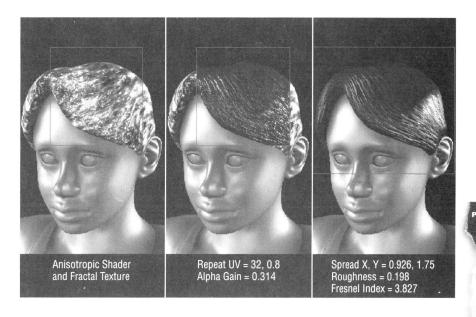

Anisotropic Shader and Fractal Texture

Repeat UV = 32, 0.8
Alpha Gain = 0.314

Spread X, Y = 0.926, 1.75
Roughness = 0.198
Fresnel Index = 3.827

T I P If you want more photorealistic hair, try scanning real hair and using it as an image file, and instead of having one surface, put layers of strips as hair. Using this technique allows you to animate strands of hair independently of the surrounding patches.

Shoe Textures

The shoes are made from simple spheres. We will need to do some fancy texturing work to make them look acceptable.

1. Assign a blinn to the shoes, and connect a ramp to the color and bump. Get rid of one of the color entries, and set Interpolation to None.

2. Start IPR and play with the position of the second color entry until it looks like (a) on the next page (and in the Color Gallery on the CD). Connect a checker texture to the bottom color entry. Set its Repeat UV to 32 and 4. Change the colors to look like the shoe in (b).

3. Add more color entries to create a lighter section in the middle of the shoe. Again, adjust the color entry positions until you see something like the shoe in (b).

4. Map another ramp to the lighter color entry in the middle, set the Type to U ramp, and set Interpolation to None. Insert color entries and set their positions to be like the shoe in (c) below.

5. Create a leather texture, change Cell Size to 5, and change the colors to something like the shoe shown in (d) below. Map the texture to the blue and yellow color entries on both the V ramp and the U ramp. You may want to perform a Convert Material to File Texture operation with the leather texture if you are concerned about the texture swimming, but that probably will not be necessary. Test to see how the texture looks as the shoe deforms.

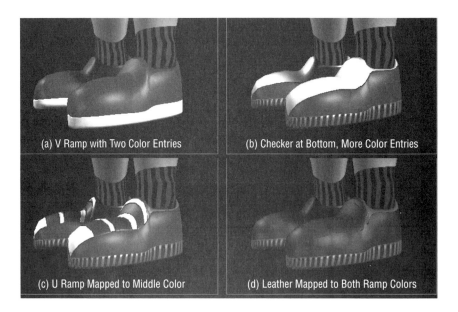

(a) V Ramp with Two Color Entries

(b) Checker at Bottom, More Color Entries

(c) U Ramp Mapped to Middle Color

(d) Leather Mapped to Both Ramp Colors

Face Textures

For our example, we will work on the mouth and eyes. However, before we get started on the mouth, it's a good idea to create a skin shader, which we can apply to all parts of the body. Leather usually makes a decent skin.

1. Start with a blinn material, increase Eccentricity to 0.4 and decrease Specular Roll Off to 0.15. Apply a leather texture as the color. For our example, a simple leather texture is being used as skin, but you may want to map other textures into the leather Cell and Crease. (Another common technique is to map an image file specifically for specularity.) In the next graphic (and in the Color Gallery on the CD) are the settings for the leather texture used, but you should experiment with the IPR to get the exact look and feel of the skin you want.

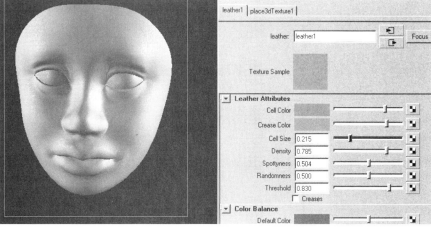

2. Assign a layered shader to the mouth. Layered shaders function essentially to allow multiple layers of materials or textures on surfaces. A green and half-transparent layer is there by default. Change the Compositing Flag to Layer Texture.

NOTE The default mode, the Layer Shaders mode, composites a bit differently from the Layer Texture mode, and it is usually less efficient in the way it calculates the layers being composited. The Layer Texture mode is the recommended setting for most situations.

3. Drag the skin material to the Layered Shader Attributes box, and MM drag it to the default layer's right side. The skin shader has now become a layer under the default layer.

4. Select the default layer and assign a blinn material to it by either dragging a new blinn material to its Color attribute or by clicking the Create button beside the Color attribute to open the Create Render Node window.

5. Decrease the Eccentricity value of the blinn to about 0.15 and its Specular Roll Off setting to about 0.4. Then assign a ramp to its color and bump. Set the Type to U Ramp, and create color entries to demarcate the lip area and a subtle light-pinkish area gradually starting just below the nose and ending before the edge. The lips should be a dark-reddish color, and the areas around the mouth and the edge should be white, as in the next graphic (and in the Color Gallery on the CD). The ramp will be used as a mask as well.

PART
5

Rendering

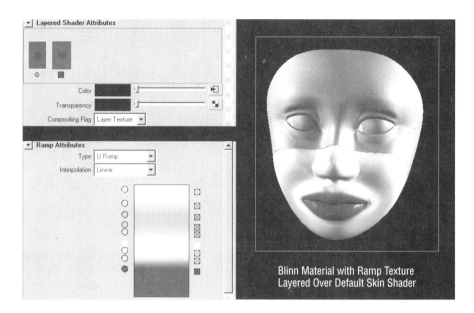

Blinn Material with Ramp Texture
Layered Over Default Skin Shader

6. Connect a fractal texture to the color entry for the lips. Set its Repeat UV to 1 and 64 and change its Color Gain and Color Offset values to make the fractal look like vertical strips of dark and darker magenta. The lips should look textured, as shown below.

7. Select the layered shader, select the top blinn layer, and drag the ramp to the blinn layer's Transparency attribute. The lighter parts of the ramp becomes a mask, masking out those sections of the ramp texture and revealing the skin material underneath. The lip color becomes lighter as well because it is doubling as a mask. You may want to readjust the fractal Color Gain. (This image is also in the Color Gallery on the CD.)

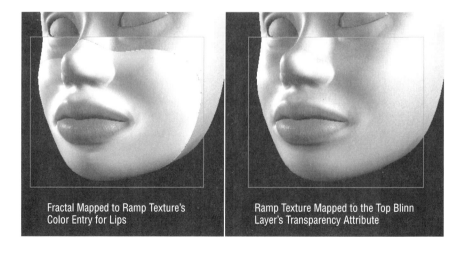

Fractal Mapped to Ramp Texture's
Color Entry for Lips

Ramp Texture Mapped to the Top Blinn
Layer's Transparency Attribute

N O T E   This kind of layered shader and ramp work we did for the mouth is pretty much what we would need to do to place the eye brows, which are typically image files.

8. You can create good-looking eyes made of simple spheres and textures. In our example, however, the eyes are made of two spheres: an inner sphere for the pupil and the iris textures and an outer sphere for specularity. Start with a layered shader, create a blinn shader layer, and assign it to the inner sphere.

9. Start an IPR process, make the blinn color light gray, decrease Eccentricity to about 0.1, and set Specular Roll Off to about 0.4.

10. Create another blinn material to be the pupil layer over the first one. Make it black, decrease its Eccentricity to 0.05, and increase Specular Roll Off to 1. Then push up the Specular Color's HSV value to 2.0. This will make the pupil shine with a tight and bright highlight. Put a ramp into the transparency and softly mask the area around the pupil, as shown in (a) below (and in the Color Gallery on the CD).

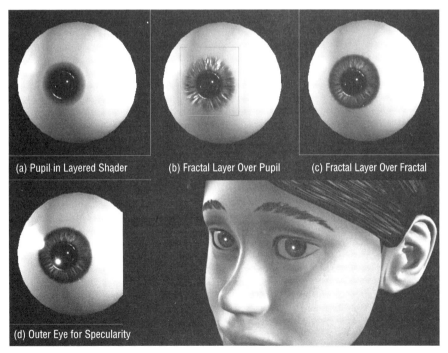

(a) Pupil in Layered Shader   (b) Fractal Layer Over Pupil   (c) Fractal Layer Over Fractal

(d) Outer Eye for Specularity

PART
5

Rendering

11. Create two more layers for texturing the iris area. Create another blinn material over the pupil layer, and map a fractal to its color and bump. Make the fractal's Repeat UV 0.1 and 1, and increase its Alpha Gain to 2.0 to intensify the bump. Put a ramp into the layer's Transparency attribute and position the color entries so the ramp won't cover the pupil or too much of the eyeball area. It should look something like (b) above.

12. Create yet another blinn layer over the third layer. But this time, turn down its specular to zero, map a fractal just to its color, and make the fractal a bit darker. Put a ramp into its Transparency attribute so it will show up only at the edge of the iris, blending with the first fractal texture. You should see something like (c).

13. Assign a blinn to the outer sphere and make it totally transparent. Decrease Eccentricity to 0.1, increase Specular Roll Off to 1.0, and push the Specular Color value to 2.0. The outer sphere basically serves to make the eyes brighter with softer specularity, as shown in (d) above, and shows the convex shape of the eye lens.

Clothes Texturing

Let's design a shirt for the child model.

1. Assign a layer shader to the shirt and the shorts, create a blinn layer, and assign cloth to its color. Below (and in the Color Gallery on the CD) are the cloth settings and the resulting pattern. Start the IPR process and experiment to see how the patterns change as you slide the cloth attributes back and forth.

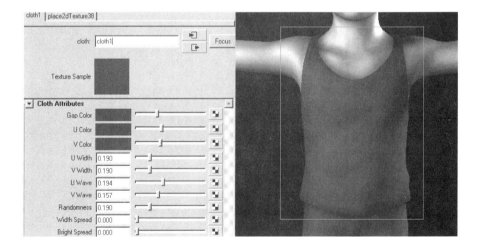

2. Create another layer on top of the cloth layer, and assign a ramp texture to the Color and Transparency attributes. Materials and textures can mix on layered shaders. Set the ramp's Type to Box Ramp and Interpolation to None. Get rid of one of the color entries. The top color entry should be white, acting as a mask, and the bottom color doesn't matter for now, because we will be mapping to it soon. Experiment with the placement node's Offset until you get a box placed on the shirt and the shorts, as shown below. (This image is also in the Color Gallery on the CD.)

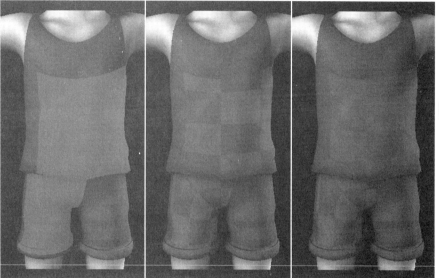

3. If we assign a checker to the ramp's bottom color, we get something like the second picture in graphic above, which is fine. But let's say we want to have a different checker color for the shorts. We can use a switch utility. Instead of assigning a checker texture to the ramp's bottom color entry, open the Switch folder inside the Utilities folder in the Visor panel, drag the Triple Shading Switch node into Hypershade, and assign it to the ramp's bottom color entry.

4. Open the Attribute Editor for the Triple Shading Switch node. You see two empty columns. The InShape column lists the surfaces being affected by the switch utility, and the InTriple column lists the triple-channel information connecting to the surfaces through the utility. Click Add Surfaces, and the shirt and short geometry names appear in the first column. Assign a checker texture to the shirt, either by dragging the checker texture from Hypershade into the appropriate row in the second column or by RM choosing over the row and opening the Create Render Node window.

5. Assign a different checker texture to the shorts, and change the color of the checker texture. The shirt and the shorts now share the same layered shader, the same ramp, but have different checker textures (as shown in the previous graphic).

Summary

In this chapter, you learned how to use the Hypershade and work with render nodes. We also covered materials and textures, their various properties and attributes, and how to work with them in shading a dog, parts of the living room scene, and parts of the child.

Shading and texturing, as we have seen working with our examples, can take the simplest objects and make them look good. But in creating these sample pictures, one essential part has been intentionally omitted from the discussion. In the next chapter, we will learn all about this other half of the equation in creating great-looking pictures. This aspect is lighting.

chapter 20

LIGHTING

Featuring

- *Types of lights and their properties*

- *Shadows*

- *Light effects*

- *Lighting techniques*

LIGHTING

A lthough this chapter follows the discussion of modeling, animation, and shading, lighting is really a circular process, and it's difficult to confine it to any one stage in the production cycle. Before you can test-render anything, whether it's a model you are building or the textures of one you've already built, you need to set up proper lights. At the same time, if you want to control precisely how the lights shine on the objects, you would want to reserve fine-tuning your lights until all the animation is finished. We will discuss proper lighting techniques later in this chapter, and conclude with some tips on optimizing the renderer once lighting is set up, but first, let's go over the four Maya lights and their attributes.

Types of Lights

You can light surfaces using ambient light, point light, directional light, or spot light. Usually you will use a combination of different lights to get the effects you want. You can create any type of light from the menu by selecting it in the Lights menu in the Rendering module, or by dragging it from the Visor panel in the Hypershade. Below are each type's icons in the Hypershade and in the modeling window.

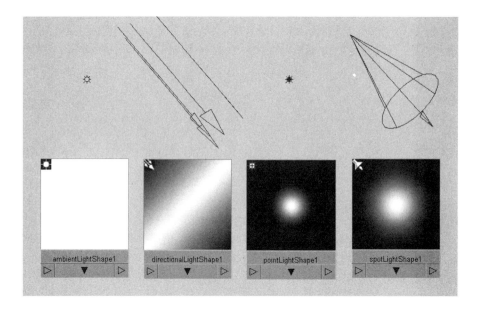

Ambient Light

Ambient light can shine, as its name suggests, everywhere uniformly—bathing all the objects in the scene from all directions. You can get similar effects from a material shader by controlling its ambient color. But ambient light can also behave as a simple point light, which shines from a specific point to different directions. These two contrasting properties of ambient light, omnidirectional and directional, can be mixed using the Ambient Shade in the Attribute Editor. When the Ambient Shade is set to 1, the Ambient light behaves exactly like a point light. Ambient light also casts shadows like point light, but only when raytraced. Below (and in the Color Gallery on the CD) you can see examples of different Ambient Shade values. The third picture is raytraced with Use Ray Trace Shadows turned on.

Directional, Point, and Spot Lights

Directional light shines in the direction the icon arrows are pointing. It imitates light coming from a distant source, such as the sun. Point light, in contrast, shines from a specific point to all directions evenly; it is ideal for imitating a light bulb or a candle. Spot light behaves exactly like a real-world spotlight, its direction defined by a beam of light that gradually widens. Spot lights are also good for imitating headlights or lamps. Below are examples of these lights.

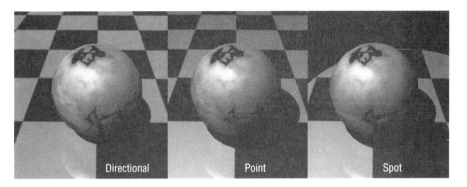

Directional   Point   Spot

Ambient and directional lights do not have Decay Rate attributes, whereas Point and Spot lights do. Spot light also has Cone Angle, Penumbra Angle, and Dropoff attributes as well. We will look at these and other light properties next.

TIP You can change a light from one type to another in the Attribute Editor. When you do that, however, only the attributes common to both types will be retained. Other attribute settings will be lost.

Light Properties

For all types of light, you can control the basic properties of color and intensity. You can also control the linkage between lights and the objects in a scene. For point and spot lights, you can vary the intensity over distance by controlling the decay rate. Spot lights have additional properties and attributes you can control. All these controls can be accessed in the light's Attribute Editor.

Color and Intensity

As with shading, you can use the Color Chooser to tint a light (usually you will want to do that subtly), or map textures, which will be projected onto the surface. When textures mask or filter certain areas of light in such a way as the second and third example pictures below, the light is called a *gobo* light. You can also change the intensity, or brightness of a light. Negative intensity values will actually take away light, which can be useful for creating shadow masks, as illustrated below (and in the Color Gallery on the CD). (You also need to change the floor to plain white color.)

TIP   A *shadow mask* is used in compositing to put shadows into a scene when objects in the scene are rendered separately. It is especially useful when computer graphic elements are being added to live footage. The shadow mask allows the compositor to blur the shadows if necessary, and adjust the HSV (hue, saturation, and value) settings of the shadow to match the shadows in the live footage.

Intensity values usually stay below 1 or 2 when the Decay Rate is set to None, but they can go up much higher when Decay Rate is turned on, as you can see here (and in the Color Gallery on the CD).

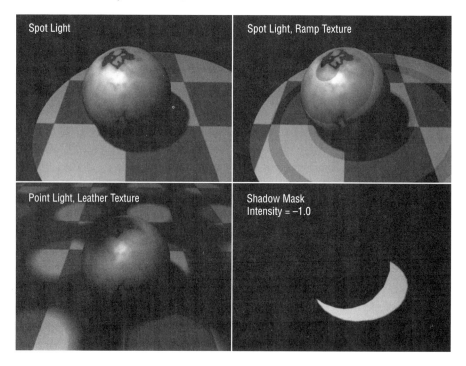

You can also control the intensity value of any light by mapping textures to it, which produces results similar to mapping texture to color. Below (and in the Color Gallery on the CD) are examples of a default grid texture mapped to the Intensity attribute of different lights with default settings. Note how the grids are translated to intensity values differently for each of the four lights.

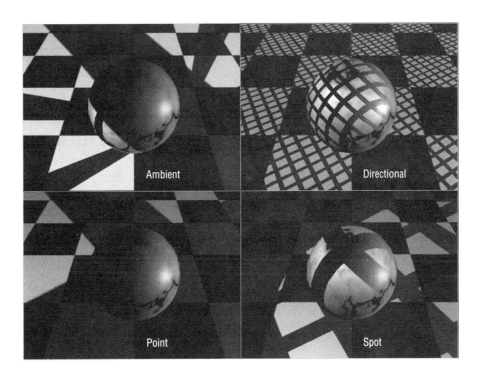

Ambient   Directional

Point   Spot

N O T E   For spot light only, you can also create Intensity and Color curves to control their values with respect to distance from the light source. To create the curves, click on the Create buttons under the Light Effects section of the Attribute Editor. You can then edit the curves in the Graph Editor.

Decay Rate

You can make the intensity of Point and Spot lights decay over a distance by turning on Decay Rate. There are three decay rates to choose from: Linear, where intensity decreases proportionally to distance; Quadratic, where intensity decreases proportionally to the square of distance (distance × distance), which is how light intensity decays in the real world; and Cubic, where intensity decreases proportionally to the cube of distance (distance × distance × distance). Below (and in the Color Gallery on the CD) you can see examples of each Decay Rate. Note how the intensity value shoots up accordingly to light the sphere. You can hardly tell the differences in the sphere itself, but the differences are noticeable on the floor.

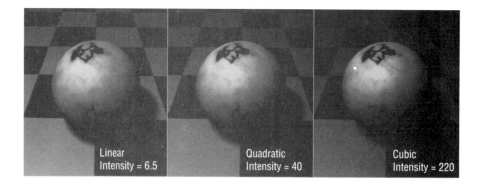

Linear
Intensity = 6.5

Quadratic
Intensity = 40

Cubic
Intensity = 220

T I P   The Decay Rate begins to affect a light's intensity only at distances greater than one unit from the light source. Inside the one-unit radius, no decrease of light intensity is possible.

Linking Lights and Objects

When a light shines on a surface, they are said to be *linked*. All the lights have a setting called Illuminates by Default, which is turned on by default and makes the light shine on all objects, which means the light is linked to all the objects in the scene. If the setting is off, the light will not shine on any object unless you manually link it to that object. You can also do the opposite and cut the link between individual objects and a light, in which case the light will not shine on those individual objects. If you are working on simple scenes, you will usually leave things at default settings and let all lights shine on all objects. As soon as the scene gets fairly complex, however, you would want to start linking lights only to the objects they need to light, as linking affects rendering time significantly.

T I P   The default light, with the Illuminates by Default setting turned on, is also called *inclusive* light. When the setting is off, the light is said to be *exclusive*.

You can link lights and objects, or sever the links, from the Lights menu in the Rendering module. Select the object(s) and light(s) in question. Select Lights ➤ Make Light Links to link them, and Lights ➤ Break Light Links to sever them. Another method is to use the Relationship Editor. You can either use what Maya calls a light-centric mode and link objects to a light, or use an object-centric mode and link lights to an object. Below is an example of using a light-centric Relationship Editor to link objects to lights. Of the three spheres in the first picture, the second and third spheres have been severed from pointLight1. In the second picture, the second sphere has also been severed from pointLight2.

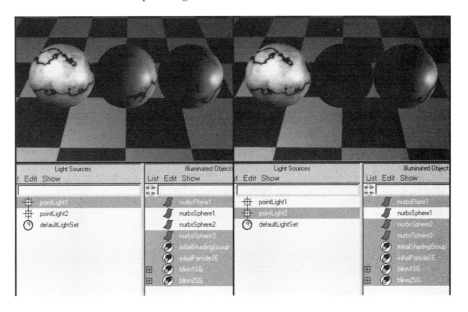

  NOTE The Lights menu also offers the Select Objects Illuminated By Light and Select Lights Illuminating Object commands. When you select a light and apply the first command all objects linked to that light are selected. When you select an object and apply the second command, all lights linked to that specific object are selected.

Spot Light Properties

Unique to spot light are the Cone Angle, Penumbra Angle, and Dropoff attributes. Cone Angle controls how much the beam will spread. It is usually sufficient to leave it at the default 40 degrees. Penumbra Angle, when given a positive value, blurs the area outside the cone to make the edge soft, and when given a negative value, blurs the area inside the edge to make it soft. Here are examples of different Cone Angle and Penumbra Angle settings.

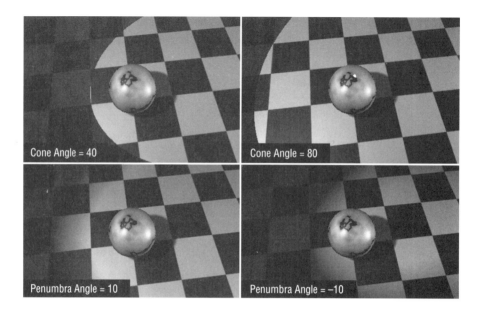

Dropoff is similar to Linear Decay Rate, but instead of decaying over a distance from the light source, it makes the intensity drop off from the center of the cone to its edge. Its results are often similar to the Penumbra Angle with a negative value. Below (and in the Color Gallery on the CD) are examples of different Dropoff values and their effects on the spot light.

Spot Light Effects

Under the Light Effects section of the Attribute Editor two more attributes, specific to spot lights, are worth mentioning: Barn Doors and Decay Regions. They are both turned off by default. Barn Doors act just like masks, or shutters, to cover the edges of the cone from four corners. The values set the angles between the spot light's center and the barn doors. The Decay Regions option, when turned on, enables you to create three regions inside the spot light beam where the light illuminates, as well as regions where the light does not illuminate. The example of Decay Regions below (and in the Color Gallery on the CD) has light fog applied to it. (The effect is similar to a smoky nightclub. You'll learn more about fog effects later in the chapter.)

PART 5

Rendering

Shadows

The default light setting in Maya produces no shadows. This is because shadows can be very computationally expensive and, in general, you want only one or two main lights to be casting shadows. All lights can be set to produce either Depth Map Shadows or Ray Trace Shadows, with the exception of Ambient light, which can only produce Ray Trace shadows. To activate shadows, go to the Shadows section of a light's Attribute Editor, where you can check Use Depth Map Shadows in the Depth Map Shadow Attributes section, or check Use Ray Trace Shadows in the Raytrace Shadow Attributes section.

Depth Map Shadows

Usually you will want to use depth map shadows, because they are much more efficient to use than ray trace shadows. When a depth map shadow is turned on, during rendering Maya creates a *depth map*, which stores the distance from the shadow casting light to the surfaces that the light is illuminating and uses this information to calculate shadows. The depth map, as you can see below, is a Z-depth (see "Render Globals Settings" in Chapter 18) image file created from the light's point of view, and it enables Maya to calculate whether one surface is behind another surface with respect to the light. In this case, areas of the floor are found to be behind the sphere and the cone, and are thus rendered as shadow. A small area of the cone is also found to be behind the sphere, and it becomes shadow.

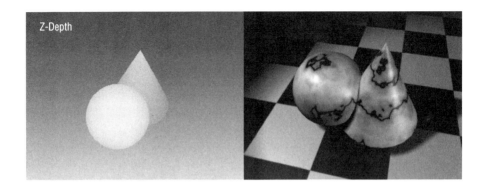

Color

The default Shadow Color setting is black, but you may want to lighten it or tint it with other colors, or even map textures to it, depending on the look you want. Mapping into color can also be a good way to fake transparency. Depth Map shadows do not recognize transparent objects; only raytraced shadows do. But for simple situations, you can often get away with clever use of Shadow Color, as in the examples below (and in the Color Gallery on the CD). In the first example, a darkened version of the marble texture was connected to the Shadow Color; in the second example, a ramp was used to create the more transparent upper area of the shadow.

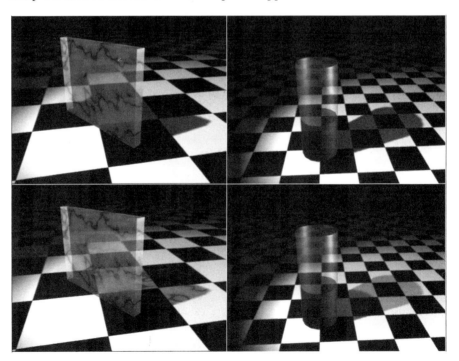

Fog Shadow Intensity and Fog Shadow Samples

When light fog is applied to the light, you can control the intensity and the graininess of the fog shadow as well. The darkness of the shadow is controlled by the Fog Shadow Intensity setting, and the graininess is controlled by Fog Shadow Samples. Increasing the value in the latter increases the rendering time, so keep its values as low as is acceptable.

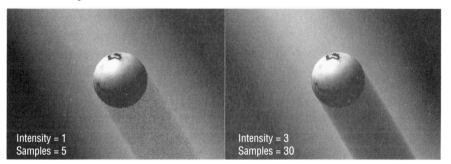

Intensity = 1
Samples = 5

Intensity = 3
Samples = 30

Dmap Resolution, Filter Size, and Bias

Dmap Resolution sets the size of the depth map that Maya creates. The default value is 512, which creates a square depth map file 512 pixels in width and height. If you need sharper shadows, you may need to increase the resolution, but for softer shadows, you can get good results with resolutions as low as 128, or even 64. The Dmap Filter Size blurs, or softens, the shadow edges. As with any filter, the higher the number the more expensive it gets, so keep the filter size as low as is acceptable. Below (and in the Color Gallery on the CD) are examples of various resolution and filter size settings and their effects.

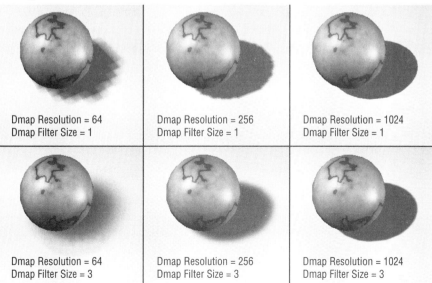

Dmap Resolution = 64
Dmap Filter Size = 1

Dmap Resolution = 256
Dmap Filter Size = 1

Dmap Resolution = 1024
Dmap Filter Size = 1

Dmap Resolution = 64
Dmap Filter Size = 3

Dmap Resolution = 256
Dmap Filter Size = 3

Dmap Resolution = 1024
Dmap Filter Size = 3

PART

5

Rendering

Dmap Bias controls how much the shadow is offset from its source. It should generally be left at its default value, except for situations where the shadow placement seems off, as in the left image below.

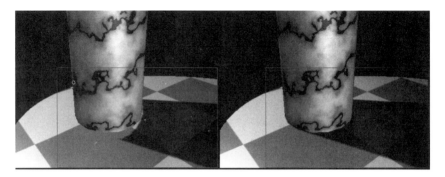

Disk Based Dmaps

The Disk Based Dmaps feature can make rendering go much faster when used properly. The default setting is Off, which means every time Maya renders, it creates depth maps for shadow calculations. But since a depth map stores as data the distance between the light and the surfaces it illuminates, as long as those relative distances in a scene do not change, you can reuse the depth map. Even if the camera and any other elements in the scene are being animated, you can still reuse the depth map.

Switch the setting to Reuse Existing Dmap(s), and the extra settings become active. The default Dmap Name is depthmap, and the Dmap Light Name is checked, which means that when the depth map is saved to disk, it will be assigned the name depthmap plus the name of the light generating the depth map. For example, for a spotlight named Spot, a depth map file named `depthmap_SpotShape1.SM.iff` is created. The first time around, Maya looks for a depth map in the current project directories; and when it doesn't find one, it creates the depth map and places it in the current project directory, under the `\depth` directory. The next time Maya renders, it uses the depth map to shadow the surfaces, thus reducing rendering time.

In cases where the distances between the light and its linked surfaces do change over time, if you will be rendering them more than once (as often happens with test renders) you can still create a sequence of depth maps and reuse them by checking Dmap Frame Ext.

The other Disk Based Dmaps setting, Overwrite Existing Dmap(s), overwrites any existing depth maps. If you have made positional changes to a light or any of its linked surfaces, you would want to overwrite the existing depth maps. Once you've rendered and created new depth maps, change the setting to Reuse Existing Dmap(s) again.

Raytraced Shadows

For many situations, you would not want to use raytraced shadows because you can get almost exactly the same quality with depth map shadows but with much more efficient render times. But when you are creating shadows for transparent objects, for example, with reflections and refractions, and photorealistic accuracy is needed, raytraced shadows are the only way to go. To use raytraced shadows, you need to turn on Use Ray Trace Shadows in the individual light's Attribute Editor, and also Raytracing in the Render Globals.

When Use Ray Trace Shadows is turned on, Shadow Radius becomes active for ambient light, Light Angle for directional light, and Light Radius for point and spot lights. These different attributes all affect the softness of the shadow edges. Zero, which is the default setting, gives you sharp, hard shadow edges, and as the values go up, the edges become softer. The value range is different for different lights.

As the shadow becomes softer, the edges at the default setting become grainier, as in the first picture below. The Shadow Rays setting blurs the graininess of the edges. Shadow Rays is render-intensive, so it is best to keep the values as low as you can.

 T I P Soft edge shadows can be much more efficiently created with depth map shadows. Raytraced shadows are more useful for creating sharp, crisp shadows.

Ray Depth Limit sets the maximum number of times, minus one, that a ray of light can be reflected or refracted and still create a shadow. If the value of the Shadows attribute in the Raytracing Quality section of the Render Globals is lower than the Ray Depth Limit value, that lower value becomes the maximum limit. In the illustration shown next (and in the Color Gallery on the CD), a Ray Depth Limit of 1 isn't showing the shadow behind the transparent sphere. By contrast, a Ray Depth Limit of 3 shows it.

Light Effects

In addition to the properties we've looked at so far, Maya offers various special effects you can apply to lights. These include fog and various optical effects such as glow, halo, and lens flare. You can access these effects from the Light Effects section of a light's Attribute Editor.

Light Fog

Light Fog can be applied to Point and Spot lights. Point light fog is spherical, whereas the spot light fog is cone shaped. When light fog is applied, a separate fog icon appears along with the light icon, which you can transform to create the size and shape of the fog you want. On the next page (top), you'll see examples of point light fog and spot light fog with different scales.

The Fog Type and Fog Radius attributes are only available for point light fog. Under Fog Type, the Normal setting lets the fog intensity remain constant regardless of the distance from the light source. The Linear setting decreases the fog intensity as the distance from the light source increases, and the Exponential setting decreases the fog intensity as the distance increases exponentially. Fog Radius determines the size of the spherical volume of the fog. On the next page (bottom) are examples of point light's fog types, and different fog radius settings.

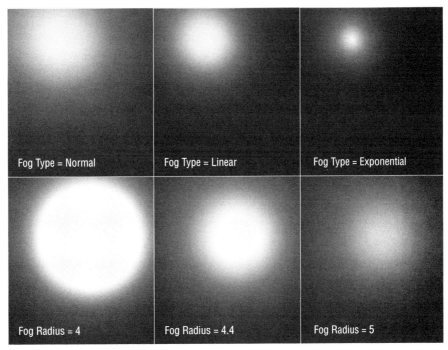

Fog Spread is an attribute available only for spot light fog. It functions very much like spot light's Dropoff attribute. It determines the decrease in fog intensity as distance from the center of the cone increases, as in the examples below. The decrease in intensity as the distance increases from the light source is determined by the spot light's Decay Rate setting.

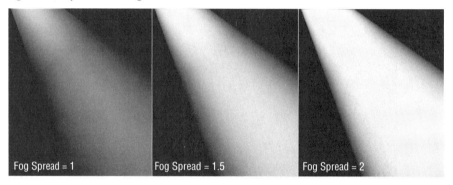

You can go to the lightFog node and adjust the Color and Density attributes of the light fog, or combine light fog with light glow (discussed next) to produce a combination effect. When using light fog, you will often also want to map textures into the light's Color attribute to imitate smoke or bigger dust particles. The example below (and in the Color Gallery on the CD) has a solid fractal texture mapped to the color attribute of spot light and point light.

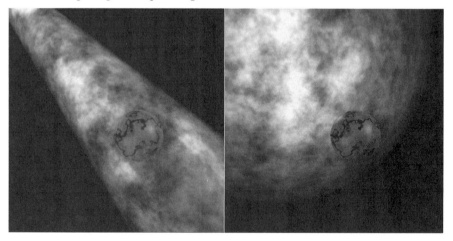

OptiF/X

Maya has an optical light effects node (called OptiF/X), which can produce glow, halo, and/or lens flare effects for point light and spot light. The light effects are useful in imitating different camera filters, stars, candles, flames, or explosions. The light sources have to be inside the camera view for the light effects to show, and the effects are all post processes, meaning they are applied after all the regular rendering is done. In the Light Effects section of a spot light's Attribute Editor, click on the box next to the Light Glow section, and an opticalFX node is created. The effects turn on when the Active box is checked, and Glow Type and Halo Type are set to something other than None. For Lens Flare, you also need to check the Lens Flare box separately. Below are examples of these three light effects.

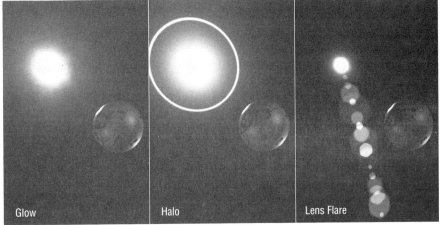

Glow   Halo   Lens Flare

Glow and Halo

Both Glow and Halo have the same list of types: Linear, Exponential, Ball, Lens Flare (which shouldn't be confused with the OpticalF/X Lens Flare effect), and Rim Halo. Below (and in the Color Gallery on the CD) are examples of the various types for glow and halo. For the glow examples, the halo type was set to None, and vice versa, but you would usually combine their effects.

Glow Linear   Glow Exponential   Glow Ball   Glow Lens Flare   Glow Rim Halo

Halo Linear   Halo Exponential   Halo Ball   Halo Lens Flare   Halo Rim Halo

Glow and Halo have the same color and intensity attributes as regular lights, and you can change their sizes through the Spread attribute. Halo Attributes are limited to those illustrated. Glow, however, has the additional Stars and Noise attributes.

Working with glow effects can get a bit confusing because these additional attributes are scattered in different sections of the Attribute Editor, with three of them in the Optical FX Attributes section, and some of the others in the Noise Attributes section. The pictures below (and in the Color Gallery on the CD) have glow beam effects with various settings. Starting from the top left, the Star Points setting determines how many regular beams will come out of the light source. Their sharpness, or width, is determined by the Glow Star Level setting, and randomness in the beams is introduced by Glow Radial Noise. Once the Radial Noise setting becomes nonzero, you can adjust the frequency of the random beams, and their width, by using the Radial Frequency attribute. The beams can be rotated with the Rotation attribute. The two last pictures show more combinations of different possible glow settings.

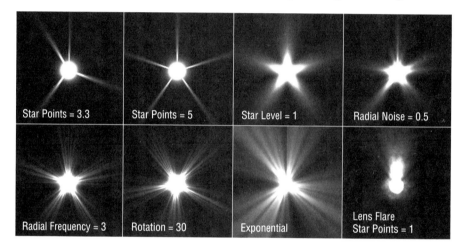

Noise attributes produce a fractalized look you can use to imitate a variety of effects such as fog or explosions, as you can see next. Glow Noise produces the fractalized glow, which should always be adjusted together with Glow Intensity and Glow Spread (among other settings) to achieve the desired look. The Noise section enables you to adjust the noise threshold, its vertical and horizontal scale and placement, as illustrated below (and in the Color Gallery on the CD).

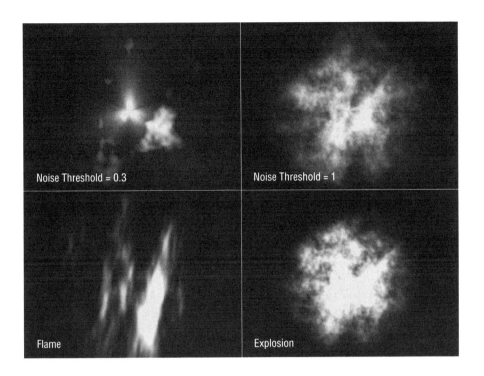

Noise Threshold = 0.3

Noise Threshold = 1

Flame

Explosion

Lens Flare

Lens Flare re-creates the effect of physical imperfections in an optical lens, which become particularly apparent as the lens is trained toward a light source. Color in Lens Flare works a bit differently from the regular color attribute in that lens flare color is a spectrum of colors, the range of which is determined by the Flare Col Spread attribute. Flare Num Circles determines how many circles (hexagons if Hexagon Flare is turned on) will show in the lens flare beam, and Flare Length determines the length of that beam. The Flare Min and Max Size attributes limit the sizes of the smallest and largest circles, and Flare Focus can blur or sharpen the flare circles. Lens Flare beam doesn't rotate but is placed in different positions with Flare Vertical and Horizontal controls. Shown next (and in the Color Gallery on the CD) are examples of lens flares with different attribute settings.

PART 5

Rendering

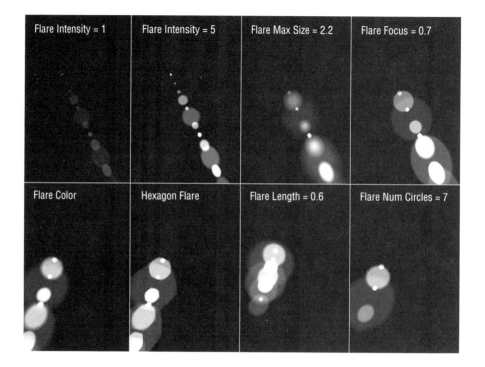

 TIP   As you've seen, lights in Maya can have many different properties and effects to manage, and a complex scene may have numerous lights. Chapter 17 shows how to build a MEL script that creates a graphical interface window for controlling all the lights in a scene.

Lighting Techniques

The art of lighting is another whole world unto itself, and studies in painting or photography will certainly be of great help. We will be able to cover only the basics in the remainder of this chapter.

The Basic Rules

One of the first things to realize about digital lighting is that there must always be a proper mixture of the real and artificial. On the one hand, lighting has to be believable. If a character is in a room, for example, you need to think about what and where the light sources are. Is there a window? Sunlight or moonlight? Are there lightbulbs or fluorescent lights? You also need to create additional lights to imitate bounce lights, or reflected lights. In the pictures below (and in the Color Gallery on the CD), the light in the first image has problems because the character's face in the shadows is totally dark, even though the room is lit. The second picture is better, as it accounts for the bounce lights in a similar brightness level as the rest of the room.

PART 5

Rendering

On the other hand, lighting is always an artificial endeavor. Stages and movie sets use many artificial lights to create the best possible lighting environment, setting the proper atmosphere and making sure the characters will be lit well. This often involves cheating reality, such as flooding characters with bright blue light for a night scene when in reality the light would be much darker, or creating a strong rim light (see the picture in the next section) on a character for a close-up, when the setting doesn't have any such strong light source coming from the character's backside. Good lighting often means that the dramatic needs of storytelling will override reality. But computer lighting also has the additional burden of making the overall result look the same as if real lights had been placed in the same spots, such as making sure the shadows look proper, that bounce lights exist, or that colors don't get washed out. You also have to worry about issues like rendering time, lighting transparent objects, linking lights only to specific objects that need the lights, and so on.

Three-Point Lighting

When it comes to lighting a person, there are no hard and fast rules to good lighting—different light setups can serve different purposes, and experimentation is often the only sure rule. Generally speaking, however, Rembrandt lighting is considered a good starting point. It is basically light hitting a subject from an angle so as to bring out the contours of the subject, as in the first picture below (and in the Color Gallery on the CD), creating a triangle of lit area on the dark side, as can be seen in many of Rembrandt's paintings. This light is usually called a *key light*. In our example, Spot lights are being used; but Point lights will work just as well. Another light is then placed to shine on the dark side of the subject, as in the second picture below, usually from the side and lower in intensity. This light is called *fill light*, because it fills the dark shadowy parts of the surface with light. The general rule is that if the key light color is warm, the fill light color should be cool, and vice versa. The third light is usually placed at the back and shining down on the subject, creating an outline of the head and shoulders. Its intensity can vary from soft to very intense, the latter creating a glow. This light is called *back light*, and it's good for separating the foreground character from the background. Some people use the term *rim light* to describe this light as well. These three lights make up what is known as *three-point lighting*, a standard lighting setup in photography. As Maya does not automatically generate the bounce lights from these three lights, you may want a fourth light to act as a low intensity, second fill light shining from the front to soften the dark areas between the key light and the first fill light, as in the fourth picture below.

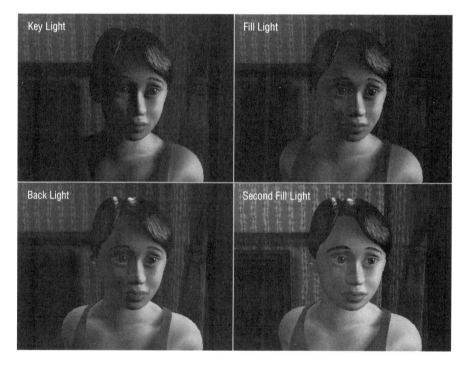

T I P   A good technique for placing lights is to select the light and then, in the modeling window, select Panels ➤ Look Through Selected. This lets you view the scene from the light's point of view. Then, as you move and rotate in the modeling window, the light position adjusts accordingly.

While three-point lighting will always give you a satisfactory setup to work with, don't fall into the trap of making it the rule for all situations. Especially with lighting, the best examples are the ones that break the rules (of course, the same can be said of the worst examples). Below are some examples of extreme lighting setups. As a general rule, you do not want the key light to be shining directly from the front, as it makes the subject look flat, but it can produce a good live video camera effect if the intensity fall off is carefully handled, as in the first picture. Hard light shining down as key light, or having two back lights as key lights, can also produce good dramatic effects, as in the second and third pictures. And there's always the "I-am-the-spawn-of-hell" lighting, the key light shining almost vertically up from under the subject, as in the fourth picture.

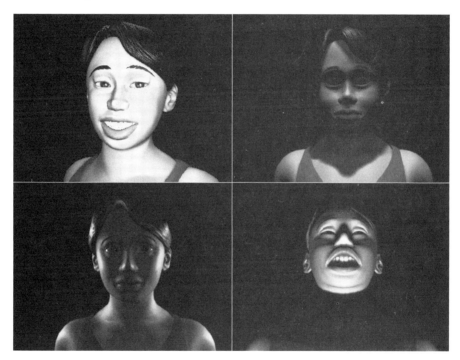

PART 5

Rendering

Render Optimization Tips

You've read through the rendering information in this book, and you've set up your scene carefully. You've put in only the lights you really need, and you've set shadow casting for most of the lights. But your render times per frame are still through the roof! What's going on?

Continued on next page

Most likely, the problem is that the render settings have not been optimized. There are many ways to do this, and modelers have their own ideas on where to compromise quality and to what extent. However, it's possible to optimize rendering without reducing the quality of your work. Here, we present some production-tested ideas to help make your scenes renderable in your lifetime.

First, and most important, you should link lights to the surfaces they will be illuminating. Linking lights causes the renderer to calculate only the rays necessary to illuminate the linked object and any shadows that are being cast by that linked object. The other objects in the scene are ignored.

For example, this technique might be helpful when you have a directional light illuminating your objects. If this light is also raytraced, the light will cast shadows from *everything*, which could take a while (to say the least). An alternative would be to create a duplicate of the directional light, exclusively link it to the objects that will not be casting shadows (don't link it to the floor, either), and make this copied light non-shadow casting. Now link the original raytraced light only to the objects that will be casting shadows (plus the floor). The result will be a faster render, with raytraced shadows for only those objects that need it.

Another way to optimize this scene would be to eliminate shadow casting for the floor itself, since we will never see the shadows it casts (which fall below the floor itself). Also, lowering the tessellation of far objects will help conserve memory. Remember that a floor (unless curved) does not need to be highly tessellated!

Maya has the ability to selectively raytrace objects and surfaces (parts of objects), which you should use.

One of the best ways to reduce render times and give yourself more flexibility is to render in layers with alpha and depth channels. Then, if you need to make adjustments later, you only need to re-render the particular objects on a specific layer, not everything else, too. The real power comes later, during compositing, because you can tweak colors, lighting (to an extent), contrast balance, layer order, and so on. These things would take far too long to adjust and test in a full-scene render, but this isn't the case with a few intelligently rendered layers. You could render separate passes for the shadow, highlights, ambient color, reflection, and so on. Then later, in the composite, you can interactively tune these parameters to your specific needs. This takes some time to set up and initially results in longer render times. However, huge time savings can be earned when you are tuning a scene in real-time, changing the amount of reflection, highlight size, shadow color, and opacity—all in a compositor, not in the renderer. An excellent example of this can be found at Jeremy Birn's Web site, http://www.3drender.com/jbirn/ea/Ant.html.

Continued on next page

(Although this rendering was done in a program other than Maya, the principle applies to any 3D application.) Here are some other render-optimization tips:

- Reduce bump maps, especially on objects far enough from the camera to not be noticed. An intelligently created color map, added to the base color map of your object's texture, can suffice to simulate the bump map from a distance, and it will greatly reduce render times.

- Only model what viewers will see. This is especially important if you are going to be raytracing—too much geometry to raytrace (in reflections and shadows on floors) will grind your render to a halt. The other reason to do this is to reduce the time you spend modeling, so that you can have more time for rendering! Don't spend time doing amazing things backstage where the audience can't see it.

- Limit your shadow map light's field of view to encompass only the objects casting shadows. This reduces the amount of computations Maya must perform and allows that savings to be applied to a larger shadow map.

- Check that only your surfaces that are supposed to be reflecting are set to have some amount of reflectivity. If the shading group was created as a phong, phongE, blinn, or anisotropic shader, these surfaces might be set to the default of 50 percent reflectivity.

- Selectively tune the render attributes of each object. Turn off Shadow Casting if you won't be seeing the object's shadow. Turn off Visible in Reflections or Refractions if that visibility isn't needed for the object. Turn off Motion Blur if the object doesn't move too fast (and if the camera doesn't fly past it too fast). Turn off Double Sided for enclosed objects that have no transparency.

- Test your render with the render diagnostics script. In the Render View window (Render ➤ Render into New Window), select File ➤ Render Diagnostics. This will alert you to any problems immediately, and it's always better to know about problems sooner than later.

- Use environment reflection maps whenever possible. They should be a size that is divisible by 2, such as 256×256. These maps also don't need to be very high resolution, if the pixels that are reflecting don't take up much screen space. You can create animated environment maps if those are needed, since the render times wouldn't be that long for each frame at the small resolution. You also can simulate blurred reflections, by running the frames through a blur filter in a compositing program first.

- Use texture maps whenever possible, because they aren't as render-intensive as procedurals are. Procedurals don't take up as much memory as image files do, but this shouldn't make a huge difference if you keep a close eye on your texture map file sizes. Don't apply texture maps bigger than you need. This is especially true for output to television, because the color space and ultimate resolution are limited to begin with.

Continued on next page

PART **5**

Rendering

- Render frames with motion blur and not fields whenever possible. The hit you take with motion blur will rarely exceed the hit you take with rendering another whole field (or frame if you are going to interlace them later in a compositor).

- Use 2D motion blur whenever and wherever you can. It is smoother than 3D motion blur, almost as accurate (as far as the human eye can tell), and the render times are a fraction of those of 3D motion blur at the same quality level.

- Last but not least, read the release notes. They can warn you of problems or slow areas of the renderer before you start pulling out your hair!

Summary

In this chapter we have gone through the four lights available in Maya and their properties, the two ways of creating shadows, and the fog, glow, halo, and lens flare effects available for point and spot lights. We have also discussed, though briefly, how to light characters in a scene using the standard three-point lighting setup. And we've discussed how to optimize rendering in relation to lighting and similar issues.

This chapter completes the coverage of all the basic stages of producing character animation in Maya, starting from the interface in Part I, and continuing through the discussions of modeling techniques (Part II), animation (Part III), the MEL scripting language (Part IV), and rendering (Part V), of which this is the last chapter. In Part VI, we will move into advanced effects in Maya, namely particles and dynamics.

PART VI

ADVANCED MAYA EFFECTS

Understand the Basics of Particle Dynamics

Use the Particle Rendering Tools

Use Particle Expressions and Ramps

Understand the Dynamics of Soft Bodies

Use the Paint Effects Tool

chapter 21

PARTICLE BASICS

Featuring

- **The Particle tool**
  ....
- **Particle emitters**
  ....
- **Fields as forces on particles**
  ....
- **Particle collisions and events**
  ....
- **Particle lifespan**
  ....
- **Particle and rigid body interactions**
  ....

PARTICLE BASICS

This chapter introduces Maya's built-in particle dynamics engine. We will begin with elementary particle systems and work our way up to more complex simulations, including particle interaction with rigid bodies. If you have not read the chapter on rigid body dynamics (Chapter 15), you might want to do that first. Particles and rigid bodies share many underlying features, so understanding one can help with understanding the other.

Although we will show you how to use particles using relatively simple examples, particles are a difficult area for most animators to grasp. Be prepared to spend some time working through the examples in this chapter and experimenting on your own.

What Are Particles?

Essentially, particles are little points (like dust, or particles in the air) that you can place in your illustrations manually or have emitted by a particle emitter. Particles, like rigid bodies, are physics simulations, not animation in the traditional sense, so you cannot manipulate them directly. To control particles, you must adjust their attributes (or the attributes of their emitters) in the Channel box or Attribute Editor. Particles can be affected by collisions and fields, and they can have their attributes altered by expressions. You can render particles in many ways, including simply as points, and they can even make up collective bodies (called soft bodies).

N O T E   We will cover using collisions and fields with particles in this chapter. Expressions, render types, and soft bodies are discussed in the next chapters.

Like (active) rigid bodies, particles themselves cannot be keyframed (although their parent emitter object can). If particles are not keyframable, and you need to use numbers to alter their behavior, why bother? As you will see, particles are a great way to create random or very large-scale behavior that would be nearly impossible to produce the traditional way. Items ranging from rocket exhaust, to dust, to human hair can be simulated using particles. If you need a plasma cannon or a fountain (our first two projects), particles come to the rescue.

Because particles (like rigid bodies) depend solely on their attributes, you need to bring along a sense of adventure to your work with particles. The best way to get to know how to do things with particles is to play (and play and play) with the numbers in the Channel box or Attribute Editor. Oddly enough, although particle simulation is based on science, it is really an art to get the particles to do what you want.

Creating Particles

Before we begin making things with particles, let's figure out how to create the particles themselves. There are a couple of basic ways to make particles: You can simply draw them into the scene using the Particle tool, or you can create an emitter to shoot them onto the scene. In the brief examples in the following sections, you'll try both methods.

Drawing Particles in a Scene

To draw a particle into a scene, create a new scene in Maya and choose Particles ➤ Particle Tool ❏ from the Dynamics menu set. This brings up the Particle Options window, as shown next.

In this option box, there are settings for creating single particles, multiple particles, random particles, and particles in grids. Let's see how they work.

1. Leave the Particle tool's default settings and click anywhere in the scene. You should see a red cross indicating where you have just created a particle. Click a few more times to create several particles in the scene (you can rotate your view to get the particles in different places), then press the Enter key to turn this bunch of particles into a group. Particles in a group all live on the same node and will share the same fields, collisions, and render types.

2. Let's create clumps of particles instead of individual ones when we click. Delete all the particles you just created. In the Particle tool option box, set the number of particles to 10, and set the maximum radius to 5. Click in the scene. You see clumps of 10 particles created in an imaginary sphere 5 units in radius. If you continue to click, the new clumps will be part of your current particle node. If you press Enter between clicks (and then Y to return to the Particle tool), you will create a new particle node each time.

PART 6

TIP The easiest way to delete particles is to drag over them using the Select tool (Q on the keyboard or the arrow in the menu) and then press Delete. You can also RM choose Select All and delete them, but the particles must be *un*selected first.

Advanced Maya Effects

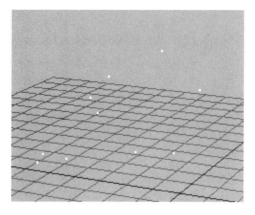

3. Now try sketching particles in a line. Delete your particles once again. Click the Reset Tool button to return to the default Particle tool settings. Then check the Sketch Particles box. In your scene window, drag to create a line of particles. Then open the Particle tool option box and reset the Number of Particles to 10 and Max Radius to 5. Sketch in the window again. You see a kind of "tube" of particles, created with a radius of 5.

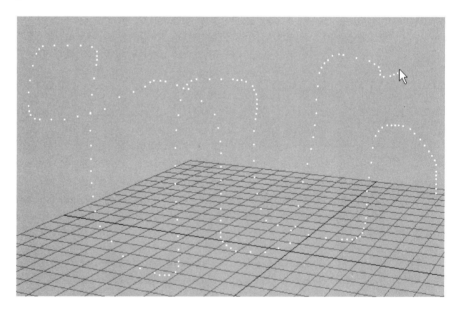

4. Finally, let's have Maya create a grid of particles for us. Delete the old particles and reset the Particle tool. Check Create Particle Grid (you can adjust the spacing between particles here as well, if you wish). Click once in the scene window, where the lower-left corner of the imaginary box around this grid would be, and then click again in the upper-right corner. You get a two-dimensional grid that looks something like the one shown below (and in the Color Gallery on the

CD). If you would rather have a 3D "box" of particles, click the With Textfields radio button in Particle Options and enter the XYZ coordinates of the corners.

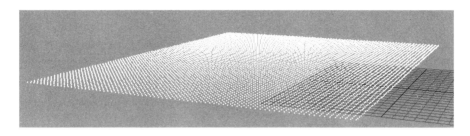

You now know how to create groups of particles by placing them with the Particle tool. The other technique for dispersing particles is through an emitter, as described in the next section.

TIP To see the difference between one particle of many parts and several smaller particle groups, try selecting one particle only. If you have created one giant particle node, all the particles in the scene will be highlighted. If you created several smaller particle nodes, only those in that particle's group will be highlighted.

Emitting Particles

Now let's see what a particle emitter does.

1. Clear your scene again and choose Particles ➤ Create Emitter ❑.

2. In the Emitter option box, select Directional for Emitter Type. In the Emission Direction section, change DirectionX (the direction the particles will be emitted) to –1. In the Emission Speed section, increase the Speed setting to 5. Then click Create and close the option box.

3. You see a small ball in the scene window and attribute options listed in the Channel box. Play back the animation. You should see a line of dots extending out from the particle emitter, as shown below.

 WARNING   To play back an animation, use the VCR-like controls at the bottom-right of the screen, or use Alt+V to play (and stop) the animation. But remember that you must *always* rewind your animation before playing it when dynamics are involved. Because all dynamics simulations are calculated based on information from the last frame, failing to rewind (or also scrubbing through the animation) will result in bizarre playback behavior. To fix this, simply rewind and play the animation from the beginning. Use the Rewind button on the Playback bar or Alt+Shift+V to rewind the animation.

4. To see the individual particles a bit more clearly, try turning down the Rate attribute in the Channel box from its default 100 to about 10 or so. Now you should see little peas shooting off into the distance.

Now that you've tried both methods for creating particles, let's see how to use them in your projects.

Working with Particles

As we've done throughout this book, we'll introduce you to the basics of particles by going through a couple of examples. In the following sections, we will build a plasma cannon and a fountain.

Making a Plasma Cannon

Every good science-fiction battle game needs at least one plasma cannon. This weapon of mass destruction shoots a blast of plasma—according to Webster's, "a collection of charged particles … containing about equal numbers of positive ions and electrons and exhibiting some properties of a gas but differing from a gas in being a good conductor of electricity." This is not something you want to have pointed at you, but it's a good workout for Maya's particle dynamics engine.

1. If you don't have an emitter from the previous example, create one with emission DirectionX set at –1, Rate at 10, and Speed at 5.

2. To make our cannon, we're going to keyframe the emitter on and off, making the particle stream "pulse," rather than emit particles continuously. With the emitter selected, set Rate to 0 in the Channel box (or Attribute Editor), and be sure you are at the first frame in the timeline.

3. With the word "rate" (to the left of the number field) selected in the Channel box, RM choose Key Selected to set the first key for the rate (at a rate of 0, which means "emit nothing"). Move to about frame 10, and key another frame at rate 0.

 T I P   If you set the Auto Key function on (click the button at the lower-right corner of your screen, so it turns red), Maya will automatically create the keys for you as you go—after you manually create the first keyframe.

4. At frame 11, set a keyframe for the rate at 50 (or more, if you want a thicker stream). At frame 18, set another keyframe at 50. At frame 19, set a keyframe at 0 again (turning off the emitter again).

5. Rewind and play back the animation. You should see a pulse of particles move away from the emitter.

6. To make the cannon pulse on and off, select all the keyframes you have made and copy them down the timeline several times. You should see a pulsed stream of particles, as shown below. (If you don't see the particles playing back properly, remember to set your playback speed to Free in the Animation Preferences dialog box.)

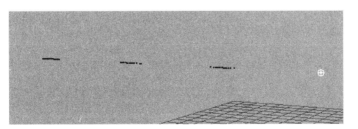

 T I P   To copy keyframes, Shift+select the keyframes in the time slider, then RM choose Copy. Move the time marker to another frame (like 25 in this case), and RM choose Paste.

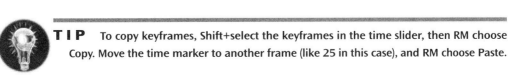

7. Let's give these pulses a bit of spread, so they're not all lined up perfectly. With the emitter still selected, set the spread attribute to 0.05 (a spread of 0 is a straight line; a spread of 1 is everywhere in a sphere around the emitter). You may also wish to increase the rate of particle emission for your keyframes to make a thicker cloud. Now when you play back the animation, the particles should look more spread out.

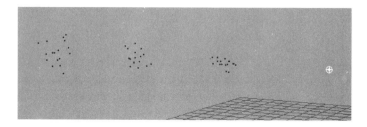

8. You will notice (if your window is large enough and if your frames are set high enough) that the particles appear to go on forever. As any true science fiction fan knows, a plasma cannon creates blasts with limited lifetimes (in other words, the particles must die off after a time). To make this happen, you must select the particle shape node itself (not the emitter). Play back your animation for a few seconds, until you see particles. Now select the particles themselves.

9. With the particle shape selected, open the Attribute Editor. In the Add Dynamic Attributes section, click the Lifespan button, check Per Object, and click Add Attribute. In the Render Attributes section, you see a new lifespan attribute. Set this to 2, and play back the animation. Now the particles should die off 2 seconds after they are emitted from the emitter.

10. Although we have created a fully functional plasma cannon, let's improve it by having it emit streaks of light rather than just particle specks. Select the particles (not the emitter) and open the Attribute Editor. Near the center of the window, there is a Render Type pop-up menu that allows you to select how you want your particles rendered. Choose MultiStreak, which makes each particle into a clump of streaks instead of a single point.

11. In the Current Render Attributes section of the Attribute Editor, click the Current Render Type button. This adds controls for new attributes associated with the MultiStreak particle type. Adjust these numbers to get a satisfactory looking streak of particles. In the example below, the settings are Line Width = 2, Multi-Count = 12, Multi-Radius = 0.165, Tail Fade = –0.5, and Tail Size = 10.5. (We also colored the particles orange, so they would stand out better, as you can see in the Color Gallery on the CD).

12. Save this project (name it plasmaCannon1.ma if you can't think of anything more original). We will use it again in the next chapter.

As you saw in step 10, there are many choices for particle styles. We will use some other types in the next examples. For a full discussion of the various types, see Chapter 22, which addresses the topic of rendering particles.

Adding Motion to Particles with Fields

In Chapter 15, you learned how to use fields with rigid bodies. Fields can also be used with particles; they simulate forces affecting the motion of particles. To demonstrate how this works, we will build a fountain using particles and fields.

1. Create a new scene in Maya. Create an emitter. In the Channel box or Attribute Editor, set the emitter's Rate to 500, DirectionX to 0, DirectionY to 1, Spread to 0.3, and Speed to 10. When you play back the animation, you should see something like the image on the next page.

2. You will notice that this image lacks an important element to make it look even remotely like a fountain: gravity. To add this element, choose Fields ≻ Create Gravity. Then select Window ≻ Animation Editors ≻ Dynamic Relationships. In the Dynamic Relationships Editor, select the emitter on the left and be sure Gravity is highlighted on the right. Now when you play back the animation, the particles will fall, as in a fountain.

TIP If you select the particles (not the emitter) before creating gravity, the two will be connected automatically. In this case, you do not need to go through the extra step of connecting them through the Dynamic Relationships Editor.

3. Add a plane across the grid. You see something like a fountain in a pool of water. To get a slightly better look for the water, change the render type of the particles to spheres (select the particles, open the Attribute Editor, and choose Spheres from the pop-up menu in the Render Attributes section of the window). Make their radii about 0.5 (so the spheres are smaller).

4. This is looking better, but everything is too smooth. To fix this, let's add a turbulence field to the fountain. Select the particles (spheres)—just grab any of the particles, and all of them will be selected. Then choose Fields ➤ Create Turbulence.

5. In the Channel box or Attribute Editor, set Magnitude to 10, Attenuation to 0.5, and Frequency to 60. Now when you play back the animation, the spheres should move in a more random pattern.

In this example, we set three of the attributes for the turbulence field:

- Magnitude sets how powerful the field is.
- Attenuation sets the falloff of the turbulence field as particles get farther from its point of origin.
- Frequency sets how often the irregularities change.

You should experiment with the settings for these attributes and discover how changing each one affects playback.

PART 6

Advanced Maya Effects

Using Collisions to Make a Splash

In the example we just finished, you probably noticed that the spheres pass right through the plane, which makes the fountain seem a bit unreal. We could use some splashing as our fountain operates. Fortunately, Maya comes to the rescue again, by providing particle "collisions." Let's see how to make particles collide.

1. Move the emitter (not the particle shape node) just a bit above the surface of the plane (otherwise, the spheres will be "trapped" in the plane and not emit properly).

2. Now select the particles (not the emitter) and Shift+select the plane. Choose Particles ➤ Make Collide. This creates a collision connection between the particles and the plane (in the Dynamic Relationships Editor, you can see—and break if you wanted to—this connection under the Collisions radio button). Play back the animation. The spheres should bounce off the plane now.

3. We have a collision, but we need something more interesting for our splashes. We need to create a bunch of smaller "splash" particles. Choose Particles ➤ Particle Collision Event. As shown below, set All Collisions on, Type to Emit, Random # Particles on, Num Particles to 5, Spread to 0.5, Target Particle to particleShape2, Inherit Velocity to 0.5, and Particle Dies on. Then click the Create Event button.

4. We now have a second group of particles, called particles2, which will "emit" when the first particles hit the plane (between 1 and 5 will be created for each collision). Set the second particle group's render type to sphere, and set its scale to 0.25 or so (so these particles are smaller than the spheres in group 1). Connect the gravity and turbulence fields to the second group of particles (see step 2 in the previous section).

5. When you play back the animation, you will see the second group of particles created, but they will simply fall through the plane. We need to create a collision event between these particles and the plane as well. Open the Dynamic Relationships Editor, select the second group of particles on the left, click the Collisions radio button, and highlight the plane in the right window.

6. Once you have connected the collision, go back to the Particle Collision Events dialog box and set the particle2 event (be sure particle2 is highlighted) as shown below. Most options are set as they were for the first particle group, but the number of particles will only be 3 and the Target Particles will be particle3 this time.

7. Return to the Dynamic Relationships Editor and connect the new particles you've just created (the particle3 group) to gravity, turbulence, and the collision with the plane. Note that here we can leave the render type as Point—these are the little splashes.

8. You could continue adding collisions and new particles, but you've probably noticed by now that playback is getting very slow because of all the calculations Maya needs to do for so many particles. Let's just make one more collision event to "kill" all the particles in group 3 when they collide with the plane. In the Particle Collision Events dialog box, select particle3 and check the Original Particle Dies box in the Event Actions section at the bottom. At the top of the Event Type section, turn off both Emit and Split (this makes sure no more particles are created). When you play back the animation, it should look something like the picture shown below.

9. Save this project (as `fountain1.ma`, or something like that). In the next chapter, we'll make the particles look a lot more like water.

This example should give you a basic idea of how to create effects with particle collisions. Just keep in mind that we used multiple collisions and did the following for *each* collision:

- Connected the particles to the collision surface (the plane)
- Connected the particles to our fields (gravity and turbulence)
- Created a collision event that either created new particles or killed the old ones

As long as you take these steps one at a time, it's really amazingly simple to create incredibly complex simulations with particles. As usual, you should play with the settings in the Particle Collision Events dialog box and watch what happens in your scene.

Tips on Speeding Up Playback

As became annoyingly apparent in our fountain example, playback can get really bogged down as you add elements, especially those that require calculations. You may want to increase playback speed, even if it sacrifices some degree of accuracy. The most obvious way to speed the playback of our fountain example is to change all the render types to simple points (you can change it back to whatever shape you wish just before you do a render). This will save a great deal of time, because Maya doesn't need to calculate the shapes of the particles.

Short of changing particle render type, there are a few other things you can do to speed up playback. If you would like your fountain to be going full force at the beginning of the animation, play it back until it is going at full volume, stop it, and type in that frame number in the Animation Start Time text field in the far-left corner of the screen (below the time slider). When you rewind and play now, you do not need to wait to see the fountain "run-up" to its full-volume state. However, you do need to start your animation at that frame.

To set the state of the objects at the current frame so you can rewind to the beginning of the animation and have them retain their current condition, select Solvers ➢ Set for Selected (or All Dynamic). This will set the current state of the selected objects (or all dynamics objects) to be their initial values when you rewind the animation to frame 1. The one problem with this method is that you can't undo it.

A better solution—especially for scrubbing—is to enable scene caching (Solvers ➢ Scene Caching ➢ Enable). It may take a while to cache the frames, but once they are cached, you can scrub back and forth in the timeline and play back the animation at much faster speeds. This solution is especially useful if there are other elements in the animation. For example, if the fountain is a background element in a character animation, not having Maya calculating the fountain's state at every frame can be a real time saver.

You can also (temporarily) disable all dynamics calculations in a scene, thereby speeding up playback of other scene elements. Simply select the particle object you wish to disable and turn isDynamic off in either the Channel box or Attribute Editor.

If you wish to see your spheres flowing, but don't want to wait for the slow speed of Maya's playback, you can try to adjust the tessellation factor to speed up playback. Select any particle shape, then select the GeoConnector tab in the Attribute Editor. Change the tessellation factor from its default of 200 to something low, like 10 or so, and see if it makes any difference in your playback speed.

PART

6

Advanced Maya Effects

Adding Particles to Objects: Plop, Plop, Fizz, Fizz

So far, we've painted particles into the scene and used emitters to make our particles for us. Another technique is to add particle emitters to objects. When you create a stand-alone emitter, it is just a point that sprays out particles; when you add a particle emitter to an object, you can tell the emitter to emit the particles from the actual surface of the object. To examine how to do this, let's recreate an image from a famous ad for a fizzy antacid: a tablet dropping in water and then bubbling.

Creating the Objects and Bubbles

We won't worry too much about our shapes right now—we just want to get the feel here.

1. Create a new scene in Maya. Create a large cylinder (the water glass) and a smaller, squashed one (the tablet). For the glass and tablet cylinders, choose Create ➤ Nurbs Primitives ➤ Cylinder ❏. To cap the ends of the cylinder for the tablet, choose the Cap Both radio button. For the glass, select the Cap Bottom button.

2. You can make the glass bluish and the tablet white if you wish. At the least, set X-ray mode on by selecting Shading ➤ Shade Options ➤ Xray. (For information about texturing objects, see Chapter 19.) Your two objects should look like those shown below (and in the Color Gallery on the CD).

3. Before we add our bubbles, let's animate the tablet falling into the water. Place the tablet a distance above the glass and keyframe all translate and rotate channels. At frame 15 or so, place the tablet just where the water starts (or at the top of the glass) and keyframe all values again. At about frame 55, place the tablet near the bottom of the glass and rotate it about. Feel free to tweak this animation as much as you wish, but at least get this basic motion. (For information about how to create a keyframed animation, see Chapter 10.)

TIP   If you don't want to bother with this animation, you can get an already animated file (glassAnimate1.ma) on the CD that accompanies this book.

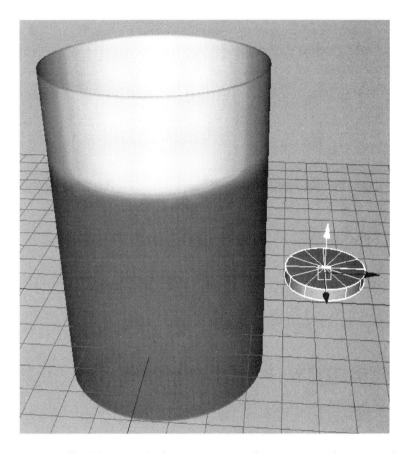

4. Now we'll *add* (instead of create) a particle emitter to the top surface of the tablet. In the Hypergraph or Outliner, be sure Show Shapes is enabled, then, from the shape nodes below the tablet shape, select the revolveTopCap2 node and choose Particles ➤ Add Emitter ❑. In the option box, change the settings to a Rate of 100, a Speed of 1, a Normal Speed of 1, and a Tangent Speed of 1.3, as shown below. Then create the emitter and close the window.

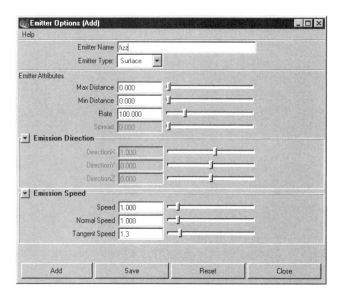

5. By adding a surface emitter to the top of the cylinder, the entire surface of the top of the tablet will act as an emitter. When you make the tangent speed of the surface emitter greater than 0 (1.3 in this case), the surface will emit particles parallel to the tablet's surface, rather than just straight out from it. (Try playing with the settings in the Channel box, and watch the results.)

6. Select Spheres as the particle render type, with a scale of about 0.25 (for small bubbles).

NOTE   You can add emitters to the side and bottom of the tablet as well. However, for this example, emitting from only the top surface will suffice. To add emitters to all surfaces at once, you can drag-select all the tablet's surfaces and add particle emitters to them using Particles ➤ Add Emitter.

7. If you have already played back the animation, you probably noticed that the particles emit very slowly and mostly just hang around. To make them rise a bit faster (as if they were air bubbles escaping from water), we'll create a weak gravity field that actually pulls the particles up instead of down. Choose Fields ➤ Create Gravity. Assign the gravity field to the bubble particles in the Dynamic Relationships Editor, and set the gravity's strength to 1 or 2 (from 9.8). Make its direction in Y +1 instead of –1 (so it pulls the particles upward).

Adjusting the Particles' Lifespan

There are a few other problems with our particles: They start emitting immediately, and they don't die! Both of these problems can be handled by keyframing either the rate or the lifespan of the particles.

1. Select the particles, go to the Attribute Editor, and choose Lifespan from the Add Dynamic Attributes section. Choose Per Object and create the new attribute.

2. Before we adjust the particles' lifespan, let's make sure that we start emitting the particles after the tablet has fallen into the water. Select the emitter (not the particles), and set a keyframe on its rate to 0 at the start frame. Create another keyframe a little after the tablet enters the water and set it to 0 as well (don't have the particle begin emitting just at the frame where it enters the water—the tablet needs time to begin dissolving). Then, at frame 35 or 40, set the rate to about 100, so the tablet is bubbling at full strength by then.

3. If you play back the animation now, you will see the particles begin emitting at the right time. However, they come shooting out of and around the glass! First, let's take care of those pesky bubbles that are escaping from the sides of the glass by making a collision between the glass and bubbles. Create the collision link between the particles and the glass, as described in the "Using Collisions to Make a Splash" section earlier in this chapter.

4. By creating a collision connection, we keep the bubbles inside the sides of the glass. However, they bubble right out of the top of the glass—talk about a head on your root beer! To keep the bubbles from popping out of the glass, we need to keyframe the *lifespan* of the particles. Because the lifespan of the particle controls how long it lives, adjusting the lifespan will change how far the particles can rise before they disappear. Getting the lifespan keyframed just right will take a bit of doing. Try the following keyframes as a starting point:

   - At 19 frames, lifespan = 0
   - At 20 frames, lifespan = 0.1
   - At 35 frames, lifespan = 0.2
   - At 50 frames, lifespan = 0.5
   - At 85 frames, lifespan = 2.5

N O T E   Unless you copied everything exactly, your mileage will vary, and you'll need to adjust your keyframes to get a good result. If you get stuck, a finished version of this particle animation is available on the **CD-ROM** that accompanies this book, (glassFizz1.ma).

PART 6

Advanced Maya Effects

5. Save this animation (as `glassfiz.ma`) for use in the next two chapters.

After you finish adjusting the lifespan of the bubble particles, you should have a fairly nice animation, although it's by no means perfect yet. Fear not, however; over the course of the next two chapters, we'll turn our fizzing antacid tablet into a really nice-looking sequence. For example, in Chapter 23, you will learn how to create a much more accurate individual lifespan.

Colliding with Rigid Bodies

You might wonder whether rigid bodies can interact with particles. Because all these objects are dynamic objects, they can interact to produce interesting and useful behavior. To examine how particles and rigid bodies interact, let's create a simple plane rigid body and turn a fire hose of particles loose on it.

1. In a new scene, make a plane, scale it out to about grid size, and rotate it 90° in the Z axis (so it stands upright).

2. Create an emitter that is directional, with a speed of about 10 and a spread of about 0.2. When you play back the animation, it should look something like the next picture. It doesn't look a lot like a hose, but it's good enough for our purposes.

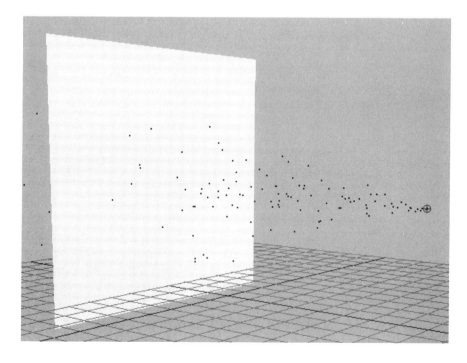

N O T E If you just used Add Particle Emitter ❏ to create the tablet particles, you probably need to go back to that option box to create the new emitter; otherwise, you'll get an error that a surface emitter cannot be created without geometry.

3. Make the plane a rigid body (select it and choose Bodies ➤ Create Active Rigid Body). When you play back the animation, it still won't show any interaction between the plane and the particles. That's because you must also create a collision event (just as in the fountain example) before the two will interact.

4. Select both the plane and the particles (not the emitter), and choose Particles ➤ Make Collide. During playback, you now see the particles ricochet off of the rigid body. This would be great, except that the rigid body isn't moving.

5. There is one last "switch" we need to throw before the rigid body will react to the particles. In the Channel box (with the plane selected), open the Rigid Body section and set Particle Collision on. When you play back the animation now, the plane goes shooting off with the first particle.

6. In order to reduce the motion of the plane, we need to do a few things: reduce the number of particles emitted, reduce the emitter's speed, and increase the mass of the rigid body. In the Channel box for the emitter, set the speed down to 1 or 2, and reduce the rate to 40. With the plane selected, change the mass to 1000 to make it heavier. Play back the animation, and you will see that the plane rotates but does not move away as quickly.

T I P Because playback of these animations can be slow, try using playblast to see your work in real time (select Windows ➤ Playblast).

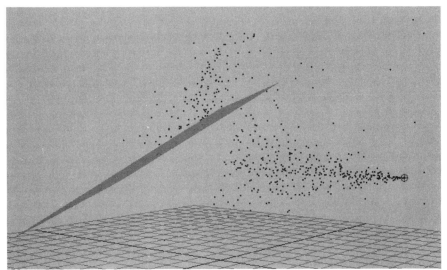

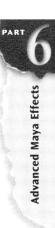

As you can imagine, in addition to creating something like a fire hose, particle/ rigid body collisions also can be useful for many other simulations—for example, space ships reacting to fire or meteors striking buildings (the buildings being made up of many smaller rigid bodies). We will use particle collisions again in Chapter 24.

 N O T E   As an exercise, try to balance a ball on a fountain of water (remember to include gravity). It's no easy task! To make things easier, try setting the initial state of the fountain after it's running at full volume.

Attaching Fields to Objects

As a final example of basic particles (if there is such a thing), let's take a look at attaching a field to a scene object and then have that object affect particles in the scene. Specifically, we'll make a UFO kick up some dust on the desert floor.

 T I P   If you don't wish to build and animate this scene, just load `ufoAnimate1.ma` from the CD-ROM that accompanies this book.

1. In a new scene, create a cone, flip it on its side, and squash it a bit (or use any UFO model you have handy). Next, place a plane a little way beneath the UFO.

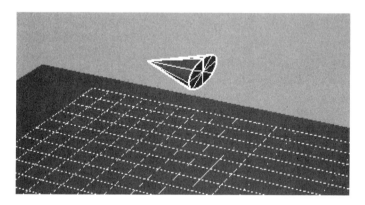

2. Animate the UFO to make a flight path across the plane. For good measure, throw in a loop and a few up-and-down moves.

3. Create a grid of particles that will be blown around by the UFO's speedy rush through the desert. Open the Particle tool option box (select Particles ➤ FR Particle Tool ❑), check the Create Grid box, and set the particle spacing to 10 (adding any more particles really slows down playback later).

4. Choose the top scene view and scale out so you can see the whole plane. Click the lower-left and upper-right corners of the plane and press Enter. You should get a grid of particle points across the plane.

5. Click the Current Render Type button and set the point size to 10 (so the particles are easily visible), then move the particle grid up on the Y axis until the particles are above the plane.

N O T E If you have a very fast computer, you can increase the density of particles in your grid. Be aware, however, that very dense grids can choke Maya, so save a backup copy of the program.

6. Now we have our UFO and particles. All we need to do is make a field to help the two interact. Select the UFO, then choose Fields ➤ Add Air ❑.

7. In the Add Air option box, click the Wake button, then try the settings shown below. Setting Direction X, Y, and Z to 1 enables the UFO to interact with the particles in all directions. Setting Inherit Rotation on allows the curving motion of the UFO to "suck up" particles. Increasing Magnitude to 10 allows the field to influence the particles, and increasing Max Distance to 10 allows the field to displace particles farther away from it. As always, try playing with these numbers to see what happens.

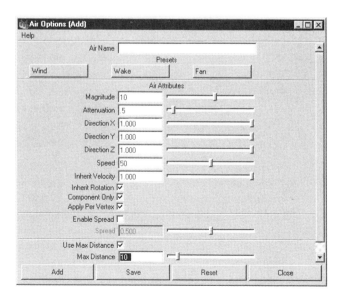

8. To connect the field to the particles, use the Dynamic Relationships Editor. Then play back the animation, and the dust particles should move around after the UFO.

9. To make this simulation look a bit more realistic (or at least appear as realistic as giant blocks moving around can), we need to add a gravity field and allow collisions between the particles and the plane, so they don't just fall through the plane. Select the particles, then choose Fields ➤ Create Gravity. You will need to drastically reduce the effect of gravity here, so the particles float back to earth as if they were light. Try setting gravity to 2 and see what happens.

10. Select the particles, and then Shift+select the plane. Choose Particles ➤ Make Collide □, and set resilience (or bounciness) to 0.2 and friction to 0.5. The frictional force will make the particles stop moving when they collide with the ground. If all worked well, you should see the dust whirl after the UFO as it passes by. (Also see this image in the Color Gallery on the CD.)

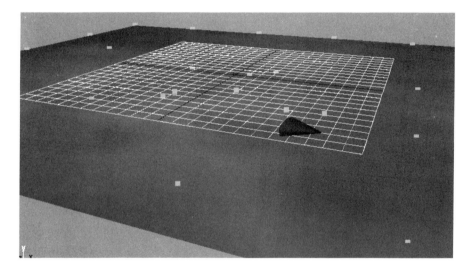

 N O T E   Finding the proper settings for gravity and the collision friction and resilience took quite a bit of tweaking. Try experimenting with the numbers and see what happens (remember to save a clean version of the project first).

11. Save your project (as UFO1.ma) for more work in the next chapter.

If you notice that the particles initially bounce off the desert floor and then settle, you may wish to set the initial condition for the particles to be after they have come to rest on the plane. First, turn off the air field (set its magnitude to 0), then run the animation until the particles have settled onto the plane. Then choose Solvers ➤ Initial State ➤ Set For All Selected.

If you want to get a better look for the dust, try setting the render type to MultiStreak, increasing the number of particles (the Multi Count), and increasing the Multi Radius. The neat thing about streaks is that they only exist when they are in motion, which means that they disappear back into the desert when they collide with the floor. This can make for a much nicer animation, although it's a bit hard to see (this effect is too subtle to be seen as reproduced in print; to see the flying dust in action, check out 22UFO.mov on the accompanying CD-ROM).

N O T E   As an exercise, try making a jet trail of particles for your UFO. Will it be affected by wind and gravity? How fast will it go? Will it be constant or pulsing?

With particles, it is often very useful initially to create sparsely packed particles that are big and blocky. This saves a great deal of time in setting up an animation. When you are ready to render the particles, simply increase the particle density and make them look more presentable.

Summary

In this chapter, we worked with particle dynamics, getting to know how to create and emit particles. You learned how to change the look and lifespan of particles, how to get them to interact with fields, how to get them to collide with objects—either standard objects or rigid bodies—and finally, how to attach fields to objects that then affect particles.

At this point, you know most of the basic elements of creating and using particles in your work. Over the next two chapters, we will take the work we started here (plus some other examples) and learn the intricacies of rendering them, as well as how to add expressions to them. So save your work and get ready to go—it just gets better from here!

PART

6

Advanced Maya Effects

PARTICLE RENDERING

Featuring

- *Hardware rendering*

- *Hardware rendering and compositing*

- *Software rendering*

- *Using sprite particles*

- *Fine-tuning your particle rendering*

PARTICLE RENDERING

 his chapter will continue work we started in the previous chapter. We will examine different particle types and how they render; specifically, we will look at how hardware rendering and software rendering differ. We will also discuss situations in which different rendering types are appropriate.

Because of the special nature of hardware-rendered particles, this chapter will also touch on compositing techniques, although that discussion will be limited. If you have not read the previous chapter on particle basics, you should be familiar with creating and using particles in a variety of situations before proceeding with this chapter. If you are not familiar with basic rendering techniques using Maya, you should first read Chapter 18.

One thing to keep in mind throughout this chapter is that rendering is truly in the eye of the beholder. You should always tweak your materials until you get a rendering you are satisfied with—even if it is quite different than our suggested material. What pleases our collective eye may not please yours, and vice versa.

When you work in Maya's workspace, you use your computer's built-in graphics card, which supports flat shading in real time. But when you tell Maya to render into a new window (Render ➤ Render into New Window) or to batch render (Render ➤ Batch Render), you are launching a separate module of the program that will render shadows, reflections, and refractions, and will generally produce a smoother, more realistic image—all at the cost of often-lengthy rendering times. In general terms, unless you are a game producer, you work in Maya's workspace (hardware rendering) and then produce your final images in the rendering module of the program (software rendering). In the preceding chapter, we examined how to create particles; this chapter will take particles to the next step of creating images that are suitable as final products.

And in This Corner: Hardware vs. Software Rendering

If you have not previously used Maya or Power Animator particles, you will discover that one of the most confusing aspects of Maya's implementation of particles is the issue of hardware rendering versus software rendering. You may have previously noticed that in the Attribute Editor for a particle shape, in the Render Attributes section, you can set Particle Render Type to Blobby Surface (s/w), Cloud (s/w), or Tube (s/w). The "s/w" indicates that the corresponding particles are software rendered, while the other particle types (like Point and MultiStreak) are hardware rendered. But what does it mean that some particles are hardware rendered and some are software rendered? Isn't all rendering part hardware and part software?

While these questions may indeed seem confusing, take comfort because there is a reasonably simple explanation. Software rendering is the type of final rendering you are already familiar with (i.e., rendering with the full power of Maya's rendering module); hardware rendering may be less familiar: it uses the power of your computer's graphics card to create flat-shaded images of your particles quickly. The main problem with understanding hardware rendering is its name, because you don't use only hardware to render the particles; you use a combination of Maya's (and the graphics card's) software and the processing power of your graphics card to create the images. Perhaps it's easier to think of this type of rendering as hybrid rendering. It's a bit of a cross between the default shading you see in your workspace and the images Maya's batch-rendering module produces.

To hardware render, Maya first creates a flat, shaded image of your particles (taking into account your preferences for rendering), and then it actually performs a screen capture to "grab" the image it just created. Because of this nifty trick, hardware-rendered particles can often be rendered in near-real time, whereas software-rendered particles can take a very long time to render.

WARNING Because hardware rendering uses a type of screen capture to create its images, you *must not* allow anything to come in front of the render window (including a screen saver). Be sure not to move any windows in front of the render window, and also be sure to turn off your screen saver if you are about to start a potentially long rendering.

The primary difficulty with hardware rendering is that you need to know and use a compositing program (like Alias|Wavefront's own Composer for IRIX, or Fusion or AfterEffects for Windows NT) to combine software and hardware renderings. This, however, can be a big advantage once you understand the technique, because you can control how your particles look independently from the way the rest of the scene looks. Compositing is such an effective and time-saving way of working with 3D animation that we often also render our software particles separately from our scenes. We will discuss some basic compositing techniques later in this chapter (see "Hardware Rendering and Compositing") to give you some insight into how powerful this technique can be.

Hardware Rendering

Let's now take a closer look at hardware rendering, using as an example the handy plasma cannon that you created in the last chapter.

TIP If you don't have a finished copy of this project from the last chapter, you can use the one on the CD-ROM that accompanies this book instead: plasma1.ma.

Open your saved project (or the one included on the CD-ROM), and play the animation until reaching a frame where you can see some of the particles. Now open the hardware rendering window by going to Window ➤ Rendering Editors ➤ Hardware Render Buffer. The Hardware Render Buffer window, showing the current frame from the workspace, will load, and you will have several menu options to choose from. The Render menu has options for test and final renderings; the Cameras menu lets you render from any camera in the scene (including an orthographic camera); and the Flipbooks menu allows you to choose or clear any flipbooks you create.

NOTE A flipbook is just Maya's term for a hardware-rendered sequence of images that are created in the *projectName*\images directory by default. Remember to set your project directory before you begin rendering images or you won't know where your images are going.

Give the hardware renderer a whirl: select Render ➤ Test Render, and you should see your particles (probably in default gray) against a black background.

Now let's adjust the render attributes for the hardware render buffer. Select Render ➤ Attributes; the Attribute Editor will open, and you will have several options for modifying your rendering.

For now, we will only look at the first section of the Attribute Editor: Image Output Files. Here, just as in the Render Globals window for software rendering, you can set filename, extension numbering (including the number of zeros in the name), start and end frame, image file type, and resolution. You can

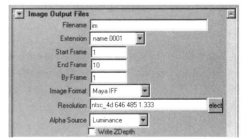

also set your alpha channel information here; you can choose None (for no alpha channel), Hardware Alpha, Luminance, or any of the RGB channels. For now, you can leave Alpha Source set to Off (the default), but be sure to turn it on (that is, use one of the other settings such as Hardware Alpha or Luminance) for final renderings that you wish to composite later.

Alpha Channels

An alpha channel (also known as a *mask* or *matte channel* or *layer*) is an outline of the rendered elements of your scene. Everything inside the outline is visible in the final image, whereas everything outside the outline is invisible (there are also semi-transparent parts at the edges of the outline, which partially show those pixels). You can think of an alpha channel as a cookie cutter that slices out the rendered pixels of an image, allowing you to place the cut image on top of another image in a compositing program. You can learn more about alpha channels in your compositing program's documentation.

If you can, use Hardware Alpha for your renderings. In the Hardware Render Buffer window (Window ➤ Rendering Editors ➤ Hardware Render Buffer), select Render ➤ Attributes and set Alpha Source to Hardware Alpha. If your graphics card doesn't support Hardware Alpha, you will see an error message in the feedback line when you try to select this option. In these cases, you will generally want to set Alpha Source to Luminance to create your alpha channel.

N O T E   You can also write the Z depth (or distance from camera) into your images. You can use this information to help you composite images, but the method is complex and beyond the scope of this book. See your compositing program's user manual for information about whether it supports Z depth compositing and how this technique works.

Be sure to set your start and end frames to the start and end frames of your animation, give your rendering a filename, and then choose Render ➤ Render Sequence from the Hardware Render Buffer window. In the window, you will see your particle animation run, and when the sequence is finished rendering, you can play back your animation in a separate (Fcheck) window by choosing Flipbooks from the Hardware Render Buffer window and then selecting your animation name. (See Chapter 18 for a quick look at the Fcheck utility.)

T I P   If you wish to stop the hardware rendering before it is complete, simply press the Esc key on your keyboard.

Upon watching the animation, you might discover that the particles are the wrong color or that they are moving too slowly or too quickly. To remedy these problems, tweak your animation for speed, tail size, and color. When the particles are moving too slowly, select the emitter, and change the speed to something like 20 instead of 5. To compensate for the resulting longer tails, change the particle's tail size to a bit shorter length by selecting the particles, changing to the Attribute Editor, and setting the tail length to 2 or so. So far, so good; the particles should now have a bit more zip to them. You can try re-rendering in the hardware buffer for verification, and, of course, tweak it some more if you are not happy with the results.

With speed and tail size under control, you can now modify the color. Make sure the particles are still selected. In the Add Dynamic Attributes section of the Attribute Editor for the particle shape, click the Color button and add a per-object color. Once you have added particle color attributes, they will be listed in the Render Attributes section. For this example, you will see Color Red, Color Green, and Color Blue listed along with the other attributes that pertain to the currently selected Particle Render Type. Try changing the color boxes (Red/Green/Blue) to suit your tastes. (For example, we liked a fiery orange, with values of 0.9, 0.2, 0.1, respectively. You can find this image in the Color Gallery on the CD.) Then you can re-render the sequence to see if you like what you have done.

PART

6

Advanced Maya Effects

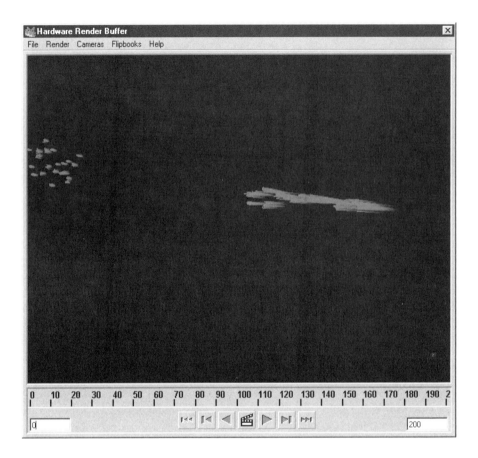

 TIP   If you keep your image sequence name the same, Maya will write over your last sequence for you, saving disk space. If you wish to keep a sequence for later use, rename your rendering something else in the Attribute Editor.

You may have noticed that you did not need a light in the scene. If you do not have any lights, Maya provides a default light for you to light the particles. Of course, you may prefer to use your own. From the Hardware Render Buffer window, select Render ➤ Attributes. In the Attribute Editor's Render Modes section, you can set Lighting Mode to Default Light, All Lights, or Selected Lights. Feel free to play with some lighting setups and see how or whether they affect the plasma cannon's appearance. (You may find that it makes no difference what lights are used with a particular particle or streak rendering type.)

Save this project for use in the next chapter.

Hardware Rendering and Compositing

Now that you have a good feeling for the basics of hardware rendering, let's create an example where we can composite the particles on top of a software-rendered scene. Open your UFO project from the previous chapter, and add a few lights to light the scene (if you didn't do this before).

TIP If you didn't complete or save the UFO project in the preceding chapter, use UFOParticles.ma **on the CD-ROM.**

You then need to open the hardware render buffer by going to Window ➤ Rendering Editors ➤ Hardware Render Buffer. Specify a filename for the image sequence in the Attribute Editor, set your beginning and ending frames, and run a test sequence. You will get an image sequence that essentially looks like a cleaner playblast rendering. (If your geometry is not included in the rendering, the Geometry Mask box is probably checked.) In this situation, however, it is best to have a software rendering of the geometry (the plane and UFO) rather than a hardware rendering of the entire scene. In order to do this, you will have to render out two individual sequences for the animation—a hardware rendering of the particles and a software rendering of the rest of the scene—and then composite them.

TIP If you do not have a compositing software package, you can still follow along until the last step.

With the Attribute Editor still open and set to the default hardware render globals, go to the Image Output Files section. Set your alpha channel (Alpha Source) to either Hardware Alpha (if your graphics card supports this) or Luminance. In order to mask out the geometry (so you can use a software rendering for it), in the Render Modes section, check the Geometry Mask box. When you now render the sequence in the render buffer, the geometry will no longer appear; only the particles will appear.

NOTE Although it is not obvious in this sequence, the geometry will still mask the particles, even though it does not appear in the rendering. If, for example, the particles pass behind an object in the scene, they will be blocked out and not rendered. This feature is very useful for later compositing.

One thing you may have noticed previously in testing particle and streak rendering types is that the particles and streaks are very sharply defined. For our desert dust being blown around by the UFO, it would be better to have a slightly more diffuse

PART
6

Advanced Maya Effects

look to the particles. Fortunately, Maya has two features that can help here: multi-pass rendering and motion blur.

When Maya does multi-pass rendering, it renders out a number of frames *in between* the frames of the animation, based on the number you select. If, for example, you select 3, the render buffer will render three "in-between" images for each frame and then average them together. This makes for a much smoother and subtler particle rendering, but it also takes much longer to render (three times as long for three rendering passes, five times as long for five, and so on).

Motion blur simulates the period of time a camera shutter is open during a picture's exposure, producing a blurring in quickly moving objects. The larger the Motion Blur number (between 0 and 1), the more blur there will be. It is often useful to keep this number small when rendering and then add a bit more blur when compositing.

To try out these options, go to the Multi-Pass Render Options section of the Attribute Editor, and check the Multi-Pass Rendering checkbox. Below it, a pop-up menu with a number (3, by default) will be enabled, allowing you to select how many Render Passes to make for each frame. Choose a fairly low number here (like 5) and also add a bit of motion blur (like 0.1 or 0.2).

Now when you do a test render, you may find the dust to be too subtle an effect (i.e., it is very difficult to see). You can adjust the number of passes, the color of the dust, the transparency of the dust, or the motion blur to make the dust stand out more, or you can make the particles highly visible and make the final adjustments in your compositing package—a much faster and more versatile method of tweaking your rendering. We often find we have to rework our renderings to make them a bit bolder in their rendered look to provide more choices when it comes time to composite, as one can easily reduce the visibility of a layer in a compositing package, but it is extremely difficult to make a layer *more* visible. When your test renders look good, select Render ➤ Render Sequence to render out an image sequence to your images folder. You can then import these images into your compositing package and combine them with your software-rendered sequence (see below).

Once your hardware render sequence is finished, you need to render your geometry out in a separate, software rendered image sequence. Open the Render Globals window (for software renderings), set your start/end frames, set your Image Format [Maya IFF (iff) is the default] to be the same as your particle rendered sequence, and then batch render the sequence.

WARNING   Do not give your geometry render sequence the same name as your particle render sequence (e.g., UFORender), or else your geometry render will erase the particle render image sequence.

N O T E   If you are not comfortable with software rendering, see Chapter 18, or read further in this chapter for more on software rendering.

Once you have your hardware and software render sequences, import them into your compositing package, but be sure to place the particle layer (with its alpha channel) as the top layer of your composition. Then, with the compositing package, you can adjust the brightness, opacity, or transform mode of the particles (and geometry) to get a high-quality final product. Save this project (as UFOParticles, perhaps) for use in the next chapter.

N O T E   For a finished example of this UFO sequence, see 22UFO.mov on the CD-ROM. (For visibility's sake, the dust has been somewhat exaggerated.)

Hardware Rendering and Compositing, Take Two

Before we leave hardware rendering and compositing, let's quickly revisit our antacid tablet project from the last chapter; the techniques we've just discussed will allow us to create much more subtle, realistic bubbles for our tablet. Open your saved file from that project, or, if you don't have a saved version of this project, use the glassFizz1.ma file on the accompanying CD-ROM. If you recall, we used the sphere rendering type for our bubble particles. The sphere type, because it's hardware rendered, doesn't support transparency, but we can make the bubbles transparent in the compositing package since they are being rendered separately. We will render all three elements (glass, tablet, and bubbles) separately and then composite the bubbles with a still shot of the glass (a nifty, time-saving trick)—plus the animated tablet.

T I P   Instead of the sphere rendering type, you can also use the cloud (software) rendering type. If you wish, you can experiment with this rendering type to see how it compares with the sphere type.

PART

6

Advanced Maya Effects

Rendering the glass, tablet, and bubbles is a bit more complex than the UFO project because the glass is supposed to be semi-transparent; thus, using the geometry mask will not work. Fortunately, there is only one extra step to this process to make it work properly: hiding geometry selectively.

Before doing that, let's first perform a little trick to save some time in the rendering process. Rewind to the first frame of the animation, select the tablet, and choose Display ➢ Hide ➢ Hide Selection (this hides the tablet). You should next change your render globals to whatever you intend to use for your tablet rendering. For example, in the Resolution section, set Render Resolution to 320 × 240 (the default), in the Anti-aliasing Quality section set Edge Anti-aliasing to Medium Quality, and in the Motion Blur section, turn Motion Blur on. Then set your start and end render frames to 1. Now batch render the "sequence" (actually just one frame), naming it something like glass. By rendering only one frame with the glass (which doesn't move during the animation, and which takes quite a while to render), we can save a great deal of time and disk space when we need to composite the elements of the tablet sequence.

NOTE   If you are unfamiliar with the method for creating software renderings, see Chapter 18, or study the software rendering section later in this chapter.

Now we can take up the process of hiding geometry selectively. Reopen the Render Globals window, and leave everything the same except for the end frame, which you should set to the final frame in your animation. Close this window, select Display ➢ Show ➢ Show Last Hidden to make your tablet visible again, and then highlight and hide the glass by selecting the glass and choosing Display ➢ Hide ➢ Hide Selection. With only the tablet now showing, batch render the complete animation, calling it something like tablet. You now have your software-rendered sequences, and it's time for the bubbles.

From the Hardware Render Buffer window, select Render ➢ Attributes. In the Image Output Files section, set Alpha Source to Hardware Alpha (if your computer supports it) or Luminance, and name the sequence something like bubbles. In the Multi-Pass Render Options section, turn Multi-Pass Rendering on (creating a multipass rendering will smooth out the bubbles just a bit),be sure Geometry Mash is on, and render the sequence.

Once the rendering is finished, import all three pieces of your project (glass, bubbles, and tablet) into your compositing package. Here, you have many options for combining your pieces. We chose to place two copies of the glass into our composition—one on top (set to low opacity and with some color adjustments) and one on the bottom (the more visible version of the glass). We then sandwiched the bubbles and the tablet between the glasses, with the bubbles above the tablet to allow them to be visible. The bubbles' opacity (or visibility) can be reduced to make them less solid looking. You can also create an opacity ramp for the bubbles so that they fade out as they rise through the water. A finished version of the animation is available as the 22glass.mov file on the CD-ROM, and you can see a still image from it in the color section of this book.

In combining Maya with your compositing package, you will surely encounter a number of problems—both artistic and technical. While it is very difficult in the context of this book to be specific about compositing Maya renderings (as there are a number of different software packages out there that perform this function, and all of them work a little differently), there are a few rules of thumb we can lay out here:

- Test single frames of your animation in your compositing package early. This way, you only have to render one frame for each composition layer to test whether the composition will work, saving you time in renderings.

- Always use alpha channels, even for those layers you don't expect to need them for. It's better to be prepared than to have to re-render.

- Render particles to be highly visible in Maya rather than going for the subtler look you intend to get in the end. Having more data (visibility) to work with can only help in the end, and it's very easy to blur or reduce the opacity of particles in your compositing package as a last step.

- Never alter your render camera once you've started final renders! If you move the camera between renderings, your particles and geometry will not match up and things will look very bad. It is often a good idea to create a separate camera (not the default perspective camera) to use for renderings. Using a separate camera reduces the chance of accidentally moving the camera as you work.

- Be sure to test-render some images in the resolution of your final project. Often things will look great at 320×240 pixels, only to look terrible when you do your final compositing at 640×480.

- Don't be afraid to try new ways of combining layers in your compositing package. Just as in Maya, you may discover a much more interesting look by doing a bit of experimentation.

Although multiple renderings and compositing may at first seem a confusing pain in the neck, once you begin to see how creatively (and often easily) you can alter the look of a particle-rendered sequence, using Maya in conjunction with a compositing package for particle sequences (and in general) will likely become your preferred method of working.

PART 6

Advanced Maya Effects

T I P   Save this project (as `glassFizz2`, perhaps) for use in the next chapter.

Software Rendering

Now that we've covered hardware rendering, let's take a look at the types of particles that Maya software-renders, and where they might be useful. In general, Maya uses hardware rendering for speed when rendering simple points and shapes; however, when it comes to complex render types like clouds, water, or fire effects, Maya sacrifices speed for the power of the software renderer to produce photorealistic images.

 T I P   Software rendering can be very slow. While doing the work for this section, you may wish to reduce the quality and size of your renderings in order to keep times reasonable. It can also be very useful to temporarily reduce the number of particles emitted while adjusting particle properties, as a few particles will give a good idea of what the final product will look like without overlong rendering times.

 N O T E   Remember that IPR renders (discussed in Chapter 18) do *not* at present work with particles, even software particles. You must re-render each image (or section thereof) manually while adjusting the look of software-rendered particles.

The three software render types are *clouds, blobby surfaces,* and *tubes.* Tubes, of course, are tubes—they can have differing beginning and ending radii and can be rendered with several special effects added to them. Tubes can be useful for everything from laser beams to hair (see the Color Gallery on the CD for a better look at this image):

Blobby surfaces are known as metaballs, spheres that blob together like drops of mercury. Blobbies can be used for water, lava, or a range of other liquid materials (again, see the Color Gallery for a better look):

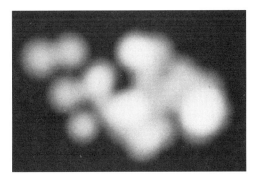

Clouds are blobby surfaces that are blurred or semi-transparent. They are very useful for airy effects such as clouds, fire, and smoke (again, see the Color Gallery for a better look):

As an exercise, let's see how blobby surfaces can be used to create the effect of water. First, either open your fountain project from the previous chapter or use the fountain1.ma project on the CD. You may wish to reduce the number of particles (currently spheres) being emitted by the fountain emitter, as blobby surfaces render slowly enough with even a few particles. We found a rate of about 200 to be sufficient for the purposes of experimentation, although using more particles allows for a smaller radius for each particle and increases the watery look. Whatever you find is a good compromise between speed and final quality is just fine.

After adjusting the particle emitter, select the particles emitted (the particle1 group, which the emitter directly emits), and change its render type to blobby surface in the Attribute Editor or Channel box. In the Attribute Editor for the particle shape (particleShape1), in the Render Attributes section, set Particle Render Type to Blobby Surface (s/w). Next, click the Current Render Type button to add blobby surface attributes to this section. The two controls you have over blobby surfaces are the Radius attribute (the size of each individual surface) and the Threshold attribute (which controls how the spheres blob together). The two controls work complementarily: as you increase the threshold from 0 (no interaction—the spheres just act like spheres) to 1 (complete meshing—spheres that are not connected will disappear), you will need to increase the radius, as the apparent size of the particles will decrease.

TIP Setting the threshold of blobby surfaces to 0 is a good way to produce software rendered spheres, allowing you to adjust materials and transparency much more carefully than hardware-rendered spheres. Slower rendering times are the price you pay for software-rendered spheres.

Like almost all other areas of Maya dynamics, a good deal of experimentation is required to get the right effect for blobby surfaces. After some tweaking, we were satisfied with a radius setting of 0.6 and a threshold of 0.9 for the particles; your tastes may vary, so try out some different settings.

Another element of blobby surfaces (like any geometry) that greatly affects the quality of the rendering is the surface type. To get something approaching a watery appearance, we used a phongE shading group, made it a very unsaturated blue and transparent, and gave it a small but very bright specular highlight. A version of the project that includes this texture is on the CD-ROM (fountain2.ma).

For the second set of particles the fountain produces (the particles that appear after the first particle group's collision event), open the Attribute Editor with the particles selected, click the Current Render Type button, and set the render type to Blobby Surface (s/w), then try a radius of 0.3 and a threshold of 0.8 for these particles for starters. You can then use the same material you created for the first set of particles for the second one—or make up a new one if you prefer.

You may remember that we set the third group of particles (those emitted when the second group collides with the plane) to be points. You can either leave them like this and then composite them in later (or leave them out entirely), or also change their type to blobby surface and then render them all together. We found the small-looking splashes created by a multi-point particle to be a nice contrast to the blobbies of the other two-particle types, so we composited them into the final rendering, producing the 22fountain.mov movie on the CD-ROM. (A still from this animation also appears in the color section of this book.)

NOTE As an exercise, try redoing your plasma cannon project using a Particle Render Type setting of Tube (s/w). Adjust the radii (that is, the Radius0 and Radius1 attributes, which are added after you click the Current Render Type button) to make the blasts grow in size as they move away from the emitter.

As with hardware rendering, there are countless ways to tweak and perfect software rendering. Although you can quickly achieve decent results with software-rendered particles, getting just the right look with them can be a very tricky and time-consuming affair, especially if you are not experienced at creating them. As you probably already know from attempting the fountain example, even minor changes to a particle's attributes or an emitter's rate often result in very different-looking renderings. Additionally, the interaction of textures, particle types, emitter rates, and so forth create a complex chain of interrelated variables that can prove frustrating to even an experienced user. Apply two rules to get your software particles to do what you want:

- Be a perfectionist; "close enough" is usually not.

- Be patient with yourself. While you want the best results, give yourself the time and freedom to make mistakes.

With a critical eye and a bit of experience, you can get excellent results out of Maya's software particles. Feel free to experiment with the Clouds and Tubes render types now that you have an understanding of what software particle rendering can do. Try creating a fuzzy beam of light with tubes, or a dissipating puff of smoke with clouds. If you have difficulty understanding one of the settings, don't forget that Maya's electronic documentation (under Dynamics) is an excellent source of information.

Save this project (as `fountain3.ma`, perhaps) for use in the next chapter.

T I P   Don't forget: it's often very useful to render software particles in a separate pass, just as is recommended for hardware particles. This way, you have a great deal of control about how the particles interact with the rest of the scene when you composite.

Pictures from Outside: Using Sprite Particles

A final particle render type that falls somewhere between hardware and software rendering is the *sprite*. Sprites are simply placeholders for an image you create somewhere else—either another 3D rendering, a computer-based image, or a scanned photograph. The image is mapped onto a two-dimensional rectangle (the sprite), and, for each particle, an instance of the image is created in the hardware renderer. Although sprites are 2D images, they are always oriented toward the camera, so they appear to have depth. You can also choose to use either one image or several images in a sequence (or animation) to map onto your sprites.

N O T E   We will discuss how to map image sequences to sprites in the next chapter.

As an example of how to use sprites, we'll revisit the UFO project—this time changing our streak particles to sprite images of leaves that the UFO can blow around. To begin, open your UFO project or `UFOParticles.ma` from the CD-ROM. In the Hypergraph, select the particle group, and then, in the Render Attributes section of the Attribute Editor, change the Particle Render Type to Sprites. There are several attributes for the

PART

6

Advanced Maya Effects

sprite render type, which are accessed by clicking the Current Render Type button in the Attribute Editor. For our purposes, check the Use Lighting box, and then set the Sprite Twist (or rotation about the Z axis) to 90. This will lay the leaves on their sides. If you desire, you can also change the Sprite Scale X and Sprite Scale Y values, altering the size of the sprites in the scene.

Once we have created the sprites, which appear as little black boxes right now, we need to create a texture for them. First, create a lambert shader group. (Lambert shaders have no specularity (or shine) to them, so they work well for sprites.)

N O T E   To create a lambert shader in the Hypershade, open the Hypershade window (Window ≻ Hypershade), and then, from the menu bar (or RM select), choose Create ≻ Materials ≻ lambert. Click anywhere on the right-hand side of the window to place the new material group.

Select the lambert materials group, and open the Attribute Editor (Ctrl+A). In the Common Material Attributes section, click the button that looks like a checkerboard to the right of the Color swatch and slider, and then in the Create Render Node window, under the Textures tab (the default), click the File button in the 2D Textures section. This creates a texture that places an image you specify on whatever object the material is applied to. Once you close this window, the Attribute Editor will be focused on the file1 texture, with an Image Name text field and a "browse" folder icon button under the File Attributes section of the Attribute Editor. Click this button, find the 22leaf.tif file from the CD, and choose it for your file texture. You should see the following in your Attribute Editor.

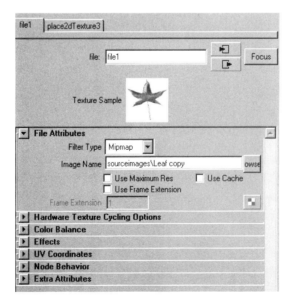

TIP You can also create your own image(s) for the file texture. Just be sure you include an alpha channel in your image in order to cut it out from the background. If you don't, you will be able to see the edges of the sprite rectangle when you apply the lambert shader to the sprite.

Now that we have a shader and a sprite, we need to connect the two. In the scene window (or Hypergraph), select the particle group; then, in the Hypershade, highlight the new lambert shader you just made. Click just below the image of the material, and RM select Assign Material to Selection, as shown here (and in the Color Gallery on the CD).

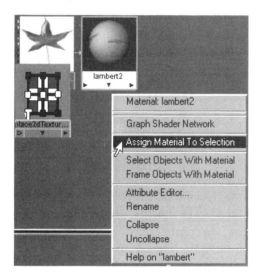

If all went well, you should now see a bunch of leaves spread across your desert floor (also check out this image in the Color Gallery on the CD):

PART

6

Advanced Maya Effects

If you now play back the animation (or, depending on how high you have placed your particles, by just looking at the first frame), you will see that the leaves fall halfway through the plane before they stop. This is because the sprites detect a collision with the plane only when their *center points* hit the plane (i.e., when they are halfway through the plane).

To get around this problem, we just need a bit of trickery. Select the plane that is the current floor, and duplicate it (Edit ➤ Duplicate). Now move the duplicate plane up just until it covers the top edges of the leaves. With the duplicate plane selected, shift-select the particle shape (using the Hypergraph or Outliner is easiest, as the duplicate plane covers the leaves in the scene window). Now make these two objects collide (Particles ➤ Make Collide).

The last step is to deselect the plane so that only the leaves are now selected, and move the leaves up until their middles are just above the new plane. Finally, select the duplicate plane, and hide it by going to Display ➤ Hide ➤ Hide Selection. The leaves will now collide with the new (invisible) plane and will, therefore, stay above the visible plane.

TIP   You may have noticed this same problem when rendering the sphere particle type for the tablet-and-glass animation. The same solution will work for that situation as well.

When you now run your animation back, the leaves should blow around in the wake of the passing UFO. You can either render this project out in hardware or just create a hardware rendering of the leaves blowing. (In the Rendering Editors ➤ Hardware Render Buffer window, select Render Attributes. In the Image Output Files section, be sure Alpha Source is set to Hardware Alpha or Luminance, not to Off. In the Render Modes section, be sure Geometry Mask is on.) You can use this new image sequence with your *old* UFO software rendering to make a new animation, saving the time and disk space of another rendering. A final composite movie is available on the CD-ROM as UFOSpriteSpin.mov. Save this project for use in the next chapter.

NOTE   As an exercise, can you use sprites for the antacid tablet project? Try to create an image of a bubble (with alpha channel), and map this to your particles. Does this method work better for this animation?

Fine-Tuning Particle Rendering

While rendering the preceding UFO leaf animation, you may have noticed that the leaves had an unrealistic lack of twirling motion as they were blown around by the UFO. This is because the sprites are always pointed at the camera. To get around this problem, you can use a nice little MEL script called `particleReplacer.mel`, which will replace selected particles with any geometry that you choose. You can then create a box or rectangle, map an image of a leaf on it, and use the script to replace the particles with that geometry and shading group, allowing the leaves to blow around more naturally. See the documentation of the script for more on how to use it. We'll use an expression in the next chapter to force the sprites to spin as they blow around.

NOTE   The `particleReplacer.mel` script is available from Alias|Wavefront's Web site (`http://www.aliaswavefront.com`) or from one of the other Web sites (like `www.high-end3D.com`) you'll find links to on the companion CD.

NOTE   If you are not familiar with using MEL scripts, refer to Chapters 16 and 17 for more on using and creating scripts.

You probably ran into a problem when you tried to composite your particles on top of your software-rendered sequence, especially if you used the Luminance alpha channel: the particles were probably close to invisible in your composition. The reason for this is that Luminance alpha takes as its alpha value the brightness (or luminance) of each particle. This is fine when the particles are very bright, but when they are darker, the alpha channel will be mostly dark too, making the particles very dim. Although it's a bit of a pain, there is an old and very effective trick to solving this problem. First, make a new copy of your scene so you won't mess up your good version. Next, create a new (lambert) shading group, and assign it to all your hardware-rendered particle groups. In the Attribute Editor, change the lambert group's color to pure white, and increase its incandescence to full. The sample should show all white.

TIP   If you are using sprites, create a file texture for the sprites with the alpha channel copied into the RGB channels of the image. (Call this something like `spriteImageWhite.tif`.) This step, combined with the complete incandescence of the shading group, will produce a good alpha channel for a sprite group.

The particles assigned to the new shading group should now all be pure white. When you render out a new hardware rendering, using luminance to create the alpha channel, you will get a rendering with white particles in exactly the same places as your colored particles from before. (Be sure to name the two sequences with different names!) Finally, in your compositing package, use the newly rendered sequence as an alpha matte for your other, colored particle layer. (See your compositing software's manuals for more on how to do this.) You will now have a much more visible set of particles to work with!

N O T E   The UFO sprite animation and still shot shown previously, as well as most of the other compositions shown in this chapter, use the "white render" trick to do their magic.

Summary

In this chapter, you took the first steps toward creating finished animations using particles. Using either hardware or software particles and employing many different techniques (and a few tricks), we were able to produce high-quality renderings. We also used multiple renders for hardware and software particles to separate out different elements of an animation, so that we could then combine them in a composting package. Although it's certainly not exhaustive, this chapter should give you a good start into the difficult-but-rewarding area of particle renderings.

In the next chapter, you will learn how to use expressions and ramp generators to create complex per-particle (rather than group-level) effects. So save your work from this chapter, and let's move on!

chapter 23

USING PARTICLE EXPRESSIONS AND RAMPS

Featuring

- *How expressions and ramps work in Maya's particle dynamics*
- *Changing color, lifespan, and radius*
- *Moving particles around*
- *Collision events and expressions*
- *Radius ramps*
- *Emitter expressions*
- *Changing opacity and rotation with motion*

USING PARTICLE EXPRESSIONS AND RAMPS

In the past two chapters, we have created, tweaked, and rendered Maya's dynamics particles. Thus far, however, we have only dealt with these particles as entire groups—now it's time to dig a little deeper into the power of Maya's dynamics and learn how to control Maya particles in very specific ways, both as entire groups and as individuals.

The tools for doing this are expressions and ramps. We've worked briefly with both of these in earlier chapters. As we explored MEL in Chapter 16, we saw how the Expression Editor allows us to define mathematical formulae that control the way objects behave. Ramps, introduced in Chapter 19, are akin to the gradients you may have created in a program like Adobe Photoshop. While these tools often overlap in functionality (and thus you can often choose your favorite method for dealing with particles), each has its strengths, as you will see during the course of this chapter.

After a general introduction to particle expressions and ramps, we'll try out various modifications of these basic techniques, though the sample of their uses presented here isn't exhaustive. While the complexity of particle expressions and ramps can at times be daunting, the power and control they bring to particle systems makes them truly worth the effort to learn.

A Simple Expression and a Simple Ramp

To explore how expressions and ramps work in Maya's particle dynamics, let's begin with a very simple example of each. Create a default emitter that shoots point particles straight up, give it a bit of spread (like 0.3), and set a fairly slow speed.

N O T E   To create an emitter, select Particles ➢ Create Emitter ❏. In the Emitter Options (Create) window, set Emitter Type to Directional. In the Emitter Attributes section, set Spread to 0.3. In the Emission Direction section, set directionY to 1, and set directionX and directionZ to 0. This ensures that the particles will shoot straight up along the workspace's Y axis. In the Emission Speed section, set Speed to 1 or 2 for a fairly slow speed. If you aren't comfortable yet with these steps for particle creation, please go back and work through Chapter 21 before you continue with this chapter, as we will move rather briskly.

To make our emitter a little more interesting, we will vary the particles' lifespan by using an expression, and we'll vary their velocity in an unusual manner by using a ramp.

Particle Expressions: Controlling Lifespan

The Lifespan attribute defines when particles disappear once they are emitted. We first worked with it in two examples in Chapter 21. In the simplest one, we created a lifespan for our plasma cannon, causing the entire plasma burst to disappear at once. Then, with our fizzing antacid tablet, we wanted bubbles to disappear as they reached the surface, so we keyframed their lifespan to the tablet's descent through the glass; bubbles emitted when it first hit the water had a shorter lifespan than those emitted when it reached the bottom. In both cases, however, every particle (emitted at a given point) had the same lifespan. Now, we will create a range of lifespans (controlling when *each* particle disappears) so that all particles will not die at the same time.

Per-Object and Per-Particle Lifespans

To see the difference between a per-object lifespan and a per-particle one, let's first create a per-object lifespan for our particles. Run the animation forward until particles come out of the emitter, then select the particles (not the emitter). In the Attribute Editor (Ctrl+A), go to the Add Dynamic Attributes section and click the Lifespan button. In the Particle Lifespan window that pops up, choose Add Per Object Attribute, click Add Attribute, and close the window. Back in the Attribute Editor, under Render Attributes, a new Lifespan field will appear, so you can control all the particles' lifespans. Enter a time of 2 (seconds) or so in the Lifespan field, and then rewind and play back the animation. All particles should die after the same amount of time, as if they are disappearing behind some invisible wall.

For some effects, this can be a good thing, but for a more random look we need… well, something more random. Return to the Attribute Editor's Add Dynamic Attributes section, and click the Lifespan button again. In the Particle Lifespan window that opens, this time choose Add Per Particle Attribute and click the Add Attribute button.

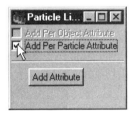

In the Render Attributes section of the Attribute Editor, the Per Object lifespan field will now be grayed out, and below, in the Per Particle (Array) Attributes section, there will now be a new field, labeled lifespanPP. If you play back the animation at this point, however, the particles still die at 2 seconds. Why? Because we have not yet defined an expression or ramp to control how long the particles live, so Maya just uses the per-object lifespan instead.

T I P   As you experiment with particle lifespans, you might decide at some point to override the per-particle lifespan calculations and use the per-object value again. To get back to the per-object lifespan calculation, simply uncheck the Use Lifespan PP checkbox in the Render Attributes section.

PART

6

Advanced Maya Effects

Defining a Particle Expression

Let's now define an expression to create randomized per-particle lifespans. But what kind of expression?

In the text field next to lifespanPP, there are two types of expressions we can choose to build: a creation expression and a runtime expression. What's the difference? A creation expression runs once for each particle (on its birth frame); a runtime expression runs for every frame (except the birth frame) for each particle. When a particle is first created (when its age is 0 frames—or its creation frame), you can have an expression that will execute once for each particle, but *only* for that frame. In other words, if a particle is created at frame 21 (its frame 0 or birth frame) and you have a creation expression for it, the creation expression will run *for that one frame*, and then the particle will go on its merry way. If you make a runtime expression, it will execute for that particle for each frame *except* the birth frame (it will execute starting at frame 1 for the particle, or frame 22 in our example). In some cases, as in lifespan, it is better to just run the expression once at the particle's birth (so it just has one lifespan value). In other cases, it is better to use a runtime expression. In yet others, you must use *both* a creation and runtime expression. We will see more of how these two types of expression work together as we proceed.

Enough theory—let's get down to business. RM choose Creation Expression from the lifespanPP drop-down list.

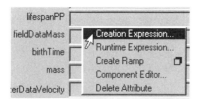

The Expression Editor will open up, ready for you to create an expression to control the lifespan of each particle. (This context-sensitivity is a convenient feature you may not have noticed when we worked with the Expression Editor in Chapter 16. Because we're launching the Expression Editor from the particle array section of the Attribute Editor, it automatically loads the proper object (particleShape1) in the Objects window.)

TIP   Also notice that the Expression Editor has two radio buttons for Particle that allow you to select either creation or runtime expressions. You therefore don't need to close and reopen the Expression Editor to create each type of expression.

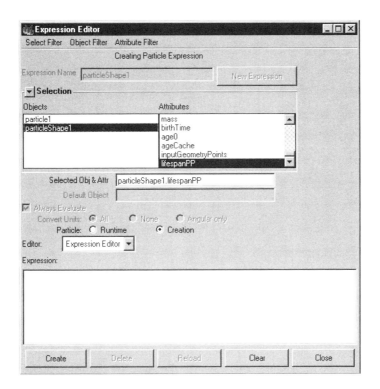

In the bottom (Expression entry) section of the Expression Editor window, type in the equation

```
lifespanPP = rand(1,3);
```

and then click the Create button at the bottom of the Expression Editor. If you entered the expression correctly, you will see the following message in the feedback line (or Script Editor): `Result: particleShape1`. If you see an error message instead, examine your expression for errors. The `rand` (or `random`) function just tells Maya to assign a random value between 1 and 3 to the particle's individual lifespan attribute. Thus, instead of each particle dying at the same time, they will all die some time between 1 and 3 seconds after their birth, creating a much more random or "real" look to the simulation. The `rand` function takes either one or two arguments. If you just use one number—like `rand(3)`—the function assumes you mean `rand(0,3)`, and produces a decimal number between 0 and 3. For more on the `rand` (and other mathematical) functions, see Maya's online help under the *MEL Command Reference: By Function*.

PART

6

Advanced Maya Effects

N O T E   Each time you rewind and play the animation, the sequence of random numbers will be different. However, you can also generate a sequence of random numbers that is the same whenever you rewind and play by using the Seed function. You might want to do this so that the animation looks the same every time you play it. By giving the Seed function a single value (like 15), you can force Maya to calculate the same sequence of random numbers each time you play back the animation. For more information, see *Using Maya: Expressions* in the Maya documentation set.

If you reopen the Expression Editor after creating your expression, you will see that Maya has updated the expression to read

```
particleShape1.lifespanPP = rand(1, 3);
```

Because you had previously selected the particleShape1 node before opening the Expression Editor, Maya knew that this was the node to apply the lifespanPP expression to. If you had not selected the particleShape1 node first, you could still create the expression, but you would have to use the full name of the attribute (such as `particleShape1.lifespanPP`).

Controlling the Velocity: Creating a Particle Ramp

Pretty neat stuff: we've quickly and (mostly) painlessly made our particles die off in a random fashion. Now let's create a ramp to control the velocity of the particles, making them move around in a circle. (Velocity is just position per unit time, so controlling particle velocity will control where in space a particle is at any given time.) First, we need to get rid of the expression that's currently controlling the lifespan, so that the lifespan per object will control how long the particles live. Reopen the Expression Editor, select the expression, and click the Delete button. (You might also wish to set the spread for the emitter to 0 for this project.)

T I P   If you don't see the expression text in the Expression subwindow, choose Select Filter ➤ By Expression Name and click the name of the expression in the Expressions subwindow.

Now return to the Attribute Editor, and, in the rampVelocity text field, RM select Create Ramp ❏.

The options window that pops up allows you to control how and where the ramp is applied.

We'll use the default options (Input U set to None, Input V set to Particle's Age, and Map To set to New Ramp), but you should be familiar with the options available here, in case you wished to map the ramp to a different set of attributes. After checking through the various settings, close the window by pressing OK. Return to the

Attribute Editor and RM select ArrayMapper1.outColorPP ➢ ArrayMapper1
.outColorPP ➢ Edit Ramp. This will focus the Attribute Editor to the ramp you have
just created.

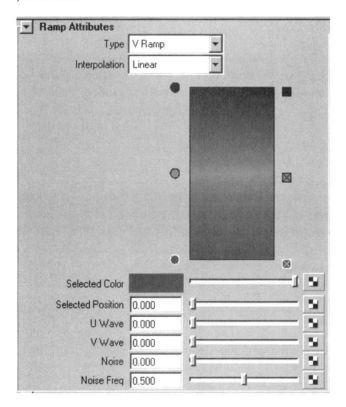

N O T E   If you used the Ramp Editor in version 1 of Maya, you will see that the editor is
now contained within the Attribute Editor, instead of in a floating window.

In the top section of the Ramp Editor is the name of the ramp (currently ramp1),
along with a texture swatch that updates as you change the options in the section
below. The swatch should be set to a ramp between red, green, and blue. For velocity,
position, and acceleration values, don't think of red, green and blue as colors, but as
values on a given axis: red is the X direction/velocity/acceleration, green is the Y
value, and blue is the Z value. (The scene window uses these colors to represent the
X, Y, and Z axes.) As the particles age, their lifespan values move up the ramp, going
from red (out the X axis) to green (up the Y axis) to blue (out the Z axis). If you play
back the animation right now, the particles will move to the right, then up, and

finally toward you, and then die. To change how quickly all this happens, set the lifespan value to a greater or lesser value.

N O T E   If there is no lifespan per object attribute set, you will not get correct behavior out of your ramp. You must have a per-object or per-particle lifespan set in order for them to "age" properly, and thus move up the ramp.

To make the particles travel in a circle, we'll need to change the default ramp, but first we must remap the array, because currently no particle can travel less than velocity 0 (no negative values). In order for our particles to travel in a circle, they must be able to go in a negative as well as a positive direction on the X and Y axes. From the menu at the top of the Attribute Editor, choose Focus ➤ ArrayMapper1. This focuses the Attribute Editor on the mapper—the part of the ramp group that tells Maya how to interpret the gradient. The Min Value field tells Maya what the minimum value for the ramp will be. For our purposes, let's make this value –1, so the particles will travel at a velocity of –1 when a certain ramp color value is 0. Leave the Max Value set to 1, so the particles will travel at a velocity of 1 when a color value is 1. Because of this remapping, a value of 0.5 for any color will translate into a velocity of 0 (halfway between –1 and 1). This remapping may be a bit confusing, but stay with us here; things should be a bit clearer when we edit the ramp.

Now that the ramp has been remapped, it's time to edit the ramp. From the Attribute Editor's menu, choose Focus ➤ ramp1, to return to the ramp. Set the first color swatch to RGB values of 0.5, 1, 0.5, by first clicking the green dot at the bottom left of the gradient, then changing to RGB (instead of HSV) mode in the color chooser, and finally entering the above values in the R, G, and B channels. The particles will now start life moving straight up the Y axis (remember that 0.5 on the color ramp equates to a 0 velocity, so there will be no motion in the X or Z directions). To make a circle, we need five points on our ramp, so, somewhere between the bottom and middle points, click in the ramp to create a new point. With the new point selected, change the Selected Position to 0.25 (one fourth of the way up the ramp), and then change the R, G, and B values of this point to 0, 0.5, and 0.5, respectively. At this point (one fourth of the way through the particle's life) the particle will be travelling in the negative X direction. Now click the middle point, be sure its Selected Position is set at 0.5, and set its RGB colors to 0.5, 0, and 0.5 (travelling straight down). Next, click above the middle point in the ramp to create a new point, set its Selected Position to 0.75, and set its RGB values to 1, 0.5, 0.5. Finally, pick the top point and set its RGB values to 0.5, 1, 0.5. When finished, your ramp should look as follows (see the Chapter 23 Color Gallery on the CD for a better look).

PART

6

Advanced Maya Effects

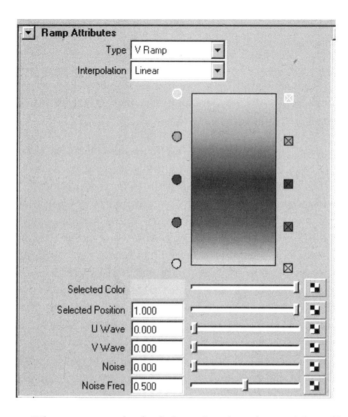

When you now play back the animation, the particles will travel around in a circle—a pretty neat effect! You can, of course, play with the ramp values to get different effects. Also try randomizing the lifespanPP values so that all particles do not have the same age. As you can see, the ramp mapper allows you to create some very interesting effects in a graphical (rather than mathematical) manner.

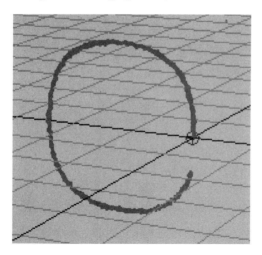

TIP You can also move points on the ramp by dragging the circle (on the left side) up and down. To delete a point, uncheck its box on the right side of the ramp.

With this introduction to particle expressions and ramps under our belts, we'll devote the rest of the chapter to trying out various modifications of these basic techniques. Sometimes we'll use one technique or the other, but often we'll use both together. The common thread in all of these exercises is that we'll be using the power of Maya to achieve more realistic—or at least more interesting—animation. The sample of uses of ramps and expressions this chapter contains is meant more to introduce you to the range of effects these two controls can produce than to be exhaustive. While you work through these examples, consider what other effects you might be able to produce with ramps and expressions, and then—using what's in this chapter as a guide—try to create what you envision.

Changing Color and Lifespan per Particle

To make our plasma cannon's blasts more realistic (or at least visually appealing), we will use expressions and ramps to modify the lifespan and the color of the plasma, respectively.

Open your saved plasma cannon project from the last chapter, or use the original `plasma1.ma` project from the CD-ROM. If you prefer, feel free to use the emitter we created above. Let's first use the same basic expression we created above to give each particle a random lifespan from 2 to 4 seconds.

NOTE As an exercise, try to make the expression to make the lifespanPP of the plasma cannon range from 2 to 4 seconds on your own. If you get stuck, the steps are the same as described in the section above.

Once you have particles that die off randomly, the plasma cannon should be getting close to production-ready. Only one thing is still missing: as the energy of the blast lessens, the color of the particles should fade from a bright blue-white to a duller orange. A ramp is a great way to accomplish this. With the particles selected, click the Color button in the Attribute Editor, check the Per Particle checkbox, and add the attribute. Next, create a ramp for the newly created rgbPP attribute, and edit the resulting default ramp (follow the steps above if you get lost).

Let's change the colors, starting at the bottom. First, click the round button to the left of the gradient (the orange one); then click the orange color swatch below it to bring up the color picker. Choose a nearly white blue color (or whatever you wish) for your first color. Choose the next point up, and make it a yellowish color, then make

PART

6

Advanced Maya Effects

the top color a darker red. One point is still missing—add a point between the yellow and red points (by clicking in the gradient), and make it orange. When you are finished, you should have something resembling the following (see the Color Gallery on the CD for a better view).

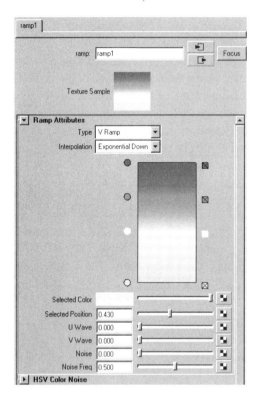

Play back your animation. You should see the particles change color as they shoot across the screen (also see this image in the Color Gallery on the CD).

Forcing a Complete Ramp Cycle

Advanced users may note that, because particle lifespans are random, many of the particles will not cycle through the complete color ramp. To force all particles, regardless of their lifespan, to go through a complete color range, you can use the following expression for both the creation and runtime expression for rgbPP instead of a color ramp (copy this expression into both the creation and runtime expressions):

```
$howOld = smoothstep (0, particleShape1.lifespanPP, particleShape1.age);
particleShape1.rgbPP = <<1.5 - $howOld, $howOld/1.2, $howOld/1.5>>;
```

The smoothstep function creates a smooth ramp from 0 (at time 0) to 1 (at time lifespan) for each particle. The rgbPP components (red, green, blue) are then assigned values between 1 (1.5 actually) and 0, based on how old the particle is compared to its full life expectancy. The numbers (1.5, 1.2, and 1.5) are just ways of adjusting the colors to make for a nice transition. (You can also find this image in the Color Gallery on the CD.)

Changing Radius by Position

Now let's see how we can change particle shape as well as lifespan by using expressions. Create a basic emitter that shoots particles up in the air, and then assign the particles a sphere render type. Next, keyframe the emitter to move up from 0 to about 10 on the Y axis over about 200 frames—we'll use this motion to make the particles' radii change.

We are now going to create an expression that ties the position of the emitter to the radius of a particle. First, we need to create a lifespanPP attribute and a radiusPP attribute for the particles. To create both attributes, click the General button in the Add Dynamic Attributes section of the Attribute Editor.

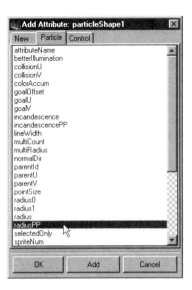

In the window that pops up, select radiusPP, click Add, and close the window. Now open the Expression Editor window by RM choosing Creation Expression from either the radiusPP or lifespanPP fields. In the creation expression, type in the following.

```
particleShape1.lifespanPP = rand(4,10);
particleShape1.radiusPP = emitter1.ty/10;
```

These two lines do two completely separate functions. One creates a random lifespan for each particle; the other gives each particle a radius based on where the emitter is at the moment of creation (the radius equals the Y position of the emitter, divided by 10). When you play back the animation, you should get something like the following image (which also appears in the Color Gallery on the CD).

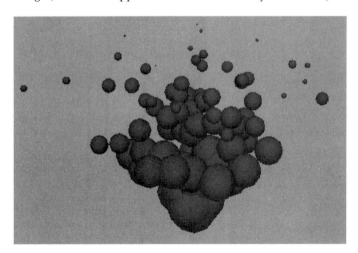

To see the difference between creation and runtime expressions, cut the second line (Ctrl+X) from the creation expression, and then click the radio button to select Runtime instead of Creation. Next just paste the line you cut from the other expression into this new one and click the Create button. When you now play back the animation, you will see the radii of all particles increase as the emitter moves up the Y axis. (You'll get a better view of this image in the Color Gallery on the CD.) Because the runtime expression is evaluated at *every* frame (except the first one), the particles' radii will constantly increase—in sync, no less—as the emitter rises.

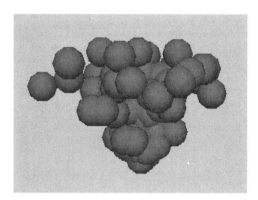

Moving Particles Around

If you happened to have looked at *Using Maya: Expressions* in the Maya 2 manual, you might have seen a picture of a spiral of particles rising from the ground. If you looked for an explanation of how to do this, however, you wouldn't find an explanation— well, here is one way to do it. We're going to create a runtime expression that uses the Sine function to place particles into a loop and push them up at the same time, so they form a spiral.

NOTE   If you are unfamiliar with the Sine function, see Chapter 16 (or a trigonometry book) for more information on what it is and how it works. (The Maya 2 manual also contains an explanation and several examples of using the Sine function—see *Using Maya: Expressions*, Chapter 7.)

First, create an emitter that emits roughly five particles per second (about one for each five frames), make the render type Spheres, and set the velocity to 0. Using an expression, we're going to place the spheres in a position based on their age, and, by virtue of the properties of the Sine function, the position of the particles will form a moving spiral. In the Attribute Editor (with the particle shape selected), RM choose

Runtime Expression in the Position field. Copy the following expression into the Expression subwindow.

```
$pX = 15 * sin(particleShape1.age);
$pZ = 15 * cos(particleShape1.age);
particleShape1.position = <<$pX, particleShape1.age, $pZ>>;
```

This expression first declares the variables $pX ad $pZ (for position X and Z), and then assigns them a value based on the Sine of their age (which starts at 0 when they are born, increasing from there).

N O T E   For more on variables, see Chapter 17.

Because Sine function values range only between –1 and 1, we multiplied the function by 15 to get a bigger number range (from –15 to 15). You will note that $pZ uses the Cosine function instead of the Sine function. This is because the Cosine is perfectly out of phase with the Sine function (that is, it is 0 when the Sine is 1, and vice versa), and, when the two are combined this way, they will make the particle travel in a circle on the X-Z plane.

The final statement of the expression does all the real work: it assigns to the X, Y, and Z positions the value of $pX, the age of the particle (forcing the spheres up in the Y direction as they age), and $pZ. As all these values change on every frame, so the particles move in a nice spiral.

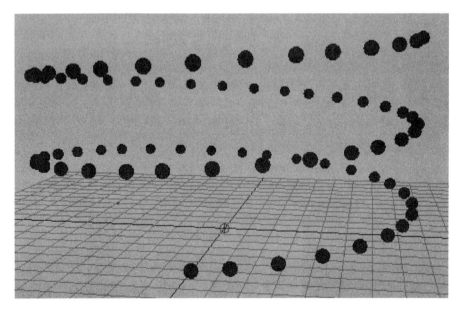

You may notice that there is a flickering at the origin as you play your animation. This is the sphere being created (at 0, 0, 0) on its first frame of life because the run-time expression does not work for a particle's birth frame. To get rid of this annoying problem, simply cut and paste the runtime expression into the Creation Expression window (switch over using the Creation/Runtime radio buttons in the Expression Editor).

As a last step, see if you can figure out how to make the spheres' colors change as they spiral up. (This is shown below and in the Chapter 23 Color Gallery on the CD.) You can use the same Sine (and Cosine) function to do this as well.

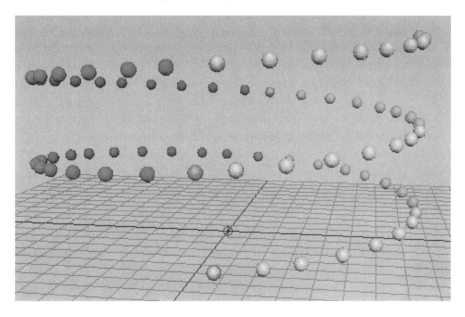

If you get stuck, try looking at this code to help you out:

```
$pX = 15 * sin(particleShape1.age);
$pZ = 15 * cos(particleShape1.age);
$cX = ($pX + 1) / 2.0;
$cZ = ($pZ + 1) / 2.0;
particleShape1.position = <<$pX, particleShape1.age, $pZ>>;
particleShape1.rgbPP = <<$cX, 0.5, $cZ>>;
```

The new variables ($cX and $cZ) reset (more properly, they renormalize) the $pX and $pZ variables to between 0 and 1 (they originally ranged from –1 to 1). The rgbPP statement just assigns these variables (plus 0.5 for green) to the spheres' red and blue color channels. Here, with just a few commands, you can create an animation that would be next to impossible to make using traditional keyframe methods.

PART 6

Advanced Maya Effects

Collision Events and Expressions

For particles, not only does Maya keep track of color, age, and other attributes; it also keeps track of events like how many times a particle has collided. Create a new scene with a fountain shooting spheres up in the air, add gravity, create a plane, and create a collision plane (if you don't want to go to the trouble of setting this up, just open the 23collide.ma project on the CD-ROM). Now let's create a runtime expression that will change each particle's color based on how many times it has collided with the plane.

We will use the event attribute (which is a per-particle attribute, even though it doesn't end in PP) to test how many collisions each particle has been through; then we'll use an if-else if-else statement to assign a different color to the particle, depending on how many collisions it has been through. To add the event attribute, you have to create a particle collision event (select the particles—not the emitter— then choose Particles ➤ Particle Collision Events, and click the Create Event button). The event attribute itself will not be listed in the Channel box or the Attribute Editor, but it will be listed in the Expression Editor's Attributes box.

NOTE   If you are not familiar with if statements, please see Chapter 17 (or a basic programming text) for more information.

NOTE   In the Maya documentation, see *Using Maya: Dynamics* for more information about creating particle collision events (Chapter 4, "Particle Collisions") and the event attribute (Chapter 13, "Advanced Particle Topics").

RM select a runtime expression for the rgbPP of the particles, type the following expression into the Expression Editor, and then click the Create button when you are finished.

```
if (event == 0)
    rgbPP = <<0,1,0>>;
else if (event == 1)
    rgbPP = <<1,0,0>>;
else if (event == 2)
    rgbPP = <<0,0,1>>;
else rgbPP = <<1,1,1>>;
```

This expression executes on every frame (except the birth frame) to see how many collisions each particle has had. If the number is 0 (no collisions), it assigns a green color to the sphere. If the number of collisions is 1 (after the first bounce), it assigns the color red to the sphere. If the number is 2 (after the second bounce), it assigns the color blue to the spheres. In all other cases (i.e., the particle has bounced more than twice), it assigns a white color (all 1s) to the sphere.

N O T E Note that the test condition is specified by a *double* equal sign (event == 0), not a single equal sign. A single equal sign tells Maya to assign a value to the left-hand side of an equation (like rgbPP = X); a double equal sign tells Maya to test whether the two sides of the equation are equivalent.

N O T E You can also use a `switch` command for cases like the expression above. A `switch` and an `if-else` statement perform the same function, but in a slightly different way. For more information about the `switch` command, see *Using Maya: Expressions* in Maya's online documentation.)

Play back the animation and watch each sphere; you will see that the individual particles change color each time they bounce, ending with a white color after it has bouncing more than twice. (The Chapter 23 Color Gallery shows the image below to better effect.) You may also notice that the spheres are emitted as completely black objects—this is (again) because a runtime expression is not evaluated on the birth frame of the particles. To solve this problem, simply copy and paste the expression into a creation expression for the rgbPP of the spheres.

Disappearing Bubbles: Radius Ramps

One problem with our antacid tablet from the previous two chapters is that the bubbles rising from the tablet have a constant radius. Let's make them shrink as they rise using a radius ramp and particles with blobby surfaces.

First, open your project from the last chapter (or, if you don't have that project, open the glassFizz.ma file on the CD-ROM). For a little different look, let's change the bubbles to software rendered ones. In the Attribute Editor, set the particle type to blobby surfaces, and set the threshold to 0. (Remember that setting the threshold of a blobby surface to 0 makes the spheres noninteractive and, thus, just spheres. For bubbles, this is exactly what we're after.) With particles selected, add a per-particle radius attribute to the bubbles, then create and edit the ramp of radiusPP to look something like this.

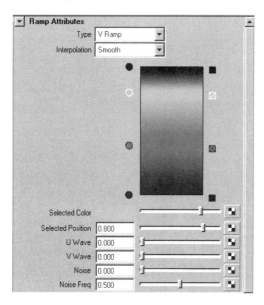

You'll probably find the bubbles created with this ramp ranging in size too much, overall, so remap their sizes using the Array Mapper (RM choose radiusPP ➤ arrayMapper1.outvaluePP ➤ arrayMapper1.outvaluePP ➤ Edit Array Mapper). A min value of 0.1 and a max of about 0.3 give a much subtler effect.

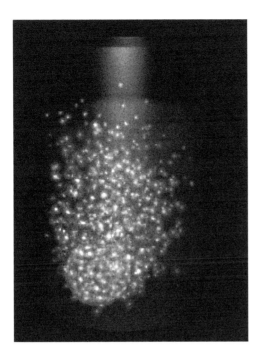

N O T E   The bubbles in this image have a material attached to them—a phongE material with high specularity and low opacity. This, of course, improves the look of the bubbles tremendously.

Emitter Expressions

We have created several ramps and expressions for particles, but it is also possible to create expressions for particle emitters. You can either create a default emitter for this example, or open your fountain project from the last chapter. It's easier to see the effects of the expression in a simpler project, so it might be advisable to first create a simple emitter and then, after you see how the expression works, copy it into the fountain project.

T I P   If you don't have the fountain project from the last chapter, use the file foun-tain3.ma on the CD-ROM.

Although emitters are random in their particle output, they tend to produce a "constant" randomness (a kind of even spread) over time. To get the emitter to create a varying number of particles and a varying amount of spread, we could keyframe these values—or we could simply create a two-line expression using the noise function.

N O T E   We could also use the rand function, but noise produces a more connected randomness (as opposed to the rand function's jumping from value to value), which looks more like the varying water pressure we might see in a fountain. For more on the noise function, see Chapter 16.

With the emitter (not the particles) selected, open the Expression Editor and type in the following expression.

```
emitter1.rate = ((noise (time) + 1) * 200) + 20;
emitter1.spread = ((noise (time) + 1)/4) + 0.1;
```

In essence, each line of this little expression tells the emitter to vary its rate (or spread amount) according to a random amount as defined by the noise function, which uses time as its input to create its numbers. The rest of the numbers are just a way to get the value output by noise into a good range for each attribute. Because noise varies between –1 and 1, we added 1 to both lines so the result would vary between 0 and 2. For the rate, we wanted the value to range between 20 and 420, so we multiplied the results of noise by 200 (giving a range of 0 to 400) and added 20. For the spread, a good range seemed to be between about 0.1 and 0.6, so we divided by 4 (giving a range of 0 to 0.5) and added 0.1. As your results should show, the noise function is a very powerful way to create a more "live" look to your particles.

The result of this expression applied to the fountain project is on your CD-ROM (23fountain.mov). If you compare this to the previous fountain movie (22fountain .mov), you can see the dramatic way the fountain looks more real (like one of those shooting fountains) in our new movie.

N O T E   As an exercise, try varying the speed of the particles in the fountain as well. What range looks best to you? Hint: to speed up the process of experimentation, try using playblast to test your motion (instead of test renders, which will be long with blobby surfaces). Also, 23fountain.mov uses variable speed, so look at it for hints as to how the final product might look.

Changing Opacity with Motion

We're now going to create a nice trick: we're going to increase the opacity of a particle based on its motion—in other words, the more it moves, the more opaque it is. To test this out, open your UFO project from the last chapter (or use UFOParticles.ma on the CD-ROM).

With the particles selected, create a per-particle opacity attribute; then open the Expression Editor and type in the following simple runtime expression.

```
if (particleShape1.velocity != 0)
    particleShape1.opacityPP = (particleShape1.velocity / 2.0);
else
particleShape1.opacityPP = 0;
```

All we do here is test whether the velocity is not 0 (the ! sign in front of a comparison operator means "not"). If the particle is moving, then its opacity is based on its speed (we divided by 2 to get a more gradual opacity fadeup—you can try other numbers if you like). If the particle is at rest (the else statement), its opacity is defined as 0, or invisible. Thus, when the "dust" is resting on our desert floor, it is invisible. As the UFO picks it up and moves it around, it becomes visible; then, as it crashes back into the ground, it becomes invisible again. A movie of this new UFO sequence is on the CD-ROM: 23UFOFade.mov.

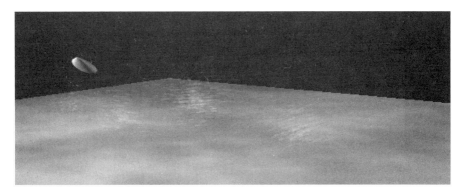

Changing Rotation with Motion

Now that we have dust blowing up, it seems only natural to visit the UFO project we did in the last chapter with sprites of leaves. This time, instead of fading the sprites up, we'll make them rotate based on their motion (so they aren't just sliding across the desert floor). Either open your UFO sprite project, or use the one on the CD-ROM (UFOSprite.ma). With the particles selected, make a spriteTwistPP attribute (click the General button in the Attribute Editor, scroll down to spriteTwistPP, highlight it, and click the Add button). In the text field next to the new spriteTwistPP attribute,

PART

6

Advanced Maya Effects

RM choose New Expression and in the Expression Editor, type in the following expression (don't press Enter after the plus sign):

```
float $speed = particleShape1.velocity;
if (particleShape1.velocity != 0)
    particleShape1.spriteTwistPP = particleShape1.spriteTwistPP +
            ($speed * noise(time) * 2);
```

The essence of this expression is the same as the last one: if the velocity isn't zero, rotate the leaves. Some of the details have changed, however. First, we created a variable (note that it is a float) called $speed, which receives the *magnitude* of the particle's velocity.

NOTE   The velocity variable is a vector quantity (with X,Y,Z values), but $speed is a scalar (just one number). When Maya sees an assignment operator (a single equal sign), it always forces the value on the right to fit that on the left if it can. In the case of a vector being converted to a float, Maya takes the magnitude of the vector (the square root of each element squared and added together), which is a single number, and assigns that number to $speed. Whew—enough math lessons for one day!

The next line checks whether the sprite's velocity is not 0; then, if that's the case, it changes the spriteTwistPP of the particle by the value of $speed. The multipliers (noise and 2) are there to make the motion of each leaf different from the others—essentially, the value of $speed is multiplied by a randomly changing number between –2 and 2, making the leaves spin in both directions by varying amounts. You will notice that there is no else statement here: if the leaf isn't moving, its rotation should just stay where it is, not suddenly jump back to some other number (like 90 degrees). A movie of the leaves is available on the CD (23UFOSpriteSpin.mov).

Animated Sprites: the UFO Again

As one last example of using expressions, let's create a more interesting, animated array of plant life for our UFO to pass over. You may have noticed how boringly static all the leaves in our desert were—now we'll remedy that situation. Open the UFOSprite .ma project (or your saved one—or the one we just worked on, though the results will be a bit harder to see with all the spinning).

Select the lambert shader that controls the sprite shape (the one with the leaf on it) and, in the Attribute Editor, click the focus button next to color (the triangle in a square) to bring up the file1 attributes. From the CD (or the directory on your hard disk where you've saved the Working_Files directories), open the LeafSequence subdirectory (you will see about 50 files in the sequence), and be sure to check the Use Frame Extension box below. This will assign the first leaf in the sequence to the shader.

T I P   For faster response time (and just to be a better user), you can copy the leaf files into your project's sourceImages folder and select them there for your shader.

Now, in the Hardware Texture Cycling Options, set the Start Cycle Extension to 1, the End Cycle Extension to 50 (for leaf1 and leaf50, respectively), and the By Cycle Increment to 1. The By Cycle Increment controls how many images are skipped before the next one is shown. For an animation (of, say, a bird flying or a rendered animation sequence you had previously made), you would set the increment to 1; for a choppier look (skipping some of the images, thus producing a more "stop motion" look as the sequence plays), an increment of 2 or 3 would work.

T I P   You might realize at this point how useful sprite sequences can be: you could play back a movie (saved out as an image sequence) in sprites, creating a dazzling array of moving images in your final scene.

If you play back the animation now, you won't see anything different. That's because we have to write an expression to alter the look of each sprite. First, add a new attribute: spriteNumPP (click the General button in the Attribute Editor and add it). Then RM choose a new runtime expression and type in the following:

```
particleShape1.spriteNumPP = (frame % 50) + 1;
```

The % sign is the modulus (or remainder) function—whatever number remains from dividing the frame number by 50 is returned (plus 1 so that the number is never 0, for which no sprite is defined). For example, on frame 1, 1 % 50 returns 1 (the remainder of 1 / 50). The second frame returns 2, and so on. At each frame, a different spriteNumPP is defined. We could also write a noise function to get each sprite to

PART 6

Advanced Maya Effects

randomly change colors, instead of all of them doing it in synch. In either case, we get all the changes of fall colors in very short order!

NOTE   As an exercise, try creating a new emitter that produces different colored leaves that then stay the same the rest of their lives. You'll need to use a creation expression this time, instead of a runtime expression. If you get stuck, see the file `differentLeaves.ma` for a clue.

Summary

In this chapter, we have discovered how to unlock the power of particle dynamics by using ramps and expressions. Using ramps, we can produce large-scale effects—be it radius, color, or even velocity—that occur over the lifetime of each particle. We learned that expressions, on the other hand, are best at breaking down groups of particles into their constituents, and allowing us to control each particle in a different but related manner. While none of the expressions were more than a couple of lines long, they produced very impressive results, ranging from positioning particles based on the Sine curve to varying their opacity based on how fast they were moving.

If you have a fairly good grasp of the past three chapters, you are now ready to create very difficult-looking effects in (most importantly!) a relatively short time. The next chapter, on soft bodies, is the final chapter on particle dynamics. You'll see that the term *soft bodies* is a slight misnomer, as they are actually collections of particles that act as bodies. While soft bodies are one of Maya's most complex and difficult features, the past three chapters have given you a very good primer for these powerful objects. When you're ready, turn the page to begin exploring soft bodies!

chapter 24

DYNAMICS OF
SOFT BODIES

Featuring

- *What are soft bodies?*
  ....

- *Creating a basic soft body*
  ....

- *Adjusting goal weights*
  ....

- *Using goal weights to create fluid motion*
  ....

- *Adding springs to soft bodies*
  ....

- *Faking a bounce*
  ....

- *Denting soft bodies*
  ....

- *Adding ripples to the fountain project*
  ....

- *Creating a watery body and face*
  ....

DYNAMICS OF SOFT BODIES

I n this chapter, you'll learn what soft bodies are, how to use them, and when you can use them to create amazing special effects. Along the way, we'll revisit the fountain example from the past several chapters, this time concentrating on the plane below the fountain. We'll also delve into an advanced use of soft bodies to create an effect similar to the famous "water head" scene in the film *The Abyss*. You will see both how soft bodies are the culmination of Maya's particle dynamics and how they allow you, the animator, to create a whole new realm of animation.

What Are Soft Bodies?

At heart, soft bodies are not particularly astounding; they are simply a collection of particles. There are a few differences, however, between standard particles and soft body particles. For one thing, soft body particles are connected to hold a shape. For another thing, they appear on the screen (and in the final render) as a solid shape rather than as a collection of points. Because of these two properties, soft bodies are special: they can appear to be a solid piece of geometry but react like a bunch of particles when forces and motions are applied to them. Creating soft bodies in Maya is easy: you simply select your model and tell Maya to make a soft body out of it.

If you have not used soft bodies, you might wonder if the trouble of learning how to use them is worth it. Our advice is to do just one of the example exercises in this chapter. You'll discover that the animation effects you have steered clear of in the past because of their apparent difficulty will now be within easy grasp. The ability to use soft bodies to create flexible, fluid objects is indeed one of Maya's most powerful features.

What's New in Maya 2

Maya 2 brings with it numerous changes to soft bodies, from their creation options, to how springs are applied to them, to many "under the hood" changes in how their dynamics are calculated. If you have used soft bodies before, you will find the new interface and workflow a huge improvement over the old. Options are now more clearly available and labeled, and springs, especially, are a far more powerful and predictable tool than in the previous version.

Creating a Basic Soft Body

Create your basic Nurbs sphere in a new scene. Now, select Bodies ➤ Create Soft Body ❏ from the Dynamics menu set. The Soft Options window will appear with your soft body options. In this window, be sure that the Make Soft option (the default option) is selected from the Creation Options pull-down menu. Now click Create, and then click Close.

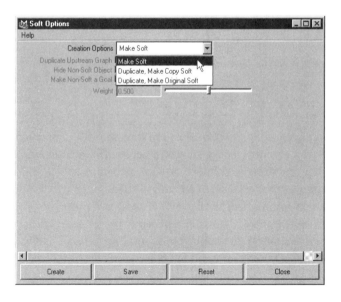

NOTE   If you used Maya 1, you will notice that this options window has changed significantly (and for the better) in Maya 2.

That's about it! You have just converted your original geometry (the sphere) into a soft body. You will see what looks like your original sphere, surrounded by a cloud of points (or particles) that actually define the shape. The number of particle points is determined by the number of isoparms (or polygon faces) in your original geometry. If you want more points (higher resolution effects), create your original shape with more isoparms. To see how this works, select the makeNurbSphere1 node and change the number of spans (or sections) to 8. You will see the number of soft body particles change to match.

Understanding the Structure of the Soft Body

Before we actually use our first soft body, let's take a quick look at its structure in the Hypergraph. Open the Hypergraph, and choose Options ➤ Display ➤ Shape Nodes. Your Hypergraph window should show something like the following.

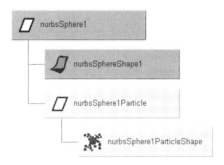

The highlighted nodes (nurbsSphere1Particle and nurbsSphere1ParticleShape) are your new soft body transform and shape nodes that have been attached to (and replace) your old sphere. If you highlight the nurbsSphere1ParticleShape node and look in the Channel box (as shown on the next page) or the Attribute Editor, you will see that the attributes listed there exactly match the attributes you'd find if you created a standard particle shape. When you finish examining the structure of your soft body, close the Hypergraph.

PART

6

Advanced Maya Effects

Channels Object	
nurbsSphere2ParticleShape	
expressionsAfterDyn	off
isDynamic	on
dynamicsWeight	1
forcesInWorld	on
conserve	1
emissionInWorld	on
maxCount	-1
levelOfDetail	1
inheritFactor	0
currentTime	1
startFrame	1
inputGeometrySpace	Geometry Lo
enforceCountFromHi	on
targetGeometrySpac	Particle Loca
goalSmoothness	3
cacheData	off
traceDepth	10
particleRenderType	Points
INPUTS	
makeNurbSphere2	

Using a Soft Body

Now that we have created a soft body, what can we do with it? First, let's create a
gravity field by which it can be affected. Select the sphere, and then choose Fields ➤
Create Gravity. Notice the gravity field now displayed in the center of the workspace.
When you play back the animation, the ball drops under the influence of gravity (just
as a rigid body would). Now, rewind the animation, move the ball up, and add a
plane to the scene (be sure to scale it large enough so that the ball will fall on it).

 WARNING   Remember that you always have to rewind a particle animation
before playing it back. If you do not, the results will look bizarre .

Select the sphere, Shift-select the plane, and then choose Particles ➤ Make Collide.
Now, as gravity forces the soft body to fall, the *particles that make up the soft body* will
collide with the plane. When you play back the animation, you should see something
like the following.

N O T E You will notice that the soft body collision is different from a rigid body collision. First, rigid bodies (the ones using the same rigid solver) will automatically collide with one another; for a soft body—as with standard particle groups—you have to define the collision. Second, each particle—not the solid surface as a whole—collides with the plane at a different time, giving rise to the sphere's distortion.

As when you created standard particle collisions (in Chapter 21), you have control over how the soft body collides with the plane. Both the soft body shape and the plane (in its geoConnector node) have controls for resilience (bounciness) and friction (how much the objects "stick" when they collide at an angle) for the collision. You cannot directly animate the soft body's resilience and friction; they are constrained to be the same values as that of the plane's geoConnector. To see how resilience works, try changing the plane's resilience attribute to a number larger than 1 (such as 1.2). When you play back the animation, the particles will bounce higher and higher (as, on each bounce, they rise 120 percent of their last height—impossible in our world, but not Maya's). If you decrease resilience to 0, the particles will simply stick to the plane when they strike it.

T I P Maya 2 supports negative resilience. With a negative value, your soft body will move through the plane and then bounce back toward it from underneath. If you use this feature with gravity, however, the particle will continue to fall (as gravity continues to pull on the object). To counteract this problem, you can keyframe gravity to change directions.

PART **6**

Advanced Maya Effects

Now move resilience back to 0.8 or so and be sure that the friction value is 0.6 or so. If there is no sideways movement to the particle (no movement tangent to the plane), you will see no difference. Try, however, adding a bit of shear to your gravity; make the directionX value of gravity 0.2 or so (select the gravity node at the center of the Maya grid or in the Hypergraph, and set directionX to about 0.2). When you play back the animation, you will see the ball move sideways under "gravity"; then, as it collides with the plane, it will slow on each collision. If the ball slides off the plane, just make the plane bigger (or enjoy the spill!). If you set friction to a large value, such as 4, the ball particles will actually bounce *backward* when you play back the animation because friction is greater than 100% (which is also impossible in the real world). If you make friction negative, the ball particles will surge forward on each collision.

 TIP   If you try to keyframe the ball's motion, you may run into a nasty little problem called double transforms. You will see the particles jump out ahead of the ball shape. To counteract this problem, simply group the soft body to itself (select the shape, and then press Ctrl+G), and keyframe the position of the ball using this new node (called group1 by default).

Adjusting Goal Weights

Now that we've created a soft body, let's make one that isn't so squishy. Make a new scene, and create a scene like the last one—a sphere above a plane (be sure to turn collisions on again by choosing Particles ➤ Make Collide). Now open the Make Soft Body options window (choose Bodies ➤ Create Soft Body ❑). Choose Duplicate, Make Copy Soft from the pull-down menu, check Make Non-Soft a Goal, and create the object (note that there is a slider for an attribute, goal weight, that is now enabled). Highlight the sphere, and create gravity. If you look in the Hypergraph now, you will see the original geometry (nurbsSphere1) and the duplicate soft body (copyOfnubsSphere1 plus the particle node).

 TIP   Generally, you want to hide the original geometry (by selecting that check box in the Create Soft Body options window). Here, we're leaving it visible so that we can see how the soft body and original geometry interact.

Play back the animation. You should see the sphere "sag," and then bounce back into nearly spherical shape. What's happening here is that soft body particles are being pulled down by gravity, but they have a "goal" to stay as close as possible to their original shape—the original sphere. Thus, they sag a bit and then try to bounce back to their original shape. We can alter how strongly attracted to its original shape a particle is simply by adjusting its goal weight. Select the particle node (you may need to do this in the Outliner or Hypergraph), and find the goalWeight[0] and goalActive[0] attributes listed there. They should be set to their default 0.5 (or 50%) and "on" settings, respectively. If you turn the goalActive attribute to "off" (by typing that in the text field), the soft body will fall away from the sphere when you play the animation, just as in our first example. Why? Because turning that attribute off tells Maya to pay no further attention to the goal weight. Now turn goalActive[0] back on.

TIP   GoalActive[0] can be keyframed, meaning that you can animate whether or not the soft body will attempt to match its original shape or simply follow the forces applied to it. The [0] for goalActive and goalWeight is a note that these attributes are for the first element in the particle array (they thus apply to the whole group). You can also alter goal weights on a per particle basis.

For more subtle control of goal weights, you can adjust the goalWeight[0] from its default 0.5. If you turn the goal weight up to 1, the soft body will no longer sag; it will now perfectly match the original shape. If you turn the goal weight down to 0, the soft body will fall away from the sphere; this is the same as turning off the goalActive attribute. Low numbers will make the soft body react strongly to gravity; high numbers will make it hold its original shape well. Try changing goalWeight's numbers, and then see how this changes playback.

Changing the Shape of a Soft Body

Now let's try changing the original shape and see how the soft body reacts. First, be sure your goal weight is about 0.3. Next, be sure you select the original shape (nurbsSphere1—not nurbsSphere1Copy!), and scale this shape out in the X axis. When you play back the animation, you will see the soft body stretch to fit the new shape of the sphere; it will overextend, however (as its goal weight isn't 1), and will "jiggle" back and forth until it finally nears the sphere's new shape. (You'll find a color version of the following image in the Color Gallery on the CD.)

PART

6

Advanced Maya Effects

Change the scale of the original shape back to 1, and then keyframe a Z rotation to the original sphere (try rotating it about 500 degrees in 40 frames). Now, as the animation plays back, the soft body shape will "balloon" out because each particle is being forced away from the original shape by centrifugal force. When the original sphere stops rotating, the soft body shape will oscillate until it adjusts back to the goal shape. (You'll find a color version of the following image in the Color Gallery on the CD.)

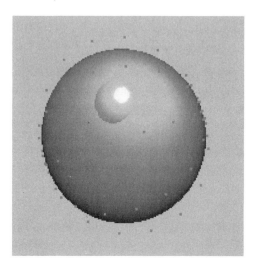

By now, you should start to see how powerful a tool soft bodies can be, so let's kick things up a notch. Not only can you adjust the soft body's goal weight as a whole, you can do it on a per particle basis. First, set your object goal weight (goalWeight[0]) to 1. With the particle node selected, in the Attribute Editor's Per Particle (Array) Attributes section, you will see a new per particle attribute called goalPP. This attribute controls the goal weight of each particle individually, just as the other per particle attributes do.

TIP   Because goal weights are now treated like other per particle attributes, you can use the methods you learned in the previous chapter to create goal weight ramps and expressions to control goal weights. You need to set your object goal weight to 1 because the object goal weight is multiplied by the particle goal weight (if a particle goal weight is 0.5 and the object goal weight is 0.6, the final goal weight of the particle will be 0.3). If the object goal weight is not 1, there will be some "play" in the entire object, and you will not see the results pictured in the next graphic.

Adjusting Goal Weights Using the Component Editor

Let's explore how to adjust goal weights using the Component Editor with our spherical soft body. In the text field next to the goalPP attribute, RM choose Component Editor. A window pops up that lets you control the value of a selected attribute. With the Component Editor around, move back into the scene window, and then switch to Select by Component mode and turn off all components but points.

N O T E   To change to Select by Component Type, select the Component Type button on the top toolbar (a cube with an arrow pointing at it). To turn off all types except points, choose All Components Off in the pop-up menu next to the button, and then click the Points button next to the menu (the black square).

Your sphere should have a cloud of blue-purple points around it. Select half the points on the sphere (the top, say), and, under the Particles tab, select all the goalPP column, and change them all to a value such as 0.2. When you play your animation, the top half should spin away from the original sphere while the bottom half stays put. (You'll find a color version of the following image in the Color Gallery on the CD.)

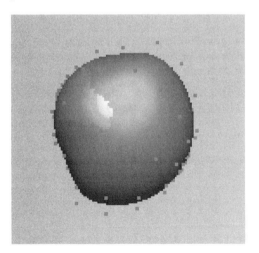

As an exercise, can you use your knowledge gained from the previous chapter to create an expression that randomizes the goal weight? If you can't figure it out, see the next section.

Using Goal Weights to Create Fluid Motion

Let's put aside our sphere test project for a moment, and create a new one. Save the sphere project for use later in the chapter.

In a new scene, create a nice, long, skinny cylinder (our tentacle), be sure that it has about 20 spans, and animate it to move back and forth on the X axis (try to make the motions happen at different speeds, including some very rapid motions). Then make the cylinder a soft body, this time hiding the original object and setting the goal weight to 1. (Note that, for space reasons, this and other images of the cylinder have been rotated sideways.)

When you play the animation, the (invisible) cylinder will move, forcing the soft body to follow. Because the soft body's goal weight is currently 1, it will move in perfect synch with the original shape—not very exciting yet. Now let's create an expression to alter the goal weights based on where each particle is. RM choose Creation Expression in the text field next to the particle's goalPP attribute. In the expression window, type the following:

```
float $scaling = 0.9;
float $offset = 0.1;

vector $pos = copyOfnurbsCylinder1ParticleShape.position;
float $posY = $pos.y;

copyOfnurbsCylinder1ParticleShape.goalPP =  ((($posY + 1) / 2) * $scaling) +
    $offset;
```

Most of the components of this expression are simply variable definitions. The one line that actually does something (the last line) tells Maya to assign each particle its goal weight based on how high up it is on the cylinder. The first two lines define a scaling and an offset constant. These variables adjust the range of values that the bottom equation will produce (in this case, 0.9 adjusts the range of goal weights to 0 to

0.9 instead of 0 to 1), and the offset of the values (in this case, the range will go from 0.1 to 1.0 instead of from 0 to 0.9). The next two lines read the (vector) particle position into a variable, $pos. This variable's Y component is then read into another variable, $posY.

T I P   You cannot directly read a single element (such as the Y component) of a vector attribute such as position into a scalar (float) variable. Thus, you have to first read the value into a vector variable and then take that variable's Y component and read it into another, scalar, variable.

The final line of the equation grabs the relative position of each particle (which is always between –1 and 1) and renormalizes it to a range of 0 to 1. The scaling and offset values are then used to further refine the range of goal weight values. When you run the animation, on the first frame, each particle is assigned a goal weight between 0.1 and 0.9, and then, depending on your cylinder's animation characteristics, the "tail" will waggle more the farther down the cylinder you go.

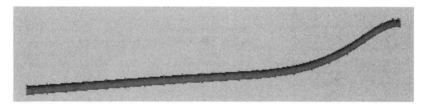

T I P   You can also paint goal weights directly onto objects like this tail using Artisan's Paint Attribute Tool. For more information on this tool, see Chapter 9, "Working with Artisan."

If your Component Editor is still open, you can look at the value of each particle by highlighting it (in component mode) and then clicking the Get Attribute button to see its value. We could, of course, have manually adjusted all the goal weights using the Component Editor, but it's sometimes nice to have Maya do the math for us. In this case, it would probably be just as fast to use the Component Editor to change the goal weights, but our expression gives us the ability (via the $scaling and $offset variables) to quickly play with the numbers to get the characteristics we want. Additionally, given a more complex shape with more points that are closer together, the above expression would be far faster than adjusting goal weights by hand. In short, use whichever way will prove faster and more flexible for your situation.

PART **6**

Advanced Maya Effects

NOTE   For more on expressions and particles, see Chapter 23.

Adding Springs to Soft Bodies

If you created violent motion on your cylinder in the last section, you probably noticed that, when you played back the animation, the bottom of your "tail" looked more like a flimsy piece of clay than a tail, because it stretched all over the place. In other words, the soft body did not maintain its length; it didn't have a kind of "bone" structure inside it, helping it to maintain its length and volume. Even more obvious, each part of the tail looked separate; what was going on at the bottom of the tail had no effect on the middle or top—not a good simulation of a tail! This is where Maya springs come in. They act (for the most part) just like little springs between each parti-cle, helping them to maintain their shape better under the stress of violent motion and allowing the motion of one particle to affect the motion of others.

Use your project from the last section (or, if you're not happy with that project, open the 24tail.ma file on your CD-ROM). Select your soft body shape in the scene window, and then choose Bodies ➢ Create Springs ❏ to open the Spring Options dia-log box.

In the Spring Methods section, set Creation Method to All (all particles are con-nected). You can leave all the other areas of this dialog box in their default state. Click the Create button, and then close the window.

TIP   You can create per spring (PS) attributes for stiffness, damping, rest length, and end weights. If you don't create per spring attributes, Maya uses per object attributes, just as with particles. Though we won't discuss modifying springs on a per spring basis, the method is the same as for per particle attributes, and the results can be extremely subtle and beautiful.

NOTE   The new wire walk length setting controls how much structure there is to your object. A walk length of 1 sets springs to each particle's closest neighbors on all sides. A walk length of 2 sets springs between the 2 closest neighbors on all sides. At higher settings the object will have more structure, but there will be an added calculation cost, as a result of the higher number of springs.

You will see a huge mess of dark dots (springs) covering your cylinder. As you play the animation, you will see the springs stretching and contracting to keep the cylinder moving in a more natural, connected motion. Once you get a look at the springs, you may want to hide them to prevent screen clutter.

NOTE   Spring calculation times have been dramatically reduced in Maya 2. Though they can still be slow in complex objects, they are now far more usable than they were in version 1.

With springs selected, you can (in the Channel box or Attribute Editor) adjust the stiffness of the springs (how resistant to bending they are) and their damping (how quickly they come back to rest after they've been moved). Although very low stiffness and damping values make the tail play back as if no springs are attached, increasing stiffness and damping can often create the rigidity that makes an object like ours appear to have a constant length. Try moving the damping up to about 0.4, and set the stiffness to 1 or a bit higher to get the tail to bend a bit more stiffly and not stretch as much. If you're lucky, you'll see your animation play back as it should. If not, you'll see the simulation go out of control.

PART

6

Advanced Maya Effects

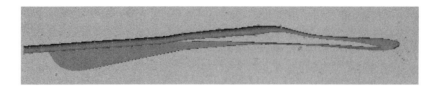

This bizarre behavior happens because Maya can't calculate the solution given its sampling rate (1 time per frame is default). The solution is to increase the sampling rate to allow Maya to better calculate the motion of the springs. From the Dynamics menu set, choose Solvers ➣ Edit Oversampling. The Attribute Editor opens with one option: Oversampling Rate (which should currently be set to 1). Try setting this number to 2 and see if that fixes the simulation. If not, move up to 3, and so on.

WARNING   Increase the oversampling rate slowly—it will severely affect your playback times! The number you put in the field is how many times longer the simulation will take to play than if the rate were set to 1, so increase by 1, and see if the simulation works; if not, increase by 1 again, and so on. Generally, very high values for stiffness and damping are not desirable anyway, so alter these numbers slowly as well.

As you can see, springs can really contribute to more realistic motion for soft bodies, so keep them in mind when your soft bodies look a bit too much like stretched taffy!

Faking a Bounce

Because of the new structure of dynamics in Maya 2, you can now create a soft body that has a rigid body as a goal—a nice new feature that was missing in Maya 1. However, there are times when, for control and accuracy (not to mention playback speed!), creating a bit of dynamics on your own can be advantageous.

TIP   The method for creating a soft body with a rigid body goal is the same as the one outlined earlier, except that you have to check the Duplicate Upstream Graph check box in the Create Soft Body Options dialog box. If you don't do this, the soft body will just go along for the ride, as if it had a goal weight of 1.

Create a new scene with a ball and a plane, and then type the following expression for motion into the Expression Editor (or just use the 24bouncerAnimated.ma file on the CD).

```
NurbsSphere1.translateY = 1 + (10 * (1 - linstep(0, 300, frame)) * abs
    (cos(time)));
```

This equation makes the ball bounce (using the cos, or Cosine, function) lower and lower, until the ball comes to rest (using the linstep function).

TIP The linstep function is useful. You give it a starting and ending value (frames here) and the "unit" it will be using (frames again), and then the function moves between 0 and 1 over that range. In this example, the value output by linstep increases from 0 to 1 over the range of 0 to 300 frames. (The smoothstep function performs the same function as the linstep function, except that it produces a smoothly varying curve instead of a straight line.)

Now we have a bouncing-ball motion. Let's add a soft body, adjust its goal weights, add some springs, and see what happens. First, add a soft body and set its goal weight to 1. Next, using the Component Editor (or the expression for goal weights given earlier), set the top points of the sphere to have a goal weight near 0.5, and set the bottom points to have a goal weight near 0. Keep playing with the values until you get a look something like this. (You'll find a color version of this image in the Color Gallery on the CD.)

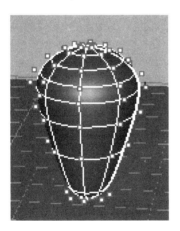

In playing back the animation, you should see the ball (the bottom especially) jiggle quite a bit. Although this could be a useful effect by itself, let's add some springs to it to give the whole ball a more connected look. Select the soft body sphere and add springs to it (you might try increasing the walk length to 2 here to give the ball more structure). When the ball bounces now, it reacts more connectedly, its sides moving in as the ball bounces away from the plane (thus imitating real life by preserving volume). Additionally, the ball now wiggles much less, because the spring dampens the extra motion—of course, this is adjustable via the damping and stiffness controls. (You'll find a color version of the following image in the Color Gallery on the CD.)

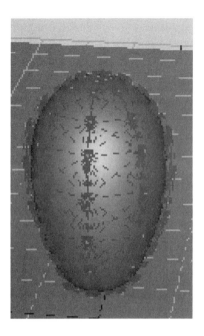

One last thing to check out with these springs is using the rest length setting (available in the Channel box or Attribute Editor). First, be sure the restLengthPS setting is off, and then try adjusting the rest length. If you set the number to 0, the ball will shrink dramatically; whereas if you set the value to 5 or 6, the ball will expand. The rest length tells the springs how far apart they should be when "resting" (in other words, when they're not being moved by forces or collisions), so the larger the number in the field, the bigger the distance between springs (and thus points), and thus the larger the sphere.

T I P   One great new feature is the ability to place springs between standard particles (not just soft bodies). You can connect a stream of emitter particles to form an interacting group, enabling you to produce anything from a simulation of molecules in a room to a "blob" that can shoot across the screen. For more information on adding springs to standard particles, see the Springs topic in the Maya 2 online reference. Also see `23cloud-srping.mov` in the CD for an example of particles using springs.

Denting Soft Bodies

To see how we can use soft bodies for modeling as well as animation, we're going to take a look at two ways to create an asteroid:

- By using a turbulence field to distort a sphere
- By using an emitter to bombard the sphere with particles

Open a new scene and create a sphere with about 32 spans and sections (so that the soft body will have lots of points on it). If you wish, you can stretch the sphere up a bit, since no one ever heard of a perfectly round asteroid!

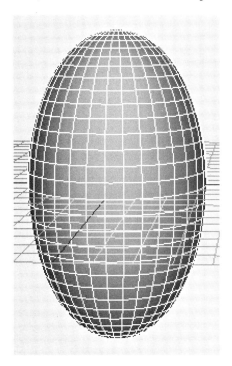

Save this project now as a separate file, because we'll use the sphere again when we create an asteroid using a particle emitter. With the sphere selected, choose Bodies ➣ Create Soft Body ❑. In the Soft Options dialog box, set the Creation Options to Make Soft.

N O T E   Choosing Make Soft tells Maya to convert the object to a soft body (there will no longer be any original geometry). Because there is no goal object, there is no goal weighting for this type of soft body.

Now, with the new soft body selected, choose Fields ➣ Create Turbulence ❑, set the magnitude (force of the turbulence) to about 5 and the frequency (the number of "waves" of turbulence) to about 20, and create the field. As you play the animation, you will see the sphere distort under the influence of the turbulence field. Since there is no goal weight to bring the sphere back, the sphere will distort too much if the

PART

6

Advanced Maya Effects

animation plays back too long. Try a few settings for magnitude and frequency, and stop the animation at a frame where you like the look of your new asteroid. (You'll find a color version of the following image in the Color Gallery on the CD.)

Now that you have the shape, getting it to be a permanent model is as easy as duplicating the shape. With the soft body selected, choose Edit ➤ Duplicate ❑. In the options window, be sure Duplicate Upstream Graph is *off*, and then duplicate the object by clicking the Duplicate button. Voilà, one ready-built asteroid!

N O T E   If you were to duplicate the upstream graph (the input connections), Maya would create another soft body that would then change with the turbulence field. By turning this option off, the model will be a standard node with no history.

T I P   If you see a group of points when you move your duplicate copy (the duplicate soft body points), you can simply delete them.

You can now either delete the original shape or alter its shape and the magnitude and frequency of the turbulence field to make a few more asteroids.

N O T E You can also turn lattices into soft bodies. As an exercise, try adding a lattice shape to your original sphere, turning the lattice into a soft body and then adding a turbulence field to the lattice. How does this alter the way the distorted sphere looks? You might like the results better.

Now that we've used a field to convert a sphere into an asteroid, let's try using an emitter plus a field (emulating lots of little meteorite collisions) to do the same thing. Open your original sphere, and make it a soft body, using the Duplicate, Make Copy Soft option, checking the Make Non-Soft a Goal box, and setting the goal weight to 0. Next, create an emitter that shoots particles at a rate of about 50 toward the sphere.

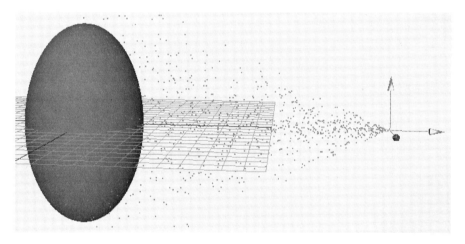

Select the particles (not the emitter), and choose Fields ➢ Add Air ❑ (be sure you choose Add, not Create). In the options window, click the Wind button, and then set the Magnitude to 20, the Directions X, Y, and Z to –1, –0.1, –0.1, respectively. Be sure Use Max Distance is on, and set it to 1; then click Add and close the window. You will now have a wind field that is owned by each particle (the air icon will move along with the particles if you play the animation). Because the Use Max Distance setting is on and because the distance is only 1 unit, each particle will create a little "ball" of wind around it that will affect any object connected to it. What we need to do now is simply attach the sphere's particles (not the emitter's) to the wind field, and the field will distort the surface of the sphere.

Select the soft body sphere, and then open the Dynamic Relationships Editor (choose Window ➢ Relationship Editors ➢ Dynamic Relationships). On the right side, highlight the airField1 text, and then close the window. Because the particles now strike the sphere, it will distort—probably more than you want it to! Never fear—we're going to use a little trick from earlier in this chapter to fix that problem. With the soft body again selected, open the Expression Editor and type in the following expression:

```
goalPP = rand (0.3, 0.6);
```

This expression simply sets the goal weights of the soft body's particles to a random number between 0.3 and 0.6. Now, as the particles (plus their air field) pass through the sphere, different parts of the sphere will react in differing amounts to the air field, creating a more interesting look to the distortion. Try adjusting the numbers for different effects.

N O T E   You will need to be sure that the per-object goal weight is set to 1 for this effect to work properly. Also, you will need to increase the magnitude of the wind field to about 500 to see results.

To get an even spread of dents, try rotating the sphere around its Y axis twice (720 degrees) over about 200 frames (select the sphere, and then key its Y rotation value between 0 and 720).

One last adjustment we can make is to force the particles to collide with the sphere. You may have noticed that, now, the particles pass through the sphere and dent it outward on the far side of the object—not what a meteorite collision would do! Select the emitted particles first, Shift-select the sphere, and then choose Particles ➤ Make Collide. Now, when the particles strike the sphere, they bounce off, creating only dents, not stretches in the sphere.

T I P   You can make a couple of adjustments to fine-tune your collisions: (1) try increasing the magnitude of the wind force to about 1000; (2) change the value of the resilience for the collision, and see what different values produce. A low resilience will keep the particles around the sphere longer, creating deeper pits.

Although playback can be a bit slow with fields and collisions turned on, you can do millions of years of damage to your asteroid in just minutes! You'll find a color version of the following image in the Color Gallery on the CD.

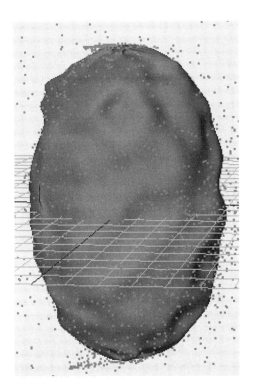

To create a permanent model from your new asteroid, simply stop on a frame you like and duplicate the object, as we did earlier. As you can see, soft bodies can be a fast way to create organic, or beat-up, shapes.

Advanced Hands-On Maya: Adding Ripples to the Fountain Project

If you thought we were finished with the fountain project after the previous three chapters, guess again. We have been leaving out an important part of our animation: the plane that the water drops strike. In real life, of course, the water in a fountain is agitated from the water that constantly falls on it—not like our flat and unassuming plane at all. To correct this, we'll make the plane a soft body and let the particles "collide" with it by having them carry an air field with them, just as we did earlier with the asteroid.

WARNING   Creating the large number of particle collisions in this project can be time-consuming. If you don't have a fast computer, you might want to just read through this section—or just attach an air field to the first group of particles.

Open your fountain project from the previous chapter (or use `fountain3.ma` on the CD-ROM). Select the plane, go to makeNurbsPlane1, and then increase the *U* and *V* spans to about 50 so there will be more points for the soft body you will create. For a more accurate simulation, you can increase this number, but remember that Maya will slow to a crawl on all but the fastest computers, even at this setting. It's going to have to do a ton of calculations for each point on the grid!

Once your plane is subdivided, make a soft body out of it, using the Duplicate, Make Copy Soft option and setting the goal weight to 0.4. Once the plane is a soft body, you need to add an air field to particles 1 and 2 (and 3, if you want even longer render times!). Select each particle group, and then add (not create) an air field, just as we did in the previous section. Set the magnitude to about 500, the X and Z directions to 0.5, and the Y direction to –1. Be sure the Use Max Distance check box is on, and set the max distance for particle1 to about 1; set the max distance for particle2 (the smaller ones) to about 0.5 so that they will make smaller "splashes." Once the air fields are created, link them to the soft body plane (choose Windows ➢ Relationship Editors ➢ Dynamic Relationships; then highlight the air fields).

You can now (attempt to) play back your animation. You will probably find, however, that the playback speed is so slow that it is difficult to see the motion of the particles and waves. To compensate for this, either playblast (choose Windows ➢ Playblast) or hardware render the scene. When you can view the motion of the plane, you should see reasonably good results. Each collision "dent," however, simply exists on its own; the waves don't connect and move. To solve this, we need—you guessed it—springs (as if playback weren't slow enough already). Here is where the real compromises begin. It would be ideal to create springs between all particles, using a large walk length (such as 3 or 4); however, unless you have a beastly computer with lots of RAM, this will not be possible, because the process of creating springs will generate a memory error (there is not enough memory to create all the springs needed). Instead, try creating springs with a wireframe setting and a walk length of 1 (so that each particle is connected only to its nearest neighbor).

TIP   If you have a fast computer with lots of RAM (512MB or so), try using a Min/Max setting, with a minimum spacing of about 0.1 (or just 0) and a max of about 2. This will produce better results, because more particles are connected, but it will be slower than the wireframe choice.

The waves will not propagate outward fully now, but the effect will still be better than it was. Set the damping value of the springs very low (at 0.05 or lower) so that the waves continue moving after the collision, and set the stiffness to a middle value such as 0.6. When you look at your playblast or hardware render of the scene, notice how the waves interact with one another and with the particles. If they don't look good enough to you, try adjusting spring stiffness and damping, as well as air field magnitude and max distance. With some patience (for the renders!) and experimentation, it is possible to get good-looking results. A final render of this scene is available on the CD-ROM (24fountain.mov).

When creating complex dynamics simulations involving soft bodies—and especially springs—the art of a successful project is often a compromise between the best settings and those that aren't quite as accurate, but will get the job done on deadline. If, for example, this fountain was a background element of your scene, it would make no sense to create such a time-consuming, accurate simulation. Simply make the plane a soft body, and add a turbulence field to simulate ripples. If, on the other hand, the fountain will be the center of attention, it is probably worth the effort to create this effect, because the inaccuracy of a simple turbulence field will call attention to itself. You, the artist, must decide where perfection and efficiency meet in these situations.

Advanced Hands-On Maya: Creating a Watery Body and Face

For the second advanced tutorial, we're going to build a long neck with a face attached to the end of it. We'll make this figure a soft body and then animate the face and goal weights, creating an effect similar to the ground-breaking effect in the film *The Abyss*. Open the file 24abyssDeformed.ma on the CD-ROM. If you play back this scene, you will see the "pseudopod" move in a bending path toward you, the face finally ending up looking at you.

Let's now use some blend shapes to alter the face's expressions (two blend shapes are built into the CD-ROM file). As the face moves through the tube, shut its eyes, and give it a neutral expression. When it stops (after about frame 160), have it go through two or three more expressions, and then return it to neutral by the end of the animation (about 400 frames).

TIP If you want your file complete with blendshapes and lighting, use the 24abyssBlended.ma **file on the CD-ROM.**

PART 6

Advanced Maya Effects

Now for the soft body stuff. We're going to turn the whole pseudopod into a soft body, adjust the goal weights on it, add a turbulence field to it, and then animate the goal weights to make the face pop out of the pseudopod. First, drag a selection marquee around the entire body; then make it a soft body with Duplicate, Make Copy Soft, and a goal weight of 1 (we'll adjust individual goal weights later). Test the soft body to be sure it animates properly (if not, go back to the saved version and try again). Because the goal weight is currently set to 1, the animation should look pretty much the same as before.

This is where things get tricky (it's an advanced tutorial, after all). Because the head is constructed of several (eight, to be exact) objects and because we need to vary the goal weight, we need to control all of them via an expression that we'll cut and paste into each particle shape's goalPP attribute. First, however, find the two long cylinder pieces, and change their global goal weights to 0.5. They will be at this goal weight constantly, so we don't need to do anything further with them.

Now, type the following into the Expression Editor, and copy it so that you can paste it into all eight goalPP runtime expressions.

```
float $goalStart = 0.6;
float $goalUp = (0.6 * smoothstep (181, 190, frame)) + 0.25;
float $goalDown = (0.6 * (1 - smoothstep (361, 385, frame))) + 0.25;

if (frame <=180)
    {
    goalPP = $goalStart;
    }
else if ((frame >180) && (frame <=360))
    {
    goalPP = $goalUp;
    }
else goalPP = $goalDown;
```

This expression sets the goal weight of each particle based on which frame it is in the animation. Early on (during the pseudopod's motion), the goal weight is lower. In the middle, during the facial expressions, the weight is higher, rising using a smoothstep function. At the end, again, the weight is lowered back down using a smoothstep function.

TIP   You could also control the goal weight for each segment of the face by keying the per object goal weight. This technique is more intuitive, but requires keyframing eight objects. Use the method that seems easier to you.

Now that the goal weights are animated, let's add a bit of turbulence. Drag-select all the soft bodies, and then choose Fields ➤ Create Turbulence ❏. Set Magnitude to about 60, Attenuation to 0, Frequency to a high number such as 100 or so (this will make for smaller waves), leave Phase as-is (at 0), and set Use Max Distance to off. As a final touch, we parented the air field to one of the head soft bodies so that the turbulence would travel along with the form. You might like the turbulence to stay in one place while the figure moves through it; try both ways and see which you prefer.

If you like your animation, all that's really left is to create and apply a water texture. Try creating a phongE shader with a pale blue color (almost white), slightly roughened, but tight and bright specular colors, and a good deal of transparency (only the highlights of water really show well). You might also add a background image or geometry and set the shader to have a refraction and reflection so that it looks more like water. A finished movie is available on the CD-ROM as 24waterHead.mov, and you can see a rendered still in the color insert.

N O T E   For more on how to create materials, see Chapter 18, "Rendering Basics."

This animation (and the fountain we developed earlier) should take you a good deal of time to get right. Work like this is the culmination of your understanding of the entire Maya dynamics package, so, when you do finish, congratulate yourself on a job well done!

Summary

In this, the final chapter on Maya dynamics, you learned what soft bodies are, how to create them, and how to use them for everything from simple animation effects, to modeling, to adding the final touch to complex projects. As a group of particles that act as a whole, soft bodies are a unique blend of form and motion, allowing us to create effects that would otherwise be so difficult to do correctly that we probably wouldn't. Although this chapter—indeed all the chapters in this section—only begin to reveal the power of Maya dynamics, we hope that you now have enough knowledge and the confidence to continue experimenting and working on your own. Think of something you always wanted to animate that has clouds of dust or jiggling, organic figures in it. Now go on and create that animation!

In the final chapter, we will look at Maya 2.5's new Paint Effects module, which provides a different way of creating organic, variable effects. Although it is not directly related to particles, Paint Effects' use of tubes, expressions, and random variability should be much easier to grasp now that you have a solid understanding of how Maya's particle system works.

PART **6**

Advanced Maya Effects

chapter 25

PAINT EFFECTS

Featuring

- *Paint Effects theory*

- *Strokes and brushes*

- *Painting on a 2D canvas*

- *Painting a 2D texture on a 3D object*

- *Painting in a 3D scene*

- *Editing previous brush strokes*

- *Adding forces and animation to brush strokes*

- *Rendering*

25

PAINT EFFECTS

Have you ever walked through a forest or a field on a beautiful fall day, and thought to yourself, "Wouldn't it be great if someday I could render a scene even half as complex and beautiful as what I'm seeing right now?" If you're a CG artist, we're sure you have many times. However, up until the release of Maya 2.5, with its new Paint Effects module, the dream of rendering a fully 3D natural environment or other organic object (like hair, plants, or food) has been an onerous task involving proprietary software and loads of difficult modeling and animation. It's little wonder that, until recently, most CG work has involved lots of spaceships and desert planets! The complexity of the problem facing the computer artist in recreating nature's many wondrous sights has been daunting, to say the least; not only are there thousands of details to recreate, they must all look natural (e.g., no straight lines or simple repetitive textures) and, ultimately, they all need to move about in a realistic fashion. This bewildering array of technical and artistic problems has kept all but the bravest CG pioneers firmly in the land of artificial objects or simple backdrops.

With Paint Effects, however, the rules have changed. Paint Effects is a brush-based paint program that lets you paint textures onto 2D objects (like the default canvas) or a texture map for a 3D object. (Its interface will feel similar to the Artisan brushes you used in Chapter 9.) More uniquely, you can paint 3D objects into your scene, fully textured and animated—all at the drag of your mouse or graphics tablet! You can paint hair, trees, grass, cornstalks, pasta, or many other default Paint Effects brushes into your scene, or you can get really creative and start making your own brushes, either using the included brushes as templates or designing them from scratch. If you paint a 3D object into your scene and wish to change its parameters (its texturing or how much it blows in the wind, for example), you simply select the node in your scene (Paint Effects brushes are node-based, just like the rest of Maya) and change whatever attributes you wish! It's hardly an exaggeration to say Paint Effects will change the way you work and even the way you think about CG work; more importantly, it will give you a huge edge over your competition, who will have to pick up their jaws off the floor when they see your work!

We introduce Paint Effects tools in a gradual, logical manner in this chapter, building your knowledge of this new feature step by step. This method will give you an excellent basic knowledge of Paint Effects, but you may wish instead to read the chapter out of order, skipping ahead to sections you are most interested in first. Feel free to read the chapter sections in any order you wish, and, most of all, play with Paint Effects as much as you can while you read this chapter. You will discover that a bit of guided interaction with a particular brush is your best instructor.

Paint Effects Theory

Paint Effects uses a "splat"-based (or tube-based)—rather than geometry-based—model for painting in both 2D and 3D. Thus, Paint Effects brushes can be rendered very quickly (compared to geometry) while still maintaining a high-quality look, plus texturing capabilities. Because the brushes are tubes (actually just curves) that can be rendered into three dimensions, you can work very interactively with the brushes (especially in wireframe mode) while producing astoundingly realistic effects. Also, because the rendering is done on the fly, you can freely move a camera (or the Paint Effects objects) in the scene, and the brushes will render properly from any angle. The combination of interactive "modeling" (though painting is closer to one's actual interaction with Paint Effects), fully 3D renders, and high-quality texturing and shadowing make Paint Effects an eminently usable feature, right out of the box! Additionally, being able to add forces like turbulence, wind, and gravity to any Paint Effects brush means that you can animate your scene in a quick, intuitive manner that looks great.

N O T E   The forces you apply to Paint Effects brushes are not actually calculated by Maya's dynamics engine, but are in fact expressions applied to the brush tubes. This means you can animate several trees, or the hairs on someone's head, with very little penalty in interactivity or rendering.

Paint Effects takes advantage of the depth buffer to do its rendering magic. The Paint Effects renderer uses the depth (or Z) buffer, in addition to six other buffers, to figure out where paint strokes should be placed in the 3D scene, then it splats the objects there, fully anti-aliased and rendered. The Paint Effects renderer is not a scan line–based rendering pass, it is actually a post process, meaning that all geometry is rendered first, and then the Paint Effects elements are added into the render. While Paint Effects is a post process, however, it allows things like transparency (which is traditionally *not* possible in depth buffer effects), out-of-order draw, glowing paint strokes, depth of field, and motion blur (both 2D and 3D). The strokes are tubes that can be fully drawn along their length and separated by gaps, and nearly all Paint Effects elements (or attributes) can be keyframed or animated—or both.

If Paint Effects sounds groundbreakingly, earth-shatteringly fantastic, just wait until you see how easy it is to use. After reading just a few pages here, you should be up and running with this feature, which is worth the price of admission to Maya 2.5 Complete all by itself. But enough superlatives, let's get painting!

Strokes and Brushes

Artists always begin by selecting their tools. To use Paint Effects, you first have to decide what line and effect you're going to produce—or, in this case, what your stroke and your brush should look like. Once you have a clear vision of the look you're after, you can create or modify the tools (strokes and brushes) to match what you want. Working with Paint Effects is a great deal like choosing a traditional paint brush and paint (the brush), and then setting down the appropriate line (or stroke) for the effect you're after.

Strokes

Strokes are the basic element that underlies all that Paint Effects does. They are, in essence, curves drawn in real time by your mouse or graphics tablet, and they can take the form of curves on a canvas, on a 3D surface, between surfaces, or even on the Maya grid plane.

Wherever they are placed (or "painted on"), strokes are the curves that either define the shape of a brush directly (as in a stroke of air-brushed paint) or "emit" brush tubes from them (as in grass blades or entire trees). While brush strokes are not particles, if they are set to emit tubes from their base curve, they can "grow" these tubes as you paint, the blades of grass, hair, or branches of a tree sprouting up from the stroke curve. In the case of trees, for instance, the strokes can emit a base branch, then sprout further branches and sub-branches, then sprout leaves, buds, or flowers. Alternatively, if you have already created a curve, you can convert it into a Paint Effects stroke, and your selected brush will be applied to the curve. If the stroke uses only the base curve you draw, paint will be applied to the curve itself. If the stroke emits tubes, the original curve will render invisible, and the paint will be applied to the tubes emitted from the curve.

T I P   Because tubes are emitted and grow (over time) from a Paint Effects brush, their growth can actually be animated, along with their other features. Thus you can create a field of flowers that grow up from the ground, or make a model's hair grow longer while the animation plays. You'll learn more about how to create this effect later in this chapter.

Brushes

Brushes are a set of growth and render options (or attributes) you set for a given curve; more simply, they are the "paint" you choose to paint with. Thus, while strokes define the shape of the curve you paint (as in a painter's brush strokes), brushes define the look of the paint.

There are nearly four hundred built-in brushes, including tube-shaped animals (snakes), animal elements (flesh, hair), natural phenomena (clouds, lightning, stars), traditional brushes (oil, felt pens, air brushes), metals and glass, plants of all varieties, and food (pastas, hamburger, corn). As you would expect from Maya, all these preset brushes are infinitely adjustable and animatible, allowing you to modify the built-in brushes to your fancy and save these new brushes for later use.

Brushes are stored in Maya2.5\brushes (on NT, the path would likely be C:\AW\ Maya2.5\brushes) and are accessible in Maya in the Visor window (Window ➤ Visor) or in the Visor subwindow of Hypershade (Window ➤ Hypershade). On opening the Visor (or Hypershade), scroll down to the bottom of the window, and click to twirl down the spin arrow next to the Maya2.5\brushes text. This allows you quick access to Paint Effects' thirty-plus folders of brush presets.

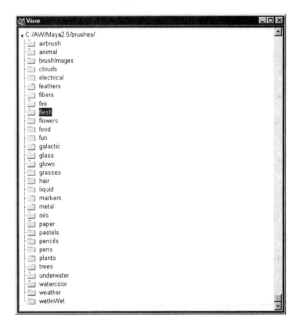

Open any folder, and inside will be brushes you can select simply by clicking on an icon. If you roll the mouse over an icon, the name of the brush will appear. Select a brush (say, Delphinium from the Flowers folder) and note that your mode is now set to the Paint Effects tool in the toolbar and that your cursor has changed to a pencil icon with a red circle under it (again, similar to the Artisan cursor).

Paint Effects Brush tool

Click inside your Scene window and paint a stroke or two. You will see the outline of several flowers appear. As soon as you release the mouse button, the flowers will reduce to a rudimentary outline, and you will see the base curve (the actual curve you drew) highlighted on the scene grid. You may also notice that the flowers are painted on the Maya scene grid; this is because the Paint Effects tool defaults to painting on the scene grid (or the X-Z plane) if no other objects are selected and set to be paintable.

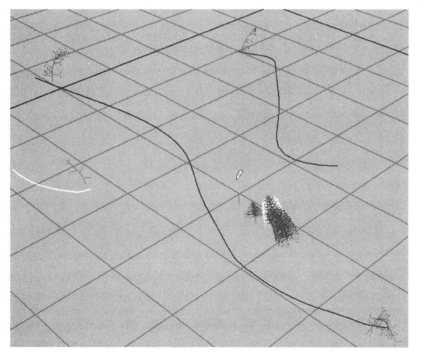

PART

6

Advanced Maya Effects

N O T E   In order to keep the scene responsive to your input, Maya automatically reduces the complexity of the curves and tubes it draws with the Paint Effects tool. You can adjust this reduction to your liking (see "Animating Brush Strokes" later in the chapter).

You may wonder why your brush strokes, while interesting, look nothing like a fully rendered flower. The answer is that, in order to see what your brush strokes will look like, you must paint in a special Paint Effects window, rather than in the default Scene windows. You can define this window to be either a 2D canvas or to mimic the perspective (or other) camera in your scene. We will begin with painting on a 2D canvas in the next section, and then move on to painting in a 3D environment later in this chapter.

Painting on a 2D Canvas

At its simplest level, Paint Effects looks a lot like traditional paint programs (Meta-Creations' Painter, for example). You simply paint on colors—or alter colors already present—and create a painterly image in two dimensions.

Start with a new Scene window (or erase the strokes you painted previously—choose Edit ➢ Delete All by Type ➢ Strokes), and then choose Window ➢ Paint Effects to open the Paint Effects window. You will probably see what appears to be your perspective view with a new set of icons at the top of the window. This is, in fact, the 3D environment for painting in Paint Effects. For now, we wish to paint on a canvas, so choose (from the panel menu bar, or RM choose) Paint ➢ Paint Canvas. You will now see a large white canvas on which to paint, with a set of new icons at the top of the window.

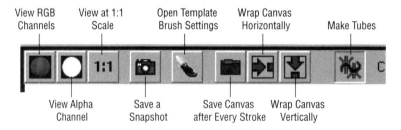

 T I P   To switch from your Scene view to the Paint Effects window and back, just press the 8 key on your keyboard (not on the number pad). As you will likely switch back and forth from the Paint Effects window to the Scene window(s) many times in a project, it is a good idea to memorize this shortcut. When you are in the Paint Effects window, you can momentarily access the Scene window (to pick an object, say) by holding down the Ctrl key and clicking in the window.

First, try painting on a few brush strokes. If you've been painting and have a brush still selected, you will see that brush painted on the canvas. If you have just opened a new session of Maya, you will see a black brush stroke (the default brush) painted on the window.

N O T E   In the 2D view, you have just one level of Undo, and it can only be accessed via the panel menu (Canvas ➢ Canvas Undo)—not by the usual Z key. You can assign this function to a hot key (like Ctrl+Z) via the Hotkey Editor (see Chapter 2 or 16 for more on assigning hotkeys).

Once you have painted a few brush strokes, you may wish to clear the canvas, so you can paint on new strokes. To do so, choose Canvas ➢ Clear, and the Canvas will be reset to its initial color (probably white). To change the background color of the canvas, choose Canvas ➢ Clear ❏, and choose a new color for the canvas from the Clear Color color chip.

Clear your canvas, choose a new brush from the Visor, and paint something interesting! You may find that on a traditional canvas like this, the more traditional brush types (oil paint, pens, air brushes, and such) look better than the organic brushes, but it's your canvas, so you get to decide. If you have a graphics tablet, you will find that many brushes have a built-in dependence on pressure, changing everything from color to size as you press harder with your stylus. You will also notice that as you move your cursor faster, many brushes will segment, not following your strokes in a continuous manner; this is because the brush strokes are merely a collection of "stamps" that the program places as you drag your mouse or stylus over the canvas. Thus, if you paint fast enough, you can "outrun" the spacing of the stamps and produce blank spaces in between. Sometimes this effect might be useful and sometimes not, so remember that Paint Effects is actually responding to the speed you draw your curves.

After you experiment a bit, clear your canvas once again (Canvas ➢ Clear) and turn on horizontal and vertical Wrap. You can choose Paint Effects ➢ Paint Effects Globals ➢ Canvas and toggle on Wrap H and Wrap V, but it's simpler just to click the Wrap icons in the Paint Effects window toolbar.

Now that you have Wrap on, try painting a brush stroke that goes beyond the edges of the canvas. You should see the stroke continue on the other side of the canvas, as if the canvas were wrapped into a ball where all sides meet together, like the canvas shown on the following page. This effect is, of course, extremely valuable for creating seamless tiles you could use as repeating textures in your Maya scene.

PART

6

Advanced Maya Effects

If you wish to see how the edges of your canvas look for this, or any set of brush strokes, you can roll the canvas in any direction using the Canvas ➢ Roll ➢ <item> commands. You can, for example, roll the canvas halfway horizontally (by selecting Canvas ➢ Roll ➢ 50% Horizontal) in order to see the vertical seam in the middle of the canvas. Another roll of 50% Horizontal and your image is back to where you started.

If you have a texture that is not currently seamless (or just for other effects), you can change the brush mode from Paint to Erase, Smear, or Blur, and alter the paint that is currently on the canvas. Choose Paint Effects ➢ Template Brush Settings (from the Rendering menu set), or click the paintbrush icon in the toolbar to bring up the Paint Effects Brush Settings window, which allows you access to all of the brush's settings. For now, just change the Brush Type pop-up to Erase (or whatever you prefer) and paint over your image. You will see that the brush stamp is now painting on an erase (or smear or blur) effect, which can make for very intricate effects, as illustrated on the next page.

To save your image (if you wanted to use the image as a texture file, for example), you can either click on the Camera (Save Snapshot) icon, or choose Paint ➢ Save Snapshot, and name the file. You can further modify the image in another program (like Adobe Photoshop) or use the file as a file texture on a scene object (see Chapter 19 for more information on using file textures).

Modifying and Saving Brushes

In addition to simply using the presets Paint Effects gives you, you can alter just about every parameter for a brush, and then save this modified brush setting for later use. There are several ways to modify the look of a brush; we'll go from the simplest method to the one that offers the most control.

Using the Toolbar Sliders

To make basic adjustments to color and transparency, you can simply change the color chips or sliders that reside on the top-right side of the Paint Effects toolbar. Clear your canvas, and then choose the Putty brush from the Oils folder. Draw a few strokes onto the canvas to see what the default brush looks like.

TIP   You may wish to scale your brush up to see the strokes better. To do so, just use the same hotkey as the outer brush radius for Artisan: the B key. By holding down the B key and dragging your mouse left and right, the brush stamp size will interactively change on the canvas, allowing you to see how large your brush will be.

For the Putty brush, you will only see two color chips and sliders in the toolbar (one pinkish, which sets color, the other a dull gray, which sets transparency). Change the pinkish color to something else by clicking on the color chip; then paint a few strokes to see your new brush in action. Next, increase the transparency (the gray color) by moving the slider to the right and paint some more. Your new strokes should look less solid (or more transparent) than before.

N O T E   You may have noticed that changing a brush setting will *not* affect your old brush strokes. Paint Effects strokes are each stored on a separate node (or, in the case of 2D work, they are just painted pixels), and thus will not automatically update when the brush profile is altered. In 3D scene painting, you can select and change old strokes, as we will see below.

If you like the brush you have created and wish to use it again in future work, you'll want to save the profile so you don't have to make the same changes over again. You can either save the brush to a shelf or in the Visor. To save the template, choose Paint Effects ➢ Save Brush Preset. In the Label field, name your brush (Blueputty, perhaps); in the Overlay Label field, type in any letters you would like to have printed on the icon overlay (this will only be visible if the brush is saved to a shelf). Choose either To Shelf or To Visor in the Save Preset box and, if you wish to save the brush to the Visor, type in the path to the directory where the brush will be saved. Finally, you can capture an image of the brush as an icon by clicking the Grab Icon button and then drawing a marquee around some strokes your brush made.

N O T E   Although Paint Effects is still a young program, most users already seem to prefer saving brush presets to a new shelf tab rather than to the Visor. This way, you can have ready access to different brushes in a convenient shelf. Of course, the choice of where to save brushes is completely up to you! For more information on creating shelves, see Chapter 2.

Blending Brushes

For broader brush control than is available through the color and transparency sliders, you can easily combine two or more brushes into a third brush that shares the qualities of both parents. Reload your basic Putty brush by selecting it again in the Visor. Now let's combine this brush with something natural, like the fernOrnament brush in the Plants folder. Be sure the Putty brush is selected first, then roll your mouse over the fernOrnament brush and RM choose Blend Brush 50% (you will see several other blend modes, which you can play with as well). Now when you paint strokes onto the canvas, you will see that your brush has become a sort of hybrid between the putty and fern brushes. If you continue to RM choose Blend Brush 50% from the fern brush, you will continue blending the brush toward the fern look, and your strokes will look more and more like the basic fern preset.

For even more control over the blending of shapes and shading between two brushes, choose Paint Effects ➤ Preset Blending, and adjust the two sliders for shape and shading. If you then choose another brush preset, it will be blended in with the other brushes according to the percentages you set. This way in just a few minutes of experimentation, you can create completely new, unique, and fun brushes for your own use. Try some blend of ferns, grass, and hair, and see what you come up with! To remove the blending effect, simply close the Brush Preset Blend window, and the next brush you pick will be loaded at 100%.

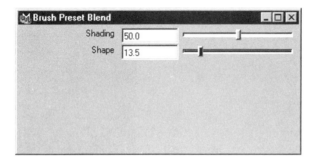

Using Brush Settings

The final way to adjust brushes is to use the Paint Effects Brush Settings window (Paint Effects ➤ Template Brush Settings). Here you have access to the "guts" of any Paint Effects brush, with control over everything from brush profile to lighting and shadowing effects to animation and forces. There are literally hundreds of settings you can adjust here (try twirling down some of the arrows to see how many nested menus there are!), so there is simply no way to cover all of them here.

TIP   If you need information about a specific setting, look in Using Maya: Paint Effects, which was included with the manuals that shipped with Maya Complete. You may also find that simply altering the setting and examining the resulting look of the brush will give you enough feedback about the purpose of this setting that you need look no further.

Instead, let's take a look at a few settings, and you can experiment with others as you go. It is no understatement to say that getting to know the Brush Settings window is paramount to becoming a skilled Paint Effects user. This window is where all the action is, and you need to understand enough to make intelligent changes to the settings in this window to control how your brushes will look.

Let's start with a simple brush. Choose the markerRed brush (in the Markers folder). Paint a few strokes to see what the marker looks like in its default setting, then clear the canvas. Open the Brush Settings window (either click the paintbrush icon in the toolbar or choose Paint Effects ➤ Template Brush Settings) and twirl down the Brush Profile settings. From this group of controls, you can set, for example, the Brush Width, Softness, and Stamp Density of the brush (how frequently the brush creates a new stamp of its image as you drag your mouse). Try setting the Brush Width bigger, the Softness very small, and the Stamp Density to a large number (like 10). You should end up with something that looks like a bunch of interconnected circles—a very different-looking brush from the default marker! The Stamp Density placed the circles very close together, the Brush Width (obviously) increased the size of the stamp, and reducing Softness created sharply defined circles instead of a blurred stroke.

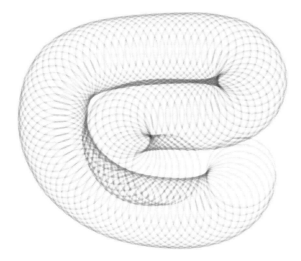

Under Shading, you can adjust the color, incandescence, and transparency of the marker brush. Illumination allows you to "light" the strokes (when Illumination On is checked), choose the light's direction (the Real Lights setting will not function in Canvas mode), and add effects like specular highlights to the brush. By setting Fake Shadow to On under Shadow Effects, you can add either a 2D offset shadow (a drop shadow) or a 3D cast shadow (the 3D cast often works best in scene painting mode). Under the Glow tab, you can set several Glow attributes. You can set Gaps in your brush, so it appears more like a dotted line than a continuous curve, via the Gaps sub-menu. Finally, under Flow Animation, you can actually animate your brush strokes (more on this under 3D painting). Experiment with any or all settings and see what your brush ends up looking like. The next illustration shows a sample of a modified brush with gaps, and you can see a color version of this in the Color Gallery on the companion CD.

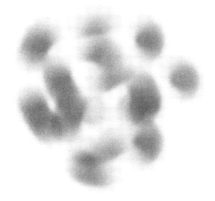

PART
6

Advanced Maya Effects

T I P   If you have a graphics tablet and want to map brush properties to stylus pressure, go to the Paint Effects Tool Settings window (Paint Effects ➤ Paint Effects Tool ❑). In this window, you have control over any three attributes you wish to map to pressure. Simply pull down the mapping pop-up, choose an attribute to map, and set the min/max values.

Now let's try a tube-based brush, to see how we can actually alter the attributes of the tubes that grow from a brush like this. Select the fernOrnament brush from the Plants folder, draw a few test strokes, and then open the Brush Settings window. You can, of course, alter any of the color, lighting, shadow, and other settings we discussed above, but here let's look at the Tubes attributes. Twirl down the Tubes settings, and then twirl down the Creation sub-menu. If you set the Tubes per Step very high (like 7 or 8), you will no longer get individual fern fronds, but a mass of fernlooking things.

While interesting, this density is calculation-intensive, so reset the Tubes per Step to a low value (like 0.2). Just a sample of the controls you have in the Creation section includes making your ferns very long by adjusting the Length Max setting, changing the tube start and end widths by adjusting the Tube Width1 and 2 settings, altering the number of Segments for each tube (more segments means more of a flowing curve) and, of course, randomizing several of the settings, so each fern doesn't look identical to its neighbor.

Creation is just the start, however; under the Growth settings, you can turn any of the following on or off, and adjust settings for them as well: Branches, Twigs, Leaves, Flowers, and Buds. The default fern only has leaves and buds turned on, so try turning on branches, twigs, and flowers, and see what happens. Without even changing the default settings, just turning on these options creates a rather interesting shrublike brush, shown in the following illustration (there's a color version of this image in the Color Gallery on the CD).

Inside each of these Growth sections, you have control over how many items will be created, at what angles they split off from their parent tubes, whether all tubes will have children (the Dropout rate), whether the new tubes will twist (and how much), how large they will be compared to their parent tubes, and several specialized settings for each element. As an experiment, let's create something that looks like a flowering wild rose tree. Our leaves and flowers are obviously too large for a tree, so we'll have to modify our Growth settings. The settings we chose for different aspects of the brush were done mostly by trial and error; we made adjustments and painted strokes until we were happy with the look of the tree. Table 25.1 lists a collection of settings that produces the rose you'll see below.

TIP   Be sure to experiment with all these settings as you go, and draw on the canvas to see how your changed settings are affecting the brush.

Table 25.1   **SETTINGS FOR A WILD ROSE TREE**

Aspect	Setting	Value
Branches	Num Branches	4
	Branch Dropout	0.15
	Middle Branch	on
Twigs	Twigs in Cluster	4

Table 25.1	SETTINGS FOR A WILD ROSE TREE (CONTINUED)	
Aspect	**Setting**	**Value**
Twigs	Num Twig Clusters	2
	Twig Dropout	0.3
	Twig Length	0.25
	Twig Base	0.9
	Tip Width	0.7
	Twig Start	0.4
	Twig Angle 1	107
	Twig Angle 2	45
	Twig Twist	0.3
Leaves	Leaves in Cluster	4
	Num Leaf Clusters	4
	Leaf Dropout	0.25
	Leaf Length	0.1
	Leaf Base	0.05
	Tip Width	0.001
	Leaf Start	0.7
	Leaf Angle 1	105
	Leaf Twist	0.5
	Leaf Flatness	1
	Leaf Size Decay	0.48
Flowers	Petals in Flower	10
	Num Flowers	5
	Petal Dropout	0.14
	Petal Length	0.03
	Petal Base	0.03
	Tip Width	0.01
	Petal Twist	0.1
Buds	Bud Size	0.02
	Bud Color	a muted red

Of course there are a multitude of possibilities here; we can't cover the effect of all of these options. To choose two examples, Twig Start sets how high up the tree the twigs will begin appearing; and Leaf Start determines how high up a tree its trunk and branches are bare. Experiment with all of the settings, and refer to *Using Maya: Paint Effects* if you want to read about a specific setting.

For the buds, choose a color that stands out from the branch color. You can also change the two base leaf colors and how the two colors are randomized—try setting the randomization values very high and see what happens. When you are finished, you should have a shrub-like tree with large reddish flowers on it. The color version of the following illustration can be found in the Color Gallery on the CD.

NOTE Because tubes are drawn using recursive, fractal algorithms, where each layer of tubes depends on the settings for the previous layer, all tube sizes, lengths, and such are relative measures, not absolute ones.

NOTE In addition to color, you can actually map texture files onto flowers, leaves, and the main object tube itself. To map the main tube, go to Shading ➢ Texturing, set Texture Type to File, and choose an image to map in the Image Name text field (to browse textures, click the folder icon to the right of the field). For Leaves and Flowers, first uncheck the Leaf (or Flower) Use Branch Tex(ture) check box, then choose an image under Image Name. See the birchBlowingLight texture in the Trees collection for a demonstration of texture mapping colors on a brush.

Painting a 2D Texture onto a 3D Object

If you would like to create a texture map for a scene object using Paint Effects, the process is fairly straightforward. First, create a side-by-side layout (Panels ➤ Layouts ➤ 2 Side by Side), make the right side the Perspective view, and the left side the Paint Effects window (still set to Paint on Canvas mode). In the Scene window, create an object you'd like to paint a texture on—for this example, a simple sphere will suffice.

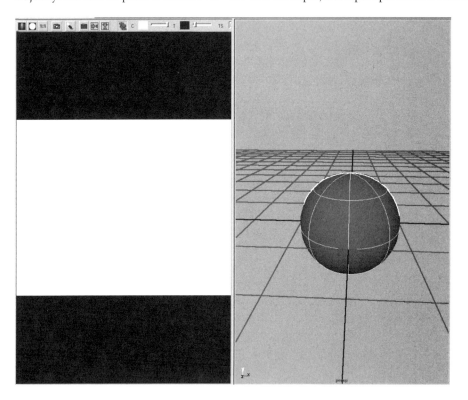

Next, open the Hypershade (or Multilister), create a new material, and assign a file texture to it. (For more on how to create textures, see Chapter 19.) From the Hypershade, first MM drag the material onto your scene object (to assign the material to it), then MM drag the file texture onto the Paint Effects canvas. A dialog box will appear, allowing you to assign the name and size (in pixels) of your texture.

Paint Effects New Texture

Image Name tempTex

X Size: 512

Y Size: 512

Apply Texture   Cancel

Click Apply Texture to File, choose Yes to save the file, and save it in your
sourceImages directory. Before painting on the canvas, choose Canvas ➢ Auto Save
and turn on Save After Each Stroke. When you release the mouse button each time,
you will see your texture updated on the scene object(s) to which the material is being
applied. Try painting with several brushes onto the canvas and see how your texture
map updates. Remember, you may wish to turn on Wrap Horizontal and Vertical to
allow your map to be seamless as it wraps around the object(s) in your scene. The
next illustration shows how Wrap appears on your canvas, and can be found in the
Color Gallery on the CD.

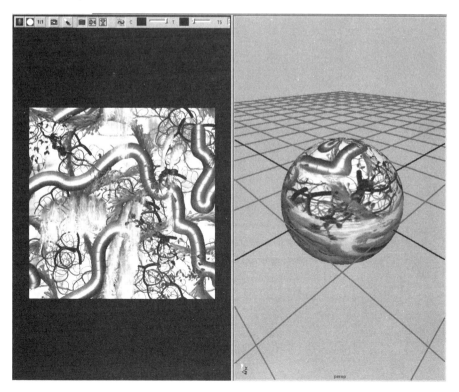

N O T E   The current version of Paint Effects has a "feature" in it that can cause a few headaches if you're not aware of it: if you choose Canvas ➤ Clear while painting a texture map, the canvas will become disconnected from the material, and you will have to assign the texture to the canvas again. To erase a canvas, then, you need to use the Erase feature of Paint Effects (under the Template Brush Settings) to erase unwanted strokes. (The reason for this feature is to keep people from accidentally erasing their file textures: with Save After Each Stroke on, clearing the canvas automatically erases the file texture, which apparently upset some Paint Effects beta testers.)

Painting in a 3D Scene

Now that we understand strokes and brushes, and how to use them in 2D, let's get on to the really interesting aspect of Paint Effects: painting in three dimensions. As all Paint Effects brushes are 3D curves that can (optionally) create tubes, you can paint in a scene as easily as on the canvas. If you open a new scene, choose a Paint Effects brush, and start painting, you will automatically paint on the scene grid (as we noted at the start of this chapter). This can work very well if you wish to paint trees, grass, or other elements on the "ground." If you wish to paint on an actual scene object, however, you need to select that object (or objects) and then tell Paint Effects that the object(s) is/are paintable.

In a new scene, create a NURBS Cylinder (be sure to cap the cylinder). In the Scene window, select the object and choose Paint Effects ➤ Make Paintable (remember, holding down the Ctrl key in the Paint Effects window momentarily enables the Scene window so you can select objects). If you are still in Canvas mode, choose Paint ➤ Paint Scene, to toggle on display of your scene.

We could choose to paint some hair on this object, but we'll wait on this until the tutorial later in this chapter. Instead, let's paint some other brushes on, like one of the grasses, an oil paint, and a waterfall (under the Liquid folder). Remember that you can alter the scale of the brush by pressing B and dragging the mouse.

 T I P   Many of the Paint Effects brushes require real lighting to appear, so you may need to add one or more lights to your scene to see your brushes in all their splendor.

 N O T E   Because painting on an object simply creates curves on the object's surface, you can select, move, modify (alter individual CVs), or offset these curves from the surface, giving you a great deal of control over the look of each curve.

If you tumble the Paint Effects window, you will notice that the brushes revert to an outline of their fully rendered selves in order to speed up redraw, so you don't have to wait for the full effect of the brushes to render each time. To change how Paint Effects simplifies the *display* of your strokes (not the actual strokes themselves), go to Template Brush Editor ➢ Tubes ➢ Creation ➢ Simplify. If you choose Tubes per Step, the redraw will remove many of the initial tubes from display (this is good for elements like hair). Choosing Segments removes portions of each tube object, but retains the initial tube for each one (this is good for trees, flowers, and the like). Choosing Tubes and Segments will (of course) reduce display of both. You can also force Paint Effects to redraw the entire window each time you move in the scene (Stroke Refresh ➢ Rendered), but this will slow your interaction with Paint Effects down a great deal. To force a redraw of the window after you have painted many strokes, click the Redraw Paint Effects View icon in the toolbar.

Redraw Paint Effects View

After some painting, your cylinder will probably look a great deal more interesting than it did in the first place! A color version of the following illustration can be found in the Color Gallery on the CD.

While painting in the Paint Effects window is great for getting the look of brushes down, it is often far more interactive to paint in the Scene view for large-scale jobs. When you switch over to the Scene window, you will be limited to painting in wireframe, but the painting will go much faster. One workflow example might be to create an interesting look for a tree brush or two in the Paint Effects window, then switch to the Scene window and paint a forest of these trees. When you create the forest, you already know what the trees look like—you just wish to paint them into the scene quickly and interactively, and the Scene window is better suited to this than the Paint Effects window.

TIP   If you wish to delete the last stroke you made in 3D paint mode, the normal Undo feature works fine. To delete selected strokes, simply select them (in the scene or the Hypergraph) and press the Backspace or Delete key. To delete all strokes in one fell swoop, simply choose Edit ≻ Delete All by Type ≻ Strokes, and all your brush strokes will magically disappear!

Take some time now to play with different brushes (altering them as you wish, or just using different defaults) and get a feel for how various brushes act in a 3D scene as opposed to a 2D canvas.

TIP   If you wish to create a curve first, and then attach a brush to the curve, select the curve in your Scene window and then choose Paint Effects ≻ Curve Utilities ≻ Attach Brush to Curve. In this manner, you can "multi-purpose" curves for brushes and other functions within your scene.

Editing Previous Brush Strokes

As you experiment with brushes, you may find yourself wishing you could go back and alter strokes you've already laid down (remember that each new stroke is a new node, so changing a brush will normally not affect older strokes). As Paint Effects strokes are just curve nodes in a 3D scene, you can choose these curves and alter any attributes you wish via the Attribute Editor.

As an example, let's choose one of the strokes you created on your scene object and modify it. You can try to select a curve via the Select tool, but you will likely choose many curves at the same time; the Hypergraph is a better way to choose an individual curve (you can also zoom in very close to a stroke and select it that way). When you open the Hypergraph, you will see dozens of nodes named stroke<*item*><*number*>, where <*item*> is the name of the brush and <*number*> is the number of that brush's stroke.

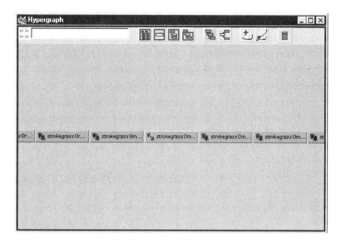

Choose one of the Grass strokes, then open the Attribute Editor (Ctrl+A). Under the grass<type> tab (the furthest right), you will have access to all the settings that were available via the Template Brush Settings window, only this time the changes will be made to the existing stroke. Try adding some flowers to the grass (under Tubes ➤ Growth), and change the color of the grass to something other than green (Shading ➤ Tube Shading). As you can see (this illustration can also be found in the Color Gallery on the CD), you have complete control over your brushes, even after you create them!

If you have several strokes that you wish to vary all at once, you can elect to "group" them so that they share one brush setting. This way, as you make adjustments to one brush, all the strokes will update simultaneously—a real time-saver. To accomplish this, select all the strokes you want to have share one brush. These strokes can have any brush attached to them, but be sure to select the one with the brush shape you want *last*, as the last stroke selected supplies the shared brush. Next, choose Paint Effects ➢ Share One Brush to make them all share the same brush settings. If you now open the Attribute Editor and change the attributes of the current brush, all the strokes you had selected will update together. If you had chosen, for example, to share the vineLeafy2 brush (in the Plants collection), you could change the default brush settings to include twigs, and all your strokes would come out looking something like the following (a color copy of which can be found in the Color Gallery on the CD).

TIP   To remove sharing between strokes, simply select the strokes, and then choose Paint Effects ➢ Remove Brush Sharing.

Adding Forces to Paint Effects Brushes

If creating still lifes isn't enough for you, don't worry; you can add dynamics to your Paint Effects brushes (at least the tube ones) and animate the brushes over time.

NOTE   Paint Effects brushes actually don't use dynamics (as do particles and rigid bodies) but use recursive expressions on the tubes nodes. While expressions aren't quite as wide-ranging as Maya's dynamics engine, using them was a very clever trade-off between speed and natural motion. Using Maya's built-in dynamics engine, even a single tree could take minutes per frame to update, whereas the expression solution allows for very fast updates, and even allows you to scrub the animation back and forth, which dynamics simulations cannot handle.

To see how to add dynamics, let's create some grass that blows in the wind. In the Visor, select the grassClump brush (in the Grasses folder), and, using the Paint Effects Template Brush Settings window, change the grass's Length Max (under Tubes ➢ Creation) to about 4, so there's a lot of grass to blow around. (There are, of course, preset grasses that include wind, but by starting with a grass that has no forces applied to it, you can build your own.) If you play back the animation now, you will see that the grass stays perfectly still as the animation plays. While you could adjust your brush settings in the Brush Settings window, and then paint a new stroke each time, it is easier to simply select the current stroke and go into the Attribute Editor and make changes. Your "sample" stroke will then update as you make changes, allowing you to see the effects of what you are doing.

With a stroke selected, click on the grassClump1 tab in the Attribute Editor, and open the Tubes ➢ Behavior subwindow. There are several menus under this: Displacement, Forces, Turbulence, Spiral, and Twist (Paint Effects is a deep program with lots of controls!). Feel free to play with any of these behavior modifiers, but we will concentrate on just a couple as examples.

First, twirl down Forces and adjust the Gravity setting. You will notice that the blades of grass bend over as if they're growing heavier and heavier as you adjust this setting. Due to the relatively few segments on the grass blade, the grass will bend at sharp angles when gravity is applied (of course you can change this by altering Tubes ➢ Creation ➢ Segments to a higher number, like 20). You can also make the grass stretch under gravity by setting the Length Flex to a number greater than 0. While a heavy, stretchy look might be great for some items, it's not particularly appropriate

PART

6

Advanced Maya Effects

for grass, so set the Length Flex back to 0. Still, we can make the grass a bit heavier by setting gravity to about 0.12). As all Paint Effects brush behaviors are based on expressions, you can either type a value for most attributes, or create an expression or a Set Driven Key to control that attribute. To create an expression or to set keys, RM choose Create New Expression (or Set Key) for an attribute; in the case of an expression, you would then write an equation that alters the value of said attribute. Try this simple equation to make the grass do "the wave." RM choose Create New Expression, then, in the expression window, type in the following:

```
Gravity = sin (time);
```

When you play back the animation, your grass should wave up and down.

N O T E   Several of the other controls in this block (like Path Follow and Attract) will be discussed in the tutorial section at the end of the chapter.

Now let's add some wind to our grass. First, delete the gravity expression from the expression editor, or RM choose Delete Expression over Gravity. Twirl down Turbulence, and choose Grass Wind from the Turbulence Type pop-up menu. Leave the Turbulence Interpolation set to Smooth over Time and Space (or feel free to experiment with the other settings), and try adjusting the Turbulence, Frequency, and Speed settings while your animation plays back. At their default settings, the grass will wave back and forth a bit, fairly quickly. To make it wave more slowly, set the Turbulence Speed to a small number. To make the grass blow more strongly, change the Turbulence slider to a large number. Turbulence Frequency controls how much space the turbulence field will vary across. In other words, setting the Turbulence Frequency to 0 will make every blade of grass blow just the same, while setting Turbulence Frequency to 1 will make them all blow independently. If you now go back and adjust the Forces ➤ Length Flex to 1, you'll get grass that stretches as it blows—an interesting, if unrealistic, effect.

T I P   If your playback speed is set to Free, you may find your animation runs too quickly, giving the illusion that your objects are moving around much faster than they will in the final render. To compensate for this, you might try setting the playback rate to Normal (Options ➤ General Preferences ➤ Animation tab) or, if your scene is complex (slowing down playback) or depends on Free playback for dynamics, just playblast the animation (Window ➤ Playblast) to get a better idea of its output speed.

Finally, once you get just the brush you were looking for, you will probably want to save it for later use. With your brush stroke still selected, choose Paint Effects ➤ Get Settings from Selected Stroke, and then save the brush to your shelf or the Visor.

NOTE The barn image included on the book cover, as well as the animation 25barn.mov on the accompanying CD-ROM, depends heavily on Paint Effects. The center color insert and CD also contain a still and an animation, respectively, of a more production-ready version of the fountain we created in the last several chapters; this fountain includes Paint Effects trees, grasses, moss, and other modified brushes (25fountain.mov). These animations (and the stills from them in the color insert) show off just a small portion of the possibilities Paint Effects opens to your modeling and animation endeavors.

Animating Brush Strokes

In addition to animating the tubes on your brush strokes, you can also animate the appearance of your strokes over time, enabling you to "grow" hair on a head, or flowers in a field. Let's do the latter, using the brush flowerTallRed (in the Flowers folder). First, make a nice long stroke in your Paint Effects or Scene window, so you have a nice bunch of flowers to work with.

To begin with, we need to change the simplification mode of the flowers (so we can see them better as we animate their growth). With the stroke selected, click the flowerTallRed1 tab in the Attribute Editor and, under Tubes ≻ Creation, set the Simplify method to Segments. Now twirl down Flow Animation to get at the settings for animating brush growth. Set the Flow Speed to a number greater than 0 (drag the slider, or, if you wish, you can set a value greater than 1 by typing in the number field). Next, check the Time Clip box, set the start time to 0 and the end time to a large number (the default is 1,000), and play back the animation. You should see all your flowers rise out of the ground at the same time, growing to full height over 40 or 50 frames.

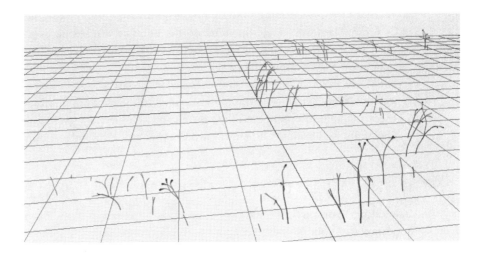

 N O T E   Setting the start time to a number greater (or less) than 0 allows the objects to begin growing after (or before) the animation starts. Setting the end time to a small number (like 1 or 2 seconds) will make the objects "decay" after that much time: they will disappear, starting at the roots. While this effect isn't quite right for flowers, it could be used in other instances (as in water drying up at its source of fireworks) to good effect.

Having all the flowers appear at once may not be what you're after. If, instead, you would like the growth pattern to follow your brush stroke, simply click the Stroke Time check box to enable the brush to remember the direction of your strokes. With both Time Clip and Stroke Time enabled for various brush strokes, you can create a field of grass and trees, or grow hair on a model's head, just as easily as drawing the curves! These flowers are growing at different rates:

Rendering

While Paint Effects is a very deep program with a great many controls, rendering is a relatively transparent process. To render a scene with Paint Effects brushes in it, all you need do is batch render (or test render into the Render View Window) as you would normally. When a render including Paint Effects brushes is launched, Maya first renders all the geometry in the scene, and then, in a post-render process, adds the brushes, fully rendered. Though Paint Effects rendering is a post-render process (after all geometry), the renderer is intelligent enough to place Paint Effects brushes properly in 3D space. In other words, a brush that is partially behind some geometry (like a cube, for instance) will render with that portion hidden from view. This way, though Paint Effects rendering is done after geometry rendering, you don't normally have to deal with the difficulties of masking and compositing the two elements together; Maya does this for you. The tutorial below covers the issue of partially occluded Paint Effects brushes in more detail.

N O T E   There is an exception to the rule that Maya precomposites Paint Effects brushes with geometry renders: refractions (for semi-transparent objects) and reflections. If you render a raytraced scene with refractions or reflections, you will not see the Paint Effects brushes in the objects that are refracting or reflecting. In order to circumvent this problem, you must render out your geometry and the Paint Effects brushes in separate passes and composite them together in a compositing package (such as Maya Composer, Maya Fusion, or AfterEffects). The fountain animation for this chapter (on the accompanying CD-ROM), as well as the still from this animation in the center color insert, use compositing to get the appropriate reflections and refractions in the water.

While most of the controls in a Paint Effects brush that have to do with rendering are fairly self-explanatory (color, textures, illumination, and so forth), two items are worth noting here. First, there is a Translucence setting for brushes (high translucence allows diffuse light to pass through an object), which can be very useful for plants, tree leaves, and hair. Second, you have two choices for shadowing: a 2D offset shadow (the drop shadow we discussed earlier in the chapter) and a 3D cast shadow. The 3D cast shadow is a "fake" shadow and thus might need some adjustment to produce proper size and density in your scene. The following tutorial discusses this issue further.

A few exceptions notwithstanding, rendering Paint Effects brushes is a very painless (and quick!) experience. With your understanding of the principles of rendering in Maya, you will find yourself producing great-looking images right from the start.

PART 6

Advanced Maya Effects

Tutorial: Painting Hair on a Head

Up until now, the boy you have created earlier in the book has been stuck with somewhat plastic hair. While you could explain it away as an overzealous use of hairspray, a better option would be to just give him some "real" hair. That's exactly what we are going to do now.

Start by opening one of your head models, or the included scene file `hair.mb`. The included project defaults to a close-up of the child's bald head. You'll notice that the rest of the child's body and IK system is hidden. We will make them visible later, but for now they would just cause unnecessary screen clutter.

Bring up the Side window fullscreen. You should be in shaded, textured mode. The hair is not very graphics-intensive, so we will be able to run at a fairly high window-display setting. This is good, because we will need the fine details to decide how and where to paint the hair. Select the head object and press the 3 key to increase the display quality.

In the Visor, go to `/AW/Maya2.5/brushes/` and open the Hair folder. Select the hairBlondeNoShape brush. Now, since the boy actually has black hair, we will blend the shading of the eyeBrowBlack brush at 100%. With your mouse over the eyeBrow-Black icon, RM choose Blend Shading 100%.

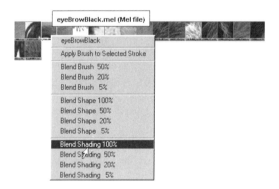

With the head still selected, choose Paint Effects ➤ Make Paintable. Now let's try a few strokes; click and hold down the mouse while drawing a line on the head. You will instantly see hair sprouting from the head, although it will probably not be long enough to give the impression that this child has much of a hairstyle. We need to change the brush size.

Interactively resize the brush with the B key (as shown previously in this chapter). You may have to experiment to get a size that works for you. Try painting different brush sizes, and once you get the hair size you want, delete all the strokes to start fresh (Edit ➤ Delete All by Type ➤ Strokes). You now have a clean head and a properly sized hair brush. The next step is to decide how the hair will be added to the child's head. There are quite a few ways to actually accomplish this. As is true with most of this book and Maya in general, the way that you should do something isn't limited to what we tell you. In fact, we encourage you to try many different ways and let us know if you find a better way. For this tutorial, many options were explored for getting hair on the head. It turns out that the most obvious, in this case, seemed to work the best for us: just paint the hair following the topology of the head model from front to back.

So, with that in mind, let's start giving this poor boy something to comb. You will notice that the included scene file contains two additional Orthographic cameras: Back and LeftSide. These are to make it easier to paint those areas of the head, since at press time Paint Effects did not have a mirror brush option as in Artisan.

Select the Side camera. We will start here, on the right side of the boy's head. Start your first stroke from the sideburn area and paint up and around the ear, to where the hair would naturally stop growing. The reason for starting here is that the more hair we add, the harder it will become to see the strokes as we make them. The area around the ear is the most critical (as it has to match the boy's sideburn and ear line), so we begin here.

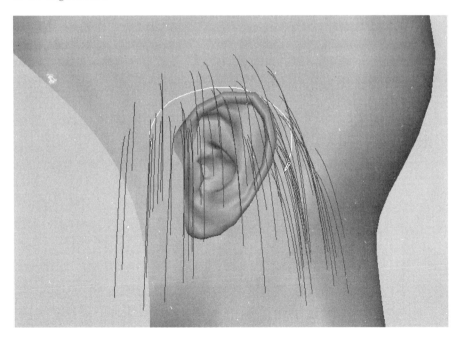

PART 6

Advanced Maya Effects

TIP   If you are painting a huge model, or one with very intricate curves, you can select your brush and, before you paint, select Paint Effects ➤ Paint Effects Tool, and change the Display Quality to 0. You will still see the hairs as you paint them, but when you lift your finger from the mouse button to get another stroke ready, they will disappear. You will be left only with the curves on surface visible, showing you where you painted without slowing your work down. Remember, this setting only affects the display, not the rendering of the strokes.

Now draw one stroke from the front to the back, but no more. Why? Because we are now going to set things up so that from this point on the hair will be shaped to the head as we paint.

 NOTE   The brush actually isn't shaping itself to the head, as much as following the direction of the curve that we are painting.

With the hair brushstroke still selected, open the Inputs for this brush in the Channel box or Attribute Editor, and scroll down until you find the attribute named Path Follow. Path Follow defaults to 0 for this brush because hairBlondeNoShape is controlling our hair's shape, while eyeBrowBlack is in control of the shading, but we need something a little different, so change the value to 0.7.

Now you will notice that the hairs that are already on the model's head have nicely aligned themselves to the shape of the head. Feel free to play with values in this field to get different results.

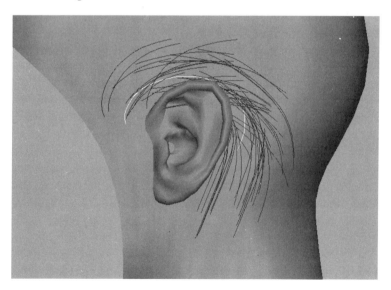

After you have a shape you like for your hair stroke, select Paint Effects ➤ Get Settings from Selected Stroke. This will ensure that as you paint each new stroke, the settings you have changed on the stroke you already have painted will be used for each subsequent stroke. Give it a try. It makes painting the hair and designing the shape of the hair style much more intuitive.

N O T E   If you also change the value of Path Attract to a non-zero number, the hairs will tend to "lean" towards the curve as well as follow its direction. This can be particularly useful when you paint braided hair and you want the hairs to be more compressed to the head in evident rows. You can also enter a negative number, to repel the hair and get an "Einstein" look.

Now start working your way up the head, drawing slow, even strokes from the front of the head towards the back. You should end up with somewhere between 10 and 15 brush strokes, which can be seen as curves on surface and show up in the Hypergraph as strokeeyeBrowBlackShape1, strokeeyeBrowBlackShape2, etc.

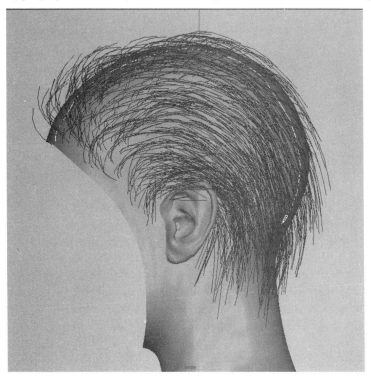

Now switch to the Orthogonal camera LeftSide and repeat the process for this side of the head. Our boy now looks as though he has a premature case of male pattern baldness, because we weren't able to paint the hair exactly on top of the head from the either of the side views. (The lines on the inside of the head model are the hairs slightly piercing the inner surface of the head. They won't be seen when the face is visible, so ignore them.)

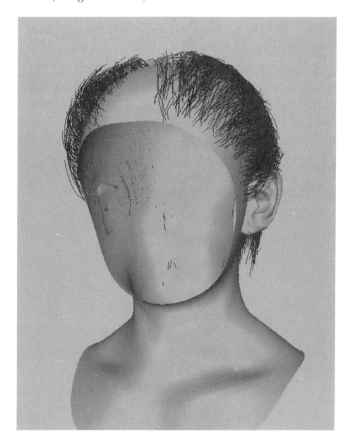

Switch to the Top camera and start at the forehead, painting towards the back of the head. Show caution here that your strokes don't touch the skin on the boy's back, as the brush will jump to that section, continuing the stroke but giving him some unwanted body hair! Finally, switch to the Back camera and finish the job.

Now, do a test render. Notice anything wrong? More than likely, the specular highlights on the hair strands are very blown out. This can be controlled for the entire head by selecting Edit ➢ Select All by Type ➢ Strokes. With all the strokes selected, go to the Channel Box and open up the Inputs for the brushes. Change the following settings, to affect the specularity: Specular to 0.085 (this sets the brightness of the specular highlight, based upon the specular color settings) and Power to 10 (this is the size of the specular highlight, where a larger number means a tighter highlight).

Do another test render. Much better! However, the hair is looking a little gray, so change the Color 1 and Color 2 settings to the following: color1 R, G, and B to 0.01 each; color2 R, G, and B to 0.02 each.

Now with another test render, you should notice more natural-looking hair color and specularity. You will find that different lighting conditions may warrant changing these settings, so feel free to experiment with them.

PART **6**

Advanced Maya Effects

There still seems to be something missing here, though; the boy looks like he received a fairly cheap hair-transplant. This is because the default settings for density on the original brush weren't high enough.

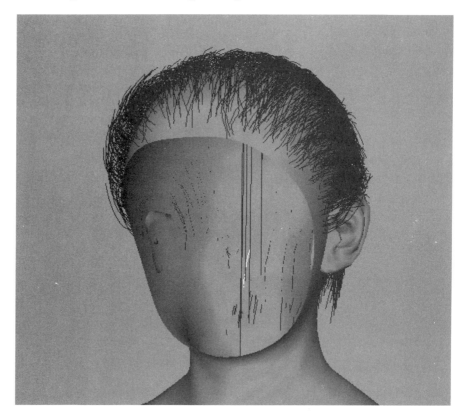

To change this, select all the strokes and, in the Channel box under Shapes, change the Density value to 5. This will give you a thicker head of hair, as the brush stroke is more densely populated by hairs along its path. Now make everything visible on the boy model and do a test render.

TIP   For even more control of the hair shape, change the number of segments for the tube (under Inputs for the stroke) to a higher number. The hair shape will not only look more realistic, but act more predictably as you paint.

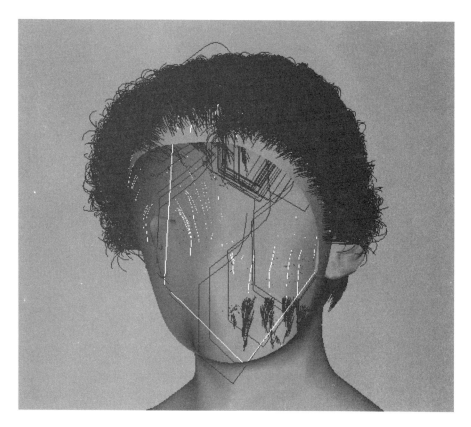

If you look closely at the render, you will notice that the hair is also casting nice fine shadows onto the boy's head. These are fake shadows, caused by Maya placing additional black strokes on the surface of the head to simulate shadows. It guesses where the surface is in 3D space, and draws a shadow paint stroke where it thinks the surface lies. This method isn't perfect, but it allows nice fine shadow details when it works. To prevent the hair from casting shadows onto other objects, or to give yourself another type of shadow option when the fake shadows aren't working, set Fake Shadow to None in the Paint Effects Brush Settings window.

NOTE   Alternatively, you can also change the shadow setting to 2D offset, but this is for creating a drop-shadow effect. While it works well for ferns that are painted on the side of a brick building, it isn't very good for hair on a curvy surface like a head.

With Fake Shadow set to None, scroll up to the top of the Inputs section and check Cast Shadows to On. Make sure your light is set to cast Depth Map Shadows. The Cast Shadows setting only works with Depth Map Shadows, as none of the Paint Effects elements can be raytraced. Compare the various shadow types shown next.

PART

6

Advanced Maya Effects

Shadow Map Shadows

3D Cast Shadows

No Shadows

On the other hand, all Paint Effects brushes can be motion-blurred, both in 2D and 3D. Most people will opt to use 2D motion blur, as it's usually faster and smoother than 3D. Also note that there will probably be some visibly chunky lines near where the stroke (hair or otherwise) is occluded by the geometry. This is because the hair is rendered into place using the Depth Buffer, and therefore there can be no anti-aliasing of the edge where they meet; depth is either true or false for a given depth. As Duncan Brinsmead (co-creator of Paint Effects) stated, "We don't have the notion of an anti-alias for the depth. It's an on or off thing. It's either at that depth or it's at a different depth for that whole pixel in the Depth Map." You must therefore take steps to compensate for this problem if it is apparent in your renders.

To alleviate this edge, we suggest you render your geometry first without the Paint Effects elements, then render the Paint Effects elements without the geometry. Using various compositing tricks, such as blurring and shrinking the elements slightly, you should be able to eliminate these chunky lines. They are really only a problem in very close shots, or when there is little to no motion. Another quick way around aliasing problems is to use 2D motion blur, which we found almost totally hid these areas.

PART

6

Advanced Maya Effects

TIP   A quick way to create your two renders is to first render only the Paint Effects elements, by choosing Windows ➢ Render Globals ➢ Renderable Objects ➢ Render Active while nothing is selected. As Paint Effects is a post-render process, it will still render, while no geometry will. Then, to render the Geometry without the Paint Effects strokes, in the Render Globals ➢ Paint Effects Rendering Options turn off Enable Stroke Rendering.

Now that you have given your model a full head of hair with shadows, take away some of his dignity and have some fun with your brush. Select all the strokes and, in the Visor, RM choose the Daisy brush, then choose Apply Brush to Selected Stroke. Do a test render. O.K., you can stop laughing now. Have fun with these experiments, and try applying several different brushes to you strokes to see what they look like.

Summary

While there is no way to fully explore the depths of Paint Effects in just one chapter (that could be the subject of another book!), this introduction should enable you to grasp the underlying elements of the Paint Effects tool set, and you should now be comfortable enough with this feature of Maya that you can experiment intelligently, using the built-in presets, or creating your own unique brushes. You have learned how to paint in both two dimensions (on a canvas) and three (in a scene), how to interactively create texture maps, how to animate your strokes, and what many of the Paint Effects options do. Furthermore, you went through a "real-world" example of using Paint Effects to create hair on a head—a process you might repeat often in a production environment. You should also have an appreciation of both the depth of

Paint Effects and how it can help you accomplish tasks that were heretofore too difficult or time-consuming to attempt.

Paint Effects is a great deal like Artisan: you will likely need to experiment with it creatively for a while before you will feel comfortable. However, you should now have enough knowledge to use simple Paint Effects elements in your scenes right away, and to understand how to experiment with the package to create even more complex and interesting effects in the future. With Paint Effects—and Maya as a whole—you should have fun recreating reality, or creating anything you can imagine. You now have the power to let your ideas take shape in the virtual world of illusion: Maya.

PART

6

Advanced Maya Effects

Appendix

INTERVIEWS

INTERVIEWS

his appendix features four interviews with luminaries from the digital graphics world. Authors Perry Harovas and John Kundert-Gibbs spoke with Mark Sylvester, Ambassador, Alias|Wavefront; Duncan Brinsmead, Principal Scientist Alias| Wavefront; Russell Owen, member of the Alias|Wavefront User Interface Team for Maya 1.0; and Habib Zargarpour, artist for Industrial Light and Magic.

Mark Sylvester: Ambassador, Alias|Wavefront

Mark Sylvester was one of the original founders of Wavefront Technologies, one of the first animation software developers, in 1984. He initially helped to develop The Advanced Visualizer, a 3D computer animation system first used at Universal Pictures. In helping to create Wavefront, Mark took a leadership role in establishing global customer support activities, which included educational relationships and user groups.

In 1995 Wavefront merged with Silicon Graphics and Alias Research, and Mark now serves as Ambassador for the new organization, Alias|Wavefront. In this role, he works closely with the development organization and the product marketing teams as a liaison between customers and the company, ensuring a close relationship between artists and developers.

Before founding Wavefront, Mark was a private chef and helped to build several restaurants in the Santa Barbara area, where he lives with his family. Mark gave us an incredible amount of his time to try to give readers a deeper understanding of Alias|Wavefront, and the tools that make up Maya.

Perry Harovas   What was the reason for creating Maya, and what were your most important goals for its first release?

Mark Sylvester   Maya is the result of an effort that was undertaken immediately upon the merger of Alias and Wavefront. At the end of 1994, Alias Research was in the midst of a next-generation, very secret product development. Wavefront, in conjunction with TDI, because we had merged with TDI three years earlier, were in the midst of a next-generation product development ourselves. The code bases at that time were about ten years old and in dramatic need of complete ground-up rewrites. Things that we did in the very beginning were a result of only being able to run on 64MB, not even that, 16MB systems with limited graphics capabilities. The operating environment of Unix at the time and the graphics library environments caused us to

do a lot of different tricks that we didn't really need anymore, so we were suffering from the inefficiencies at an architectural level. That is why we had started those rewriting efforts. Because of the merger, we were faced with a couple of issues. One was a business problem which was, can we continue to effectively support and put research and development dollars into the Advanced Visualizer, which was Wavefront's product line; Explore, which was the TDI product line; and PowerAnimator, which was the Alias product line? Management at the time said, "You know that really doesn't make sense because not only would we have those three lines, we have a next-generation effort at Wavefront and a next-generation effort at Alias. So that's really several teams that are working, and that's painfully expensive. Let's figure it out." The president at the time challenged the technical team to come up with a unified product agenda that would unify the requirements of the Wavefront users, the Alias users, and the TDI users into one next-generation product that we could deliver in a year. Absolutely overly ambitious, but I believe our heart was in the right place.

So you had this really interesting challenge because the Alias developers really knew how to think along the lines that they had been accustomed to thinking for 10 years as was the same with Wavefront developers and the Parisian developers. The first year was really spent understanding the requirements of the various installed bases because they were all very, very different. We also spent a great deal of time learning how to work together, across continents and language barriers.

It is somewhat interesting that three graphic systems were all started within three months of one another in 1984. They all had modeling, animation, rendering and display capabilities. They all attracted a certain kind of user. There was the Californian approach; there was the Canadian approach; and there was the Parisian approach. They had their own zealots who felt that their given approach was the right way to do it. Yet, at the end of the day, we all made pictures and got pixels up on the screen.

Perry Harovas How did you get to be known as "The Ambassador"?

Mark Sylvester My role at the company has always been interesting. At the merger, the management was predominantly Alias management and they did not believe in titles for people. So, at the merger, we found out that there would be no titles; no one would have a title. I was going to Japan two weeks later to head up a delegation that was going to assure all of our customers in the Pacific rim that everything was going to be fine and the merger was going to be good for them; just to kind of calm them down. I said, "Listen, I cannot go to Japan without a title. It's not acceptable. They will not know how to deal with me. It's a culturally significant issue." They said, "OK, that's fine." So they called me one day and said, "We think we have got a title. How does 'Ambassador' sound?" And instantly, it hit me chemically. I said, "That's it. That's absolutely it." And while we were on the phone I jumped on the Net and looked up the definition of "ambassador" and in reading it, I thought that's a perfect job description for me because it would allow me to exercise the kind of mission that I've always had, which focuses more on back channel kind of relationships. A role that is clearly focused on customers. My favorite line was when I was meeting with a vice president at NBC. He likes to walk me through [the facility] and as he introduces me, he loves to give my title and he says that I am the only guy he knows that outranks an entire room of vice presidents.

Perry Harovas What area of Maya do you think doesn't get enough attention?

Mark Sylvester Wow, that's a great question! Boy, that's a hard one. My first thought is the dynamics. I think that that's the most unexplored territory. I think people naturally gravitate toward particle system work and they're starting to understand the soft body dynamics more. But I think the whole area of dynamics gives a look to modeling that there's no other way to achieve; and it gives a feel to standard key frame animation that's exquisite and can produce effects in the renderer that are impossible any other way, yet none of it is readily apparent. It does take experimentation and so I'm very sensitive to the fact that most users don't have a lot of time to experiment—they're busy! They're busy getting work done and it's hard enough to learn what the software does as it's designed to do, much less to say, "what would happen if I did this; if I hooked up this emitter to the transparency feature in a shader?" You know, that kind of thing. "What would happen; what if?" That's the part of the software where I spend most of my time; I like to get in and play with the dynamics almost exclusively. I just think you can get to unusual-looking images quicker than any other way. I see myself artistically as a surrealist, not a photorealist.

Perry Harovas Are there tangible results from relationships with places like ILM, Pixar, and Santa Barbara Studios?

Mark Sylvester Oh, absolutely. The relationship that we have with these customers is what we call "Design Partnerships." It goes beyond beta testing and it precedes beta testing by at least a year. We work with customers, not just in film but video, game development, and industrial design, to help us understand what the new requirements are that they're starting to see from *their* customers. Remember, we're tool builders, and the best tool builders are the ones that have forged strong relationships with the people who use the tools. They're the ones that are sitting in the meetings with the visionaries and the directors and the avant-garde designers and the game developers saying, "Wouldn't it be cool if we could do this?" And then they look at the software to determine whether they can do that or not.

It takes a long time to develop software, and places like ILM are going to want to be able to respond to their own customers' requirements as quickly as possible. Now, they can come back to us and say, "We need to be able to do this," whatever it is and we will take that under advisement, as we do with all requests, and we can produce those requests at a given speed—a given rate of innovation. That's where open architecture comes in and that's where an API that's extremely robust and touches all aspects of the code becomes probably the single most important feature for those customers. Because it allows the customers to add these features themselves, especially if they do not have time to wait for us.

I think it's the most important aspect of Maya for the high end of the market. It's certainly not the most important part to the low end of the marketplace. The high end of the market wants to be able to open the hood and fine-tune the engine. The lower end of the market just wants to get in the car and go to the store. They don't want to understand the ignition system, they just want to turn the key and go.

Perry Harovas   And they want to do it fast!

Mark Sylvester   Exactly! I would say we probably have an order of magnitude of work to do in the ease-of-use, ease-of-learning piece of Maya in the next couple of years.

Perry Harovas   What do you see as the single most important thing next to tackle?

Mark Sylvester   I'm going to say ease of learning. I think that continuing education in a software package is extremely underrated as to its importance. Software is not static, and so once or twice a year you get a major update of software and you have a challenge in front of you, which is to be able to assimilate that technology into your pipeline, your workflow, into the way that you produce images. We don't produce gratuitous features. We produce features that are specific to solving problems, and yet we'll find that once someone gets a version update, they tend to load the CD into the computer, the software gets loaded, the manual goes onto the bookshelf and sometimes doesn't even get opened. Maybe the

release notes will get read. But to be able to assimilate that newly installed software takes an investment of time in what I call "continuing education." You constantly have to be thinking about improving your skills and learning more about the software that you already have. So, given that condition, I think that's the next major area that has to be resolved.

I'd like to also say that the other area that I think is ready—and it's one of our goals—is to create *Synthespians*. Jeff Kleiser coined that term 10 years ago. We have created photorealistic humans and creatures; we've created surrealistic humans and creatures, aliens and the like, and they move realistically and they look realistic, but they're dumb as rocks! I think there is a real opportunity to build intelligence into these characters that would absolutely help our ability to tell stories if we didn't have to worry about hand-animating walk cycles. Yet, you want to have the individuality that every organic creature has. Nothing walks the same or flies the same.

So you can't really solve this problem with motion capture and you can't really solve the problem with procedurally generated motion, and I don't really know how to solve the problem. I think that's one of the great things about audacious goals is that you don't really know how you're going to solve it, but I would love to have directable characters. I would love to be able to feed a script into the system and be able to direct the system by voice much as a director would and not have to be concerned as much with hand animating walk cycles.

Perry Harovas   Yet one of the difficult things for artists is changing the way they work, especially when it comes to doing the same thing they have always done, but approaching it in a vastly different way.

Mark Sylvester   Yes. That is very hard. It takes openness and willingness, and people are very resistant to change. That is a core human condition. No matter how high-tech we envision ourselves, no matter how advanced and cutting edge we think we are, we don't like to change. This whole ability to just have your eyes opened to the idea that there might be another way of doing it. And again, I don't know how to do that yet. I'm looking at it. I'm trying to figure out how can I help capture the little stolen moments in a day and use those for education. While you're waiting for a render to happen or you're waiting for a file to load, could you get a little 3-minute lesson on lighting or could you listen to someone during lunch? Could you download a ten-minute brown bag lesson by some lighting director? I think it's an area that we haven't spent as much time as I think we need to, and I know for sure that Alias|Wavefront is devoting a tremendous amount of time now into this whole area of continuing education. It's clear that we're not completely meeting the needs of the broader professional market until we have a level of ease that will show users how to learn online, quickly and easily.

Perry Harovas It's very interesting that applications like 3D Studio MAX and Lightwave, which are obviously very complex programs in their own right—although compared to Maya, a percentage of Maya's complexity—have all this education out there to explain them! Then you have all these users of Maya that are scratching their heads saying, "I don't know what I'm going to do next; I guess I'm out here on my own trying to figure this out." A main sour point with Alias|Wavefront has always been the Web site and the amount of information that's on the Web site to help people. Recently the LISTSERV has been probably the most fertile ground for some of this stuff, but I think there needs to be something else.

Mark Sylvester The importance of continuing education; the importance of ease of use and ease of learning is one of the number one priorities for the Maya team. We will not have the success that we need in a broader professional market and with casual users and with this coming tidal wave of new users unless we address this specific issue.

These users, they know all the features are there but like you said, it's access to help, access to information, access to tips and tricks, that kind of stuff. We know that historically we've not been as successful in this area, so I expect that to change, probably not dramatically at first, but with real strong incremental steps along the way.

Perry Harovas Well that's good to hear. Who do you see as your primary competition in the 3D world?

Mark Sylvester Oh, Studio MAX, without a doubt!

Perry Harovas So, was that what you had up on your bulletin board when you were developing Maya?

Mark Sylvester No, at the beginning it was SoftImage. I think neither Alias nor Wavefront had strong character animation tools. SoftImage did, and as the trend toward character animation grew, so did their business. So that was one of the principle areas that we wanted to focus on in 1.0, which we did—the whole character building-character modeling, IK, puppetry, the digital puppets, all of that stuff. All of it was to be able to respond to the needs that our customers had, which was for strong character animation tools. We wanted to break the paradigm of "model in Alias, animate in Soft, render in Renderman." That had to go away. So now many shops are strictly Maya. We want to be able to have the entire workflow be within Maya. So that was one goal. I think after 1.0 we absolutely hit that target dead on. And consequently Softimage is not the main competitor anymore.

Now we have a challenge that there are thousands of MAX users out there and they, for a long time, really gave Maya a hard time saying, "Well, I can do 80% of it for 20% of the cost." Well, now with Maya Complete being $7500, *less* than the cost of comparable Studio MAX with the plug-ins to bring it up to the functionality of Maya, it's easy for them to switch; very easy for them to switch. So now it's a matter of getting out there and appealing to the Max users who would really love to have Maya and felt it was out of reach and I don't think we did a very good job with letting people know we were not $50,000, but that we're $7500.

Perry Harovas   Because that was a huge change, and you're right, there was not a lot of press about that.

Mark Sylvester   Huge! So that's another thing that we're going to work on changing is that whole perception.

Perry Harovas   I think everybody was really angry for a long time that they were paying a lot for what could be considered in MAX, a plug-in. But now with the price drop, people started saying, "I can't believe they finally did that. It looks like they've taken what we've said seriously."

Mark Sylvester   We have, we have. We were doing a lot of things that weren't effective. We read the LISTSERV, we get the mail, we know. We're out there talking to customers all the time.

Perry Harovas   In terms of specific tools, what would you like to see Maya do better, as a user?

Mark Sylvester   My personal weakness is in modeling and so anything that we can do in the area of making it easier to do will be appreciated. I think that one of the goals as a visual artist is to create very complex worlds, with scenes and environments that tend to require lots of detail. Look what Paint Effects has done. I mean, try modeling a palm tree and try modeling it within a year. It's a lot of work to make it look real. Yet, we can do a palm tree in what amount of time with Paint Effects? Two seconds, three seconds—with dynamics on it even! So tools that help us model complexity are very important because to make things visually interesting, they've got to have a lot of detail in them and that can be very, very time-consuming, especially for someone who is not real gifted as a modeler, and that's certainly me!

Perry Harovas   I've always said, I don't know if it's the Moore's law of 3D graphics—I haven't

come up with a name for it yet—but this is the core idea: once you get a new tool that lets you do something that you've never been able to do before, all of sudden you're excited and then you're interested in doing things which you never would have attempted, and it becomes voracious and you start to attempt things that slow down your system again and you work towards the point where you can actually get back up to functionality. The systems come up to speed again and then another tool is introduced which bogs you down again. And I don't think with the complexity of what we're trying to do as artists, we're ever going to have the computing horsepower to achieve everything we can see in our heads.

Mark Sylvester   Right. Absolutely! It's the same with disk space; you never have enough. I had thought that one of the things that we could invent that would be really helpful would be a, I don't know what you would call it, but it would be a Complexity Meter that you could have turned on, and as you are doing things the Complexity Meter starts to rise so that you know that that thing you just did just added 33% more to the render time, for instance. You put the shadow button on in a shader and this meter goes up another 50% or whatever.

This is something that I've talked with our broadcast clients about. They would like to be able to say, "I need to get something done in an hour...just bam, bam, bam get it done!" Now I want to turn up the quality knob by another 50%. What does that mean? Now I can use this level of shaders; I can add this much more geometry and this many more lights and now...because it doesn't have to be ready until the 6 o'clock news, I can turn the quality meter up again. It's going to be something that's going to go on a weekly event that's going to happen and I've three or four more days so I can turn that quality knob up even more.

How many times have you just start working, you're doing this, doing that, and all of sudden you've got a one-hour render and you're like, "Oh-h-h!" As I was working had this, whatever that meter was, had it shown me as I was glibly adding more and more complexity, that's where I think we can help users. That isn't on the planning boards anywhere. But it is a great idea and would really be helpful. Especially to help us in the case where you are bidding a job—to be able to say that I can complete this job and keep my quality meter on at 2 and be able to deliver it at so many dollars a second. And if the budget goes up I can crank, crank, crank it up and now I know I can add volumetric clouds or hundreds of lights and still make my budget.

Perry Harovas   Well, it becomes very easy to do things like paint in complexity with Paint Effects where it's casual. It's kind of going back to the other statement I made where you would never even think that you could paint a field of grass, yet I've done at least six animations of fields of grass, with trees and every blade of grass casting shadows. I mean…

Mark Sylvester   You never would have done it.

Perry Harovas   I would have laughed in your face if you would have even suggested it to me and now you just casually do it, so you keep adding complexity to it and now all of a sudden you're surprised when you see an hour-long render! Look at things like radiosity. People want to have radiosity or global illumination and don't care how long it's going to take if it's a choice between a long render time or not having it at all. Of course they'd rather have less render time *and* the feature, but they don't want to be limited at all. That must be very difficult for you when you decide what features to put in there; when you have to balance it against how much time and money it's going to take to develop this and how much return on our investment you are going to get.

Mark Sylvester   Correct. That's absolutely correct. When we look at any given release there's three big audiences that have to be appeased. One of them is our own developers. There are things that need to be done in any given release that are architectural or are things that are done under the hood that never show up on a list of new features added. And there are things that you didn't get done in a prior release or things that you know that you need to do to get ready for the next release. Or it's just under-the-hood kind of stuff that if you ignore, it will come back and bite you *bad* in a release or two down the road. Because you will have no flexibility. That's very important, to listen to those engineers when they say, "We've got to do this."

The second group is the marketing group. They're out there talking to new customers about things that need to be in the software that aren't there. They're looking at the competition; seeing what the competition is doing; what they're working on; what their future stuff is going to be; to make sure that we're competitive on a check list basis and that we don't lose business because we don't have the key features for given markets that we're trying to grow into. If you don't grow your business, you go out of business and then no one is happy.

The third group is customers. And customers are just users—me and you. Our needs and our focus are all on what we're doing right now, today, our current projects and the projects in our immediate future. That's really what our whole field of view is, really focused on the job that we're doing day to day. We're the ones that are going to report bugs because we're the ones that are using the software most aggressively. We're the ones who probably use competitive packages as well and can say, "Well, I really like the way this package handles this particular problem."

So, you've got that group's advice and suggestions as well, but you can't listen to any one of those groups exclusively or to the exclusion of the others. The trick is to come up with a balance—and a good balance so that you add new features, fix bugs, put things in to remain competitive, and also work on your architectural underpinnings. This becomes a real balancing act because you have to add a business wrapper on that whole topic and say, "OK, that looks good. Now how much of that can we do in a short enough time to continue our momentum, and not so long that we get out of phase?"

So, that's one of the hardest things to do as a software company is to figure out what do you do now, what do you do later. What do you put on the list for later? How do you make your dates? Making your dates or not being late is something that we've intermittently been very good at and very poor at. I think we are much better at time commitments now than we've ever have been in the past. I think it's due to maturity in the team and a commitment to keep our commitments. So, it will be the case that not everything gets in but releases get out on a regular basis.

Perry Harovas   I think you as a company need to let the users, the people on the LISTSERV who are very vocal and maybe are or are not coming from an informed view, know your struggles and why certain things are in there and why certain things aren't. Why you're making these engineering leaps and they're "under the hood," as you say, and nobody even knows about them. I think people's assumptions are that the majority or all of your work is spent on new tools. So naturally they start to say "Why isn't tool X in this new release of Maya?" I think there is a lack of that knowledge for the casual users. ILM certainly is aware of it, but Joe Animator doesn't know what your challenges are as Alias|Wavefront and what you have to do day in and day out, so that might be an area to work on.

Mark Sylvester   Maybe you can help by getting a little bit of that flavor in the book.

Perry Harovas   I would love to. Just to give them an idea, and not to shut them up, certainly, but just to get them more informed so that…

Mark Sylvester   Yes, exactly. Don't shut them up at all. That's where we get our best ideas! But we get our ideas lots of different ways. That's what is important. If I just listened to one guy, then what do I do about my guys at NASA? What do I do

about my guys at NBC? What do I do about my guys at Pixar, or the ones that are just a few guys in a garage working on feature films?

That's the deal. And how do we keep it up? Even though we've gotten to be a pretty good size company, I don't want to lose that kind of interaction. We're actively listening to customers. We're paying attention to these kinds of things. I hope that we never get too big where we don't have that personal touch. We can't get out and get to every customer, but I know that we are extremely proactive in going out on customer visits in all areas of the company. And that once we do have a chance to have these kinds of conversations, people will come away with a strong appreciation for the challenges we have and a respect for the way that we go about running our business. At least, I hope so.

Duncan Brinsmead: Principal Scientist, Alias|Wavefront

Duncan Brinsmead is a principal scientist at Alias|Wavefront headquarters in Toronto. His inspired experiments are things that make our lives as 3D artists more fun, easier, and give us more realistic results in the final render. He has written some of the most popular and widely used parts of PowerAnimator (Maya's precursor), and has now created what will probably be regarded as a significant advancement in 3D graphics, Paint Effects. We spoke with Duncan at length about Paint Effects, and what he sees as some of the possibilities still left to be conquered in CGI. It was a wonderful conversation—you could just hear the excitement in his voice. It was unmistakable: this man loves what he does for a living.

Perry Harovas   Where did the impetus come from for you to start down this path which resulted in Paint Effects?

Duncan Brinsmead   Well, actually, I got into doing Paint Effects when I was working on the

Balloon Girl's hair in Bingo. I had an old paint system I'd written long ago that did 2D where you could brush trees and other objects, but it was in 2D. I had an anisotropic shader that I wrote for Maya, and with that shader, I wanted to have texture maps of hair that gave not only Alpha and brightness but also direction to the hair. I rewrote some routines in my paint system to produce some images that had 3 dimensions— they kind of encoded the twist and the direction of the hairs, right? So I kind of coded and colored it all in one image, which looked kind of nutty, but then I could take that texture and use it to control the anisotropic direction on the surface so that it matched the hairs and all the different parts worked together.

Then I started to realize that while I can paint these hair streaks, I wanted to get a little more elaborate—I wanted it to be 3D and coming out at you so that I could encode not just the 2D direction of the hair but the 3D, and use that for texture maps. You could have hairs curling around or twisting under each other and get the correct highlights on them. I wrote a little stand-alone to help me do that, and then as I was writing the stand-alone, I thought, "Well, gee, you know, to actually draw the hairs, I could use the line renderer I used for the PowerAnimator toon shader," which essentially could paint anti-aliased lines in three dimensions so that foreground fat lines will occlude lines behind them and have a nice anti-alias on the edge. I just modified that so then it would work properly with the perspective camera, and I then realized, well, "Gee, I can draw the lines now—I don't just have to draw them in kind of a 2D sense, I can really draw them coming off an object." And so it kind of started from that and kept snowballing and I kept adding more and more. Which is usually actually how most ideas kind of go with me, I'll start something and then just keep adding on bits incrementally.

Perry Harovas Do you try to do as much animating as possible to try to figure out what the problems that need solving are?

Duncan Brinsmead Yeah. I think that's one of the reasons that people seem to like the stuff I do as much as they do. Since I tend to use it, not quite the same as in a production environment, but it provides more flexibility and gives me more time than a production environment would. I tend to be after a particular effect, and I'll create some new parameter. When it doesn't do what I want it to, I'll change the parameter, or change the way it works. Where most people in software development tend to write up UVR, or User View Requirement, documents that plan everything out on paper and then have people go over and review it multiple times, I tend to work more in just a continuous stream. I just code and I try things out, I add parameters on the fly and I reconfigure the user interface if I don't like it. I find I can't go from a User View document because it changes so much for me as I'm developing it. What I end up with might be a completely different product than what I started out with in the first place. I think of it as being Opportunistic Programming, where you see some neat effect or something that you're doing work on, and then you exploit that. If you're bound doing a particular requirement that's been set down for you, then you don't have the ability to take advantage of those kinds of opportunities.

Perry Harovas Well, I know that all of us in production have said for years "They don't understand"—"they" meaning any software company—"they don't understand what our real needs are, or the fact that we don't know what our needs are, sometimes, until we actually need them." So, it's interesting that you and the people on Chris Landreth's team are some of the only people in software development, in 3D anyway, that seem to be doing any kind of production-worthy stuff. And I think that's what your advantage is.

Duncan Brinsmead Well, yeah. A lot of the programmers I've met over the years don't necessarily have the art background to appreciate a lot of the problems, and I think also that if you've done any animation work, you know how frustrating it can be. You know when the software doesn't behave the way you think or you can't get the effect you want. People will get it so that it looks good on paper sometimes, but if it can't take you all the way to the final effect that you're after, with all the little subtleties and nuances that you have to do for that effect to work properly, then it's not as useful. At the same time, I do like to explore doing and creating things that are not necessarily something I definitely know users are going to need. With Paint Effects I saw some useful things that can be done as I was starting out on it, but you know there was a lot of time where I didn't know what people were going to do with it because I'd never seen anything quite like it before. You know, some people might prefer some more traditional kinds of paradigms. Maya Fur is a more traditional way of doing hair where you use attribute maps. Some people may prefer that for certain kinds of jobs, so there's a certain amount of experimenting and risk-taking to see if it will yield something that's useful. Sometimes you have to look at things, things that nobody has done before, and that's very hard if I have to present something to a manager and get it approved as a project and nobody's ever done it before! It's very hard to get anyone to agree on that, but those kinds of things, I find I tend to just pursue them on my own, and then when they're ready I show them to people.

Perry Harovas   Exactly how does Paint Effects work in Maya?

Duncan Brinsmead   Okay, let's see. If I'm describing it, I'd say that basically in Maya, most of the modeling you'll do would be in terms of NURBS surfaces or polygons. The normal way of rendering that we use is a scan-line rendering for the finished rendering. Paint Effects kind of occupies an interim area where we're rendering to a Depth Buffer, but it's actually a complicated set of buffers where we can handle transparencies and stuff, which normal Depth Buffering can't handle. We also handle anti-aliasing of fine lines. If people are thinking in terms of particles, they could think of

being sort of halfway in-between the software particle render and the hardware particle render that we have in Maya. I personally find this ground, this sort of halfway between, very fertile for a lot of effects that you can't traditionally achieve—in particular, things where you have enormous complexity and millions of hairs, grass, a forest full of trees, these kinds of things that are normally beyond the range of a scan line–based rendering of triangles. Where the memory requirements would be too great traditionally, Paint Effects allows you to creatively get around that because we throw everything away as we render so that the memory costs are fixed. The memory requirement is for the buffer or the set of buffers we use; we have about six or seven buffers, and if you're on a really giant image, that might take up a fair bit of memory. I know a guy who's doing an image, something unwieldy like 13000 pixels by 2000 or something, and he just went into swap at that point on the image size.

The great thing about it is that you can render the Paint Effects if you want without any object memory. You can pre-render your scene without the Paint Effects saving a Depth Buffer, and then you just load the Depth Buffer and the image buffer in the Paint Effects. Then you can render Paint Effects on that and the Paint Effects during that render will integrate with those objects as naturally as if you'd done them together. At any rate, it happens at the end of the render and some of the memory space is freed up by the time we get to the Paint Effects phase. Then, even if you've got a fairly big scene with a lot of objects, it might not conflict too much with the memory in Paint Effects (normally the memory isn't that bad anyway). The memory needed to do one blade of grass or a million blades of grass is the same, because it's dealing with the buffer memory and not so much the memory per tube.

Perry Harovas   You see, that's beautiful because— I mean, as an animator, I've said for years as I walk through a forest that this world is much more complex than we ever have time or memory to handle. I mean, if you just look at the falling leaves in the forest, you couldn't possibly count how many leaves there are just in your field of view! Never mind if you did a pan. I noticed in some of the hair renders, that the shadow of the hair is bigger than the actual tube. Is this because...?

Duncan Brinsmead Well, I can tell you that. The Depth Map that's used by the light for the shadow map: let's say it's at a low resolution, and a hair covers a pixel even though the hair is only 1/10th of a pixel in width; it sets the Depth in the Depth Map for that pixel. We don't have the notion of an anti-alias for the depth. It's an on or off thing. It's either at that depth or it's at a different depth for that whole pixel in the Depth Map. So, what this means is that if you have stuff like very fine fur or hair, the width of the hair is grossly exaggerated in the Depth Buffer. One way around that is to make your Depth Buffer resolution very high (I mean your Depth Map on the light really large, which is kind of heavy on memory).

Another thing you can do that helps is to focus in the range of the Depth Map using the placement parameters of the Depth Map. Another trick that I sometimes use is to make the shadow color on the light not black so that the shadows aren't quite so heavy. If you want you can try fake shadowing on the tubes. This will give you very, very fine shadows. So if you've got bangs or something and you want to see the very fine shadows of the individual hairs on the forehead, you can do that a bit with fake shadows (although this trick is not perfect because it tries to guess where the surface is). And it's not a true cast shadow, it's basically another paint stroke that's painted in 3D into the scene. It's just a black stroke. In some cases that can work pretty well. If you have a tree and you want to give it a sharp base and have all the branches really sharp on the ground, that can work for those kinds of things as well.

Perry Harovas One of the things that really shocked me, in a good way, was that you could 2D and 3D motion blur with Paint Effects, and I think a lot of the people in the field were really surprised and really happy that you decided, "Well, we're not going to limit you to one kind of motion blur."

Duncan Brinsmead Yeah, we realized that it was important to do both, especially when it comes to hair. We initially did 3D, which was difficult, and once we had all that in place, it was pretty easy to add the 2D. I think the 2D is actually the one a lot of people might end up using more because it's faster and in some cases, it's also smoother.

Perry Harovas I prefer it almost 80 to 20%.

Duncan Brinsmead Yeah. There are just a few cases where some people might want 3D just for their objects, not necessarily the Paint Effects elements. Again, you can render the different elements separately if you want. But, yeah, I thought just having motion blur in general was pretty important for Paint Effects, because if you want to do hair or these kinds of things and moving objects, they need to blur, and motion blur has become really important.

Perry Harovas Do you get excited about images to the point where you can't wait to show somebody, or are you more low-key about it, like, animators hate what they do because it's never perfect?

Duncan Brinsmead I guess I'm more the show-off type. I always like having people into my office and, in fact, I get some of the managers around here pacing around my office checking to see if I have anyone demo'ing and showing off stuff to them. I'm pretty bad that way. [laughs] I like to create images and then bring people in and ask them what they think.

Perry Harovas What did you not get to do with this release of Paint Effects that, just because of trying to get it out the door, you think you'd like to implement in the future?

Duncan Brinsmead There are a few little clunky odds and ends here and there in the interface that we didn't get time to do or implement. But you know, all in all, I'm really happy with this release. We got a lot more in than I'd originally planned on, and we extended a lot of stuff. I wanted to have the time after SIGGRAPH to put in some presets and the way it worked out, I ended up putting in 400 presets!

Perry Harovas   The presets are even more extensive than they were at SIGGRAPH. I was really surprised to see things like waterfalls and, quite frankly, hands! Which I still haven't found a use for, but I'm dying to find a use for that one. [laughs]

Duncan Brinsmead   Yeah. I did a waterfall awhile back that we showed at SIGGRAPH using the PowerAnimator particles, and people liked that at the time, but it was difficult to set up and to create. There were a lot of things that I wanted to do that I just couldn't do in the PowerAnimator particles, so I tried to make sure I put the kind of elements I wanted into the Paint Effects particles. The volumetric self-shadowing in Paint Effects isn't as good yet as it is in the PowerAnimator software particles, although with the Depth Map shadowing you can do half-decent stuff that way. The nice thing in the Paint Effects particles is the way you can texture down the flow of the particles (I shouldn't call them particles I guess, they're tubes that you define in Paint Effects). Using the gaps (of the tubes) you can simulate a kind of particle motion through them, and you can simulate at very slow speed. If you wanted a waterfall that had connected tubes, a really big flow coming out through it, each tube has to move very slowly. If you're using particles in PowerAnimator, because of the way that the streaks have to fit the motion to make tubes, you'd have to have so many particles to move slowly, like the more slowly you move, the more particles you'd have to have because of their speed. You know they connect to their last position, so you'd end up raytracing billions of particles if you wanted to do a really slow big waterfall. You can do that kind of thing in Paint Effects. I haven't really experimented enough with it to get a good waterfall, but I think you should be able to get a pretty decent effect. It doesn't do the collisions with objects but you can

sort of paint that in, I think. Waterfalls are rather static anyway.

Something I did as an experiment recently, that I think works out really well, is to take a cylinder— take a simple 1 degree curve 2 points on the cylinder curve-on-surface, and make it so that the U on one of the points is like 1000. Essentially what you get is a spiral going down the cylinder. It's like scan lines going down the cylinder, and then you assign a Paint Effects stroke to that, and this essentially gives you a surface that's a Paint Effects surface so you can make it fuzzy. It's like a surface where you set the stamp densities to get an even grid of stamps bound to the surface. If you want to be fancy about it, you can turn on a tube and just have one tube that exactly follows the stroke with the Path Follow of 1 and a Length Flex of 1 and a large number of points on it. I did this and then added a little turbulence to it and then moved this around so that you have your cylinder, but you're going to apply a turbulent wind to deform it. There are all kinds of neat things you can do with that, and one of the nice things about the Paint Effects is that it's not a flat surface. Doing it this way you create a kind of volumetric surface that, as objects are penetrated, it will kind of softly emerge out of it.

Perry Harovas   What type of things, kind of along those lines, do you wish people would do with Paint Effects beyond just landscapes and hair and things like that?

Duncan Brinsmead   I think when people get it out of the box, they will just use it for grass, probably. [laughs]

Perry Harovas   Yeah, because it's so much fun!

Duncan Brinsmead   I've seen a lot of people using it for hair and stuff too. I'd like to see somebody try and tackle some really long hair, like using the control curves and maybe soft-body dynamics or maybe just keyframing. Try doing something like a woman with long flowing hair that kind of blows around. It might not be easy, but it would be interesting to see because I don't think anyone's really done anything like that,… that looks half-decent. Something else I think might be a neat way of using it is in areas where you might previously have thought of using a post-effect. For instance, when you just want to blur a part of a scene for example, you know you can essentially paint a brush on the object that'll blur that object or smear it a bit. There are these kinds of uses for it. It's not like a canned effect. I think these possibilities are really great. Let's say you have a seam on an object, and I don't say this is the best way of doing it right now, but you've got very crude triangulation. So you see this gap along the joint and you want to get rid of that gap. You can up the triangulations really high, but your renders get really slow. Or you can create a Paint Effects stroke that has tubes on with Randomize at 0 and you have these little tiny, tiny short tubes that are very even and go sideways to the direction of the stroke. Then you paint them right along the edge of one surface and they essentially kind of smear the edge of the triangles onto the next surface so that it closes up the gap. There might be problems when you get an object going in front of it—it might pull in a little of that into the smear something and not look quite right—but if it's really subtle stuff, it might help make certain renders faster. I'd certainly consider using Paint Effects.

Let's take the flow of gas over a car hood for example (I've seen people struggle with that). It's not too hard now with Maya. You can have curves, the particles can flow along the curve, so that's not too hard to do anymore. Still, with the particles in Maya, trying to get a good-looking, coherent flow of a stroke where you're using a texture that flows nicely along it, that might still be difficult whereas with Paint Effects you can select one of these brushes, Jet Trail for example. You can take a brush like that and you can either stroke it along the surface and then just do a little surface offset to position the stroke up, or you could just take a curve and attach it to the curve and then just animate the path follow. I think

there are a lot of cases where you can use a simple kind of flow along the curve instead of the dynamic behavior particles, and it's much easier to control that kind of animation than it would be a particle animation.

Perry Harovas   Are there any plans to incorporate it into IPR?

Duncan Brinsmead   It's sort of its own IPR in a way because it's a post-process. If you want, one way of visualizing in an IPR-like setting is to take your IPR image, load it in as an image plane, and then just modify the Paint Effects window. If you pre-render your scene, and then you save up the scene in the Depth Buffer, there's a mode of rendering where you can load that Depth Buffer and then the image as an image plane. You can render the Paint Effects onto that so it renders onto that Depth Buffer. So if you do that and then you tweak something and then you update the Paint Effects window, that's about as fast an update as you'll get. Since it's not scan line–based the way IPR is, we can't just render one scan line of Paint Effects. We can render one object in Paint Effects, but you can't render just that one object and then have all the other objects in the scene. You do get kind of a fast feedback if you go into Render Shaded stroke and then turn Active on, so it's only rendering the active stroke. Then when you go in to modify it in the Attribute Editor, it will redraw the Paint Effects for you fairly quickly. So, in a way, the Paint Effects panel is sort of an IPR window of its own, but it's a different kind of IPR.

Perry Harovas   What are the areas in CGI that you still see as needing a lot of work? Things that you would love to tackle, or things you would love somebody else to tackle because you just don't have the time?

Duncan Brinsmead   There are a lot of great things that people here are currently working on. One thing I think that needs work is rendering Global Illumination; a lot of good effort went into that, and a lot of people putting that into renderers, etc. I think it's more important than some people think for certain aspects of animation, like for facial rendering. I've looked a lot at different shading models for doing facial rendering, and you know, of course if you take a scan of a face, you can make it look pretty realistic, but it doesn't hold up well under different lighting conditions, right? One of the key aspects, I think, of white skin is the global illumination effects of light scattering in multiple bounces, say between the lower eyelids and the cheek, because it's white and the skin is very transparent and it scatters the light a lot. It's a very directional type of scattering, and there are certain cases where you need to show the way light bounces around or it doesn't look quite right. People fake it a lot with clever use of ambient lights and they kind of paint the radiosity effects into their textures, but it would be nice to have something that automatically did that. You get some interesting packages, some of the ones for simulating dirt. One of the neat effects is that it actually simulates the way light is hidden by certain areas. So as you get closer to a crevice or something, it gets darker and darker because less light can get into that region. And then more dirt tends to get into that region as well, and I think a lot of times the reasons images look good when you apply these dirt algorithms isn't because it's adding the dirt, but because it's adding the effect of Global Illumination. It just jumps out—it is so much more real than the typical plastic kind of graphics rendering that you see. To me, the key difference between reality and most computer graphics renderings is Global Illumination effects. When a novice sits down at a machine and their first renders come out, usually the ambient light is all wrong, the shadows are blown out, it's flat, and it is all due basically to the lack of Global Illumination. If you're using a program that uses radiosity or something, it doesn't let you make those kinds of mistakes. You might make it look like an over-exposed picture, if the software works well, but you shouldn't be able to make it look unrealistic. The real problem is that Global Illumination is incredibly expensive computationally. So it's just

a very difficult problem to make it fast and easy to use. You have to do a lot of work just to set it up to make it optimal so you can use it. I think it will be a long time before it just becomes something that's automatically on in a scene.

Perry Harovas   And people thought the same thing about raytracing. To a degree it is almost fast enough where you can use it all the time because of the machines. It's not really because of the algorithm, but it'd be nice, because it's still such a huge problem if people figured it out on the algorithm side first, and then we could use it now instead of waiting five years for machines to catch up to it.

Duncan Brinsmead   One of the nice things about Paint Effects is that everything is on one node, which is kind of one of the bad things too, I suppose, depending on how you look at it. I sort of wanted it where the animation, the modeling, and the rendering are all there together and you can get at it very quickly. If it were a network of nodes all linked together, it would be a lot more complicated to do (brush) blending and to make iterative changes on it. An L systems approach would've required that I go to some kind of multi-nodal thing and it would've made it more flexible, I think, on defining the shapes, but it would've made it more difficult to use and I wanted something that was very simple.

Perry Harovas   Well, it seems like you have a type of L system in there kind of already, at least with the trees and branching.

Duncan Brinsmead   Yeah. It's not really the same, it's a different method. It's a parametric definition of an object just with a very large parameter space. I suppose you can look at L systems as being that way, and there are rules involved so they're not totally different, but they're certainly different.

Perry Harovas   Did you have any Beta testers out there that were using it in production?

Duncan Brinsmead   Yes, quite a few. I don't know if I want to mention who or what they're working on though. We had lots of people using Beta, including companies using it in movies. Some people were working in very high resolution; for example, one shop was working on an enormous project for some kind of theme park where they had multiple screens set up.

Perry Harovas I mean, you'd never ever think of doing something that large in a traditional way. Even the particle render for hair in Power-Animator was incredibly memory-intensive.

Duncan Brinsmead I know! I wrote that, and it really wasn't initially designed to do hair; we kind of tricked it into doing hair and as a result there were a few things I meant to change later [but] just never got around to doing. But even that alone—doing millions of hairs is incredibly memory-inefficient if you want to raytrace them. Just trying to raytrace millions of anything gets to be very difficult. With Paint Effects, if you want to do 10 million hairs, you can just let your renderer run that much longer. Whereas in PowerAnimator it's more like an exponential curve, and there's a point where you hit the slope, where the curve just suddenly shoots off into swap space, and then forget it.

Perry Harovas Besides you, how many people actually went into the Paint Effects effort?

Duncan Brinsmead It was really a team effort—where myself and Andrew Pearce did most of the programming. We had help from others on the team on UI development (including parameter wording, porting to NT, and then some miscellaneous bug fixing near the end.) We had product specialists testing Paint Effects, and they also offered suggestions on parameter names. We did quite a bit of work initially getting down the set of parameters on the brushes after usability testing. This usability testing profiled the fact that we needed to change our layouts in windows. Honestly, putting the toolbar in the Paint Effects window is an effort to try and help people distinguish between the Paint Effects panel and the modeling window, because initially these people were thinking, "Oh, it's just another display model in my modeling window," and then they got confused when they tried to tumble or pick

objects. I think the toolbar helped a bit with that, because it makes it look more like an IPR sort of window, which is closer to what it is in fact. That was a difficult part of Paint Effects, because we had no precedent in the interface for this kind of interaction mode.

Perry Harovas Thank you for all you have done to help further the tools we use everyday, and thank you for taking so much time to give us a behind-the-scenes look at Paint Effects.

Duncan Brinsmead Sure! You're welcome.

Russell Owen: Alias|Wavefront User Interface Team Member for Maya 1.0

Russell Owen earned his B.A. from the University of Toronto, majoring in Computer Science and Cultural Anthropology. His research projects there included using computers to teach reading. Russell joined Alias (soon to be Alias|Wavefront) in 1994, initially to work in coding; he was later switched to interface design and development for the nascent Maya, and worked specifically on right-mouse-button context menus and the device control interface for the program. As the interview took place, he was working with Duncan Brinsmead on Maya's new Paint Effects tool.

John Kundert-Gibbs What were your early, guiding goals when the interface team first talked of creating the Maya GUI?

Russell Owen First, we wanted to allow users to work as much as possible in perspective mode. We placed the axis reminder directly in the view, then we made sure all the manipulators (for moving, scaling, and rotating) were also in the scene window, rather than in their own windows. As the manipulators can be accessed by pressing the QWERTY menu keys, the user doesn't even have to move the mouse outside the scene window to change tools. The goal was to keep users from having to look all over the interface to find the most basic tools—especially the manipulator tools, the time line, and keyframing.

We also wanted to give over as much screen as possible to the scene window, so we built in the ability to remove any or all of the menus, toolbars, and even the Channel box. An experienced user will often work in just one big scene window with nothing else showing. To allow this space savings to happen, we created the hotbox and other contextual menus (usually accessed via the right mouse button), which give users the information and control they need when they need it but don't clutter up the screen the rest of the time.

John Kundert-Gibbs Was building the interface entirely out of MEL (Maya Embedded Language) scripts a technical issue, or one driven by user interface concerns?

Russell Owen The decision was actually a combination of technical and interface needs. We wanted to give our interface engineers the ability to tear down and rebuild the interface without needing to go into the C++ (base) code. Building the interface on MEL also allows users with little technical experience to rebuild the interface themselves without having to either hire a techie to rework the interface or wait for the next release of the software.

John Kundert-Gibbs Above, you alluded to creating a better workflow as a guiding principle for the Maya interface. How does the Maya interface optimize workflow for the expert user?

Russell Owen Around here [A|W headquarters], we like to joke that the "out of the box" Maya user interface hardly resembles an expert's interface. This is because the interface is very open to optimization, allowing the expert user to do away with screen clutter in favor of a more streamlined interface and workflow.

We spent some time working with human–computer interaction experts, determining the cognitive load limits of a typical user; then we tried to reduce the complexity of the interface to

fit within these parameters. In addition to the cognitive grouping of manipulator tools we discussed above, we tried to reduce the user's need to pay attention to modes (a common hurdle in other programs). For example, you're almost always in select mode, meaning that, whatever tool is selected, you can still click or drag an object to select it. Not having to switch back and forth between select and manipulation modes may seem like a simple idea, but it has reduced the difficulty of learning Maya a great deal.

Another way we tried to increase the information that is "obvious" to the user (thereby reducing the cognitive load) was to make the last selected object green, while all other selected objects are white. Because many of Maya's functions (like Stitch, Blend, and Make Collide) depend on the order you select objects, having a visual reminder of which object was selected last can really help in using some of these complex tools.

Habib Zargarpour: Associate Visual Effects Supervisor, Industrial Light and Magic

Habib Zargarpour of George Lucas's visual effects firm Industrial Light & Magic (ILM) has been instrumental in helping to create some of the most stunning visual effects ever seen on film. His credits include *The Mask, Twister, Spawn,* and *Star Wars: Episode I " The Phantom Menace,"* and he is currently working on *The Perfect Storm.* He has been a frequent Maya enthusiast, giving speeches two years in a row at the Alias|Wavefront Global Users Association meetings during the SIGGRAPH convention. He is also one of the nicest and most knowledgeable people working in visual effects today. We spoke with him at length about the way Maya was used in *Star Wars,* and how it integrated into the ILM production pipeline.

Perry Harovas The things you've done with Maya are amazing! How long have you been using Maya?

Habib Zargarpour I'm actually coming onto two years with Maya.

Perry Harovas And did you start from nothing? Were you going through the tutorials and all that, or did you just dive in?

Habib Zargarpour I kind of dove in and tried to figure things out. I'm more like a self-hacker rather than reading manuals. So, unfortunately that means that sometimes there are a lot of features that I don't find out about until other people tell me, but I do look at online documentation a lot. I like doing searches through the documentation, the global index, and especially the MEL commands. So, that stuff is really helpful.

Perry Harovas What version of Maya did you run on Star Wars?

Habib Zargarpour We started with Maya 1.0 and then we were able to get additions like the emit command, which we use heavily in animation, and the curve emitter, so then it was called version 1.1 Alpha 3, which is pretty much like the 1.5 release.

Perry Harovas Did you have any trepidation about upgrading the software in the middle of production?

Habib Zargarpour We had a concern, but it went very painlessly. We got the new version and basically switched over lunch. It was fine.

Perry Harovas How did Maya get implemented into your pipeline at ILM, with all the other applications that you use all having to talk to each other?

Habib Zargarpour When we started out, we wanted to look at rigid body dynamics to use on the show and also to replace any particle effects we had to do instead of using Dynamation. But the particular application for me was to use it for crashing the pods and as we were doing R&D for that, we tripped into doing the pod flying with it, which is simulating how they fly and animate. So, we ended up making a really nice setup where all the pod animations were, for the most part, done as rigid body simulations in Maya, and in the same scene we were able to set up the animation for dust for the pods and exhaust animations for the pods. Sometimes pods affecting each other, or hitting each other.

Animators were trained to use the package and to use the dynamic controls that they needed. If they wanted to keyframe they could go ahead and keyframe shots. And then we created a Maya pipeline that would take the Maya scene through our in-house software so that we can render it in Renderman. So, it was actually a pretty smooth setup, and the replacing of the geometry to higher resolution was done in our in-house pipeline.

Perry Harovas Did you have any problems converting Maya's scene files, animations, and things like trims that are specific to Maya, over to Renderman to render?

Habib Zargarpour We did have a problem initially, through the in-house pipeline, dealing with NURBS because we were previously just dealing with B-Spline surfaces from Softimage. Other than that, I believe trims made their way through okay and all the other kinds of geometry made their way okay. We wrote our own converter so that so we could add things that were missing or we could decide what would happen to certain types of nodes that weren't recognized.

But I think as far as the use we had for it, it kind of started growing from when we were doing the pods to doing things like bubbles in the underwater sequence or suspended algae, doing the effect in the underwater city when Quigon and Obi Wan walked through the membrane.

We used it for doing some flock animation of different places and then, of course, eventually it got used for doing the people animation in the stadium—people sitting on the seats and also in the end battle sequence where the Gungans and Droids are battling. That whole choreography of running and simulating the crowds all used Maya. So as we started out, we didn't think we would end up with such a large usage of the software, but because of the expandability and the way we could put our own plug-ins into it, we could make it fast and efficient. We were able to take advantage of it for a lot of uses. And I have to say, it's thanks to our supervisor John Knoll, who's open to new ideas and new methodologies and not afraid to dive into doing that.

Perry Harovas   Was there extensive testing going on to decide what you were going to do in what specific application and what you were actually going to shoot on-set as a real element to comp in?

Habib Zargarpour   Yeah. Each Visual Effects Supervisor was using their own experience to decide what elements should be filmed and what should be CG. But sometimes George would have an opinion about that and he would want it one way or the other.

But the scope of the project and all the different shots that had to be accomplished was really vast, so a lot of times approaching it wouldn't be as obvious as you would think because you would say, "Well this might make sense normally to shoot an element, but then we'd need hundreds of them from different angles." The Rotunda is an example, with all the people sitting in the boxes, trying to get that kind of footage.

Perry Harovas   I know that muticolored Q-tips were photographed in the models of the stadium to simulate thousands of people in the stands. Were all those shots eventually replaced with CG?

Habib Zargarpour   No. There were shots where the Q-tips were left in. Mostly shots where you were not within the stadium or from a distance. The shots where you can see people waving their arms, those pretty much were replaced with CG crowd or footage with a compositing technique.

Perry Harovas   I believe I remember you saying at the Alias|Wavefront Users Group that you can make them do the wave if you wanted to! Did you do any shots where you just had fun with them?

Habib Zargarpour   We actually had blooper takes of them doing very funny stuff. But we had some people running blooper shots on their own. What I wanted to do was have a Battle Droid riding one of the pod engines.

Perry Harovas   How did the MelBots get started?

Habib Zargarpour   We were doing all kinds of work with dynamics and expressions, and a couple of in-house people were experimenting with them. I started using them for the pods, and that year I think the real robot wars got canceled. So in the back of my mind I was always saying, "It's really sad because John Knoll also participates in that, in the robot world, you know, the robot he built in the lightweight category." So the real stuff was always in our minds, so it was only a matter of time to connect the virtual stuff to say, I think Mike Ludlum had run some preliminary tests of rigid bodies that moved around.

So I took that idea and took the real robot world idea and I thought, hey if you could build robots actually with rigid bodies, then they'll have expressions so they can fight each other. Then we actually made a sample case with it. We were having a riot with how fun it was to watch these things go at it. I had some really preliminary tests where they would just attack a cube or something. It grew from there to build more intelligence in them. Like the first arena I had didn't have a border so they kept falling off the edge. So I had them build in that experience so that they avoided the edges.

Perry Harovas   Does it ever threaten to be addictive?

Habib Zargarpour   Oh yeah, definitely! Each time we run it, people start piling up and looking and cheering for one side or the other. If you had a new robot, you'd want to run some test battles first and fine tune your expressions first and then you'll be ready. It's kind of like an evolution thing, it grows. With more experience you can improve your robot. It would pretty unfair if you didn't have battle experience and you just put it in there. You'd probably get run over pretty quickly the first time!

Perry Harovas   I like the rules: you can't delete your opponent, you can't change your robot's size on the fly, and things like that.

Habib Zargarpour   Right. I still have people coming up to me saying, "Hey, you know you can do this…" and then you think, "Well, that's cheating." The rules are getting longer and longer.

Perry Harovas Have you put up a Web site devoted to this yet?

Habib Zargarpour I'm just in the process of sending that to Alias|Wavefront. We're going to co-host a Web site, I guess, and have a sample scene, probably very preliminary basic rules and a digital scale, a rigid body scale that you put your robot on it, and measure how much it weighs.

Perry Harovas Have you ever just said, "You know what, I'm going to stay here late, I'm going to work on something just for fun because it's what I want to do and nobody else has to have a say on how it looks or how it moves"? It doesn't have to be anything big or anything anybody ever sees, but just something that make you happy as an artist.

Habib Zargarpour I find myself thinking constantly about things that are possible to do or things I want to be able to do and it becomes like a little test pilot. Kind of like if you're in a restaurant and you have a napkin and you find yourself sketching on it, but as ideas come you think to yourself, "I wonder if I can make something like *this* and hook it up to *that*?"

To me the interesting part of the package is when you have these different modular features in it, then you can combine them. You can combine rigid bodies with particles; you can combine relational modeling with animation. All these different things can talk to each other, so then you start thinking in your head about tinkering with different inventions, basically, building them in Maya, and that's the curiosity factor for me. You build things to see if you can make it work a certain way. Or someone else can throw you a challenge, saying, "I bet you can't make a locomotive drive chain with an IK skeleton," or something like that, you know? I have lots of scenes that are just little proof of concepts of different effects or inventions.

Perry Harovas And I'm sure all of those end up getting funneled back into production when you need an idea, and you remember you did something 6 months ago for fun?

Habib Zargarpour Yeah, absolutely. And that's where good naming conventions come in. You want to name something *exactly* what you think it should be called when you want to look for it again.

Perry Harovas What do you see as the most difficult part of using a commercial application like Maya in production?

Habib Zargarpour That's a heavy question. [Pause] Learning it, I guess.

Perry Harovas Having the time to learn it or just *learning* it in the first place?

Habib Zargarpour Both. I think there's so much there that you want to be able to continuously learn. That's true with any package, but specifically, to really harness the power you need good training on a package like Maya to be aware of all the different possibilities. And also to take advantage of the expressions.

I think it is a voyage of discovery. You cannot be afraid of going into different places or menus. I think that anyone who has fear of what's new is going to have trouble in general in the land of computer graphics. Things change so fast that you have to accept that change is going to happen. I went through this when I had learned Alias and then Softimage came around and I had to [learn that]. Initially I was really angry and bitter that here's a whole new thing I have to learn after becoming good with Alias. I think at that point I decided to accept change and decided that if there's something new, I'm going to dive into it. You just have to change your attitude around.

Perry Harovas When you open yourself up to things like that, sometimes there's the danger of being into everything new and it affects what you're trying to do if you're excited about the new thing and get lost in it. I imagine you have to scale yourself back sometimes so that you can meet your schedules?

Habib Zargarpour Yeah. You don't jump into everything that's new; you have to use your judgment to say, "This particular thing looks very promising, so it seems like it's worth checking out." As you check it out, you find pretty quickly if you made a good decision or not. You know, at some points it was more fun to make the [MEL] scripts than to do the work. I think that's the danger with Maya—it's really fun to make those buttons and make the icons for them and make them do stuff! I thought that was just extremely fun. We have over 200 of them, some of which I've made and some of which the rest of the crew did. I think we've been very successful in integrating it into our pipeline, customizing it for what we do.

Perry Harovas There is only so far you can go with MEL and at some point you have to do a plug-in either for speed or just to get it done at all. Did your R&D department write a lot of plug-ins as well?

Habib Zargarpour Yes. Actually, our R&D TD's (Technical Directors) would write plug-ins; the software department would handle things like stand-alone tools.

Perry Harovas Are you able to write at that level of programming or are you happier and most confident in things like expressions and MEL?

Habib Zargarpour I have a software background in mechanical engineering. I learned it there and I have been writing code on various platforms, as well as some custom code on *Twister* and some of the programs we use in-house. I wouldn't say I'm totally confident with it. I'm much better at editing than writing it from scratch, and I'm certainly much more comfortable with the scripting language, having done a lot of Dynamation work before. Thanks to the speed [Maya] has, there are very few times you need to go to the plug-in level. The cases where you have to go to the plug-in level are if you want to create a primitive and have it deform and have it all be part of the Hypergraph pipeline, the live relational things. I'm most likely

to hand that stuff out to people that are more capable than me and much faster than me in the actual programming language.

Perry Harovas Maya Fur and Maya Cloth are part of the package and they're really well integrated, but I imagine that there was some reason that you made a decision not to use those, and to instead use your own in-house tools for those things?

Habib Zargarpour Those weren't decisions I had to make, as I wasn't working on that creature portion of the show. The people that were doing the creatures were developing in-house cloth and were open to using any other packages' cloth that was available to test, but it just so happened that we finished our cloth and made it very robust before the Maya cloth was ready. At that point, when the Maya cloth was ready and we saw it, I think our dynamics were still ahead in terms of robustness and realism. They still had improvements to make, which they did by SIGGRAPH last year. The people who were deciding which methodology to use were happy with what we already had.

In terms of Fur, we've had a long history of doing fur kind of projects here, and they've been going through different evolutions with every show. The first use, I think, was in *The Flintstones*, believe it or not. Then we used it on the monkeys in *Jumanji*, and on the lion. Then the latest resurrection of it is in *Mighty Joe Young* with the gorilla fur, where we added dynamics to it.

Perry Harovas Is it the same in-house renderer as your particle renderer?

Habib Zargarpour It used to be separate, but now both are integrated into the same. I don't know if the people responsible for doing that work had a chance to look at Maya Fur or not. Certainly, what they saw with the Paint Effects, they were very impressed with this year at SIGGRAPH.

Perry Harovas Did you get a chance to see Paint Effects after your speech at the Alias|Wavefront User's Group?

Habib Zargarpour Unfortunately not. I'd seen it last year, but it was an independent unit; it wasn't integrated into the package and I don't think he [Duncan Brinsmead] had all the animation features. But I heard people talk about it. It sounded really promising.

Perry Harovas   At SIGGRAPH, ILM presented a technical paper that described how you were able to keyframe the dynamics, which is a fascinating concept. Have you tried to implement any of that in Maya?

Habib Zargarpour   We implemented that concept. In the Rigid Bodies, we were using impulses to add our own guidance into what we wanted to do. In some ways, the way pod rigs were set up was pretty much that you have human input into a dynamics system to guide it, to tell it where to go. But basically, the bottom line would be that the simulation is going to decide where it's going based on its own characteristics of mass, momentum—all these different things. So, in a way, that setup is entirely an input into a dynamic system, as opposed to letting it run purely based on fields, like we do on particles. With particles, there are so many of them that you have to come up with *global* controls.

Perry Harovas   So the cage you set up, with the different springs attached to the engines of the pods, that was your input device, by keyframing that, then letting the dynamics of the springs on top of it take over under that?

Habib Zargarpour   Exactly.

Perry Harovas   How, if you can tell me this without killing me, did you implement denting in the pieces of the engine that hit the ground?

Habib Zargarpour   [Laughs] We had several different R&D projects at the same time looking into that, and one of the methodologies was to take expressions and use lattices to deform them based on impact. To deform the object, you have to do all kinds of tricky things to the rigid bodies for them to recognize that they got deformed, but I won't go into that! It was a combination of what's in the package and some expressions and plug-ins that we managed to get the airframe technique

working so it would automatically dent as it hit and deform to whatever object it was impacting.

It was very exciting for us, for example, to get the front ring of the engine hitting the ground. If that was a solid piece, it would just hit the ground and fly out, whereas if it's an airframe, the bottom starts to take the impact and warp backwards and causes a distortion to go through it. It behaves more like a piece of sheet metal would, that could deform, as opposed to a hard piece that would just fly off.

The last technique was something we had developed as a plug-in, which was a deformation node. We could hand-place and animate them as a live relational node in the Hypergraph. We would just dial in how much deformation we wanted. That technique was used when the wrench goes into the Marpod engine, for example. You see dents coming out of the different spots on the engine. That way, it was real easy for us to just place them in different spots, and if George wanted more or less of them or different timing on them, [we could do that]. So it was very simple for us to place the deformers manually and just hand-animate them coming on. Because they were relational it was animatable, so it wasn't like we were permanently deforming it.

Perry Harovas   Were there any instances where the dynamics were not working, or taking much too long to calculate?

Habib Zargarpour   There were a few shots where the animators were trying to get the pod rigs to move a certain way, and there would be maybe some really fast turn that they couldn't do, or a specific action. So for the most part, they would make the simulation so that most of the pieces' were moving physically correctly, and then they could go in and hand-edit some of the keyframes. Like, if an engine went a little too high in a certain frame, they could bring it down and basically post-edit it as if it was motion capture. But that didn't happen very often.

Perry Harovas   How long did it take you to develop the cages that surrounded the pods and engines?

Habib Zargarpour   That's a good question. That process took about three to four months. And the reason being that it was basically an engineering project trying to make an airplane and fly it. You need test pilots and you need mechanical configurations. We ran into all kinds of interesting discoveries, like dealing with moving rigid body hierarchies. It was not only a matter of building it, but also making tools that could handle it. In Maya 1.0 you couldn't do rigid body hierarchies, so we had to come up with a way to do the hierarchies and then a way to move them and rotate them.

But it wasn't four months of full-time work for me. As I was doing the pod crashes, I was also doing this research. As an example, if you weren't real precise with your Pod rope configuration, let's say like where the pins would go, you would end up with some high-frequency problems at high speed causing the cockpit to break off or something. That's why I keep saying it's like dealing with a real craft—it physically *has* to function that way. A lot of the time was spent trying to get the right configuration. What is the best way to grab an engine? Do you grab it from the front, which is the first thing we tried, or do you grab it from all four corners? Each decision has its own repercussions and efficiency.

One of the difficulties in doing the pod race was we weren't able to tell them any details about what we were doing with the rigid bodies. We just had to say, "Look, we're trying to go really fast and it's misbehaving or doing this or that." Not having the luxury of sending [Alias|Wavefront] a scene and ask "Why doesn't this work?"—that's always a frustrating thing not to be able to do that.

Perry Harovas   I think it's maybe everybody's misperception that ILM has a really, really fast machine on everybody's desk.

Habib Zargarpour   Right, that's what I thought before I came here! I thought everyone would be doing real-time renders on big machines.

Perry Harovas   Were you given something that could do the calculations in our lifetime so that you wouldn't have to be there all day and all night to wait for the simulation?

Habib Zargarpour   I just used my [SGI] O2. What you had to do is use the tools in the package to *make* efficiencies happen. If two objects are really heavy, you put them on different layers. Those kinds of things you have to constantly watch for and take advantage of. But yeah, it would be really nice if they multi-threaded the package as far as dynamics go, not just rendering, so that you could run the simulation on an Origin or do massive parallel processing on fast machines. Nowadays, even desktops are coming with four processors!

Perry Harovas   Is there a concern about using commercial packages, which change often, and sometimes go away?

Habib Zargarpour   Yeah, that's always a concern. I feel like we need to take full advantage as much as we can from vendor software because there are so many developers involved with it. There's only so much manpower you have in-house, and we do have amazing programmers here. But I find that if we are able to harness some or both of those rather than making it exclusive, there are huge benefits in that kind of relationship. As users, we end up benefiting from developers and dedicated companies who make tools for you. And more and more, I guess, packages are opening up with APIs and plug-ins, and it's creating this interesting gray area where code is code, and it's almost like it doesn't make any difference what it's called or where it's running. Put one package into another or vice versa. But then what's important is the user interface and the design, right?

Perry Harovas   Do the other users of Maya out there ever benefit from things that you've developed in ILM, or do they just not let anything go to Alias|Wavefront?

Habib Zargarpour   That's a good question. We have a lot of suggestions for them on improving the package, and most of those changes get put into the official package.

Perry Harovas   Thank you for a such a wonderful conversation, and for all your thoughts and ideas and excitement.

Habib Zargarpour   You're welcome!

INDEX

Note to Reader: In this index, **boldfaced** page numbers refer to primary discussions of the topic; *italics* page numbers refer to figures.

N

O

HIGHEND3D.COM
YOUR HIGH-END 3D RESOURCE AND COMMUNITY WEB SITE
art by
Nick Savy / Will McCullough

What's on the CD-ROM

Mastering Maya 2 Complete fully embraces the philosophy of "learn by doing," and the companion CD is an integral part of that approach. It contains all the project files, sketches, and MEL (Maya Embedded Language) scripts you'll need to get started with the hands-on exercises and tutorials we've used to teach Maya techniques and concepts. As you work through the chapters, you'll also be directed to this CD to view animation clips or high-resolution images that look their best when seen in color.

Besides the material that's related to specific book contents, the CD contains plenty of bonus items. All of the authors are highly skilled animators and 3D graphic artists, and they've provided extra images and animations that will fire your imagination and inspire you to create great Maya work of your own.

Here's a quick list of the folders you'll find on the CD:

Bonus Gallery Here you'll find an assortment of movies and images from authors Perry Harovas, John Kundert-Gibbs, and Peter Lee.

Color Gallery Here we have provided you with color images from throughout *Mastering Maya Complete 2* that use color to convey important information and are best viewed onscreen. To view these files, go to the Color_Gallery folder and find the folder for the chapter you're studying. Then double-click on the .tif file of your choice; each file has been named to match its description in the text.

Sample Animations Here you will find the animation clips that supplement various chapters. See for yourself the power and sophistication of Maya's dynamics engines and be inspired to create work of your own that is just as dazzling. To run the animation clips, go to the SampleAnimations folder and click on the chapter folder of your choice, and then double-click the .mov file of your choice.

Scripts Here you'll find the scripts from Chapters 16 and 17. You can work through the MEL source code presented in these chapters without typing it yourself. To install the scripts, go to the Scripts folder, and double-click Scripts.exe. The default path is C:\Maya\Scripts. You will then be able to open these scripts in Maya's Script Editor.

Working Files Most chapters present their essential concepts and features by directing you through exercises and tutorials—some simple, some quite ambitious. Here you'll find the project (.mb and .ma) files and sketches to get you started with the exercises. To install the working files, go to the Working_Files folder, and double-click on WorkingFiles.exe. The default path is C:\Maya\WorkingFiles.

Web Links: In the Sybex folder you'll find links to some of today's most important 3D graphics and animation sites.

QuickTime: Finally, as a convenience for anyone who doesn't already own it, the Xtras folder contains QuickTime 4 so you can run the animations from any machine.

The CD is designed to run using Windows NT 4. It uses the Sybex Clickme interface as a convenient way to install or copy the various files, but you can also access them directly through NT's Explorer. You may find that many of the animation and project files run or load faster once you've copied them to your hard disk. Also note that you need QuickTime 4 installed to run the .mov files. Except for the Chapter 25 working file, which was specifically created for the Maya 2.5 Paint Effects module, all of the Maya files on the CD can be used in either Maya Complete 2.0 or Maya Complete 2.5.